Constitutional Law and Human Rights in Hong Kong

Constitutional Law and Human Rights in Hong Kong
A Sourcebook

Edited by

Guobin Zhu

Mark Kielsgard

Surya Deva

香港城市大學出版社
City University of Hong Kong Press

ISBN: 978-962-937-615-4

Published by
City University of Hong Kong Press
Tat Chee Avenue
Kowloon, Hong Kong
Website: www.cityu.edu.hk/upress
E-mail: upress@cityu.edu.hk

Printed in Hong Kong

TABLE OF CONTENTS

Preface

The resumption of the exercise of sovereignty over Hong Kong by the People's Republic of China (PRC) on 1 July 1997 and the establishment of the Hong Kong Special Administrative Region (HKSAR) marked the creation of a new constitutional order for Hong Kong. While "the laws previously in force in Hong Kong, that is, the common law, rules of equity, ordinances, subordinate legislation and customary law shall be maintained" (Basic Law, Article 8), constitutional law built upon the Basic Law of the HKSAR has been implemented in the HKSAR ever since. Under the principle of "One Country, Two Systems", the court system and "the legal system and principles previously in force in Hong Kong" have indeed been basically maintained (Basic Law, Article 19). Moreover, Article 39 of the Basic Law provides that the "provisions of the International Covenant on Civil and Political Rights, the International Covenant on Economic, Social and Cultural Rights, and international labour conventions as applied to Hong Kong shall remain in force and shall be implemented through the laws of the Hong Kong Special Administrative Region".

With the enactment of the National Security Law in 2020, the current constitutional system in the HKSAR as well as the effect of the international framework of human rights applicable to Hong Kong is undergoing changes as we write this preface. Although it is not yet fully known how the National Security Law will impact the enjoyment of human rights and freedoms in Hong Kong in the long run, it is widely expected to have a significant impact on the contours of rights and freedoms.

We have been teaching several undergraduate and postgraduate courses in the School of Law at the City University of Hong Kong which are related to constitutional law and human rights in Hong Kong. As professors and legal scholars, we have felt the need for a convenient sourcebook containing the relevant primary materials most often referenced in the field. This book is an attempt to fill this gap. It includes materials in the form of selected core statutes and international instruments, and it will be an essential reference for courses such as Constitutional Law, Basic Law, Public Law of Hong Kong, The Law of Human Rights of Hong Kong, International Human Rights Law, International Criminal Law, International Labour Law, International Environmental Law, Law and Gender, Business and Human Rights, and Discrimination Law. As such, we hope that this sourcebook benefits both students and teachers by providing them key materials all in one place. The book will be equally of interest to researchers, lawyers, and judges engaging with issues concerning constitutional law and human rights in Hong Kong as well as for teach and research in the fields of political science, Asian studies, business, social sciences, and international studies. However, while it is not possible to include all the relevant primary resources that would be useful for such a wide range of courses and fields because of space constraints, we have done our best to pick those most relevant and exercised our discretion to create a bouquet of materials. It includes legal instruments updated as of April 2021, and it will undoubtedly need to be periodically revised to cater for changing teaching and learning needs. Lastly, the documents have been formatted to appear in a consistent style. This includes light editing of heading structure as well as changes in spelling (Oxford) and term capitalization for clarity. However, these changes do not in any way affect the content or meaning of the text.

We would like thank HU Taige, TSE Long Hei Ronnie, NG Lok Yi Jasmine, and Eric Yang for providing us with excellent research assistance in completing this book project. We also wish to express our gratitude to the City University of Hong Kong Press for their professional assistance, and in particular, to Dr Abby Manthey, the English editor at the Press, for her efficient and meticulous editing, without which it would not have been possible to publish this work on time.

Guobin Zhu
Mark Kielsgard
Surya Deva
4 June 2021

PART I

CONSTITUTIONAL LAW OF THE HKSAR

Introduction

Section I The Basic Law of the HKSAR

Section I contains the first group of key legal instruments forming the constitutional system of Hong Kong: the Basic Law.

On 1 July 1997, Hong Kong formally transformed from a dependent territory of the United Kingdom to become the Hong Kong Special Administrative Region (HKSAR) of the People's Republic of China (PRC). With China's resumption of sovereignty over Hong Kong, a "New Constitutional Order" (*per* Yash Ghai [*]) was thereby established.

According to Article 31 of the PRC Constitution, China's national legislature — the National People's Congress (NPC) — adopted the Basic Law of the Hong Kong Special Administrative Region ("the Basic Law") on 4 April 1990, laying down the political, social, and economic systems to be practised in post-1997 Hong Kong. As explained by former Chief Justice Andrew Li, the Basic Law is both "a national law" of the PRC as well as the "constitution of the Region".[†]

Section II NPC Decisions and Interpretations

Section II contains the second group of key legal instruments forming the constitutional system of Hong Kong: the Decisions of the NPC and its Standing Committee (the NPCSC). Notably, the Instruments listed in this section follow a numbering scheme that does not adhere to the informal numbering patterns used by some government sources. Nor is the numbering scheme chorological one, rather it is based on the nature, kind, and category of the documents concerned, making it more conducive for teaching and learning.

In the years leading up to 1997, the NPC and the NPCSC adopted a series of "Decisions" (Instruments 1–6) to supplement the Basic Law and to ensure a seamless transition to the "New Constitutional Order". These include a Decision on the constitutionality of the Basic Law (Instrument 1), the formal establishment of the HKSAR (Instrument 2), the method of the formation of the First Government and the First Legislative Council of the HKSAR (Instrument 3), the establishment of a Committee for the Basic Law under the NPCSC (Instrument 4), the legal effect of the English text of the Basic Law (Instrument 5), and the treatment of the laws previously in force in Hong Kong (Instrument 6). The State Council also promulgated an "Order" (Instrument 7) to set out the boundary of the new Special Administrative Region.

The Basic Law contains three Annexes: Annex I "Method for the Selection of the Chief Executive of the Hong Kong Special Administrative Region", Annex II "Method for the Formation of the Legislative Council of the Hong Kong Special Administrative Region and Its Voting Procedures", and Annex III "National Laws to be Applied in the Hong Kong Special Administrative Region". Under the procedures stipulated in the Basic Law, Annexes I and II were amended in 2010 as part of a constitutional reform to increase democratic participation in the elections of the Chief Executive and the Legislative Councillors (Instruments 8–9).

Under Article 18 of the Basic Law, national laws of the PRC shall not be applied in Hong Kong except for those listed in Annex III to the Basic Law, and the NPCSC may add to or delete from the list of laws in Annex III through prescribed legal procedures. By 2020, a total of 14 national laws had been applied to the HKSAR through Annex III by the NPCSC (Instruments 10–14), with the most recent one

---

* Yash Ghai, *Hong Kong's New Constitutional Order: The Resumption of Chinese Sovereignty and the Basic Law* (2nd edition, Hong Kong University Press 1999).

† *Ng Ka Ling v The Director of Immigration* [1999] 1 HKC 323, para. F.

being the *Law on Safeguarding National Security in the Hong Kong Special Administrative Region*. The laws listed in Annex III shall be applied locally by way of promulgation or legislation by the HKSAR.

After the Handover, the NPC and the NPCSC also adopted eight stand-alone Decisions on Hong Kong-related legal issues. The first group of these Decisions (Instruments 15–18) concerns the democratic reform to achieve "universal suffrage" in both Chief Executive and Legislative Council elections. In 2017, the NPCSC approved a co-location arrangement between Guangdong Province and the HKSAR for establishing a Mainland Port Area in Hong Kong (Instrument 19). In May 2020, the NPC decided to authorize the NPCSC to enact a national security law for Hong Kong (Instrument 20). Finally, in August and November 2020, the NPCSC adopted two Decisions regarding the postponement of the Legislative Council election and the qualification of certain Legislative Councillors (Instruments 21–22).

Apart from issuing legally-binding "Decisions", the PRC Constitution also confers on the NPCSC the power to interpret laws with both retrospective and prospective effects.* Article 158(1) of the Basic Law again sets out that "[t]he power of interpretation of this Law shall be vested in the [NPCSC]". Before 1997, the NPCSC had already adopted an interpretation concerning the implementation of the Nationality Law in Hong Kong (Instrument 23). After the establishment of the HKSAR, the NPCSC has issued five interpretations to the Basic Law (Instruments 24–28), examining issues ranging from the right of abode (Instrument 24) to the oath-taking requirement for public officers (Instrument 28).

Section III The Constitution of the PRC

Section III contains the Constitution of the PRC. Last amended in 2018, it is the direct source of authority for establishing the HKSAR and for enacting the Basic Law of Hong Kong. Apart from the provisions directly related to the SAR, including Article 31 and Article 62(14), scholars have doubted whether the rest of the PRC Constitution is also applicable in Hong Kong. However, according to a White Paper released by the State Council in 2014, the Central People's Government took the view that "[a]s the fundamental law of the country, the Constitution, with supreme legal status and the highest legal authority, is applicable throughout the territory of the People's Republic of China, including the HKSAR".†

Section IV Selected National Laws as Applied in the HKSAR

Section IV includes the full text of two important national laws that have been applied in the HKSAR by way of promulgation through Annex III of the Basic Law.

The Law on the Garrisoning of the Hong Kong Special Administrative Region ("Garrison Law") was adopted by the NPCSC on 30 December 1996. Pursuing to Article 14 of the Basic Law, the Garrison Law was enacted to "ensure the lawful performance of functions and responsibilities by the military forces stationed by the Central People's Government in the [HKSAR] for defence, and to maintain the sovereignty, unity and territorial integrity of the State and the security of Hong Kong". It consists of 6 Chapters and 30 Articles.

The Law of the People's Republic of China on Safeguarding National Security in the Hong Kong Special Administrative Region ("Hong Kong National Security Law") was adopted by the NPCSC on 30 June 2020 and took effect on the same day. It was enacted according to the NPC Decision in May 2020 (see Section II, Instrument 20) to establish and improve the "legal system and enforcement mechanisms" for the HKSAR to safeguard national security in light of the Anti-Extradition Bill Protests

* Constitution of the People's Republic of China, Art. 67(4).

† Information Office of the State Council, *The Practice of the "One Country, Two Systems" Policy in the Hong Kong Special Administrative Region* (June 2014).

in 2019 and the failure of the HKSAR Government to enact a national security law on its own under Article 23 of the Basic Law.

Section V Sino-British Joint Declaration

Lastly, Section V contains the Joint Declaration on the Question of Hong Kong. It was signed by the governments of the PRC and the United Kingdom on 19 December 1984 and came into effect on 27 May 1985. In the Joint Declaration, China declares that it will "resume the exercise of sovereignty over Hong Kong" with effect from 1 July 1997 and lists out its basic policies regarding Hong Kong, which will later be stipulated in the Basic Law. The Joint Declaration includes three Annexes: Annex I (Elaboration by the Government of the People's Republic of China of its Basic Policies Regarding Hong Kong), Annex II (Sino-British Joint Liaison Group), and Annex III (Land Leases). It also contains two memoranda exchanged between the parties. While the Chinese side insists that the Joint Declaration is a "historical document" that lost its practical significance following the enactment of the Basic Law,[*] the British government still views it as a legally valid treaty.[†]

---

* *Reuters*, "China says Sino-British Joint Declaration on Hong Kong no longer has meaning", 30 June 2017, available online at: www.reuters.com/article/us-hongkong-anniversary-china-idUSKBN19L1J1.

† Ibid.

SECTION I

THE BASIC LAW OF THE HONG KONG SPECIAL ADMINISTRATIVE REGION OF THE PEOPLE'S REPUBLIC OF CHINA*

(Adopted at the Third Session of the Seventh National People's Congress on 4 April 1990; Promulgated by Order No. 26 of the President of the People's Republic of China on 4 April 1990; Effective as of 1 July 1997)

Contents

---

* Please also see —

a. Decision of the National People's Congress on the Basic Law of the Hong Kong Special Administrative Region of the People's Republic of China (Adopted at the Third Session of the Seventh National People's Congress on 4 April 1990) (see Instrument 1 in Part I, Section II of this volume); and

b. Decision of the Standing Committee of the National People's Congress on the English Text of the Basic Law of the Hong Kong Special Administrative Region of the People's Republic of China (Adopted on 28 June 1990) (see Instrument 5 in Part I, Section II of this volume).

Annex I:	Method for the Selection of the Chief Executive of the Hong Kong Special Administrative Region
Annex II:	Method for the Formation of the Legislative Council of the Hong Kong Special Administrative Region and Its Voting Procedures
Annex III:	National Laws to be Applied in the Hong Kong Special Administrative Region

Preamble

Hong Kong has been part of the territory of China since ancient times; it was occupied by Britain after the Opium War in 1840. On 19 December 1984, the Chinese and British Governments signed the Joint Declaration on the Question of Hong Kong, affirming that the Government of the People's Republic of China will resume the exercise of sovereignty over Hong Kong with effect from 1 July 1997, thus fulfilling the long-cherished common aspiration of the Chinese people for the recovery of Hong Kong.

Upholding national unity and territorial integrity, maintaining the prosperity and stability of Hong Kong, and taking account of its history and realities, the People's Republic of China has decided that upon China's resumption of the exercise of sovereignty over Hong Kong, a Hong Kong Special Administrative Region will be established in accordance with the provisions of Article 31 of the Constitution of the People's Republic of China, and that under the principle of "one country, two systems", the socialist system and policies will not be practised in Hong Kong. The basic policies of the People's Republic of China regarding Hong Kong have been elaborated by the Chinese Government in the Sino-British Joint Declaration.

In accordance with the Constitution of the People's Republic of China, the National People's Congress hereby enacts the Basic Law of the Hong Kong Special Administrative Region of the People's Republic of China, prescribing the systems to be practised in the Hong Kong Special Administrative Region, in order to ensure the implementation of the basic policies of the People's Republic of China regarding Hong Kong.

Chapter I
General Principles

Article 1

The Hong Kong Special Administrative Region is an inalienable part of the People's Republic of China.

Article 2

The National People's Congress authorizes the Hong Kong Special Administrative Region to exercise a high degree of autonomy and enjoy executive, legislative and independent judicial power, including that of final adjudication, in accordance with the provisions of this Law.

Article 3

The executive authorities and legislature of the Hong Kong Special Administrative Region shall be composed of permanent residents of Hong Kong in accordance with the relevant provisions of this Law.

Article 4

The Hong Kong Special Administrative Region shall safeguard the rights and freedoms of the residents of the Hong Kong Special Administrative Region and of other persons in the Region in accordance with law.

Article 5

The socialist system and policies shall not be practised in the Hong Kong Special Administrative Region, and the previous capitalist system and way of life shall remain unchanged for 50 years.

Article 6

The Hong Kong Special Administrative Region shall protect the right of private ownership of property in accordance with law.

Article 7

The land and natural resources within the Hong Kong Special Administrative Region shall be State property. The Government of the Hong Kong Special Administrative Region shall be responsible for their management, use and development and for their lease or grant to individuals, legal persons or organizations for use or development. The revenues derived therefrom shall be exclusively at the disposal of the government of the Region.

Article 8

The laws previously in force in Hong Kong, that is, the common law, rules of equity, ordinances, subordinate legislation and customary law shall be maintained, except for any that contravene this Law, and subject to any amendment by the legislature of the Hong Kong Special Administrative Region.

Article 9

In addition to the Chinese language, English may also be used as an official language by the executive authorities, legislature and judiciary of the Hong Kong Special Administrative Region.

Article 10

Apart from displaying the national flag and national emblem of the People's Republic of China, the Hong Kong Special Administrative Region may also use a regional flag and regional emblem.

The regional flag of the Hong Kong Special Administrative Region is a red flag with a bauhinia highlighted by five star-tipped stamens.

The regional emblem of the Hong Kong Special Administrative Region is a bauhinia in the centre highlighted by five star-tipped stamens and encircled by the words "Hong Kong Special Administrative Region of the People's Republic of China" in Chinese and "HONG KONG" in English.

Article 11

In accordance with Article 31 of the Constitution of the People's Republic of China, the systems and policies practised in the Hong Kong Special Administrative Region, including the social and economic systems, the system for safeguarding the fundamental rights and freedoms of its residents, the executive, legislative and judicial systems, and the relevant policies, shall be based on the provisions of this Law.

No law enacted by the legislature of the Hong Kong Special Administrative Region shall contravene this Law.

Chapter II
Relationship between the Central Authorities and the Hong Kong Special Administrative Region

Article 12

The Hong Kong Special Administrative Region shall be a local administrative region of the People's Republic of China, which shall enjoy a high degree of autonomy and come directly under the Central People's Government.

Article 13

The Central People's Government shall be responsible for the foreign affairs relating to the Hong Kong Special Administrative Region.*

The Ministry of Foreign Affairs of the People's Republic of China shall establish an office in Hong Kong to deal with foreign affairs.

The Central People's Government authorizes the Hong Kong Special Administrative Region to conduct relevant external affairs on its own in accordance with this Law.

Article 14

The Central People's Government shall be responsible for the defence of the Hong Kong Special Administrative Region.

The Government of the Hong Kong Special Administrative Region shall be responsible for the maintenance of public order in the Region.

Military forces stationed by the Central People's Government in the Hong Kong Special Administrative Region for defence shall not interfere in the local affairs of the Region. The Government of the Hong Kong Special Administrative Region may, when necessary, ask the Central People's Government for assistance from the garrison in the maintenance of public order and in disaster relief.

In addition to abiding by national laws, members of the garrison shall abide by the laws of the Hong Kong Special Administrative Region.

Expenditure for the garrison shall be borne by the Central People's Government.

Article 15

The Central People's Government shall appoint the Chief Executive and the principal officials of the executive authorities of the Hong Kong Special Administrative Region in accordance with the provisions of Chapter IV of this Law.

Article 16

The Hong Kong Special Administrative Region shall be vested with executive power. It shall, on its own, conduct the administrative affairs of the Region in accordance with the relevant provisions of this Law.

Article 17

The Hong Kong Special Administrative Region shall be vested with legislative power.

Laws enacted by the legislature of the Hong Kong Special Administrative Region must be reported to the Standing Committee of the National People's Congress for the record. The reporting for record shall not affect the entry into force of such laws.

If the Standing Committee of the National People's Congress, after consulting the Committee for the Basic Law of the Hong Kong Special Administrative Region under it, considers that any law enacted by the legislature of the Region is not in conformity with the provisions of this Law regarding affairs within the responsibility of the Central Authorities or regarding the relationship between the Central Authorities and the Region, the Standing Committee may return the law in question but shall not amend it. Any law returned by the Standing Committee of the National People's Congress shall immediately be invalidated. This invalidation shall not have retroactive effect, unless otherwise provided for in the laws of the Region.

---

* See Interpretation of Paragraph 1, Article 13 and Article 19 of the Basic Law of the Hong Kong Special Administrative Region of the People's Republic of China by the Standing Committee of the National People's Congress (Adopted at the Twenty Second Session of the Standing Committee of the Eleventh National People's Congress on 26 August 2011) (see Instrument 27 in Part I, Section II of this volume).

Article 18

The laws in force in the Hong Kong Special Administrative Region shall be this Law, the laws previously in force in Hong Kong as provided for in Article 8 of this Law, and the laws enacted by the legislature of the Region.

National laws shall not be applied in the Hong Kong Special Administrative Region except for those listed in Annex III to this Law. The laws listed therein shall be applied locally by way of promulgation or legislation by the Region.

The Standing Committee of the National People's Congress may add to or delete from the list of laws in Annex III after consulting its Committee for the Basic Law of the Hong Kong Special Administrative Region and the government of the Region. Laws listed in Annex III to this Law shall be confined to those relating to defence and foreign affairs as well as other matters outside the limits of the autonomy of the Region as specified by this Law.

In the event that the Standing Committee of the National People's Congress decides to declare a state of war or, by reason of turmoil within the Hong Kong Special Administrative Region which endangers national unity or security and is beyond the control of the government of the Region, decides that the Region is in a state of emergency, the Central People's Government may issue an order applying the relevant national laws in the Region.

Article 19

The Hong Kong Special Administrative Region shall be vested with independent judicial power, including that of final adjudication.

The courts of the Hong Kong Special Administrative Region shall have jurisdiction over all cases in the Region, except that the restrictions on their jurisdiction imposed by the legal system and principles previously in force in Hong Kong shall be maintained.

The courts of the Hong Kong Special Administrative Region shall have no jurisdiction over acts of state such as defence and foreign affairs. The courts of the Region shall obtain a certificate from the Chief Executive on questions of fact concerning acts of state such as defence and foreign affairs whenever such questions arise in the adjudication of cases. This certificate shall be binding on the courts. Before issuing such a certificate, the Chief Executive shall obtain a certifying document from the Central People's Government.*

Article 20

The Hong Kong Special Administrative Region may enjoy other powers granted to it by the National People's Congress, the Standing Committee of the National People's Congress or the Central People's Government.

Article 21

Chinese citizens who are residents of the Hong Kong Special Administrative Region shall be entitled to participate in the management of state affairs according to law.

In accordance with the assigned number of seats and the selection method specified by the National People's Congress, the Chinese citizens among the residents of the Hong Kong Special Administrative Region shall locally elect deputies of the Region to the National People's Congress to participate in the work of the highest organ of state power.

---

* See Interpretation of Paragraph 1, Article 13 and Article 19 of the Basic Law of the Hong Kong Special Administrative Region of the People's Republic of China by the Standing Committee of the National People's Congress (Adopted at the Twenty Second Session of the Standing Committee of the Eleventh National People's Congress on 26 August 2011) (see Instrument 27 in Part I, Section II of this volume).

Article 22

No department of the Central People's Government and no province, autonomous region, or municipality directly under the Central Government may interfere in the affairs which the Hong Kong Special Administrative Region administers on its own in accordance with this Law.

If there is a need for departments of the Central Government, or for provinces, autonomous regions, or municipalities directly under the Central Government to set up offices in the Hong Kong Special Administrative Region, they must obtain the consent of the government of the Region and the approval of the Central People's Government.

All offices set up in the Hong Kong Special Administrative Region by departments of the Central Government, or by provinces, autonomous regions, or municipalities directly under the Central Government, and the personnel of these offices shall abide by the laws of the Region.

For entry into the Hong Kong Special Administrative Region, people from other parts of China must apply for approval. Among them, the number of persons who enter the Region for the purpose of settlement shall be determined by the competent authorities of the Central People's Government after consulting the government of the Region.*

The Hong Kong Special Administrative Region may establish an office in Beijing.

Article 23

The Hong Kong Special Administrative Region shall enact laws on its own to prohibit any act of treason, secession, sedition, subversion against the Central People's Government, or theft of state secrets, to prohibit foreign political organizations or bodies from conducting political activities in the Region, and to prohibit political organizations or bodies of the Region from establishing ties with foreign political organizations or bodies.

Chapter III
Fundamental Rights and Duties of the Residents

Article 24

Residents of the Hong Kong Special Administrative Region ("Hong Kong residents") shall include permanent residents and non-permanent residents.

The permanent residents of the Hong Kong Special Administrative Region shall be:

(1) Chinese citizens born in Hong Kong before or after the establishment of the Hong Kong Special Administrative Region;

(2) Chinese citizens who have ordinarily resided in Hong Kong for a continuous period of not less than seven years before or after the establishment of the Hong Kong Special Administrative Region;

* See The Interpretation by the Standing Committee of the National People's Congress of Articles 22(4) and 24(2)(3) of the Basic Law of the Hong Kong Special Administrative Region of the People's Republic of China (Adopted at the Tenth Session of the Standing Committee of the Ninth National People's Congress on 26 June 1999) (see Instrument 24 in Part I, Section II of this volume).

(3) Persons of Chinese nationality born outside Hong Kong of those residents listed in categories (1) and (2);*

(4) Persons not of Chinese nationality who have entered Hong Kong with valid travel documents, have ordinarily resided in Hong Kong for a continuous period of not less than seven years and have taken Hong Kong as their place of permanent residence before or after the establishment of the Hong Kong Special Administrative Region;

(5) Persons under 21 years of age born in Hong Kong of those residents listed in category (4) before or after the establishment of the Hong Kong Special Administrative Region; and

(6) Persons other than those residents listed in categories (1) to (5), who, before the establishment of the Hong Kong Special Administrative Region, had the right of abode in Hong Kong only.

The above-mentioned residents shall have the right of abode in the Hong Kong Special Administrative Region and shall be qualified to obtain, in accordance with the laws of the Region, permanent identity cards which state their right of abode.

The non-permanent residents of the Hong Kong Special Administrative Region shall be persons who are qualified to obtain Hong Kong identity cards in accordance with the laws of the Region but have no right of abode.

Article 25

All Hong Kong residents shall be equal before the law.

Article 26

Permanent residents of the Hong Kong Special Administrative Region shall have the right to vote and the right to stand for election in accordance with law.

Article 27

Hong Kong residents shall have freedom of speech, of the press and of publication; freedom of association, of assembly, of procession and of demonstration; and the right and freedom to form and join trade unions, and to strike.

Article 28

The freedom of the person of Hong Kong residents shall be inviolable.

No Hong Kong resident shall be subjected to arbitrary or unlawful arrest, detention or imprisonment. Arbitrary or unlawful search of the body of any resident or deprivation or restriction of the freedom of the person shall be prohibited. Torture of any resident or arbitrary or unlawful deprivation of the life of any resident shall be prohibited.

Article 29

The homes and other premises of Hong Kong residents shall be inviolable. Arbitrary or unlawful search of, or intrusion into, a resident's home or other premises shall be prohibited.

Article 30

The freedom and privacy of communication of Hong Kong residents shall be protected by law. No department or individual may, on any grounds, infringe upon the freedom and privacy of communication

* See The Interpretation by the Standing Committee of the National People's Congress of Articles 22(4) and 24(2)(3) of the Basic Law of the Hong Kong Special Administrative Region of the People's Republic of China (Adopted at the Tenth Session of the Standing Committee of the Ninth National People's Congress on 26 June 1999) (see Instrument 24 in Part I, Section II of this volume).

of residents except that the relevant authorities may inspect communication in accordance with legal procedures to meet the needs of public security or of investigation into criminal offences.

Article 31

Hong Kong residents shall have freedom of movement within the Hong Kong Special Administrative Region and freedom of emigration to other countries and regions. They shall have freedom to travel and to enter or leave the Region. Unless restrained by law, holders of valid travel documents shall be free to leave the Region without special authorization.

Article 32

Hong Kong residents shall have freedom of conscience.

Hong Kong residents shall have freedom of religious belief and freedom to preach and to conduct and participate in religious activities in public.

Article 33

Hong Kong residents shall have freedom of choice of occupation.

Article 34

Hong Kong residents shall have freedom to engage in academic research, literary and artistic creation, and other cultural activities.

Article 35

Hong Kong residents shall have the right to confidential legal advice, access to the courts, choice of lawyers for timely protection of their lawful rights and interests or for representation in the courts, and to judicial remedies.

Hong Kong residents shall have the right to institute legal proceedings in the courts against the acts of the executive authorities and their personnel.

Article 36

Hong Kong residents shall have the right to social welfare in accordance with law. The welfare benefits and retirement security of the labour force shall be protected by law.

Article 37

The freedom of marriage of Hong Kong residents and their right to raise a family freely shall be protected by law.

Article 38

Hong Kong residents shall enjoy the other rights and freedoms safeguarded by the laws of the Hong Kong Special Administrative Region.

Article 39

The provisions of the International Covenant on Civil and Political Rights, the International Covenant on Economic, Social and Cultural Rights, and international labour conventions as applied to Hong Kong shall remain in force and shall be implemented through the laws of the Hong Kong Special Administrative Region.

The rights and freedoms enjoyed by Hong Kong residents shall not be restricted unless as prescribed by law. Such restrictions shall not contravene the provisions of the preceding paragraph of this Article.

Article 40

The lawful traditional rights and interests of the indigenous inhabitants of the "New Territories" shall be protected by the Hong Kong Special Administrative Region.

Article 41

Persons in the Hong Kong Special Administrative Region other than Hong Kong residents shall, in accordance with law, enjoy the rights and freedoms of Hong Kong residents prescribed in this Chapter.

Article 42

Hong Kong residents and other persons in Hong Kong shall have the obligation to abide by the laws in force in the Hong Kong Special Administrative Region.

Chapter IV
Political Structure

Section 1 The Chief Executive

Article 43

The Chief Executive of the Hong Kong Special Administrative Region shall be the head of the Hong Kong Special Administrative Region and shall represent the Region.

The Chief Executive of the Hong Kong Special Administrative Region shall be accountable to the Central People's Government and the Hong Kong Special Administrative Region in accordance with the provisions of this Law.

Article 44

The Chief Executive of the Hong Kong Special Administrative Region shall be a Chinese citizen of not less than 40 years of age who is a permanent resident of the Region with no right of abode in any foreign country and has ordinarily resided in Hong Kong for a continuous period of not less than 20 years.

Article 45

The Chief Executive of the Hong Kong Special Administrative Region shall be selected by election or through consultations held locally and be appointed by the Central People's Government.

The method for selecting the Chief Executive shall be specified in the light of the actual situation in the Hong Kong Special Administrative Region and in accordance with the principle of gradual and orderly progress. The ultimate aim is the selection of the Chief Executive by universal suffrage upon nomination by a broadly representative nominating committee in accordance with democratic procedures.

The specific method for selecting the Chief Executive is prescribed in Annex I "Method for the Selection of the Chief Executive of the Hong Kong Special Administrative Region".

Article 46

The term of office of the Chief Executive of the Hong Kong Special Administrative Region shall be five years. He or she may serve for not more than two consecutive terms.

Article 47

The Chief Executive of the Hong Kong Special Administrative Region must be a person of integrity, dedicated to his or her duties.

The Chief Executive, on assuming office, shall declare his or her assets to the Chief Justice of the Court of Final Appeal of the Hong Kong Special Administrative Region. This declaration shall be put on record.

Article 48

The Chief Executive of the Hong Kong Special Administrative Region shall exercise the following powers and functions:

(1) To lead the government of the Region;

(2) To be responsible for the implementation of this Law and other laws which, in accordance with this Law, apply in the Hong Kong Special Administrative Region;

(3) To sign bills passed by the Legislative Council and to promulgate laws;

To sign budgets passed by the Legislative Council and report the budgets and final accounts to the Central People's Government for the record;

(4) To decide on government policies and to issue executive orders;

(5) To nominate and to report to the Central People's Government for appointment the following principal officials: Secretaries and Deputy Secretaries of Departments, Directors of Bureaux, Commissioner Against Corruption, Director of Audit, Commissioner of Police, Director of Immigration and Commissioner of Customs and Excise; and to recommend to the Central People's Government the removal of the above-mentioned officials;

(6) To appoint or remove judges of the courts at all levels in accordance with legal procedures;

(7) To appoint or remove holders of public office in accordance with legal procedures;

(8) To implement the directives issued by the Central People's Government in respect of the relevant matters provided for in this Law;

(9) To conduct, on behalf of the Government of the Hong Kong Special Administrative Region, external affairs and other affairs as authorized by the Central Authorities;

(10) To approve the introduction of motions regarding revenues or expenditure to the Legislative Council;

(11) To decide, in the light of security and vital public interests, whether government officials or other personnel in charge of government affairs should testify or give evidence before the Legislative Council or its committees;

(12) To pardon persons convicted of criminal offences or commute their penalties; and

(13) To handle petitions and complaints.

Article 49

If the Chief Executive of the Hong Kong Special Administrative Region considers that a bill passed by the Legislative Council is not compatible with the overall interests of the Region, he or she may return it to the Legislative Council within three months for reconsideration. If the Legislative Council passes the original bill again by not less than a two-thirds majority of all the members, the Chief Executive must sign and promulgate it within one month, or act in accordance with the provisions of Article 50 of this Law.

Article 50

If the Chief Executive of the Hong Kong Special Administrative Region refuses to sign a bill passed the second time by the Legislative Council, or the Legislative Council refuses to pass a budget or any other important bill introduced by the government, and if consensus still cannot be reached after consultations, the Chief Executive may dissolve the Legislative Council.

The Chief Executive must consult the Executive Council before dissolving the Legislative Council. The Chief Executive may dissolve the Legislative Council only once in each term of his or her office.

Article 51

If the Legislative Council of the Hong Kong Special Administrative Region refuses to pass the budget introduced by the government, the Chief Executive may apply to the Legislative Council for provisional appropriations. If appropriation of public funds cannot be approved because the Legislative Council has already been dissolved, the Chief Executive may, prior to the election of the new Legislative Council, approve provisional short-term appropriations according to the level of expenditure of the previous fiscal year.

Article 52

The Chief Executive of the Hong Kong Special Administrative Region must resign under any of the following circumstances:

(1) When he or she loses the ability to discharge his or her duties as a result of serious illness or other reasons;

(2) When, after the Legislative Council is dissolved because he or she twice refuses to sign a bill passed by it, the new Legislative Council again passes by a two-thirds majority of all the members the original bill in dispute, but he or she still refuses to sign it; and

(3) When, after the Legislative Council is dissolved because it refuses to pass a budget or any other important bill, the new Legislative Council still refuses to pass the original bill in dispute.

Article 53

If the Chief Executive of the Hong Kong Special Administrative Region is not able to discharge his or her duties for a short period, such duties shall temporarily be assumed by the Administrative Secretary, Financial Secretary or Secretary of Justice in this order of precedence.

In the event that the office of Chief Executive becomes vacant, a new Chief Executive shall be selected within six months in accordance with the provisions of Article 45 of this Law. During the period of vacancy, his or her duties shall be assumed according to the provisions of the preceding paragraph.*

Article 54

The Executive Council of the Hong Kong Special Administrative Region shall be an organ for assisting the Chief Executive in policy-making.

Article 55

Members of the Executive Council of the Hong Kong Special Administrative Region shall be appointed by the Chief Executive from among the principal officials of the executive authorities, members of the Legislative Council and public figures. Their appointment or removal shall be decided by the Chief Executive. The term of office of members of the Executive Council shall not extend beyond the expiry of the term of office of the Chief Executive who appoints them.

Members of the Executive Council of the Hong Kong Special Administrative Region shall be Chinese citizens who are permanent residents of the Region with no right of abode in any foreign country.

The Chief Executive may, as he or she deems necessary, invite other persons concerned to sit in on meetings of the Council.

Article 56

The Executive Council of the Hong Kong Special Administrative Region shall be presided over by the Chief Executive.

---

* See Interpretation of Paragraph 2, Article 53 of the Basic Law of the Hong Kong Special Administrative Region of the People's Republic of China by the Standing Committee of the National People's Congress (Adopted at the Fifteenth Session of the Standing Committee of the Tenth National People's Congress on 27 April 2005) (see Instrument 26 in Part I, Section II of this volume).

Except for the appointment, removal and disciplining of officials and the adoption of measures in emergencies, the Chief Executive shall consult the Executive Council before making important policy decisions, introducing bills to the Legislative Council, making subordinate legislation, or dissolving the Legislative Council.

If the Chief Executive does not accept a majority opinion of the Executive Council, he or she shall put the specific reasons on record.

Article 57

A Commission Against Corruption shall be established in the Hong Kong Special Administrative Region. It shall function independently and be accountable to the Chief Executive.

Article 58

A Commission of Audit shall be established in the Hong Kong Special Administrative Region. It shall function independently and be accountable to the Chief Executive.

Section 2 The Executive Authorities

Article 59

The Government of the Hong Kong Special Administrative Region shall be the executive authorities of the Region.

Article 60

The head of the Government of the Hong Kong Special Administrative Region shall be the Chief Executive of the Region.

A Department of Administration, a Department of Finance, a Department of Justice, and various bureaux, divisions and commissions shall be established in the Government of the Hong Kong Special Administrative Region.

Article 61

The principal officials of the Hong Kong Special Administrative Region shall be Chinese citizens who are permanent residents of the Region with no right of abode in any foreign country and have ordinarily resided in Hong Kong for a continuous period of not less than 15 years.

Article 62

The Government of the Hong Kong Special Administrative Region shall exercise the following powers and functions:

(1) To formulate and implement policies;

(2) To conduct administrative affairs;

(3) To conduct external affairs as authorized by the Central People's Government under this Law;

(4) To draw up and introduce budgets and final accounts;

(5) To draft and introduce bills, motions and subordinate legislation; and

(6) To designate officials to sit in on the meetings of the Legislative Council and to speak on behalf of the government.

Article 63

The Department of Justice of the Hong Kong Special Administrative Region shall control criminal prosecutions, free from any interference.

Article 64

The Government of the Hong Kong Special Administrative Region must abide by the law and be accountable to the Legislative Council of the Region: it shall implement laws passed by the Council and already in force; it shall present regular policy addresses to the Council; it shall answer questions raised by members of the Council; and it shall obtain approval from the Council for taxation and public expenditure.

Article 65

The previous system of establishing advisory bodies by the executive authorities shall be maintained.

Section 3 The Legislature

Article 66

The Legislative Council of the Hong Kong Special Administrative Region shall be the legislature of the Region.

Article 67

The Legislative Council of the Hong Kong Special Administrative Region shall be composed of Chinese citizens who are permanent residents of the Region with no right of abode in any foreign country. However, permanent residents of the Region who are not of Chinese nationality or who have the right of abode in foreign countries may also be elected members of the Legislative Council of the Region, provided that the proportion of such members does not exceed 20 percent of the total membership of the Council.

Article 68

The Legislative Council of the Hong Kong Special Administrative Region shall be constituted by election.

The method for forming the Legislative Council shall be specified in the light of the actual situation in the Hong Kong Special Administrative Region and in accordance with the principle of gradual and orderly progress. The ultimate aim is the election of all the members of the Legislative Council by universal suffrage.

The specific method for forming the Legislative Council and its procedures for voting on bills and motions are prescribed in Annex II: "Method for the Formation of the Legislative Council of the Hong Kong Special Administrative Region and Its Voting Procedures".

Article 69

The term of office of the Legislative Council of the Hong Kong Special Administrative Region shall be four years, except the first term which shall be two years.

Article 70

If the Legislative Council of the Hong Kong Special Administrative Region is dissolved by the Chief Executive in accordance with the provisions of this Law, it must, within three months, be reconstituted by election in accordance with Article 68 of this Law.

Article 71

The President of the Legislative Council of the Hong Kong Special Administrative Region shall be elected by and from among the members of the Legislative Council.

The President of the Legislative Council of the Hong Kong Special Administrative Region shall be a Chinese citizen of not less than 40 years of age, who is a permanent resident of the Region with no right of abode in any foreign country and has ordinarily resided in Hong Kong for a continuous period of not less than 20 years.

Article 72

The President of the Legislative Council of the Hong Kong Special Administrative Region shall exercise the following powers and functions:

(1) To preside over meetings;

(2) To decide on the agenda, giving priority to government bills for inclusion in the agenda;

(3) To decide on the time of meetings;

(4) To call special sessions during the recess;

(5) To call emergency sessions on the request of the Chief Executive; and

(6) To exercise other powers and functions as prescribed in the rules of procedure of the Legislative Council.

Article 73

The Legislative Council of the Hong Kong Special Administrative Region shall exercise the following powers and functions:

(1) To enact, amend or repeal laws in accordance with the provisions of this Law and legal procedures;

(2) To examine and approve budgets introduced by the government;

(3) To approve taxation and public expenditure;

(4) To receive and debate the policy addresses of the Chief Executive;

(5) To raise questions on the work of the government;

(6) To debate any issue concerning public interests;

(7) To endorse the appointment and removal of the judges of the Court of Final Appeal and the Chief Judge of the High Court;

(8) To receive and handle complaints from Hong Kong residents;

(9) If a motion initiated jointly by one-fourth of all the members of the Legislative Council charges the Chief Executive with serious breach of law or dereliction of duty and if he or she refuses to resign, the Council may, after passing a motion for investigation, give a mandate to the Chief Justice of the Court of Final Appeal to form and chair an independent investigation committee. The committee shall be responsible for carrying out the investigation and reporting its findings to the Council. If the committee considers the evidence sufficient to substantiate such charges, the Council may pass a motion of impeachment by a two-thirds majority of all its members and report it to the Central People's Government for decision; and

(10) To summon, as required when exercising the above-mentioned powers and functions, persons concerned to testify or give evidence.

Article 74

Members of the Legislative Council of the Hong Kong Special Administrative Region may introduce bills in accordance with the provisions of this Law and legal procedures. Bills which do not relate to public expenditure or political structure or the operation of the government may be introduced individually or jointly by members of the Council. The written consent of the Chief Executive shall be required before bills relating to government policies are introduced.

Article 75

The quorum for the meeting of the Legislative Council of the Hong Kong Special Administrative Region shall be not less than one half of all its members.

The rules of procedure of the Legislative Council shall be made by the Council on its own, provided that they do not contravene this Law.

Article 76

A bill passed by the Legislative Council of the Hong Kong Special Administrative Region may take effect only after it is signed and promulgated by the Chief Executive.

Article 77

Members of the Legislative Council of the Hong Kong Special Administrative Region shall be immune from legal action in respect of their statements at meetings of the Council.

Article 78

Members of the Legislative Council of the Hong Kong Special Administrative Region shall not be subjected to arrest when attending or on their way to a meeting of the Council.

Article 79

The President of the Legislative Council of the Hong Kong Special Administrative Region shall declare that a member of the Council is no longer qualified for the office under any of the following circumstances:

(1) When he or she loses the ability to discharge his or her duties as a result of serious illness or other reasons;

(2) When he or she, with no valid reason, is absent from meetings for three consecutive months without the consent of the President of the Legislative Council;

(3) When he or she loses or renounces his or her status as a permanent resident of the Region;

(4) When he or she accepts a government appointment and becomes a public servant;

(5) When he or she is bankrupt or fails to comply with a court order to repay debts;

(6) When he or she is convicted and sentenced to imprisonment for one month or more for a criminal offence committed within or outside the Region and is relieved of his or her duties by a motion passed by two-thirds of the members of the Legislative Council present; and

(7) When he or she is censured for misbehaviour or breach of oath by a vote of two-thirds of the members of the Legislative Council present.

Section 4 The Judiciary

Article 80

The courts of the Hong Kong Special Administrative Region at all levels shall be the judiciary of the Region, exercising the judicial power of the Region.

Article 81

The Court of Final Appeal, the High Court, district courts, magistrates' courts and other special courts shall be established in the Hong Kong Special Administrative Region. The High Court shall comprise the Court of Appeal and the Court of First Instance.

The judicial system previously practised in Hong Kong shall be maintained except for those changes consequent upon the establishment of the Court of Final Appeal of the Hong Kong Special Administrative Region.

Article 82

The power of final adjudication of the Hong Kong Special Administrative Region shall be vested in the Court of Final Appeal of the Region, which may as required invite judges from other common law jurisdictions to sit on the Court of Final Appeal.

Article 83

The structure, powers and functions of the courts of the Hong Kong Special Administrative Region at all levels shall be prescribed by law.

Article 84

The courts of the Hong Kong Special Administrative Region shall adjudicate cases in accordance with the laws applicable in the Region as prescribed in Article 18 of this Law and may refer to precedents of other common law jurisdictions.

Article 85

The courts of the Hong Kong Special Administrative Region shall exercise judicial power independently, free from any interference. Members of the judiciary shall be immune from legal action in the performance of their judicial functions.

Article 86

The principle of trial by jury previously practised in Hong Kong shall be maintained.

Article 87

In criminal or civil proceedings in the Hong Kong Special Administrative Region, the principles previously applied in Hong Kong and the rights previously enjoyed by parties to proceedings shall be maintained.

Anyone who is lawfully arrested shall have the right to a fair trial by the judicial organs without delay and shall be presumed innocent until convicted by the judicial organs.

Article 88

Judges of the courts of the Hong Kong Special Administrative Region shall be appointed by the Chief Executive on the recommendation of an independent commission composed of local judges, persons from the legal profession and eminent persons from other sectors.

Article 89

A judge of a court of the Hong Kong Special Administrative Region may only be removed for inability to discharge his or her duties, or for misbehaviour, by the Chief Executive on the recommendation of a tribunal appointed by the Chief Justice of the Court of Final Appeal and consisting of not fewer than three local judges.

The Chief Justice of the Court of Final Appeal of the Hong Kong Special Administrative Region may be investigated only for inability to discharge his or her duties, or for misbehaviour, by a tribunal appointed by the Chief Executive and consisting of not fewer than five local judges and may be removed by the Chief Executive on the recommendation of the tribunal and in accordance with the procedures prescribed in this Law.

Article 90

The Chief Justice of the Court of Final Appeal and the Chief Judge of the High Court of the Hong Kong Special Administrative Region shall be Chinese citizens who are permanent residents of the Region with no right of abode in any foreign country.

In the case of the appointment or removal of judges of the Court of Final Appeal and the Chief Judge of the High Court of the Hong Kong Special Administrative Region, the Chief Executive shall, in addition to following the procedures prescribed in Articles 88 and 89 of this Law, obtain the endorsement of the Legislative Council and report such appointment or removal to the Standing Committee of the National People's Congress for the record.

Article 91

The Hong Kong Special Administrative Region shall maintain the previous system of appointment and removal of members of the judiciary other than judges.

Article 92

Judges and other members of the judiciary of the Hong Kong Special Administrative Region shall be chosen on the basis of their judicial and professional qualities and may be recruited from other common law jurisdictions.

Article 93

Judges and other members of the judiciary serving in Hong Kong before the establishment of the Hong Kong Special Administrative Region may all remain in employment and retain their seniority with pay, allowances, benefits and conditions of service no less favourable than before.

The Government of the Hong Kong Special Administrative Region shall pay to judges and other members of the judiciary who retire or leave the service in compliance with regulations, including those who have retired or left the service before the establishment of the Hong Kong Special Administrative Region, or to their dependants, all pensions, gratuities, allowances and benefits due to them on terms no less favourable than before, irrespective of their nationality or place of residence.

Article 94

On the basis of the system previously operating in Hong Kong, the Government of the Hong Kong Special Administrative Region may make provisions for local lawyers and lawyers from outside Hong Kong to work and practise in the Region.

Article 95

The Hong Kong Special Administrative Region may, through consultations and in accordance with law, maintain juridical relations with the judicial organs of other parts of the country, and they may render assistance to each other.

Article 96

With the assistance or authorization of the Central People's Government, the Government of the Hong Kong Special Administrative Region may make appropriate arrangements with foreign states for reciprocal juridical assistance.

Section 5 District Organizations

Article 97

District organizations which are not organs of political power may be established in the Hong Kong Special Administrative Region, to be consulted by the government of the Region on district administration and other affairs, or to be responsible for providing services in such fields as culture, recreation and environmental sanitation.

Article 98

The powers and functions of the district organizations and the method for their formation shall be prescribed by law.

Section 6 Public Servants

Article 99

Public servants serving in all government departments of the Hong Kong Special Administrative Region must be permanent residents of the Region, except where otherwise provided for in Article 101 of this Law regarding public servants of foreign nationalities and except for those below a certain rank as prescribed by law.

Public servants must be dedicated to their duties and be responsible to the Government of the Hong Kong Special Administrative Region.

Article 100

Public servants serving in all Hong Kong government departments, including the police department, before the establishment of the Hong Kong Special Administrative Region, may all remain in employment and retain their seniority with pay, allowances, benefits and conditions of service no less favourable than before.

Article 101

The Government of the Hong Kong Special Administrative Region may employ British and other foreign nationals previously serving in the public service in Hong Kong, or those holding permanent identity cards of the Region, to serve as public servants in government departments at all levels, but only Chinese citizens among permanent residents of the Region with no right of abode in any foreign country may fill the following posts: the Secretaries and Deputy Secretaries of Departments, Directors of Bureaux, Commissioner Against Corruption, Director of Audit, Commissioner of Police, Director of Immigration and Commissioner of Customs and Excise.

The Government of the Hong Kong Special Administrative Region may also employ British and other foreign nationals as advisers to government departments and, when required, may recruit qualified candidates from outside the Region to fill professional and technical posts in government departments. These foreign nationals shall be employed only in their individual capacities and shall be responsible to the government of the Region.

Article 102

The Government of the Hong Kong Special Administrative Region shall pay to public servants who retire or who leave the service in compliance with regulations, including those who have retired or who have left the service in compliance with regulations before the establishment of the Hong Kong Special Administrative Region, or to their dependants, all pensions, gratuities, allowances and benefits due to them on terms no less favourable than before, irrespective of their nationality or place of residence.

Article 103

The appointment and promotion of public servants shall be on the basis of their qualifications, experience and ability. Hong Kong's previous system of recruitment, employment, assessment, discipline, training and management for the public service, including special bodies for their appointment, pay and conditions of service, shall be maintained, except for any provisions for privileged treatment of foreign nationals.

Article 104

When assuming office, the Chief Executive, principal officials, members of the Executive Council and of the Legislative Council, judges of the courts at all levels and other members of the judiciary in the Hong Kong Special Administrative Region must, in accordance with law, swear to uphold the Basic Law of the Hong Kong Special Administrative Region of the People's Republic of China and swear allegiance to the Hong Kong Special Administrative Region of the People's Republic of China.*

* See Interpretation of Article 104 of the Basic Law of the Hong Kong Special Administrative Region of the People's Republic of China by the Standing Committee of the National People's Congress (Adopted by the Standing Committee of the Twelfth National People's Congress at its Twenty-fourth Session on 7 November 2016) (see Instrument 28 in Part I, Section II of this volume).

Chapter V
Economy

Section 1 Public Finance, Monetary Affairs, Trade, Industry and Commerce

Article 105

The Hong Kong Special Administrative Region shall, in accordance with law, protect the right of individuals and legal persons to the acquisition, use, disposal and inheritance of property and their right to compensation for lawful deprivation of their property.

Such compensation shall correspond to the real value of the property concerned at the time and shall be freely convertible and paid without undue delay.

The ownership of enterprises and the investments from outside the Region shall be protected by law.

Article 106

The Hong Kong Special Administrative Region shall have independent finances.

The Hong Kong Special Administrative Region shall use its financial revenues exclusively for its own purposes, and they shall not be handed over to the Central People's Government.

The Central People's Government shall not levy taxes in the Hong Kong Special Administrative Region.

Article 107

The Hong Kong Special Administrative Region shall follow the principle of keeping expenditure within the limits of revenues in drawing up its budget, and strive to achieve a fiscal balance, avoid deficits and keep the budget commensurate with the growth rate of its gross domestic product.

Article 108

The Hong Kong Special Administrative Region shall practise an independent taxation system.

The Hong Kong Special Administrative Region shall, taking the low tax policy previously pursued in Hong Kong as reference, enact laws on its own concerning types of taxes, tax rates, tax reductions, allowances and exemptions, and other matters of taxation.

Article 109

The Government of the Hong Kong Special Administrative Region shall provide an appropriate economic and legal environment for the maintenance of the status of Hong Kong as an international financial centre.

Article 110

The monetary and financial systems of the Hong Kong Special Administrative Region shall be prescribed by law.

The Government of the Hong Kong Special Administrative Region shall, on its own, formulate monetary and financial policies, safeguard the free operation of financial business and financial markets, and regulate and supervise them in accordance with law.

Article 111

The Hong Kong dollar, as the legal tender in the Hong Kong Special Administrative Region, shall continue to circulate.

The authority to issue Hong Kong currency shall be vested in the Government of the Hong Kong Special Administrative Region. The issue of Hong Kong currency must be backed by a 100 percent reserve fund.

The system regarding the issue of Hong Kong currency and the reserve fund system shall be prescribed by law.

The Government of the Hong Kong Special Administrative Region may authorize designated banks to issue or continue to issue Hong Kong currency under statutory authority, after satisfying itself that any issue of currency will be soundly based and that the arrangements for such issue are consistent with the object of maintaining the stability of the currency.

Article 112

No foreign exchange control policies shall be applied in the Hong Kong Special Administrative Region. The Hong Kong dollar shall be freely convertible. Markets for foreign exchange, gold, securities, futures and the like shall continue.

The Government of the Hong Kong Special Administrative Region shall safeguard the free flow of capital within, into and out of the Region.

Article 113

The Exchange Fund of the Hong Kong Special Administrative Region shall be managed and controlled by the government of the Region, primarily for regulating the exchange value of the Hong Kong dollar.

Article 114

The Hong Kong Special Administrative Region shall maintain the status of a free port and shall not impose any tariff unless otherwise prescribed by law.

Article 115

The Hong Kong Special Administrative Region shall pursue the policy of free trade and safeguard the free movement of goods, intangible assets and capital.

Article 116

The Hong Kong Special Administrative Region shall be a separate customs territory.

The Hong Kong Special Administrative Region may, using the name "Hong Kong, China", participate in relevant international organizations and international trade agreements (including preferential trade arrangements), such as the General Agreement on Tariffs and Trade and arrangements regarding international trade in textiles.

Export quotas, tariff preferences and other similar arrangements, which are obtained or made by the Hong Kong Special Administrative Region or which were obtained or made and remain valid, shall be enjoyed exclusively by the Region.

Article 117

The Hong Kong Special Administrative Region may issue its own certificates of origin for products in accordance with prevailing rules of origin.

Article 118

The Government of the Hong Kong Special Administrative Region shall provide an economic and legal environment for encouraging investments, technological progress and the development of new industries.

Article 119

The Government of the Hong Kong Special Administrative Region shall formulate appropriate policies to promote and co-ordinate the development of various trades such as manufacturing, commerce, tourism, real estate, transport, public utilities, services, agriculture and fisheries, and pay regard to the protection of the environment.

Section 2 Land Leases

Article 120

All leases of land granted, decided upon or renewed before the establishment of the Hong Kong Special Administrative Region which extend beyond 30 June 1997, and all rights in relation to such leases, shall continue to be recognized and protected under the law of the Region.

Article 121

As regards all leases of land granted or renewed where the original leases contain no right of renewal, during the period from 27 May 1985 to 30 June 1997, which extend beyond 30 June 1997 and expire not later than 30 June 2047, the lessee is not required to pay an additional premium as from 1 July 1997, but an annual rent equivalent to 3 percent of the rateable value of the property at that date, adjusted in step with any changes in the rateable value thereafter, shall be charged.

Article 122

In the case of old schedule lots, village lots, small houses and similar rural holdings, where the property was on 30 June 1984 held by, or, in the case of small houses granted after that date, where the property is granted to, a lessee descended through the male line from a person who was in 1898 a resident of an established village in Hong Kong, the previous rent shall remain unchanged so long as the property is held by that lessee or by one of his lawful successors in the male line.

Article 123

Where leases of land without a right of renewal expire after the establishment of the Hong Kong Special Administrative Region, they shall be dealt with in accordance with laws and policies formulated by the Region on its own.

Section 3 Shipping

Article 124

The Hong Kong Special Administrative Region shall maintain Hong Kong's previous systems of shipping management and shipping regulation, including the system for regulating conditions of seamen.

The Government of the Hong Kong Special Administrative Region shall, on its own, define its specific functions and responsibilities in respect of shipping.

Article 125

The Hong Kong Special Administrative Region shall be authorized by the Central People's Government to continue to maintain a shipping register and issue related certificates under its legislation, using the name "Hong Kong, China".

Article 126

With the exception of foreign warships, access for which requires the special permission of the Central People's Government, ships shall enjoy access to the ports of the Hong Kong Special Administrative Region in accordance with the laws of the Region.

Article 127

Private shipping businesses and shipping-related businesses and private container terminals in the Hong Kong Special Administrative Region may continue to operate freely.

Section 4 Civil Aviation

Article 128

The Government of the Hong Kong Special Administrative Region shall provide conditions and take measures for the maintenance of the status of Hong Kong as a centre of international and regional aviation.

Article 129

The Hong Kong Special Administrative Region shall continue the previous system of civil aviation management in Hong Kong and keep its own aircraft register in accordance with provisions laid down by the Central People's Government concerning nationality marks and registration marks of aircraft.

Access of foreign state aircraft to the Hong Kong Special Administrative Region shall require the special permission of the Central People's Government.

Article 130

The Hong Kong Special Administrative Region shall be responsible on its own for matters of routine business and technical management of civil aviation, including the management of airports, the provision of air traffic services within the flight information region of the Hong Kong Special Administrative Region, and the discharge of other responsibilities allocated to it under the regional air navigation procedures of the International Civil Aviation Organization.

Article 131

The Central People's Government shall, in consultation with the Government of the Hong Kong Special Administrative Region, make arrangements providing air services between the Region and other parts of the People's Republic of China for airlines incorporated in the Hong Kong Special Administrative Region and having their principal place of business in Hong Kong and other airlines of the People's Republic of China.

Article 132

All air service agreements providing air services between other parts of the People's Republic of China and other states and regions with stops at the Hong Kong Special Administrative Region and air services between the Hong Kong Special Administrative Region and other states and regions with stops at other parts of the People's Republic of China shall be concluded by the Central People's Government.

In concluding the air service agreements referred to in the first paragraph of this Article, the Central People's Government shall take account of the special conditions and economic interests of the Hong Kong Special Administrative Region and consult the government of the Region.

Representatives of the Government of the Hong Kong Special Administrative Region may, as members of the delegations of the Government of the People's Republic of China, participate in air service consultations conducted by the Central People's Government with foreign governments concerning arrangements for such services referred to in the first paragraph of this Article.

Article 133

Acting under specific authorizations from the Central People's Government, the Government of the Hong Kong Special Administrative Region may:

(1) renew or amend air service agreements and arrangements previously in force;

(2) negotiate and conclude new air service agreements providing routes for airlines incorporated in the Hong Kong Special Administrative Region and having their principal place of business in Hong Kong and providing rights for over-flights and technical stops; and

(3) negotiate and conclude provisional arrangements with foreign states or regions with which no air service agreements have been concluded.

All scheduled air services to, from or through Hong Kong, which do not operate to, from or through the mainland of China shall be regulated by the air service agreements or provisional arrangements referred to in this Article.

Article 134

The Central People's Government shall give the Government of the Hong Kong Special Administrative Region the authority to:

(1) negotiate and conclude with other authorities all arrangements concerning the implementation of the air service agreements and provisional arrangements referred to in Article 133 of this Law;

(2) issue licences to airlines incorporated in the Hong Kong Special Administrative Region and having their principal place of business in Hong Kong;

(3) designate such airlines under the air service agreements and provisional arrangements referred to in Article 133 of this Law; and

(4) issue permits to foreign airlines for services other than those to, from or through the mainland of China.

Article 135

Airlines incorporated and having their principal place of business in Hong Kong and businesses related to civil aviation functioning there prior to the establishment of the Hong Kong Special Administrative Region may continue to operate.

Chapter VI
Education, Science, Culture, Sports, Religion, Labour and Social Services

Article 136

On the basis of the previous educational system, the Government of the Hong Kong Special Administrative Region shall, on its own, formulate policies on the development and improvement of education, including policies regarding the educational system and its administration, the language of instruction, the allocation of funds, the examination system, the system of academic awards and the recognition of educational qualifications.

Community organizations and individuals may, in accordance with law, run educational undertakings of various kinds in the Hong Kong Special Administrative Region.

Article 137

Educational institutions of all kinds may retain their autonomy and enjoy academic freedom. They may continue to recruit staff and use teaching materials from outside the Hong Kong Special Administrative Region. Schools run by religious organizations may continue to provide religious education, including courses in religion.

Students shall enjoy freedom of choice of educational institutions and freedom to pursue their education outside the Hong Kong Special Administrative Region.

Article 138

The Government of the Hong Kong Special Administrative Region shall, on its own, formulate policies to develop Western and traditional Chinese medicine and to improve medical and health services.

Community organizations and individuals may provide various medical and health services in accordance with law.

Article 139

The Government of the Hong Kong Special Administrative Region shall, on its own, formulate policies on science and technology and protect by law achievements in scientific and technological research, patents, discoveries and inventions.

The Government of the Hong Kong Special Administrative Region shall, on its own, decide on the scientific and technological standards and specifications applicable in Hong Kong.

Article 140

The Government of the Hong Kong Special Administrative Region shall, on its own, formulate policies on culture and protect by law the achievements and the lawful rights and interests of authors in their literary and artistic creation.

Article 141

The Government of the Hong Kong Special Administrative Region shall not restrict the freedom of religious belief, interfere in the internal affairs of religious organizations or restrict religious activities which do not contravene the laws of the Region.

Religious organizations shall, in accordance with law, enjoy the rights to acquire, use, dispose of and inherit property and the right to receive financial assistance. Their previous property rights and interests shall be maintained and protected.

Religious organizations may, according to their previous practice, continue to run seminaries and other schools, hospitals and welfare institutions and to provide other social services.

Religious organizations and believers in the Hong Kong Special Administrative Region may maintain and develop their relations with religious organizations and believers elsewhere.

Article 142

The Government of the Hong Kong Special Administrative Region shall, on the basis of maintaining the previous systems concerning the professions, formulate provisions on its own for assessing the qualifications for practice in the various professions.

Persons with professional qualifications or qualifications for professional practice obtained prior to the establishment of the Hong Kong Special Administrative Region may retain their previous qualifications in accordance with the relevant regulations and codes of practice.

The Government of the Hong Kong Special Administrative Region shall continue to recognize the professions and the professional organizations recognized prior to the establishment of the Region, and these organizations may, on their own, assess and confer professional qualifications.

The Government of the Hong Kong Special Administrative Region may, as required by developments in society and in consultation with the parties concerned, recognize new professions and professional organizations.

Article 143

The Government of the Hong Kong Special Administrative Region shall, on its own, formulate policies on sports. Non-governmental sports organizations may continue to exist and develop in accordance with law.

Article 144

The Government of the Hong Kong Special Administrative Region shall maintain the policy previously practised in Hong Kong in respect of subventions for non-governmental organizations in fields such as education, medicine and health, culture, art, recreation, sports, social welfare and social work. Staff members previously serving in subvented organizations in Hong Kong may remain in their employment in accordance with the previous system.

Article 145

On the basis of the previous social welfare system, the Government of the Hong Kong Special Administrative Region shall, on its own, formulate policies on the development and improvement of this system in the light of the economic conditions and social needs.

Article 146

Voluntary organizations providing social services in the Hong Kong Special Administrative Region may, on their own, decide their forms of service, provided that the law is not contravened.

Article 147

The Hong Kong Special Administrative Region shall on its own formulate laws and policies relating to labour.

Article 148

The relationship between non-governmental organizations in fields such as education, science, technology, culture, art, sports, the professions, medicine and health, labour, social welfare and social work as well as religious organizations in the Hong Kong Special Administrative Region and their counterparts on the Mainland shall be based on the principles of non-subordination, non-interference and mutual respect.

Article 149

Non-governmental organizations in fields such as education, science, technology, culture, art, sports, the professions, medicine and health, labour, social welfare and social work as well as religious organizations in the Hong Kong Special Administrative Region may maintain and develop relations with their counterparts in foreign countries and regions and with relevant international organizations. They may, as required, use the name "Hong Kong, China" in the relevant activities.

Chapter VII
External Affairs

Article 150

Representatives of the Government of the Hong Kong Special Administrative Region may, as members of delegations of the Government of the People's Republic of China, participate in negotiations at the diplomatic level directly affecting the Region conducted by the Central People's Government.

Article 151

The Hong Kong Special Administrative Region may on its own, using the name "Hong Kong, China", maintain and develop relations and conclude and implement agreements with foreign states and regions and relevant international organizations in the appropriate fields, including the economic, trade, financial and monetary, shipping, communications, tourism, cultural and sports fields.

Article 152

Representatives of the Government of the Hong Kong Special Administrative Region may, as members of delegations of the People's Republic of China, participate in international organizations or conferences in appropriate fields limited to states and affecting the Region, or may attend in such other capacity as may be permitted by the Central People's Government and the international organization or conference concerned, and may express their views, using the name "Hong Kong, China".

The Hong Kong Special Administrative Region may, using the name "Hong Kong, China", participate in international organizations and conferences not limited to states.

The Central People's Government shall take the necessary steps to ensure that the Hong Kong Special Administrative Region shall continue to retain its status in an appropriate capacity in those international organizations of which the People's Republic of China is a member and in which Hong Kong participates in one capacity or another.

The Central People's Government shall, where necessary, facilitate the continued participation of the Hong Kong Special Administrative Region in an appropriate capacity in those international organizations in which Hong Kong is a participant in one capacity or another, but of which the People's Republic of China is not a member.

Article 153

The application to the Hong Kong Special Administrative Region of international agreements to which the People's Republic of China is or becomes a party shall be decided by the Central People's Government, in accordance with the circumstances and needs of the Region, and after seeking the views of the government of the Region.

International agreements to which the People's Republic of China is not a party but which are implemented in Hong Kong may continue to be implemented in the Hong Kong Special Administrative Region. The Central People's Government shall, as necessary, authorize or assist the government of the Region to make appropriate arrangements for the application to the Region of other relevant international agreements.

Article 154

The Central People's Government shall authorize the Government of the Hong Kong Special Administrative Region to issue, in accordance with law, passports of the Hong Kong Special Administrative Region of the People's Republic of China to all Chinese citizens who hold permanent identity cards of the Region, and travel documents of the Hong Kong Special Administrative Region of the People's Republic of China to all other persons lawfully residing in the Region. The above passports and documents shall be valid for all states and regions and shall record the holder's right to return to the Region.

The Government of the Hong Kong Special Administrative Region may apply immigration controls on entry into, stay in and departure from the Region by persons from foreign states and regions.

Article 155

The Central People's Government shall assist or authorize the Government of the Hong Kong Special Administrative Region to conclude visa abolition agreements with foreign states or regions.

Article 156

The Hong Kong Special Administrative Region may, as necessary, establish official or semi-official economic and trade missions in foreign countries and shall report the establishment of such missions to the Central People's Government for the record.

Article 157

The establishment of foreign consular and other official or semi-official missions in the Hong Kong Special Administrative Region shall require the approval of the Central People's Government.

Consular and other official missions established in Hong Kong by states which have formal diplomatic relations with the People's Republic of China may be maintained.

According to the circumstances of each case, consular and other official missions established in Hong Kong by states which have no formal diplomatic relations with the People's Republic of China may be permitted either to remain or be changed to semi-official missions.

States not recognized by the People's Republic of China may only establish non-governmental institutions in the Region.

Chapter VIII
Interpretation and Amendment of the Basic Law

Article 158

The power of interpretation of this Law shall be vested in the Standing Committee of the National People's Congress.

The Standing Committee of the National People's Congress shall authorize the courts of the Hong Kong Special Administrative Region to interpret on their own, in adjudicating cases, the provisions of this Law which are within the limits of the autonomy of the Region.

The courts of the Hong Kong Special Administrative Region may also interpret other provisions of this Law in adjudicating cases. However, if the courts of the Region, in adjudicating cases, need to interpret the provisions of this Law concerning affairs which are the responsibility of the Central People's Government, or concerning the relationship between the Central Authorities and the Region, and if such interpretation will affect the judgments on the cases, the courts of the Region shall, before making their final judgments which are not appealable, seek an interpretation of the relevant provisions from the Standing Committee of the National People's Congress through the Court of Final Appeal of the Region. When the Standing Committee makes an interpretation of the provisions concerned, the courts of the Region, in applying those provisions, shall follow the interpretation of the Standing Committee. However, judgments previously rendered shall not be affected.

The Standing Committee of the National People's Congress shall consult its Committee for the Basic Law of the Hong Kong Special Administrative Region before giving an interpretation of this Law.

Article 159

The power of amendment of this Law shall be vested in the National People's Congress.

The power to propose bills for amendments to this Law shall be vested in the Standing Committee of the National People's Congress, the State Council and the Hong Kong Special Administrative Region. Amendment bills from the Hong Kong Special Administrative Region shall be submitted to the National People's Congress by the delegation of the Region to the National People's Congress after obtaining the consent of two-thirds of the deputies of the Region to the National People's Congress, two-thirds of all the members of the Legislative Council of the Region, and the Chief Executive of the Region.

Before a bill for amendment to this Law is put on the agenda of the National People's Congress, the Committee for the Basic Law of the Hong Kong Special Administrative Region shall study it and submit its views.

No amendment to this Law shall contravene the established basic policies of the People's Republic of China regarding Hong Kong.

Chapter IX
Supplementary Provisions

Article 160

Upon the establishment of the Hong Kong Special Administrative Region, the laws previously in force in Hong Kong shall be adopted as laws of the Region except for those which the Standing Committee of the National People's Congress declares to be in contravention of this Law. If any laws are later discovered to be in contravention of this Law, they shall be amended or cease to have force in accordance with the procedure as prescribed by this Law.

Documents, certificates, contracts, and rights and obligations valid under the laws previously in force in Hong Kong shall continue to be valid and be recognized and protected by the Hong Kong Special Administrative Region, provided that they do not contravene this Law.

Annex I: Method for the Selection of the Chief Executive of the Hong Kong Special Administrative Region

(Adopted at the Third Session of the Seventh National People's Congress on 4 April 1990, amended, as approved at the Sixteenth Meeting of the Standing Committee of the Eleventh National People's Congress on 28 August 2010, and amended at the Twenty-Seventh Meeting of the Standing Committee of the Thirteenth National People's Congress on 30 March 2021)

(1) The Chief Executive shall be elected in accordance with this Law by an Election Committee which is broadly representative, suited to the actual situation of the Hong Kong Special Administrative Region (HKSAR), and represents the overall interests of society, and shall be appointed by the Central People's Government.

(2) The Election Committee shall be composed of 1,500 members from the following sectors:

First Sector: Industrial, commercial and financial sectors	300
Second Sector: The professions	300
Third Sector: Grassroots, labour, religious and other sectors	300
Fourth Sector: Members of the Legislative Council, representatives of district organizations and other organizations	300
Fifth Sector: HKSAR deputies to the National People's Congress (NPC), HKSAR members of the National Committee of the Chinese People's Political Consultative Conference (CPPCC), and representatives of Hong Kong members of relevant national organizations	300

Members of the Election Committee must be permanent residents of the HKSAR.

The term of office of the Election Committee shall be five years.

(3) The delimitation of and the number of seats allocated to each sector of the Election Committee are as follows:

The First Sector shall be composed of the following 18 subsectors:

Industrial (first)	17
Industrial (second)	17

Textiles and garment	17
Commercial (first)	17
Commercial (second)	17
Commercial (third)	17
Finance	17
Financial services	17
Insurance	17
Real estate and construction	17
Transport	17
Import and export	17
Tourism	17
Hotel	16
Catering	16
Wholesale and retail	17
Employers' Federation of Hong Kong	15
Small and medium enterprises	15

The Second Sector shall be composed of the following 10 subsectors:

Technology and innovation	30
Engineering	30
Architectural, surveying, planning and landscape	30
Accountancy	30
Legal	30
Education	30
Sports, performing arts, culture and publication	30
Medical and health services	30
Chinese medicine	30
Social welfare	30

The Third Sector shall be composed of the following five subsectors:

Agriculture and fisheries	60
Labour	60
Grassroots associations	60
Associations of Chinese fellow townsmen	60
Religious	60

The Fourth Sector shall be composed of the following five subsectors:

Members of the Legislative Council	90
Heung Yee Kuk	27
Representatives of members of Area Committees, District Fight Crime Committees, and District Fire Safety Committees of Hong Kong Island and Kowloon	76

Representatives of members of Area Committees, District Fight Crime Committees, and District Fire Safety Committees of the New Territories	80
Representatives of associations of Hong Kong residents in the Mainland	27

The Fifth Sector shall be composed of the following two subsectors:

HKSAR deputies to the NPC and HKSAR members of the CPPCC National Committee	190
Representatives of Hong Kong members of relevant national organizations	110

(4) The Election Committee shall be constituted in the following manner:

(a) HKSAR deputies to the NPC, HKSAR members of the CPPCC National Committee, Hong Kong members of the Committee for the Basic Law of the HKSAR under the NPC Standing Committee, members of the Legislative Council, university presidents or chairpersons of the board of governors or the council of universities, and responsible persons of statutory bodies, advisory bodies and relevant associations of the subsectors of engineering (15), architectural, surveying, planning and landscape (15), education (5), medical and health services (15) and social welfare (15) shall be Election Committee members of the corresponding subsectors.

An HKSAR deputy to the NPC or an HKSAR member of the CPPCC National Committee may choose to register as an Election Committee member in a subsector other than one in the Fifth Sector with which he or she has a substantial connection. If an HKSAR deputy to the NPC or an HKSAR member of the CPPCC National Committee is registered as an Election Committee member in a subsector other than one in the Fifth Sector, his or her seat shall be counted as one in that subsector and the number of members to be returned by that subsector in accordance with paragraph (c) of this subsection shall be reduced accordingly. After the registration of HKSAR deputies to the NPC and HKSAR members of the CPPCC National Committee as Election Committee members of the relevant subsectors, the number of members to be returned by those subsectors in accordance with paragraphs (a), (b) and (c) of this subsection, as determined by the provision in this subparagraph, shall remain unchanged within the term of office of the Election Committee.

(b) Election Committee members of the religious subsector shall be nominated;

- 15 members of the technology and innovation subsector shall be nominated from among Hong Kong academicians of the Chinese Academy of Sciences and the Chinese Academy of Engineering;
- 15 members of the accountancy subsector shall be nominated from among Hong Kong Accounting Advisors appointed by the Ministry of Finance;
- 9 members of the legal subsector shall be nominated from among Hong Kong members of the Council of the China Law Society;
- 15 members of the sports, performing arts, culture and publication subsector shall be nominated respectively by the Sports Federation and Olympic Committee of Hong Kong, China, China Federation of Literary and Art Circles Hong Kong Member Association and Hong Kong Publishing Federation;
- 15 members of the Chinese medicine subsector shall be nominated from among Hong Kong members of the Council of the World Federation of Chinese Medicine Societies; and
- 27 members of the subsector of representatives of associations of Hong Kong residents in the Mainland shall be nominated by such associations.

(c) Election Committee members of a subsector, except for those specified in paragraphs (a) and (b) of this subsection, shall be elected by eligible corporate voters for the corresponding subsector. Eligible corporate voters for subsectors shall be composed of institutions, organizations, associations or enterprises which are representative and specified by law. Unless specified in the electoral law of the HKSAR, an association or enterprise may become a corporate voter for a subsector only if it has been operating for not less than three years after acquiring relevant qualifications for that subsector. Election Committee members of subsectors — the Heung Yee Kuk, representatives of members of Area Committees, District Fight Crime Committees, and District Fire Safety Committees of Hong Kong Island and Kowloon, and representatives of members of Area Committees, District Fight Crime Committees, and District Fire Safety Committees of the New Territories in the Fourth Sector and representatives of Hong Kong members of relevant national organizations in the Fifth Sector may be elected by individual voters. A candidate for Election Committee member of a subsector shall be nominated by five voters for the subsector. The number of candidates each voter for a subsector may nominate shall not exceed the number of seats allocated to the subsector. Voters for a subsector of the Election Committee shall elect Election Committee members of that subsector from the list of nominations by secret ballot.

The specific method for returning the Election Committee members referred to in the preceding subsection, including the definition of statutory bodies, advisory bodies, relevant associations and eligible corporate voters for relevant subsectors, the method for nomination of candidates and the method for voting shall be prescribed by the electoral law of the HKSAR.

(5) There shall be a system of conveners for the Election Committee. The conveners shall be responsible for convening meetings of the Election Committee as necessary and handle relevant matters. A chief convener shall be an Election Committee member who holds an office of state leadership. The chief convener shall designate a number of conveners for each sector of the Election Committee.

(6) A candidate for the office of Chief Executive shall be nominated by not less than 188 members of the Election Committee, with not less than 15 members from each of the five sectors. Each Election Committee member may nominate one candidate only.

(7) The Election Committee shall elect the Chief Executive designate from the list of nominations by secret ballot on a one-person-one-vote basis. The Chief Executive designate must obtain more than 750 votes. The specific election method shall be prescribed by the electoral law of the HKSAR.

(8) The Candidate Eligibility Review Committee of the HKSAR shall be responsible for reviewing and confirming the eligibility of candidates for Election Committee members and for the office of Chief Executive. The Committee for Safeguarding National Security of the HKSAR shall, on the basis of the review by the department for safeguarding national security of the Police Force of the HKSAR, make findings as to whether a candidate for Election Committee member or for the office of Chief Executive meets the legal requirements and conditions of upholding the Basic Law of the Hong Kong Special Administrative Region of the People's Republic of China and swearing allegiance to the Hong Kong Special Administrative Region of the People's Republic of China, and issue an opinion to the Candidate Eligibility Review Committee of the HKSAR in respect of a candidate who fails to meet such legal requirements and conditions.

No legal proceedings may be instituted in respect of a Decision made by the Candidate Eligibility Review Committee of the HKSAR on the eligibility of a candidate for Election Committee member or for the office of Chief Executive pursuant to the opinion of the Committee for Safeguarding National Security of the HKSAR.

(9) The HKSAR shall, in accordance with the law, take measures against acts of manipulating or undermining election.

(10) The NPC Standing Committee exercises in accordance with the law the power to amend this method. Prior to making any amendment, the NPC Standing Committee shall solicit views of various sectors of Hong Kong by appropriate means.

(11) The term of office of the Election Committee constituted under the method previously in force shall terminate upon the commencement of term of office of the Election Committee constituted under this method.

(12) This method shall come into force on 31 March 2021. Annex I and its amendment previously in force shall cease to apply.

Annex II: Method for the Formation of the Legislative Council of the Hong Kong Special Administrative Region and Its Voting Procedures

(Adopted at the Third Session of the Seventh National People's Congress on 4 April 1990, amended, as recorded at the Sixteenth Meeting of the Standing Committee of the Eleventh National People's Congress on 28 August 2010, and amended at the Twenty-Seventh Meeting of the Standing Committee of the Thirteenth National People's Congress on 30 March 2021)

(1) The Legislative Council of the Hong Kong Special Administrative Region (HKSAR) shall be composed of 90 members for each term. The composition of the Legislative Council shall be as follows:

Members returned by the Election Committee	40
Members returned by functional constituencies	30
Members returned by geographical constituencies through direct elections	20

The above-mentioned Election Committee refers to the one provided for in Annex I to this Law.

(2) Candidates for members of the Legislative Council returned by the Election Committee shall be nominated by at least 10 but no more than 20 members of the Election Committee, with at least 2 but no more than 4 members from each sector. Any eligible voter in an election of the Legislative Council may be nominated as a candidate. Each Election Committee member may nominate one candidate only.

The Election Committee shall elect members of the Legislative Council from the list of nominations by secret ballot. A ballot paper is valid only if the number of candidates voted for is equal to the number of members of the Legislative Council to be returned. The 40 candidates who obtain the highest numbers of votes shall be elected.

(3) There shall be 28 functional constituencies for election of members of the Legislative Council:

Agriculture and fisheries
Heung Yee Kuk
Industrial (first)
Industrial (second)
Textiles and garment
Commercial (first)
Commercial (second)
Commercial (third)
Finance
Financial services

Insurance

Real estate and construction

Transport

Import and export

Tourism

Catering

Wholesale and retail

Technology and innovation

Engineering

Architectural, surveying, planning and landscape

Accountancy

Legal

Education

Sports, performing arts, culture and publication

Medical and health services

Social welfare

Labour

HKSAR deputies to the National People's Congress (NPC),

HKSAR members of the National Committee of the Chinese People's Political Consultative Conference (CPPCC), and representatives of relevant national organizations

Three members shall be returned by the labour functional constituency, and one member shall be returned by each of the other functional constituencies.

Members of the Legislative Council returned by the following functional constituencies shall be elected by individual voters:

Heung Yee Kuk

Engineering

Architectural, surveying, planning and landscape

Accountancy

Legal

Education

Medical and health services

Social welfare

HKSAR deputies to the NPC, HKSAR members of the CPPCC National Committee and representatives of relevant national organizations

Members of the Legislative Council returned by the other functional constituencies shall be elected by eligible corporate voters. Eligible corporate voters for functional constituencies shall be composed of institutions, organizations, associations or enterprises which are representative and specified by law. Unless specified in the electoral law of the HKSAR, an association or enterprise may become a corporate voter for a functional constituency only if it has been operating for not less than three years after acquiring relevant qualifications for that functional constituency.

A candidate for a functional constituency shall be nominated by at least 10 but no more than 20 voters for the functional constituency as well as at least 2 but no more than 4 members from each sector of the Election Committee. Each Election Committee member may nominate one candidate only for the election of members of the Legislative Council returned by functional constituencies.

Voters for a functional constituency shall elect Legislative Council member for that functional constituency from the list of nominations by secret ballot.

The delimitation of corporate bodies and the definition of eligible corporate voters for functional constituencies, and the election method shall be prescribed by the electoral law of the HKSAR.

(4) There shall be 10 geographical constituencies for returning members of the Legislative Council through direct elections. Two members shall be returned by each geographical constituency. A candidate for a geographical constituency shall be nominated by at least 100 but no more than 200 voters for the geographical constituency as well as at least 2 but no more than 4 members from each sector of the Election Committee. Each Election Committee member may nominate one candidate only for direct election of members of the Legislative Council returned by geographical constituencies.

For each geographical constituency, a voter may vote for one candidate on the list of nominations by secret ballot. The two candidates who obtain the highest numbers of votes shall be elected.

The delineation of geographical constituencies and the voting method shall be prescribed by the electoral law of the HKSAR.

(5) The Candidate Eligibility Review Committee of the HKSAR shall be responsible for reviewing and confirming the eligibility of candidates for members of the Legislative Council. The Committee for Safeguarding National Security of the HKSAR shall, on the basis of the review by the department for safeguarding national security of the Police Force of the HKSAR, make findings as to whether a candidate for member of the Legislative Council meets the legal requirements and conditions of upholding the Basic Law of the Hong Kong Special Administrative Region of the People's Republic of China and swearing allegiance to the Hong Kong Special Administrative Region of the People's Republic of China, and issue an opinion to the Candidate Eligibility Review Committee of the HKSAR in respect of a candidate who fails to meet such legal requirements and conditions.

No legal proceedings may be instituted in respect of a Decision made by the Candidate Eligibility Review Committee of the HKSAR on the eligibility of a candidate for member of the Legislative Council pursuant to the opinion of the Committee for Safeguarding National Security of the HKSAR.

(6) The HKSAR shall, in accordance with the law, take measures against acts of manipulating or undermining election.

(7) Unless otherwise provided for in this Law, the Legislative Council shall adopt the following procedures for voting on bills and motions:

- The passage of bills introduced by the government shall require a simple majority of votes of the members of the Legislative Council present.
- The passage of motions, bills or amendments to government bills introduced by individual members of the Legislative Council shall require a simple majority of votes of each of the two groups of members present (i.e., members returned by the Election Committee, and those returned by functional constituencies and by geographical constituencies through direct elections).

(8) The NPC Standing Committee exercises in accordance with the law the power to amend this method and the procedures for voting on bills and motions. Prior to making any amendment, the NPC Standing Committee shall solicit views of various sectors of Hong Kong by appropriate means.

(9) This method and the procedures for voting on bills and motions shall come into force on 31 March 2021. Annex II and its amendment previously in force shall cease to apply.

Annex III: National Laws to be Applied in the Hong Kong Special Administrative Region*

The following national laws shall be applied locally with effect from 1 July 1997 by way of promulgation or legislation by the Hong Kong Special Administrative Region:

(1) Resolution on the Capital, Calendar, National Anthem and National Flag of the People's Republic of China

(2) Resolution on the National Day of the People's Republic of China

(3) Order on the National Emblem of the People's Republic of China Proclaimed by the Central People's Government

Attached: Design of the national emblem, notes of explanation and instructions for use

(4) Declaration of the Government of the People's Republic of China on the Territorial Sea

(5) Nationality Law of the People's Republic of China

(6) Regulations of the People's Republic of China Concerning Diplomatic Privileges and Immunities

Appendix: Explanations on "The Basic Law of the Hong Kong Special Administrative Region of the People's Republic of China (Draft)" and Its Related Documents

(Addressing the Third Session of the Seventh National People's Congress on 28 March 1990)†

Ji Pengfei

Chairman of the Drafting Committee for the Basic Law of the Hong Kong Special Administrative Region of the People's Republic of China

---

* For addition to and deletion from the list of laws in Annex III, please see:

a. Decision of the Standing Committee of the National People's Congress on the addition to or deletion from the list of national laws in Annex III to the Basic Law of the Hong Kong Special Administrative Region of the People's Republic of China (Adopted at the Twenty Sixth Session of the Standing Committee of the Eighth National People's Congress on 1 July 1997) (see Instrument 10 in Part I, Section II of this volume);

b. Decision of the Standing Committee of the National People's Congress on the addition to the list of national laws in Annex III to the Basic Law of the Hong Kong Special Administrative Region of the People's Republic of China (Adopted on 4 November 1998) (see Instrument 11 in Part I, Section II of this volume);

c. Decision of the Standing Committee of the National People's Congress on the addition to the list of national laws in Annex III to the Basic Law of the Hong Kong Special Administrative Region of the People's Republic of China (Adopted on 27 October 2005) (see Instrument 12 in Part I, Section II of this volume);

d. Decision of the Standing Committee of the National People's Congress on the addition to the list of national laws in Annex III to the Basic Law of the Hong Kong Special Administrative Region of the People's Republic of China (Adopted on 4 November 2017) (see Instrument 13 in Part I, Section II of this volume); and

e. Decision of the Standing Committee of the National People's Congress on the addition to the list of national laws in Annex III to the Basic Law of the Hong Kong Special Administrative Region of the People's Republic of China (Adopted at the Twentieth Session of the Standing Committee of the Thirteenth National People's Congress on 30 June 2020) (see Instrument 14 in Part I, Section II of this volume).

† This is an English translation of the original Instrument in Chinese and is published for the reader's information.

Fellow Deputies,

Through four years and eight months of effort, the Drafting Committee for The Basic Law of the Hong Kong Special Administrative Region of the People's Republic of China has completed the work of drafting the Basic Law. The Standing Committee of the National People's Congress has submitted to the current session of the National People's Congress for examination "The Basic Law of the Hong Kong Special Administrative Region of the People's Republic of China (Draft)" and three Annexes; the draft designs of the regional flag and regional emblem for the Hong Kong Special Administrative Region: "The Decision of the National People's Congress of the People's Republic of China on the Method for the Formation of the First Government and the First Legislative Council of the Hong Kong Special Administrative Region (Draft)," which has been worked out by the Drafting Committee on behalf of the National People's Congress; and "The Proposal by the Drafting Committee for the Basic Law of the Hong Kong Special Administrative Region on the Establishment of the Committee for the Basic Law of the Hong Kong Special Administrative Region under the Standing Committee of the National People's Congress." I have been entrusted by the Drafting Committee for the Basic Law of the Hong Kong Special Administrative Region to make the following explanations concerning this legal document.

In accordance with "The Decision of the Third Session of the Sixth National People's Congress on the Establishment of the Drafting Committee for the Basic Law of the Hong Kong Special Administrative Region of the People's Republic of China," at its 11th session the Standing Committee of the Sixth National People's Congress appointed the members of the Hong Kong Basic Law Drafting Committee. On 1 July 1985, the Drafting Committee was officially established and began its work. After mapping out its work plans and deciding upon the structure of the Basic Law, the Drafting Committee set up five special groups consisting of committee members from both the Mainland and Hong Kong. The five groups, namely, the Special Group Concerned with the Relationship between the Central Authorities and the Hong Kong Special Administrative Region; the Special Group Concerned with Fundamental Rights and Duties of Residents; the Special Group Concerned with the Political Structure; the Special Group Concerned with the Economy; and the Special Group Concerned with Education, Science, Technology, Culture, Sports and Religion, were responsible for the drafting work. After these special groups worked out their first draft of provisions of the Basic Law, the General Working Group was set up to make overall adjustment and revision of the draft provisions. In April 1988, the seventh plenary session of the Hong Kong Basic Law Drafting Committee issued "The Draft Basic Law of the Hong Kong Special Administrative Region of the People's Republic of China for Solicitation of Opinions." In the next five months, the Committee widely collected opinions from Hong Kong and the provinces, autonomous regions, municipalities directly under the Central Government and relevant departments on the Mainland and, based on the collected opinions, the Committee made more than 100 revisions in the draft version. In January 1989, at its eighth plenary session, the Drafting Committee voted by secret ballot on the draft Hong Kong Basic Law and its Annexes and related documents to be submitted to the Standing Committee of the National People's Congress, Article by Article and document by document. Except for Article 19 in the draft Basic Law, all other provisions, Annexes and related documents were adopted by a two-thirds majority. At its sixth session held in February 1989, the Standing Committee of the Seventh National People's Congress decided to promulgate the Hong Kong Basic Law (Draft), its Annexes and other related documents to widely solicit opinions from Hong Kong; from the provinces, autonomous regions and municipalities directly under the Central Government on the Mainland; and from central government departments, democratic parties, mass organizations and experts as well as from the general departments of the People's Liberation Army. After an eight-month opinion-soliciting period followed by a careful study of the opinions collected from all circles, the special groups jointly put forward 24 amendment bills, including the one regarding Article 19 in the Hong Kong Basic Law (Draft). At the ninth plenary session of the Drafting Committee in February this year, those amendment bills were voted upon by secret ballot one by one and all of them were passed by an over two-thirds majority. Then, all relevant provisions in the original draft were replaced by provisions recommended by the amendment bills. With this, the work of drawing up the Hong Kong Basic Law (Draft), its Annexes and other related documents was complete.

The collection and selection of designs for the regional flag and regional emblem of the Hong Kong Special Administrative Region was the responsibility of the Committee for Selecting Designs for the

Regional Flag and Regional Emblem of the Hong Kong Special Administrative Region, consisting of five drafters of the Basic Law and six experts from both Hong Kong and the Mainland. After the selecting committee conducted the first and second rounds of selection from the 7,147 contributed designs, the Basic Law Drafting Committee examined and appraised the candidates recommended by the selecting committee. Since the Drafting Committee failed to decide upon a single set of designs for the regional flag and regional emblem to be submitted to the National People's Congress for examination, the selecting committee again worked out three sets of candidate designs of the regional flag and regional emblem for the Hong Kong Special Administrative Region through collective modification of certain contributed designs. The draft designs of the regional flag and regional emblem to be submitted to the National People's Congress for examination were finally selected at the ninth plenary session of the Basic Law Drafting Committee through a secret ballot. Also at the session, the second and third paragraphs under Article 10 of the draft Basic Law regarding the regional flag and regional emblem of the Special Administrative Region were passed.

Over this period of more than four years, the Drafting Committee has held nine plenary sessions, 25 meetings of the Chairman and Vice-Chairmen and two enlarged meetings of the Chairman and Vice-Chairmen; the General Working Group held three meetings; the Special Groups met 73 times; and even the Committee for Selecting Designs for the Regional Flag and Regional Emblem of the Hong Kong Special Administrative Region held five meetings.

In reviewing the work done over this period of more than four years, we must say that drafting of this legal document was conducted in a very democratic and open manner. During the process of drafting the Basic Law, members of the Drafting Committee worked together with one heart and pooled their wisdom and efforts; and each and every Article of the document was worked out after investigation, study and full discussion in which views of the majority were followed and those of the minority respected. After every meeting, reporters covering the event were briefed and the Consultative Committee for the Basic Law of the Hong Kong Special Administrative Region was immediately informed of its proceedings. The work of drafting the Basic Law was completed with the close attention and broad participation of the entire nation, especially the compatriots and people from all circles in Hong Kong. What is especially noteworthy here is that the Hong Kong Basic Law Consultative Committee, formed by people from all walks of life in Hong Kong, collected a great amount of opinions and suggestions in Hong Kong on the Basic Law and promptly referred them to the Drafting Committee and has rendered active and effective assistance to the work of drafting the Basic Law from the very beginning. The work of the Consultative Committee has been praised by the drafters.

Fellow Deputies,

The draft Basic Law that has been submitted to the current session of the National People's Congress for examination includes a Preamble and 160 Articles in nine Chapters. The nine Chapters are: Chapter I, General Principles; Chapter II, Relationship Between the Central Authorities and the Hong Kong Special Administrative Region; Chapter III, Fundamental Rights and Duties of the Residents; Chapter IV, Political Structure; Chapter V, Economy; Chapter VI, Education, Science, Culture, Sports, Religion, Labour and Social Services; Chapter VII, External Affairs; Chapter VIII, Interpretation and Amendment of the Basic Law; and Chapter IX, Supplementary Provisions. There are also three Annexes, namely, Annex I: Method for the Selection of the Chief Executive of the Hong Kong Special Administrative Region; Annex II: Method for the Formation of the Legislative Council of the Hong Kong Special Administrative Region and Its Voting Procedures; and Annex III: National Laws to be Applied in the Hong Kong Special Administrative Region.

I *On the Guiding Principle of Drafting the Hong Kong Basic Law*

"One country, two systems" is the fundamental policy of the Chinese Government for bringing about the country's reunification. In line with this policy, the Chinese Government has formulated a series of principles and policies regarding Hong Kong. The main point is to establish a special administrative region directly under the Central People's Government when China resumes its sovereignty over Hong Kong. Except for national defence and foreign affairs, which are to be administered by the Central Government, the Hong Kong Special Administrative Region will exercise a high degree of autonomy; no socialist system or policies will be practised in the Region, the original capitalist society, economic system and way of life will remain unchanged and the laws previously in force in Hong Kong will remain basically the same; Hong Kong's status as an international financial centre and free port will be maintained; and the economic interests of Britain and other countries in Hong Kong will be taken into consideration. The Chinese Government has written the above principles and policies into the Sino-British Joint Declaration on the Question of Hong Kong and proclaimed that all the principles and policies regarding Hong Kong will remain unchanged for 50 years, which is to be codified in the Basic Law. The concept of "one country, two systems" and all the principles and policies regarding Hong Kong formulated on the basis of this concept provide the fundamental guarantee for the resumption of China's sovereignty over Hong Kong and the maintenance of Hong Kong's stability and prosperity; they also conform to the basic interests of the Chinese people, particularly those of the Hong Kong compatriots.

Article 31 of China's Constitution stipulates that "the state may establish special administrative regions when necessary. The systems to be instituted in special administrative regions shall be prescribed by law enacted by the National People's Congress in the light of the specific conditions." China is a socialist country and socialism is China's basic system. To realize China's reunification, however, another kind of social system, namely, the capitalist system, may be practised in individual regions of the country. It is on the basis of China's Constitution and with "one country, two systems" as the guiding principle that all the state principles and policies regarding Hong Kong have been established in the draft Hong Kong Basic Law, which has been submitted to the present session of the National People's Congress for examination.

II On the Relationship between the Central Authorities and the Hong Kong Special Administrative Region

The relationship between the Central Authorities and the Hong Kong Special Administrative Region is one of the important issues defined by the Basic Law and is touched upon not only in Chapter II but also in Chapter I, Chapter VII, Chapter VIII and other Chapters.

Article 12 of the draft stipulates, "The Hong Kong Special Administrative Region shall be a local administrative region of the People's Republic of China, which shall enjoy a high degree of autonomy and come directly under the Central People's Government." This stipulation defines the legal status of the Hong Kong Special Administrative Region and constitutes the basis for specifying the Region's limits of power and its relationship with the Central Authorities. The Hong Kong Special Administrative Region, as an inalienable part of the People's Republic of China, will be a local administrative region directly under the Central People's Government and at the same time, it will be a special administrative region enjoying a high degree of autonomy and practising a system and executing policies different from those of the Mainland. Therefore, the draft Basic Law contains both provisions embodying the unity and sovereignty of the country and provisions empowering the Special Administrative Region with a high degree of autonomy in the light of Hong Kong's special circumstances.

The power to be exercised by, or the affairs which are the responsibility of the Standing Committee of the National People's Congress or the Central People's Government, as prescribed in the draft law, is indispensable to maintaining the state sovereignty. For example, the Central People's Government will be responsible for the Special Administrative Region's defence and foreign affairs and the Chief Executive and other principal officials of the Special Administrative Region will be appointed by the Central People's Government; a small number of national laws relating to defence and foreign affairs as well as other matters beyond the limits of the autonomy of the Special Administrative Region will be applied locally by way of promulgation or legislation by the Special Administrative Region; and in the event that the National People's Congress Standing Committee decides to declare a state of war or, by reason of turmoil within the Hong Kong Special Administrative Region which endangers national unity or security and is beyond the control of the Special Administrative Region Government, decides that the Region is in a state of emergency, the Central People's Government may issue an order applying the relevant national laws in Hong Kong. The draft law also stipulates that the Hong Kong Special Administrative Region shall enact laws on its own to prohibit any act of treason, secession, sedition, or subversion against the Central People's Government, or theft of state secret, to prohibit foreign political organizations or bodies from conducting political activities in the Region, and to prohibit political organizations or bodies of the Region from establishing ties with foreign political organizations or bodies. These stipulations are entirely necessary for maintaining the state sovereignty, unity and territorial integrity as well as for preserving Hong Kong's long-term stability and prosperity.

The high degree of autonomy to be enjoyed by the Special Administrative Region, as stipulated in the draft, embodies executive, legislative and independent judicial power, including that of final adjudication. The Special Administrative Region, authorized by the Central People's Government, also has the power to conduct relevant external affairs on its own. This shows that the Hong Kong Special Administrative Region will enjoy extensive autonomy.

Regarding the executive power, the draft law, while stipulating that the Special Administrative Region shall, on its own, conduct the administrative affairs of Hong Kong in accordance with the Basic Law, specifically defines the Special Administrative Region's autonomy in areas such as finance, economy, industry and commerce, trade, transport and communications, development and management of land and natural resources, education, science and technology, culture, sports, public order and control of entry and exit activities. For instance, the draft law stipulates that the Special Administrative Region shall have independent finances, its revenues shall not be handed over to the Central Government, and the Central Government shall not levy taxes in the Region; and the Special Administrative Region may, on its own, formulate monetary and financial policies, the Hong Kong dollar shall be the legal tender in the Region, and the authority to issue Hong Kong currency shall be vested in the Special Administrative Region Government. Also, the draft stipulates that representatives of the Special Administrative Region Government may act as members of delegations of the Chinese Government to participate in negotiations at the diplomatic level affecting Hong Kong; the Special Administrative Region may on its own, using the name "Hong Kong, China," maintain and develop relations and conclude and implement agreements with foreign states and regions and relevant international organizations in economic, trade, financial and monetary, shipping, communications, tourism, cultural, sports and other appropriate fields.

Regarding the legislative power, the draft stipulates that laws enacted by the Hong Kong Special Administrative Region legislature shall take effect upon the signature and promulgation by the Chief Executive. The laws shall be reported to the National People's Congress Standing Committee for the record, but they will go into force without being affected by this reporting. The draft also stipulates that only when it considers that any law enacted by the Special Administrative Region legislature is not in conformity with the provisions of the Basic Law regarding affairs within the responsibility of the Central Authorities or regarding the relationship between the Central Authorities and the Region, shall the National People's Congress Standing Committee return the law in question; the Standing Committee shall not amend it. Any law returned by the National People's Congress Standing Committee shall immediately be invalidated. These stipulations not only conform with the "one country, two systems" principle and are in line with provisions of the Constitution, but also take into full consideration the need for Hong Kong to enjoy a high degree of autonomy.

According to the Constitution, interpretation of laws is among the powers and functions of the National People's Congress Standing Committee. To take into account Hong Kong's special circumstances, the draft Basic Law, while stipulating that the power of interpretation of the Basic Law shall be vested in the National People's Congress Standing Committee, provides that the National People's Congress Standing Committee shall authorizes the courts of the Hong Kong Special Administrative Region to interpret on their own, in adjudicating cases, the provisions of the Basic Law which are within the limits of the autonomy of the Region. This stipulation will guarantee the power of the National People's Congress Standing Committee and also facilitate the Hong Kong Special

Administrative Region in exercising its autonomy. According to the draft, the Hong Kong Special Administrative Region courts may also interpret other provisions of the Basic Law in adjudicating cases. However, if the courts, in adjudicating cases, need to interpret the provisions of the Basic Law concerning affairs which are the responsibility of the Central People's Government, or the relationship between the Central Authorities and the Region, and if such interpretation will affect their final judgements on the cases, the courts shall seek an interpretation of the relevant provisions from the National People's Congress Standing Committee through the Court of Final Appeal of the Region. The courts, in applying those provisions, shall follow the interpretation of the National People's Congress Standing Committee. This stipulation will provide the basis for the Region's courts, in adjudicating cases, to comprehend the provisions of the Basic Law concerning affairs which are the responsibility of the Central Government or the relationship between the Central Authorities and the Hong Kong Special Administrative Region, and prevent the courts from making erroneous judgements due to inaccurate understanding.

The draft vests the courts of the Special Administrative Region with independent judicial power, including that of final adjudication. This is certainly a very special situation wherein courts in a local administrative region enjoy the power of final adjudication. Nevertheless, in view of the fact that Hong Kong will practise social and legal systems different from the Mainland's, this provision is necessary. Under the current judicial system and principles, the Hong Kong authorities have never exercised jurisdiction over acts of state such as defence and foreign affairs. While preserving the above principle, the draft stipulates that the courts of the Hong Kong Special Administrative Region shall obtain a certificate from the Chief Executive on questions of fact concerning acts of state such as defence and foreign affairs wherever such questions arise in the adjudication of cases. This certificate shall be binding on the courts. However, before issuing such a certificate, the Chief Executive shall obtain a certifying document from the Central People's Government. This stipulation not only appropriately solves the question of jurisdiction over acts of state, but also guarantees that the courts of the Region can conduct their functions in a normal way.

In addition, in order to enable the National People's Congress Standing Committee to heed fully the opinions of the people from all walks of life in Hong Kong when it makes Decisions on whether a law enacted by the Special Administrative Region legislature conforms to the provisions concerning affairs within the responsibility of the Central Authorities or to the provisions concerning the relationship between the Central Authorities and the Special Administrative Region, Decisions on adding to or deleting from the list of national laws which are applicable in the Hong Kong Special Administrative Region in Annex III and Decisions on the interpretation of and amendment to the Basic Law, the drafters have recommended that when the Basic Law comes into force, a working committee be set up under the National People's Congress Standing Committee to submit its views regarding the above questions to the National People's Congress Standing Committee. The working committee shall be composed of people from the Mainland and Hong Kong. To this end, the Hong Kong Basic Law Drafting Committee has drafted the "Proposal by the Drafting Committee for the Basic Law of the Hong Kong Special Administrative Region on the Establishment of the Committee for the Basic Law of the Hong Kong Special Administrative Region under the Standing Committee of the National People's Congress."

III On the Fundamental Rights and Duties of Hong Kong Residents

The extensive rights and freedoms enjoyed by the residents of the Hong Kong Special Administrative Region and other people residing in the Region as prescribed in Chapter III of the draft Basic Law include political, economic, cultural, social and family rights and freedoms and the freedom of person. The special features in the provisions concerning Hong Kong residents' rights and freedoms in the draft Basic Law boil down to the following two basic points:

(1) The draft provides multi-level protection for Hong Kong residents' rights and freedoms. In accordance with the characteristics of the composition of Hong Kong residents, the draft stipulates not only the general rights and freedoms enjoyed by Hong Kong residents, but

also the rights of the permanent residents and Chinese citizens living among them. It also stipulates that people other than Hong Kong residents also enjoy the rights and freedoms of Hong Kong residents in accordance with the law. In addition, while stipulating in explicit terms the fundamental rights and freedoms of Hong Kong residents, the draft also stipulates that Hong Kong residents shall enjoy the other rights and freedoms safeguarded by the laws of the Hong Kong Special Administrative Region. In view of the application in Hong Kong of the International Covenant on Civil and Political Rights, the International Covenant on Economic, Social and Cultural Rights, and international labour conventions, the draft stipulates that those provisions shall remain in force and be implemented through the laws of the Special Administrative Region. In addition to a Chapter specially devoted to Hong Kong residents' rights and freedoms, there are also provisions concerning the issue in other relevant Chapters and Articles. Thus, extensive, comprehensive and multi-level protection is provided for safeguarding Hong Kong residents' rights and freedoms.

(2) The rights, freedoms and duties of Hong Kong residents are prescribed in the draft in accordance with the principle of "one country, two systems" and in the light of Hong Kong's actual situation. They include such specific provisions as protection of private ownership of property, the freedom of movement and freedom to enter or leave the Region, the right to raise a family freely and protection of private persons' and legal entities' property. The draft also provides that the systems to safeguard the fundamental rights and freedoms of Hong Kong residents shall all be based on the Basic Law.

IV *On the Political Structure*

Chapter IV of the draft Basic Law mainly defines the formation and powers of and inter-relationship among the executive, legislature and judiciary, as well as the qualifications, powers and functions of and relevant policies regarding the Chief Executive, principal officials, members of the executive and legislative councils, judges of the courts at all levels and other members of the judiciary, and public servants of the Hong Kong Special Administrative Region. It also provides that district organizations which are not organs of political power may be established in the Region.

The political structure of the Hong Kong Special Administrative Region should accord with the principle of "one country, two systems" and aim to maintain stability and prosperity in Hong Kong in line with its legal status and actual situation. To this end, consideration must be given to the interests of the different sectors of society and the structure must facilitate the development of the capitalist economy in the Region. While the part of the existing political structure proven to be effective will be maintained, a democratic system that suits Hong Kong's reality should gradually be introduced. In accordance with this principle, Chapter IV and Annexes I and II of the Basic Law contain the following major provisions concerning the political structure of the Hong Kong Special Administrative Region:

(1) The relationship between the executive authorities and the legislature. The executive authorities and the legislature should regulate each other as well as co-ordinate their activities. To maintain Hong Kong's stability and administrative efficiency, the Chief Executive must have real power which, at the same time, should be subject to some restrictions. The draft provides for the Chief Executive to be the head of the Hong Kong Special Administrative Region and accountable to the Central People's Government and the Hong Kong Special Administrative Region. He or she is to lead the government of the Region, sign bills and budgets and promulgate laws. If the Chief Executive considers a bill passed by the Legislative Council to be not compatible with the overall interests of the Region, he or she may return it to the Legislative Council for reconsideration. If the Chief Executive refuses to sign a bill passed the second time by the Legislative Council, or the Legislative Council refuses to pass a budget or any other important bill introduced by the government, and if consensus still cannot be reached after consultations, the

Chief Executive may dissolve the Legislative Council. On the other hand, the Basic Law provides that the government of the Region must abide by the law and be accountable to the Legislative Council. It must implement laws passed by the Legislative Council and already in force, present regular policy addresses to the Council, answer questions raised by members of the Council and obtain approval from the Council for taxation and public expenditure. The Chief Executive must consult the Executive Council before making important policy decisions, introducing bills to the Legislative Council, enacting subordinate legislation, or dissolving the Legislative Council. The Basic Law also stipulates that if the bill returned by the Chief Executive is passed again by the Legislative Council with at least a two-thirds majority, the Chief Executive must sign and promulgate it within one month, unless he or she dissolves the Legislative Council. If the newly elected Legislative Council, after the old one has been dissolved, again passes by a two-thirds majority the original bill in dispute, or it still refuses to pass the original budget or any other important bill introduced by the government, the Chief Executive must resign. If the Chief Executive is found to have committed a serious breach of law or dereliction of duty and if he or she still refuses to resign, the Legislative Council may pass a motion of impeachment through the specified procedures and refer it to the Central People's Government for Decision. The provisions mentioned above embody the relationship of regulation and co-ordination between the executive authorities and the legislature.

(2) The method for the selection of the Chief Executive. The draft stipulates that the Chief Executive shall be selected by election or through consultations and be appointed by the Central People's Government. The method for selecting the Chief Executive shall be worked out in the light of the actual situation in Hong Kong and applied in a gradual and orderly way. The ultimate goal is the selection of the Chief Executive by universal suffrage upon nomination by a broadly representative nominating committee in accordance with democratic procedures. Based on these provisions, Annex I provides specific rules on selecting the Chief Executive. In the ten years between 1997 and 2007, the Chief Executive will be elected by a broadly representative Election Committee. If there is need to amend this method of election after that period, such amendments must be made with the endorsement of a two-thirds majority of all the members of the Legislative Council and the consent of the Chief Executive, and they must be submitted to the Standing Committee of the National People's Congress for approval. The method for selecting the Chief Executive is provided in an Annex to make it more amenable to revision when necessary.

(3) The method for forming the Legislative Council and its procedures for voting on bills and motions. According to the draft Basic Law, the Legislative Council will be constituted by election. The method for forming the Legislative Council will be worked out in the light of the actual situation in Hong Kong and applied in a gradual and orderly way. The ultimate goal is the election of all the members of the Legislative Council by universal suffrage. In accordance with these provisions, Annex II provides specific rules on formation of the Legislative Council. The first and second Legislative Council will be formed by members elected by functional constituencies, by the Election Committee or by geographical constituencies through direct elections. During the first 10 years after the Special Administrative Region is established, the number of seats in the Legislative Council for members elected by geographical constituencies through direct elections will be increased with each passing council, and the number of seats elected by the Election Committee will be gradually reduced. When the third Legislative Council is formed, members elected by functional constituencies and geographical constituencies through direct elections will each share half the seats of the Legislative Council. These rules accord with the principle of developing the election system in a gradual and orderly way. Annex II also stipulates that different voting procedures shall be adopted by the Legislative Council in handling bills introduced by the government and motions and bills introduced by individual members

of the Legislative Council. The passage of bills introduced by the government requires a simple majority vote of the members of the Legislative Council present. The passage of motions, bills or amendments to government bills introduced by individual members of the Legislative Council requires at least a simple majority vote by each of the two groups of members present (i.e., members returned by functional constituencies and those returned by geographical constituencies through direct elections and by the Election Committee). Such provisions take into consideration the interests of all social strata and will prevent endless debates over government bills, thus helping the government work with efficiency. Ten years after the establishment of the Special Administrative Region, if there is a need to improve the method for forming the Legislative Council and its procedures for voting on bills and motions, such improvements shall be made with the endorsement of a two-thirds majority of all the members of the Legislative Council and the consent of the Chief Executive, and they must be reported to the Standing Committee of the National People's Congress for the record. The method for forming the Legislative Council and the Council's procedures for voting on bills and motions are provided in an Annex because it is more amenable to revision when necessary.

(4) Qualifications for the Chief Executive of the Hong Kong Special Administrative Region, members of the Executive Council, the President of the Legislative Council, principal government officials, the chief justice of the Court of Final Appeal and the chief judges of the High Court, as well as Hong Kong members of the Basic Law Committee. Relevant provisions in the draft Basic Law stipulate that these posts must be held by Chinese citizens who are permanent residents of the Region with no right of abode in any foreign country. This helps define state sovereignty and reflects the principle of managing Hong Kong by the Hong Kong people. Only in this way can those maintaining the posts mentioned above hold themselves responsible to the State, the Region and the residents of Hong Kong. Based on the same considerations, relevant Articles stipulate that the Region's Legislative Council must be composed of Chinese citizens who are permanent residents of the Region with no right of abode in any foreign country. However, in view of Hong Kong's specific conditions, permanent residents of the Region who are not of Chinese nationality or who have the right of abode in foreign countries may also be elected members of the Legislative Council of the Region, provided that the proportion of such members does not exceed 20 percent of the total membership of the Council.

(5) The method for the formation of the first Government and the first Legislative Council of the Hong Kong Special Administrative Region. In line with the principles of state sovereignty and for the benefit of smooth transition, the establishment of the Special Administrative Region will be presided over by a Preparatory Committee set up by the National People's Congress. Since preparations must be made before the establishment of the first Government and the first Legislative Council and since the Basic Law will not go into effect until 1 July 1997, the Drafting Committee has suggested that the National People's Congress make a special Decision on the method for the formation of the first Government and Legislative Council and that the Decision be made public together with the Basic Law. The Drafting Committee has therefore worked out a draft of the Decision on behalf of the National People's Congress. According to this Decision, the candidate for the first Chief Executive of the Hong Kong Special Administrative Region will be recommended by a selection committee composed entirely of Hong Kong residents and then referred to the Central People's Government for appointment. If the composition of the last Hong Kong Legislative Council before the establishment of the Special Administrative Region is in conformity with the provisions of the Decision made by the National People's Congress on the method for the formation of the first Government and the first Legislative Council, those of its members who uphold the Basic Law and pledge allegiance to the Hong Kong Special Administrative Region and who meet the requirements set forth in the

> Basic Law may, upon confirmation by the Preparatory Committee, become members of the first Legislative Council of the Region. This arrangement is designed to ensure stability throughout the transition period and make the two governments dovetail without a hitch.

According to the Decision, when assuming office, the Chief Executive, principal officials, members of the Executive Council and the Legislative Council, judges of the courts at all levels and other members of the judiciary must swear to uphold the Basic Law and swear allegiance to the Hong Kong Special Administrative Region of the People's Republic of China.

V *On Economy, Education, Science, Culture, Sports, Religion, Labour and Social Services*

Chapter V of the Basic Law contains stipulations on the economic system and policies of the Hong Kong Special Administrative Region, divided into eight fields of endeavour: public finance, monetary affairs, trade, industry, commerce, land leases, shipping and civil aviation. These stipulations are indispensable to ensuring the normal operation of Hong Kong's capitalist economic mechanism and maintaining its status as an international financial centre and free port. Concerning monetary affairs, for instance, the draft Basic Law stipulates that no foreign exchange control policies shall be applied in the Hong Kong Special Administrative Region and that markets for foreign exchange, gold, securities, futures and the like shall continue. The free flow of capital within, into and out of Region as well as the free operation of financial businesses and financial markets are safeguarded. It also stipulates that the Hong Kong dollar is the legal tender in the Region and shall be freely convertible and that the authority for its issuance shall be vested in the Government of the Hong Kong Special Administrative Region. As for foreign trade, the draft Basic Law stipulates that all investments from outside the Region shall be protected by law, and the free movement of goods, intangible assets and capital shall be safeguarded. Unless otherwise prescribed by law, no tariff shall be imposed. As a separate customs territory, the Region may, using the name "Hong Kong, China," participate in relevant international organizations and trade agreements (including preferential trade arrangements), such as the General Agreement on Tariffs and Trade and arrangements regarding international trade in textiles. Export quotas, tariff preferences and other similar arrangements obtained or made by the Hong Kong Special Administrative Region shall be enjoyed exclusively by the Region. The draft Basic Law also stipulates that the Hong Kong Special Administrative Region shall strive to achieve a fiscal balance and avoid deficits in drawing up its budget. The Region may also enact laws on its own concerning the taxation system, using the previously pursued low tax policy as reference. The draft Basic Law also carries detailed stipulations concerning the major trades, land leases, shipping, civil aviation and the like.

Chapter VI of the draft Basic Law carries stipulations on the maintenance and development of Hong Kong's current systems and policies concerning education, science, culture, sports, religion, labour and social services. These stipulations involve the interests of Hong Kong residents in many aspects of public life and are important for social stability and development.

There are quite a number of Articles concerning policies in Chapter V and VI of the draft Basic Law. The Chinese Government has undertaken, in the Sino-British Joint Declaration, to write its basic principles and policies on Hong Kong and their detailed explanations as given in Annex I of the Joint Declaration into Basic Law, and Hong Kong residents from all walks of life have a strong desire for the Basic Law to reflect and protect their interests. Therefore, it was decided in the end that these Articles concerning policies should remain in the draft Basic Law, despite the differing opinions expressed over the brevity of Articles during the drafting of the law.

Finally, I should like to explain a few points about the draft designs of the regional flag and regional emblem of the Hong Kong Special Administrative Region. The regional flag carries a design of five bauhinia petals, each with a star in the middle, on a red background. The red flag represents the motherland and the bauhinia represents Hong Kong. The design implies that Hong Kong is an inalienable part of China and prospers in the embrace of the motherland. The five stars on the flower symbolize the fact that all Hong Kong compatriots love their motherland, while the red and white colours embody the principle of "one country, two systems." The regional emblem is round and bears a design similar to the one on the flag, with five red stars on a white bauhinia against a red background, which also symbolizes the principle of "one country, two systems" by the use of red and white. The outer ring of the emblem carries the words "Hong Kong Special Administrative Region of the People's Republic of China" in Chinese, and "HONG KONG" in English.

Fellow Deputies,

I hereby present my explanations concerning "The Basic Law of the Hong Kong Special Administrative Region of the People's Republic of China (Draft)," its Annexes and other relevant documents and concerning the draft designs of the regional flag and regional emblem of the Special Administrative Region, to the National People's Congress for examination.

SECTION II
NATIONAL PEOPLE'S CONGRESS AND STANDING COMMITTEE DECISIONS AND INTERPRETATIONS

Instrument 1
NPC Decision on the Basic Law of the Hong Kong Special Administrative Region of the People's Republic of China

(Adopted at the Third Session of the Seventh National People's Congress on 4 April 1990)

The Third Session of the Seventh National People's Congress adopts the Basic Law of the Hong Kong Special Administrative Region of the People's Republic of China, including Annex I: Method for the Selection of the Chief Executive of the Hong Kong Special Administrative Region, Annex II: Method for the Formation of the Legislative Council of the Hong Kong Special Administrative Region and Its Voting Procedures, Annex III: National Laws to be Applied in the Hong Kong Special Administrative Region, and the designs of the regional flag and regional emblem of the Hong Kong Special Administrative Region. Article 31 of the Constitution of the People's Republic of China provides: "The State may establish special administrative regions when necessary. The systems to be instituted in special administrative regions shall be prescribed by law enacted by the National People's Congress in the light of the specific conditions." The Basic Law of the Hong Kong Special Administrative Region is constitutional as it is enacted in accordance with the Constitution of the People's Republic of China and in the light of the specific conditions of Hong Kong. The systems, policies and laws to be instituted after the establishment of the Hong Kong Special Administrative Region shall be based on the Basic Law of the Hong Kong Special Administrative Region.

The Basic Law of the Hong Kong Special Administrative Region of the People's Republic of China shall be put into effect as of 1 July 1997

Instrument 2
NPC Decision on the Establishment of the Hong Kong Special Administrative Region

(Adopted at the Third Session of the Seventh National People's Congress on 4 April 1990)

In accordance with the provisions of Article 31 and subparagraph (13) of Article 62 of the Constitution of the People's Republic of China, the Third Session of the Seventh National People's Congress decides:

(1) The Hong Kong Special Administrative Region is to be established on 1 July 1997.

(2) The area of the Hong Kong Special Administrative Region covers the Hong Kong Island, the Kowloon Peninsula, and the islands and adjacent waters under its jurisdiction. The map of the administrative division of the Hong Kong Special Administrative Region will be published by the State Council separately.

Instrument 3
NPC Decision on the Method for the Formation of the First Government and the First Legislative Council of the Hong Kong Special Administrative Region

(Adopted at the Third Session of the Seventh National People's Congress on 4 April 1990)

(1) The first Government and the first Legislative Council of the Hong Kong Special Administrative Region shall be formed in accordance with the principles of State sovereignty and smooth transition.

(2) Within the year 1996, the National People's Congress shall establish a Preparatory Committee for the Hong Kong Special Administrative Region, which shall be responsible for preparing the establishment of the Hong Kong Special Administrative Region and shall prescribe the specific method for the formation of the first Government and the first Legislative Council in accordance with this Decision. The Preparatory Committee shall be composed of Mainland members and of Hong Kong members who shall constitute not less than 50 percent of its membership. Its chairman and members shall be appointed by the Standing Committee of the National People's Congress.

(3) The Preparatory Committee for the Hong Kong Special Administrative Region shall be responsible for preparing the establishment of the Selection Committee for the First Government of the Hong Kong Special Administrative Region (hereinafter referred to as the Selection Committee).

The Selection Committee shall be composed entirely of permanent residents of Hong Kong and must be broadly representative. It shall include Hong Kong deputies to the National People's Congress, representatives of Hong Kong members of the National Committee of the Chinese People's Political Consultative Conference, persons with practical experience who have served in Hong Kong's executive, legislative and advisory organs prior to the establishment of the Hong Kong Special Administrative Region, and persons representative of various strata and sectors of society.

The Selection Committee shall be composed of 400 members in the following proportions:

Industrial, commercial and financial sectors	25 percent
The professions	25 percent
Labour, grass-roots, religious and other sectors	25 percent
Former political figures, Hong Kong deputies to the National People's Congress, and representatives of Hong Kong members of the National Committee of the Chinese People's Political Consultative Conference	25 percent

(4) The Selection Committee shall recommend the candidate for the first Chief Executive through local consultations or through nomination and election after consultations, and report the recommended candidate to the Central People's Government for appointment. The term of office of the first Chief Executive shall be the same as the regular term.

(5) The Chief Executive of the Hong Kong Special Administrative Region shall be responsible for preparing the formation of the first Government of the Region in accordance with the Basic Law of the Hong Kong Special Administrative Region.

(6) The first Legislative Council of the Hong Kong Special Administrative Region shall be composed of 60 members, with 20 members returned by geographical constituencies through direct elections, 10 members returned by an Election Committee, and 30 members returned by functional constituencies. If the composition of the last Hong Kong Legislative Council before the establishment of the Hong Kong Special Administrative Region is in conformity with the relevant

provisions of this Decision and the Basic Law of the Hong Kong Special Administrative Region, those of its members who uphold the Basic Law of the Hong Kong Special Administrative Region of the People's Republic of China and pledge allegiance to the Hong Kong Special Administrative Region of the People's Republic of China, and who meet the requirements set forth in the Basic Law of the Region may, upon confirmation by the Preparatory Committee, become members of the first Legislative Council of the Region.

The term of office of members of the first Legislative Council of the Hong Kong Special Administrative Region shall be two years.

Instrument 4
NPC Decision on Approving the Proposal by the Drafting Committee for the Basic Law of the Hong Kong Special Administrative Region on the Establishment of the Committee for the Basic Law of the Hong Kong Special Administrative Region under the Standing Committee of the National People's Congress

(Adopted at the Third Session of the Seventh National People's Congress on 4 April 1990)

The Third Session of the Seventh National People's Congress decides:

(1) to approve the proposal by the Drafting Committee for the Basic Law of the Hong Kong Special Administrative Region on the Establishment of the Committee for the Basic Law of the Hong Kong Special Administrative Region under the Standing Committee of the National People's Congress; and

(2) to establish the Committee for the Basic Law of the Hong Kong Special Administrative Region under the Standing Committee of the National People's Congress when the Basic Law of the Hong Kong Special Administrative Region of the People's Republic of China is put into effect.

Appendix: Proposal by the Drafting Committee for the Basic Law of the Hong Kong Special Administrative Region on the Establishment of the Committee for the Basic Law of the Hong Kong Special Administrative Region under the Standing Committee of the National People's Congress

(1) Name: The Committee for the Basic Law of the Hong Kong Special Administrative Region under the Standing Committee of the National People's Congress.

(2) Affiliation: To be a working committee under the Standing Committee of the National People's Congress.

(3) Function: To study questions arising from the implementation of Articles 17, 18, 158 and 159 of the Basic Law of the Hong Kong Special Administrative Region and submit its views thereon to the Standing Committee of the National People's Congress.

(4) Composition: Twelve members, six from the Mainland and six from Hong Kong, including persons from the legal profession, appointed by the Standing Committee of the National People's

Congress for a term of office of five years. Hong Kong members shall be Chinese citizens who are permanent residents of the Hong Kong Special Administrative Region with no right of abode in any foreign country and shall be nominated jointly by the Chief Executive, President of the Legislative Council and Chief Justice of the Court of Final Appeal of the Region for appointment by the Standing Committee of the National People's Congress.

Instrument 5
NPCSC Decision on the English Text of the Basic Law of the Hong Kong Special Administrative Region of the People's Republic of China

(Adopted at the Fourteenth Session of the Standing Committee of the Seventh National People's Congress on 28 June 1990)

The 14th Meeting of the Standing Committee of the Seventh National People's Congress decides: the English translation of the Basic Law of the Hong Kong Special Administrative Region of the People's Republic of China, examined and approved under the aegis of the Law Committee of the National People's Congress, shall be the official English text and shall be equally authentic as the Chinese text. In case of any discrepancy in the meaning of wording between the English text and the Chinese text, the Chinese text shall prevail.

Instrument 6
NPCSC Decision on Treatment of the Laws Previously in Force in Hong Kong in Accordance with Article 160 of the Basic Law of the Hong Kong Special Administrative Region of the People's Republic of China

(Adopted at the Twenty Fourth Session of the Standing Committee of the Eighth National People's Congress on 23 February 1997)

Article 160 of the Basic Law of the Hong Kong Special Administrative Region of the People's Republic of China (hereinafter referred to as "the Basic Law") stipulates:

"Upon the establishment of the Hong Kong Special Administrative Region, the laws previously in force in Hong Kong shall be adopted as laws of the Region except for those which the Standing Committee of the National People's Congress declares to be in contravention of this Law. If any laws are later discovered to be in contravention of this Law, they shall be amended or cease to have force in accordance with the procedure as prescribed by this Law."

Article 8 stipulates:

"The laws previously in force in Hong Kong, that is, the common law, rules of equity, ordinances, subordinate legislation and customary law shall be maintained, except for any that contravene this Law, and subject to any amendment by the legislature of the Hong Kong Special Administrative Region."

In accordance with the above provisions, the Standing Committee of the Eighth National People's Congress examined the proposals made by the Preparatory Committee of the Hong Kong Special Administrative Region on treatment of issues relating to the laws previously in force in Hong Kong, and decides at its Twenty Fourth Session as follows:

(1) The laws previously in force in Hong Kong, which include the common law, rules of equity, ordinances, subordinate legislation and customary law, except for those which are in contravention of the Basic Law, are adopted as the laws of the Hong Kong Special Administrative Region.

(2) Such of the ordinances and subordinate legislation previously in force in Hong Kong as set out in Annex 1 to this Decision are in contravention of the Basic Law and are not adopted as the laws of the Hong Kong Special Administrative Region.

(3) Such provisions of the ordinances and subordinate legislation previously in force in Hong Kong as set out in Annex 2 to this Decision are in contravention of the Basic Law and those provisions are not adopted as the laws of the Hong Kong Special Administrative Region.

(4) Such of the laws previously in force in Hong Kong which have been adopted as the laws of the Hong Kong Special Administrative Region shall, as from 1 July 1997, be applied subject to such modifications, adaptations, limitations or exceptions as are necessary so as to bring them into conformity with the status of Hong Kong after resumption by the People's Republic of China of the exercise of sovereignty over Hong Kong as well as to be in conformity with the relevant provisions of the Basic Law. For example, the New Territories Land (Exemption) Ordinance should conform with the above principles in its application.

Apart from conforming with the above principles, the following shall be observed, that is to say, in the ordinances and subordinate legislation previously in force:

(1) laws relating to foreign affairs in respect of the Hong Kong Special Administrative Region which are inconsistent with the national laws applied in the Hong Kong Special Administrative Region shall be subject to the national laws and shall be consistent with the international rights and obligations of the Central People's Government;

(2) provisions conferring privileges on the United Kingdom or other Commonwealth countries or territories, other than provisions relating to reciprocal arrangements between Hong Kong and the United Kingdom or other Commonwealth countries or territories, are not retained;

(3) provisions relating to the rights, exemptions and obligations of military forces stationed in Hong Kong by the United Kingdom are retained subject to the provisions of the Basic Law and the Law of the People's Republic of China on the Garrisoning of the Hong Kong Special Administrative Region of the People's Republic of China, and shall apply to the military forces stationed in the Hong Kong Special Administrative Region by the Central People's Government of the People's Republic of China;

(4) provisions relating to the superior legal status of the English language as compared with the Chinese language shall be construed as providing that both the Chinese and English languages are to be official languages;

(5) provisions applying any English law may continue to be applicable by reference thereto as a transitional arrangement pending their amendment by the Hong Kong Special Administrative Region, provided that they are not prejudicial to the sovereignty of the People's Republic of China and do not contravene the provisions of the Basic Law.

(6) Subject to the provisions of paragraph (4), the names or expressions appearing in the laws previously in force in Hong Kong that are adopted as the laws of the Hong Kong Special Administrative Region shall, unless the context otherwise requires, be construed or applied in accordance with the principles of substitution provided for in Annex 3 to this Decision.

(7) If any laws previously in force in Hong Kong which have been adopted as the laws of the Hong Kong Special Administrative Region are later discovered to be in contravention of

the Basic Law, they shall be amended or shall cease to have force in accordance with the procedure as prescribed by the Basic Law.

Annex 1

The following ordinances and subordinate legislation previously in force in Hong Kong, which contravene the Basic Law, are not adopted as the laws of the Hong Kong Special Administrative Region:

(1) Trustees (Hong Kong Government Securities) Ordinance (Cap. 77, Laws of Hong Kong);

(2) Application of English Law Ordinance (Cap. 88, Laws of Hong Kong);

(3) Foreign Marriage Ordinance (Cap. 180, Laws of Hong Kong);

(4) Chinese Extradition Ordinance (Cap. 235, Laws of Hong Kong);

(5) Colony Armorial Bearings (Protection) Ordinance (Cap. 315, Laws of Hong Kong);

(6) Secretary of State for Defence (Succession to Property) Ordinance (Cap. 193, Laws of Hong Kong);

(7) Royal Hong Kong Regiment Ordinance (Cap. 199, Laws of Hong Kong);

(8) Compulsory Service Ordinance (Cap. 246, Laws of Hong Kong);

(9) Army and Royal Air Force Legal Services Ordinance (Cap. 286, Laws of Hong Kong);

(10) British Nationality (Miscellaneous Provisions) Ordinance (Cap. 186, Laws of Hong Kong);

(11) British Nationality Act 1981 (Consequential Amendments) Ordinance (Cap. 373, Laws of Hong Kong);

(12) Electoral Provisions Ordinance (Cap. 367, Laws of Hong Kong);

(13) Legislative Council (Electoral Provisions) Ordinance (Cap. 381, Laws of Hong Kong);

(14) Boundary and Election Commission Ordinance (Cap. 432, Laws of Hong Kong).

Annex 2

The following provisions in ordinances and subordinate legislation previously in force in Hong Kong, which are in contravention of the Basic Law, are not adopted as the laws of the Hong Kong Special Administrative Region:

(1) the definition of "Hong Kong permanent resident" in Section 2 of the Immigration Ordinance (Cap. 115, Laws of Hong Kong) and the provisions relating to "Hong Kong permanent residents" in Schedule 1 to that Ordinance;

(2) any provision giving effect to the British Nationality Act as applied in Hong Kong;

(3) provisions relating to election in the Urban Council Ordinance (Cap. 101, Laws of Hong Kong);

(4) provisions relating to election in the Regional Council Ordinance (Cap. 385, Laws of Hong Kong);

(5) provisions relating to election in the District Boards Ordinance (Cap. 366, Laws of Hong Kong);

(6) the Urban Council, Regional Council and District Board Election Expenses Order (sub. leg. A) and the Resolution of the Legislative Council (sub. leg. C) made under the Corrupt and Illegal Practices Ordinance (Cap. 288, Laws of Hong Kong);

(7) provisions relating to the interpretation and application of the Ordinance in Section 2(3), the effect on pre-existing legislation in Section 3 and the interpretation of subsequent

legislation in Section 4 of the Hong Kong Bill of Rights Ordinance (Cap. 383, Laws of Hong Kong);

(8) provisions relating to the overriding status of the Personal Data (Privacy) Ordinance (Cap. 486, Laws of Hong Kong) in Section 3(2) of that Ordinance;

(9) major amendments to the Societies Ordinance (Cap. 151, Laws of Hong Kong) since 17 July 1992;

(10) major amendments to the Public Order Ordinance (Cap. 245, Laws of Hong Kong) since 27 July 1995.

Annex 3

Names or expressions in the laws previously in force in Hong Kong that are adopted as the laws of the Hong Kong Special Administrative Region shall generally be construed or applied in accordance with the following principles of substitution:

(1) In the case of any provision in which any reference is made to "Her Majesty", "the Crown", "the British Government" or "the Secretary of State" or to a similar name or expression, where the content of the provision relates to title to land in Hong Kong or involves affairs provided for in the Basic Law for which the Central People's Government is responsible or involves the relationship between the Central People's Government and the Hong Kong Special Administrative Region, the name or expression shall be construed as the Central People's Government or other competent authorities of the People's Republic of China. In other cases, the name or expression shall be construed as the Government of the Hong Kong Special Administrative Region.

(2) In the case of any provision in which any reference is made to "Her Majesty in Council" or "the Privy Council", where the content of the provision relates to appellate jurisdiction, the name or expression shall be construed as the Court of Final Appeal of the Hong Kong Special Administrative Region. In other cases, the name or expression shall be dealt with in accordance with the provisions of paragraph (1) hereof.

(3) In the case of a Government agency or a semi-official agency bearing a name with the word "Royal", the word "Royal" shall be removed from its name and the agency shall be construed as the corresponding agency of the Hong Kong Special Administrative Region

(4) Any reference to "the Colony" shall be construed as a reference to the Hong Kong Special Administrative Region and any description of the territories of Hong Kong shall be construed and applied by reference to the map of the administrative division of the Hong Kong Special Administrative Region published by the State Council.

(5) Any reference to such name or expression as "the Supreme Court" or "the High Court" shall be construed respectively as a reference to the High Court or the Court of First Instance of the High Court.

(6) Any reference to such name or expression as "the Governor", "the Governor in Council", "the Chief Secretary", "the Attorney General", "the Chief Justice", "the Secretary for Home Affairs", "the Secretary for Constitutional Affairs", "the Commissioner of Customs and Excise" and "Justice" shall be construed respectively as a reference to the Chief Executive of the Hong Kong Special Administrative Region, the Chief Executive in Council, the Administrative Secretary, the Secretary for Justice, the Chief Justice of the Court of Final Appeal or Chief Judge of the High Court, the Secretary for Home Affairs, the Secretary for Constitutional Affairs, the Commissioner of Customs and Excise or Judge of the High Court.

(7) Any reference in the Chinese text of any law previously in force in Hong Kong to such name or expression as the Legislative Council, the Judiciary or the Executive Authorities or

the officers of those bodies shall be construed and applied in accordance with the relevant provisions of the Basic Law.

(8) In the case of any provision in which any reference is made to "the People's Republic of China" or "China" or to a similar name or expression, such reference shall be construed as a reference to the People's Republic of China as including Taiwan, Hong Kong and Macau; and in the case of any provision in which any reference is made to such name or expression as the Mainland, Taiwan, Hong Kong or Macau, whether separately or concurrently, such reference shall be construed respectively as a reference to the Mainland, Taiwan, Hong Kong or Macau, as a part of the People's Republic of China.

(9) In the case of any provision in which any reference is made to "foreign state" or "foreign country" or to a similar term or expression, such reference shall be construed as a reference to any state, country or territory other than the People's Republic of China, or as a reference to "any place other than the Hong Kong Special Administrative Region", as the context of the relevant law or provision requires; and in the case of any provision in which any reference is made to "alien" or to a similar term or expression, such reference shall be construed as a reference to a person other than a citizen of the People's Republic of China.

(10) Any reference in any provision to "nothing in this Ordinance shall affect or be deemed to affect the rights of Her Majesty the Queen, Her heirs or successors" shall be construed as a reference to "nothing in this Ordinance shall affect or be deemed to affect the rights of the Central People's Government or the Government of the Hong Kong Special Administrative Region under the Basic law or other laws".

Instrument 7
Order of the State Council of the People's Republic of China No. 221

It is hereby promulgated that in accordance with the Decision of the National People's Congress on the Establishment of the Hong Kong Special Administrative Region adopted at the Third Session of the Seventh National People's Congress on 4 April 1990, the map of the administrative division of the Hong Kong Special Administrative Region of the People's Republic of China was approved at the 56th Executive Meeting of the State Council on 7 May 1997.*

Appendix: Description of the boundary of the administrative division of the Hong Kong Special Administrative Region of the People's Republic of China

LI Peng
Premier
1 July 1997

Appendix: Description of the Boundary of the Administrative Division of the Hong Kong Special Administrative Region of the People's Republic of China

The boundary comprises a land and sea sector.

---

* See page 63 of this volume for the approved map.

I The Land Sector

The land sector comprises three sections as follows:

1 *Sha Tau Kok Town*

(1) The boundary starts at the eastern corner of the base of the Sha Tau Kok pier ("Point 1", Latitude 22°32'37.21" North, Longitude 114°13'34.85" East). From there, it runs directly to the mouth of the ditch running along the eastern side of San Lau Street. It then follows the centre line of the ditch, as far as the point where that line meets the centre line of Chung Ying Street ("Point 2", Latitude 22°32'45.42" North, Longitude 114°13'32.40" East).

(2) From Point 2, the boundary follows the centre line of Chung Ying Street as far as the point where that line meets the centre line of Bubu Street ("Point 3", Latitude 22°32'52.26" North, Longitude 114°13'36.91" East).

(3) From Point 3, the boundary follows a straight line to the western tip of the base of the foundation of Sha Tau Kok River Bridge in the middle of the river ("Point 4", Latitude 22°32'52.83" North, Longitude 114°13'36.86" East).

2 *Sha Tau Kok Town to Pak Kung Au*

From Point 4, the boundary runs upstream along the centre line of the Sha Tau Kok River and thence along the bottom line of the valley east of Pak Kung Au until it reaches the middle of the Pak Kung Au saddle point ("Point 5", Latitude 22°33'23.49" North, Longitude 114°12'24.25" East).

3 *Pak Kung Au to the Mouth of the Shenzhen River*

The boundary runs from Point 5 along the bottom line of the main valley west of Pak Kung Au as far as the source of the Shenzhen River at Pak Kung Au. It continues along the centre line of the Shenzhen River to the mouth of the river at Shenzhen Bay (otherwise known as Deep Bay).

After the realignment of the Shenzhen River, the boundary will follow the new centre line of the river.

II The Sea Sector

The sea sector comprises three sections as follows:

1 *Shenzhen Bay*

From the mouth of the Shenzhen River, the boundary runs along the middle of the southern navigable channel as far as Beacon 84 (otherwise known as "B" Beacon) ("Point 6", Latitude 22°30'36.23" North, Longitude 113°59'42.20" East). From there, it follows straight lines in sequence through the following two points:

(1) Beacon 83 (otherwise known as "A" Beacon) in Shenzhen Bay ("Point 7", Latitude 22°28'20.49" North, Longitude 113°56'52.10" East); and

(2) "Point 8", (Latitude 22°25'43.7" North, Longitude 113°52'08.8" East), defined as the point where the line between Point 7 and Dongjiaozui at the southernmost tip of Neilingding Island intersects the meridian line of Longitude 113°52'08.8" East.

2 *Southern Sea Section*

From Point 8, the boundary follows a series of straight lines sequentially through the following thirteen points:

(1) The boundary first runs southwards along the meridian line of Longitude 113°52'08.8" East until it reaches Latitude 22°20' North ("Point 9", Latitude 22°20' North, Longitude 113°52'08.8" East). The boundary runs thence in sequence to:

(2) "Point 10" (Latitude 22°16'23.2" North, Longitude 113°50'50.6" East), defined as the point one nautical mile northwest of the most northerly point on the coastline of Tai O;

(3) "Point 11" (Latitude 22°16'03.8" North, Longitude 113°50'20.4" East), defined as the point one nautical mile northwest of the most westerly point on the coastline of Tai O;

(4) "Point 12" (Latitude 22°14'21.4" North, Longitude 113°49'35.0" East), defined as the point one nautical mile northwest of the tip of the protruding point on the Lantau coastline southwest of Kai Kung Shan;

(5) "Point 13" (Latitude 22°13'01.4" North, Longitude 113°49'01.6" East), defined as the point one nautical mile west of the most westerly point on Kai Yet Kok off Lantau Island;

(6) "Point 14" (Latitude 22°11'01.9" North, Longitude 113°49'56.6" East), defined as the point one nautical mile southwest of the most southwesterly point on the coastline at Fan Lau Kok on Lantau Island;

(7) "Point 15" (Latitude 22°08'33.1" North, Longitude 113°53'47.6" East), defined as the mid-point of a straight line between the most southerly point on the coastline of Tai A Chau in the Soko Islands and the tip of the protruding point at Yinjiaozui on the northern coastline of Dazhizhou;

(8) "Point 16" (Latitude 22°08'12.2" North, Longitude 113°55'20.6" East), defined as the point one nautical mile south of the most southerly point on the coastline of Tau Lo Chau in the Soko Islands;

(9) "Point 17" (Latitude 22°08'54.5" North, Longitude 113°56'22.4" East), defined as the eastern point of intersection between the parallel of Latitude 22°08'54.5" North and an arc sector of one nautical mile radius centred on the most southerly point on the coastline of Tau Lo Chau in the Soko Islands;

(10) "Point 18" (Latitude 22°08'54.5" North, Longitude 114°14'09.6" East), defined as the western point of intersection between the parallel of Latitude 22°08'54.5" North and an arc sector of one nautical mile radius centred on the most southwesterly point on the coastline of Mat Chau in the Po Toi Islands;

(11) "Point 19" (Latitude 22°08'18.8" North, Longitude 114°15'18.6" East), defined as the point one nautical mile due south of Nam Kok Tsui on Po Toi Island;

(12) "Point 20" (Latitude 22°08'54.5" North, Longitude 114°17'02.4" East), defined as the eastern point of intersection between the parallel of Latitude 22°08'54.5" North and an arc sector of one nautical mile radius centred on the most southeasterly point at Tai Kok Tau on Po Toi Island;

(13) "Point 21", defined by the coordinates Latitude 22°08'54.5" North, Longitude 114°30'08.8" East.

3 *Mirs Bay*

From Point 21, the boundary then runs in sequential straight lines through the following ten points, then back to Point 1:

(1) "Point 22", defined by the coordinates Latitude 22°21'54.5" North, Longitude 114°30'08.8" East;

The Map of the Hong Kong Special Administrative Region of the People's Republic of China

1:500,000

(2) "Point 23" (Latitude 22°28'07.4" North, Longitude 114°27'17.6" East), defined as the mid-point of a straight line between the tip of the protruding point on the coastline north of Daluwan and the beacon on Shek Ngau Chau;

(3) "Point 24" (Latitude 22°32'41.9" North, Longitude 114°27'18.5" East), defined as the mid-point of a straight line between the tip of the protruding point on the coastline southwest of Shuitousha and Kang Lau Shek on Ping Chau Island;

(4) "Point 25" (Latitude 22°33'43.2" North, Longitude 114°26'02.3" East), defined as the mid-point of a straight line between Chengtoujiao and Chau Mei Kok on Ping Chau Island;

(5) "Point 26" (Latitude 22°34'06.0" North, Longitude 114°19'58.7" East), defined as the mid-point of a straight line between the tip of the protruding point on the coastline at Beizaijiao and the most northerly point on the coastline of Round Island;

(6) "Point 27" (Latitude 22°34'00.0" North, Longitude 114°18'32.7" East), defined as the mid-point of a straight line between the tip of the protruding point on the coastline at Zhengjiaozui and the most easterly point on the coastline at Kai Kung Tau on Crooked Island;

(7) "Point 28" (Latitude 22°33'55.8" North, Longitude 114°16'33.7" East), defined as the mid-point of a straight line between the tip of the protruding point on the coastline at Tangyuanchong and the most northerly point on the coastline of Crooked Island;

(8) "Point 29" (Latitude 22°33'20.6" North, Longitude 114°14'55.2" East), defined as the mid-point of a straight line between the point where the stream south of Enshang meets the sea and Cheung Pai Tau;

(9) "Point 30" (Latitude 22°33'02.6" North, Longitude 114°14'13.4" East), defined as the mid-point of a straight line between the point where the stream at Guanluxia meets the sea and Sam Kuk Tsui; and

(10) "Point 31" (Latitude 22°32'37.2" North, Longitude 114°14'01.1" East), defined as the mid-point of a straight line running due east from Point 1 to the opposite shoreline.

Note: The above geographical co-ordinates are represented by WGS84.

Instrument 8
NPCSC Decision on Approving the "Amendment to Annex I to the Basic Law of the Hong Kong Special Administrative Region of the People's Republic of China Concerning the Method for the Selection of the Chief Executive of the Hong Kong Special Administrative Region"

(Adopted at the Sixteenth Session of the Standing Committee of the Eleventh National People's Congress on 28 August 2010)

The Standing Committee of the Eleventh National People's Congress at its Sixteenth Session decides as follows:

Pursuant to Annex I to the Basic Law of the Hong Kong Special Administrative Region of the People's Republic of China, "The Interpretation by the Standing Committee of the National People's Congress of Article 7 of Annex I and Article III of Annex II to the Basic Law of the Hong Kong Special Administrative Region of the People's Republic of China" and the "Decision of the Standing Committee of the National People's Congress on Issues Relating to the Methods for Selecting the Chief Executive of the Hong

Kong Special Administrative Region and for Forming the Legislative Council of the Hong Kong Special Administrative Region in the Year 2012 and on Issues Relating to Universal Suffrage", the "Amendment to Annex I to the Basic Law of the Hong Kong Special Administrative Region of the People's Republic of China Concerning the Method for the Selection of the Chief Executive of the Hong Kong Special Administrative Region proposed by the Hong Kong Special Administrative Region" is approved.

The "Amendment to Annex I to the Basic Law of the Hong Kong Special Administrative Region of the People's Republic of China Concerning the Method for the Selection of the Chief Executive of the Hong Kong Special Administrative Region" comes into effect on the date of approval.

Appendix: Amendment to Annex I to the Basic Law of the Hong Kong Special Administrative Region of the People's Republic of China Concerning the Method for the Selection of the Chief Executive of the Hong Kong Special Administrative Region

(Approved at the Sixteenth Session of the Standing Committee of the Eleventh National People's Congress on 28 August 2010)

(1) The Election Committee for electing the fourth term Chief Executive in 2012 shall be composed of 1,200 members from the following sectors:

Industrial, commercial and financial sectors	300
The professions	300
Labour, social services, religious and other sectors	300
Members of the Legislative Council, representatives of members of the District Councils, representatives of the Heung Yee Kuk, Hong Kong deputies to the National People's Congress, and representatives of Hong Kong members of the National Committee of the Chinese People's Political Consultative Conference	300

The term of office of the Election Committee shall be five years.

(2) Candidates for the office of Chief Executive may be nominated jointly by not less than 150 members of the Election Committee. Each member may nominate only one candidate.

Instrument 9
NPCSC Proclamation No. 15

It is promulgated that pursuant to Annex II to the Basic Law of the Hong Kong Special Administrative Region of the People's Republic of China, "The Interpretation by the Standing Committee of the National People's Congress of Article 7 of Annex I and Article III of Annex II to the Basic Law of the Hong Kong Special Administrative Region of the People's Republic of China" and the "Decision of the Standing Committee of the National People's Congress on Issues Relating to the Methods for Selecting the Chief Executive of the Hong Kong Special Administrative Region and for Forming the Legislative Council of the Hong Kong Special Administrative Region in the Year 2012 and on Issues Relating to Universal Suffrage", the "Amendment to Annex II to the Basic Law of the Hong Kong Special Administrative Region of the People's Republic of China Concerning the Method for the Formation of the Legislative Council of the Hong Kong Special Administrative Region and Its Voting Procedures" is recorded by the Standing Committee of the National People's Congress.

The "Amendment to Annex II to the Basic Law of the Hong Kong Special Administrative Region of the People's Republic of China Concerning the Method for the Formation of the Legislative Council of the Hong Kong Special Administrative Region and Its Voting Procedures" comes into effect on the date of promulgation.

This proclamation is hereby made.

Standing Committee of the National People's Congress
28 August 2010

Appendix: Amendment to Annex II to the Basic Law of the Hong Kong Special Administrative Region of the People's Republic of China Concerning the Method for the Formation of the Legislative Council of the Hong Kong Special Administrative Region and Its Voting Procedures

(Recorded at the Sixteenth Session of the Standing Committee of the Eleventh National People's Congress on 28 August 2010)

The fifth term Legislative Council in the year 2012 shall be composed of 70 members, and the composition shall be as follows:

Members returned by functional constituencies	35
Members returned by geographical constituencies through direct elections	35

Instrument 10
NPCSC Decision on the Addition to or Deletion from the List of National Laws in Annex III to the Basic Law of the Hong Kong Special Administrative Region of the People's Republic of China

(Adopted at the Twenty Sixth Session of the Standing Committee of the Eighth National People's Congress on 1 July 1997)

(I) The following national laws are added to the list of laws in Annex III to the Basic Law of the Hong Kong Special Administrative Region of the People's Republic of China:

(1) Law of the People's Republic of China on the National Flag;

(2) Regulations of the People's Republic of China concerning Consular Privileges and Immunities;

(3) Law of the People's Republic of China on the National Emblem;

(4) Law of the People's Republic of China on the Territorial Sea and the Contiguous Zone;

(5) Law of the People's Republic of China on the Garrisoning of the Hong Kong Special Administrative Region.

The above national laws shall be applied with effect from 1 July 1997 by way of promulgation or legislation by the Hong Kong Special Administrative Region.

(II) The following national law is deleted from Annex III to the Basic Law of the Hong Kong Special Administrative Region:

Order on the National Emblem of the People's Republic of China Proclaimed by the Central People's Government.

Attached: Design of the national emblem, notes of explanation and instructions for use.

Instrument 11
NPCSC Decision on the Addition to the List of National Laws in Annex III to the Basic Law of the Hong Kong Special Administrative Region of the People's Republic of China

(Adopted at the Fifth Session of the Standing Committee of the Ninth National People's Congress on 4 November 1998)

The Fifth meeting of the Standing Committee of the Ninth National People's Congress decides: the national law being the "Law of the People's Republic of China on the Exclusive Economic Zone and the Continental Shelf" is added to the list of laws in Annex III to the Basic Law of the Hong Kong Special Administrative Region of the People's Republic of China.

Instrument 12
NPCSC Decision on the Addition to the List of National Laws in Annex III to the Basic Law of the Hong Kong Special Administrative Region of the People's Republic of China

(Adopted at the Eighteenth Session of the Standing Committee of the Tenth National People's Congress on 27 October 2005)

The Eighteenth meeting of the Standing Committee of the Tenth National People's Congress decides: the national law being the "Law of the People's Republic of China on Judicial Immunity from Compulsory Measures Concerning the Property of Foreign Central Banks" is added to the list of laws in Annex III to the Basic Law of the Hong Kong Special Administrative Region of the People's Republic of China.

Instrument 13
NPCSC Decision on the Addition to the List of National Laws in Annex III to the Basic Law of the Hong Kong Special Administrative Region of the People's Republic of China

(Adopted at the Thirtieth Session of the Standing Committee of the Twelfth National People's Congress on 4 November 2017)

The Thirtieth meeting of the Standing Committee of the Twelfth National People's Congress decides: the national law being the "Law of the People's Republic of China on the National Anthem" is added to the list of laws in Annex III to the Basic Law of the Hong Kong Special Administrative Region of the People's Republic of China.

Instrument 14
NPCSC Decision on the Addition to the List of National Laws in Annex III to the Basic Law of the Hong Kong Special Administrative Region of the People's Republic of China

(Adopted at the Twentieth Session of the Standing Committee of the Thirteenth National People's Congress on 30 June 2020)

In accordance with the "Decision of the National People's Congress on Establishing and Improving the Legal System and Enforcement Mechanism for the Hong Kong Special Administrative Region to Safeguard National Security", the Twentieth Session of the Standing Committee of the Thirteenth National People's Congress decides: the national law being the "Law of the People's Republic of China on Safeguarding National Security in the Hong Kong Special Administrative Region" is added to the list of laws in Annex III to the Basic Law of the Hong Kong Special Administrative Region of the People's Republic of China, and shall be applied locally by way of promulgation by the Region.

Instrument 15
NPCSC Decision on Issues Relating to the Methods for Selecting the Chief Executive of the Hong Kong Special Administrative Region in the Year 2007 and for Forming the Legislative Council of the Hong Kong Special Administrative Region in the Year 2008

(Adopted at the Ninth Session of the Standing Committee of the Tenth National People's Congress on 26 April 2004)

The Standing Committee of the Tenth National People's Congress examined at its Ninth Session the "Report on whether there is a need to amend the methods for selecting the Chief Executive of the Hong Kong Special Administrative Region in 2007 and for forming the Legislative Council of the Hong Kong Special Administrative Region in 2008" submitted by Tung Chee-hwa, the Chief Executive of the Hong Kong Special Administrative Region, on 15 April 2004 and, before the Session, had consulted the Hong Kong deputies to the National People's Congress, the Hong Kong members of the National Committee of the Chinese People's Political Consultative Conference, different sectors of Hong Kong, the Hong Kong members of the Committee for the Basic Law of the Hong Kong Special Administrative Region under the Standing Committee of the National People's Congress, and the Constitutional Development Task Force of the Government of the Hong Kong Special Administrative Region, and had also sought the views of the Hong Kong and Macao Affairs Office of the State Council. The Standing Committee of the National People's Congress was, in the course of the examination, fully aware of the recent concerns of the Hong Kong society about the methods for selecting the Chief Executive and for forming the

Legislative Council after the year 2007, including the views of some bodies and people that they wish to see the selection of the Chief Executive by universal suffrage in the year 2007 and the election of all the members of the Legislative Council by universal suffrage in the year 2008.

The Session is of the view that Articles 45 and 68 of the Basic Law of the Hong Kong Special Administrative Region of the People's Republic of China (hereinafter referred to as "Hong Kong Basic Law") already expressly provide that the methods for selecting the Chief Executive of the Hong Kong Special Administrative Region and for forming the Legislative Council of the Hong Kong Special Administrative Region shall be specified in the light of the actual situation in the Hong Kong Special Administrative Region and in accordance with the principle of gradual and orderly progress, and that the ultimate aims are the selection of the Chief Executive by universal suffrage upon nomination by a broadly representative nominating committee in accordance with democratic procedures and the election of all the members of the Legislative Council by universal suffrage. The methods for selecting the Chief Executive of the Hong Kong Special Administrative Region and for forming the Legislative Council of the Hong Kong Special Administrative Region shall conform to the above principles and provisions of the Hong Kong Basic Law. Any change relating to the methods for selecting the Chief Executive of the Hong Kong Special Administrative Region and for forming the Legislative Council of the Hong Kong Special Administrative Region shall conform to principles such as being compatible with the social, economic, political development of Hong Kong, being conducive to the balanced participation of all sectors and groups of the society, being conducive to the effective operation of the executive-led system, being conducive to the maintenance of the long-term prosperity and stability of Hong Kong.

The Session is of the view that since the establishment of the Hong Kong Special Administrative Region, Hong Kong residents have enjoyed democratic rights that they have never had before. The first Chief Executive was elected by the Selection Committee, which was composed of 400 members. The second Chief Executive was elected by the Election Committee, which was composed of 800 members. Out of the 60 members of the Legislative Council, the number of members returned by geographical constituencies through direct elections increased from 20 in the Legislative Council in the first term to 24 in the Legislative Council in the second term and will reach 30 in the Legislative Council in the third term to be formed this September. Hong Kong does not have a long history of practising democratic elections. Until now, Hong Kong residents have exercised the democratic right to participate in the selection of the Chief Executive of the Special Administrative Region for less than 7 years. Since the reunification of Hong Kong with the motherland, the number of members of the Legislative Council returned by geographical constituencies through direct elections has already substantially increased. When the set-up is such that half of the members are returned by geographical constituencies through direct elections and half of the members are returned by functional constituencies, the impact on the operation of the Hong Kong society as a whole, especially the impact on the executive-led system, remains to be examined through practice. Further, at present, different sectors of the Hong Kong society still have considerable differences on how to determine the methods for selecting the Chief Executive and for forming the Legislative Council after the year 2007 and have not come to a broad consensus. In the circumstances, conditions do not exist for the selection of the Chief Executive by universal suffrage upon nomination by a broadly representative nominating committee in accordance with democratic procedures as provided for in Article 45 of the Hong Kong Basic Law and the election of all the members of the Legislative Council by universal suffrage as provided for in Article 68 of the Hong Kong Basic Law.

In the light of the above and pursuant to the relevant provisions of the Hong Kong Basic Law and "The Interpretation by the Standing Committee of the National People's Congress of Article 7 of Annex I and Article III of Annex II to the Basic Law of the Hong Kong Special Administrative Region of the People's Republic of China", the Standing Committee of the National People's Congress makes the following Decision on the methods for selecting the Chief Executive of the Hong Kong Special Administrative Region in the year 2007 and for forming the Legislative Council of the Hong Kong Special Administrative Region in the year 2008:

(1) The election of the third Chief Executive of the Hong Kong Special Administrative Region to be held in the year 2007 shall not be by means of universal suffrage. The election of the

Legislative Council of the Hong Kong Special Administrative Region in the fourth term in the year 2008 shall not be by means of an election of all the members by universal suffrage. The ratio between members returned by functional constituencies and members returned by geographical constituencies through direct elections, who shall respectively occupy half of the seats, is to remain unchanged. The procedures for voting on bills and motions in the Legislative Council are to remain unchanged.

(2) Subject to Article 1 of this Decision not being contravened, appropriate amendments that conform to the principle of gradual and orderly progress may be made to the specific method for selecting the third Chief Executive of the Hong Kong Special Administrative Region in the year 2007 and the specific method for forming the Legislative Council of the Hong Kong Special Administrative Region in the fourth term in the year 2008 according to the provisions of Articles 45 and 68 of the Hong Kong Basic Law and the provisions of Article 7 of Annex I and Article III of Annex II to the Hong Kong Basic Law.

The Session is of the view that developing democracy in the Hong Kong Special Administrative Region in the light of the actual situation and in a gradual and orderly manner according to the provisions of the Hong Kong Basic Law has all along been the resolute and firm stance of the Central Authorities. With the development and progress in all aspects of the Hong Kong society and through the joint endeavours of the Government of the Hong Kong Special Administrative Region and Hong Kong residents, the democratic system of the Hong Kong Special Administrative Region will certainly be able to progress forward incessantly, and ultimately attain the aims of selecting the Chief Executive by universal suffrage upon nomination by a broadly representative nominating committee in accordance with democratic procedures and electing all the members of the Legislative Council by universal suffrage provided for in the Hong Kong Basic Law.

Instrument 16

NPCSC Decision on Issues Relating to the Methods for Selecting the Chief Executive of the Hong Kong Special Administrative Region and for Forming the Legislative Council of the Hong Kong Special Administrative Region in the Year 2012 and on Issues Relating to Universal Suffrage

(Adopted at the Twenty First Session of the Standing Committee of the Tenth National People's Congress on 29 December 2007)

The Standing Committee of the Tenth National People's Congress considered at its Thirty-first Session the "Report on the Public Consultation on Constitutional Development and on whether there is a need to amend the methods for selecting the Chief Executive of the Hong Kong Special Administrative Region and for forming the Legislative Council of the Hong Kong Special Administrative Region in 2012" submitted by Tsang Yam-kuen, the Chief Executive of the Hong Kong Special Administrative Region, on 12 December 2007. The Session is of the view that appropriate amendments may be made to the specific method for selecting the fourth Chief Executive and the specific method for forming the fifth term Legislative Council of the Hong Kong Special Administrative Region in the year 2012; that the election of the fifth Chief Executive of the Hong Kong Special Administrative Region in the year 2017 may be implemented by the method of universal suffrage; that after the Chief Executive is selected by universal suffrage, the election of the Legislative Council of the Hong Kong Special Administrative Region may be implemented by the method of electing all the members by universal suffrage. Pursuant to the relevant provisions of the Basic Law of the Hong Kong Special Administrative Region of the People's Republic of China and "The Interpretation by the Standing Committee of the National People's Congress of Article 7 of Annex I and Article III of Annex II to the Basic Law of the Hong Kong Special Administrative Region of the People's Republic of China", the Standing Committee of the National People's Congress hereby makes the following Decision:

(1) The election of the fourth Chief Executive of the Hong Kong Special Administrative Region in the year 2012 shall not be implemented by the method of universal suffrage. The election of the fifth term Legislative Council of the Hong Kong Special Administrative Region in the year 2012 shall not be implemented by the method of electing all the members by universal suffrage. The half-and-half ratio between members returned by functional constituencies and members returned by geographical constituencies through direct elections shall remain unchanged. The procedures for voting on bills and motions in the Legislative Council shall remain unchanged. Subject to the aforementioned, appropriate amendments conforming to the principle of gradual and orderly progress may be made to the specific method for selecting the fourth Chief Executive of the Hong Kong Special Administrative Region in the year 2012 and the specific method for forming the fifth term Legislative Council of the Hong Kong Special Administrative Region in the year 2012 in accordance with the provisions of Articles 45 and 68, and those of Article 7 of Annex I and Article III of Annex II to the Basic Law of the Hong Kong Special Administrative Region of the People's Republic of China.

(2) At an appropriate time prior to the selection of the Chief Executive of the Hong Kong Special Administrative Region by universal suffrage, the Chief Executive shall make a report to the Standing Committee of the National People's Congress as regards the issue of amending the method for selecting the Chief Executive in accordance with the relevant provisions of the Hong Kong Basic Law and "The Interpretation by the Standing Committee of the National People's Congress of Article 7 of Annex I and Article III of Annex II to the Basic Law of the Hong Kong Special Administrative Region of the People's Republic of China"; a determination thereon shall be made by the Standing Committee of the National People's Congress. The bills on the amendments to the method for selecting the Chief Executive and the proposed amendments to such bills shall be introduced by the Government of the Hong Kong Special Administrative Region to the Legislative Council; such amendments must be made with the endorsement of a two-thirds majority of all the members of the Legislative Council and the consent of the Chief Executive and they shall be reported to the Standing Committee of the National People's Congress for approval.

(3) At an appropriate time prior to the election of all the members of the Legislative Council of the Hong Kong Special Administrative Region by universal suffrage, the Chief Executive shall make a report to the Standing Committee of the National People's Congress as regards the issue of amending the method for forming the Legislative Council and the issue of whether any corresponding amendment should be made to the procedures for voting on bills and motions in the Legislative Council in accordance with the relevant provisions of the Hong Kong Basic Law and "The Interpretation by the Standing Committee of the National People's Congress of Article 7 of Annex I and Article III of Annex II to the Basic Law of the Hong Kong Special Administrative Region of the People's Republic of China"; a determination thereon shall be made by the Standing Committee of the National People's Congress. The bills on the amendments to the method for forming the Legislative Council and its procedures for voting on bills and motions and the proposed amendments to such bills shall be introduced by the Government of the Hong Kong Special Administrative Region to the Legislative Council; such amendments must be made with the endorsement of a two-thirds majority of all the members of the Legislative Council and the consent of the Chief Executive and they shall be reported to the Standing Committee of the National People's Congress for the record.

(4) If no amendment is made to the method for selecting the Chief Executive, the method for forming the Legislative Council or its procedures for voting on bills and motions in

accordance with the legal procedures, the method for selecting the Chief Executive used for the preceding term shall continue to apply, and the method for forming the Legislative Council and the procedures for voting on bills and motions used for the preceding term shall continue to apply.

The Session is of the view that in accordance with the provisions of Article 45 of the Hong Kong Basic Law, in selecting the Chief Executive of the Hong Kong Special Administrative Region by the method of universal suffrage, a broadly representative nominating committee shall be formed. The nominating committee may be formed with reference to the current provisions regarding the Election Committee in Annex I to the Hong Kong Basic Law. The nominating committee shall in accordance with democratic procedures nominate a certain number of candidates for the office of the Chief Executive, who is to be elected through universal suffrage by all registered electors of the Hong Kong Special Administrative Region, and to be appointed by the Central People's Government.

The Session is of the view that with the joint efforts of the Government of the Hong Kong Special Administrative Region and the people of Hong Kong, the democratic system of the Hong Kong Special Administrative Region will definitely make progress continuously, and that the aim of the selection of the Chief Executive and the election of all the members of the Legislative Council by universal suffrage will be realized in accordance with the Hong Kong Basic Law and this Decision.

Instrument 17
NPCSC Decision on Issues Relating to the Selection of the Chief Executive of the Hong Kong Special Administrative Region by Universal Suffrage and on the Method for Forming the Legislative Council of the Hong Kong Special Administrative Region in the Year 2016

(Adopted at the Tenth Session of the Standing Committee of the Twelfth National People's Congress on 31 August 2014)

The Standing Committee of the Twelfth National People's Congress considered at its Tenth Session the Report on whether there is a need to amend the methods for selecting the Chief Executive of the Hong Kong Special Administrative Region in 2017 and for forming the Legislative Council of the Hong Kong Special Administrative Region in 2016 submitted by Leung Chun-ying, the Chief Executive of the Hong Kong Special Administrative Region, on 15 July 2014. In the course of deliberation, the relevant views and suggestions of the Hong Kong community were given full consideration.

The Session points out that according to the Decision of the Standing Committee of the National People's Congress on Issues Relating to the Methods for Selecting the Chief Executive of the Hong Kong Special Administrative Region and for Forming the Legislative Council of the Hong Kong Special Administrative Region in the Year 2012 and on Issues Relating to Universal Suffrage adopted by the Standing Committee of the Tenth National People's Congress at its Thirty-first Session on 29 December 2007, the election of the fifth Chief Executive of the Hong Kong Special Administrative Region in the year 2017 may be implemented by the method of universal suffrage; at an appropriate time prior to the selection of the Chief Executive of the Hong Kong Special Administrative Region by universal suffrage, the Chief Executive shall make a report to the Standing Committee of the National People's Congress as regards the issue of amending the method for selecting the Chief Executive in accordance with the relevant provisions of the Hong Kong Basic Law and the Interpretation by the Standing Committee of the National People's Congress of Article 7 of Annex I and Article III of Annex II to the Basic Law of the Hong Kong Special Administrative Region of the People's Republic of China, and a determination thereon shall be made by the Standing Committee of the National People's Congress. From 4 December 2013 to 3 May 2014, the Government of the Hong Kong Special Administrative Region conducted an extensive and in-depth public consultation on the methods for selecting the Chief Executive in 2017 and for forming the Legislative Council in 2016. In the course of consultation, the Hong Kong community generally expressed the hope to see the selection of the Chief Executive by universal suffrage in 2017, and broad consensus was reached on important principles such as: the method for selecting the Chief Executive by universal suffrage shall comply with the Hong Kong Basic Law and the relevant Decisions of the Standing Committee of the National People's Congress and the Chief Executive shall be a person who loves the country and loves Hong Kong. With respect to the methods for selecting the Chief Executive by universal suffrage in 2017 and for forming the Legislative Council in 2016, the Hong Kong community put forward various views and suggestions. It was on this basis that the Chief Executive of the Hong Kong Special Administrative Region made a report to the Standing Committee of the National People's Congress on issues relating to amending the methods for selecting the Chief Executive in 2017 and for forming the Legislative Council in 2016. The Session is of the view that the report complies with the requirements of the Hong Kong Basic Law, the Interpretation by the Standing Committee of the National People's Congress of Article 7 of Annex I and Article III of Annex II to the Hong Kong Basic Law and the relevant Decisions of the Standing Committee of the National People's Congress, and reflects comprehensively and objectively the views collected during the public consultation; and is thus a positive, responsible and pragmatic report.

The Session is of the view that implementing universal suffrage for the selection of the Chief Executive represents a historic progress in Hong Kong's democratic development and a significant change in the political structure of the Hong Kong Special Administrative Region. Since the long-term prosperity and stability of Hong Kong and the sovereignty, security and development interests of the country are at stake, there is a need to proceed in a prudent and steady manner. The selection of the Chief Executive of the Hong Kong Special Administrative Region by universal suffrage has its origin in paragraph 2 of Article 45 of the Hong Kong Basic Law: "The method for selecting the Chief Executive shall be specified in the light of the actual situation in the Hong Kong Special Administrative Region and in accordance with the principle of gradual and orderly progress. The ultimate aim is the selection of the Chief Executive by universal suffrage upon nomination by a broadly representative nominating committee in accordance with democratic procedures." The formulation of the method for selecting the Chief Executive by universal suffrage must strictly comply with the relevant provisions of the Hong Kong Basic Law, accord with the principle of "one country, two systems", and befit the legal status of the Hong Kong Special Administrative Region. It must meet the interests of different sectors of the society, achieve balanced participation, be conducive to the development of the capitalist economy, and make gradual and orderly progress in developing a democratic system that suits the actual situation in Hong Kong. Given the divergent views within the Hong Kong community on how to implement the Hong Kong Basic Law provisions on universal suffrage for selecting the Chief Executive, and in light of the constitutional responsibility of the Standing Committee of the National People's Congress for the proper implementation of the Hong Kong Basic Law and for deciding on the method for the selection of the Chief Executive, the Standing Committee of the National People's Congress finds it necessary to make provisions on certain core issues concerning the method for selecting the Chief Executive by universal suffrage, so as to facilitate the building of consensus within the Hong Kong community and the attainment of universal suffrage for the selection of the Chief Executive smoothly and in accordance with law.

The Session is of the view that since the Chief Executive of the Hong Kong Special Administrative Region shall be accountable to both the Hong Kong Special Administrative Region and the Central People's Government in accordance with the provisions of the Hong Kong Basic Law, the principle that the Chief Executive has to be a person who loves the country and loves Hong Kong must be upheld. This is a basic requirement of the policy of "one country, two systems". It is determined by the legal status as well as important functions and duties of the Chief Executive, and is called for by the actual need to maintain long-term prosperity and stability of Hong Kong and uphold the sovereignty, security and development interests of the country. The method for selecting the Chief Executive by universal suffrage must provide corresponding institutional safeguards for this purpose.

The Session is of the view that the amendments made to the method for forming the fifth term Legislative Council in 2012 represented major strides towards the direction of enhancing democracy. The existing formation method and voting procedures for the Legislative Council as prescribed in Annex II to the Hong Kong Basic Law will not be amended, and will continue to apply in respect of the sixth term Legislative Council in 2016. This is consistent with the principle of gradual and orderly progress in developing a democratic system that suits Hong Kong's actual situation and conforms to the majority view in the Hong Kong community. It also helps the various sectors of the Hong Kong community to focus their efforts on addressing the issues concerning universal suffrage for selecting the Chief Executive first, thus creating the conditions for attaining the aim of electing all the members of the Legislative Council by universal suffrage after the implementation of universal suffrage for the selection of the Chief Executive.

Accordingly, pursuant to the relevant provisions of the Basic Law of the Hong Kong Special Administrative Region of the People's Republic of China, the Interpretation by the Standing Committee of the National People's Congress of Article 7 of Annex I and Article III of Annex II to the Basic Law of the Hong Kong Special Administrative Region of the People's Republic of China and the Decision of the Standing Committee of the National People's Congress on Issues Relating to the Methods for Selecting the Chief Executive of the Hong Kong Special Administrative Region and for Forming the Legislative Council of the Hong Kong Special Administrative Region in the Year 2012 and on Issues Relating to Universal Suffrage, the Standing Committee of the National People's Congress makes the following Decision:

(I) Starting from 2017, the selection of the Chief Executive of the Hong Kong Special Administrative Region may be implemented by the method of universal suffrage.

(II) When the selection of the Chief Executive of the Hong Kong Special Administrative Region is implemented by the method of universal suffrage:

 (1) A broadly representative nominating committee shall be formed. The provisions for the number of members, composition and formation method of the nominating committee shall be made in accordance with the number of members, composition and formation method of the Election Committee for the Fourth Chief Executive.

 (2) The nominating committee shall nominate two to three candidates for the office of Chief Executive in accordance with democratic procedures. Each candidate must have the endorsement of more than half of all the members of the nominating committee.

 (3) All eligible electors of the Hong Kong Special Administrative Region have the right to vote in the election of the Chief Executive and elect one of the candidates for the office of Chief Executive in accordance with law.

 (4) The Chief Executive-elect, after being selected through universal suffrage, will have to be appointed by the Central People's Government.

(III) The specific method of universal suffrage for selecting the Chief Executive shall be prescribed in accordance with legal procedures through amending Annex I to the Basic Law of the Hong Kong Special Administrative Region of the People's Republic of China: The Method for the Selection of the Chief Executive of the Hong Kong Special Administrative Region. The bill on the amendments and the proposed amendments to such bill shall be introduced by the Hong Kong Special Administrative Region Government to the Legislative Council of the Hong Kong Special Administrative Region in accordance with the Hong Kong Basic Law and the provisions of this Decision. Such amendments shall obtain the endorsement of a two-thirds majority of all the members of the Legislative Council and the consent of the Chief Executive before being submitted to the Standing Committee of the National People's Congress for approval.

(IV) If the specific method of universal suffrage for selecting the Chief Executive is not adopted in accordance with legal procedures, the method used for selecting the Chief Executive for the preceding term shall continue to apply.

(V) The existing formation method and voting procedures for the Legislative Council as prescribed in Annex II to the Hong Kong Basic Law will not be amended. The formation method and procedures for voting on bills and motions of the fifth term Legislative Council will continue to apply to the sixth term Legislative Council of the Hong Kong Special Administrative Region in 2016. After the election of the Chief Executive by universal suffrage, the election of all the members of the Legislative Council of the Hong Kong Special Administrative Region may be implemented by the method of universal suffrage. At an appropriate time prior to the election of the Legislative Council by universal suffrage, the Chief Executive elected by universal suffrage shall submit a report to the Standing Committee of the National People's Congress in accordance with the relevant provisions of the Hong Kong Basic Law and the Interpretation by the Standing Committee of the National People's Congress of Article 7 of Annex I and Article III of Annex II to the Basic Law of the Hong Kong Special Administrative Region of the People's Republic of China as regards the issue of amending the method for forming the Legislative Council. A determination thereon shall be made by the Standing Committee of the National People's Congress.

The Session stresses that it is the consistent position of the central authorities to implement resolutely and firmly the principles of "one country, two systems", "Hong Kong people administering Hong Kong" and a high degree of autonomy, strictly adhere to the Hong Kong Basic Law and steadily take forward the selection of the Chief Executive by universal suffrage in 2017. It is hoped that the Hong Kong Special Administrative Region Government and all sectors of the Hong Kong community will act in accordance with the provisions of the Hong Kong Basic Law and this Decision and jointly work towards the attainment of the aim of selecting the Chief Executive by universal suffrage.

Instrument 18
NPC Decision on Improving the Electoral System of the Hong Kong Special Administrative Region*

(Adopted at the Fourth Session of the Thirteenth National People's Congress on 11 March 2021)

The Fourth Session of the Thirteenth National People's Congress deliberated the motion regarding the request for examination of the "Draft Decision of the National People's Congress on Improving the Electoral System of the Hong Kong Special Administrative Region" submitted by the Standing Committee of the National People's Congress. The Session is of the view that the return of Hong Kong to the motherland puts the region once again under the overall governance system of the country, and the Constitution of the People's Republic of China and the Basic Law of the Hong Kong Special Administrative Region of the People's Republic of China jointly form the constitutional basis of the Hong Kong Special Administrative Region. The electoral system practised in the Hong Kong Special Administrative Region, which includes the methods for the selection of the Chief Executive and for the formation of the Legislative Council, is an important part of the political structure of the Hong Kong

* This document does not currently have an official English translation. The text below is an unofficial translation by the editors at the time of publication.

Special Administrative Region. The electoral system should conform to the policy of "one country, two systems", meet the realities in the Hong Kong Special Administrative Region, and serve to ensure that Hong Kong is administered by people who love the country and love Hong Kong. The electoral system should be conducive to safeguarding China's national sovereignty, security, and development interests and help maintain the long-term prosperity and stability of Hong Kong. To improve the electoral system of the Hong Kong Special Administrative Region and develop a democratic system suited to the realities in the Hong Kong Special Administrative Region, the National People's Congress has made the following Decision pursuant to Articles 31, 62(2), 62(14), and 62(16) of the Constitution of the People's Republic of China and the relevant provisions of the Basic Law of the Hong Kong Special Administrative Region of the People's Republic of China and the Law on Safeguarding National Security in the Hong Kong Special Administrative Region of the People's Republic of China:

(1) Improving the electoral system of the Hong Kong Special Administrative Region must fully and faithfully implement the policy of "one country, two systems" under which the people of Hong Kong administer Hong Kong with a high degree of autonomy, uphold the constitutional order in the Hong Kong Special Administrative Region as established by the Constitution of the People's Republic of China and the Basic Law of the Hong Kong Special Administrative Region of the People's Republic of China, ensure the administration of Hong Kong by Hong Kong people with patriots as the main body, effectively improve the governance efficacy of the Hong Kong Special Administrative Region, and safeguard the right to vote and the right to stand for election of permanent residents of the Hong Kong Special Administrative Region.

(2) The Hong Kong Special Administrative Region shall establish an Election Committee which is broadly representative, suited to the realities in the Hong Kong Special Administrative Region, and representative of the overall interests of its society. The Election Committee shall be responsible for electing the Chief Executive designate and part of the members of the Legislative Council. The Election Committee shall also be responsible for nominating candidates for the Chief Executive and members of the Legislative Council, as well as for other matters.

The Election Committee shall be composed of 1,500 members from the following five sectors: industrial, commercial, and financial sectors; the professions; grassroots, labour, religious, and other sectors; members of the Legislative Council and representatives of district organizations; Hong Kong deputies to the National People's Congress, Hong Kong members of the National Committee of the Chinese People's Political Consultative Conference, and representatives of Hong Kong members of related national organizations.

(3) The Chief Executive of the Hong Kong Special Administrative Region shall be elected by the Election Committee and appointed by the Central People's Government.

Candidates for the office of the Chief Executive shall be nominated jointly by not less than 188 members of the Election Committee, among whom the number of members of each sector should be not less than 15. The Election Committee shall elect the Chief Executive designate by secret ballot on a one-person-one-vote basis. The election of the Chief Executive designate shall require a simple majority vote of all the members of the Election Committee.

(4) The Legislative Council of the Hong Kong Special Administrative Region shall be composed of 90 members in each term. Members of the Legislative Council shall include members returned by the Election Committee, those returned by functional constituencies, and those by geographical constituencies through direct elections.

(5) A candidate qualification review committee of the Hong Kong Special Administrative Region shall be established. The committee shall be responsible for reviewing and confirming the qualifications of candidates for the Election Committee members, the Chief Executive, and the members of the Legislative Council. The Hong Kong Special

Administrative Region shall improve the system and mechanisms related to qualification review to ensure that the qualifications of candidates are in conformity with the Basic Law of the Hong Kong Special Administrative Region of the People's Republic of China, the Law on Safeguarding National Security in the Hong Kong Special Administrative Region of the People's Republic of China, the Interpretation by the Standing Committee of the National People's Congress on Article 104 of the Basic Law of the Hong Kong Special Administrative Region of the People's Republic of China, the Decision of the Standing Committee of the National People's Congress on the Qualification of Members of the Legislative Council of the Hong Kong Special Administrative Region, and provisions of relevant local laws of the Hong Kong Special Administrative Region.

(6) The Standing Committee of the National People's Congress is authorized to, in accordance with this Decision, amend Annex I: Method for the Selection of the Chief Executive of the Hong Kong Special Administrative Region and Annex II: Method for the Formation of the Legislative Council of the Hong Kong Special Administrative Region and Its Voting Procedures, to the Basic Law of the Hong Kong Special Administrative Region of the People's Republic of China.

(7) In accordance with this Decision and Annex I: Method for the Selection of the Chief Executive of the Hong Kong Special Administrative Region and Annex II: Method for the Formation of the Legislative Council of the Hong Kong Special Administrative Region and Its Voting Procedures, to the Basic Law of the Hong Kong Special Administrative Region of the People's Republic of China as amended by the Standing Committee of the National People's Congress, the Hong Kong Special Administrative Region shall amend relevant local laws, and organize and regulate election activities accordingly.

(8) The Chief Executive of the Hong Kong Special Administrative Region shall submit in a timely manner reports to the Central People's Government on relevant important situations including the institutional arrangements for elections of the Hong Kong Special Administrative Region and the organization of the elections.

(9) The Decision shall go into effect as of the date of promulgation.

Instrument 19
NPCSC Decision on Approving the Co-operation Arrangement between the Mainland and the Hong Kong Special Administrative Region on the Establishment of the Port at the West Kowloon Station of the Guangzhou-Shenzhen-Hong Kong Express Rail Link for Implementing Co-location Arrangement

(Adopted at the Thirty-first Session of the Standing Committee of the Twelfth National People's Congress on 27 December 2017)

The Standing Committee of the Twelfth National People's Congress examined at its Thirty-first Session the motion submitted by the State Council requesting examination of the Draft Decision on Approving the Co-operation Arrangement between the Mainland and the Hong Kong Special Administrative Region on the Establishment of the Port at the West Kowloon Station of the Guangzhou-Shenzhen-Hong Kong Express Rail Link for Implementing Co-location Arrangement. In the course of its examination, the Standing Committee of the National People's Congress has fully considered the views of relevant parties of the Hong Kong Special Administrative Region and the Mainland concerning the establishment of the port juxtaposed at the Guangzhou-Shenzhen-Hong Kong Express Rail Link and the mode of conducting clearance and inspection.

The Session is of the view that the construction of the Guangzhou-Shenzhen-Hong Kong Express Rail Link and the realization of the inter-connection and mutual access between the Hong Kong Special Administrative Region and the national high-speed rail network are conducive to promoting interactions between the people of, and economic and trade activities between, the Hong Kong Special Administrative Region and the Mainland; conducive to the deepening of mutually beneficial co-operation between the Hong Kong Special Administrative Region and the Mainland; and conducive to the Hong Kong Special Administrative Region's further integration into the macro picture of national development. These have great significance for maintaining the long-term prosperity and stability of the Hong Kong Special Administrative Region. To fully unleash the high-speed rail's advantages of high speed and great efficiency, enable the vast number of passengers to fully enjoy fast and convenient service, and ensure the transport, economic and social benefits and efficiency of the Hong Kong Section of the Guangzhou-Shenzhen-Hong Kong Express Rail Link, it is necessary to implement co-location arrangement at the West Kowloon Station of the Guangzhou-Shenzhen-Hong Kong Express Rail Link in the Hong Kong Special Administrative Region ("West Kowloon Station") and to establish the Mainland Port Area for the specific purpose of conducting clearance and inspection on high-speed rail passengers and their personal belongings and luggage.

The Session is of the view that the Co-operation Arrangement is consistent with the principle of "one country, two systems" and is consistent with the Constitution and the Basic Law of the Hong Kong Special Administrative Region. Pursuant to the Constitution, the Basic Law of the Hong Kong Special Administrative Region authorizes the Hong Kong Special Administrative Region to exercise a high degree of autonomy, including implementing a separate immigration controls system, etc. The making of an appropriate arrangement through consultation on issues relating to the establishment of a port at the West Kowloon Station and the implementation of co-location arrangement thereat by the Government of the Hong Kong Special Administrative Region with the relevant parties of the Mainland is a clear demonstration of the exercise of a high degree of autonomy by the Hong Kong Special Administrative Region in accordance with law. The establishment of the Mainland Port Area at the West Kowloon Station does not alter the boundary of the administrative division of the Hong Kong Special Administrative Region, does not affect the high degree of autonomy enjoyed by the Hong Kong Special Administrative Region in accordance with law, and does not undermine the rights and freedoms enjoyed by the residents of the Hong Kong Special Administrative Region in accordance with law. Out of the need to implement co-location arrangement at the West Kowloon Station, it is appropriate that the Co-operation Arrangement makes provisions for the delineation of jurisdiction (including jurisdiction of the courts) and the application of laws of the Mainland and the Hong Kong Special Administrative Region and expressly provides for the West Kowloon Station Mainland Port Area to be regarded as being situated in the Mainland. The authorities stationed by the Mainland at the West Kowloon Station Mainland Port Area will perform their duties and functions in accordance with the laws of the Mainland, strictly confined to the Mainland Port Area. This is different from the application of national laws in the entire Hong Kong Special Administrative Region under Article 18 of the Basic Law of the Hong Kong Special Administrative Region. The acquisition of the right to use the areas of the West Kowloon Station Mainland Port Area, the duration and the fees will be provided for in a contract to be entered into by the Government of the Hong Kong Special Administrative Region and the relevant Mainland authorities, and this is consistent with the provisions of Article 7 of the Basic Law of the Hong Kong Special Administrative Region regarding the ownership of the land of the Hong Kong Special Administrative Region and the management of its uses. The implementation of co-location arrangement at the West Kowloon Station is consistent with the requirements of the Basic Law of the Hong Kong Special Administrative Region that the Government of the Hong Kong Special Administrative Region should formulate appropriate policies to promote and co-ordinate the development of various trades and provide an appropriate economic and legal environment for promoting economic developments, etc., and is consistent with the fundamental purposes of the "one country, two systems" principle and of the Basic Law of the Hong Kong Special Administrative Region.

Pursuant to the Constitution of the People's Republic of China and the Basic Law of the Hong Kong Special Administrative Region of the People's Republic of China, the Standing Committee of the National People's Congress decides as follows:

(1) The Co-operation Arrangement signed by the People's Government of Guangdong Province and the Government of the Hong Kong Special Administrative Region on 18 November 2017 is hereby approved, and it is also hereby confirmed that the Co-operation Arrangement is consistent with the Constitution and the Basic Law of the Hong Kong Special Administrative Region.

The Hong Kong Special Administrative Region should enact legislation to ensure the implementation of the Co-operation Arrangement.

(2) The establishment of the West Kowloon Station Mainland Port Area and its specific area are to be approved by the State Council.

The Mainland will exercise jurisdiction over the West Kowloon Station Mainland Port Area in accordance with the laws of the Mainland and the Co-operation Arrangement with effect from its commissioning date, and will station immigration inspection authority, customs authority, inspection and quarantine authority, integrated port administration authority and railway police authority thereat to perform duties and functions in accordance with law. The above-mentioned authorities and their personnel shall not enforce the law in any area outside the West Kowloon Station Mainland Port Area.

(3) After the commissioning of the West Kowloon Station Port, any amendment to the Co-operation Arrangement shall be approved by the State Council and shall be reported to the Standing Committee of the National People's Congress for record.

Instrument 20
NPC Decision on Establishing and Improving the Legal System and Enforcement Mechanisms for the Hong Kong Special Administrative Region to Safeguard National Security

(Adopted at the Third Session of the Thirteenth National People's Congress on 28 May 2020)

The Third Session of the Thirteenth National People's Congress (NPC) deliberated the motion regarding the request for examination of the "Draft Decision of the National People's Congress on Establishing and Improving the Legal System and Enforcement Mechanisms for the Hong Kong Special Administrative Region to Safeguard National Security" submitted by the Standing Committee of the NPC. The session considered that the risks for national security in the Hong Kong Special Administrative Region (HKSAR) have become notable in recent years. Various unlawful activities such as advocacy for "Hong Kong independence" as well as acts of secession, violence and terrorism, etc. have seriously jeopardized national sovereignty, unity and territorial integrity. Certain foreign or external forces have flagrantly interfered in Hong Kong's affairs and utilized Hong Kong to carry out activities endangering national security. To safeguard national sovereignty, security and development interests, uphold and improve the "one country, two systems" regime, safeguard the long-term prosperity and stability of Hong Kong, and safeguard the legitimate rights and interests of Hong Kong residents, the NPC has made the following Decision pursuant to Articles 31, 62(2), 62(14) and 62(16) of the

Constitution of the People's Republic of China (PRC) and the relevant provisions of the Basic Law of the HKSAR of the PRC:

(1) The country unswervingly, fully and faithfully implements the principles of "one country, two systems", "Hong Kong people administering Hong Kong" and a high degree of autonomy; upholds that Hong Kong be administered in strict accordance with the law; upholds the Constitution and the constitutional order in the HKSAR established by the Basic Law of the HKSAR; takes necessary measures to establish and improve the legal system and enforcement mechanisms for the HKSAR to safeguard national security, as well as to prevent, stop and punish in accordance with the law acts and activities endangering national security.

(2) The country resolutely opposes interference in the HKSAR's affairs by any foreign or external forces in any form, and will take necessary countermeasures to prevent, stop and punish in accordance with the law activities of secession, subversion, infiltration and sabotage carried out by foreign or external forces in Hong Kong.

(3) It is the HKSAR's constitutional responsibilities to safeguard national sovereignty, unity and territorial integrity. The HKSAR must complete the national security legislation stipulated in the Basic Law of the HKSAR at an earlier date. The HKSAR's administrative, legislative and judicial organs must, in accordance with relevant laws and regulations, effectively prevent, stop and punish acts and activities endangering national security.

(4) The HKSAR must establish and improve the institutions and enforcement mechanisms for safeguarding national security, strengthen the enforcement forces for safeguarding national security, and step up enforcement to safeguard national security. When needed, relevant national security organs of the Central People's Government (CPG) will set up agencies in the HKSAR to fulfil relevant duties to safeguard national security in accordance with the law.

(5) The Chief Executive of the HKSAR must regularly report to the CPG on the HKSAR's performance of the duty to safeguard national security, carry out national security education, and forbid acts and activities of endangering national security in accordance with the law, etc.

(6) The NPC Standing Committee is entrusted to formulate relevant laws on establishing and improving the legal system and enforcement mechanisms for the HKSAR to safeguard national security, in order to effectively prevent, stop and punish acts and activities to split the country, subvert state power, organize and carry out terrorist activities and other behaviours that seriously endanger national security, as well as activities of foreign or external forces interfering in the affairs of the HKSAR. The NPC Standing Committee decides on including relevant laws into Annex III of the Basic Law of the HKSAR of the PRC to be promulgated and implemented by the HKSAR locally.

(7) The Decision shall go into effect as of the date of promulgation.

Instrument 21
NPCSC Decision on the Continuing Discharge of Duties by the Sixth Term Legislative Council of the Hong Kong Special Administrative Region

(Adopted at the Twenty-first Session of the Standing Committee of the Thirteenth National People's Congress on 11 August 2020)

The Standing Committee of the Thirteenth National People's Congress deliberated at its Twenty-first Session the motion submitted by the State Council requesting a Decision by the Standing Committee of the National People's Congress on the continuing operation of the sixth term Legislative Council of the Hong Kong Special Administrative Region. The motion was moved following the relevant report submitted by the Chief Executive of the Hong Kong Special Administrative Region to the Central People's Government. In response to the severe local situation of the novel coronavirus epidemic, the Chief Executive of the Hong Kong Special Administrative Region in consultation with the Executive Council had decided to postpone the election for the seventh term Legislative Council of the Hong Kong Special Administrative Region for one year. As such, there will be a lacuna in the legislature of the Hong Kong Special Administrative Region. To safeguard the constitutional order and order of the rule of law in the Hong Kong Special Administrative Region and to ensure the normal governmental administration of the Government of the Hong Kong Special Administrative Region and the normal operation of the society, the Standing Committee of the National People's Congress decides, pursuant to the relevant provisions of the Constitution of the People's Republic of China and the Basic Law of the Hong Kong Special Administrative Region of the People's Republic of China, as follows:

After 30 September 2020, the sixth term Legislative Council of the Hong Kong Special Administrative Region is to continue to discharge duties for not less than one year until the seventh term of office of the Legislative Council of the Hong Kong Special Administrative Region begins. After the seventh term Legislative Council of the Hong Kong Special Administrative Region is formed in accordance with the law, its term of office remains to be four years.

The Decision is hereby announced.

Instrument 22
NPCSC Decision on Issues Relating to the Qualification of the Members of the Legislative Council of the Hong Kong Special Administrative Region*

(Adopted at the Twenty-third Session of the Standing Committee of the Thirteenth National People's Congress on 11 November 2020)

The Standing Committee of the Thirteenth National People's Congress deliberated at its Twenty-third Session the motion submitted by the State Council requesting a Decision by the Standing Committee of the National People's Congress on Issues Relating to the Qualification of the Members of the Legislative Council of the Hong Kong Special Administrative Region. The motion was moved following the request by the Chief Executive of the Hong Kong Special Administrative Region. The Session is of the view that in order to fully and faithfully implement the principle of "one country, two systems" and the Basic Law of the Hong Kong Special Administrative Region of the People's Republic of China, safeguard national sovereignty, security and development interests, and maintain long-term prosperity and stability in Hong Kong, it shall be ensured that the relevant public officers of the Hong Kong Special Administrative Region, including members of the Legislative Council, are in compliance with the legal requirements and preconditions on upholding the Basic Law of the Hong Kong Special Administrative Region of the People's Republic of China and pledging allegiance to the Hong Kong Special Administrative Region of the People's Republic of China. Accordingly, the Standing Committee of the Thirteenth National

* This document does not currently have an official English translation. The text below is an unofficial translation by the editors at the time of publication.

People's Congress approves the motion submitted by the State Council on 7 November 2020 and decides, pursuant to Articles 52, 54, and 67(1) of the Constitution of the People's Republic of China, the relevant provisions of the Basic Law of the Hong Kong Special Administrative Region of the People's Republic of China, the Decision of the National People's Congress on Establishing and Improving the Legal System and Enforcement Mechanisms for the Hong Kong Special Administrative Region to Safeguard National Security, and the Law of the People's Republic of China on Safeguarding National Security in the Hong Kong Special Administrative Region, as well as the Interpretation of the Standing Committee of the National People's Congress of Article 104 of the Basic Law of the Hong Kong Special Administrative Region of the People's Republic of China and the Decision of the Standing Committee of the National People's Congress on the Continuing Discharge of Duties by the Sixth Term Legislative Council of the Hong Kong Special Administrative Region, as follows:

A member of the Legislative Council of the Hong Kong Special Administrative Region does not fulfil the legal requirements and preconditions on upholding the Basic Law of the Hong Kong Special Administrative Region of the People's Republic of China and pledging allegiance to the Hong Kong Special Administrative Region of the People's Republic of China if the member advocates or supports the idea of "Hong Kong independence", refuses to recognize the holding and exercise of sovereignty over Hong Kong by the state, solicits intervention of foreign or external forces in the affairs of the Hong Kong Special Administrative Region, or conducts other activities endangering national security. When the above is so confirmed in accordance with law, the member will be immediately disqualified from the Legislative Council.

The Decision is applicable to the members of the sixth term Legislative Council whose nominations were concluded to be invalid in accordance with the law by the Hong Kong Special Administrative Region based on their non-conformance with the requirements outlined above during the nomination period of the election for the seventh term Legislative Council of the Hong Kong Special Administrative Region which was originally scheduled for 6 September 2020.

The Decision is applicable to any person standing for election in respect of or taking up the office of members of the Legislative Council in future where adherence to the provisions above is required.

The disqualification of members of the Legislative Council pursuant to the above provisions is to be announced by the Government of the Hong Kong Special Administrative Region.

Instrument 23
NPCSC Explanations of Some Questions Concerning the Implementation of the Nationality Law of the People's Republic of China in the Hong Kong Special Administrative Region

(Adopted at the Nineteenth Session of the Standing Committee of the Eighth National People's Congress on 15 May 1996)

According to Article 18 of and Annex III to the Basic Law of the Hong Kong Special Administrative Region of the People's Republic of China, the Nationality Law of the People's Republic of China shall be applied in the Hong Kong Special Administrative Region from 1 July 1997. Taking account of the historical background and the existing circumstances of Hong Kong, the Standing Committee gives the following explanations concerning the implementation in the Hong Kong Special Administrative Region of the Nationality Law of the People's Republic of China-

(1) Where a Hong Kong resident is of Chinese descent and was born in the Chinese territories (including Hong Kong), or where a person satisfies the criteria laid down in the

Nationality Law of the People's Republic of China for having Chinese nationality, he is a Chinese national.

(2) All Hong Kong Chinese compatriots are Chinese nationals, whether or not they are holders of the "British Dependent Territories Citizens passport" or "British Nationals (Overseas) passport". With effect from 1 July 1997, Chinese nationals mentioned above may, for the purpose of travelling to other countries and territories, continue to use the valid travel documents issued by the Government of the United Kingdom. However, they shall not be entitled to British consular protection in the Hong Kong Special Administrative Region and other parts of the People's Republic of China on account of their holding the above mentioned British travel documents.

(3) According to the Nationality Law of the People's Republic of China, the British Citizenship acquired by Chinese nationals in Hong Kong through the "British Nationality Selection Scheme" will not be recognized. They are still Chinese nationals and will not be entitled to British consular protection in the Hong Kong Special Administrative Region and other parts of the People's Republic of China.

(4) Chinese nationals of the Hong Kong Special Administrative Region with right of abode in foreign countries may, for the purpose of travelling to other countries and territories, use the relevant documents issued by the foreign governments. However, they will not be entitled to consular protection in the Hong Kong Special Administrative Region and other parts of the People's Republic of China on account of their holding the above mentioned documents.

(5) If there is a change in the nationality of a Chinese national of the Hong Kong Special Administrative Region, he may, with valid documents in support, make a declaration at the authority of the Hong Kong Special Administrative Region responsible for nationality applications.

(6) The Government of the Hong Kong Special Administrative Region is authorized to designate its Immigration Department as the authority of the Hong Kong Special Administrative Region responsible for nationality applications. The Immigration Department of the Hong Kong Special Administrative Region shall handle all nationality applications in accordance with the Nationality Law of the People's Republic of China and the foregoing provisions.

Instrument 24
NPCSC Interpretation of Articles 22(4) and 24(2)(3) of the Basic Law of the Hong Kong Special Administrative Region of the People's Republic of China

(Adopted at the Tenth Session of the Standing Committee of the Ninth National People's Congress on 26 June 1999)

The Standing Committee of the Ninth National People's Congress examined at its Tenth Session the "Motion Regarding the Request for an Interpretation of Articles 22(4) and 24(2)(3) of the Basic Law of the Hong Kong Special Administrative Region of the People's Republic of China" submitted by the State Council. The motion of the State Council was submitted upon the report furnished by the Chief Executive of the Hong Kong Special Administrative Region under the relevant provisions of Articles 43 and 48(2) of the Basic Law of the Hong Kong Special Administrative Region of the People's Republic of China. The issue raised in the Motion concerns the interpretation of the relevant provisions of the Basic

Law of the Hong Kong Special Administrative Region of the People's Republic of China by the Court of Final Appeal of the Hong Kong Special Administrative Region in its judgment dated 29 January 1999. Those relevant provisions concern affairs which are the responsibility of the Central People's Government and concern the relationship between the Central Authorities and the Hong Kong Special Administrative Region. Before making its judgment, the Court of Final Appeal had not sought an interpretation of the Standing Committee of the National People's Congress in compliance with the requirement of Article 158(3) of the Basic Law of the Hong Kong Special Administrative Region of the People's Republic of China. Moreover, the interpretation of the Court of Final Appeal is not consistent with the legislative intent. Therefore, having consulted the Committee for the Basic Law of the Hong Kong Special Administrative Region under the Standing Committee of the National People's Congress, the Standing Committee of the National People's Congress has decided to make, under the provisions of Article 67(4) of the Constitution of the People's Republic of China and Article 158(1) of the Basic Law of the Hong Kong Special Administrative Region of the People's Republic of China, an interpretation of the provisions of Articles 22(4) and 24(2)(3) of the Basic Law of the Hong Kong Special Administrative Region of the People's Republic of China as follows:

(1) The provisions of Article 22(4) of the Basic Law of the Hong Kong Special Administrative Region of the People's Republic of China regarding "For entry into the Hong Kong Special Administrative Region, people from other parts of China must apply for approval" mean as follows: People from all provinces, autonomous regions, or municipalities directly under the Central Government, including those persons of Chinese nationality born outside Hong Kong of Hong Kong permanent residents, who wish to enter the Hong Kong Special Administrative Region for whatever reason, must apply to the relevant authorities of their residential districts for approval in accordance with the relevant national laws and administrative regulations, and must hold valid documents issued by the relevant authorities before they can enter the Hong Kong Special Administrative Region. It is unlawful for people from all provinces, autonomous regions, or municipalities directly under the Central Government, including persons of Chinese nationality born outside Hong Kong of Hong Kong permanent residents, to enter the Hong Kong Special Administrative Region without complying with the appropriate approval procedure prescribed by the relevant national laws and administrative regulations.

(2) It is stipulated in the first three categories of Article 24(2) of the Basic Law of the Hong Kong Special Administrative Region of the People's Republic of China that the "permanent residents of the Hong Kong Special Administrative Region shall be:

(a) Chinese citizens born in Hong Kong before or after the establishment of the Hong Kong Special Administrative Region;

(b) Chinese citizens who have ordinarily resided in Hong Kong for a continuous period of not less than seven years before or after the establishment of the Hong Kong Special Administrative Region;

(c) Persons of Chinese nationality born outside Hong Kong of those residents listed in categories (a) and (b);".

The provisions of category (c) regarding the "persons of Chinese nationality born outside Hong Kong of those residents listed in categories (a) and (b)" mean both parents of such persons, whether born before or after the establishment of the Hong Kong Special Administrative Region, or either of such parents must have fulfilled the condition prescribed by category (1) or (2) of Article 24(2) of the Basic Law of the Hong Kong Special Administrative Region of the People's Republic of China at the time of their birth. The legislative intent as stated by this Interpretation, together with the legislative intent of all other categories of Article 24(2) of the Basic Law of the Hong Kong Special Administrative Region of the People's Republic of China, have been reflected in the "Opinions on the Implementation of Article 24(2) of the Basic Law of the Hong Kong Special Administrative Region of the People's Republic of China" adopted at the Fourth Plenary Meeting of the Preparatory Committee for the Hong Kong Special Administrative Region of the National People's Congress on 10 August 1996.

As from the promulgation of this Interpretation, the courts of the Hong Kong Special Administrative Region, when referring to the relevant provisions of the Basic Law of the Hong Kong Special Administrative Region of the People's Republic of China, shall adhere to this Interpretation. This Interpretation does not affect the right of abode in the Hong Kong Special Administrative Region which has been acquired under the judgment of the Court of Final Appeal on the relevant cases dated 29 January 1999 by the parties concerned in the relevant legal proceedings. Other than that, the question whether any other person fulfils the conditions prescribed by Article 24(2)(3) of the Basic Law of the Hong Kong Special Administrative Region of the People's Republic of China shall be determined by reference to this Interpretation.

Instrument 25
NPCSC Interpretation of Article 7 of Annex I and Article 3 of Annex II to the Basic Law of the Hong Kong Special Administrative Region of the People's Republic of China

(Adopted at the Eighth Session of the Standing Committee of the Tenth National People's Congress on 6 April 2004)

The Standing Committee of the Tenth National People's Congress examined at its Eighth Session the motion regarding the request for examination of "The Draft Interpretation of Article 7 of Annex I and Article III of Annex II to the Basic Law of the Hong Kong Special Administrative Region of the People's Republic of China" submitted by the Council of Chairmen. Having consulted the Committee for the Basic Law of the Hong Kong Special Administrative Region under the Standing Committee of the National People's Congress, the Standing Committee of the National People's Congress has decided to make, under the provisions of Article 67(4) of the Constitution of the People's Republic of China and Article 158(1) of the Basic Law of the Hong Kong Special Administrative Region of the People's Republic of China, an interpretation of the provisions of Article 7 of Annex I "Method for the Selection of the Chief Executive of the Hong Kong Special Administrative Region" to the Basic Law of the Hong Kong Special Administrative Region of the People's Republic of China regarding "If there is a need to amend the method for selecting the Chief Executives for the terms subsequent to the year 2007, such amendments must be made with the endorsement of a two-thirds majority of all the members of the Legislative Council and the consent of the Chief Executive, and they shall be reported to the Standing Committee of the National People's Congress for approval" and the provisions of Article III of Annex II "Method for the Formation of the Legislative Council of the Hong Kong Special Administrative Region and Its Voting Procedures" regarding "With regard to the method for forming the Legislative Council of the Hong Kong Special Administrative Region and its procedures for voting on bills and motions after 2007, if there is a need to amend the provisions of this Annex, such amendments must be made with the endorsement of a two-thirds majority of all the members of the Council and the consent of the Chief Executive, and they shall be reported to the Standing Committee of the National People's Congress for the record" as follows:

(1) The phrases "subsequent to the year 2007" and "after 2007" stipulated in the two above-mentioned Annexes include the year 2007.

(2) The provisions in the two above-mentioned Annexes that "if there is a need" to amend the method for selecting the Chief Executives for the terms subsequent to the year 2007 or the method for forming the Legislative Council and its procedures for voting on bills and motions after 2007 mean they may be amended or remain unamended.

(3) The provisions in the two above-mentioned Annexes that any amendment must be made with the endorsement of a two-thirds majority of all the members of the Legislative Council and the consent of the Chief Executive and shall be reported to the Standing Committee of the National People's Congress for approval or for the record mean the requisite legislative process through which the method for selecting the Chief Executive and the method for forming the Legislative Council and its procedures for voting on bills and motions are amended. Such an amendment may take effect only if it has gone through the said process, including the approval or recording ultimately given or made by the Standing Committee of the National People's Congress in accordance with law. The Chief Executive of the Hong Kong Special Administrative Region shall make a report to the Standing Committee of the National People's Congress as regards whether there is a need to make an amendment; and the Standing Committee of the National People's Congress shall, in accordance with the provisions of Articles 45 and 68 of the Basic Law of the Hong Kong Special Administrative Region of the People's Republic of China, make a determination in the light of the actual situation in the Hong Kong Special Administrative Region and in accordance with the principle of gradual and orderly progress. The bills on the amendments to the method for selecting the Chief Executive and the method for forming the Legislative Council and its procedures for voting on bills and motions and the proposed amendments to such bills shall be introduced by the Government of the Hong Kong Special Administrative Region into the Legislative Council.

(4) If no amendment is made to the method for selecting the Chief Executive, the method for forming the Legislative Council and its procedures for voting on bills and motions as stipulated in the two above-mentioned Annexes, the provisions relating to the method for selecting the Chief Executive in Annex I will still be applicable to the method for selecting the Chief Executive, and the provisions relating to the method for forming the third term of the Legislative Council in Annex II and the provisions relating to its procedures for voting on bills and motions in Annex II will still be applicable to the method for forming the Legislative Council and its procedures for voting on bills and motions.

This Interpretation is hereby proclaimed.

Instrument 26

NPCSC Interpretation of Paragraph 2, Article 53 of the Basic Law of the Hong Kong Special Administrative Region of the People's Republic of China

(Adopted at the Fifteenth Session of the Standing Committee of the Tenth National People's Congress on 27 April 2005)

The Standing Committee of the Tenth National People's Congress at its 15th session deliberated the State Council's Proposal on Requesting Interpretation of Paragraph 2, Article 53 of the Basic Law of the Hong Kong Special Administrative Region of the People's Republic of China. In accordance with item 4, Article 67 of the Constitution of the People's Republic of China and paragraph 1, Article 158 of the Basic Law of the Hong Kong Special Administrative Region of the People's Republic of China, and after consulting the Committee for the Basic Law of the HKSAR under the NPC Standing Committee, the Standing Committee of the National People's Congress hereby makes the following interpretation on paragraph 2, Article 53 of the Basic Law of the Hong Kong Special Administrative Region of the People's Republic of China.

Paragraph 2, Article 53 of the Basic Law stipulates, "In the event that the office of Chief Executive becomes vacant, a new Chief Executive shall be selected within six months in accordance with the provisions of Article 45 of this Law." The phrase "a new Chief Executive shall be selected ... in accordance with the provisions of Article 45 of this Law" implies that both the method of selecting and the term of office of the new Chief Executive shall be as prescribed and determined by the said Article.

Paragraph 3, Article 45 of the Basic Law stipulates, "The specific method for selecting the Chief Executive is prescribed in Annex I 'Method for the Selection of the Chief Executive of the Hong Kong Special Administrative Region'." Clause 1 of Annex I stipulates, "The Chief Executive shall be elected by a broadly representative Election Committee in accordance with this Law and appointed by the Central People's Government." Clause 2 of Annex I stipulates, "The term of office of the Election Committee shall be five years." Clause 7 of Annex I stipulates, "If there is a need to amend the method for selecting the Chief Executives for the terms subsequent to the year 2007, such amendments must be made with the endorsement of a two-thirds majority of all the members of the Legislative Council and the consent of the Chief Executive, and they shall be reported to the Standing Committee of the National People's Congress for approval." These provisions make it clear that prior to the year 2007, when the Chief Executive is selected by the Election Committee with a five-year term of office, in the event that the office of Chief Executive becomes vacant as he (she) fails to serve the full term of office of five years as prescribed by Article 46 of the Basic Law, the term of office of the new Chief Executive shall be the remainder of the previous Chief Executive; and that after 2007, the above-mentioned method for selecting the Chief Executives could be amended, and should the office of the Chief Executive then become vacant, the term of office of the new Chief Executive shall be determined in accordance with the amended method for the selection of the Chief Executive.

This Interpretation is hereby announced.

Instrument 27
NPCSC Interpretation of Paragraph 1, Article 13 and Article 19 of the Basic Law of the Hong Kong Special Administrative Region of the People's Republic of China

(Adopted at the Twenty Second Session of the Standing Committee of the Eleventh National People's Congress on 26 August 2011)

The Standing Committee of the Eleventh National People's Congress examined at its Twenty-second Session the motion regarding the request for examination of The Draft Interpretation of Paragraph 1, Article 13 and Article 19 of the Basic Law of the Hong Kong Special Administrative Region of the People's Republic of China by the Standing Committee of the National People's Congress submitted by the Council of Chairmen. The motion of the Council of Chairmen was submitted upon the report by the Court of Final Appeal of the Hong Kong Special Administrative Region requesting the Standing Committee of the National People's Congress to interpret the relevant provisions of the Basic Law of the Hong Kong Special Administrative Region of the People's Republic of China, in accordance with the provisions of paragraph 3, Article 158 of the Basic Law of the Hong Kong Special Administrative Region of the People's Republic of China.

The Court of Final Appeal of the Hong Kong Special Administrative Region needs to ascertain, in adjudicating a case involving the Democratic Republic of the Congo, whether the Hong Kong Special Administrative Region should apply the rules or policies on state immunity as determined by the Central People's Government. For this purpose, in accordance with the provisions of paragraph 3, Article 158 of the Basic Law of the Hong Kong Special Administrative Region of the People's Republic of China, the

Court of Final Appeal of the Hong Kong Special Administrative Region, seeks an interpretation from the Standing Committee of the National People's Congress on the following questions: "(1) whether on the true interpretation of paragraph 1, Article 13, the Central People's Government has the power to determine the rule or policy of the People's Republic of China on state immunity; (2) if so, whether, on the true interpretation of paragraph 1, Article 13 and Article 19, the Hong Kong Special Administrative Region (HKSAR), including the courts of the HKSAR: (1) is bound to apply or give effect to the rule or policy on state immunity determined by the Central People's Government under paragraph 1, Article 13; or (2) on the other hand, is at liberty to depart from the rule or policy on state immunity determined by the Central People's Government under paragraph 1, Article 13 and to adopt a different rule; (3) whether the determination by the Central People's Government as to the rule or policy on state immunity falls within 'acts of state such as defence and foreign affairs' in the first sentence of paragraph 3, Article 19 of the Basic Law; and (4) whether, upon the establishment of the HKSAR, the effect of paragraph 1, Article 13, Article 19 and the status of Hong Kong as a Special Administrative Region of the People's Republic of China upon the common law on state immunity previously in force in Hong Kong (that is, before 1 July 1997), to the extent that such common law was inconsistent with the rule or policy on state immunity as determined by the Central People's Government pursuant to paragraph 1, Article 13, was to require such common law to be applied subject to such modifications, adaptations, limitations or exceptions as were necessary to ensure that such common law is consistent with the rule or policy on state immunity as determined by the Central People's Government, in accordance with Articles 8 and 160 of the Basic Law and the Decision of the Standing Committee of the National People's Congress dated 23 February 1997 made pursuant to Article 160." The above request for interpretation by the Court of Final Appeal of the Hong Kong Special Administrative Region complies with the provisions of paragraph 3, Article 158 of the Basic Law of the Hong Kong Special Administrative Region of the People's Republic of China.

In accordance with subparagraph (4), Article 67 of the Constitution of the People's Republic of China and Article 158 of the Basic Law of the Hong Kong Special Administrative Region of the People's Republic of China, and after consulting the Committee for the Basic Law of the Hong Kong Special Administrative Region under the Standing Committee of the National People's Congress, the Standing Committee of the National People's Congress, in relation to the request for interpretation by the Court of Final Appeal of the Hong Kong Special Administrative Region, hereby makes the following interpretation of the provisions of paragraph 1, Article 13 and Article 19 of the Basic Law of the Hong Kong Special Administrative Region of the People's Republic of China and related issues:

(1) On question (1) on which an interpretation is sought by the Court of Final Appeal of the Hong Kong Special Administrative Region. According to subparagraph (9), Article 89 of the Constitution of the People's Republic of China, the State Council as the Central People's Government exercises the function and power to conduct the foreign affairs of the State; as the rules or policies on state immunity fall within diplomatic affairs in the realm of the foreign affairs of the state, the Central People's Government has the power to determine the rules or policies of the People's Republic of China on state immunity to be given effect to uniformly in the territory of the People's Republic of China. Based on the above, in accordance with the provisions of paragraph 1, Article 13 of the Basic Law of the Hong Kong Special Administrative Region of the People's Republic of China that "[t]he Central People's Government shall be responsible for the foreign affairs relating to the Hong Kong Special Administrative Region", the conduct of the foreign affairs relating to the Hong Kong Special Administrative Region falls within the power of the Central People's Government. The Central People's Government has the power to determine the rules or policies on state immunity to be applied in the Hong Kong Special Administrative Region.

(2) On question (2) on which an interpretation is sought by the Court of Final Appeal of the Hong Kong Special Administrative Region. According to the provisions of paragraph 1, Article 13 of the Basic Law of the Hong Kong Special Administrative Region of the People's Republic of China and Article 1 of this Interpretation, the Central People's Government has

the power to determine the rules or policies on state immunity to be applied in the Hong Kong Special Administrative Region. According to the provision of Article 19 of the Basic Law of the Hong Kong Special Administrative Region of the People's Republic of China and Article 3 of this Interpretation, the courts of the Hong Kong Special Administrative Region have no jurisdiction over the act of the Central People's Government in determining the rules or policies on state immunity. Therefore, when questions of immunity from jurisdiction and immunity from execution of foreign states and their properties arise in the adjudication of cases, the courts of the Hong Kong Special Administrative Region must apply and give effect to the rules or policies on state immunity determined by the Central People's Government as being applicable to the Hong Kong Special Administrative Region. Based on the above, in accordance with the provisions of paragraph 1, Article 13 and Article 19 of the Basic Law of the Hong Kong Special Administrative Region of the People's Republic of China, the Hong Kong Special Administrative Region, including the courts of the Hong Kong Special Administrative Region, is under a duty to apply or give effect to the rules or policies on state immunity that the Central People's Government has determined, and must not depart from the abovementioned rules or policies nor adopt a rule that is inconsistent with the abovementioned rules or policies.

(3) On question (3) on which an interpretation is sought by the Court of Final Appeal of the Hong Kong Special Administrative Region. State immunity concerns whether the courts of a state have jurisdiction over foreign states and their properties and whether foreign states and their properties enjoy immunity in the courts of a state. It directly relates to the state's foreign relations and international rights and obligations. Therefore, the determination as to the rules or policies on state immunity is an act of state involving foreign affairs. Based on the above, "acts of state such as defence and foreign affairs" as stipulated in paragraph 3, Article 19 of the Basic Law of the Hong Kong Special Administrative Region of the People's Republic of China includes the act of determination by the Central People's Government as to the rules or policies on state immunity.

(4) On question (4) on which an interpretation is sought by the Court of Final Appeal of the Hong Kong Special Administrative Region. According to the provisions of Articles 8 and 160 of the Basic Law of the Hong Kong Special Administrative Region of the People's Republic of China, the laws previously in force in Hong Kong shall be maintained only if there is no contravention of the Basic Law of the Hong Kong Special Administrative Region of the People's Republic of China. In accordance with the provisions of paragraph 4 of the Decision of the Standing Committee of the National People's Congress on Treatment of the Laws Previously in Force in Hong Kong in accordance with Article 160 of the Basic Law of the Hong Kong Special Administrative Region of the People's Republic of China, such of the laws previously in force in Hong Kong which have been adopted as the laws of the Hong Kong Special Administrative Region shall, as from 1 July 1997, be applied subject to such modifications, adaptations, limitations or exceptions as are necessary so as to bring them into conformity with the status of Hong Kong after resumption by the People's Republic of China of the exercise of sovereignty over Hong Kong as well as to be in conformity with the relevant provisions of the Basic Law. The Hong Kong Special Administrative Region, as a local administrative region of the People's Republic of China that enjoys a high degree of autonomy and comes directly under the Central People's Government, must give effect to the rules or policies on state immunity as determined by the Central People's Government. The laws previously in force in Hong Kong relating to the rules on state immunity may continue to be applied after 1 July 1997 only if they comply with the above requirements. Based on the above, in accordance with the provisions of paragraph 1, Article 13 and Article 19 of the Basic Law of the Hong Kong Special Administrative Region of the People's Republic of China, such of the laws previously in force in Hong Kong concerning the rules on state immunity which have been adopted as the laws of the Hong Kong Special

Administrative Region according to the Decision of the Standing Committee of the National People's Congress on Treatment of the Laws Previously in Force in Hong Kong in accordance with Article 160 of the Basic Law of the Hong Kong Special Administrative Region of the People's Republic of China, when applied as from 1 July 1997, must be subject to such modifications, adaptations, limitations or exceptions as are necessary so as to be consistent with the rules or policies on state immunity that the Central People's Government has determined.

The interpretation is hereby announced.

Instrument 28
NPCSC Interpretation of Article 104 of the Basic Law of the Hong Kong Special Administrative Region of the People's Republic of China

(Adopted by the Standing Committee of the Twelfth National People's Congress at its Twenty-fourth Session on 7 November 2016)

The Standing Committee of the Twelfth National People's Congress examined at its Twenty-fourth Session the motion regarding the request for examination of the Draft Interpretation of Article 104 of the Basic Law of the Hong Kong Special Administrative Region of the People's Republic of China submitted by the Council of Chairmen. Having consulted the Committee for the Basic Law of the Hong Kong Special Administrative Region under the Standing Committee of the National People's Congress, the Standing Committee of the National People's Congress has decided to make, under the provisions of Article 67(4) of the Constitution of the People's Republic of China and Article 158(1) of the Basic Law of the Hong Kong Special Administrative Region of the People's Republic of China, an interpretation of the provisions of Article 104 of the Basic Law of the Hong Kong Special Administrative Region of the People's Republic of China regarding "When assuming office, the Chief Executive, principal officials, members of the Executive Council and of the Legislative Council, judges of the courts at all levels and other members of the judiciary in the Hong Kong Special Administrative Region must, in accordance with law, swear to uphold the Basic Law of the Hong Kong Special Administrative Region of the People's Republic of China and swear allegiance to the Hong Kong Special Administrative Region of the People's Republic of China" as follows:

(1) "To uphold the Basic Law of the Hong Kong Special Administrative Region of the People's Republic of China" and to bear "allegiance to the Hong Kong Special Administrative Region of the People's Republic of China" as stipulated in Article 104 of the Basic Law of the Hong Kong Special Administrative Region of the People's Republic of China, are not only the legal content which must be included in the oath prescribed by the Article, but also the legal requirements and preconditions for standing for election in respect of or taking up the public office specified in the Article.

(2) The provisions in Article 104 of the Basic Law of the Hong Kong Special Administrative Region of the People's Republic of China that "When assuming office", the relevant public officers "must, in accordance with law, swear" bear the following meaning:

(a) Oath taking is the legal prerequisite and required procedure for public officers specified in the Article to assume office. No public office shall be assumed, no corresponding powers and functions shall be exercised, and no corresponding entitlements shall be enjoyed by anyone who fails to lawfully and validly take the oath or who declines to take the oath.

(b) Oath taking must comply with the legal requirements in respect of its form and content. An oath taker must take the oath sincerely and solemnly, and must accurately, completely and solemnly read out the oath prescribed by law, the content of which includes "will uphold the Basic Law of the Hong Kong Special Administrative Region of the People's Republic of China, bear allegiance to the Hong Kong Special Administrative Region of the People's Republic of China".

(c) An oath taker is disqualified forthwith from assuming the public office specified in the Article if he or she declines to take the oath. An oath taker who intentionally reads out words which do not accord with the wording of the oath prescribed by law, or takes the oath in a manner which is not sincere or not solemn, shall be treated as declining to take the oath. The oath so taken is invalid and the oath taker is disqualified forthwith from assuming the public office specified in the Article.

(d) The oath must be taken before the person authorized by law to administer the oath. The person administering the oath has the duty to ensure that the oath is taken in a lawful manner. He or she shall determine that an oath taken in compliance with this Interpretation and the requirements under the laws of the Hong Kong Special Administrative Region is valid, and that an oath which is not taken in compliance with this Interpretation and the requirements under the laws of the Hong Kong Special Administrative Region is invalid. If the oath taken is determined as invalid, no arrangement shall be made for retaking the oath.

(3) The taking of the oath stipulated by Article 104 of the Basic Law of the Hong Kong Special Administrative Region of the People's Republic of China is a legal pledge made by the public officers specified in the Article to the People's Republic of China and its Hong Kong Special Administrative Region, and is legally binding. The oath taker must sincerely believe in and strictly abide by the relevant oath prescribed by law. An oath taker who makes a false oath, or, who, after taking the oath, engages in conduct in breach of the oath, shall bear legal responsibility in accordance with law.

This Interpretation is hereby announced.

SECTION III
THE CONSTITUTION OF THE PEOPLE'S REPUBLIC OF CHINA

(1982, with 1988, 1993, 1999, 2004, 2018 amendments)

(Adopted at the Fifth Session of the Fifth National People's Congress and promulgated by the Announcement of the National People's Congress on 4 December 1982; amended in accordance with the Amendment to the Constitution of the People's Republic of China adopted at the First Session of the Seventh National People's Congress on 12 April 1988, the Amendment to the Constitution of the People's Republic of China adopted at the First Session of the Eighth National People's Congress on 29 March 1993, the Amendment to the Constitution of the People's Republic of China adopted at the Second Session of the Ninth National People's Congress on 15 March 1999, the Amendment to the Constitution of the People's Republic of China adopted at the Second Session of the Tenth National People's Congress on 14 March 2004, and the Amendment to the Constitution of the People's Republic of China adopted at the First Session of the Thirteenth National People's Congress on 11 March 2018)

Contents

Preamble

China is one of the countries with the longest histories in the world. The Chinese people of all ethnic groups jointly created its magnificent culture and have a proud revolutionary tradition.

After 1840, feudal China gradually became a semi-colonial, semi-feudal country. The Chinese people, wave upon wave, waged heroic struggles for national independence and liberation and for democracy and freedom.

In the 20th century, momentous historical changes took place in China.

The Revolution of 1911, led by Dr. Sun Yat-sen, abolished the feudal monarchy and gave birth to the Republic of China. However, the historic mission of the Chinese people to oppose imperialism and feudalism was not yet accomplished.

In 1949, after engaging in protracted, arduous and tortuous struggles, armed and in other forms, the Chinese people of all ethnic groups led by the Communist Party of China with Chairman Mao Zedong as its leader finally overthrew the rule of imperialism, feudalism and bureaucratic-capitalism, won a great victory in the New Democratic Revolution, and founded the People's Republic of China. The Chinese people thus secured power and became masters of their own country.

After the founding of the People's Republic of China, our country gradually achieved the transition from a new democratic society to a socialist society. The socialist transformation of private ownership of the means of production has been completed, the system of exploitation of man by man abolished, and a socialist system established. The people's democratic dictatorship led by the working class and based on an alliance of workers and peasants, which in essence is a dictatorship of the proletariat, has been consolidated and developed. The Chinese people and the Chinese People's Liberation Army have defeated imperialist and hegemonist aggression, sabotage and armed provocations, safeguarded national independence and security, and strengthened national defence.

Major achievements have been made in economic development. An independent and relatively complete socialist industrial system has now basically been established, and agricultural output has markedly increased. Significant advances have been made in education, science, culture and other fields, and education about socialist thought has made notable progress. The lives of the people have been considerably improved.

Both the victory in China's New Democratic Revolution and the successes in its socialist cause have been achieved by the Chinese people of all ethnic groups under the leadership of the Communist Party of China and the guidance of Marxism-Leninism and Mao Zedong Thought by upholding truth, correcting errors, and surmounting many difficulties and obstacles. Our country will long remain in the primary stage of socialism. The fundamental task for our country is to concentrate on achieving socialist modernization along the road of socialism with Chinese characteristics. We the Chinese people of all ethnic groups will continue, under the leadership of the Communist Party of China and the guidance of Marxism-Leninism, Mao Zedong Thought, Deng Xiaoping Theory, the Theory of Three Represents, the Scientific Outlook on Development and Xi Jinping Thought on Socialism with Chinese Characteristics for a New Era, to uphold the people's democratic dictatorship, stay on the socialist road, carry out reform and opening up, steadily improve the socialist institutions, develop the socialist market economy and socialist democracy, improve socialist rule of law, apply the new development philosophy, and work hard in a spirit of self-reliance to modernize step by step the country's industry, agriculture, national defence, and science and technology and promote coordinated material, political, cultural-ethical, social and ecological advancement, in order to build China into a great modern socialist country that is prosperous, strong, democratic, culturally advanced, harmonious and beautiful, and realize the great rejuvenation of the Chinese nation.

In our country the exploiting class, as a class, has been eliminated, but class struggle will continue to exist within a certain scope for a long time to come. The people of China must fight against those domestic and foreign forces and elements that are hostile to and undermine our country's socialist system.

Taiwan is part of the sacred territory of the People's Republic of China. It is the sacred duty of all the Chinese people, including our fellow Chinese in Taiwan, to achieve the great reunification of the motherland.

The cause of building socialism must rely on workers, peasants and intellectuals and unite all forces that can be united. Through the long process of revolution, development and reform, a broad patriotic united front has formed under the leadership of the Communist Party of China, with the participation of other political parties and people's organizations and including all socialist working people, people involved in building socialism, patriots who support socialism, and patriots who support China's reunification and are dedicated to the rejuvenation of the Chinese nation. This united front will continue to be consolidated and developed. The Chinese People's Political Consultative Conference is a broadly representative organization of the united front, and has played a significant historical role. In the future, it will play an even more important role in the country's political and social life and its friendly foreign activities, in socialist modernization and in safeguarding the unity and solidarity of the country. The system of multiparty cooperation and political consultation under the leadership of the Communist Party of China will continue and develop long into the future.

The People's Republic of China is a unified multi-ethnic state founded by the Chinese people of all ethnic groups. Socialist ethnic relations of equality, unity, mutual assistance and harmony are established and will continue to be strengthened. In the struggle to safeguard ethnic unity, we should oppose major ethnic group chauvinism, which mainly refers to Han chauvinism, and local ethnic chauvinism. The state makes every effort to promote the shared prosperity of all the country's ethnic groups.

The achievements of China's revolution, development and reform would have been impossible without the support of the world's people. The future of China is closely bound up with the future of the world. China pursues an independent foreign policy, observes the five principles of mutual respect for sovereignty and territorial integrity, mutual nonaggression, mutual non-interference in internal affairs, equality and mutual benefit, and peaceful coexistence, keeps to a path of peaceful development, follows a mutually beneficial strategy of opening up, works to develop diplomatic relations and economic and cultural exchanges with other countries, and promotes the building of a human community with a shared future. China consistently opposes imperialism, hegemonism and colonialism, works to strengthen its solidarity with the people of all other countries, supports oppressed peoples and other developing countries in their just struggles to win and safeguard their independence and develop their economies, and strives to safeguard world peace and promote the cause of human progress.

This Constitution affirms, in legal form, the achievements of the struggles of the Chinese people of all ethnic groups and stipulates the fundamental system and task of the state. It is the fundamental law of the state and has supreme legal force. The people of all ethnic groups, all state organs and armed forces, all political parties and social organizations, and all enterprises and public institutions in the country must treat the Constitution as the fundamental standard of conduct; they have a duty to uphold the sanctity of the Constitution and ensure its compliance.

Chapter I
General Principles

Article 1

The People's Republic of China is a socialist state governed by a people's democratic dictatorship that is led by the working class and based on an alliance of workers and peasants.

The socialist system is the fundamental system of the People's Republic of China. Leadership by the Communist Party of China is the defining feature of socialism with Chinese characteristics. It is prohibited for any organization or individual to damage the socialist system.

Article 2

All power in the People's Republic of China belongs to the people.

The organs through which the people exercise state power are the National People's Congress and the local people's congresses at all levels.

The people shall, in accordance with the provisions of law, manage state affairs, economic and cultural undertakings, and social affairs through various channels and in various ways.

Article 3

The state institutions of the People's Republic of China shall practise the principle of democratic centralism.

The National People's Congress and the local people's congresses at all levels shall be created through democratic election and shall be responsible to the people and subject to their oversight.

All administrative, supervisory, adjudicatory and procuratorial organs of the state shall be created by the people's congresses and shall be responsible to them and subject to their oversight.

The division of functions and powers between the central and local state institutions shall honour the principle of giving full play to the initiative and motivation of local authorities under the unified leadership of the central authorities.

Article 4

All ethnic groups of the People's Republic of China are equal. The state shall protect the lawful rights and interests of all ethnic minorities and uphold and promote relations of equality, unity, mutual assistance and harmony among all ethnic groups. Discrimination against and oppression of any ethnic group are prohibited; any act that undermines the unity of ethnic groups or creates divisions among them is prohibited.

The state shall, in light of the characteristics and needs of all ethnic minorities, assist all ethnic minority areas in accelerating their economic and cultural development.

All areas inhabited by ethnic minorities shall practise regional autonomy, establish autonomous organs, and exercise the power to self-govern. All ethnic autonomous areas are inseparable parts of the People's Republic of China.

All ethnic groups shall have the freedom to use and develop their own spoken and written languages and to preserve or reform their own traditions and customs.

Article 5

The People's Republic of China shall practise law-based governance and build a socialist state under the rule of law.

The state shall safeguard the unity and sanctity of the socialist legal system.

No law, administrative regulation or local regulation shall be in conflict with the Constitution.

All state organs and armed forces, all political parties and social organizations, and all enterprises and public institutions must abide by the Constitution and the law. Accountability must be enforced for all acts that violate the Constitution or laws.

No organization or individual shall have any privilege beyond the Constitution or the law.

Article 6

The foundation of the socialist economic system of the People's Republic of China is socialist public ownership of the means of production, that is, ownership by the whole people and collective ownership by the working people. The system of socialist public ownership has eradicated the system of exploitation of man by man, and practises the principle of "from each according to his ability, to each according to his work."

In the primary stage of socialism, the state shall uphold a fundamental economic system under which public ownership is the mainstay and diverse forms of ownership develop together, and shall uphold an income distribution system under which distribution according to work is the mainstay, while multiple forms of distribution exist alongside it.

Article 7

The state sector of the economy, that is, the sector of the socialist economy under ownership by the whole people, shall be the leading force in the economy. The state shall ensure the consolidation and development of the state sector of the economy.

Article 8

Rural collective economic organizations shall practise a two-tiered system of both unified and separate operations with household contract management as its basis. Rural economic cooperatives — producer, supply and marketing, credit and consumer cooperatives — are part of the socialist economy under collective ownership by the working people. Working people who belong to rural collective economic organizations shall have the right, within the scope prescribed by law, to farm cropland and hillsides allotted to them for their private use, engage in household sideline production, and raise privately owned livestock.

The various forms of cooperative economic activities in cities and towns, such as those in the handicraft, industrial, building, transport, commercial and service trades, shall all be part of the socialist economy under collective ownership by the working people.

The state shall protect the lawful rights and interests of urban and rural collective economic organizations and shall encourage, guide and assist the growth of the collective sector of the economy.

Article 9

All mineral resources, waters, forests, mountains, grasslands, unreclaimed land, mudflats and other natural resources are owned by the state, that is, by the whole people, except for the forests, mountains, grasslands, unreclaimed land and mudflats that are owned by collectives as prescribed by law.

The state shall ensure the rational use of natural resources and protect rare animals and plants. It is prohibited for any organization or individual to seize or damage natural resources by any means.

Article 10

Land in cities is owned by the state.

Land in rural and suburban areas is owned by collectives except for that which belongs to the state as prescribed by law; housing sites and cropland and hillsides allotted for private use are also owned by collectives.

The state may, in order to meet the demands of the public interest and in accordance with the provisions of law, expropriate or requisition land and furnish compensation.

No organization or individual shall unlawfully transfer land through seizure, sale and purchase, or in any other form. Land-use rights may be transferred in accordance with the provisions of law.

All organizations and individuals using land must use it in an appropriate manner.

Article 11

Non-public economic sectors that are within the scope prescribed by law, such as individually owned and private businesses, are an important component of the socialist market economy.

The state shall protect the lawful rights and interests of non-public economic sectors such as individually owned and private businesses. The state shall encourage, support and guide the development of non-public economic sectors and exercise oversight and regulation over non-public economic sectors in accordance with law.

Article 12

Socialist public property is sacred and inviolable.

The state shall protect socialist public property. It is prohibited for any organization or individual to seize or damage state or collective property by any means.

Article 13

Citizens' lawful private property is inviolable.

The state shall protect the right of citizens to own and inherit private property in accordance with the provisions of law.

The state may, in order to meet the demands of the public interest and in accordance with the provisions of law, expropriate or requisition citizens' private property and furnish compensation.

Article 14

The state shall continually raise labour productivity and improve economic performance to develop productive forces by increasing working people's motivation and level of technical skill, promoting advanced science and technology, improving the systems of economic management and enterprise operation and management, practising different forms of socialist responsibility system and improving the organization of work.

The state shall practise strict economy and combat waste.

The state shall appropriately handle accumulation and consumption, give due consideration at once to the interests of the state, collectives and individuals and, based on the development of production, gradually improve the material and cultural wellbeing of the people.

The state shall establish a sound social security system compatible with the level of economic development.

Article 15

The state shall practise a socialist market economy.

The state shall strengthen economic legislation and improve macro regulation.

The state shall, in accordance with law, prohibit disruption of the socioeconomic order by any organization or individual.

Article 16

State-owned enterprises shall, within the scope prescribed by law, have the right to operate autonomously.

State-owned enterprises shall, in accordance with the provisions of law, practise democratic management through employee congresses and other means.

Article 17

Collective economic organizations shall, on the condition that they abide by relevant laws, have the autonomy to independently conduct economic activities.

Collective economic organizations shall practise democratic management and shall, in accordance with the provisions of law, elect and remove their management personnel and decide on major issues concerning their operations and management.

Article 18

The People's Republic of China shall permit foreign enterprises, other economic organizations and individuals, to invest in China and to enter into various forms of economic cooperation with Chinese enterprises or other economic organizations in accordance with the provisions of law of the People's Republic of China.

All foreign enterprises, other foreign economic organizations and Chinese-foreign joint ventures in the territory of China shall abide by the law of the People's Republic of China. Their lawful rights and interests shall be protected by the law of the People's Republic of China.

Article 19

The state shall develop socialist education to raise the scientific and cultural level of the whole nation.

The state shall run schools of all types, provide universal compulsory primary education, develop secondary, vocational and higher education, and also develop preschool education.

The state shall develop different types of educational facilities, eliminate illiteracy, provide political, cultural, scientific, technical and field-specific education for workers, peasants, state employees and other working people, and encourage people to become accomplished individuals through self-study.

The state shall encourage collective economic organizations, state enterprises, public institutions and other social actors to run education programs of various types in accordance with the provisions of law.

The state shall promote the common speech — *Putonghua* — used nationwide.

Article 20

The state shall develop the natural and social sciences, disseminate scientific and technological knowledge, and commend and award research achievements and technological discoveries and inventions.

Article 21

To protect the people's health, the state shall develop medical and health care, develop modern medicine and traditional Chinese medicine, encourage and support the running of various medical and health facilities by rural collective economic organizations, state enterprises, public institutions and neighbourhood organizations, and promote public health activities.

To improve the people's physical fitness, the state shall develop sports and promote public sports activities.

Article 22

The state shall develop art and literature, the press, radio and television broadcasting, publishing, libraries, museums and cultural centres, and other cultural undertakings that serve the people and socialism; and shall promote public cultural activities.

The state shall protect places of scenic beauty and historical interest, valuable cultural relics and other forms of important historical and cultural heritage.

Article 23

The state shall train all kinds of specialized personnel to serve socialism, expand the ranks of intellectuals, and create the conditions for giving full play to their role in socialist modernization.

Article 24

The state shall promote socialist cultural-ethical advancement through widely accessible education on ideals, morality, culture, discipline and law, and through the formulation and observance of different forms of rules of conduct and public pledges among different urban and rural populations.

The state shall champion core socialist values; advocate the civic virtues of love for the motherland, for the people, for work, for science and for socialism; educate the people in patriotism and collectivism, in internationalism and communism, and in dialectical and historical materialism; and combat capitalist, feudal and other forms of decadent thought.

Article 25

The state shall promote family planning to see that population growth is consistent with economic and social development plans.

Article 26

The state shall protect and improve living environments and the ecological environment, and prevent and control pollution and other public hazards.

The state shall organize and encourage afforestation and protect forests.

Article 27

All state organs shall practise the principle of lean and efficient administration, a work responsibility system, and a system of employee training and evaluation in order to keep improving the quality and efficiency of their work and combat bureaucratism.

All state organs and state employees must rely on the support of the people, stay engaged with them, listen to their opinions and suggestions, accept their oversight, and work hard to serve them.

State employees, when assuming office, should make a public pledge of allegiance to the Constitution in accordance with the provisions of law.

Article 28

The state shall maintain public order, suppress treason and other criminal activities that jeopardize national security, punish criminal activities, including those that endanger public security or harm the socialist economy, and punish and reform criminals.

Article 29

The armed forces of the People's Republic of China belong to the people. Their missions are to strengthen national defence, resist aggression, defend the motherland, safeguard the people's peaceful work, participate in national development, and work hard to serve the people.

The state shall make the armed forces more revolutionary, more modernized and better regulated in order to strengthen national defence capabilities.

Article 30

The administrative areas of the People's Republic of China shall be delineated as follows:

(1) The country consists of provinces, autonomous regions and cities directly under central government jurisdiction;

(2) Provinces and autonomous regions consist of autonomous prefectures, counties, autonomous counties and cities; and

(3) Counties and autonomous counties consist of townships, ethnic townships and towns.

Cities directly under central government jurisdiction and other large cities consist of districts and counties. Autonomous prefectures consist of counties, autonomous counties and cities.

All autonomous regions, autonomous prefectures and autonomous counties are ethnic autonomous areas.

Article 31

The state may establish special administrative regions when necessary. The systems instituted in special administrative regions shall, in light of specific circumstances, be prescribed by laws enacted by the National People's Congress.

Article 32

The People's Republic of China shall protect the lawful rights and interests of foreigners in the territory of China; foreigners in the territory of China must abide by the law of the People's Republic of China.

The People's Republic of China may grant asylum to foreigners who request it on political grounds.

Chapter II
Fundamental Rights and Obligations of Citizens

Article 33

All persons holding the nationality of the People's Republic of China are citizens of the People's Republic of China.

All citizens of the People's Republic of China are equal before the law.

The state shall respect and protect human rights.

Every citizen shall enjoy the rights prescribed by the Constitution and the law and must fulfil the obligations prescribed by the Constitution and the law.

Article 34

All citizens of the People's Republic of China who have reached the age of 18, regardless of ethnicity, race, gender, occupation, family background, religious belief, level of education, property status or length of residence, shall have the right to vote and stand for election; persons deprived of political rights in accordance with law shall be an exception.

Article 35

Citizens of the People's Republic of China shall enjoy freedom of speech, the press, assembly, association, procession and demonstration.

Article 36

Citizens of the People's Republic of China shall enjoy freedom of religious belief.

No state organ, social organization or individual shall coerce citizens to believe in or not to believe in any religion, nor shall they discriminate against citizens who believe in or do not believe in any religion.

The state shall protect normal religious activities. No one shall use religion to engage in activities that disrupt public order, impair the health of citizens or interfere with the state's education system.

Religious groups and religious affairs shall not be subject to control by foreign forces.

Article 37

The personal freedom of citizens of the People's Republic of China shall not be violated.

No citizen shall be arrested unless with the approval or by the decision of a people's procuratorate or by the decision of a people's court, and arrests must be made by a public security organ.

Unlawful detention, or the unlawful deprivation or restriction of a citizen's personal freedom by other means, is prohibited; the unlawful search of a citizen's person is prohibited.

Article 38

The personal dignity of citizens of the People's Republic of China shall not be violated. It is prohibited to use any means to insult, libel or falsely accuse citizens.

Article 39

The homes of citizens of the People's Republic of China are inviolable. The unlawful search of or unlawful intrusion into a citizen's home is prohibited.

Article 40

Freedom and confidentiality of correspondence of citizens of the People's Republic of China shall be protected by law. Except in cases necessary for national security or criminal investigation, when public security organs or procuratorial organs shall examine correspondence in accordance with procedures prescribed by law, no organization or individual shall infringe on a citizen's freedom and confidentiality of correspondence for any reason.

Article 41

Citizens of the People's Republic of China shall have the right to criticize and make suggestions regarding any state organ or state employee, and have the right to file with relevant state organs complaints, charges or reports against any state organ or state employee for violations of the law or dereliction of duty, but they shall not fabricate or distort facts to make false accusations.

The state organ concerned must ascertain the facts concerning the complaints, charges or reports made by citizens and take responsibility for their handling. No one shall suppress such complaints, charges or reports or take retaliatory action.

Persons who have suffered losses resulting from infringement of their civil rights by any state organ or state employee shall have the right to receive compensation in accordance with the provisions of law.

Article 42

Citizens of the People's Republic of China shall have the right and the obligation to work.

The state shall, in various ways, create employment opportunities, strengthen worker protections, improve working conditions and, based on the development of production, increase remuneration for work and work-related benefits.

Work is an honourable duty for every citizen who is able to work. All working people in state owned enterprises and in urban and rural collective economic organizations should approach their own work as masters of their country. The state shall encourage socialist work contests and commend and award model workers and advanced workers. The state shall encourage citizens to participate in voluntary work.

The state shall provide necessary pre-employment training for its citizens.

Article 43

Working people in the People's Republic of China shall have the right to rest.

The state shall develop rest and recuperation facilities for working people and stipulate systems for employee working hours and vacations.

Article 44

The state shall, in accordance with the provisions of law, implement a retirement system for employees of enterprises, public institutions and state organs. The livelihood of retirees shall be ensured by the state and society.

Article 45

Citizens of the People's Republic of China shall have the right to material assistance from the state and society when they are aged, ill or have lost the capacity to work. The state shall develop the social insurance, social relief, and medical and health services necessary for citizens to enjoy this right.

The state and society shall guarantee the livelihood of disabled military personnel, provide pensions to the families of martyrs, and give preferential treatment to the family members of military personnel.

The state and society shall assist arrangements for the work, livelihood and education of citizens who are blind, deaf, mute or have other disabilities.

Article 46

Citizens of the People's Republic of China shall have the right and the obligation to receive education.

The state shall foster the all-round moral, intellectual and physical development of young adults, youths and children.

Article 47

Citizens of the People's Republic of China shall enjoy the freedom to engage in scientific research, literary and artistic creation, and other cultural pursuits. The state shall encourage and assist creative work that is beneficial to the people of citizens engaged in education, science, technology, literature, art and other cultural activities.

Article 48

Women in the People's Republic of China shall enjoy equal rights with men in all spheres of life: political, economic, cultural, social and familial.

The state shall protect the rights and interests of women, implement a system of equal pay for equal work, and train and select female officials.

Article 49

Marriage, families, mothers and children shall be protected by the state.

Both husband and wife shall have the obligation to practise family planning.

Parents shall have the obligation to raise and educate their minor children; adult children shall have the obligation to support and assist their parents.

Infringement of the freedom of marriage is prohibited; mistreatment of senior citizens, women and children is prohibited.

Article 50

The People's Republic of China shall protect the legitimate rights and interests of Chinese nationals overseas as well as the lawful rights and interests of Chinese nationals who have returned from overseas and of the family members in China of Chinese nationals overseas.

Article 51

When exercising their freedoms and rights, citizens of the People's Republic of China shall not undermine the interests of the state, society or collectives, or infringe upon the lawful freedoms and rights of other citizens.

Article 52

Citizens of the People's Republic of China shall have the obligation to safeguard national unity and the solidarity of all the country's ethnic groups.

Article 53

Citizens of the People's Republic of China must abide by the Constitution and the law, keep state secrets, protect public property, observe discipline in the workplace, observe public order, and respect social morality.

Article 54

Citizens of the People's Republic of China shall have the obligation to safeguard the security, honour and interests of the motherland; they must not behave in any way that endangers the motherland's security, honour or interests.

Article 55

It is the sacred duty of every citizen of the People's Republic of China to defend the motherland and resist aggression.

It is an honourable obligation of citizens of the People's Republic of China to perform military service or join the militia in accordance with law.

Article 56

Citizens of the People's Republic of China shall have the obligation to pay taxes in accordance with law.

Chapter III
State Institutions

Section 1 The National People's Congress

Article 57

The National People's Congress of the People's Republic of China is the highest state organ of power. Its permanent organ is the National People's Congress Standing Committee.

Article 58

The National People's Congress and the National People's Congress Standing Committee exercise the legislative power of the state.

Article 59

The National People's Congress shall be composed of deputies elected from the provinces, autonomous regions, cities directly under central government jurisdiction, special administrative regions and armed forces. All ethnic minorities should have an appropriate number of deputies.

The election of deputies to the National People's Congress shall be presided over by the National People's Congress Standing Committee.

The number of deputies to the National People's Congress and the procedures for their election shall be prescribed by law.

Article 60

Each National People's Congress shall have a term of five years.

The National People's Congress Standing Committee must complete the election of deputies to the next National People's Congress two months prior to the completion of the term of office of the current National People's Congress. If extraordinary circumstances prevent an election from going ahead, the election may be postponed and the term of office of the current National People's Congress may be extended by a Resolution supported by at least two-thirds of the members of the current National People's Congress Standing Committee. The election of deputies to the next National People's Congress must be completed within one year of said extraordinary circumstances coming to an end.

Article 61

A session of the National People's Congress shall be held once every year and shall be convened by the National People's Congress Standing Committee. If the National People's Congress Standing Committee deems it necessary, or one-fifth or more of National People's Congress deputies so propose, a session of the National People's Congress may be convened in the interim.

When the National People's Congress holds a session, it shall elect a presidium to conduct that session.

Article 62

The National People's Congress shall exercise the following functions and powers:

(1) amending the Constitution;

(2) overseeing the enforcement of the Constitution;

(3) enacting and amending criminal, civil, state institutional and other basic laws;

(4) electing the president and the vice president of the People's Republic of China;

(5) deciding, based on nomination by the president of the People's Republic of China, on the successful candidate for the premier of the State Council; deciding, based on nominations by the premier of the State Council, on the successful candidates for vice premiers, state councillors, ministers of ministries, ministers of commissions, the auditor general and the secretary general of the State Council;

(6) electing the chairperson of the Central Military Commission and deciding, based on nominations by the chairperson of the Central Military Commission, on the successful candidates for other members of the Central Military Commission;

(7) electing the chairperson of the National Commission of Supervision;

(8) electing the president of the Supreme People's Court;

(9) electing the procurator general of the Supreme People's Procuratorate;

(10) reviewing and approving the plan for national economic and social development and the report on its implementation;

(11) reviewing and approving the state budget and the report on its implementation;

(12) changing or revoking inappropriate Decisions of the National People's Congress Standing Committee;

(13) approving the establishment of provinces, autonomous regions and cities directly under central government jurisdiction;

(14) deciding on the establishment of special administrative regions and the systems to be instituted there;

(15) deciding on issues concerning war and peace; and

(16) other functions and powers that the highest state organ of power should exercise.

Article 63

The National People's Congress shall have the power to remove from office the following personnel:

(1) the president and the vice president of the People's Republic of China;

(2) the premier, vice premiers, state councillors, ministers of ministries, ministers of commissions, the auditor general and the secretary general of the State Council;

(3) the chairperson of the Central Military Commission and other members of the Central Military Commission;

(4) the chairperson of the National Commission of Supervision;

(5) the president of the Supreme People's Court; and

(6) the procurator general of the Supreme People's Procuratorate.

Article 64

Amendments to the Constitution must be proposed by the National People's Congress Standing Committee or by one-fifth or more of National People's Congress deputies and be adopted by a vote of at least two-thirds of National People's Congress deputies.

Laws and other proposals shall be adopted by a majority vote of the National People's Congress deputies.

Article 65

The National People's Congress Standing Committee shall be composed of the following personnel:

a chairperson,

vice chairpersons,

a secretary general, and

members.

There should be an appropriate number of ethnic minority deputies who sit as members on the National People's Congress Standing Committee.

The National People's Congress shall elect, and have the power to remove from office, the members of the National People's Congress Standing Committee.

Members of the National People's Congress Standing Committee shall not hold office in an administrative, supervisory, adjudicatory or procuratorial organ of the state.

Article 66

Each National People's Congress Standing Committee shall have the same term of office as that of the National People's Congress; it shall exercise its functions and powers until a new Standing Committee is elected by the next National People's Congress.

The chairperson and vice chairpersons of the Standing Committee shall serve no more than two consecutive terms.

Article 67

The National People's Congress Standing Committee shall exercise the following functions and powers:

(1) interpreting the Constitution and overseeing its enforcement;

(2) enacting and amending laws other than those that should be enacted by the National People's Congress;

(3) when the National People's Congress is out of session, partially supplementing and amending laws enacted by the National People's Congress but without conflicting with the basic principles of those laws;

(4) interpreting laws;

(5) when the National People's Congress is out of session, reviewing and approving partial adjustments to the plan for national economic and social development and the state budget that must be made in the course of implementation;

(6) overseeing the work of the State Council, the Central Military Commission, the National Commission of Supervision, the Supreme People's Court and the Supreme People's Procuratorate;

(7) revoking administrative regulations, decisions and orders formulated by the State Council that are in conflict with the Constitution or laws;

(8) revoking local regulations and resolutions formulated by the state organs of power in provinces, autonomous regions and cities directly under central government jurisdiction that are in conflict with the Constitution, laws, or administrative regulations;

(9) when the National People's Congress is out of session, deciding, based on nominations by the premier of the State Council, on successful candidates for ministers of ministries, ministers of commissions, the auditor general and the secretary general of the State Council;

(10) when the National People's Congress is out of session, deciding, based on nominations by the chairperson of the Central Military Commission, on successful candidates for other members of the Central Military Commission;

(11) appointing or removing, based on recommendations by the chairperson of the National Commission of Supervision, vice chairpersons and members of the National Commission of Supervision;

(12) appointing or removing, based on recommendations by the president of the Supreme People's Court, vice presidents, judges and Adjudicatory Committee members of the Supreme People's Court, and the president of the Military Court;

(13) appointing or removing, based on recommendations by the procurator general of the Supreme People's Procuratorate, deputy procurators general, procurators and Procuratorial Committee members of the Supreme People's Procuratorate, and the chief procurator of the Military Procuratorate; and approving the appointment or removal of chief procurators of the people's procuratorates of provinces, autonomous regions and cities directly under central government jurisdiction;

(14) deciding on the appointment or removal of plenipotentiary representatives abroad;

(15) deciding on the ratification or abrogation of treaties and important agreements concluded with foreign countries;

(16) stipulating systems of titles and ranks for military and diplomatic personnel and other field-specific title and ranking systems;

(17) stipulating national medals and titles of honour and deciding on their conferment;

(18) deciding on the granting of special pardons;

(19) when the National People's Congress is out of session, in the event of an armed attack on the country or in fulfilment of international treaty obligations concerning common defence against aggression, deciding on declaring a state of war;

(20) deciding on national or local mobilization;

(21) deciding on entering a state of emergency nationwide or in particular provinces, autonomous regions or cities directly under central government jurisdiction; and

(22) other functions and powers accorded to it by the National People's Congress.

Article 68

The chairperson of the National People's Congress Standing Committee shall preside over the work of the National People's Congress Standing Committee and convene meetings of the National People's Congress Standing Committee. The vice chairpersons and the secretary general shall assist the chairperson in his or her work.

The chairperson, vice chairpersons and the secretary general constitute a Council of Chairpersons, which handles the important day-to-day work of the National People's Congress Standing Committee.

Article 69

The National People's Congress Standing Committee shall be responsible to the National People's Congress and shall report to the Congress on its work.

Article 70

The National People's Congress shall establish an Ethnic Affairs Committee, a Constitution and Law Committee, a Financial and Economic Committee, an Education, Science, Culture and Public Health Committee, a Foreign Affairs Committee, an Overseas Chinese Affairs Committee and such other special committees as are necessary. When the National People's Congress is out of session, all special committees shall work under the leadership of the National People's Congress Standing Committee.

The special committees shall research, discuss and draw up relevant proposals under the leadership of the National People's Congress and the National People's Congress Standing Committee.

Article 71

When the National People's Congress and the National People's Congress Standing Committee deem it necessary, they may organize investigation committees on specific issues and, based on investigation committee reports, adopt appropriate resolutions.

When an investigation committee is conducting an investigation, all state organs, social organizations and citizens concerned shall have the obligation to provide the committee with the necessary data.

Article 72

Deputies to the National People's Congress and members of the National People's Congress Standing Committee shall have the power, in accordance with procedures prescribed by law, to submit proposals within the scope of the respective functions and powers of the National People's Congress and the National People's Congress Standing Committee.

Article 73

Deputies to the National People's Congress, when the Congress is in session, and members of the National People's Congress Standing Committee, when the Standing Committee is meeting, shall have the power, in accordance with procedures prescribed by law, to submit inquiries to the State Council or the ministries and commissions under it. Organs that receive such inquiries must take responsibility for answering them.

Article 74

Deputies to the National People's Congress shall not be arrested or placed on criminal trial without the consent of the presidium of the current session of the National People's Congress or, when the Congress is out of session, the consent of the National People's Congress Standing Committee.

Article 75

The statements and votes of National People's Congress deputies at meetings of the National People's Congress shall not be subject to legal liability.

Article 76

Deputies to the National People's Congress must play an exemplary role in abiding by the Constitution and the law and keeping state secrets and, in the production, work and public activities they participate in, assist in the enforcement of the Constitution and the law.

Deputies to the National People's Congress should maintain close contact with the organizations and people that elected them, listen to and convey the opinions and demands of the people, and work hard to serve them.

Article 77

Deputies to the National People's Congress shall be subject to the oversight of the organizations that elected them. Organizations that have elected deputies shall have the power to remove them from office in accordance with procedures prescribed by law.

Article 78

The organization and working procedures of the National People's Congress and the National People's Congress Standing Committee shall be prescribed by law.

Section 2 The President of the People's Republic of China

Article 79

The president and the vice president of the People's Republic of China shall be elected by the National People's Congress.

Citizens of the People's Republic of China who have the right to vote and stand for election and who have reached the age of 45 are eligible for election as president or vice president of the People's Republic of China.

The president and the vice president of the People's Republic of China shall have the same term of office as that of the National People's Congress.

Article 80

The president of the People's Republic of China, pursuant to Decisions of the National People's Congress and the National People's Congress Standing Committee, promulgates laws, appoints or removes the premier, vice premiers, state councillors, ministers of ministries, ministers of commissions, the auditor general and the secretary general of the State Council, confers national medals and titles of honour, issues orders of special pardon, declares a state of emergency, declares a state of war, and issues mobilization orders.

Article 81

The president of the People's Republic of China engages in affairs of state and receives foreign diplomatic envoys on behalf of the People's Republic of China and, pursuant to Decisions of the National People's Congress Standing Committee, appoints or recalls plenipotentiary representatives abroad and ratifies or abrogates treaties and important agreements concluded with foreign countries.

Article 82

The vice president of the People's Republic of China shall assist the president in his or her work.

The vice president of the People's Republic of China may, when so entrusted by the president, exercise part of the functions and powers of the president on his or her behalf.

Article 83

The president and the vice president of the People's Republic of China shall exercise their functions and powers until the president and the vice president elected by the next National People's Congress assume office.

Article 84

In the event that the office of president of the People's Republic of China becomes vacant the vice president shall succeed to the office of president.

In the event that the office of vice president of the People's Republic of China becomes vacant the National People's Congress shall elect a new vice president to fill the vacancy.

In the event that the offices of both president and vice president of the People's Republic of China become vacant the National People's Congress shall elect a new president and a new vice president; prior to their election, the chairperson of the National People's Congress Standing Committee shall temporarily act as the president.

Section 3 The State Council

Article 85

The State Council of the People's Republic of China, namely, the Central People's Government, is the executive organ of the highest state organ of power; it is the highest state administrative organ.

Article 86

The State Council is composed of the following personnel:

a premier,

vice premiers,

state councillors,

ministers of ministries,

ministers of commissions,

an auditor general, and

a secretary general.

The State Council shall practise a premier responsibility system. The ministries and commissions shall each practise a minister responsibility system

The organization of the State Council shall be prescribed by law.

Article 87

The State Council shall have the same term of office as that of the National People's Congress.

The premier, vice premiers and state councillors shall serve no more than two consecutive terms.

Article 88

The premier shall direct the work of the State Council. The vice premiers and state councillors shall assist the premier in his or her work.

The premier, vice premiers, state councillors and the secretary general shall attend State Council executive meetings.

The premier shall convene and preside over State Council executive meetings and State Council plenary meetings.

Article 89

The State Council shall exercise the following functions and powers:

(1) stipulating administrative measures, formulating administrative regulations and issuing decisions and orders in accordance with the Constitution and the law;

(2) submitting proposals to the National People's Congress or the National People's Congress Standing Committee;

(3) stipulating the missions and responsibilities of the ministries and commissions, exercising unified leadership over their work, and directing national administrative work that does not fall within the responsibilities of the ministries and commissions;

(4) exercising unified leadership over the work of local state administrative organs at all levels nationwide and stipulating the detailed division of functions and powers between the Central Government and state administrative organs in provinces, autonomous regions and cities directly under central government jurisdiction;

(5) drawing up and implementing plans for national economic and social development and state budgets;

(6) directing and managing economic work, urban and rural development and ecological conservation;

(7) directing and managing education, science, culture, health, sports and family planning work;

(8) directing and managing work such as civil affairs, public security and judicial administration;

(9) managing foreign affairs and concluding treaties and agreements with foreign countries;

(10) directing and managing the development of national defence;

(11) directing and managing ethnic affairs and protecting the equal rights of ethnic minorities and the power to self-govern of ethnic autonomous areas;

(12) protecting the legitimate rights and interests of Chinese nationals overseas and protecting the lawful rights and interests of returned overseas Chinese nationals and the family members in China of Chinese nationals overseas;

(13) changing or revoking inappropriate orders, directives and regulations issued by ministries or commissions;

(14) changing or revoking inappropriate decisions and orders issued by local state administrative organs at all levels;

(15) approving the geographic division of provinces, autonomous regions and cities directly under central government jurisdiction and approving the establishment and geographic division of autonomous prefectures, counties, autonomous counties and cities;

(16) deciding, in accordance with the provisions of law, on entering a state of emergency in parts of provinces, autonomous regions and cities directly under central government jurisdiction;

(17) reviewing and deciding on the staff size of administrative organs and, in accordance with the provisions of law, appointing or removing, training, evaluating, and awarding or punishing administrative personnel; and

(18) other functions and powers accorded to it by the National People's Congress and the National People's Congress Standing Committee.

Article 90

State Council ministers of ministries and ministers of commissions shall be responsible for the work of their departments, and shall convene and preside over ministerial meetings or general and executive commission meetings to discuss and decide on major issues in their departments' work.

Ministries and commissions shall, in accordance with the law and the administrative regulations, decisions and orders of the State Council, issue orders and directives and promulgate regulations within the scope of their authority.

Article 91

The State Council shall establish an audit office to conduct auditing oversight over the revenue and expenditure of all State Council departments and local governments at all levels, and over the revenue and expenditure of all state financial institutions, enterprises and public institutions.

The audit office shall, under the leadership of the premier of the State Council, independently exercise the power to conduct auditing oversight in accordance with the provisions of law, and shall not be subject to interference from other administrative organs, social organizations or individuals.

Article 92

The State Council shall be responsible to the National People's Congress and shall report to the Congress on its work; when the National People's Congress is out of session it shall be responsible to the National People's Congress Standing Committee and shall report to the Standing Committee on its work.

Section 4 The Central Military Commission

Article 93

The Central Military Commission of the People's Republic of China shall lead the country's armed forces.

The Central Military Commission is composed of the following personnel:

a chairperson,

vice chairpersons, and

members.

The Central Military Commission shall practise a chairperson responsibility system.

The Central Military Commission shall have the same term of office as that of the National People's Congress.

Article 94

The chairperson of the Central Military Commission shall be responsible to the National People's Congress and the National People's Congress Standing Committee.

Section 5 Local People's Congresses at All Levels and Local People's Governments at All Levels

Article 95

Provinces, cities directly under central government jurisdiction, counties, cities, municipal districts, townships, ethnic townships and towns shall establish people's congresses and people's governments.

The organization of local people's congresses at all levels and local people's governments at all levels shall be prescribed by law.

Autonomous regions, autonomous prefectures and autonomous counties shall establish autonomous organs. The organization and work of autonomous organs shall be prescribed by law in accordance with the basic principles laid down in Chapter III Sections 5 and 6 of the Constitution.

Article 96

Local people's congresses at all levels are local state organs of power.

Local people's congresses at and above the county level shall establish standing committees.

Article 97

Deputies to the people's congresses of provinces, cities directly under central government jurisdiction and cities divided into districts shall be elected by the people's congresses at the next level down; deputies to the people's congresses of counties, cities not divided into districts, municipal districts, townships, ethnic townships and towns shall be directly elected by their constituencies.

The number of deputies to local people's congresses at all levels and the procedures of their election shall be prescribed by law.

Article 98

Local people's congresses at all levels shall have a term of five years.

Article 99

Local people's congresses at all levels shall, within their administrative areas, ensure the observance and enforcement of the Constitution, laws and administrative regulations; they shall, according to the authority invested in them as prescribed by law, adopt and issue resolutions, and review and decide on local economic, cultural and public service development plans.

Local people's congresses at and above the county level shall review and approve the economic and social development plans and budgets of their administrative areas as well as reports on their implementation; they shall have the power to change or revoke inappropriate decisions made by their own standing committees.

The people's congresses of ethnic townships may, according to the authority invested in them as prescribed by law, take specific measures suited to ethnic characteristics.

Article 100

The people's congresses of provinces and cities directly under central government jurisdiction and their standing committees may, provided there is no conflict with the Constitution, laws or administrative regulations, formulate local regulations, which shall be reported to the National People's Congress Standing Committee to be placed on record.

The people's congresses of cities divided into districts and their standing committees may, provided there is no conflict with the Constitution, laws or administrative regulations, or with the local regulations of their province or autonomous region, formulate local regulations in accordance with the provisions of law, which shall go into force after submission to the standing committee of the people's congress of their province or autonomous region and the receipt of approval.

Article 101

Local people's congresses shall, at their respective levels, elect and have the power to remove from office governors and deputy governors, mayors and deputy mayors, county heads and deputy heads, municipal district heads and deputy heads, township heads and deputy heads, and town heads and deputy heads.

Local people's congresses at and above the county level shall elect, and have the power to remove from office, chairpersons of the commissions of supervision, presidents of the people's courts and chief procurators of the people's procuratorates at their respective levels. The election or removal of chief procurator of the people's procuratorate must be reported to the chief procurator of the people's procuratorate at the next level up for submission to the standing committee of the people's congress at that level for approval.

Article 102

Deputies to the people's congresses of provinces, cities directly under central government jurisdiction and cities divided into districts shall be subject to oversight by the organizations that elected them; deputies to the people's congresses of counties, cities not divided into districts, municipal districts, townships, ethnic townships and towns shall be subject to oversight by their constituencies.

The organizations and constituencies that elect deputies to local people's congresses at all levels shall have the power to remove them from office in accordance with procedures prescribed by law.

Article 103

The standing committees of local people's congresses at and above the county level shall be composed of a chairperson, vice chairpersons and members; they shall be responsible to the people's congresses at their respective levels and shall report to them on their work.

Local people's congresses at and above the county level shall elect, and have the power to remove from office, members of their standing committees.

Members of the standing committee of a local people's congress at or above the county level shall not hold office in an administrative, supervisory, adjudicatory or procuratorial organ of the state.

Article 104

The standing committees of local people's congresses at and above the county level shall discuss and decide on major issues in all areas of work in their administrative areas; oversee the work of the people's government, the commission of supervision, the people's court and the people's procuratorate at their respective levels; revoke inappropriate decisions and orders made by the people's government at the same level; revoke inappropriate resolutions adopted by the people's congress at the next level down; decide on the appointment or removal of employees of state organs according to the authority invested in them as prescribed by law; and, when people's congresses at their level are out of session, remove from office and elect to fill vacancies individual deputies to the people's congress at the next level up.

Article 105

Local people's governments at all levels are the executive organs of the local state organs of power at their respective levels; they are the local state administrative organs at their respective levels.

Local people's governments at all levels shall practise a governor, mayor, county head, municipal district head, township head or town head responsibility system.

Article 106

Local people's governments at all levels shall have the same term of office as that of the people's congresses at their respective levels.

Article 107

Local people's governments at and above the county level shall, according to the authority invested in them as prescribed by law, manage administrative work related to the economy, education, science, culture, public health, sports, urban and rural development, finance, civil affairs, public security, ethnic affairs, judicial administration, family planning, etc., within their administrative areas; and shall issue decisions and orders, appoint or remove, train, evaluate, and award or punish administrative employees.

The people's governments of townships, ethnic townships and towns shall implement the resolutions of the people's congresses at their level and the decisions and orders of state administrative organs at the next level up; they shall manage the administrative work of their respective administrative areas.

The people's governments of provinces and cities directly under central government jurisdiction shall decide on the establishment of townships, ethnic townships and towns and their geographic division.

Article 108

Local people's governments at and above the county level shall direct the work of their subordinate departments and of the people's governments at the next level down and shall have the power to change or revoke inappropriate decisions made by their subordinate departments and the people's governments at the next level down.

Article 109

Local people's governments at and above the county level shall establish audit offices. Local audit offices at all levels shall, in accordance with the provisions of law, independently exercise the power to conduct auditing oversight; they shall be responsible to the people's government at their level and to the audit office at the next level up.

Article 110

Local people's governments at all levels shall be responsible to the people's congresses at their levels and shall report to them on their work. Local people's governments at and above the county level shall, when the people's congresses at their level are out of session, be responsible to the standing committees of the people's congresses at their level and shall report to them on their work.

Local people's governments at all levels shall be responsible to state administrative organs at the next level up and shall report to them on their work. Local people's governments at all levels nationwide are state administrative organs under the unified leadership of the State Council; they shall all be subordinate to the State Council.

Article 111

Residents committees and villagers committees, established among urban and rural residents on the basis of their place of residence, are primary-level people's organizations for self-governance. Residents committee and villagers' committee chairpersons, vice chairpersons and members shall be elected by residents. The relations between residents committees and villagers committees and primary-level state bodies shall be prescribed by law.

Residents committees and villagers committees shall establish people's mediation, public security, public health and other subcommittees to handle public affairs and public services in the residential areas to which they belong, mediate civil disputes and help maintain public order; they shall convey residents' opinions and demands and make proposals to the people's government.

Section 6 Autonomous Organs of Ethnic Autonomous Areas

Article 112

The autonomous organs of ethnic autonomous areas are the people's congresses and the people's governments of autonomous regions, autonomous prefectures and autonomous counties.

Article 113

In the people's congresses of autonomous regions, autonomous prefectures and autonomous counties, aside from deputies of the ethnic group that exercises regional autonomy, other ethnic groups resident in that administrative area should also have an appropriate number of deputies.

On the standing committees of people's congresses of autonomous regions, autonomous prefectures and autonomous counties, there should be citizens of the ethnic group that exercises regional autonomy in office as chairperson or vice chairperson.

Article 114

The offices of governor of an autonomous region, prefect of an autonomous prefecture and head of an autonomous county shall be filled by a citizen belonging to the ethnic group that exercises regional autonomy there.

Article 115

The autonomous organs of autonomous regions, autonomous prefectures and autonomous counties shall exercise the functions and powers of local state organs as specified in Chapter III Section 5 of the Constitution; at the same time, they shall exercise the power to self-govern according to the authority invested in them as prescribed by the Constitution and the Law on Regional Ethnic Autonomy and other laws, and, based on local circumstances, shall implement the laws and policies of the state.

Article 116

The people's congresses of ethnic autonomous areas shall have the power to formulate autonomous regulations and local-specific regulations in accordance with the political, economic and cultural characteristics of the ethnic groups in their areas. The autonomous regulations and local-specific regulations of autonomous regions shall go into effect after submission to the National People's Congress Standing Committee and receipt of approval. The autonomous regulations and local-specific regulations of autonomous prefectures and autonomous counties shall go into effect after submission to the standing committees of the people's congresses of their provinces or autonomous regions and receipt of approval, and shall be reported to the National People's Congress Standing Committee to be placed on record.

Article 117

Autonomous organs of ethnic autonomous areas shall have the autonomy to manage their local finances. All fiscal revenue which, according to the state financial system, belongs to an ethnic autonomous area should be autonomously allocated and used by the autonomous organs of that ethnic autonomous area.

Article 118

Autonomous organs of ethnic autonomous areas shall, under the guidance of state plans, autonomously plan for and manage local economic development.

When the state is exploiting resources or establishing enterprises in an ethnic autonomous area, it should be attentive to the interests of that area.

Article 119

Autonomous organs of ethnic autonomous areas shall autonomously manage the educational, scientific, cultural, health and sports undertakings of their areas, protect and restore the cultural heritage of their ethnic groups, and promote the development and a thriving of ethnic cultures.

Article 120

Autonomous organs of ethnic autonomous areas may, in accordance with the military system of the state and local needs, and with the approval of the State Council, organize local public security units to maintain public order.

Article 121

In performing their duties, autonomous organs of ethnic autonomous areas shall, in accordance with the autonomous regulations of that ethnic autonomous area, use the spoken and written language or languages commonly used in that area.

Article 122

The state shall provide financial, material and technical assistance to ethnic minorities to accelerate their economic and cultural development.

The state shall assist ethnic autonomous areas in training on a large scale officials at all levels, different types of specialized personnel and technical workers from among that area's ethnic groups.

Section 7 Commissions of Supervision

Article 123

Commissions of supervision of the People's Republic of China at all levels are the supervisory organs of the state.

Article 124

The People's Republic of China shall establish a National Commission of Supervision and local commissions of supervision at all levels.

A commission of supervision shall be composed of the following personnel:

a chairperson,

vice chairpersons, and

members.

The chairperson of a commission of supervision shall have the same term of office as that of the people's congress at the same level. The chairperson of the National Commission of Supervision shall serve no more than two consecutive terms.

The organization, functions and powers of the commissions of supervision shall be prescribed by law.

Article 125

The National Commission of Supervision of the People's Republic of China is the highest supervisory organ.

The National Commission of Supervision shall direct the work of local commissions of supervision at all levels; commissions of supervision at higher levels shall direct the work of those at lower levels.

Article 126

The National Commission of Supervision shall be responsible to the National People's Congress and the National People's Congress Standing Committee. Local commissions of supervision at all levels shall be responsible to the state organs of power that created them and to the commissions of supervision at the next level up.

Article 127

Commissions of supervision shall, in accordance with the provisions of law, independently exercise supervisory power, and shall not be subject to interference from any administrative organ, social organization or individual.

The supervisory organs, in handling cases of duty-related malfeasance or crime, shall work together with adjudicatory organs, procuratorial organs and law enforcement departments; they shall act as a mutual check on each other.

Section 8 People's Courts and People's Procuratorates

Article 128

The people's courts of the People's Republic of China are the adjudicatory organs of the state.

Article 129

The People's Republic of China shall establish a Supreme People's Court and local people's courts at all levels, military courts and other special people's courts.

The president of the Supreme People's Court shall have the same term of office as that of the National People's Congress and shall serve no more than two consecutive terms.

The organization of the people's courts shall be prescribed by law.

Article 130

Except in special circumstances as prescribed by law, all cases in the people's courts shall be tried in public. The accused shall have the right to defence.

Article 131

The people's courts shall, in accordance with the provisions of law, independently exercise adjudicatory power, and shall not be subject to interference from any administrative organ, social organization or individual.

Article 132

The Supreme People's Court is the highest adjudicatory organ.

The Supreme People's Court shall oversee the adjudicatory work of local people's courts at all levels and of special people's courts; people's courts at higher levels shall oversee the adjudicatory work of those at lower levels.

Article 133

The Supreme People's Court shall be responsible to the National People's Congress and the National People's Congress Standing Committee. Local people's courts at all levels shall be responsible to the state organs of power that created them.

Article 134

The people's procuratorates of the People's Republic of China are the legal oversight organs of the state.

Article 135

The People's Republic of China shall establish a Supreme People's Procuratorate, local people's procuratorates at all levels, military procuratorates and other special people's procuratorates.

The procurator general of the Supreme People's Procuratorate shall have the same term of office as that of the National People's Congress and shall serve no more than two consecutive terms.

The organization of the people's procuratorates shall be prescribed by law.

Article 136

The people's procuratorates shall, in accordance with the provisions of law, independently exercise procuratorial power, and shall not be subject to interference from any administrative organ, social organization or individual.

Article 137

The Supreme People's Procuratorate is the highest procuratorial organ.

The Supreme People's Procuratorate shall direct the work of local people's procuratorates at all levels and of special people's procuratorates; people's procuratorates at higher levels shall direct the work of those at lower levels.

Article 138

The Supreme People's Procuratorate shall be responsible to the National People's Congress and the National People's Congress Standing Committee. Local people's procuratorates at all levels shall be responsible to the state organs of power that created them and to the people's procuratorates at higher levels.

Article 139

Citizens of all ethnic groups shall have the right to use their own ethnic group's spoken and written languages in court proceedings. The people's courts and the people's procuratorates should provide translation services for any party to court proceedings who does not have a good command of the spoken or written languages commonly used in the locality.

In areas inhabited by people of an ethnic minority or by a number of ethnic groups living together, court hearings should be conducted in the language or languages commonly used in the locality; indictments, judgments, notices and other documents should be written in the language or languages commonly used in the locality according to actual needs.

Article 140

In handling criminal cases, the people's courts, the people's procuratorates and public security organs should each be responsible for their respective tasks, work together with each other, and act as checks on each other to ensure the faithful and effective enforcement of the law.

Chapter IV
The National Flag, National Anthem, National Emblem and the Capital

Article 141

The national flag of the People's Republic of China is a red flag with five stars.

The national anthem of the People's Republic of China is the March of the Volunteers.

Article 142

The national emblem of the People's Republic of China consists of an image of Tiananmen Gate in the centre illuminated by five stars and encircled by spikes of grain and a cogwheel.

Article 143

The capital of the People's Republic of China is Beijing.

SECTION IV
SELECTED NATIONAL LAWS AS APPLIED IN HONG KONG

This Section includes two national laws as applied in Hong Kong. They are:

(1) The Law of the People's Republic of China on the Garrisoning of the Hong Kong Special Administrative Region

(2) The Law of the People's Republic of China on Safeguarding National Security in the Hong Kong Special Administrative Region

THE LAW OF THE PEOPLE'S REPUBLIC OF CHINA ON THE GARRISONING OF THE HONG KONG SPECIAL ADMINISTRATIVE REGION

(Adopted at the 23rd Meeting of the Standing Committee of the Eighth National People's Congress on 30 December 1996, promulgated by Order No. 80 of the President of the People's Republic of China on 30 December 1996, and effective as of 1 July 1997)

Contents

Chapter I
General Provisions

Article 1

This Law is enacted in accordance with the Constitution and the Basic Law of the Hong Kong Special Administrative Region to ensure the lawful performance of functions and responsibilities by the military forces stationed by the Central People's Government in the Hong Kong Special Administrative Region for defence, and to maintain the sovereignty, unity and territorial integrity of the State and the security of Hong Kong.

Article 2

The military forces stationed by the Central People's Government in the Hong Kong Special Administrative Region for defence shall be composed of forces from the Army, the Navy and the Air Force of the Chinese People's Liberation Army, and be designated as the Hong Kong Garrison of the Chinese People's Liberation Army (hereinafter referred to as the Hong Kong Garrison).

Article 3

The Hong Kong Garrison shall be subject to the direction of the Central Military Commission of the People's Republic of China. The number of its members shall be determined according to the need for the defence of the Hong Kong Special Administrative Region.

The Hong Kong Garrison shall practise a system of rotation of its members.

Article 4

Expenditure for the Hong Kong Garrison shall be borne by the Central People's Government.

Chapter II
Functions and Responsibilities of the Hong Kong Garrison

Article 5

The Hong Kong Garrison shall perform the following defence functions and responsibilities:

(1) preparing against and resisting aggression, and safeguarding the security of the Hong Kong Special Administrative Region;

(2) carrying out defence duties;

(3) controlling military facilities, and

(4) handling foreign-related military affairs.

Article 6

In the event that the Standing Committee of the National People's Congress decides to declare a state of war or, by reason of turmoil within the Hong Kong Special Administrative Region which endangers national unity or security and is beyond the control of the Government of the Region, decides that the Region is in a state of emergency, the Hong Kong Garrison shall perform its duties in accordance with the provisions of the national laws that the Central People's Government decides to apply in the Region.

Article 7

No weapon and equipment, such as aircraft and vessels, and no material of the Hong Kong Garrison, and no member or vehicle of the Garrison that bears a certificate or a document of certification issued by the Hong Kong Garrison showing that the bearer is on official duty, shall be inspected, searched, seized or detained by any law-enforcing officer of the Hong Kong Special Administrative Region.

The Hong Kong Garrison and its members shall also enjoy other rights and immunities prescribed by the laws in force in the Hong Kong Special Administrative Region.

Article 8

Members of the Hong Kong Garrison may, in accordance with the provisions of the laws in force in the Hong Kong Special Administrative Region, take measures to stop any act which obstructs their performance of official duties.

Chapter III
Relationship between the Hong Kong Garrison and the Government of the Hong Kong Special Administrative Region

Article 9

The Hong Kong Garrison shall not interfere in the local affairs of the Hong Kong Special Administrative Region.

Article 10

The Government of the Hong Kong Special Administrative Region shall support the Hong Kong Garrison in its performance of defence functions and responsibilities and guarantee the lawful rights and interests of the Hong Kong Garrison and its members.

The Hong Kong Special Administrative Region shall consult the Hong Kong Garrison when formulating any policy or drafting any legislation which concerns the Hong Kong Garrison.

Article 11

The Hong Kong Garrison shall notify in advance the Government of the Hong Kong Special Administrative Region of any military activities it is to conduct such as training exercises and manoeuvres which may affect the public interests of the Hong Kong Special Administrative Region.

Article 12

The Hong Kong Garrison and the Government of the Hong Kong Special Administrative Region shall jointly protect the military facilities within the Hong Kong Special Administrative Region.

The Hong Kong Garrison shall delimit military restricted zones in conjunction with the Government of the Hong Kong Special Administrative Region. The locations and boundaries of the military restricted zones shall be declared by the Government of the Hong Kong Special Administrative Region.

The Government of the Hong Kong Special Administrative Region shall assist the Hong Kong Garrison in maintaining the security of the military restricted zones.

Without permission of the Commander of the Hong Kong Garrison or other officers as he may authorize to give such permission, no person, vehicle, ship or aircraft other than the ones of the Hong Kong Garrison shall enter the military restricted zones. Guards of the military restricted zones shall have the right to stop according to law any unauthorized entry into any military restricted zone or any act which damages or endangers any military facilities.

The Hong Kong Garrison shall protect the natural resources, historical relics and monuments, and other non-military rights and interests within the military restricted zones in accordance with the laws of the Hong Kong Special Administrative Region.

Article 13

Any land used by the Hong Kong Garrison for military purposes, when approved by the Central People's Government to be no longer needed for defence purposes, shall be turned over without compensation to the Government of the Hong Kong Special Administrative Region for disposal.

If the Government of the Hong Kong Special Administrative Region needs for public use any part of the land used for military purposes by the Hong Kong Garrison, it shall seek approval of the Central People's Government; where approval is obtained, the Government of the Hong Kong Special Administrative Region shall in return provide land and military facilities for the Hong Kong Garrison at such sites as agreed to by the Central People's Government, and shall bear all the expenses and costs entailed.

Article 14

Pursuant to the provisions of the Basic Law of the Hong Kong Special Administrative Region, the Government of the Hong Kong Special Administrative Region may, when necessary, ask the Central

People's Government for assistance from the Hong Kong Garrison in the maintenance of public order or in disaster relief.

After the request of the Government of the Hong Kong Special Administrative Region is approved by the Central People's Government, the Hong Kong Garrison shall call out troops in accordance with the order of the Central Military Commission to carry out tasks of assistance in the maintenance of public order or in disaster relief, and upon completion of the tasks, the troops shall return to their barracks immediately.

The troops of the Hong Kong Garrison who are called out to assist in the maintenance of public order or in disaster relief shall, under the arrangement of the Government of the Hong Kong Special Administrative Region, be directed by the Commander of the Hong Kong Garrison or the officer authorized by him.

Members of the Hong Kong Garrison may exercise the powers conferred by the laws of the Hong Kong Special Administrative Region in the course of rendering assistance in the maintenance of public order or in disaster relief.

Article 15

The Hong Kong Garrison and the Government of the Hong Kong Special Administrative Region shall establish necessary liaison to deal with matters concerning the Hong Kong Garrison through consultation.

Chapter IV
Obligations of and Discipline for Members of the Hong Kong Garrison

Article 16

Members of the Hong Kong Garrison shall fulfil the following obligations:

(1) to be loyal to their motherland, perform their functions and responsibilities, maintain the security, honour and interests of their motherland, and safeguard the security of Hong Kong;

(2) to abide by national laws and the laws of the Hong Kong Special Administrative Region, and observe military discipline;

(3) to respect the organs of political power, the social system and the ways of life of the Hong Kong Special Administrative Region;

(4) to cherish the public property of the Hong Kong Special Administrative Region and the private property of Hong Kong residents and other persons, and

(5) to observe public ethics and cultivate civility and courtesy.

Article 17

Members of the Hong Kong Garrison shall not join any political, religious or public organization in Hong Kong.

Article 18

The Hong Kong Garrison or its members shall not engage in any form of profit-making business activities. Members of the Hong Kong Garrison shall not engage in any other activity incompatible with their functions and responsibilities as servicemen.

Article 19

Any member of the Hong Kong Garrison who contravenes any national law or law of the Hong Kong Special Administrative Region shall be investigated for legal responsibility according to law.

Any member of the Hong Kong Garrison who breaches military discipline shall be subject to disciplinary sanction.

Chapter V
Judicial Jurisdiction over Members of the Hong Kong Garrison

Article 20

Criminal offences committed by members of the Hong Kong Garrison shall be under the jurisdiction of the military judicial organs; but acts committed by members of the Hong Kong Garrison, when not performing their official duties, in violation of the personal right or property right of Hong Kong residents or other persons not of the Hong Kong Garrison and other offences committed in violation of the laws of the Hong Kong Special Administrative Region, which constitute crimes shall be subject to jurisdiction of the courts and the relevant law-enforcing organs of the Hong Kong Special Administrative Region.

The military judicial organ and the court or the relevant law-enforcing organ of the Hong Kong Special Administrative Region may transfer to the other party the criminal cases of members of the Hong Kong Garrison under their respective jurisdiction if they consider it to be more appropriate for the other party to exercise jurisdiction, provided that consensus is reached through consultation.

Hong Kong residents or other persons not of the Hong Kong Garrison involved as defendants in the criminal cases of members of the Hong Kong Garrison under the jurisdiction of the military judicial organs shall be tried by the courts of the Hong Kong Special Administrative Region.

Article 21

Any person who is lawfully arrested as a suspected offender by law-enforcing officers of the Hong Kong Special Administrative Region, once confirmed upon investigation to be a member of the Hong Kong Garrison, shall be handed over to the Hong Kong Garrison for custody. Jurisdiction over the case involving the person in custody shall be determined in accordance with the provisions in Article 20 of this Law.

Article 22

Any member of the Hong Kong Garrison sentenced by a court of the Hong Kong Special Administrative Region to criminal punishment which deprives him of or restricts his personal freedom shall be delivered for sentence enforcement according to the provisions of the laws of the Hong Kong Special Administrative Region, except for the case in which the place of sentence enforcement is determined otherwise by a relevant law-enforcing organ of the Hong Kong Special Administrative Region and the military judicial organ through consultation.

Article 23

Where any member of the Hong Kong Garrison, in contravention of the laws of the Hong Kong Special Administrative Region, infringes the civil rights of any Hong Kong resident or other person not of the Hong Kong Garrison, the parties concerned may seek settlement through consultation or mediation; if they are unwilling or fail to reach settlement through consultation or mediation, the infringed party may bring an action in the court. Cases of tort arising from acts committed by members of the Hong Kong Garrison when not performing their official duties shall be subject to the jurisdiction of the courts of the Hong Kong Special Administrative Region; cases of tort arising from acts committed by members of the Hong Kong Garrison when performing their official duties shall be subject to the jurisdiction of the Supreme People's Court of the People's Republic of China, and compensation for any loss or injury incurred by acts of tort shall be governed by the laws of the Hong Kong Special Administrative Region.

Article 24

Where any contractual dispute arises within the Hong Kong Special Administrative Region between any organ or unit of the Hong Kong Garrison and any Hong Kong resident or other person not of the Hong Kong Garrison, the parties concerned may settle their dispute through consultation or mediation; if the parties are unwilling or fail to reach settlement through consultation or mediation, they may submit the dispute to the arbitration agency for arbitration in accordance with the arbitration clause contained in the contract or with a written arbitration agreement reached by the parties afterwards. If no arbitration clause is contained in the contract and no written arbitration agreement is reached afterwards, the parties may institute proceedings in a court of the Hong Kong Special Administrative Region, except that the parties agree otherwise as to the court for instituting proceedings.

Article 25

Certificates issued by the Hong Kong Garrison regarding facts such as identity of membership of the Hong Kong Garrison and acts in performance of official duties shall be valid evidence in proceedings in the courts of the Hong Kong Special Administrative Region, unless the contrary is proved.

Article 26

Acts of State, such as actions for defence taken by the Hong Kong Garrison, shall not be subject to the jurisdiction of the courts of the Hong Kong Special Administrative Region.

Article 27

Organs or units of the Hong Kong Garrison shall comply with the judgments or orders issued by the courts of the Hong Kong Special Administrative Region concerning arrangement of their property; but the said courts shall not enforce judgments or orders on any weapon, equipment, material or other property of the Hong Kong Garrison.

Article 28

The military judicial organs may, through consultation, maintain juridical relations with the courts and the relevant law-enforcing organs of the Hong Kong Special Administrative Region, and they may render assistance to each other.

Chapter VI
Supplementary Provisions

Article 29

The power of interpretation of this Law shall be vested in the Standing Committee of the National People's Congress.

Article 30

This Law shall come into force as of 1 July 1997.

THE LAW OF THE PEOPLE'S REPUBLIC OF CHINA ON SAFEGUARDING NATIONAL SECURITY IN THE HONG KONG SPECIAL ADMINISTRATIVE REGION

(Adopted at the Twentieth Session of the Standing Committee of the Thirteenth National People's Congress on 30 June 2020)

Contents

Chapter I
General Principles

Article 1

This Law is enacted, in accordance with the Constitution of the People's Republic of China, the Basic Law of the Hong Kong Special Administrative Region of the People's Republic of China, and the Decision of the National People's Congress on Establishing and Improving the Legal System and Enforcement Mechanisms for Safeguarding National Security in the Hong Kong Special Administrative Region, for the purpose of:

(1) ensuring the resolute, full and faithful implementation of the policy of One Country, Two Systems under which the people of Hong Kong administer Hong Kong with a high degree of autonomy;

(2) safeguarding national security;

(3) preventing, suppressing and imposing punishment for the offences of secession, subversion, organization and perpetration of terrorist activities, and collusion with a foreign country or with external elements to endanger national security in relation to the Hong Kong Special Administrative Region;

(4) maintaining prosperity and stability of the Hong Kong Special Administrative Region; and

(5) protecting the lawful rights and interests of the residents of the Hong Kong Special Administrative Region.

Article 2

The provisions in Articles 1 and 12 of the Basic Law of the Hong Kong Special Administrative Region on the legal status of the Hong Kong Special Administrative Region are the fundamental provisions in the Basic Law. No institution, organization or individual in the Region shall contravene these provisions in exercising their rights and freedoms.

Article 3

The Central People's Government has an overarching responsibility for national security affairs relating to the Hong Kong Special Administrative Region.

It is the duty of the Hong Kong Special Administrative Region under the Constitution to safeguard national security and the Region shall perform the duty accordingly.

The executive authorities, legislature and judiciary of the Region shall effectively prevent, suppress and impose punishment for any act or activity endangering national security in accordance with this Law and other relevant laws.

Article 4

Human rights shall be respected and protected in safeguarding national security in the Hong Kong Special Administrative Region. The rights and freedoms, including the freedoms of speech, of the press, of publication, of association, of assembly, of procession and of demonstration, which the residents of the Region enjoy under the Basic Law of the Hong Kong Special Administrative Region and the provisions of the International Covenant on Civil and Political Rights and the International Covenant on Economic, Social and Cultural Rights as applied to Hong Kong, shall be protected in accordance with the law.

Article 5

The principle of the rule of law shall be adhered to in preventing, suppressing, and imposing punishment for offences endangering national security. A person who commits an act which constitutes an offence under the law shall be convicted and punished in accordance with the law. No one shall be convicted and punished for an act which does not constitute an offence under the law.

A person is presumed innocent until convicted by a judicial body. The right to defend himself or herself and other rights in judicial proceedings that a criminal suspect, defendant, and other parties in judicial proceedings are entitled to under the law shall be protected. No one shall be liable to be tried or punished again for an offence for which he or she has already been finally convicted or acquitted in judicial proceedings.

Article 6

It is the common responsibility of all the people of China, including the people of Hong Kong, to safeguard the sovereignty, unification and territorial integrity of the People's Republic of China.

Any institution, organization or individual in the Hong Kong Special Administrative Region shall abide by this Law and the laws of the Region in relation to the safeguarding of national security, and shall not engage in any act or activity which endangers national security.

A resident of the Region who stands for election or assumes public office shall confirm in writing or take an oath to uphold the Basic Law of the Hong Kong Special Administrative Region of the People's Republic of China and swear allegiance to the Hong Kong Special Administrative Region of the People's Republic of China in accordance with the law.

Chapter II
The Duties and the Government Bodies of the Hong Kong Special Administrative Region for Safeguarding National Security

Part 1 Duties

Article 7

The Hong Kong Special Administrative Region shall complete, as early as possible, legislation for safeguarding national security as stipulated in the Basic Law of the Hong Kong Special Administrative Region and shall refine relevant laws.

Article 8

In order to safeguard national security effectively, the law enforcement and judicial authorities of the Hong Kong Special Administrative Region shall fully enforce this Law and the laws in force in the Region concerning the prevention of, suppression of, and imposition of punishment for acts and activities endangering national security.

Article 9

The Hong Kong Special Administrative Region shall strengthen its work on safeguarding national security and prevention of terrorist activities. The Government of the Hong Kong Special Administrative Region shall take necessary measures to strengthen public communication, guidance, supervision and regulation over matters concerning national security, including those relating to schools, universities, social organizations, the media, and the internet.

Article 10

The Hong Kong Special Administrative Region shall promote national security education in schools and universities and through social organizations, the media, the internet and other means to raise the awareness of Hong Kong residents of national security and of the obligation to abide by the law.

Article 11

The Chief Executive of the Hong Kong Special Administrative Region shall be accountable to the Central People's Government for affairs relating to safeguarding national security in the Hong Kong Special Administrative Region and shall submit an annual report on the performance of duties of the Region in safeguarding national security.

The Chief Executive shall, at the request of the Central People's Government, submit in a timely manner a report on specific matters relating to safeguarding national security.

Part 2 Government Bodies

Article 12

The Hong Kong Special Administrative Region shall establish the Committee for Safeguarding National Security. The Committee shall be responsible for affairs relating to and assume primary responsibility for safeguarding national security in the Region. It shall be under the supervision of and accountable to the Central People's Government.

Article 13

The Chief Executive shall be the chairperson of the Committee for Safeguarding National Security of the Hong Kong Special Administrative Region. The other members of the Committee shall be the Chief Secretary for Administration, the Financial Secretary, the Secretary for Justice, the Secretary for Security, the Commissioner of Police, the head of the department for safeguarding national security of the Hong Kong Police Force established under Article 16 of this Law, the Director of Immigration, the Commissioner of Customs and Excise, and the Director of the Chief Executive's Office.

A secretariat headed by a Secretary-General shall be established under the Committee. The Secretary-General shall be appointed by the Central People's Government upon nomination by the Chief Executive.

Article 14

The duties and functions of the Committee for Safeguarding National Security of the Hong Kong Special Administrative Region shall be:

(1) analysing and assessing developments in relation to safeguarding national security in the Hong Kong Special Administrative Region, making work plans, and formulating policies for safeguarding national security in the Region;

(2) advancing the development of the legal system and enforcement mechanisms of the Region for safeguarding national security; and

(3) coordinating major work and significant operations for safeguarding national security in the Region.

No institution, organization or individual in the Region shall interfere with the work of the Committee. Information relating to the work of the Committee shall not be subject to disclosure. Decisions made by the Committee shall not be amenable to judicial review.

Article 15

The Committee for Safeguarding National Security of the Hong Kong Special Administrative Region shall have a National Security Adviser, who shall be designated by the Central People's Government and provide advice on matters relating to the duties and functions of the Committee. The National Security Adviser shall sit in on meetings of the Committee.

Article 16

The Police Force of the Hong Kong Special Administrative Region shall establish a department for safeguarding national security with law enforcement capacity.

The head of the department for safeguarding national security of the Hong Kong Police Force shall be appointed by the Chief Executive. The Chief Executive shall seek in writing the opinion of the Office established under Article 48 of this Law before making the appointment. When assuming office, the head of the department for safeguarding national security of the Hong Kong Police Force shall swear to uphold the Basic Law of the Hong Kong Special Administrative Region of the People's Republic of China, swear allegiance to the Hong Kong Special Administrative Region of the People's Republic of China, and swear to abide by the law and to observe the obligation of secrecy.

The department for safeguarding national security of the Hong Kong Police Force may recruit qualified professionals and technical personnel from outside the Hong Kong Special Administrative Region to provide assistance in the performance of duties for safeguarding national security.

Article 17

The duties and functions of the department for safeguarding national security of the Hong Kong Police Force shall be:

(1) collecting and analysing intelligence and information concerning national security;

(2) planning, coordinating and enforcing measures and operations for safeguarding national security;

(3) investigating offences endangering national security;

(4) conducting counter-interference investigation and national security review;

(5) carrying out tasks of safeguarding national security assigned by the Committee for Safeguarding National Security of the Hong Kong Special Administrative Region; and

(6) performing other duties and functions necessary for the enforcement of this Law.

Article 18

The Department of Justice of the Hong Kong Special Administrative Region shall establish a specialized prosecution division responsible for the prosecution of offences endangering national security and other related legal work. The prosecutors of this division shall be appointed by the Secretary for Justice after obtaining the consent of the Committee for Safeguarding National Security of the Hong Kong Special Administrative Region.

The head of the specialized prosecution division of the Department of Justice shall be appointed by the Chief Executive, who shall seek in writing the opinion of the Office established under Article 48 of this Law before making the appointment. When assuming office, the head of the specialized prosecution division shall swear to uphold the Basic Law of the Hong Kong Special Administrative Region of the People's Republic of China, swear allegiance to the Hong Kong Special Administrative Region of the People's Republic of China, and swear to abide by the law and to observe the obligation of secrecy.

Article 19

The Financial Secretary of the Hong Kong Special Administrative Region shall, upon approval of the Chief Executive, appropriate from the general revenue a special fund to meet the expenditure for safeguarding national security and approve the establishment of relevant posts, which are not subject to any restrictions in the relevant provisions of the laws in force in the Region. The Financial Secretary shall submit an annual report on the control and management of the fund for this purpose to the Legislative Council of the Hong Kong Special Administrative Region.

Chapter III
Offences and Penalties

Part 1 Secession

Article 20

A person who organizes, plans, commits or participates in any of the following acts, whether or not by force or threat of force, with a view to committing secession or undermining national unification shall be guilty of an offence:

(1) separating the Hong Kong Special Administrative Region or any other part of the People's Republic of China from the People's Republic of China;

(2) altering by unlawful means the legal status of the Hong Kong Special Administrative Region or of any other part of the People's Republic of China; or

(3) surrendering the Hong Kong Special Administrative Region or any other part of the People's Republic of China to a foreign country.

A person who is a principal offender or a person who commits an offence of a grave nature shall be sentenced to life imprisonment or fixed-term imprisonment of not less than ten years; a person who actively participates in the offence shall be sentenced to fixed-term imprisonment of not less than three years but not more than ten years; and other participants shall be sentenced to fixed-term imprisonment of not more than three years, short-term detention or restriction.

Article 21

A person who incites, assists in, abets or provides pecuniary or other financial assistance or property for the commission by other persons of the offence under Article 20 of this Law shall be guilty of an offence. If the circumstances of the offence committed by a person are of a serious nature, the person shall be sentenced to fixed-term imprisonment of not less than five years but not more than ten years; if the circumstances of the offence committed by a person are of a minor nature, the person shall be sentenced to fixed-term imprisonment of not more than five years, short-term detention or restriction.

Part 2 Subversion

Article 22

A person who organizes, plans, commits or participates in any of the following acts by force or threat of force or other unlawful means with a view to subverting the State power shall be guilty of an offence:

(1) overthrowing or undermining the basic system of the People's Republic of China established by the Constitution of the People's Republic of China;

(2) overthrowing the body of central power of the People's Republic of China or the body of power of the Hong Kong Special Administrative Region;

(3) seriously interfering in, disrupting, or undermining the performance of duties and functions in accordance with the law by the body of central power of the People's Republic of China or the body of power of the Hong Kong Special Administrative Region; or

(4) attacking or damaging the premises and facilities used by the body of power of the Hong Kong Special Administrative Region to perform its duties and functions, rendering it incapable of performing its normal duties and functions.

A person who is a principal offender or a person who commits an offence of a grave nature shall be sentenced to life imprisonment or fixed-term imprisonment of not less than ten years; a person who actively participates in the offence shall be sentenced to fixed-term imprisonment of not less than three years but not more than ten years; and other participants shall be sentenced to fixed-term imprisonment of not more than three years, short-term detention or restriction.

Article 23

A person who incites, assists in, abets or provides pecuniary or other financial assistance or property for the commission by other persons of the offence under Article 22 of this Law shall be guilty of an offence. If the circumstances of the offence committed by a person are of a serious nature, the person shall be sentenced to fixed-term imprisonment of not less than five years but not more than ten years; if the circumstances of the offence committed by a person are of a minor nature, the person shall be sentenced to fixed-term imprisonment of not more than five years, short-term detention or restriction.

Part 3 Terrorist Activities

Article 24

A person who organizes, plans, commits, participates in or threatens to commit any of the following terrorist activities causing or intended to cause grave harm to the society with a view to coercing the Central People's Government, the Government of the Hong Kong Special Administrative Region or an international organization or intimidating the public in order to pursue political agenda shall be guilty of an offence:

(1) serious violence against a person or persons;

(2) explosion, arson, or dissemination of poisonous or radioactive substances, pathogens of infectious diseases or other substances;

(3) sabotage of means of transport, transport facilities, electric power or gas facilities, or other combustible or explosible facilities;

(4) serious interruption or sabotage of electronic control systems for providing and managing public services such as water, electric power, gas, transport, telecommunications and the internet; or

(5) other dangerous activities which seriously jeopardize public health, safety or security.

A person who commits the offence causing serious bodily injury, death or significant loss of public or private property shall be sentenced to life imprisonment or fixed-term imprisonment of not less than ten years; in other circumstances, a person who commits the offence shall be sentenced to fixed-term imprisonment of not less than three years but not more than ten years.

Article 25

A person who organizes or takes charge of a terrorist organization shall be guilty of an offence and shall be sentenced to life imprisonment or fixed-term imprisonment of not less than ten years, and shall be subject to confiscation of property; a person who actively participates in a terrorist organization shall be sentenced to fixed-term imprisonment of not less than three years but not more than ten years and shall be imposed with a criminal fine; and other participants shall be sentenced to fixed-term imprisonment of not more than three years, short-term detention or restriction, and shall be liable to a criminal fine.

For the purpose of this Law, a terrorist organization means an organization which commits or intends to commit the offence under Article 24 of this Law or participates or assists in the commission of the offence.

Article 26

A person who provides support, assistance or facility such as training, weapons, information, funds, supplies, labour, transport, technologies or venues to a terrorist organization or a terrorist, or for the commission of a terrorist activity; or manufactures or illegally possesses substances such as explosive, poisonous or radioactive substances and pathogens of infectious diseases or uses other means to prepare for the commission of a terrorist activity, shall be guilty of an offence. If the circumstances of the offence committed by a person are of a serious nature, the person shall be sentenced to fixed-term imprisonment of not less than five years but not more than ten years, and shall be imposed with a criminal fine or subject to confiscation of property; in other circumstances, a person shall be sentenced to fixed-term imprisonment of not more than five years, short-term detention or restriction, and shall be imposed with a criminal fine.

If the act referred to in the preceding paragraph also constitutes other offences, the person who commits the act shall be convicted and sentenced for the offence that carries a more severe penalty.

Article 27

A person who advocates terrorism or incites the commission of a terrorist activity shall be guilty of an offence. If the circumstances of the offence committed by a person are of a serious nature, the person shall be sentenced to fixed-term imprisonment of not less than five years but not more than ten years, and shall be imposed with a criminal fine or subject to confiscation of property; in other circumstances, a person shall be sentenced to fixed-term imprisonment of not more than five years, short-term detention or restriction, and shall be imposed with a criminal fine.

Article 28

The provisions of this Part shall not affect the prosecution of terrorist offences committed in other forms or the imposition of other measures such as freezing of property in accordance with the laws of the Hong Kong Special Administrative Region.

Part 4 Collusion with a Foreign Country or with External Elements to Endanger National Security

Article 29

A person who steals, spies, obtains with payment, or unlawfully provides State secrets or intelligence concerning national security for a foreign country or an institution, organization or individual outside the mainland, Hong Kong, and Macao of the People's Republic of China shall be guilty of an offence; a person who requests a foreign country or an institution, organization or individual outside the mainland, Hong Kong, and Macao of the People's Republic of China, or conspires with a foreign country or an institution, organization or individual outside the mainland, Hong Kong, and Macao of the People's Republic of China, or directly or indirectly receives instructions, control, funding or other kinds of support from a foreign country or an institution, organization or individual outside the mainland, Hong Kong, and Macao of the People's Republic of China, to commit any of the following acts shall be guilty of an offence:

(1) waging a war against the People's Republic of China, or using or threatening to use force to seriously undermine the sovereignty, unification and territorial integrity of the People's Republic of China;

(2) seriously disrupting the formulation and implementation of laws or policies by the Government of the Hong Kong Special Administrative Region or by the Central People's Government, which is likely to cause serious consequences;

(3) rigging or undermining an election in the Hong Kong Special Administrative Region, which is likely to cause serious consequences;

(4) imposing sanctions or blockade, or engaging in other hostile activities against the Hong Kong Special Administrative Region or the People's Republic of China; or

(5) provoking by unlawful means hatred among Hong Kong residents towards the Central People's Government or the Government of the Region, which is likely to cause serious consequences.

A person who commits the offence shall be sentenced to fixed-term imprisonment of not less than three years but not more than ten years; a person who commits an offence of a grave nature shall be sentenced to life imprisonment or fixed-term imprisonment of not less than ten years.

The institution, organization and individual outside the mainland, Hong Kong, and Macao of the People's Republic of China referred to in the first paragraph of this Article shall be convicted and punished for the same offence.

Article 30

A person who conspires with or directly or indirectly receives instructions, control, funding or other kinds of support from a foreign country or an institution, organization, or individual outside the mainland, Hong Kong, and Macao of the People's Republic of China to commit the offences under Article 20 or 22 of this Law shall be liable to a more severe penalty in accordance with the provisions therein respectively.

Part 5 Other Provisions on Penalty

Article 31

An incorporated or unincorporated body such as a company or an organization which commits an offence under this Law shall be imposed with a criminal fine.

The operation of an incorporated or unincorporated body such as a company or an organization shall be suspended or its licence or business permit shall be revoked if the body has been punished for committing an offence under this Law.

Article 32

Proceeds obtained from the commission of an offence under this Law including financial aid, gains and rewards, and funds and tools used or intended to be used in the commission of the offence shall be seized and confiscated.

Article 33

A lighter penalty may be imposed, or the penalty may be reduced or, in the case of a minor offence, exempted, if an offender, criminal suspect, or defendant:

(1) in the process of committing an offence, voluntarily discontinues the commission of the offence or voluntarily and effectively forestalls its consequences;

(2) voluntarily surrenders himself or herself and gives a truthful account of the offence; or

(3) reports on the offence committed by other person, which is verified to be true, or provides material information which assists in solving other criminal case.

Subparagraph (2) of the preceding paragraph shall apply to a criminal suspect or defendant who is subjected to mandatory measures and provides a truthful account of other offences committed by him or her under this Law which are unknown to the law enforcement or judicial authorities.

Article 34

A person who is not a permanent resident of the Hong Kong Special Administrative Region may be subject to deportation as the sole or an additional punishment if he or she commits an offence under this Law.

A person who is not a permanent resident of the Region may be subject to deportation if he or she contravenes the provisions of this Law but is not prosecuted for any reason.

Article 35

A person who is convicted of an offence endangering national security by a court shall be disqualified from standing as a candidate in the elections of the Legislative Council and district councils of the Hong Kong Special Administrative Region, holding any public office in the Region, or serving as a member of the Election Committee for electing the Chief Executive. If a person so convicted is a member of the Legislative Council, a government official, a public servant, a member of the Executive Council, a judge or a judicial officer, or a member of the district councils, who has taken an oath or made a declaration to uphold the Basic Law of the Hong Kong Special Administrative Region of the People's Republic of China and swear allegiance to the Hong Kong Special Administrative Region of the People's Republic of China, he or she shall be removed from his or her office upon conviction, and shall be disqualified from standing for the aforementioned elections or from holding any of the aforementioned posts.

The disqualification and removal from offices referred to in the preceding paragraph shall be announced by the authorities responsible for organizing and managing the relevant elections or for the appointment and removal of holders of public office.

Part 6 Scope of Application

Article 36

This Law shall apply to offences under this Law which are committed in the Hong Kong Special Administrative Region by any person. An offence shall be deemed to have been committed in the Region if an act constituting the offence or the consequence of the offence occurs in the Region.

This Law shall also apply to offences under this Law committed on board a vessel or aircraft registered in the Region.

Article 37

This Law shall apply to a person who is a permanent resident of the Hong Kong Special Administrative Region or an incorporated or unincorporated body such as a company or an organization which is set up in the Region if the person or the body commits an offence under this Law outside the Region.

Article 38

This Law shall apply to offences under this Law committed against the Hong Kong Special Administrative Region from outside the Region by a person who is not a permanent resident of the Region.

Article 39

This Law shall apply to acts committed after its entry into force for the purpose of conviction and imposition of punishment.

Chapter IV
Jurisdiction, Applicable Law and Procedure

Article 40

The Hong Kong Special Administrative Region shall have jurisdiction over cases concerning offences under this Law, except under the circumstances specified in Article 55 of this Law.

Article 41

This Law and the laws of the Hong Kong Special Administrative Region shall apply to procedural matters, including those related to criminal investigation, prosecution, trial, and execution of penalty, in respect of cases concerning offence endangering national security over which the Region exercises jurisdiction.

No prosecution shall be instituted in respect of an offence endangering national security without the written consent of the Secretary for Justice. This provision shall not prejudice the arrest and detention of a person who is suspected of having committed the offence or the application for bail by the person in accordance with the law.

Cases concerning offence endangering national security within the jurisdiction of the Hong Kong Special Administrative Region shall be tried on indictment.

The trial shall be conducted in an open court. When circumstances arise such as the trial involving State secrets or public order, all or part of the trial shall be closed to the media and the public but the judgment shall be delivered in an open court.

Article 42

When applying the laws in force in the Hong Kong Special Administrative Region concerning matters such as the detention and time limit for trial, the law enforcement and judicial authorities of the Region shall ensure that cases concerning offence endangering national security are handled in a fair and timely manner so as to effectively prevent, suppress and impose punishment for such offence.

No bail shall be granted to a criminal suspect or defendant unless the judge has sufficient grounds for believing that the criminal suspect or defendant will not continue to commit acts endangering national security.

Article 43

When handling cases concerning offence endangering national security, the department for safeguarding national security of the Police Force of the Hong Kong Special Administrative Region may take measures that law enforcement authorities, including the Hong Kong Police Force, are allowed to apply under the laws in force in the Hong Kong Special Administrative Region in investigating serious crimes, and may also take the following measures:

(1) search of premises, vehicles, vessels, aircraft and other relevant places and electronic devices that may contain evidence of an offence;

(2) ordering any person suspected of having committed an offence endangering national security to surrender travel documents, or prohibiting the person concerned from leaving the Region;

(3) freezing of, applying for restraint order, charging order and confiscation order in respect of, and forfeiture of property used or intended to be used for the commission of the offence, proceeds of crime, or other property relating to the commission of the offence;

(4) requiring a person who published information or the relevant service provider to delete the information or provide assistance;

(5) requiring a political organization of a foreign country or outside the mainland, Hong Kong, and Macao of the People's Republic of China, or an agent of authorities or a political organization of a foreign country or outside the mainland, Hong Kong, and Macao of the People's Republic of China, to provide information;

(6) upon approval of the Chief Executive, carrying out interception of communications and conducting covert surveillance on a person who is suspected, on reasonable grounds, of having involved in the commission of an offence endangering national security; and

(7) requiring a person, who is suspected, on reasonable grounds, of having in possession information or material relevant to investigation, to answer questions and furnish such information or produce such material.

The Committee for Safeguarding National Security of the Hong Kong Special Administrative Region shall be responsible for supervising the implementation of the measures stipulated in the first paragraph of this Article by law enforcement authorities including the department for safeguarding national security of the Hong Kong Police Force.

The Chief Executive shall be authorized, in conjunction with the Committee for Safeguarding National Security of the Hong Kong Special Administrative Region, to make relevant implementation rules for the purpose of applying the measures under the first paragraph of this Article.

Article 44

The Chief Executive shall designate a number of judges from the magistrates, the judges of the District Court, the judges of the Court of First Instance and the Court of Appeal of the High Court, and the judges of the Court of Final Appeal, and may also designate a number of judges from deputy judges or recorders, to handle cases concerning offence endangering national security. Before making such designation, the Chief Executive may consult the Committee for Safeguarding National Security of the Hong Kong Special Administrative Region and the Chief Justice of the Court of Final Appeal. The term of office of the aforementioned designated judges shall be one year.

A person shall not be designated as a judge to adjudicate a case concerning offence endangering national security if he or she has made any statement or behaved in any manner endangering national security. A designated judge shall be removed from the designation list if he or she makes any statement or behaves in any manner endangering national security during the term of office.

The proceedings in relation to the prosecution for offences endangering national security in the magistrates' courts, the District Court, the High Court and the Court of Final Appeal shall be handled by the designated judges in the respective courts.

Article 45

Unless otherwise provided by this Law, magistrates' courts, the District Court, the High Court and the Court of Final Appeal shall handle proceedings in relation to the prosecution for offences endangering national security in accordance with the laws of the Hong Kong Special Administrative Region.

Article 46

In criminal proceedings in the Court of First Instance of the High Court concerning offences endangering national security, the Secretary for Justice may issue a certificate directing that the case shall be tried without a jury on the grounds of, among others, the protection of State secrets, involvement of foreign factors in the case, and the protection of personal safety of jurors and their family members. Where the Secretary for Justice has issued the certificate, the case shall be tried in the Court of First Instance without a jury by a panel of three judges.

Where the Secretary for Justice has issued the certificate, the reference to "a jury" or "a verdict of the jury" in any provision of the laws of the Hong Kong Special Administrative Region applicable to the related proceedings shall be construed as referring to the judges or the functions of the judge as a judge of fact.

Article 47

The courts of the Hong Kong Special Administrative Region shall obtain a certificate from the Chief Executive to certify whether an act involves national security or whether the relevant evidence involves State secrets when such questions arise in the adjudication of a case. The certificate shall be binding on the courts.

Chapter V
Office for Safeguarding National Security of the Central People's Government in the Hong Kong Special Administrative Region

Article 48

The Central People's Government shall establish in the Hong Kong Special Administrative Region an office for safeguarding national security. The Office for Safeguarding National Security of the Central People's Government in the Hong Kong Special Administrative Region shall perform its mandate for safeguarding national security and exercise relevant powers in accordance with the law.

The staff of the Office shall be jointly dispatched by relevant national security authorities under the Central People's Government.

Article 49

The Office for Safeguarding National Security of the Central People's Government in the Hong Kong Special Administrative Region shall perform the following mandate:

(1) analysing and assessing developments in relation to safeguarding national security in the Hong Kong Special Administrative Region, and providing opinions and making proposals on major strategies and important policies for safeguarding national security;

(2) overseeing, guiding, coordinating with, and providing support to the Region in the performance of its duties for safeguarding national security;

(3) collecting and analysing intelligence and information concerning national security; and

(4) handling cases concerning offence endangering national security in accordance with the law.

Article 50

The Office for Safeguarding National Security of the Central People's Government in the Hong Kong Special Administrative Region shall perform its mandate in strict compliance with the law and be subject to supervision in accordance with the law. It shall not infringe upon the lawful rights and interests of any individual or organization.

The staff of the Office shall abide by the laws of the Hong Kong Special Administrative Region as well as national laws.

The staff of the Office shall be subject to the supervision of the national supervisory authorities in accordance with the law.

Article 51

The Office for Safeguarding National Security of the Central People's Government in the Hong Kong Special Administrative Region shall be funded by the Central People's Government.

Article 52

The Office for Safeguarding National Security of the Central People's Government in the Hong Kong Special Administrative Region shall strengthen working relations and cooperation with the Liaison Office of the Central People's Government in the Hong Kong Special Administrative Region, the Office of the Commissioner of the Ministry of Foreign Affairs in the Hong Kong Special Administrative Region, and the Hong Kong Garrison of the Chinese People's Liberation Army.

Article 53

The Office for Safeguarding National Security of the Central People's Government in the Hong Kong Special Administrative Region shall establish a mechanism of coordination with the Committee for Safeguarding National Security of the Hong Kong Special Administrative Region to oversee and provide guidance on the work of the Hong Kong Special Administrative Region for safeguarding national security.

The working departments of the Office shall establish mechanisms for collaboration with the relevant authorities of the Region responsible for safeguarding national security to enhance information sharing and operations coordination.

Article 54

The Office for Safeguarding National Security of the Central People's Government in the Hong Kong Special Administrative Region and the Office of the Commissioner of the Ministry of Foreign Affairs in the Hong Kong Special Administrative Region shall, together with the Government of the Hong Kong Special Administrative Region, take necessary measures to strengthen the management of and services for organs of foreign countries and international organizations in the Region, as well as non-governmental organizations and news agencies of foreign countries and from outside the mainland, Hong Kong, and Macao of the People's Republic of China in the Region.

Article 55

The Office for Safeguarding National Security of the Central People's Government in the Hong Kong Special Administrative Region shall, upon approval by the Central People's Government of a request made by the Government of the Hong Kong Special Administrative Region or by the Office itself, exercise jurisdiction over a case concerning offence endangering national security under this Law, if:

(1) the case is complex due to the involvement of a foreign country or external elements, thus making it difficult for the Region to exercise jurisdiction over the case;

(2) a serious situation occurs where the Government of the Region is unable to effectively enforce this Law; or

(3) a major and imminent threat to national security has occurred.

Article 56

In exercising jurisdiction over a case concerning offence endangering national security pursuant to Article 55 of this Law, the Office for Safeguarding National Security of the Central People's Government in the Hong Kong Special Administrative Region shall initiate investigation into the case, the Supreme People's Procuratorate shall designate a prosecuting body to prosecute it, and the Supreme People's Court shall designate a court to adjudicate it.

Article 57

The Criminal Procedure Law of the People's Republic of China and other related national laws shall apply to procedural matters, including those related to criminal investigation, examination and prosecution, trial, and execution of penalty, in respect of cases over which jurisdiction is exercised pursuant to Article 55 of this Law.

When exercising jurisdiction over cases pursuant to Article 55 of this Law, the law enforcement and judicial authorities referred to in Article 56 of this Law shall exercise powers in accordance with the law. The legal documents issued by these authorities on their decisions to take mandatory and investigation measures and on their judicial decisions shall have legal force in the Hong Kong Special Administrative Region. The institutions, organizations and individuals concerned must comply with measures taken by the Office for Safeguarding National Security of the Central People's Government in the Hong Kong Special Administrative Region in accordance with the law.

Article 58

In a case over which jurisdiction is exercised pursuant to Article 55 of this Law, a criminal suspect shall have the right to retain a lawyer to represent him or her from the day he or she first receives inquiry made by the Office for Safeguarding National Security of the Central People's Government in the Hong Kong Special Administrative Region or from the day a mandatory measure is taken against him or her. A defence lawyer may provide legal assistance to a criminal suspect or defendant in accordance with the law.

A criminal suspect or defendant who is arrested in accordance with the law shall be entitled to a fair trial before a judicial body without undue delay.

Article 59

In a case over which jurisdiction is exercised pursuant to Article 55 of this Law, any person who has information pertaining to an offence endangering national security under this Law is obliged to testify truthfully.

Article 60

The acts performed in the course of duty by the Office for Safeguarding National Security of the Central People's Government in the Hong Kong Special Administrative Region and its staff in accordance with this Law shall not be subject to the jurisdiction of the Hong Kong Special Administrative Region.

In the course of performing duty, a holder of an identification document or a document of certification issued by the Office and the Articles including vehicles used by the holder shall not be subject to inspection, search or detention by law enforcement officers of the Region.

The Office and its staff shall enjoy other rights and immunities provided by laws of the Region.

Article 61

The relevant departments of the Government of the Hong Kong Special Administrative Region shall provide necessary facilitation and support to the Office for Safeguarding National Security of the Central People's Government in the Hong Kong Special Administrative Region in performing its mandate in accordance with this Law, and shall stop any act obstructing the performance of such mandate and hold those who commit such act liable in accordance with the law.

Chapter VI
Supplementary Provisions

Article 62

This Law shall prevail where provisions of the local laws of the Hong Kong Special Administrative Region are inconsistent with this Law.

Article 63

The law enforcement and judicial authorities and their staff who handle cases concerning offence endangering national security under this Law, or the law enforcement and judicial authorities of the Hong Kong Special Administrative Region and their staff who handle other cases concerning offence endangering national security, shall keep confidential State secrets, trade secrets or personal information which they come to know in the process of handling such cases.

A lawyer who serves as defence counsel or legal representative shall keep confidential State secrets, trade secrets or personal information which he or she comes to know in the practice of law.

The relevant institutions, organizations and individuals who assist with the handling of a case shall keep confidential any information pertaining to the case.

Article 64

In the application of this Law in the Hong Kong Special Administrative Region, the terms "fixed-term imprisonment", "life imprisonment", "confiscation of property" and "criminal fine" in this Law respectively mean "imprisonment", "imprisonment for life",

"confiscation of proceeds of crime" and "fine"; "short-term detention" shall be construed, with reference to the relevant laws of the Region, as "imprisonment", "detention in a detention centre" or "detention in a training centre"; "restriction" shall be construed, with reference to the relevant laws of the Region, as "community service" or "detention in a reformatory school"; and "revoke licence or business permit" means "revoke registration or exemption from registration, or revoke licence" as provided for in the relevant laws of the Region.

Article 65

The power of interpretation of this Law shall be vested in the Standing Committee of the National People's Congress.

Article 66

This Law shall come into force on the date of its promulgation.

SECTION V
SINO-BRITISH JOINT DECLARATION

Joint Declaration of the Government of the United Kingdom of Great Britain and Northern Ireland and the Government of the People's Republic of China on the Question of Hong Kong

The Government of the United Kingdom of Great Britain and Northern Ireland and the Government of the People's Republic of China have reviewed with satisfaction the friendly relations existing between the two Governments and peoples in recent years and agreed that a proper negotiated settlement of the question of Hong Kong, which is left over from the past, is conducive to the maintenance of the prosperity and stability of Hong Kong and to the further strengthening and development of the relations between the two countries on a new basis. To this end, they have, after talks between the delegations of the two Governments, agreed to declare as follows:*

1 The Government of the People's Republic of China declares that to recover the Hong Kong area (including Hong Kong Island, Kowloon and the New Territories, hereinafter referred to as Hong Kong) is the common aspiration of the entire Chinese people, and that it has decided to resume the exercise of sovereignty over Hong Kong with effect from 1 July 1997.

2 The Government of the United Kingdom declares that it will restore Hong Kong to the People's Republic of China with effect from 1 July 1997.

3 The Government of the People's Republic of China declares that the basic policies of the People's Republic of China regarding Hong Kong are as follows:

(1) Upholding national unity and territorial integrity and taking account of the history of Hong Kong and its realities, the People's Republic of China has decided to establish, in accordance with the provisions of Article 31 of the Constitution of the People's Republic of China, a Hong Kong Special Administrative Region upon resuming the exercise of sovereignty over Hong Kong.

(2) The Hong Kong Special Administrative Region will be directly under the authority of the Central People's Government of the People's Republic of China. The Hong Kong Special Administrative Region will enjoy a high degree of autonomy, except in foreign and defence affairs which are the responsibilities of the Central People's Government.

(3) The Hong Kong Special Administrative Region will be vested with executive, legislative and independent judicial power, including that of final adjudication. The laws currently in force in Hong Kong will remain basically unchanged.

(4) The Government of the Hong Kong Special Administrative Region will be composed of local inhabitants. The chief executive will be appointed by the Central People's Government on the basis of the results of elections or consultations to be held locally. Principal officials will be nominated by the chief executive of the Hong Kong Special Administrative Region for appointment by the Central People's Government. Chinese and foreign nationals previously working in the public and police services

* Please note that the numbering in this section has not been standardized and instead follows that used in the original document in order to maintain easy identification of the widely known "12 Policies" in the third declaration.

in the government departments of Hong Kong may remain in employment. British and other foreign nationals may also be employed to serve as advisers or hold certain public posts in government departments of the Hong Kong Special Administrative Region.

(5) The current social and economic systems in Hong Kong will remain unchanged, and so will the life-style. Rights and freedoms, including those of the person, of speech, of the press, of assembly, of association, of travel, of movement, of correspondence, of strike, of choice of occupation, of academic research and of religious belief will be ensured by law in the Hong Kong Special Administrative Region. Private property, ownership of enterprises, legitimate right of inheritance and foreign investment will be protected by law.

(6) The Hong Kong Special Administrative Region will retain the status of a free port and a separate customs territory.

(7) The Hong Kong Special Administrative Region will retain the status of an international financial centre, and its markets for foreign exchange, gold, securities and futures will continue. There will be free flow of capital. The Hong Kong dollar will continue to circulate and remain freely convertible.

(8) The Hong Kong Special Administrative Region will have independent finances. The Central People's Government will not levy taxes on the Hong Kong Special Administrative Region.

(9) The Hong Kong Special Administrative Region may establish mutually beneficial economic relations with the United Kingdom and other countries, whose economic interests in Hong Kong will be given due regard.

(10) Using the name of "Hong Kong, China", the Hong Kong Special Administrative Region may on its own maintain and develop economic and cultural relations and conclude relevant agreements with states, regions and relevant international organizations.

The Government of the Hong Kong Special Administrative Region may on its own issue travel documents for entry into and exit from Hong Kong.

(11) The maintenance of public order in the Hong Kong Special Administrative Region will be the responsibility of the Government of the Hong Kong Special Administrative Region.

(12) The above-stated basic policies of the People's Republic of China regarding Hong Kong and the elaboration of them in Annex I to this Joint Declaration will be stipulated, in a Basic Law of the Hong Kong Special Administrative Region of the People's Republic of China, by the National People's Congress of the People's Republic of China, and they will remain unchanged for 50 years.

4 The Government of the United Kingdom and the Government of the People's Republic of China declare that, during the transitional period between the date of the entry into force of this Joint Declaration and 30 June 1997, the Government of the United Kingdom will be responsible for the administration of Hong Kong with the object of maintaining and preserving its economic prosperity and social stability; and that the Government of the People's Republic of China will give its co-operation in this connection.

5 The Government of the United Kingdom and the Government of the People's Republic of China declare that, in order to ensure a smooth transfer of government in 1997, and with a view to the effective implementation of this Joint Declaration, a Sino-British Joint Liaison Group will be set up when this Joint Declaration enters into force; and that it will be established and will function in accordance with the provisions of Annex II to this Joint Declaration.

6 The Government of the United Kingdom and the Government of the People's Republic of China declare that land leases in Hong Kong and other related matters will be dealt with in accordance with the provisions of Annex III to this Joint Declaration.

7 The Government of the United Kingdom and the Government of the People's Republic of China agree to implement the preceding declarations and the Annexes to this Joint Declaration.

8 This Joint Declaration is subject to ratification and shall enter into force on the date of the exchange of instruments of ratification,* which shall take place in Beijing before 30 June 1985. This Joint Declaration and its Annexes shall be equally binding.

Done in duplicate at Beijing on 19 December 1984 in the English and Chinese languages, both texts being equally authentic.

For the Government of the United Kingdom of Great Britain and Northern Ireland	For the Government of the People's Republic of China
Margaret Thatcher	[ZHAO ZIYANG]

Annex I: Elaboration by the Government of the People's Republic of China of its Basic Policies Regarding Hong Kong

The Government of the People's Republic of China elaborates the basic policies of the People's Republic of China regarding Hong Kong as set out in paragraph (3) of the Joint Declaration of the Government of the United Kingdom of Great Britain and Northern Ireland and the Government of the People's Republic of China on the Question of Hong Kong as follows:

I

The Constitution of the People's Republic of China stipulates in Article 31 that "the state may establish special administrative regions when necessary. The systems to be instituted in special administrative regions shall be prescribed by laws enacted by the National People's Congress in the light of the specific conditions." In accordance with this Article, the People's Republic of China shall, upon the resumption of the exercise of sovereignty over Hong Kong on 1 July 1997, establish the Hong Kong Special Administrative Region of the People's Republic of China. The National People's Congress of the People's Republic of China shall enact and promulgate a Basic Law of the Hong Kong Special Administrative Region of the People's Republic of China (hereinafter referred to as the Basic Law) in accordance with the Constitution of the People's Republic of China, stipulating that after the establishment of the Hong Kong Special Administrative Region the socialist system and socialist policies shall not be practised in the Hong Kong Special Administrative Region and that Hong Kong's previous capitalist system and life-style shall remain unchanged for 50 years.

The Hong Kong Special Administrative Region shall be directly under the authority of the Central People's Government of the People's Republic of China and shall enjoy a high degree of autonomy. Except for foreign and defence affairs which are the responsibilities of the Central People's Government, the Hong Kong Special Administrative Region shall be vested with executive, legislative and independent judicial power, including that of final adjudication. The Central People's Government shall authorize

* The Joint Declaration and Annexes entered into force on 27 May 1985.

the Hong Kong Special Administrative Region to conduct on its own those external affairs specified in Section XI of this Annex.

The government and legislature of the Hong Kong Special Administrative Region shall be composed of local inhabitants. The chief executive of the Hong Kong Special Administrative Region shall be selected by election or through consultations held locally and be appointed by the Central People's Government. Principal officials (equivalent to Secretaries) shall be nominated by the chief executive of the Hong Kong Special Administrative Region and appointed by the Central People's Government. The legislature of the Hong Kong Special Administrative Region shall be constituted by elections. The executive authorities shall abide by the law and shall be accountable to the legislature.

In addition to Chinese, English may also be used in organs of government and in the courts in the Hong Kong Special Administrative Region.

Apart from displaying the national flag and national emblem of the People's Republic of China, the Hong Kong Special Administrative Region may use a regional flag and emblem of its own.

II

After the establishment of the Hong Kong Special Administrative Region, the laws previously in force in Hong Kong (i.e., the common law, rules of equity, ordinances, subordinate legislation and customary law) shall be maintained, save for any that contravene the Basic Law and subject to any amendment by the Hong Kong Special Administrative Region legislature.

The legislative power of the Hong Kong Special Administrative Region shall be vested in the legislature of the Hong Kong Special Administrative Region. The legislature may on its own authority enact laws in accordance with the provisions of the Basic Law and legal procedures, and report them to the Standing Committee of the National People's Congress for the record. Laws enacted by the legislature which are in accordance with the Basic Law and legal procedures shall be regarded as valid.

The laws of the Hong Kong Special Administrative Region shall be the Basic Law, and the laws previously in force in Hong Kong and laws enacted by the Hong Kong Special Administrative Region legislature as above.

III

After the establishment of the Hong Kong Special Administrative Region, the judicial system previously practised in Hong Kong shall be maintained except for those changes consequent upon the vesting in the courts of the Hong Kong Special Administrative Region of the power of final adjudication.

Judicial power in the Hong Kong Special Administrative Region shall be vested in the courts of the Hong Kong Special Administrative Region. The courts shall exercise judicial power independently and free from any interference. Members of the judiciary shall be immune from legal action in respect of their judicial functions. The courts shall decide cases in accordance with the laws of the Hong Kong Special Administrative Region and may refer to precedents in other common law jurisdictions.

Judges of the Hong Kong Special Administrative Region courts shall be appointed by the chief executive of the Hong Kong Special Administrative Region acting in accordance with the recommendation of an independent commission composed of local judges, persons from the legal profession and other eminent persons. Judges shall be chosen by reference to their judicial qualities and may be recruited from other common law jurisdictions. A judge may only be removed for inability to discharge the functions of his office, or for misbehaviour, by the chief executive of the Hong Kong Special Administrative Region acting in accordance with the recommendation of a tribunal appointed by the chief judge of the court of final appeal, consisting of not fewer than three local judges. Additionally, the appointment or removal of principal judges (i.e., those of the highest rank) shall be made by the chief executive with the endorsement of the Hong Kong Special Administrative Region legislature and reported to the Standing Committee of the National People's Congress for the record. The system of appointment and removal of judicial officers other than judges shall be maintained.

The power of final judgment of the Hong Kong Special Administrative Region shall be vested in the court of final appeal in the Hong Kong Special Administrative Region, which may as required invite judges from other common law jurisdictions to sit on the court of final appeal.

A prosecuting authority of the Hong Kong Special Administrative Region shall control criminal prosecutions free from any interference.

On the basis of the system previously operating in Hong Kong, the Hong Kong Special Administrative Region Government shall on its own make provision for local lawyers and lawyers from outside the Hong Kong Special Administrative Region to work and practise in the Hong Kong Special Administrative Region.

The Central People's Government shall assist or authorize the Hong Kong Special Administrative Region Government to make appropriate arrangements for reciprocal juridical assistance with foreign states.

IV

After the establishment of the Hong Kong Special Administrative Region, public servants previously serving in Hong Kong in all government departments, including the police department, and members of the judiciary may all remain in employment and continue their service with pay, allowances, benefits and conditions of service no less favourable than before. The Hong Kong Special Administrative Region Government shall pay to such persons who retire or complete their contracts, as well as to those who have retired before 1 July 1997, or to their dependants, all pensions, gratuities, allowances and benefits due to them on terms no less favourable than before, and irrespective of their nationality or place of residence.

The Hong Kong Special Administrative Region Government may employ British and other foreign nationals previously serving in the public service in Hong Kong, and may recruit British and other foreign nationals holding permanent identity cards of the Hong Kong Special Administrative Region to serve as public servants at all levels, except as heads of major government departments (corresponding to branches or departments at Secretary level) including the police department, and as deputy heads of some of those departments. The Hong Kong Special Administrative Region Government may also employ British and other foreign nationals as advisers to government departments and, when there is a need, may recruit qualified candidates from outside the Hong Kong Special Administrative Region to professional and technical posts in government departments. The above shall be employed only in their individual capacities and, like other public servants, shall be responsible to the Hong Kong Special Administrative Region Government.

The appointment and promotion of public servants shall be on the basis of qualifications, experience and ability. Hong Kong's previous system of recruitment, employment, assessment, discipline, training and management for the public service (including special bodies for appointment, pay and conditions of service) shall, save for any provisions providing privileged treatment for foreign nationals, be maintained.

V

The Hong Kong Special Administrative Region shall deal on its own with financial matters, including disposing of its financial resources and drawing up its budgets and its final accounts. The Hong Kong Special Administrative Region shall report its budgets and final accounts to the Central People's Government for the record.

The Central People's Government shall not levy taxes on the Hong Kong Special Administrative Region. The Hong Kong Special Administrative Region shall use its financial revenues exclusively for its own purposes and they shall not be handed over to the Central People's Government. The systems by which taxation and public expenditure must be approved by the legislature, and by which there is accountability to the legislature for all public expenditure, and the system for auditing public accounts shall be maintained.

VI

The Hong Kong Special Administrative Region shall maintain the capitalist economic and trade systems previously practised in Hong Kong. The Hong Kong Special Administrative Region Government shall decide its economic and trade policies on its own. Rights concerning the ownership of property, including those relating to acquisition, use, disposal, inheritance and compensation for lawful deprivation (corresponding to the real value of the property concerned, freely convertible and paid without undue delay) shall continue to be protected by law.

The Hong Kong Special Administrative Region shall retain the status of a free port and continue a free trade policy, including the free movement of goods and capital. The Hong Kong Special Administrative Region may on its own maintain and develop economic and trade relations with all states and regions.

The Hong Kong Special Administrative Region shall be a separate customs territory. It may participate in relevant international organizations and international trade agreements (including preferential trade arrangements), such as the General Agreement on Tariffs and Trade* and arrangements regarding international trade in textiles. Export quotas, tariff preferences and other similar arrangements obtained by the Hong Kong Special Administrative Region shall be enjoyed exclusively by the Hong Kong Special Administrative Region. The Hong Kong Special Administrative Region shall have authority to issue its own certificates of origin for products manufactured locally, in accordance with prevailing rules of origin.

The Hong Kong Special Administrative Region may, as necessary, establish official and semi-official economic and trade missions in foreign countries, reporting the establishment of such missions to the Central People's Government for the record.

VII

The Hong Kong Special Administrative Region shall retain the status of an international financial centre. The monetary and financial systems previously practised in Hong Kong, including the systems of regulation and supervision of deposit taking institutions and financial markets, shall be maintained.

The Hong Kong Special Administrative Region Government may decide its monetary and financial policies on its own. It shall safeguard the free operation of financial business and the free flow of capital within, into and out of the Hong Kong Special Administrative Region. No exchange control policy shall be applied in the Hong Kong Special Administrative Region. Markets for foreign exchange, gold, securities and futures shall continue.

The Hong Kong dollar, as the local legal tender, shall continue to circulate and remain freely convertible. The authority to issue Hong Kong currency shall be vested in the Hong Kong Special Administrative Region Government. The Hong Kong Special Administrative Region Government may authorize designated banks to issue or continue to issue Hong Kong currency under statutory authority, after satisfying itself that any issue of currency will be soundly based and that the arrangements for such issue are consistent with the object of maintaining the stability of the currency. Hong Kong currency bearing references inappropriate to the status of Hong Kong as a Special Administrative Region of the People's Republic of China shall be progressively replaced and withdrawn from circulation.

The Exchange Fund shall be managed and controlled by the Hong Kong Special Administrative Region Government, primarily for regulating the exchange value of the Hong Kong dollar.

---

* Basic Instruments and Selected Documents, General Agreement on Tariffs and Trade, Volume IV, Text of the General Agreement (Sales No. GATT/1969-1, available through Agency Section, Her Majesty's Stationery Office, PO Box 276, London SW8 5DT).

VIII

The Hong Kong Special Administrative Region shall maintain Hong Kong's previous systems of shipping management and shipping regulation, including the system for regulating conditions of seamen. The specific functions and responsibilities of the Hong Kong Special Administrative Region Government in the field of shipping shall be defined by the Hong Kong Special Administrative Region Government on its own. Private shipping businesses and shipping-related businesses and private container terminals in Hong Kong may continue to operate freely.

The Hong Kong Special Administrative Region shall be authorized by the Central People's Government to continue to maintain a shipping register and issue related certificates under its own legislation in the name of "Hong Kong, China".

With the exception of foreign warships, access for which requires the permission of the Central People's Government, ships shall enjoy access to the ports of the Hong Kong Special Administrative Region in accordance with the laws of the Hong Kong Special Administrative Region.

IX

The Hong Kong Special Administrative Region shall maintain the status of Hong Kong as a centre of international and regional aviation. Airlines incorporated and having their principal place of business in Hong Kong and civil aviation related businesses may continue to operate. The Hong Kong Special Administrative Region shall continue the previous system of civil aviation management in Hong Kong, and keep its own aircraft register in accordance with provisions laid down by the Central People's Government concerning nationality marks and registration marks of aircraft. The Hong Kong Special Administrative Region shall be responsible on its own for matters of routine business and technical management of civil aviation, including the management of airports, the provision of air traffic services within the flight information region of the Hong Kong Special Administrative Region, and the discharge of other responsibilities allocated under the regional air navigation procedures of the International Civil Aviation Organization.

The Central People's Government shall, in consultation with the Hong Kong Special Administrative Region Government, make arrangements providing for air services between the Hong Kong Special Administrative Region and other parts of the People's Republic of China for airlines incorporated and having their principal place of business in the Hong Kong Special Administrative Region and other airlines of the People's Republic of China. All Air Service Agreements providing for air services between other parts of the People's Republic of China and other states and regions with stops at the Hong Kong Special Administrative Region and air services between the Hong Kong Special Administrative Region and other states and regions with stops at other parts of the People's Republic of China shall be concluded by the Central People's Government. For this purpose, the Central People's Government shall take account of the special conditions and economic interests of the Hong Kong Special Administrative Region and consult the Hong Kong Special Administrative Region Government. Representatives of the Hong Kong Special Administrative Region Government may participate as members of delegations of the Government of the People's Republic of China in air service consultations with foreign governments concerning arrangements for such services.

Acting under specific authorizations from the Central People's Government, the Hong Kong Special Administrative Region Government may:

- renew or amend Air Service Agreements and arrangements previously in force; in principle, all such Agreements and arrangements may be renewed or amended with the rights contained in such previous Agreements and arrangements being as far as possible maintained;
- negotiate and conclude new Air Service Agreements providing routes for airlines incorporated and having their principal place of business in the Hong Kong Special Administrative Region and rights for overflights and technical stops; and

– negotiate and conclude provisional arrangements where no Air Service Agreement with a foreign state or other region is in force.

All scheduled air services to, from or through the Hong Kong Special Administrative Region which do not operate to, from or through the mainland of China shall be regulated by Air Service Agreements or provisional arrangements referred to in this paragraph.

The Central People's Government shall give the Hong Kong Special Administrative Region Government the authority to:

– negotiate and conclude with other authorities all arrangements concerning the implementation of the above Air Service Agreements and provisional arrangements;
– issue licences to airlines incorporated and having their principal place of business in the Hong Kong Special Administrative Region;
– designate such airlines under the above Air Service Agreements and provisional arrangements; and
– issue permits to foreign airlines for services other than those to, from or through the mainland of China.

X

The Hong Kong Special Administrative Region shall maintain the educational system previously practised in Hong Kong. The Hong Kong Special Administrative Region Government shall on its own decide policies in the fields of culture, education, science and technology, including policies regarding the educational system and its administration, the language of instruction, the allocation of funds, the examination system, the system of academic awards and the recognition of educational and technological qualifications. Institutions of all kinds, including those run by religious and community organizations, may retain their autonomy. They may continue to recruit staff and use teaching materials from outside the Hong Kong Special Administrative Region. Students shall enjoy freedom of choice of education and freedom to pursue their education outside the Hong Kong Special Administrative Region.

XI

Subject to the principle that foreign affairs are the responsibility of the Central People's Government, representatives of the Hong Kong Special Administrative Region Government may participate, as members of delegations of the Government of the People's Republic of China, in negotiations at the diplomatic level directly affecting the Hong Kong Special Administrative Region conducted by the Central People's Government. The Hong Kong Special Administrative Region may on its own, using the name "Hong Kong, China", maintain and develop relations and conclude and implement agreements with states, regions and relevant international organizations in the appropriate fields, including the economic, trade, financial and monetary, shipping, communications, touristic, cultural and sporting fields. Representatives of the Hong Kong Special Administrative Region Government may participate, as members of delegations of the Government of the People's Republic of China, in international organizations or conferences in appropriate fields limited to states and affecting the Hong Kong Special Administrative Region, or may attend in such other capacity as may be permitted by the Central People's Government and the organization or conference concerned, and may express their views in the name of "Hong Kong, China". The Hong Kong Special Administrative Region may, using the name "Hong Kong, China", participate in international organizations and conferences not limited to states.

The application to the Hong Kong Special Administrative Region of international agreements to which the People's Republic of China is or becomes a party shall be decided by the Central People's Government, in accordance with the circumstances and needs of the Hong Kong Special Administrative Region, and after seeking the views of the Hong Kong Special Administrative Region Government. International agreements to which the People's Republic of China is not a party but which are implemented in Hong Kong may remain implemented in the Hong Kong Special Administrative

Region. The Central People's Government shall, as necessary, authorize or assist the Hong Kong Special Administrative Region Government to make appropriate arrangements for the application to the Hong Kong Special Administrative Region of other relevant international agreements. The Central People's Government shall take the necessary steps to ensure that the Hong Kong Special Administrative Region shall continue to retain its status in an appropriate capacity in those international organizations of which the People's Republic of China is a member and in which Hong Kong participates in one capacity or another. The Central People's Government shall, where necessary, facilitate the continued participation of the Hong Kong Special Administrative Region in an appropriate capacity in those international organizations in which Hong Kong is a participant in one capacity or another, but of which the People's Republic of China is not a member.

Foreign consular and other official or semi-official missions may be established in the Hong Kong Special Administrative Region with the approval of the Central People's Government. Consular and other official missions established in Hong Kong by states which have established formal diplomatic relations with the People's Republic of China, may be maintained. According to the circumstances of each case, consular and other official missions of states having no formal diplomatic relations with the People's Republic of China may either be maintained or changed to semi-official missions. States not recognized by the People's Republic of China can only establish non-governmental institutions.

The United Kingdom may establish a Consulate-General in the Hong Kong Special Administrative Region.

XII

The maintenance of public order in the Hong Kong Special Administrative Region shall be the responsibility of the Hong Kong Special Administrative Region Government. Military forces sent by the Central People's Government to be stationed in the Hong Kong Special Administrative Region for the purpose of defence shall not interfere in the internal affairs of the Hong Kong Special Administrative Region. Expenditure for these military forces shall be borne by the Central People's Government.

XIII

The Hong Kong Special Administrative Region Government shall protect the rights and freedoms of inhabitants and other persons in the Hong Kong Special Administrative Region according to law. The Hong Kong Special Administrative Region Government shall maintain the rights and freedoms as provided for by the laws previously in force in Hong Kong, including freedom of the person, of speech, of the press, of assembly, of association, to form and join trade unions, of correspondence, of travel, of movement, of strike, of demonstration, of choice of occupation, of academic research, of belief, inviolability of the home, the freedom to marry and the right to raise a family freely.

Every person shall have the right to confidential legal advice, access to the courts, representation in the courts by lawyers of his choice, and to obtain judicial remedies. Every person shall have the right to challenge the actions of the executive in the courts.

Religious organizations and believers may maintain their relations with religious organizations and believers elsewhere, and schools, hospitals and welfare institutions run by religious organizations may be continued. The relationship between religious organizations in the Hong Kong Special Administrative Region and those in other parts of the People's Republic of China shall be based on the principles of non-subordination, non-interference and mutual respect.

The provisions of the International Covenant on Civil and Political Rights* and the International Covenant on Economic, Social and Cultural Rights† as applied to Hong Kong shall remain in force.

---

* Treaty Series No. 6 (1977), Cmnd 6702.

† Treaty Series No. 6 (1977), Cmnd 6702.

XIV

The following categories of persons shall have the right of abode in the Hong Kong Special Administrative Region, and, in accordance with the law of the Hong Kong Special Administrative Region, be qualified to obtain permanent identity cards issued by the Hong Kong Special Administrative Region Government, which state their right of abode:

- all Chinese nationals who were born or who have ordinarily resided in Hong Kong before or after the establishment of the Hong Kong Special Administrative Region for a continuous period of 7 years or more, and persons of Chinese nationality born outside Hong Kong of such Chinese nationals;
- all other persons who have ordinarily resided in Hong Kong before or after the establishment of the Hong Kong Special Administrative Region for a continuous period of 7 years or more and who have taken Hong Kong as their place of permanent residence before or after the establishment of the Hong Kong Special Administrative Region, and persons under 21 years of age who were born of such persons in Hong Kong before or after the establishment of the Hong Kong Special Administrative Region;
- any other persons who had the right of abode only in Hong Kong before the establishment of the Hong Kong Special Administrative Region.

The Central People's Government shall authorize the Hong Kong Special Administrative Region Government to issue, in accordance with the law, passports of the Hong Kong Special Administrative Region of the People's Republic of China to all Chinese nationals who hold permanent identity cards of the Hong Kong Special Administrative Region, and travel documents of the Hong Kong Special Administrative Region of the People's Republic of China to all other persons lawfully residing in the Hong Kong Special Administrative Region. The above passports and documents shall be valid for all states and regions and shall record the holder's right to return to the Hong Kong Special Administrative Region.

For the purpose of travelling to and from the Hong Kong Special Administrative Region, residents of the Hong Kong Special Administrative Region may use travel documents issued by the Hong Kong Special Administrative Region Government, or by other competent authorities of the People's Republic of China, or of other states. Holders of permanent identity cards of the Hong Kong Special Administrative Region may have this fact stated in their travel documents as evidence that the holders have the right of abode in the Hong Kong Special Administrative Region.

Entry into the Hong Kong Special Administrative Region of persons from other parts of China shall continue to be regulated in accordance with the present practice.

The Hong Kong Special Administrative Region Government may apply immigration controls on entry, stay in and departure from the Hong Kong Special Administrative Region by persons from foreign states and regions.

Unless restrained by law, holders of valid travel documents shall be free to leave the Hong Kong Special Administrative Region without special authorization.

The Central People's Government shall assist or authorize the Hong Kong Special Administrative Region Government to conclude visa abolition agreements with states or regions.

Annex II: Sino-British Joint Liaison Group

(1) In furtherance of their common aim and in order to ensure a smooth transfer of government in 1997, the Government of the United Kingdom and the Government of the People's Republic of China have agreed to continue their discussions in a friendly spirit and to develop the co-operative relationship which already exists between the two Governments over Hong Kong with a view to the effective implementation of the Joint Declaration.

(2) In order to meet the requirements for liaison, consultation and the exchange of information, the two Governments have agreed to set up a Joint Liaison Group.

(3) The functions of the Joint Liaison Group shall be:

(a) to conduct consultations on the implementation of the Joint Declaration;

(b) to discuss matters relating to the smooth transfer of government in 1997;

(c) to exchange information and conduct consultations on such subjects as may be agreed by the two sides.

Matters on which there is disagreement in the Joint Liaison Group shall be referred to the two Governments for solution through consultations.

(4) Matters for consideration during the first half of the period between the establishment of the Joint Liaison Group and 1 July 1997 shall include:

(a) action to be taken by the two Governments to enable the Hong Kong Special Administrative Region to maintain its economic relations as a separate customs territory, and in particular to ensure the maintenance of Hong Kong's participation in the General Agreement on Tariffs and Trade, the Multifibre Arrangement and other international arrangements; and

(b) action to be taken by the two Governments to ensure the continued application of international rights and obligations affecting Hong Kong.

(5) The two Governments have agreed that in the second half of the period between the establishment of the Joint Liaison Group and 1 July 1997 there will be need for closer co-operation, which will therefore be intensified during that period. Matters for consideration during this second period shall include:

(a) procedures to be adopted for the smooth transition in 1997;

(b) action to assist the Hong Kong Special Administrative Region to maintain and develop economic and cultural relations and conclude agreements on these matters with states, regions and relevant international organizations.

(6) The Joint Liaison Group shall be an organ for liaison and not an organ of power. It shall play no part in the administration of Hong Kong or the Hong Kong Special Administrative Region. Nor shall it have any supervisory role over that administration. The members and supporting staff of the Joint Liaison Group shall only conduct activities with the scope of the functions of the Joint Liaison Group.

(7) Each side shall designate a senior representative, who shall be of Ambassadorial rank, and four other members of the group. Each side may send up to 20 supporting staff.

(8) The Joint Liaison Group shall be established on the entry into force of the Joint Declaration. From 1 July 1988 the Joint Liaison Group shall have its principal base in Hong Kong. The Joint Liaison Group shall continue its work until 1 January 2000.

(9) The Joint Liaison Group shall meet in Beijing, London and Hong Kong. It shall meet at least once in each of the three locations in each year. The venue for each meeting shall be agreed between the two sides.

(10) Members of the Joint Liaison Group shall enjoy diplomatic privileges and immunities as appropriate when in the three locations. Proceedings of the Joint Liaison Group shall remain confidential unless otherwise agreed between the two sides.

(11) The Joint Liaison Group may by agreement between the two sides decide to set up specialist sub-groups to deal with particular subjects requiring expert assistance.

(12) Meetings of the Joint Liaison Group and sub-groups may be attended by experts other than the members of the Joint Liaison Group. Each side shall determine the composition of its delegation

to particular meetings of the Joint Liaison Group or sub-group in accordance with the subjects to be discussed and the venue chosen.

(13) The working procedures of the Joint Liaison Group shall be discussed and decided upon by the two sides within the guidelines laid down in this Annex.

Annex III: Land Leases

The Government of the United Kingdom and the Government of the People's Republic of China have agreed that, with effect from the entry into force of the Joint Declaration, land leases in Hong Kong and other related matters shall be dealt with in accordance with the following provisions:

(1) All leases of land granted or decided upon before the entry into force of the Joint Declaration and those granted thereafter in accordance with paragraph (2) or (3) of this Annex, and which extend beyond 30 June 1997, and all rights in relation to such leases shall continue to be recognized and protected under the law of the Hong Kong Special Administrative Region.

(2) All leases of land granted by the British Hong Kong Government not containing a right of renewal that expire before 30 June 1997, except short term tenancies and leases for special purposes, may be extended if the lessee so wishes for a period expiring not later than 30 June 2047 without payment of an additional premium. An annual rent shall be charged from the date of extension equivalent to 3 percent of the rateable value of the property at that date, adjusted in step with any changes in the rateable value thereafter. In the case of old schedule lots, village lots, small houses and similar rural holdings, where the property was on 30 June 1984 held by, or, in the case of small houses granted after that date, the property is granted to, a person descended through the male line from a person who was in 1898 a resident of an established village in Hong Kong, the rent shall remain unchanged so long as the property is held by that person or by one of his lawful successors in the male line. Where leases of land not having a right of renewal expire after 30 June 1997, they shall be dealt with in accordance with the relevant land laws and policies of the Hong Kong Special Administrative Region.

(3) From the entry into force of the Joint Declaration until 30 June 1997, new leases of land may be granted by the British Hong Kong Government for terms expiring not later than 30 June 2047. Such leases shall be granted at a premium and nominal rental until 30 June 1997, after which date they shall not require payment of an additional premium but an annual rent equivalent to 3 percent of the rateable value of the property at that date, adjusted in step with changes in the rateable value thereafter, shall be charged.

(4) The total amount of new land to be granted under paragraph (3) of this Annex shall be limited to 50 hectares a year (excluding land to be granted to the Hong Kong Housing Authority for public rental housing) from the entry into force of the Joint Declaration until 30 June 1997.

(5) Modifications of the conditions specified in leases granted by the British Hong Kong Government may continue to be granted before 1 July 1997 at a premium equivalent to the difference between the value of the land under the previous conditions and its value under the modified conditions.

(6) From the entry into force of the Joint Declaration until 30 June 1997, premium income obtained by the British Hong Kong Government from land transactions shall, after deduction of the average cost of land production, be shared equally between the British Hong Kong Government and the future Hong Kong Special Administrative Region Government. All the income obtained by the British Hong Kong Government, including the amount of the above mentioned deduction, shall be put into the Capital Works Reserve

Fund for the financing of land development and public works in Hong Kong. The Hong Kong Special Administrative Region Government's share of the premium income shall be deposited in banks incorporated in Hong Kong and shall not be drawn on except for the financing of land development and public works in Hong Kong in accordance with the provisions of paragraph (7)(d) of this Annex.

(7) A Land Commission shall be established in Hong Kong immediately upon the entry into force of the Joint Declaration. The Land Commission shall be composed of an equal number of officials designated respectively by the Government of the United Kingdom and the Government of the People's Republic of China together with necessary supporting staff. The officials of the two sides shall be responsible to their respective governments. The Land Commission shall be dissolved on 30 June 1997.

The terms of reference of the Land Commission shall be:

(a) to conduct consultations on the implementation of this Annex;

(b) to monitor observance of the limit specified in paragraph (4) of this Annex, the amount of land granted to the Hong Kong Housing Authority for public rental housing, and the division and use of premium income referred to in paragraph (6) of this Annex;

(c) to consider and decide on proposals from the British Hong Kong Government for increasing the limit referred to in paragraph (4) of this Annex;

(d) to examine proposals for drawing on the Hong Kong Special Administrative Region Government's share of premium income referred to in paragraph (6) of this Annex and to make recommendations to the Chinese side for decision.

Matters on which there is disagreement in the Land Commission shall be referred to the Government of the United Kingdom and the Government of the People's Republic of China for decision.

(8) Specific details regarding the establishment of the Land Commission shall be finalized separately by the two sides through consultations.

Exchange of Memoranda

United Kingdom Memorandum

In connection with the Joint Declaration of the Government of the United Kingdom of Great Britain and Northern Ireland and the Government of the People's Republic of China on the question of Hong Kong to be signed this day, the Government of the United Kingdom declares that, subject to the completion of the necessary amendments to the relevant United Kingdom legislation:

(a) All persons who on 30 June 1997 are, by virtue of a connection with Hong Kong, British Dependent Territories citizens (BDTCs) under the law in force in the United Kingdom will cease to be BDTCs with effect from 1 July 1997, but will be eligible to retain an appropriate status which, without conferring the right of abode in the United Kingdom, will entitle them to continue to use passports issued by the Government of the United Kingdom. This status will be acquired by such persons only if they hold or are included in such a British passport issued before 1 July 1997, except that eligible persons born on or after 1 January 1997 but before 1 July 1997 may obtain or be included in such a passport up to 31 December 1997.

(b) No person will acquire BDTC status on or after 1 July 1997 by virtue of a connection with Hong Kong. No person born on or after 1 July 1997 will acquire the status referred to as being appropriate in subparagraph (a).

(c) United Kingdom consular officials in the Hong Kong Special Administrative Region and elsewhere may renew and replace passports of persons mentioned in subparagraph (a) and may also issue them to persons, born before 1 July 1997 of such persons, who had previously been included in the passport of their parent.

(d) Those who have obtained or been included in passports issued by the Government of the United Kingdom under subparagraphs (a) and (c) will be entitled to receive, upon request, British consular services and protection when in third countries.

Beijing, 19 December 1984.

Chinese Memorandum

The Government of the People's Republic of China has received the memorandum from the Government of the United Kingdom of Great Britain and Northern Ireland dated 19 December 1984.

Under the Nationality Law of the People's Republic of China, all Hong Kong Chinese compatriots, whether they are holders of the "British Dependent Territories citizens' Passport" or not, are Chinese nationals.

Taking account of the historical background of Hong Kong and its realities, the competent authorities of the Government of the People's Republic of China will, with effect from 1 July 1997, permit Chinese nationals in Hong Kong who were previously called "British Dependent Territories citizens" to use travel documents issued by the Government of the United Kingdom for the purpose of travelling to other states and regions.

The above Chinese nationals will not be entitled to British consular protection in the Hong Kong Special Administrative Region and other parts of the People's Republic of China on account of their holding the above-mentioned British travel documents.

Beijing, 19 December 1984.

PART II

INTERNATIONAL HUMAN RIGHTS INSTRUMENTS

Introduction

Part II contains the text of selected human rights instruments in force in the HKSAR. This compilation is designed to assist scholars, students, human rights lawyers, civil society actors, and others in their work related to human rights in Hong Kong. The instruments included are designed to provide a representative list of primary materials within the space constraints of this sourcebook. A complete list of multilateral agreements (including international human rights instruments) in force in Hong Kong is available on the HKSAR's Department of Justice website.*

We have taken the term "human rights" in a broad sense to include instruments in several related fields. For more efficient access, human rights instruments in this part are divided into five Sections. In addition to the core instruments — the Universal Declaration of Human Rights (UDHR) and seven of the nine core human rights treaties in force in the HKSAR — other selective instruments in four thematic areas — criminal law, labour rights, environment and climate, and business and human rights — are also included in the following Sections.

Section I Core Instruments

This Section provides the core international human rights instruments applicable to the HKSAR. It includes the 1948 United Nations General Assembly Resolution on the UDHR, which though not a binding treaty, nonetheless reflects customary international law in many of its Articles. Containing both civil and political rights as well as economic, social, and cultural rights, the UDHR also served as a pathway towards the development of the International Convention on Civil and Political Rights (ICCPR) and the International Covenant on Economic, Social and Cultural Rights (ICESCR). These three instruments are colloquially known as the International Bill of Rights.

In addition to these three instruments, this Section contains key treaties that seek to (i) eliminate discrimination against women or on the basis of race; (ii) protect rights of children, migrant workers, and persons with disability; and (iii) provide protection against torture and other cruel, inhuman, or degrading treatment or punishment.

Where applicable, treaty reservations and general comments or recommendations have been included after the text of each instrument. These show the year or full date of publication or adoption in parentheses whenever available.

Section II Criminal Law

The instruments in this Section include a representative list of three treaties applicable to Hong Kong concerning the international crime of genocide, transnational organized crime, and suppression of the financing of terrorism. These instruments are designed to ensure the human rights of Hong Kong people by guaranteeing them protection from international crimes and more effectively cooperating with other states to combat sophisticated criminal networks. These treaties focus on transnational cooperation in investigations, extradition, and resource sharing on international criminal enterprises, such as organized crime cartels and terrorist groups. They also include liability for international crimes and eradication of impunity, regardless of the official status of the perpetrator. These treaties are in place to deter international criminal activity and to punish transgressions when they occur.

Section III Labour Rights

Despite debates about the relationship between "human rights" and "labour rights" and separate institutional arrangements at the international level for the protection of these two sets of rights, this book

* Department of Justice website: www.doj.gov.hk/en/external/treaties.html.

treats labour rights as human rights because of deep interlinkages between the two. For example, the freedom of association and the right to collective bargaining are recognized not only in the International Labour Organization (ILO) conventions but also under the ICCPR. Similarly, the protection against discrimination and the rights of children against exploitation are enshrined in international instruments related to both human rights and labour rights. Moreover, the fulfilment of labour rights will contribute to the realization of human rights and vice versa. The relation of the payment of minimum/living wage to the enjoyment of civil, political, economic, social, and cultural rights is a case in point.

Out of about 40 conventions concerning international labour rights which are applicable to the HKSAR, this Section includes the text of seven conventions related to minimum age for work, maternity protection, forced labour, child labour, and freedom of association and collective bargaining. Because of space constraints, it was not possible to include various other conventions concerning labour rights related to, for example, occupational health and safety, workmen compensation, or protection of workers in special settings.

This Section also includes the text of the 1998 ILO Declaration on Fundamental Principles and Rights at Work, which delinks the protection of certain core labour rights from the ratification of relevant conventions. This Declaration commits all ILO member states — irrespective of whether they have ratified the relevant conventions or not — to respect and promote principles and rights in the following four categories: freedom of association and the effective recognition of the right to collective bargaining; the elimination of forced or compulsory labour; the abolition of child labour; and the elimination of discrimination in respect of employment and occupation. The ILO Declaration on Fundamental Principles is also relevant in the context of business and human rights, because of its reference in Principle 12 of the United Nation's Guiding Principles on Business and Human Rights (UNGPs).

There is one unique aspect about the international institutional arrangement for the protection of labour rights: unlike other UN agencies, the ILO is a tripartite institution with governments, employers' organizations, and workers' organization taking decisions collectively about labour standards and policies.

Section IV Environment and Climate

Environmental pollution and climate change are increasingly becoming relevant in the context of human rights for two main reasons: first, there is growing momentum for an explicit recognition of the right to a safe, clean, healthy, and sustainable environment at the international level; and second, the realization of all human rights is inextricably linked to the preservation of the environment and the planet.

This Section contains a few key conventions concerning the disposal of hazardous wastes (Basel Convention on the Control of Transboundary Movement of Hazardous Wastes and Their Disposal), climate change (UN Framework Convention on Climate Change along with the Kyoto Protocol and the Paris Agreement), and preservation of fauna and flora (Convention on International Trade in Endangered Species of Wild Fauna and Flora). Considering Hong Kong's status a shipping hub, the text of the International Convention for the Prevention of Pollution from Ships has also been included. While not exhaustive, these instruments will provide readers a flavour of international instruments aimed at protecting the environment and limiting global warming.

Section V Business and Human Rights

Historically, human rights predominantly evolved in a vertical (state versus individuals) setting. International human rights law mostly imposed obligations on states to "respect, protect, and fulfil" human rights. However, this vertical understanding of human rights has been undergoing changes over the years in proportion to the rise in the power and functions of corporations in a globalized free market economy. Apart from a horizontal application of constitutional rights, international human rights law has started taking small steps to conceive human rights obligations or responsibilities of non-state actors such as business enterprises. The field concerning human rights responsibilities and obligations of business enterprises is now known as "business and human rights" and is often differentiated from a much older field of "corporate social responsibility".

Although the quest to adopt human rights standards applicable to (transnational) corporations has been continuing at the UN level since the early 1970s, the UN Human Rights Council's endorsement of the UNGPs in June 2011 was a watershed moment. This Section contains the text of the UNGPs, which lay down the respective duties of states and responsibilities of business enterprises to prevent, mitigate, and remedy business-related human rights abuses. As soft international standards accepted by all states and other stakeholders, the UNGPs have proved to be highly influential in shaping laws and policies in the business and human rights field at the national, regional, and international levels. For example, in addition to triggering mandatory human rights due diligence legislation in Europe, they are also informing the content of a proposed legally binding international instrument currently being negotiated in the Human Rights Council.

The Section also contains the text of the ILO Tripartite Declaration concerning Multinational Enterprises and Social Policy. This Declaration, which was originally adopted in 1977, was most recently revised in 2017 to align with the UNGPs. Because of space constraints, it was not possible to include many other business and human rights standards which may apply to business enterprises operating in Hong Kong, such as the UN Global Compact, the OECD Guidelines for Multinational Enterprises, modern slavery legislation of the United Kingdom and Australia, the Principles for Responsible Investment, the Children's Rights and Business Principles, ISO 26000: Social Responsibility, the International Code of Conduct for Private Security Service Providers, and LGBTI Standards of Conduct for Business.

SECTION I
THE CORE INSTRUMENTS

This Section includes eight international human rights instruments as applied in Hong Kong. They are:

(1) The Universal Declaration of Human Rights

(2) The International Covenant on Civil and Political Rights

(3) The International Covenant on Economic, Social and Cultural Rights

(4) The International Convention on the Elimination of All Forms of Racial Discrimination

(5) The Convention against Torture and Other Cruel, Inhuman or Degrading Treatment or Punishment

(6) The Convention on the Elimination of All Forms of Discrimination against Women

(7) The Convention on the Rights of the Child

(8) The Convention on the Rights of Persons with Disabilities

UNIVERSAL DECLARATION OF HUMAN RIGHTS

(Adopted: 10 December 1948)

Preamble

Whereas recognition of the inherent dignity and of the equal and inalienable rights of all members of the human family is the foundation of freedom, justice and peace in the world,

Whereas disregard and contempt for human rights have resulted in barbarous acts which have outraged the conscience of mankind, and the advent of a world in which human beings shall enjoy freedom of speech and belief and freedom from fear and want has been proclaimed as the highest aspiration of the common people,

Whereas it is essential, if man is not to be compelled to have recourse, as a last resort, to rebellion against tyranny and oppression, that human rights should be protected by the rule of law,

Whereas it is essential to promote the development of friendly relations between nations,

Whereas the peoples of the United Nations have in the Charter reaffirmed their faith in fundamental human rights, in the dignity and worth of the human person and in the equal rights of men and women and have determined to promote social progress and better standards of life in larger freedom,

Whereas Member States have pledged themselves to achieve, in co-operation with the United Nations, the promotion of universal respect for and observance of human rights and fundamental freedoms,

Whereas a common understanding of these rights and freedoms is of the greatest importance for the full realization of this pledge,

Now, therefore,

The General Assembly,

Proclaims this Universal Declaration of Human Rights as a common standard of achievement for all peoples and all nations, to the end that every individual and every organ of society, keeping this Declaration constantly in mind, shall strive by teaching and education to promote respect for these rights and freedoms and by progressive measures, national and international, to secure their universal and effective recognition and observance, both among the peoples of Member States themselves and among the peoples of territories under their jurisdiction.

Article 1

All human beings are born free and equal in dignity and rights. They are endowed with reason and conscience and should act towards one another in a spirit of brotherhood.

Article 2

Everyone is entitled to all the rights and freedoms set forth in this Declaration, without distinction of any kind, such as race, colour, sex, language, religion, political or other opinion, national or social origin, property, birth or other status. Furthermore, no distinction shall be made on the basis of the political, jurisdictional or international status of the country or territory to which a person belongs, whether it be independent, trust, non-self-governing or under any other limitation of sovereignty.

Article 3

Everyone has the right to life, liberty and the security of person.

Article 4

No one shall be held in slavery or servitude; slavery and the slave trade shall be prohibited in all their forms.

Article 5

No one shall be subjected to torture or to cruel, inhuman or degrading treatment or punishment.

Article 6

Everyone has the right to recognition everywhere as a person before the law.

Article 7

All are equal before the law and are entitled without any discrimination to equal protection of the law. All are entitled to equal protection against any discrimination in violation of this Declaration and against any incitement to such discrimination.

Article 8

Everyone has the right to an effective remedy by the competent national tribunals for acts violating the fundamental rights granted him by the constitution or by law.

Article 9

No one shall be subjected to arbitrary arrest, detention or exile.

Article 10

Everyone is entitled in full equality to a fair and public hearing by an independent and impartial tribunal, in the determination of his rights and obligations and of any criminal charge against him.

Article 11

(1) Everyone charged with a penal offence has the right to be presumed innocent until proved guilty according to law in a public trial at which he has had all the guarantees necessary for his defence.

(2) No one shall be held guilty of any penal offence on account of any act or omission which did not constitute a penal offence, under national or international law, at the time when it was committed.

Nor shall a heavier penalty be imposed than the one that was applicable at the time the penal offence was committed.

Article 12

No one shall be subjected to arbitrary interference with his privacy, family, home or correspondence, nor to attacks upon his honour and reputation. Everyone has the right to the protection of the law against such interference or attacks.

Article 13

(1) Everyone has the right to freedom of movement and residence within the borders of each State.

(2) Everyone has the right to leave any country, including his own, and to return to his country.

Article 14

(1) Everyone has the right to seek and to enjoy in other countries asylum from persecution.

(2) This right may not be invoked in the case of prosecutions genuinely arising from non-political crimes or from acts contrary to the purposes and principles of the United Nations.

Article 15

(1) Everyone has the right to a nationality.

(2) No one shall be arbitrarily deprived of his nationality nor denied the right to change his nationality.

Article 16

(1) Men and women of full age, without any limitation due to race, nationality or religion, have the right to marry and to found a family. They are entitled to equal rights as to marriage, during marriage and at its dissolution.

(2) Marriage shall be entered into only with the free and full consent of the intending spouses.

(3) The family is the natural and fundamental group unit of society and is entitled to protection by society and the State.

Article 17

(1) Everyone has the right to own property alone as well as in association with others.

(2) No one shall be arbitrarily deprived of his property.

Article 18

Everyone has the right to freedom of thought, conscience and religion; this right includes freedom to change his religion or belief, and freedom, either alone or in community with others and in public or private, to manifest his religion or belief in teaching, practice, worship and observance.

Article 19

Everyone has the right to freedom of opinion and expression; this right includes freedom to hold opinions without interference and to seek, receive and impart information and ideas through any media and regardless of frontiers.

Article 20

(1) Everyone has the right to freedom of peaceful assembly and association.

(2) No one may be compelled to belong to an association.

Article 21

(1) Everyone has the right to take part in the government of his country, directly or through freely chosen representatives.

(2) Everyone has the right to equal access to public service in his country.

(3) The will of the people shall be the basis of the authority of government; this will shall be expressed in periodic and genuine elections which shall be by universal and equal suffrage and shall be held by secret vote or by equivalent free voting procedures.

Article 22

Everyone, as a member of society, has the right to social security and is entitled to realization, through national effort and international co-operation and in accordance with the organization and resources of each State, of the economic, social and cultural rights indispensable for his dignity and the free development of his personality.

Article 23

(1) Everyone has the right to work, to free choice of employment, to just and favourable conditions of work and to protection against unemployment.

(2) Everyone, without any discrimination, has the right to equal pay for equal work.

(3) Everyone who works has the right to just and favourable remuneration ensuring for himself and his family an existence worthy of human dignity, and supplemented, if necessary, by other means of social protection.

(4) Everyone has the right to form and to join trade unions for the protection of his interests.

Article 24

Everyone has the right to rest and leisure, including reasonable limitation of working hours and periodic holidays with pay.

Article 25

(1) Everyone has the right to a standard of living adequate for the health and well-being of himself and of his family, including food, clothing, housing and medical care and necessary social services, and the right to security in the event of unemployment, sickness, disability, widowhood, old age or other lack of livelihood in circumstances beyond his control.

(2) Motherhood and childhood are entitled to special care and assistance. All children, whether born in or out of wedlock, shall enjoy the same social protection.

Article 26

(1) Everyone has the right to education. Education shall be free, at least in the elementary and fundamental stages. Elementary education shall be compulsory. Technical and professional education shall be made generally available and higher education shall be equally accessible to all on the basis of merit.

(2) Education shall be directed to the full development of the human personality and to the strengthening of respect for human rights and fundamental freedoms. It shall promote understanding, tolerance and friendship among all nations, racial or religious groups, and shall further the activities of the United Nations for the maintenance of peace.

(3) Parents have a prior right to choose the kind of education that shall be given to their children.

Article 27

(1) Everyone has the right freely to participate in the cultural life of the community, to enjoy the arts and to share in scientific advancement and its benefits.

(2) Everyone has the right to the protection of the moral and material interests resulting from any scientific, literary or artistic production of which he is the author.

Article 28

Everyone is entitled to a social and international order in which the rights and freedoms set forth in this Declaration can be fully realized.

Article 29

(1) Everyone has duties to the community in which alone the free and full development of his personality is possible.

(2) In the exercise of his rights and freedoms, everyone shall be subject only to such limitations as are determined by law solely for the purpose of securing due recognition and respect for the rights and freedoms of others and of meeting the just requirements of morality, public order and the general welfare in a democratic society.

(3) These rights and freedoms may in no case be exercised contrary to the purposes and principles of the United Nations.

Article 30

Nothing in this Declaration may be interpreted as implying for any State, group or person any right to engage in any activity or to perform any act aimed at the destruction of any of the rights and freedoms set forth herein.

INTERNATIONAL COVENANT ON CIVIL AND POLITICAL RIGHTS

(Adopted: 16 December 1966; Entry into force: 23 March 1976, in accordance with Article 49)

Preamble

The States Parties to the present Covenant,

Considering that, in accordance with the principles proclaimed in the Charter of the United Nations, recognition of the inherent dignity and of the equal and inalienable rights of all members of the human family is the foundation of freedom, justice and peace in the world,

Recognizing that these rights derive from the inherent dignity of the human person,

Recognizing that, in accordance with the Universal Declaration of Human Rights, the ideal of free human beings enjoying civil and political freedom and freedom from fear and want can only be achieved if conditions are created whereby everyone may enjoy his civil and political rights, as well as his economic, social and cultural rights,

Considering the obligation of States under the Charter of the United Nations to promote universal respect for, and observance of, human rights and freedoms,

Realizing that the individual, having duties to other individuals and to the community to which he belongs, is under a responsibility to strive for the promotion and observance of the rights recognized in the present Covenant,

Agree upon the following Articles:

Part I

Article 1

(1) All peoples have the right of self-determination. By virtue of that right they freely determine their political status and freely pursue their economic, social and cultural development.

(2) All peoples may, for their own ends, freely dispose of their natural wealth and resources without prejudice to any obligations arising out of international economic co-operation, based upon the principle of mutual benefit, and international law. In no case may a people be deprived of its own means of subsistence.

(3) The States Parties to the present Covenant, including those having responsibility for the administration of Non-Self-Governing and Trust Territories, shall promote the realization of the right of self-determination, and shall respect that right, in conformity with the provisions of the Charter of the United Nations.

Part II

Article 2

(1) Each State Party to the present Covenant undertakes to respect and to ensure to all individuals within its territory and subject to its jurisdiction the rights recognized in the present Covenant, without distinction of any kind, such as race, colour, sex, language, religion, political or other opinion, national or social origin, property, birth or other status.

(2) Where not already provided for by existing legislative or other measures, each State Party to the present Covenant undertakes to take the necessary steps, in accordance with its constitutional processes and with the provisions of the present Covenant, to adopt such legislative or other measures as may be necessary to give effect to the rights recognized in the present Covenant.

(3) Each State Party to the present Covenant undertakes:

(a) To ensure that any person whose rights or freedoms as herein recognized are violated shall have an effective remedy, notwithstanding that the violation has been committed by persons acting in an official capacity;

(b) To ensure that any person claiming such a remedy shall have his right thereto determined by competent judicial, administrative or legislative authorities, or by any other competent authority provided for by the legal system of the State, and to develop the possibilities of judicial remedy;

(c) To ensure that the competent authorities shall enforce such remedies when granted.

Article 3

The States Parties to the present Covenant undertake to ensure the equal right of men and women to the enjoyment of all civil and political rights set forth in the present Covenant.

Article 4

(1) In time of public emergency which threatens the life of the nation and the existence of which is officially proclaimed, the States Parties to the present Covenant may take measures derogating from their obligations under the present Covenant to the extent strictly required by the exigencies of the situation, provided that such measures are not inconsistent with their other obligations under international law and do not involve discrimination solely on the ground of race, colour, sex, language, religion or social origin.

(2) No derogation from Articles 6, 7, 8 (paragraphs (1) and (2)), 11, 15, 16 and 18 may be made under this provision.

(3) Any State Party to the present Covenant availing itself of the right of derogation shall immediately inform the other States Parties to the present Covenant, through the intermediary of the Secretary-General of the United Nations, of the provisions from which it has derogated and of the reasons by which it was actuated. A further communication shall be made, through the same intermediary, on the date on which it terminates such derogation.

Article 5

(1) Nothing in the present Covenant may be interpreted as implying for any State, group or person any right to engage in any activity or perform any act aimed at the destruction of any of the rights and freedoms recognized herein or at their limitation to a greater extent than is provided for in the present Covenant.

(2) There shall be no restriction upon or derogation from any of the fundamental human rights recognized or existing in any State Party to the present Covenant pursuant to law, conventions, regulations or custom on the pretext that the present Covenant does not recognize such rights or that it recognizes them to a lesser extent.

Part III

Article 6

(1) Every human being has the inherent right to life. This right shall be protected by law. No one shall be arbitrarily deprived of his life.

(2) In countries which have not abolished the death penalty, sentence of death may be imposed only for the most serious crimes in accordance with the law in force at the time of the commission of the crime and not contrary to the provisions of the present Covenant and to the Convention on the Prevention and Punishment of the Crime of Genocide. This penalty can only be carried out pursuant to a final judgement rendered by a competent court.

(3) When deprivation of life constitutes the crime of genocide, it is understood that nothing in this Article shall authorize any State Party to the present Covenant to derogate in any way from any obligation assumed under the provisions of the Convention on the Prevention and Punishment of the Crime of Genocide.

(4) Anyone sentenced to death shall have the right to seek pardon or commutation of the sentence. Amnesty, pardon or commutation of the sentence of death may be granted in all cases.

(5) Sentence of death shall not be imposed for crimes committed by persons below eighteen years of age and shall not be carried out on pregnant women.

(6) Nothing in this Article shall be invoked to delay or to prevent the abolition of capital punishment by any State Party to the present Covenant.

Article 7

No one shall be subjected to torture or to cruel, inhuman or degrading treatment or punishment. In particular, no one shall be subjected without his free consent to medical or scientific experimentation.

Article 8

(1) No one shall be held in slavery; slavery and the slave-trade in all their forms shall be prohibited.

(2) No one shall be held in servitude.

(3)

- (a) No one shall be required to perform forced or compulsory labour;
- (b) Paragraph (3)(a) shall not be held to preclude, in countries where imprisonment with hard labour may be imposed as a punishment for a crime, the performance of hard labour in pursuance of a sentence to such punishment by a competent court;
- (c) For the purpose of this paragraph the term "forced or compulsory labour" shall not include:
  - (i) Any work or service, not referred to in subparagraph (b), normally required of a person who is under detention in consequence of a lawful order of a court, or of a person during conditional release from such detention;

(ii) Any service of a military character and, in countries where conscientious objection is recognized, any national service required by law of conscientious objectors;

(iii) Any service exacted in cases of emergency or calamity threatening the life or well-being of the community;

(iv) Any work or service which forms part of normal civil obligations.

Article 9

(1) Everyone has the right to liberty and security of person. No one shall be subjected to arbitrary arrest or detention. No one shall be deprived of his liberty except on such grounds and in accordance with such procedure as are established by law.

(2) Anyone who is arrested shall be informed, at the time of arrest, of the reasons for his arrest and shall be promptly informed of any charges against him.

(3) Anyone arrested or detained on a criminal charge shall be brought promptly before a judge or other officer authorized by law to exercise judicial power and shall be entitled to trial within a reasonable time or to release. It shall not be the general rule that persons awaiting trial shall be detained in custody, but release may be subject to guarantees to appear for trial, at any other stage of the judicial proceedings, and, should occasion arise, for execution of the judgement.

(4) Anyone who is deprived of his liberty by arrest or detention shall be entitled to take proceedings before a court, in order that court may decide without delay on the lawfulness of his detention and order his release if the detention is not lawful.

(5) Anyone who has been the victim of unlawful arrest or detention shall have an enforceable right to compensation.

Article 10

(1) All persons deprived of their liberty shall be treated with humanity and with respect for the inherent dignity of the human person.

(2)

(a) Accused persons shall, save in exceptional circumstances, be segregated from convicted persons and shall be subject to separate treatment appropriate to their status as unconvicted persons;

(b) Accused juvenile persons shall be separated from adults and brought as speedily as possible for adjudication.

(3) The penitentiary system shall comprise treatment of prisoners the essential aim of which shall be their reformation and social rehabilitation. Juvenile offenders shall be segregated from adults and be accorded treatment appropriate to their age and legal status.

Article 11

No one shall be imprisoned merely on the ground of inability to fulfil a contractual obligation.

Article 12

(1) Everyone lawfully within the territory of a State shall, within that territory, have the right to liberty of movement and freedom to choose his residence.

(2) Everyone shall be free to leave any country, including his own.

(3) The above-mentioned rights shall not be subject to any restrictions except those which are provided by law, are necessary to protect national security, public order (ordre public), public health or morals or the rights and freedoms of others, and are consistent with the other rights recognized in the present Covenant.

(4) No one shall be arbitrarily deprived of the right to enter his own country.

Article 13

An alien lawfully in the territory of a State Party to the present Covenant may be expelled therefrom only in pursuance of a decision reached in accordance with law and shall, except where compelling reasons of national security otherwise require, be allowed to submit the reasons against his expulsion and to have his case reviewed by, and be represented for the purpose before, the competent authority or a person or persons especially designated by the competent authority.

Article 14

(1) All persons shall be equal before the courts and tribunals. In the determination of any criminal charge against him, or of his rights and obligations in a suit at law, everyone shall be entitled to a fair and public hearing by a competent, independent and impartial tribunal established by law. The press and the public may be excluded from all or part of a trial for reasons of morals, public order (ordre public) or national security in a democratic society, or when the interest of the private lives of the parties so requires, or to the extent strictly necessary in the opinion of the court in special circumstances where publicity would prejudice the interests of justice; but any judgement rendered in a criminal case or in a suit at law shall be made public except where the interest of juvenile persons otherwise requires or the proceedings concern matrimonial disputes or the guardianship of children.

(2) Everyone charged with a criminal offence shall have the right to be presumed innocent until proved guilty according to law.

(3) In the determination of any criminal charge against him, everyone shall be entitled to the following minimum guarantees, in full equality:

- (a) To be informed promptly and in detail in a language which he understands of the nature and cause of the charge against him;
- (b) To have adequate time and facilities for the preparation of his defence and to communicate with counsel of his own choosing;
- (c) To be tried without undue delay;
- (d) To be tried in his presence, and to defend himself in person or through legal assistance of his own choosing; to be informed, if he does not have legal assistance, of this right; and to have legal assistance assigned to him, in any case where the interests of justice so require, and without payment by him in any such case if he does not have sufficient means to pay for it;
- (e) To examine, or have examined, the witnesses against him and to obtain the attendance and examination of witnesses on his behalf under the same conditions as witnesses against him;
- (f) To have the free assistance of an interpreter if he cannot understand or speak the language used in court;
- (g) Not to be compelled to testify against himself or to confess guilt.

(4) In the case of juvenile persons, the procedure shall be such as will take account of their age and the desirability of promoting their rehabilitation.

(5) Everyone convicted of a crime shall have the right to his conviction and sentence being reviewed by a higher tribunal according to law.

(6) When a person has by a final decision been convicted of a criminal offence and when subsequently his conviction has been reversed or he has been pardoned on the ground that a new or newly discovered fact shows conclusively that there has been a miscarriage of justice, the person who has suffered punishment as a result of such conviction shall be compensated according to law, unless it is proved that the non-disclosure of the unknown fact in time is wholly or partly attributable to him.

(7) No one shall be liable to be tried or punished again for an offence for which he has already been finally convicted or acquitted in accordance with the law and penal procedure of each country.

Article 15

(1) No one shall be held guilty of any criminal offence on account of any act or omission which did not constitute a criminal offence, under national or international law, at the time when it was committed. Nor shall a heavier penalty be imposed than the one that was applicable at the time when the criminal offence was committed. If, subsequent to the commission of the offence, provision is made by law for the imposition of the lighter penalty, the offender shall benefit thereby.

(2) Nothing in this Article shall prejudice the trial and punishment of any person for any act or omission which, at the time when it was committed, was criminal according to the general principles of law recognized by the community of nations.

Article 16

Everyone shall have the right to recognition everywhere as a person before the law.

Article 17

(1) No one shall be subjected to arbitrary or unlawful interference with his privacy, family, home or correspondence, nor to unlawful attacks on his honour and reputation.

(2) Everyone has the right to the protection of the law against such interference or attacks.

Article 18

(1) Everyone shall have the right to freedom of thought, conscience and religion. This right shall include freedom to have or to adopt a religion or belief of his choice, and freedom, either individually or in community with others and in public or private, to manifest his religion or belief in worship, observance, practice and teaching.

(2) No one shall be subject to coercion which would impair his freedom to have or to adopt a religion or belief of his choice.

(3) Freedom to manifest one's religion or beliefs may be subject only to such limitations as are prescribed by law and are necessary to protect public safety, order, health, or morals or the fundamental rights and freedoms of others.

(4) The States Parties to the present Covenant undertake to have respect for the liberty of parents and, when applicable, legal guardians to ensure the religious and moral education of their children in conformity with their own convictions.

Article 19

(1) Everyone shall have the right to hold opinions without interference.

(2) Everyone shall have the right to freedom of expression; this right shall include freedom to seek, receive and impart information and ideas of all kinds, regardless of frontiers, either orally, in writing or in print, in the form of art, or through any other media of his choice.

(3) The exercise of the rights provided for in paragraph (2) of this Article carries with it special duties and responsibilities. It may therefore be subject to certain restrictions, but these shall only be such as are provided by law and are necessary:

  (a) For respect of the rights or reputations of others;

  (b) For the protection of national security or of public order (ordre public), or of public health or morals.

Article 20

(1) Any propaganda for war shall be prohibited by law.

(2) Any advocacy of national, racial or religious hatred that constitutes incitement to discrimination, hostility or violence shall be prohibited by law.

Article 21

The right of peaceful assembly shall be recognized. No restrictions may be placed on the exercise of this right other than those imposed in conformity with the law and which are necessary in a democratic society in the interests of national security or public safety, public order (ordre public), the protection of public health or morals or the protection of the rights and freedoms of others.

Article 22

(1) Everyone shall have the right to freedom of association with others, including the right to form and join trade unions for the protection of his interests.

(2) No restrictions may be placed on the exercise of this right other than those which are prescribed by law and which are necessary in a democratic society in the interests of national security or public safety, public order (ordre public), the protection of public health or morals or the protection of the rights and freedoms of others. This Article shall not prevent the imposition of lawful restrictions on members of the armed forces and of the police in their exercise of this right.

(3) Nothing in this Article shall authorize States Parties to the International Labour Organization Convention of 1948 concerning Freedom of Association and Protection of the Right to Organize to take legislative measures which would prejudice, or to apply the law in such a manner as to prejudice, the guarantees provided for in that Convention.

Article 23

(1) The family is the natural and fundamental group unit of society and is entitled to protection by society and the State.

(2) The right of men and women of marriageable age to marry and to found a family shall be recognized.

(3) No marriage shall be entered into without the free and full consent of the intending spouses.

(4) States Parties to the present Covenant shall take appropriate steps to ensure equality of rights and responsibilities of spouses as to marriage, during marriage and at its dissolution. In the case of dissolution, provision shall be made for the necessary protection of any children.

Article 24

(1) Every child shall have, without any discrimination as to race, colour, sex, language, religion, national or social origin, property or birth, the right to such measures of protection as are required by his status as a minor, on the part of his family, society and the State.

(2) Every child shall be registered immediately after birth and shall have a name.

(3) Every child has the right to acquire a nationality.

Article 25

Every citizen shall have the right and the opportunity, without any of the distinctions mentioned in Article 2 and without unreasonable restrictions:

(a) To take part in the conduct of public affairs, directly or through freely chosen representatives;

(b) To vote and to be elected at genuine periodic elections which shall be by universal and equal suffrage and shall be held by secret ballot, guaranteeing the free expression of the will of the electors;

(c) To have access, on general terms of equality, to public service in his country.

Article 26

All persons are equal before the law and are entitled without any discrimination to the equal protection of the law. In this respect, the law shall prohibit any discrimination and guarantee to all persons equal and effective protection against discrimination on any ground such as race, colour, sex, language, religion, political or other opinion, national or social origin, property, birth or other status.

Article 27

In those States in which ethnic, religious or linguistic minorities exist, persons belonging to such minorities shall not be denied the right, in community with the other members of their group, to enjoy their own culture, to profess and practise their own religion, or to use their own language.

Part IV

Article 28

(1) There shall be established a Human Rights Committee (hereafter referred to in the present Covenant as the Committee). It shall consist of eighteen members and shall carry out the functions hereinafter provided.

(2) The Committee shall be composed of nationals of the States Parties to the present Covenant who shall be persons of high moral character and recognized competence in the field of human rights, consideration being given to the usefulness of the participation of some persons having legal experience.

(3) The members of the Committee shall be elected and shall serve in their personal capacity.

Article 29

(1) The members of the Committee shall be elected by secret ballot from a list of persons possessing the qualifications prescribed in Article 28 and nominated for the purpose by the States Parties to the present Covenant.

(2) Each State Party to the present Covenant may nominate not more than two persons. These persons shall be nationals of the nominating State.

(3) A person shall be eligible for renomination.

Article 30

(1) The initial election shall be held no later than six months after the date of the entry into force of the present Covenant.

(2) At least four months before the date of each election to the Committee, other than an election to fill a vacancy declared in accordance with Article 34, the Secretary-General of the United Nations shall address a written invitation to the States Parties to the present Covenant to submit their nominations for membership of the Committee within three months.

(3) The Secretary-General of the United Nations shall prepare a list in alphabetical order of all the persons thus nominated, with an indication of the States Parties which have nominated them, and shall submit it to the States Parties to the present Covenant no later than one month before the date of each election.

(4) Elections of the members of the Committee shall be held at a meeting of the States Parties to the present Covenant convened by the Secretary General of the United Nations at the Headquarters of the United Nations. At that meeting, for which two thirds of the States Parties to the present Covenant shall constitute a quorum, the persons elected to the Committee shall be those nominees who obtain the largest number of votes and an absolute majority of the votes of the representatives of States Parties present and voting.

Article 31

(1) The Committee may not include more than one national of the same State.

(2) In the election of the Committee, consideration shall be given to equitable geographical distribution of membership and to the representation of the different forms of civilization and of the principal legal systems.

Article 32

(1) The members of the Committee shall be elected for a term of four years. They shall be eligible for re-election if renominated. However, the terms of nine of the members elected at the first election shall expire at the end of two years; immediately after the first election, the names of these nine members shall be chosen by lot by the Chairman of the meeting referred to in Article 30, paragraph (4).

(2) Elections at the expiry of office shall be held in accordance with the preceding Articles of this part of the present Covenant.

Article 33

(1) If, in the unanimous opinion of the other members, a member of the Committee has ceased to carry out his functions for any cause other than absence of a temporary character, the Chairman of the Committee shall notify the Secretary-General of the United Nations, who shall then declare the seat of that member to be vacant.

(2) In the event of the death or the resignation of a member of the Committee, the Chairman shall immediately notify the Secretary-General of the United Nations, who shall declare the seat vacant from the date of death or the date on which the resignation takes effect.

Article 34

(1) When a vacancy is declared in accordance with Article 33 and if the term of office of the member to be replaced does not expire within six months of the declaration of the vacancy, the Secretary-General of the United Nations shall notify each of the States Parties to the present Covenant, which may within two months submit nominations in accordance with Article 29 for the purpose of filling the vacancy.

(2) The Secretary-General of the United Nations shall prepare a list in alphabetical order of the persons thus nominated and shall submit it to the States Parties to the present Covenant. The election to fill the vacancy shall then take place in accordance with the relevant provisions of this part of the present Covenant.

(3) A member of the Committee elected to fill a vacancy declared in accordance with Article 33 shall hold office for the remainder of the term of the member who vacated the seat on the Committee under the provisions of that Article.

Article 35

The members of the Committee shall, with the approval of the General Assembly of the United Nations, receive emoluments from United Nations resources on such terms and conditions as the General Assembly may decide, having regard to the importance of the Committee's responsibilities.

Article 36

The Secretary-General of the United Nations shall provide the necessary staff and facilities for the effective performance of the functions of the Committee under the present Covenant.

Article 37

(1) The Secretary-General of the United Nations shall convene the initial meeting of the Committee at the Headquarters of the United Nations.

(2) After its initial meeting, the Committee shall meet at such times as shall be provided in its rules of procedure.

(3) The Committee shall normally meet at the Headquarters of the United Nations or at the United Nations Office at Geneva.

Article 38

Every member of the Committee shall, before taking up his duties, make a solemn declaration in open committee that he will perform his functions impartially and conscientiously.

Article 39

(1) The Committee shall elect its officers for a term of two years. They may be re-elected.

(2) The Committee shall establish its own rules of procedure, but these rules shall provide, inter alia, that:

(a) Twelve members shall constitute a quorum;

(b) Decisions of the Committee shall be made by a majority vote of the members present.

Article 40

(1) The States Parties to the present Covenant undertake to submit reports on the measures they have adopted which give effect to the rights recognized herein and on the progress made in the enjoyment of those rights:

(a) Within one year of the entry into force of the present Covenant for the States Parties concerned;

(b) Thereafter whenever the Committee so requests.

(2) All reports shall be submitted to the Secretary-General of the United Nations, who shall transmit them to the Committee for consideration. Reports shall indicate the factors and difficulties, if any, affecting the implementation of the present Covenant.

(3) The Secretary-General of the United Nations may, after consultation with the Committee, transmit to the specialized agencies concerned copies of such parts of the reports as may fall within their field of competence.

(4) The Committee shall study the reports submitted by the States Parties to the present Covenant. It shall transmit its reports, and such General Comments as it may consider appropriate, to the States Parties. The Committee may also transmit to the Economic and Social Council these comments along with the copies of the reports it has received from States Parties to the present Covenant.

(5) The States Parties to the present Covenant may submit to the Committee observations on any comments that may be made in accordance with paragraph (4) of this Article.

Article 41

(1) A State Party to the present Covenant may at any time declare under this Article that it recognizes the competence of the Committee to receive and consider communications to the effect that a State Party claims that another State Party is not fulfilling its obligations under the present Covenant. Communications under this Article may be received and considered only if submitted by a State Party which has made a declaration recognizing in regard to itself the competence of the Committee. No communication shall be received by the Committee if it concerns a State Party which has not made such a declaration. Communications received under this Article shall be dealt with in accordance with the following procedure:

(a) If a State Party to the present Covenant considers that another State Party is not giving effect to the provisions of the present Covenant, it may, by written communication, bring the matter to the attention of that State Party. Within three months after the receipt of the communication the receiving State shall afford the State which sent the communication an explanation, or any other statement in writing clarifying the matter which should include, to the extent possible and pertinent, reference to domestic procedures and remedies taken, pending, or available in the matter;

(b) If the matter is not adjusted to the satisfaction of both States Parties concerned within six months after the receipt by the receiving State of the initial communication, either State shall have the right to refer the matter to the Committee, by notice given to the Committee and to the other State;

(c) The Committee shall deal with a matter referred to it only after it has ascertained that all available domestic remedies have been invoked and exhausted in the matter, in conformity with the generally recognized principles of international law. This shall not be the rule where the application of the remedies is unreasonably prolonged;

(d) The Committee shall hold closed meetings when examining communications under this Article;

(e) Subject to the provisions of subparagraph (c), the Committee shall make available its good offices to the States Parties concerned with a view to a friendly solution of the matter on the basis of respect for human rights and fundamental freedoms as recognized in the present Covenant;

(f) In any matter referred to it, the Committee may call upon the States Parties concerned, referred to in subparagraph (b), to supply any relevant information;

(g) The States Parties concerned, referred to in subparagraph (b), shall have the right to be represented when the matter is being considered in the Committee and to make submissions orally and/or in writing;

(h) The Committee shall, within twelve months after the date of receipt of notice under subparagraph (b), submit a report:

(i) If a solution within the terms of subparagraph (e) is reached, the Committee shall confine its report to a brief statement of the facts and of the solution reached;

(ii) If a solution within the terms of subparagraph (e) is not reached, the Committee shall confine its report to a brief statement of the facts; the written submissions and record of the oral submissions made by the States Parties concerned shall be attached to the report.

In every matter, the report shall be communicated to the States Parties concerned.

(2) The provisions of this Article shall come into force when ten States Parties to the present Covenant have made declarations under paragraph (1) of this Article. Such declarations shall be deposited by the States Parties with the Secretary-General of the United Nations, who shall transmit copies thereof to the other States Parties. A declaration may be withdrawn at any time by notification to the Secretary-General. Such a withdrawal shall not prejudice the consideration of any matter which is the subject of a communication already transmitted under this Article; no further communication by any State Party shall be received after the notification of withdrawal of the declaration has been received by the Secretary-General, unless the State Party concerned has made a new declaration.

Article 42

(1)

(a) If a matter referred to the Committee in accordance with Article 41 is not resolved to the satisfaction of the States Parties concerned, the Committee may, with the prior consent of the States Parties concerned, appoint an ad hoc Conciliation Commission (hereinafter referred to as the Commission). The good offices of the Commission shall be made available to the States Parties concerned with a view to an amicable solution of the matter on the basis of respect for the present Covenant;

(b) The Commission shall consist of five persons acceptable to the States Parties concerned. If the States Parties concerned fail to reach agreement within three months on all or part of the composition of the Commission, the members of the Commission concerning whom no agreement has been reached shall be elected by secret ballot by a two-thirds majority vote of the Committee from among its members.

(2) The members of the Commission shall serve in their personal capacity. They shall not be nationals of the States Parties concerned, or of a State not Party to the present Covenant, or of a State Party which has not made a declaration under Article 41.

(3) The Commission shall elect its own Chairman and adopt its own rules of procedure.

(4) The meetings of the Commission shall normally be held at the Headquarters of the United Nations or at the United Nations Office at Geneva. However, they may be held at such other convenient places as the Commission may determine in consultation with the Secretary-General of the United Nations and the States Parties concerned.

(5) The secretariat provided in accordance with Article 36 shall also service the commissions appointed under this Article.

(6) The information received and collated by the Committee shall be made available to the Commission and the Commission may call upon the States Parties concerned to supply any other relevant information.

(7) When the Commission has fully considered the matter, but in any event not later than twelve months after having been seized of the matter, it shall submit to the Chairman of the Committee a report for communication to the States Parties concerned:

  (a) If the Commission is unable to complete its consideration of the matter within twelve months, it shall confine its report to a brief statement of the status of its consideration of the matter;

  (b) If an amicable solution to the matter on tie [*sic*] basis of respect for human rights as recognized in the present Covenant is reached, the Commission shall confine its report to a brief statement of the facts and of the solution reached;

  (c) If a solution within the terms of subparagraph (b) is not reached, the Commission's report shall embody its findings on all questions of fact relevant to the issues between the States Parties concerned, and its views on the possibilities of an amicable solution of the matter. This report shall also contain the written submissions and a record of the oral submissions made by the States Parties concerned;

  (d) If the Commission's report is submitted under subparagraph (c), the States Parties concerned shall, within three months of the receipt of the report, notify the Chairman of the Committee whether or not they accept the contents of the report of the Commission.

(8) The provisions of this Article are without prejudice to the responsibilities of the Committee under Article 41.

(9) The States Parties concerned shall share equally all the expenses of the members of the Commission in accordance with estimates to be provided by the Secretary-General of the United Nations.

(10) The Secretary-General of the United Nations shall be empowered to pay the expenses of the members of the Commission, if necessary, before reimbursement by the States Parties concerned, in accordance with paragraph (9) of this Article.

Article 43

The members of the Committee, and of the ad hoc conciliation commissions which may be appointed under Article 42, shall be entitled to the facilities, privileges and immunities of experts on mission for the United Nations as laid down in the relevant Sections of the Convention on the Privileges and Immunities of the United Nations.

Article 44

The provisions for the implementation of the present Covenant shall apply without prejudice to the procedures prescribed in the field of human rights by or under the constituent instruments and the conventions of the United Nations and of the specialized agencies and shall not prevent the States Parties to the present Covenant from having recourse to other procedures for settling a dispute in accordance with general or special international agreements in force between them.

Article 45

The Committee shall submit to the General Assembly of the United Nations, through the Economic and Social Council, an annual report on its activities.

Part V

Article 46

Nothing in the present Covenant shall be interpreted as impairing the provisions of the Charter of the United Nations and of the constitutions of the specialized agencies which define the respective responsibilities of the various organs of the United Nations and of the specialized agencies in regard to the matters dealt with in the present Covenant.

Article 47

Nothing in the present Covenant shall be interpreted as impairing the inherent right of all peoples to enjoy and utilize fully and freely their natural wealth and resources.

Part VI

Article 48

(1) The present Covenant is open for signature by any State Member of the United Nations or member of any of its specialized agencies, by any State Party to the Statute of the International Court of Justice, and by any other State which has been invited by the General Assembly of the United Nations to become a Party to the present Covenant.

(2) The present Covenant is subject to ratification. Instruments of ratification shall be deposited with the Secretary-General of the United Nations.

(3) The present Covenant shall be open to accession by any State referred to in paragraph (1) of this Article.

(4) Accession shall be effected by the deposit of an instrument of accession with the Secretary-General of the United Nations.

(5) The Secretary-General of the United Nations shall inform all States which have signed this Covenant or acceded to it of the deposit of each instrument of ratification or accession.

Article 49

(1) The present Covenant shall enter into force three months after the date of the deposit with the Secretary-General of the United Nations of the thirty-fifth instrument of ratification or instrument of accession.

(2) For each State ratifying the present Covenant or acceding to it after the deposit of the thirty-fifth instrument of ratification or instrument of accession, the present Covenant shall enter into force three months after the date of the deposit of its own instrument of ratification or instrument of accession.

Article 50

The provisions of the present Covenant shall extend to all parts of federal States without any limitations or exceptions.

Article 51

(1) Any State Party to the present Covenant may propose an amendment and file it with the Secretary-General of the United Nations. The Secretary-General of the United Nations shall thereupon communicate any proposed amendments to the States Parties to the present Covenant with a request that they notify him whether they favour a conference of States Parties for the purpose of considering and voting upon the proposals. In the event that at least one third of the States Parties favours such a conference, the Secretary-General shall convene the conference under the auspices of the United Nations. Any amendment adopted by a majority of the States Parties present and voting at the conference shall be submitted to the General Assembly of the United Nations for approval.

(2) Amendments shall come into force when they have been approved by the General Assembly of the United Nations and accepted by a two-thirds majority of the States Parties to the present Covenant in accordance with their respective constitutional processes.

(3) When amendments come into force, they shall be binding on those States Parties which have accepted them, other States Parties still being bound by the provisions of the present Covenant and any earlier amendment which they have accepted.

Article 52

Irrespective of the notifications made under Article 48, paragraph (5), the Secretary-General of the United Nations shall inform all States referred to in paragraph (1) of the same Article of the following particulars:

(a) Signatures, ratifications and accessions under Article 48;

(b) The date of the entry into force of the present Covenant under Article 49 and the date of the entry into force of any amendments under Article 51.

Article 53

(1) The present Covenant, of which the Chinese, English, French, Russian and Spanish texts are equally authentic, shall be deposited in the archives of the United Nations.

(2) The Secretary-General of the United Nations shall transmit certified copies of the present Covenant to all States referred to in Article 48.

Application of the Covenant to the Hong Kong Special Administrative Region

In 1976, the Government of the United Kingdom ratified the International Covenant on Civil and Political Rights with certain reservations and declarations, and extended the Covenant to 10 British dependent territories including Hong Kong.

On 20 June 1997, the Government of the People's Republic of China notified the United Nations Secretary-General in a Note that-

> "In accordance with the Joint Declaration of the Government of the United Kingdom of Great Britain and North Ireland and the Government of the People's Republic of China on the Question of Hong Kong signed on 19 December 1984 (hereinafter referred to as the Joint Declaration), the People's Republic of China will resume the exercise of sovereignty over Hong Kong with effect from 1 July 1997. Hong Kong will, with effect from that date, become a Special Administrative Region of the People's Republic of China. ... Furthermore, it is provided both in Section XI of Annex I to the Joint Declaration and Article 153 of the Basic Law that international agreements

to which the People's Republic of China is not a party but which are implemented in Hong Kong may continue to be implemented in the Hong Kong Special Administrative Region."

In this connection, the Government of the People's Republic of China informed the United Nations Secretary-General that the provisions of the International Covenant on Civil and Political Rights as applied to Hong Kong shall remain in force beginning from 1 July 1997. The application of the Covenant is also provided for in Article 39 of the Basic Law.

The reservations and declarations in the Covenant which continue to apply to the Hong Kong Special Administrative Region are as follows-

Declaration Made on Signing the Covenant

First, the Government of the United Kingdom declare their understanding that, by virtue of Article 103 of the Charter of the United Nations, in the event of any conflict between their obligations under Article 1 of the Covenant and their obligations under the Charter (in particular, under Articles 1, 2 and 73 thereof) their obligations under the Charter shall prevail.

Declarations and Reservations Made on Depositing the Instrument of Ratification of the Covenant

Firstly the Government of the United Kingdom maintain their declaration in respect of Article 1 made at the time of signature of the Covenant.

The Government of the United Kingdom reserve the right to apply to members of and persons serving with the armed forces of the Crown and to persons lawfully detained in penal establishments of whatever character such laws and procedures as they may from time to time deem to be necessary for the preservation of service and custodial discipline and their acceptance of the provisions of the Covenant is subject to such restrictions as may for these purposes from time to time be authorized by law.

Where at any time there is a lack of suitable prison facilities or where the mixing of adults and juveniles is deemed to be mutually beneficial, the Government of the United Kingdom reserve the right not to apply Article 10.2(b) and 10.3 so far as those provisions require juveniles who are detained to be accommodated separately from adults, [...]

The Government of the United Kingdom reserve the right to interpret the provisions of Article 12.1 relating to the territory of a State as applying separately to each of the territories comprising the United Kingdom and its dependencies.

The Government of the United Kingdom reserve the right to continue to apply such immigration legislation governing entry into, stay in and departure from the United Kingdom as they may deem necessary from time to time and, accordingly, their acceptance of Article 12.4 and of the other provisions of the Covenant is subject to the provisions of any such legislation as regards persons not at the time having the right under the law of the United Kingdom to enter and remain in the United Kingdom. The United Kingdom also reserves a similar right in regard to each of its dependent territories.

The Government of the United Kingdom reserve the right not to apply Article 13 in Hong Kong in so far as it confers a right of review of a decision to deport an alien and a right to be represented for this purpose before the competent authority.

The Government of the United Kingdom interpret Article 20 consistently with the rights conferred by Articles 19 and 21 of the Covenant and having legislated in matters of practical concern in the interests of public order (ordre public) reserve the right not to introduce any further legislation. The United Kingdom also reserve a similar right in regard to each of its dependent territories.

The Government of the United Kingdom reserve the right to enact such nationality legislation as they may deem necessary from time to time to reserve the acquisition and possession of citizenship under such legislation to those having sufficient connection with the United Kingdom or any of its dependent territories and accordingly their acceptance of Article 24.3 and of the other provisions of the Covenant is subject to the provisions of any such legislation.

The Government of the United Kingdom reserve the right not to apply subparagraph (b) of Article 25 in so far as it may require the establishment of an elected Executive or Legislative Council in Hong Kong [...].

Declaration under Article 41 Dated 17 May 1976

The Government of the United Kingdom declares under Article 41 of this Covenant that it recognizes the competence of the Human Rights Committee to receive and consider communications submitted by another State Party, provided that such other State Party has, not less than twelve months prior to the submission by it of a communication relating to the United Kingdom, made a declaration under Article 41 recognizing the competence of the Committee to receive and consider communications relating to itself.

Reservations Applicable to Hong Kong *

United Kingdom of Great Britain and Northern Ireland †

Signed on 16 September 1968
Ratified on 20 May 1976

Upon signature:

[...]

(c) In relation to Article 25 of the Covenant, they must reserve the right not to apply:

(i) Subparagraph (b) in so far as it may require the establishment of an elected legislature in Hong Kong and the introduction of equal suffrage, as between different electoral rolls, for elections in Fiji; and

* With regard to the application of the Covenant to Hong Kong, the Secretary-General received communications concerning the status of Hong Kong from the United Kingdom and China (see note 2 under "United Kingdom of Great Britain and Northern Ireland" and note 2 under "China" in the "Historical Information" Section at https://treaties.un.org/Pages/HistoricalInfo.aspx?clang=_en#, which has been reproduced in the footnotes to the following sections). Upon resuming the exercise of sovereignty over Hong Kong, China notified the Secretary-General that the Covenant will also apply to the Hong Kong Special Administrative Region.

† The following is reproduced from note 2 in the "Historical Information" Section for United Kingdom of Great Britain and Northern Ireland, which can be found at https://treaties.un.org/Pages/HistoricalInfo.aspx?clang=_en#UnitedKingdomofGreatBritainandNorthernIreland.

Note 2: On 10 June 1997, the Government of the United Kingdom of Great Britain and Northern Ireland notified the Secretary-General of the following: "In accordance with the Joint Declaration of the United Kingdom of Great Britain and Northern Ireland and the Government of the People's Republic of China on the Question of Hong Kong signed on 19 December 1984, the Government of the United Kingdom will restore Hong Kong to the People's Republic of China with effect from 1 July 1997. The Government of the United Kingdom will continue to have international responsibility for Hong Kong until that date. Therefore, from that date the Government of the United Kingdom will cease to be responsible for the international rights and obligations arising from the application of [Conventions] to Hong Kong." See also note 2 under "China", which is reproduced in the footnote of the following section.

(ii) Subparagraph (c) in so far as it applies to jury service in the Isle of Man and to the employment of married women in the Civil Service of Northern Ireland, Fiji, and Hong Kong.

Upon ratification:

[...]

The Government of the United Kingdom reserve the right not to apply Article 13 in Hong Kong in so far as it confers a right of review of a decision to deport an alien and a right to be represented for this purpose before the competent authority.

The Government of the United Kingdom reserve the right not to apply subparagraph (b) of Article 25 in so far as it may require the establishment of an elected Executive or Legislative Council in Hong Kong [...].

The Government of the United Kingdom reserve the right not to apply subparagraph (b) of Article 25 in so far as it may require the establishment of an elected Executive or Legislative Council in Hong Kong [...].

China *

* The following is reproduced from note 2 in the "Historical Information" Section for China, which can be found at https://treaties.un.org/Pages/HistoricalInfo.aspx?clang=_en#China.

Note 2: By a notification on 20 June 1997, the Government of China informed the Secretary-General of the status of Hong Kong in relation to treaties deposited with the Secretary-General. The notification, in pertinent part, reads as follows: "In accordance with the Joint Declaration of the Government of the United Kingdom of Great Britain and Northern Ireland and the Government of the People's Republic of China on the Question of Hong Kong, signed on 19 December 1984 (hereinafter referred to as the Joint Declaration), the People's Republic of China will resume the exercise of sovereignty over Hong Kong with effect from 1 July 1997. Hong Kong will, with effect from that date, become a Special Administrative Region of the People's Republic of China. [For the full text of the Joint Declaration of the Government of the United Kingdom of Great Britain and Northern Ireland and the Government of the People's Republic of China on the Question of Hong Kong, 19 December 1984, see United Nation Treaty Series volume No. 1399, p. 61, (registration number I-23391)].

It is provided in Section 1 of Annex I to the Joint Declaration, "Elaboration by the Government of the People's Republic of China of its Basic Policies Regarding Hong Kong" and in Articles 12, 13 and 14 of the Basic Law of the Hong Kong Special Administrative Region of the People's Republic of China, which was adopted on 4 April 1990 by the National People's Congress of the People's Republic of China (hereinafter referred to as the Basic Law), that the Hong Kong Special Administrative Region will enjoy a high degree of autonomy, except in foreign and defence affairs which are the responsibility of the Central People's Government of the People's Republic of China. Furthermore, it is provided both in Section XI of Annex I to the Joint Declaration and Article 153 of the Basic Law that international agreements to which the People's Republic of China is not a party but which are implemented in Hong Kong may continue to be implemented in the Hong Kong Administrative Region.

In this connection, on behalf of the Government of the People's Republic of China, I would like to inform Your Excellency as follows:

I. The treaties listed in Annex I to this Note [herein under], to which the People's Republic of China is a party, will be applied to the Hong Kong Special Administrative Region with effect from 1 July 1997 as they:

(i) are applied to Hong Kong before 1 July 1997; or

(ii) fall within the category of foreign affairs or defence or, owing to their nature and provisions, must apply to the entire territory of a State; or

[footnote continued]

(iii) are not applied to Hong Kong before 1 July 1997 but with respect to which it has been decided to apply them to Hong Kong with effect from that date (denoted by an asterisk in Annex I).

II. The treaties listed in Annex II to this Note [herein under], to which the People's Republic of China is not yet a party and which apply to Hong Kong before 1 July 1997, will continue to apply to the Hong Kong Special Administrative Region with effect from 1 July 1997.

The provisions of the International Covenant on Civil and Political Rights and the International Covenant on Economic, Social and Cultural Rights as applied to Hong Kong shall remain in force beginning from 1 July 1997.

III. The Government of the People's Republic of China has already carried out separately the formalities required for the application of the treaties listed in the aforesaid Annexes, including all the related amendments, protocols, reservations and declarations, to the Hong Kong Special Administrative Region with effect from 1 July 1997.

IV. With respect to any other treaty not listed in the Annexes to this Note, to which the People's Republic of China is or will become a party, in the event that it is decided to apply such treaty to the Hong Kong Special Administrative Region, the Government of the People's Republic of China will carry out separately the formalities for such application. For the avoidance of doubt, no separate formalities will need to be carried out by the Government of the People's Republic of China with respect to treaties which fall within in the category of foreign affairs or defence or which, owing to their nature and provisions, must apply to the entire territory of a State."

The treaties listed in Annexes I and II, referred to in the notification, are reproduced below.

Information regarding reservations and/or declarations made by China with respect to the application of treaties to the Hong Kong Special Administrative Region can be found in the footnotes to the treaties concerned as published herein. Footnote indicators are placed against China's entry in the status list of those treaties.

Moreover, with regard to treaty actions undertaken by China after 1 July 1997, the Chinese Government confirmed that the territorial scope of each treaty action would be specified. As such, declarations concerning the territorial scope of the relevant treaties with regard to the Hong Kong Special Administrative Region can be found in the footnotes to the treaties concerned as published herein. Footnote indicators are placed against China's entry in the status list of those treaties.

Annex I (The treaties are listed in the order that they published in these volumes.)

Charter of the United Nations and Statute of the International Court of Justice:

- Charter of the United Nations, 26 June 1945;
- Statute of the International Court of Justice, 26 June 1945;
- Amendment to Article 61 of the Charter of the United Nations, adopted by the General Assembly of the United Nations in resolution 2847 (XXVI) of 20 December 1971.

Privileges and Immunities, Diplomatic and Consular Relations:

- Convention on the Privileges and Immunities of the United Nations, 13 February 1946;
- Convention on the Privileges and Immunities of the Specialized Agencies of the United Nations, 21 November 1947;
- Vienna Convention on Diplomatic Relations, 18 April 1961;
- Vienna Convention on Consular Relations, 24 April 1963.

Human Rights:

- Convention on the Prevention and Punishment of the Crime of Genocide, 9 December 1948;
- International Convention on the Elimination of All Forms of Racial Discrimination, 7 March 1966;
- Convention on the Elimination of All Forms of Discrimination against Women, 18 December 1979;
- Convention against Torture and Other Cruel, Inhuman or Degrading Treatment or Punishment, 10 December 1984;
- Convention on the Rights of the Child, 20 November 1989.

[footnote continued]

Narcotic Drugs and Psychotropic Substances:
- Convention on psychotropic substances, 21 February 1971;
- Single Convention on Narcotic Drugs, 1961, as amended by the Protocol amending the Single Convention on Narcotic Drugs, 1961, 8 August 1975;
- United Nations Convention against Illicit Traffic in Narcotic Drugs and Psychotropic Substances, 20 December 1988.

Health:
- Constitution of the World Health Organization, 22 July 1946.

International Trade and Development:
- Agreement establishing the Asian Development Bank, 4 December 1965;
- Charter of the Asian and Pacific Development Centre, 1 April 1982

Transport and Communications — Customs matters:
- Customs Convention on Containers, 2 December 1972*.

Navigation:
- Convention on the International Maritime Organization, 6 March 1948;
- Convention on a Code of Conduct for Liner Conferences, 6 April 1974.

Educational and Cultural Matters:
- Convention for the Protection of Products of Phonograms Against Unauthorized Duplication of their Phonograms, 29 October 1971.

Penal Matters:
- International Convention against the taking of hostages, 17 December 1979;
- Convention on the Prevention and Punishment of Crimes against Internationally Protected Persons, including Diplomatic Agents, 14 December 1973.

Law of the Sea:
- United Nations Convention on the Law of the Sea, 10 December 1982.

Commercial Arbitration:
- Convention on the Recognition and Enforcement of Foreign Arbitral Awards, 10 June 1958.

Outer Space:
- Convention on the Registration of Objects Launched into Outer Space, 12 November 1974.

Telecommunications:
- Constitution of the Asia-Pacific Telecommunity, 27 March 1976.

Disarmament:
- Convention on Prohibitions or restrictions on the Use of Certain Conventional Weapons which may be deemed to be Excessively Injurious or to have Indiscriminate Effects (with Protocols I, II and III), 10 October 1980;
- Convention on the Prohibition of the Development, Production and Stockpiling and Use of Chemical Weapons and on their Destruction, 3 September 1992.

Environment:
- Vienna Convention for the Protection of the Ozone Layer, 22 March 1985;
- Montreal Protocol on Substances that Deplete the Ozone Layer, 16 September 1987;
- Amendment to the Montreal Protocol on Substances that Deplete the Ozone Layer, 29 June 1990;
- Basel Convention on the Control of Transboundary Movement of Hazardous Wastes and their Disposal, 22 March 1989.

Annex II (The treaties are listed in the order that they are published in these volumes.)

Refugees and Stateless Persons:
- Convention relating to the Status of Stateless Persons, 28 September 1954.

[footnote continued]

Traffic in Persons:

- International Convention for the Suppression of the Traffic in Women and Children, 30 September 1921;
- Protocol amending the International Agreement for the Suppression of the White Slave Traffic, signed at Paris on 18 May 1904, and the International Convention for the Suppression of the White Slave Traffic, signed at Paris on 4 May 1910, 4 May 1949;
- International Agreement for the Suppression of the "White Slave Traffic", 18 May 1904;
- International Convention for the Suppression of the White Slave Traffic, 4 May 1910.

Obscene Publications:

- Protocol to amend the Convention for the suppression of the circulation of, and traffic in, obscene publications, concluded at Geneva on 12 September 1923, 12 November 1947;
- International Convention for the Suppression of the Circulation of, and Traffic in Obscene Publications, 12 September 1923;
- Protocol amending the Agreement for the Suppression of the Circulation of Obscene Publications, signed at Paris on 4 May 1910, 4 May 1949;
- Agreement for the Repression of Obscene Publications, 4 May 1910.

Transport and Communications — Custom matters:

- International Convention to Facilitate the Importation of Commercial Samples and Advertising Materials, 7 November 1952;
- Convention concerning Customs Facilities for Touring, 4 June 1954;
- Additional Protocol to the Convention concerning Customs Facilities for Touring, relating to the Importation of Tourist Publicity Documents and Material, 4 June 1954;
- Customs Convention on the Temporary Importation of Private Road Vehicles, 4 June 1954;
- Customs Convention on the Temporary Importation of Commercial Road Vehicles, 18 May 1956;
- Customs Convention on the Temporary Importation for Private Use of Aircraft and Pleasure Boats, 18 May 1956;
- European Convention on Customs Treatment of Pallets Used in International Transport, 9 December 1960.

Transport and Communications — Road Traffic:

- Convention on Road Traffic, 19 September 1949.

Educational and Cultural Matters:

- Agreement of the Importation of Educational, Scientific and Cultural materials, 22 November 1950.

Status of Women:

- Convention on the Political Rights of Women, 31 March 1953;
- Convention on Consent to Marriage, Minimum Age for Marriage and Registration of Marriages, 10 December 1962.

Penal Matters:

- Protocol amending the Slavery Convention signed at Geneva 25 September 1926, 7 December 1953;
- Slavery Convention, 25 September 1926;
- Supplementary Convention on the Abolition of Slavery, the Slave Trade and Institutions and Practices Similar to Slavery, 7 September 1956.

Environment:

- Amendment to the Montreal Protocol on Substances that Deplete the Ozone Layer, Copenhagen, 25 November 1992.

League of Nations:

- Convention and Statute on Freedom of Transit, 20 April 1921;
- Convention and Statute on the Regime of Navigable Waterways of International Concern, 20 April 1921;
- Declaration Recognizing the Right to a Flag of States Having no Sea-coast, 20 April 1921;
- Convention and Statute on the International Regime of Maritime Ports, 9 December 1923 ;
- International Convention relating to the Simplification of Customs Formalities, 3 November 1923.

See also note 2 under "United Kingdom of Great Britain and Northern Ireland".

General Comments

(1) General Comment No. 1: Reporting obligation (27 July 1981) [General Comment No. 1 has been replaced by General Comment No. 30]

(2) General Comment No. 2: Reporting guidelines (28 July 1981) [Has been superseded by CCPR/C/66/GUI, Consolidated guidelines for State reports under the International Covenant on Civil and Political Rights, dated 29 September 1999]

(3) General Comment No. 3: Article 2 (Implementation at the national level) [General Comment No. 3 has been replaced by General Comment No. 31] (29 July 1981)

(4) General Comment No. 4: Article 3 (Equal right of men and women to the enjoyment of all civil and political rights) (30 July 1981) [General Comment No. 4 has been replaced by General Comment No. 28]

(5) General Comment No. 5: Article 4 (Derogations) (1981)

(6) General Comment No. 6: Article 6 (Right to life) (30 April 1982)

(7) General Comment No. 7: Article 7 (Prohibition of torture or cruel, inhuman or degrading treatment or punishment) (30 May 1982)

(8) General Comment No. 8: Article 9 (Right to liberty and security of persons) (30 June 1982)

(9) General Comment No. 9: Article 10 (Humane treatment of person deprived of their liberty) (1982)

(10) General Comment No. 10: Article 19 (Freedom of opinion) (1983)

(11) General Comment No. 11: Article 20 (1983)

(12) General Comment No. 12: Article 1 (Right to self-determination) (1984)

(13) General Comment No. 13: Article 14 (Administration of justice) (1984)

(14) General Comment No. 14: Article 6 (Right to life) (1984)

(15) General Comment No. 15: The position of aliens under the Covenant (1986)

(16) General Comment No. 16: Article 17 (Right to privacy) (1988)

(17) General Comment No. 17: Article 24 (Rights of the child) (1989)

(18) General Comment No. 18: Non-discrimination (1989)

(19) General Comment No. 19: Article 23 (The family) (1992)

(20) General Comment No. 20: Article 7 (Prohibition of torture, or other cruel, inhuman or degrading treatment or punishment) (1992)

(21) General Comment No. 21: Article 10 (Humane treatment of persons deprived of their liberty) (1992)

(22) General Comment No. 22: Article 18 (Freedom of thought, conscience or religion) (30 July 1993)

(23) General Comment No. 23: Article 27 (Rights of minorities) (8 April 1994)

(24) General Comment No. 24: Issues relating to reservations made upon ratification or accession to the Covenant or the Optional Protocols thereto, or in relation to declarations under Article 41 of the Covenant (4 November 1994)

(25) General Comment No. 25: Article 25 (Participation in public affairs and the right to vote) (12 July 1996)

(26) General Comment No. 26: Continuity of obligations (8 December 1997)

(27) General Comment No. 27: Article 12 (Freedom of movement) (2 November 1999)

(28) General Comment No. 28: Article 3 (The equality of rights between men and women) (29 March 2000)

(29) General Comment No. 29: Article 4 (Derogations during a state of emergency) (31 August 2001)

(30) General Comment No. 30: Reporting obligations of States parties under Article 40 of the Covenant (18 September 2002)

(31) General Comment No. 31: The Nature of the General Legal Obligation Imposed on States Parties to the Covenant (26 May 2004)

(32) General Comment No. 32: Right to equality before courts and tribunals and to a fair trial (23 August 2007)

(33) General Comment No.33: Obligations of States parties under the Optional Protocol to the International Covenant on Civil and Political Rights (25 June 2009)

(34) General Comment No. 34: Article 19 (Freedoms of opinion and expression) (12 September 2011)

(35) General Comment No. 35: Article 9 (Liberty and security of person) (23 October 2014)

(36) General Comment No. 36: Article 6 (the right to life) (3 September 2019)

(37) General Comment No. 37 on Article 21 (Right of peaceful assembly) (17 September 2020)

INTERNATIONAL COVENANT ON ECONOMIC, SOCIAL AND CULTURAL RIGHTS

(Adopted: 16 December 1966; Entry into force: 3 January 1976, in accordance with Article 27)

Preamble

The States Parties to the present Covenant,

Considering that, in accordance with the principles proclaimed in the Charter of the United Nations, recognition of the inherent dignity and of the equal and inalienable rights of all members of the human family is the foundation of freedom, justice and peace in the world,

Recognizing that these rights derive from the inherent dignity of the human person,

Recognizing that, in accordance with the Universal Declaration of Human Rights, the ideal of free human beings enjoying freedom from fear and want can only be achieved if conditions are created whereby everyone may enjoy his economic, social and cultural rights, as well as his civil and political rights,

Considering the obligation of States under the Charter of the United Nations to promote universal respect for, and observance of, human rights and freedoms,

Realizing that the individual, having duties to other individuals and to the community to which he belongs, is under a responsibility to strive for the promotion and observance of the rights recognized in the present Covenant,

Agree upon the following Articles:

Part I

Article 1

(1) All peoples have the right of self-determination. By virtue of that right they freely determine their political status and freely pursue their economic, social and cultural development.

(2) All peoples may, for their own ends, freely dispose of their natural wealth and resources without prejudice to any obligations arising out of international economic co-operation, based upon the principle of mutual benefit, and international law. In no case may a people be deprived of its own means of subsistence.

(3) The States Parties to the present Covenant, including those having responsibility for the administration of Non-Self-Governing and Trust Territories, shall promote the realization of the right of self-determination, and shall respect that right, in conformity with the provisions of the Charter of the United Nations.

Part II

Article 2

(1) Each State Party to the present Covenant undertakes to take steps, individually and through international assistance and co-operation, especially economic and technical, to the maximum of its available resources, with a view to achieving progressively the full realization of the rights recognized in the present Covenant by all appropriate means, including particularly the adoption of legislative measures.

(2) The States Parties to the present Covenant undertake to guarantee that the rights enunciated in the present Covenant will be exercised without discrimination of any kind as to race, colour, sex, language, religion, political or other opinion, national or social origin, property, birth or other status.

(3) Developing countries, with due regard to human rights and their national economy, may determine to what extent they would guarantee the economic rights recognized in the present Covenant to non-nationals.

Article 3

The States Parties to the present Covenant undertake to ensure the equal right of men and women to the enjoyment of all economic, social and cultural rights set forth in the present Covenant.

Article 4

The States Parties to the present Covenant recognize that, in the enjoyment of those rights provided by the State in conformity with the present Covenant, the State may subject such rights only to such limitations as are determined by law only in so far as this may be compatible with the nature of these rights and solely for the purpose of promoting the general welfare in a democratic society.

Article 5

(1) Nothing in the present Covenant may be interpreted as implying for any State, group or person any right to engage in any activity or to perform any act aimed at the destruction of any of the rights or freedoms recognized herein, or at their limitation to a greater extent than is provided for in the present Covenant.

(2) No restriction upon or derogation from any of the fundamental human rights recognized or existing in any country in virtue of law, conventions, regulations or custom shall be admitted on the pretext that the present Covenant does not recognize such rights or that it recognizes them to a lesser extent.

Part III

Article 6

(1) The States Parties to the present Covenant recognize the right to work, which includes the right of everyone to the opportunity to gain his living by work which he freely chooses or accepts, and will take appropriate steps to safeguard this right.

(2) The steps to be taken by a State Party to the present Covenant to achieve the full realization of this right shall include technical and vocational guidance and training programmes, policies and techniques to

achieve steady economic, social and cultural development and full and productive employment under conditions safeguarding fundamental political and economic freedoms to the individual.

Article 7

The States Parties to the present Covenant recognize the right of everyone to the enjoyment of just and favourable conditions of work which ensure, in particular:

(a) Remuneration which provides all workers, as a minimum, with:

(i) Fair wages and equal remuneration for work of equal value without distinction of any kind, in particular women being guaranteed conditions of work not inferior to those enjoyed by men, with equal pay for equal work;

(ii) A decent living for themselves and their families in accordance with the provisions of the present Covenant;

(b) Safe and healthy working conditions;

(c) Equal opportunity for everyone to be promoted in his employment to an appropriate higher level, subject to no considerations other than those of seniority and competence;

(d) Rest, leisure and reasonable limitation of working hours and periodic holidays with pay, as well as remuneration for public holidays

Article 8

(1) The States Parties to the present Covenant undertake to ensure:

(a) The right of everyone to form trade unions and join the trade union of his choice, subject only to the rules of the organization concerned, for the promotion and protection of his economic and social interests. No restrictions may be placed on the exercise of this right other than those prescribed by law and which are necessary in a democratic society in the interests of national security or public order or for the protection of the rights and freedoms of others;

(b) The right of trade unions to establish national federations or confederations and the right of the latter to form or join international trade-union organizations;

(c) The right of trade unions to function freely subject to no limitations other than those prescribed by law and which are necessary in a democratic society in the interests of national security or public order or for the protection of the rights and freedoms of others;

(d) The right to strike, provided that it is exercised in conformity with the laws of the particular country.

(2) This Article shall not prevent the imposition of lawful restrictions on the exercise of these rights by members of the armed forces or of the police or of the administration of the State.

(3) Nothing in this Article shall authorize States Parties to the International Labour Organization Convention of 1948 concerning Freedom of Association and Protection of the Right to Organize to take legislative measures which would prejudice, or apply the law in such a manner as would prejudice, the guarantees provided for in that Convention.

Article 9

The States Parties to the present Covenant recognize the right of everyone to social security, including social insurance.

Article 10

The States Parties to the present Covenant recognize that:

(1) The widest possible protection and assistance should be accorded to the family, which is the natural and fundamental group unit of society, particularly for its establishment and while it is responsible for the care and education of dependent children. Marriage must be entered into with the free consent of the intending spouses.

(2) Special protection should be accorded to mothers during a reasonable period before and after childbirth. During such period working mothers should be accorded paid leave or leave with adequate social security benefits.

(3) Special measures of protection and assistance should be taken on behalf of all children and young persons without any discrimination for reasons of parentage or other conditions. Children and young persons should be protected from economic and social exploitation. Their employment in work harmful to their morals or health or dangerous to life or likely to hamper their normal development should be punishable by law. States should also set age limits below which the paid employment of child labour should be prohibited and punishable by law.

Article 11

(1) The States Parties to the present Covenant recognize the right of everyone to an adequate standard of living for himself and his family, including adequate food, clothing and housing, and to the continuous improvement of living conditions. The States Parties will take appropriate steps to ensure the realization of this right, recognizing to this effect the essential importance of international co-operation based on free consent.

(2) The States Parties to the present Covenant, recognizing the fundamental right of everyone to be free from hunger, shall take, individually and through international co-operation, the measures, including specific programmes, which are needed:

(a) To improve methods of production, conservation and distribution of food by making full use of technical and scientific knowledge, by disseminating knowledge of the principles of nutrition and by developing or reforming agrarian systems in such a way as to achieve the most efficient development and utilization of natural resources;

(b) Taking into account the problems of both food-importing and food-exporting countries, to ensure an equitable distribution of world food supplies in relation to need.

Article 12

(1) The States Parties to the present Covenant recognize the right of everyone to the enjoyment of the highest attainable standard of physical and mental health.

(2) The steps to be taken by the States Parties to the present Covenant to achieve the full realization of this right shall include those necessary for:

(a) The provision for the reduction of the stillbirth-rate and of infant mortality and for the healthy development of the child;

(b) The improvement of all aspects of environmental and industrial hygiene;

(c) The prevention, treatment and control of epidemic, endemic, occupational and other diseases;

(d) The creation of conditions which would assure to all medical service and medical attention in the event of sickness.

Article 13

(1) The States Parties to the present Covenant recognize the right of everyone to education. They agree that education shall be directed to the full development of the human personality and the sense of its dignity, and shall strengthen the respect for human rights and fundamental freedoms. They further agree that education shall enable all persons to participate effectively in a free society, promote understanding, tolerance and friendship among all nations and all racial, ethnic or religious groups, and further the activities of the United Nations for the maintenance of peace.

(2) The States Parties to the present Covenant recognize that, with a view to achieving the full realization of this right:

(a) Primary education shall be compulsory and available free to all;

(b) Secondary education in its different forms, including technical and vocational secondary education, shall be made generally available and accessible to all by every appropriate means, and in particular by the progressive introduction of free education;

(c) Higher education shall be made equally accessible to all, on the basis of capacity, by every appropriate means, and in particular by the progressive introduction of free education;

(d) Fundamental education shall be encouraged or intensified as far as possible for those persons who have not received or completed the whole period of their primary education;

(e) The development of a system of schools at all levels shall be actively pursued, an adequate fellowship system shall be established, and the material conditions of teaching staff shall be continuously improved.

(3) The States Parties to the present Covenant undertake to have respect for the liberty of parents and, when applicable, legal guardians to choose for their children schools, other than those established by the public authorities, which conform to such minimum educational standards as may be laid down or approved by the State and to ensure the religious and moral education of their children in conformity with their own convictions.

(4) No part of this Article shall be construed so as to interfere with the liberty of individuals and bodies to establish and direct educational institutions, subject always to the observance of the principles set forth in paragraph (1) of this Article and to the requirement that the education given in such institutions shall conform to such minimum standards as may be laid down by the State.

Article 14

Each State Party to the present Covenant which, at the time of becoming a Party, has not been able to secure in its metropolitan territory or other territories under its jurisdiction compulsory primary education, free of charge, undertakes, within two years, to work out and adopt a detailed plan of action for the progressive implementation, within a reasonable number of years, to be fixed in the plan, of the principle of compulsory education free of charge for all.

Article 15

(1) The States Parties to the present Covenant recognize the right of everyone:

(a) To take part in cultural life;

(b) To enjoy the benefits of scientific progress and its applications;

(c) To benefit from the protection of the moral and material interests resulting from any scientific, literary or artistic production of which he is the author.

(2) The steps to be taken by the States Parties to the present Covenant to achieve the full realization of this right shall include those necessary for the conservation, the development and the diffusion of science and culture.

(3) The States Parties to the present Covenant undertake to respect the freedom indispensable for scientific research and creative activity.

(4) The States Parties to the present Covenant recognize the benefits to be derived from the encouragement and development of international contacts and co-operation in the scientific and cultural fields.

Part IV

Article 16

(1) The States Parties to the present Covenant undertake to submit in conformity with this part of the Covenant reports on the measures which they have adopted and the progress made in achieving the observance of the rights recognized herein.

(2)

(a) All reports shall be submitted to the Secretary-General of the United Nations, who shall transmit copies to the Economic and Social Council for consideration in accordance with the provisions of the present Covenant;

(b) The Secretary-General of the United Nations shall also transmit to the specialized agencies copies of the reports, or any relevant parts therefrom, from States Parties to the present Covenant which are also members of these specialized agencies in so far as these reports, or parts therefrom, relate to any matters which fall within the responsibilities of the said agencies in accordance with their constitutional instruments.

Article 17

(1) The States Parties to the present Covenant shall furnish their reports in stages, in accordance with a programme to be established by the Economic and Social Council within one year of the entry into force of the present Covenant after consultation with the States Parties and the specialized agencies concerned.

(2) Reports may indicate factors and difficulties affecting the degree of fulfilment of obligations under the present Covenant.

(3) Where relevant information has previously been furnished to the United Nations or to any specialized agency by any State Party to the present Covenant, it will not be necessary to reproduce that information, but a precise reference to the information so furnished will suffice.

Article 18

Pursuant to its responsibilities under the Charter of the United Nations in the field of human rights and fundamental freedoms, the Economic and Social Council may make arrangements with the specialized agencies in respect of their reporting to it on the progress made in achieving the observance of the provisions of the present Covenant falling within the scope of their activities. These reports may include particulars of decisions and recommendations on such implementation adopted by their competent organs.

Article 19

The Economic and Social Council may transmit to the Commission on Human Rights for study and General Recommendation or, as appropriate, for information the reports concerning human rights submitted by States in accordance with Articles 16 and 17, and those concerning human rights submitted by the specialized agencies in accordance with Article 18.

Article 20

The States Parties to the present Covenant and the specialized agencies concerned may submit comments to the Economic and Social Council on any General Recommendation under Article 19 or reference to such General Recommendation in any report of the Commission on Human Rights or any documentation referred to therein.

Article 21

The Economic and Social Council may submit from time to time to the General Assembly reports with recommendations of a general nature and a summary of the information received from the States Parties to the present Covenant and the specialized agencies on the measures taken and the progress made in achieving general observance of the rights recognized in the present Covenant.

Article 22

The Economic and Social Council may bring to the attention of other organs of the United Nations, their subsidiary organs and specialized agencies concerned with furnishing technical assistance any matters arising out of the reports referred to in this part of the present Covenant which may assist such bodies in deciding, each within its field of competence, on the advisability of international measures likely to contribute to the effective progressive implementation of the present Covenant.

Article 23

The States Parties to the present Covenant agree that international action for the achievement of the rights recognized in the present Covenant includes such methods as the conclusion of conventions, the adoption of recommendations, the furnishing of technical assistance and the holding of regional meetings and technical meetings for the purpose of consultation and study organized in conjunction with the Governments concerned.

Article 24

Nothing in the present Covenant shall be interpreted as impairing the provisions of the Charter of the United Nations and of the constitutions of the specialized agencies which define the respective responsibilities of the various organs of the United Nations and of the specialized agencies in regard to the matters dealt with in the present Covenant.

Article 25

Nothing in the present Covenant shall be interpreted as impairing the inherent right of all peoples to enjoy and utilize fully and freely their natural wealth and resources.

Part V

Article 26

(1) The present Covenant is open for signature by any State Member of the United Nations or member of any of its specialized agencies, by any State Party to the Statute of the International Court of Justice, and by any other State which has been invited by the General Assembly of the United Nations to become a party to the present Covenant.

(2) The present Covenant is subject to ratification. Instruments of ratification shall be deposited with the Secretary-General of the United Nations.

(3) The present Covenant shall be open to accession by any State referred to in paragraph (1) of this Article.

(4) Accession shall be effected by the deposit of an instrument of accession with the Secretary-General of the United Nations.

(5) The Secretary-General of the United Nations shall inform all States which have signed the present Covenant or acceded to it of the deposit of each instrument of ratification or accession.

Article 27

(1) The present Covenant shall enter into force three months after the date of the deposit with the Secretary-General of the United Nations of the thirty-fifth instrument of ratification or instrument of accession.

(2) For each State ratifying the present Covenant or acceding to it after the deposit of the thirty-fifth instrument of ratification or instrument of accession, the present Covenant shall enter into force three months after the date of the deposit of its own instrument of ratification or instrument of accession.

Article 28

The provisions of the present Covenant shall extend to all parts of federal States without any limitations or exceptions.

Article 29

(1) Any State Party to the present Covenant may propose an amendment and file it with the Secretary-General of the United Nations. The Secretary-General shall thereupon communicate any proposed amendments to the States Parties to the present Covenant with a request that they notify him whether they favour a conference of States Parties for the purpose of considering and voting upon the proposals. In the event that at least one third of the States Parties favours such a conference, the Secretary-General shall convene the conference under the auspices of the United Nations. Any amendment adopted by a majority of the States Parties present and voting at the conference shall be submitted to the General Assembly of the United Nations for approval.

(2) Amendments shall come into force when they have been approved by the General Assembly of the United Nations and accepted by a two-thirds majority of the States Parties to the present Covenant in accordance with their respective constitutional processes.

(3) When amendments come into force they shall be binding on those States Parties which have accepted them, other States Parties still being bound by the provisions of the present Covenant and any earlier amendment which they have accepted.

Article 30

Irrespective of the notifications made under Article 26, paragraph (5), the Secretary-General of the United Nations shall inform all States referred to in paragraph (1) of the same Article of the following particulars:

(a) Signatures, ratifications and accessions under Article 26;

(b) The date of the entry into force of the present Covenant under Article 27 and the date of the entry into force of any amendments under Article 29.

Article 31

(1) The present Covenant, of which the Chinese, English, French, Russian and Spanish texts are equally authentic, shall be deposited in the archives of the United Nations.

(2) The Secretary-General of the United Nations shall transmit certified copies of the present Covenant to all States referred to in Article 26.

Reservations Applicable to Hong Kong

*United Kingdom of Great Britain and Northern Ireland**

* With regard to the application of the Covenant to Hong Kong, the Secretary-General received communications concerning the status of Hong Kong from China and the United Kingdom (see note 2 under "China" and note 2 under "United Kingdom of Great Britain and Northern Ireland" concerning Hong Kong in the "Historical Information" Section at https://treaties.un.org/Pages/HistoricalInfo.aspx?clang=_en#, which have been reproduced in the footnotes on pages 180–184 of this volume). Upon resuming the exercise of sovereignty over Hong Kong, China notified the Secretary-General that the Covenant with the reservation made by China will also apply to the Hong Kong Special Administrative Region.

Further, on 20 April 2001, the Secretary-General received from the Government of China the following communication:

1. Article 6 of the Covenant does not preclude the formulation of regulations by the HKSAR for employment restrictions, based on place of birth or residence qualifications, for the purpose of safeguarding the employment opportunities of local workers in the HKSAR
2. "National federations or confederations" in Article 8.1(b) of the Covenant shall be interpreted, in this case, as "federations or confederations in the HKSAR", and this Article does not imply the right of trade union federations or confederations to form or join political organizations or bodies established outside the HKSAR.

Upon signature:

[...]

Thirdly, the Government of the United Kingdom declare that, in relation to Article 8 of the Covenant, they must reserve the right not to apply subparagraph (b) of paragraph (1) in Hong Kong, in so far as it may involve the right of trade unions not engaged in the same trade or industry to establish federations or confederations.

Upon ratification:

[...]

The Government of the United Kingdom reserve the right to postpone the application of subparagraph (i) of paragraph (a) of Article 7, in so far as it concerns the provision of equal pay to men and women for equal work in the private sector in Jersey, Guernsey, the Isle of Man, Bermuda, Hong Kong and the Solomon Islands.

The Government of the United Kingdom reserve the right not to apply subparagraph (1)(b) of Article 8 in Hong Kong.

China

Statement made upon ratification:

In accordance with the Decision made by the Standing Committee of the Ninth National People's Congress of the People's Republic of China at its Twentieth Session, the President of the People's Republic of China hereby ratifies The International Covenant on Economic, Social and Cultural Rights, which was signed by Mr. Qin Huasun on behalf of the People's Republic of China on 27 October 1997, and declares the following:

[...]

2. In accordance with the official notes addressed to the Secretary-General of the United Nations by the Permanent Representative of the People's Republic of China to the United Nations on 20 June 1997 and 2 December 1999 respectively, the International Covenant on Economic, Social and Cultural Rights shall be applicable to the Hong Kong Special Administrative Region of the People's Republic of China and the Macao Special Administrative Region of the People's Republic of China and shall, pursuant to the provisions of the Basic Law of the Hong Kong Special Administrative Region of the People's Republic of China and the Basic Law of the Macao Special Administrative Region of the People's Republic of China, be implemented through the respective laws of the two special administrative regions.

General Comments

(1) General Comment No. 1: Reporting by States parties (1989)

(2) General Comment No. 2: International technical assistance measures (Art. 22 of the Covenant) (1990)

(3) General Comment No. 3: The nature of States parties obligations (Art. 2, para. 1 of the Covenant) (1990)

(4) General Comment No. 4: The right to adequate housing (Art. 11(1) of the Covenant) (1991)

(5) General Comment No. 5: Persons with disabilities (1994)

(6) General Comment No. 6: The economic, social and cultural rights of older persons (24 November 1995)

(7) General Comment No. 7: The right to adequate housing (Art. 11(1) of the Covenant): Forced evictions (1997)

(8) General Comment No. 8: The relationship between economic sanctions and respect for economic, social and cultural rights (4 December 1997

(9) General Comment No. 9: The domestic application of the Covenant (3 December 1998)

(10) General Comment No. 10: The role of national human rights institutions in the protection of economic, social and cultural rights (10 December 1998)

(11) General Comment No. 11: Plans of action for primary education (Art. 14 of the Covenant) (10 May 1999)

(12) General Comment No. 12: The right to adequate food (Art. 11 of the Covenant) (12 May 1999)

(13) General Comment No. 13: The right to education (Art. 13 of the Covenant) (8 December 1999)

(14) General Comment No. 14: The right to the highest attainable standard of health (Art. 12 of the Covenant) (11 August 2000)

(15) General Comment No. 15: The right to water (Arts. 11 and 12 of the Covenant) (20 January 2003)

(16) General Comment No. 16: The equal right of men and women to the enjoyment of all economic, social and cultural rights (Art. 3 of the Covenant) (11 August 2005)

(17) General Comment No. 17: The right of everyone to benefit from the protection of the moral and material interests resulting from any scientific, literary or artistic production of which he or she is the author (Art. 15, para. 1(c) of the Covenant) (12 January 2006)

(18) General Comment No. 18: The right to work (Art. 6 of the Covenant) (6 February 2006)

(19) [Observation générale No. 16: Droit égal de l'homme et de la femme au bénéfice de tous les droits économiques, sociaux et culturels — Rectificatif] (16 March 2006)

(20) General Comment No. 19: The right to social security (Art. 9 of the Covenant) (4 February 2008)

(21) General Comment No. 20: Non-discrimination in economic, social and cultural rights (Art. 2, para. 2 of the Covenant) (2 July 2009)

(22) General Comment No. 21: Right of everyone to take part in cultural life (Art. 15, para. 1(a) of the Covenant) (21 December 2009)

(23) [Observación general N° 21: Derecho de toda persona a participar en la vida cultural (artículo 15, párrafo 1 a), del Pacto Internacional de Derechos Económicos, Sociales y Culturas)] (17 May 2010)

(24) General Comment No. 23 on the right to just and favourable conditions of work (Art. 7 of the Covenant) (27 April 2016)

(25) General Comment No. 22 on the right to sexual and reproductive health (Art. 12 of the Covenant) (2 May 2016)

(26) General Comment No. 24: on State Obligations under the International Covenant on Economic, Social and Cultural Rights in the Context of Business Activities (10 August 2017)

(27) General Comment No. 25 on science and economic, social and cultural rights (Arts. 15(1)(b), (2), (3) and (4) of the Covenant) (30 April 2020)

INTERNATIONAL CONVENTION ON THE ELIMINATION OF ALL FORMS OF RACIAL DISCRIMINATION

(Adopted: 21 December 1965; Entry into force: 4 January 1969, in accordance with Article 19)

The States Parties to this Convention,

Considering that the Charter of the United Nations is based on the principles of the dignity and equality inherent in all human beings, and that all Member States have pledged themselves to take joint and separate action, in co-operation with the Organization, for the achievement of one of the purposes of the United Nations which is to promote and encourage universal respect for and observance of human rights and fundamental freedoms for all, without distinction as to race, sex, language or religion,

Considering that the Universal Declaration of Human Rights proclaims that all human beings are born free and equal in dignity and rights and that everyone is entitled to all the rights and freedoms set out therein, without distinction of any kind, in particular as to race, colour or national origin,

Considering that all human beings are equal before the law and are entitled to equal protection of the law against any discrimination and against any incitement to discrimination,

Considering that the United Nations has condemned colonialism and all practices of segregation and discrimination associated therewith, in whatever form and wherever they exist, and that the Declaration on the Granting of Independence to Colonial Countries and Peoples of 14 December 1960 (General Assembly Resolution 1514(XV)) has affirmed and solemnly proclaimed the necessity of bringing them to a speedy and unconditional end,

Considering that the United Nations Declaration on the Elimination of All Forms of Racial Discrimination of 20 November 1963 (General Assembly Resolution 1904(XVIII)) solemnly affirms the necessity of speedily eliminating racial discrimination throughout the world in all its forms and manifestations and of securing understanding of and respect for the dignity of the human person,

Convinced that any doctrine of superiority based on racial differentiation is scientifically false, morally condemnable, socially unjust and dangerous, and that there is no justification for racial discrimination, in theory or in practice, anywhere,

Reaffirming that discrimination between human beings on the grounds of race, colour or ethnic origin is an obstacle to friendly and peaceful relations among nations and is capable of disturbing peace and security among peoples and the harmony of persons living side by side even within one and the same State,

Convinced that the existence of racial barriers is repugnant to the ideals of any human society,

Alarmed by manifestations of racial discrimination still in evidence in some areas of the world and by governmental policies based on racial superiority or hatred, such as policies of apartheid, segregation or separation,

Resolved to adopt all necessary measures for speedily eliminating racial discrimination in all its forms and manifestations, and to prevent and combat racist doctrines and practices in order to promote understanding between races and to build an international community free from all forms of racial segregation and racial discrimination,

Bearing in mind the Convention concerning Discrimination in respect of Employment and Occupation adopted by the International Labour Organization in 1958, and the Convention against Discrimination in Education adopted by the United Nations Educational, Scientific and Cultural Organization in 1960,

Desiring to implement the principles embodied in the United Nations Declaration on the Elimination of Al 1 Forms of Racial Discrimination and to secure the earliest adoption of practical measures to that end,

Have agreed as follows:

Part I

Article 1

(1) In this Convention, the term "racial discrimination" shall mean any distinction, exclusion, restriction or preference based on race, colour, descent, or national or ethnic origin which has the purpose or effect of nullifying or impairing the recognition, enjoyment or exercise, on an equal footing, of human rights and fundamental freedoms in the political, economic, social, cultural or any other field of public life.

(2) This Convention shall not apply to distinctions, exclusions, restrictions or preferences made by a State Party to this Convention between citizens and non-citizens.

(3) Nothing in this Convention may be interpreted as affecting in any way the legal provisions of States Parties concerning nationality, citizenship or naturalization, provided that such provisions do not discriminate against any particular nationality.

(4) Special measures taken for the sole purpose of securing adequate advancement of certain racial or ethnic groups or individuals requiring such protection as may be necessary in order to ensure such groups or individuals equal enjoyment or exercise of human rights and fundamental freedoms shall not be deemed racial discrimination, provided, however, that such measures do not, as a consequence, lead to the maintenance of separate rights for different racial groups and that they shall not be continued after the objectives for which they were taken have been achieved.

Article 2

(1) States Parties condemn racial discrimination and undertake to pursue by all appropriate means and without delay a policy of eliminating racial discrimination in all its forms and promoting understanding among all races, and, to this end:

  (a) Each State Party undertakes to engage in no act or practice of racial discrimination against persons, groups of persons or institutions and to ensure that all public authorities and public institutions, national and local, shall act in conformity with this obligation;

  (b) Each State Party undertakes not to sponsor, defend or support racial discrimination by any persons or organizations;

  (c) Each State Party shall take effective measures to review governmental, national and local policies, and to amend, rescind or nullify any laws and regulations which have the effect of creating or perpetuating racial discrimination wherever it exists;

  (d) Each State Party shall prohibit and bring to an end, by all appropriate means, including legislation as required by circumstances, racial discrimination by any persons, group or organization;

  (e) Each State Party undertakes to encourage, where appropriate, integrationist multiracial organizations and movements and other means of eliminating barriers between races, and to discourage anything which tends to strengthen racial division.

(2) States Parties shall, when the circumstances so warrant, take, in the social, economic, cultural and other fields, special and concrete measures to ensure the adequate development and protection of certain racial groups or individuals belonging to them, for the purpose of guaranteeing them the full and equal enjoyment of human rights and fundamental freedoms. These measures shall in no case entail as a consequence the maintenance of unequal or separate rights for different racial groups after the objectives for which they were taken have been achieved.

Article 3

States Parties particularly condemn racial segregation and apartheid and undertake to prevent, prohibit and eradicate all practices of this nature in territories under their jurisdiction.

Article 4

States Parties condemn all propaganda and all organizations which are based on ideas or theories of superiority of one race or group of persons of one colour or ethnic origin, or which attempt to justify or promote racial hatred and discrimination in any form, and undertake to adopt immediate and positive measures designed to eradicate all incitement to, or acts of, such discrimination and, to this end, with due regard to the principles embodied in the Universal Declaration of Human Rights and the rights expressly set forth in Article 5 of this Convention, inter alia:

(a) Shall declare an offence punishable by law all dissemination of ideas based on racial superiority or hatred, incitement to racial discrimination, as well as all acts of violence or incitement to such acts against any race or group of persons of another colour or ethnic origin, and also the provision of any assistance to racist activities, including the financing thereof;

(b) Shall declare illegal and prohibit organizations, and also organized and all other propaganda activities, which promote and incite racial discrimination, and shall recognize participation in such organizations or activities as an offence punishable by law;

(c) Shall not permit public authorities or public institutions, national or local, to promote or incite racial discrimination.

Article 5

In compliance with the fundamental obligations laid down in Article 2 of this Convention, States Parties undertake to prohibit and to eliminate racial discrimination in all its forms and to guarantee the right of everyone, without distinction as to race, colour, or national or ethnic origin, to equality before the law, notably in the enjoyment of the following rights:

(a) The right to equal treatment before the tribunals and all other organs administering justice;

(b) The right to security of person and protection by the State against violence or bodily harm, whether inflicted by government officials or by any individual group or institution;

(c) Political rights, in particular the right to participate in elections-to vote and to stand for election-on the basis of universal and equal suffrage, to take part in the Government as well as in the conduct of public affairs at any level and to have equal access to public service;

(d) Other civil rights, in particular:

    (i) The right to freedom of movement and residence within the border of the State;

    (ii) The right to leave any country, including one's own, and to return to one's country;

    (iii) The right to nationality;

    (iv) The right to marriage and choice of spouse;

    (v) The right to own property alone as well as in association with others;

    (vi) The right to inherit;

    (vii) The right to freedom of thought, conscience and religion;

    (viii) The right to freedom of opinion and expression;

    (ix) The right to freedom of peaceful assembly and association;

(e) Economic, social and cultural rights, in particular:

    (i) The rights to work, to free choice of employment, to just and favourable conditions of work, to protection against unemployment, to equal pay for equal work, to just and favourable remuneration;

    (ii) The right to form and join trade unions;

    (iii) The right to housing;

    (iv) The right to public health, medical care, social security and social services;

    (v) The right to education and training;

(vi) The right to equal participation in cultural activities;

(f) The right of access to any place or service intended for use by the general public, such as transport hotels, restaurants, cafes, theatres and parks.

Article 6

States Parties shall assure to everyone within their jurisdiction effective protection and remedies, through the competent national tribunals and other State institutions, against any acts of racial discrimination which violate his human rights and fundamental freedoms contrary to this Convention, as well as the right to seek from such tribunals just and adequate reparation or satisfaction for any damage suffered as a result of such discrimination.

Article 7

States Parties undertake to adopt immediate and effective measures, particularly in the fields of teaching, education, culture and information, with a view to combating prejudices which lead to racial discrimination and to promoting understanding, tolerance and friendship among nations and racial or ethnical groups, as well as to propagating the purposes and principles of the Charter of the United Nations, the Universal Declaration of Human Rights, the United Nations Declaration on the Elimination of All Forms of Racial Discrimination, and this Convention.

Part II

Article 8

(1) There shall be established a Committee on the Elimination of Racial Discrimination (hereinafter referred to as the Committee) consisting of eighteen experts of high moral standing and acknowledged impartiality elected by States Parties from among their nationals, who shall serve in their personal capacity, consideration being given to equitable geographical distribution and to the representation of the different forms of civilization as well as of the principal legal systems.

(2) The members of the Committee shall be elected by secret ballot from a list of persons nominated by the States Parties. Each State Party may nominate one person from among its own nationals.

(3) The initial election shall be held six months after the date of the entry into force of this Convention. At least three months before the date of each election the Secretary-General of the United Nations shall address a letter to the States Parties inviting them to submit their nominations within two months. The Secretary-General shall prepare a list in alphabetical order of all persons thus nominated, indicating the States Parties which have nominated them, and shall submit it to the States Parties.

(4) Elections of the members of the Committee shall be held at a meeting of States Parties convened by the Secretary-General at United Nations Headquarters. At that meeting, for which two thirds of the States Parties shall constitute a quorum, the persons elected to the Committee shall be nominees who obtain the largest number of votes and an absolute majority of the votes of the representatives of States Parties present and voting.

(5)

(a) The members of the Committee shall be elected for a term of four years. However, the terms of nine of the members elected at the first election shall expire at the end of two years; immediately after the first election the names of these nine members shall be chosen by lot by the Chairman of the Committee;

(b) For the filling of casual vacancies, the State Party whose expert has ceased to function as a member of the Committee shall appoint another expert from among its nationals, subject to the approval of the Committee.

(6) States Parties shall be responsible for the expenses of the members of the Committee while they are in performance of Committee duties.

Article 9

(1) States Parties undertake to submit to the Secretary-General of the United Nations, for consideration by the Committee, a report on the legislative, judicial, administrative or other measures which they have adopted and which give effect to the provisions of this Convention: (a) within one year after the entry into force of the Convention for the State concerned; and (b) thereafter every two years and whenever the Committee so requests. The Committee may request further information from the States Parties.

(2) The Committee shall report annually, through the Secretary General, to the General Assembly of the United Nations on its activities and may make suggestions and General Recommendations based on the examination of the reports and information received from the States Parties. Such suggestions and General Recommendations shall be reported to the General Assembly together with comments, if any, from States Parties.

Article 10

(1) The Committee shall adopt its own rules of procedure.

(2) The Committee shall elect its officers for a term of two years.

(3) The secretariat of the Committee shall be provided by the Secretary General of the United Nations.

(4) The meetings of the Committee shall normally be held at United Nations Headquarters.

Article 11

(1) If a State Party considers that another State Party is not giving effect to the provisions of this Convention, it may bring the matter to the attention of the Committee. The Committee shall then transmit the communication to the State Party concerned. Within three months, the receiving State shall submit to the Committee written explanations or statements clarifying the matter and the remedy, if any, that may have been taken by that State.

(2) If the matter is not adjusted to the satisfaction of both parties, either by bilateral negotiations or by any other procedure open to them, within six months after the receipt by the receiving State of the initial communication, either State shall have the right to refer the matter again to the Committee by notifying the Committee and also the other State.

(3) The Committee shall deal with a matter referred to it in accordance with paragraph (2) of this Article after it has ascertained that all available domestic remedies have been invoked and exhausted in the case, in conformity with the generally recognized principles of international law. This shall not be the rule where the application of the remedies is unreasonably prolonged.

(4) In any matter referred to it, the Committee may call upon the States Parties concerned to supply any other relevant information.

(5) When any matter arising out of this Article is being considered by the Committee, the States Parties concerned shall be entitled to send a representative to take part in the proceedings of the Committee, without voting rights, while the matter is under consideration.

Article 12

(1)

(a) After the Committee has obtained and collated all the information it deems necessary, the Chairman shall appoint an ad hoc Conciliation Commission (hereinafter referred to as the Commission) comprising five persons who may or may not be members of the Committee. The members of the Commission shall be appointed with the unanimous consent of the parties to the dispute, and its good offices shall be made available to the States concerned with a view to an amicable solution of the matter on the basis of respect for this Convention;

(b) If the States parties to the dispute fail to reach agreement within three months on all or part of the composition of the Commission, the members of the Commission not agreed upon by the States parties to the dispute shall be elected by secret ballot by a two-thirds majority vote of the Committee from among its own members.

(2) The members of the Commission shall serve in their personal capacity. They shall not be nationals of the States parties to the dispute or of a State not Party to this Convention.

(3) The Commission shall elect its own Chairman and adopt its own rules of procedure.

(4) The meetings of the Commission shall normally be held at United Nations Headquarters or at any other convenient place as determined by the Commission.

(5) The secretariat provided in accordance with Article 10, paragraph (3), of this Convention shall also service the Commission whenever a dispute among States Parties brings the Commission into being.

(6) The States parties to the dispute shall share equally all the expenses of the members of the Commission in accordance with estimates to be provided by the Secretary-General of the United Nations.

(7) The Secretary-General shall be empowered to pay the expenses of the members of the Commission, if necessary, before reimbursement by the States parties to the dispute in accordance with paragraph (6) of this Article.

(8) The information obtained and collated by the Committee shall be made available to the Commission, and the Commission may call upon the States concerned to supply any other relevant information.

Article 13

(1) When the Commission has fully considered the matter, it shall prepare and submit to the Chairman of the Committee a report embodying its findings on all questions of fact relevant to the issue between the parties and containing such recommendations as it may think proper for the amicable solution of the dispute.

(2) The Chairman of the Committee shall communicate the report of the Commission to each of the States parties to the dispute. These States shall, within three months, inform the Chairman of the Committee whether or not they accept the recommendations contained in the report of the Commission.

(3) After the period provided for in paragraph (2) of this Article, the Chairman of the Committee shall communicate the report of the Commission and the declarations of the States Parties concerned to the other States Parties to this Convention.

Article 14

(1) A State Party may at any time declare that it recognizes the competence of the Committee to receive and consider communications from individuals or groups of individuals within its jurisdiction claiming to be victims of a violation by that State Party of any of the rights set forth in this Convention. No communication shall be received by the Committee if it concerns a State Party which has not made such a declaration.

(2) Any State Party which makes a declaration as provided for in paragraph (1) of this Article may establish or indicate a body within its national legal order which shall be competent to receive and consider petitions from individuals and groups of individuals within its jurisdiction who claim to be victims of a violation of any of the rights set forth in this Convention and who have exhausted other available local remedies.

(3) A declaration made in accordance with paragraph (1) of this Article and the name of any body established or indicated in accordance with paragraph (2) of this Article shall be deposited by the State Party concerned with the Secretary-General of the United Nations, who shall transmit copies thereof to the other States Parties. A declaration may be withdrawn at any time by notification to

the Secretary-General, but such a withdrawal shall not affect communications pending before the Committee.

(4) A register of petitions shall be kept by the body established or indicated in accordance with paragraph (2) of this Article, and certified copies of the register shall be filed annually through appropriate channels with the Secretary-General on the understanding that the contents shall not be publicly disclosed.

(5) In the event of failure to obtain satisfaction from the body established or indicated in accordance with paragraph (2) of this Article, the petitioner shall have the right to communicate the matter to the Committee within six months.

(6)

(a) The Committee shall confidentially bring any communication referred to it to the attention of the State Party alleged to be violating any provision of this Convention, but the identity of the individual or groups of individuals concerned shall not be revealed without his or their express consent. The Committee shall not receive anonymous communications;

(b) Within three months, the receiving State shall submit to the Committee written explanations or statements clarifying the matter and the remedy, if any, that may have been taken by that State.

(7)

(a) The Committee shall consider communications in the light of all information made available to it by the State Party concerned and by the petitioner. The Committee shall not consider any communication from a petitioner unless it has ascertained that the petitioner has exhausted all available domestic remedies. However, this shall not be the rule where the application of the remedies is unreasonably prolonged;

(b) The Committee shall forward its suggestions and recommendations, if any, to the State Party concerned and to the petitioner.

(8) The Committee shall include in its annual report a summary of such communications and, where appropriate, a summary of the explanations and statements of the States Parties concerned and of its own suggestions and recommendations.

(9) The Committee shall be competent to exercise the functions provided for in this Article only when at least ten States Parties to this Convention are bound by declarations in accordance with paragraph (1) of this Article.

Article 15

(1) Pending the achievement of the objectives of the Declaration on the Granting of Independence to Colonial Countries and Peoples, contained in General Assembly Resolution 1514(XV) of 14 December 1960, the provisions of this Convention shall in no way limit the right of petition granted to these peoples by other international instruments or by the United Nations and its specialized agencies.

(2)

(a) The Committee established under Article 8, paragraph (1), of this Convention shall receive copies of the petitions from, and submit expressions of opinion and recommendations on these petitions to, the bodies of the United Nations which deal with matters directly related to the principles and objectives of this Convention in their consideration of petitions from the inhabitants of Trust and Non-Self-Governing Territories and all other territories to which General Assembly Resolution 1514(XV) applies, relating to matters covered by this Convention which are before these bodies;

(b) The Committee shall receive from the competent bodies of the United Nations copies of the reports concerning the legislative, judicial, administrative or other measures directly related to the principles and objectives of this Convention applied by the administering

Powers within the Territories mentioned in subparagraph (a) of this paragraph, and shall express opinions and make recommendations to these bodies.

(3) The Committee shall include in its report to the General Assembly a summary of the petitions and reports it has received from United Nations bodies, and the expressions of opinion and recommendations of the Committee relating to the said petitions and reports.

(4) The Committee shall request from the Secretary-General of the United Nations all information relevant to the objectives of this Convention and available to him regarding the Territories mentioned in paragraph (2)(a) of this Article.

Article 16

The provisions of this Convention concerning the settlement of disputes or complaints shall be applied without prejudice to other procedures for settling disputes or complaints in the field of discrimination laid down in the constituent instruments of, or conventions adopted by, the United Nations and its specialized agencies, and shall not prevent the States Parties from having recourse to other procedures for settling a dispute in accordance with general or special international agreements in force between them.

Part III

Article 17

(1) This Convention is open for signature by any State Member of the United Nations or member of any of its specialized agencies, by any State Party to the Statute of the International Court of Justice, and by any other State which has been invited by the General Assembly of the United Nations to become a Party to this Convention.

(2) This Convention is subject to ratification. Instruments of ratification shall be deposited with the Secretary-General of the United Nations.

Article 18

(1) This Convention shall be open to accession by any State referred to in Article 17, paragraph (1), of the Convention.

(2) Accession shall be effected by the deposit of an instrument of accession with the Secretary-General of the United Nations.

Article 19

(1) This Convention shall enter into force on the thirtieth day after the date of the deposit with the Secretary-General of the United Nations of the twenty-seventh instrument of ratification or instrument of accession.

(2) For each State ratifying this Convention or acceding to it after the deposit of the twenty-seventh instrument of ratification or instrument of accession, the Convention shall enter into force on the thirtieth day after the date of the deposit of its own instrument of ratification or instrument of accession.

Article 20

(1) The Secretary-General of the United Nations shall receive and circulate to all States which are or may become Parties to this Convention reservations made by States at the time of ratification or accession. Any State which objects to the reservation shall, within a period of ninety days from the date of the said communication, notify the Secretary-General that it does not accept it.

(2) A reservation incompatible with the object and purpose of this Convention shall not be permitted, nor shall a reservation the effect of which would inhibit the operation of any of the bodies

established by this Convention be allowed. A reservation shall be considered incompatible or inhibitive if at least two thirds of the States Parties to this Convention object to it.

(3) Reservations may be withdrawn at any time by notification to this effect addressed to the Secretary-General. Such notification shall take effect on the date on which it is received.

Article 21

A State Party may denounce this Convention by written notification to the Secretary-General of the United Nations. Denunciation shall take effect one year after the date of receipt of the notification by the Secretary General.

Article 22

Any dispute between two or more States Parties with respect to the interpretation or application of this Convention, which is not settled by negotiation or by the procedures expressly provided for in this Convention, shall, at the request of any of the parties to the dispute, be referred to the International Court of Justice for decision, unless the disputants agree to another mode of settlement.

Article 23

(1) A request for the revision of this Convention may be made at any time by any State Party by means of a notification in writing addressed to the Secretary-General of the United Nations.

(2) The General Assembly of the United Nations shall decide upon the steps, if any, to be taken in respect of such a request.

Article 24

The Secretary-General of the United Nations shall inform all States referred to in Article 17, paragraph (1), of this Convention of the following particulars:

(a) Signatures, ratifications and accessions under Articles 17 and 18;

(b) The date of entry into force of this Convention under Article 19;

(c) Communications and declarations received under Articles 14, 20 and 23;

(d) Denunciations under Article 21.

Article 25

(1) This Convention, of which the Chinese, English, French, Russian and Spanish texts are equally authentic, shall be deposited in the archives of the United Nations.

(2) The Secretary-General of the United Nations shall transmit certified copies of this Convention to all States belonging to any of the categories mentioned in Article 17, paragraph (1), of the Convention.

Reservations Applicable to Hong Kong

China

On 10 June 1997, the Secretary-General received communications concerning the status of Hong Kong from the Governments of the United Kingdom and China (see also note 2 under "China" and note 2 under "United Kingdom of Great Britain and Northern Ireland" regarding Hong Kong in the "Historical Information" Section).* Upon resuming the exercise of sovereignty over Hong Kong, China notified the

* These notes can be accessed at https://treaties.un.org/Pages/HistoricalInfo.aspx?clang=_en#. They have also been reproduced in the footnotes on pages 180–184 of this volume.

Secretary-General that the Convention with the reservation made by China will also apply to the Hong Kong special Administrative Region.

In addition, the notification made by the Government of China contained the following declarations:

(1) [...]

(2) The reservation of the People's Republic of China on behalf of the Hong Kong Special Administrative Region interprets the requirement in Article 6 concerning "reparation and satisfaction" as being fulfilled if one or other of these forms of redress is made available and interprets "satisfaction" as including any form of redress effective to bring the discriminatory conduct to an end.

Reservation:

The People's Republic of China has reservations on the provisions of Article 22 of the Convention and will not be bound by it. (The reservation was circulated by the Secretary-General on 13 January 1982.)

Declaration:

The signing and ratification of the said Convention by the Taiwan authorities in the name of China are illegal and null and void.

General Recommendations

(1) General Recommendation No. 1 concerning States parties' obligations (Art. 4 of the Convention) (1972)

(2) General Recommendation No. 2 concerning States parties' obligations (1972)

(3) General Recommendation No. 3 concerning reporting by States parties (1972)

(4) General Recommendation No. 4 concerning reporting by States parties (Art. 1 of the Convention) (1973)

(5) General Recommendation No. 5 concerning reporting by States parties (Art. 7 of the Convention) (1977)

(6) General Recommendation No. 6 concerning overdue reports (1982)

(7) General Recommendation No. 7 relating to the implementation of Article 4 (1985)

(8) General Recommendation No. 8 concerning the interpretation and application of Article 1, paragraphs (1) and (4) of the Convention (1990)

(9) General Recommendation No. 9 concerning the application of Article 8, paragraph (1), of the Convention (1990)

(10) General Recommendation No. 10 concerning technical assistance (1991)

(11) General Recommendation No. 11 on non-citizens (1993)

(12) General Recommendation No. 12 on successor States (1993)

(13) General Recommendation No. 13 on the training of law enforcement officials in the protection of human rights (1993)

(14) General Recommendation No. 14 on Article 1, paragraph (1), of the Convention (199)3

(15) General Recommendation No. 15 on Article 4 of the Convention (1993)

(16) General Recommendation No. 16 concerning the application of Article 9 of the Convention (1993)

(17) General Recommendation No. 17 on the establishment of national institutions to facilitate the implementation of the Convention (1993)

(18) General Recommendation No. 18 on the establishment of an international tribunal to prosecute crimes against humanity (1994)

(19) General Recommendation No. 19 on Article 3 of the Convention (1995)

(20) General Recommendation No. 20 on Article 5 of the Convention (1996)

(21) General Recommendation No. 21 on the right to self-determination (1996)

(22) General Recommendation No. 22 on Article 5 of the Convention on refugees and displaced persons (1996)

(23) General Recommendation No. 23 on the rights of indigenous peoples (1997)

(24) General Recommendation No. 24 concerning Article 1 of the Convention (1999)

(25) General Recommendation No. 25 on gender-related dimensions of racial discrimination (20 March 2000)

(26) General Recommendation No. 26 on Article 6 of the Convention (24 March 2000)

(27) General Recommendation No. 27 on discrimination against Roma (16 August 2000)

(28) General Recommendation No. 28 on the follow-up to the World Conference against Racism, Racial Discrimination, Xenophobia and Related Intolerance (19 March 2002)

(29) General Recommendation No. 29 on Article 1, paragraph (1), of the Convention (Descent) (2002)

(30) General Recommendation No. 30 on discrimination against non-citizens (2005)

(31) General Recommendation No. 31 on the prevention of racial discrimination in the administration and functioning of the criminal justice system (2005)

(32) General Recommendation No. 32: The meaning and scope of special measures in the International Convention on the Elimination of All Forms Racial Discrimination (24 September 2009)

(33) General Recommendation No. 33: Follow-up to the Durban Review Conference (29 September 2009)

(34) General Recommendation No. 34: Racial discrimination against people of African descent (3 October 2011)

(35) General Recommendation No. 35: Combatting racist hate speech (26 September 2013)

(36) General Recommendation No. 36: Corr.1 (14 February 2014)

(37) General Recommendation No. 37: Preventing and Combating Racial Profiling by Law Enforcement Officials (24 November 2020)

CONVENTION AGAINST TORTURE AND OTHER CRUEL, INHUMAN OR DEGRADING TREATMENT OR PUNISHMENT

(Adopted: 10 December 1984; Entry into force: 26 June 1987, in accordance with Article 27(1))

The States Parties to this Convention,

Considering that, in accordance with the principles proclaimed in the Charter of the United Nations, recognition of the equal and inalienable rights of all members of the human family is the foundation of freedom, justice and peace in the world,

Recognizing that those rights derive from the inherent dignity of the human person,

Considering the obligation of States under the Charter, in particular Article 55, to promote universal respect for, and observance of, human rights and fundamental freedoms,

Having regard to Article 5 of the Universal Declaration of Human Rights and Article 7 of the International Covenant on Civil and Political Rights, both of which provide that no one shall be subjected to torture or to cruel, inhuman or degrading treatment or punishment,

Having regard also to the Declaration on the Protection of All Persons from Being Subjected to Torture and Other Cruel, Inhuman or Degrading Treatment or Punishment, adopted by the General Assembly on 9 December 1975,

Desiring to make more effective the struggle against torture and other cruel, inhuman or degrading treatment or punishment throughout the world,

Have agreed as follows:

Part I

Article 1

(1) For the purposes of this Convention, the term "torture" means any act by which severe pain or suffering, whether physical or mental, is intentionally inflicted on a person for such purposes as obtaining from him or a third person information or a confession, punishing him for an act he or a third person has committed or is suspected of having committed, or intimidating or coercing him or a third person, or for any reason based on discrimination of any kind, when such pain or suffering is inflicted by or at the instigation of or with the consent or acquiescence of a public official or other person acting in an official capacity. It does not include pain or suffering arising only from, inherent in or incidental to lawful sanctions.

(2) This Article is without prejudice to any international instrument or national legislation which does or may contain provisions of wider application.

Article 2

(1) Each State Party shall take effective legislative, administrative, judicial or other measures to prevent acts of torture in any territory under its jurisdiction.

(2) No exceptional circumstances whatsoever, whether a state of war or a threat of war, internal political in stability or any other public emergency, may be invoked as a justification of torture.

(3) An order from a superior officer or a public authority may not be invoked as a justification of torture.

Article 3

(1) No State Party shall expel, return ("refouler") or extradite a person to another State where there are substantial grounds for believing that he would be in danger of being subjected to torture.

(2) For the purpose of determining whether there are such grounds, the competent authorities shall take into account all relevant considerations including, where applicable, the existence in the State concerned of a consistent pattern of gross, flagrant or mass violations of human rights.

Article 4

(1) Each State Party shall ensure that all acts of torture are offences under its criminal law. The same shall apply to an attempt to commit torture and to an act by any person which constitutes complicity or participation in torture.

(2) Each State Party shall make these offences punishable by appropriate penalties which take into account their grave nature.

Article 5

(1) Each State Party shall take such measures as may be necessary to establish its jurisdiction over the offences referred to in Article 4 in the following cases:

(a) When the offences are committed in any territory under its jurisdiction or on board a ship or aircraft registered in that State;

(b) When the alleged offender is a national of that State;

(c) When the victim is a national of that State if that State considers it appropriate.

(2) Each State Party shall likewise take such measures as may be necessary to establish its jurisdiction over such offences in cases where the alleged offender is present in any territory under its jurisdiction and it does not extradite him pursuant to Article 8 to any of the States mentioned in paragraph (1) of this Article.

(3) This Convention does not exclude any criminal jurisdiction exercised in accordance with internal law.

Article 6

(1) Upon being satisfied, after an examination of information available to it, that the circumstances so warrant, any State Party in whose territory a person alleged to have committed any offence referred to in Article 4 is present shall take him into custody or take other legal measures to ensure his presence. The custody and other legal measures shall be as provided in the law of that State but may be continued only for such time as is necessary to enable any criminal or extradition proceedings to be instituted.

(2) Such State shall immediately make a preliminary inquiry into the facts.

(3) Any person in custody pursuant to paragraph (1) of this Article shall be assisted in communicating immediately with the nearest appropriate representative of the State of which he is a national, or, if he is a stateless person, with the representative of the State where he usually resides.

(4) When a State, pursuant to this Article, has taken a person into custody, it shall immediately notify the States referred to in Article 5, paragraph (1), of the fact that such person is in custody and of the circumstances which warrant his detention. The State which makes the preliminary inquiry contemplated in paragraph (2) of this Article shall promptly report its findings to the said States and shall indicate whether it intends to exercise jurisdiction.

Article 7

(1) The State Party in the territory under whose jurisdiction a person alleged to have committed any offence referred to in Article 4 is found shall in the cases contemplated in Article 5, if it does not extradite him, submit the case to its competent authorities for the purpose of prosecution.

(2) These authorities shall take their decision in the same manner as in the case of any ordinary offence of a serious nature under the law of that State. In the cases referred to in Article 5, paragraph (2), the standards of evidence required for prosecution and conviction shall in no way be less stringent than those which apply in the cases referred to in Article 5, paragraph (1).

(3) Any person regarding whom proceedings are brought in connection with any of the offences referred to in Article 4 shall be guaranteed fair treatment at all stages of the proceedings.

Article 8

(1) The offences referred to in Article 4 shall be deemed to be included as extraditable offences in any extradition treaty existing between States Parties. States Parties undertake to include such offences as extraditable offences in every extradition treaty to be concluded between them.

(2) If a State Party which makes extradition conditional on the existence of a treaty receives a request for extradition from another State Party with which it has no extradition treaty, it may consider this Convention as the legal basis for extradition in respect of such offences. Extradition shall be subject to the other conditions provided by the law of the requested State.

(3) States Parties which do not make extradition conditional on the existence of a treaty shall recognize such offences as extraditable offences between themselves subject to the conditions provided by the law of the requested State.

(4) Such offences shall be treated, for the purpose of extradition between States Parties, as if they had been committed not only in the place in which they occurred but also in the territories of the States required to establish their jurisdiction in accordance with Article 5, paragraph (1).

Article 9

(1) States Parties shall afford one another the greatest measure of assistance in connection with criminal proceedings brought in respect of any of the offences referred to in Article 4, including the supply of all evidence at their disposal necessary for the proceedings.

(2) States Parties shall carry out their obligations under paragraph (1) of this Article in conformity with any treaties on mutual judicial assistance that may exist between them.

Article 10

(1) Each State Party shall ensure that education and information regarding the prohibition against torture are fully included in the training of law enforcement personnel, civil or military, medical personnel, public officials and other persons who may be involved in the custody, interrogation or treatment of any individual subjected to any form of arrest, detention or imprisonment.

(2) Each State Party shall include this prohibition in the rules or instructions issued in regard to the duties and functions of any such person.

Article 11

Each State Party shall keep under systematic review interrogation rules, instructions, methods and practices as well as arrangements for the custody and treatment of persons subjected to any form of arrest, detention or imprisonment in any territory under its jurisdiction, with a view to preventing any cases of torture.

Article 12

Each State Party shall ensure that its competent authorities proceed to a prompt and impartial investigation, wherever there is reasonable ground to believe that an act of torture has been committed in any territory under its jurisdiction.

Article 13

Each State Party shall ensure that any individual who alleges he has been subjected to torture in any territory under its jurisdiction has the right to complain to, and to have his case promptly and impartially examined by, its competent authorities. Steps shall be taken to ensure that the complainant and witnesses are protected against all ill-treatment or intimidation as a consequence of his complaint or any evidence given.

Article 14

(1) Each State Party shall ensure in its legal system that the victim of an act of torture obtains redress and has an enforceable right to fair and adequate compensation, including the means for as full rehabilitation as possible. In the event of the death of the victim as a result of an act of torture, his dependants shall be entitled to compensation.

(2) Nothing in this Article shall affect any right of the victim or other persons to compensation which may exist under national law.

Article 15

Each State Party shall ensure that any statement which is established to have been made as a result of torture shall not be invoked as evidence in any proceedings, except against a person accused of torture as evidence that the statement was made.

Article 16

(1) Each State Party shall undertake to prevent in any territory under its jurisdiction other acts of cruel, inhuman or degrading treatment or punishment which do not amount to torture as defined in Article 1, when such acts are committed by or at the instigation of or with the consent or acquiescence of a public official or other person acting in an official capacity. In particular, the obligations contained in Articles 10, 11, 12 and 13 shall apply with the substitution for references to torture of references to other forms of cruel, inhuman or degrading treatment or punishment.

(2) The provisions of this Convention are without prejudice to the provisions of any other international instrument or national law which prohibits cruel, inhuman or degrading treatment or punishment or which relates to extradition or expulsion.

Part II

Article 17

(1) There shall be established a Committee against Torture (hereinafter referred to as the Committee) which shall carry out the functions hereinafter provided. The Committee shall consist of ten experts of high moral standing and recognized competence in the field of human rights, who shall serve in their personal capacity. The experts shall be elected by the States Parties, consideration being given to equitable geographical distribution and to the usefulness of the participation of some persons having legal experience.

(2) The members of the Committee shall be elected by secret ballot from a list of persons nominated by States Parties. Each State Party may nominate one person from among its own nationals. States Parties shall bear in mind the usefulness of nominating persons who are also members of the Human Rights Committee established under the International Covenant on Civil and Political Rights and who are willing to serve on the Committee against Torture.

(3) Elections of the members of the Committee shall be held at biennial meetings of States Parties convened by the Secretary-General of the United Nations. At those meetings, for which two thirds of the States Parties shall constitute a quorum, the persons elected to the Committee shall be those who obtain the largest number of votes and an absolute majority of the votes of the representatives of States Parties present and voting.

(4) The initial election shall be held no later than six months after the date of the entry into force of this Convention. At least four months before the date of each election, the Secretary-General of the United Nations shall address a letter to the States Parties inviting them to submit their nominations within three months. The Secretary-General shall prepare a list in alphabetical order of all persons thus nominated, indicating the States Parties which have nominated them, and shall submit it to the States Parties.

(5) The members of the Committee shall be elected for a term of four years. They shall be eligible for re-election if renominated. However, the term of five of the members elected at the first election shall expire at the end of two years; immediately after the first election the names of these five members shall be chosen by lot by the chairman of the meeting referred to in paragraph (3) of this Article.

(6) If a member of the Committee dies or resigns or for any other cause can no longer perform his Committee duties, the State Party which nominated him shall appoint another expert from among

its nationals to serve for the remainder of his term, subject to the approval of the majority of the States Parties. The approval shall be considered given unless half or more of the States Parties respond negatively within six weeks after having been informed by the Secretary-General of the United Nations of the proposed appointment.

(7) States Parties shall be responsible for the expenses of the members of the Committee while they are in performance of Committee duties.*

Article 18

(1) The Committee shall elect its officers for a term of two years. They may be re-elected.

(2) The Committee shall establish its own rules of procedure, but these rules shall provide, inter alia, that:

(a) Six members shall constitute a quorum;

(b) Decisions of the Committee shall be made by a majority vote of the members present.

(3) The Secretary-General of the United Nations shall provide the necessary staff and facilities for the effective performance of the functions of the Committee under this Convention.

(4) The Secretary-General of the United Nations shall convene the initial meeting of the Committee. After its initial meeting, the Committee shall meet at such times as shall be provided in its rules of procedure.

(5) The States Parties shall be responsible for expenses incurred in connection with the holding of meetings of the States Parties and of the Committee, including reimbursement to the United Nations for any expenses, such as the cost of staff and facilities, incurred by the United Nations pursuant to paragraph (3) of this Article.*

Article 19

(1) The States Parties shall submit to the Committee, through the Secretary-General of the United Nations, reports on the measures they have taken to give effect to their undertakings under this Convention, within one year after the entry into force of the Convention for the State Party concerned. Thereafter the States Parties shall submit supplementary reports every four years on any new measures taken and such other reports as the Committee may request.

(2) The Secretary-General of the United Nations shall transmit the reports to all States Parties.

(3) Each report shall be considered by the Committee which may make such General Comments on the report as it may consider appropriate and shall forward these to the State Party concerned. That State Party may respond with any observations it chooses to the Committee.

(4) The Committee may, at its discretion, decide to include any comments made by it in accordance with paragraph (3) of this Article, together with the observations thereon received from the State Party concerned, in its annual report made in accordance with Article 24. If so requested by the State Party concerned, the Committee may also include a copy of the report submitted under paragraph (1) of this Article.

Article 20

(1) If the Committee receives reliable information which appears to it to contain well-founded indications that torture is being systematically practised in the territory of a State Party, the Committee shall invite that State Party to co-operate in the examination of the information and to this end to submit observations with regard to the information concerned.

(2) Taking into account any observations which may have been submitted by the State Party concerned, as well as any other relevant information available to it, the Committee may, if it

* Amendment (see General Assembly Resolution 47/111 of 16 December 1992); status of ratification.

decides that this is warranted, designate one or more of its members to make a confidential inquiry and to report to the Committee urgently.

(3) If an inquiry is made in accordance with paragraph (2) of this Article, the Committee shall seek the co-operation of the State Party concerned. In agreement with that State Party, such an inquiry may include a visit to its territory.

(4) After examining the findings of its member or members submitted in accordance with paragraph (2) of this Article, the Commission shall transmit these findings to the State Party concerned together with any comments or suggestions which seem appropriate in view of the situation.

(5) All the proceedings of the Committee referred to in paragraphs (1) to (4) of this Article shall be confidential, and at all stages of the proceedings the co-operation of the State Party shall be sought. After such proceedings have been completed with regard to an inquiry made in accordance with paragraph (2), the Committee may, after consultations with the State Party concerned, decide to include a summary account of the results of the proceedings in its annual report made in accordance with Article 24.

Article 21

(1) A State Party to this Convention may at any time declare under this Article that it recognizes the competence of the Committee to receive and consider communications to the effect that a State Party claims that another State Party is not fulfilling its obligations under this Convention. Such communications may be received and considered according to the procedures laid down in this Article only if submitted by a State Party which has made a declaration recognizing in regard to itself the competence of the Committee. No communication shall be dealt with by the Committee under this Article if it concerns a State Party which has not made such a declaration. Communications received under this Article shall be dealt with in accordance with the following procedure;

(a) If a State Party considers that another State Party is not giving effect to the provisions of this Convention, it may, by written communication, bring the matter to the attention of that State Party. Within three months after the receipt of the communication the receiving State shall afford the State which sent the communication an explanation or any other statement in writing clarifying the matter, which should include, to the extent possible and pertinent, reference to domestic procedures and remedies taken, pending or available in the matter;

(b) If the matter is not adjusted to the satisfaction of both States Parties concerned within six months after the receipt by the receiving State of the initial communication, either State shall have the right to refer the matter to the Committee, by notice given to the Committee and to the other State;

(c) The Committee shall deal with a matter referred to it under this Article only after it has ascertained that all domestic remedies have been invoked and exhausted in the matter, in conformity with the generally recognized principles of international law. This shall not be the rule where the application of the remedies is unreasonably prolonged or is unlikely to bring effective relief to the person who is the victim of the violation of this Convention;

(d) The Committee shall hold closed meetings when examining communications under this Article;

(e) Subject to the provisions of subparagraph (e), the Committee shall make available its good offices to the States Parties concerned with a view to a friendly solution of the matter on the basis of respect for the obligations provided for in this Convention. For this purpose, the Committee may, when appropriate, set up an ad hoc conciliation commission;

(f) In any matter referred to it under this Article, the Committee may call upon the States Parties concerned, referred to in subparagraph (b), to supply any relevant information;

(g) The States Parties concerned, referred to in subparagraph (b), shall have the right to be represented when the matter is being considered by the Committee and to make submissions orally and/or in writing;

(h) The Committee shall, within twelve months after the date of receipt of notice under subparagraph (b), submit a report:

(i) If a solution within the terms of subparagraph (e) is reached, the Committee shall confine its report to a brief statement of the facts and of the solution reached;

(ii) If a solution within the terms of subparagraph (e) is not reached, the Committee shall confine its report to a brief statement of the facts; the written submissions and record of the oral submissions made by the States Parties concerned shall be attached to the report.

In every matter, the report shall be communicated to the States Parties concerned.

(2) The provisions of this Article shall come into force when five States Parties to this Convention have made declarations under paragraph (1) of this Article. Such declarations shall be deposited by the States Parties with the Secretary-General of the United Nations, who shall transmit copies thereof to the other States Parties. A declaration may be withdrawn at any time by notification to the Secretary-General. Such a withdrawal shall not prejudice the consideration of any matter which is the subject of a communication already transmitted under this Article; no further communication by any State Party shall be received under this Article after the notification of withdrawal of the declaration has been received by the Secretary-General, unless the State Party concerned has made a new declaration.

Article 22

(1) A State Party to this Convention may at any time declare under this Article that it recognizes the competence of the Committee to receive and consider communications from or on behalf of individuals subject to its jurisdiction who claim to be victims of a violation by a State Party of the provisions of the Convention. No communication shall be received by the Committee if it concerns a State Party which has not made such a declaration.

(2) The Committee shall consider inadmissible any communication under this Article which is anonymous or which it considers to be an abuse of the right of submission of such communications or to be incompatible with the provisions of this Convention.

(3) Subject to the provisions of paragraph (2), the Committee shall bring any communications submitted to it under this Article to the attention of the State Party to this Convention which has made a declaration under paragraph (1) and is alleged to be violating any provisions of the Convention. Within six months, the receiving State shall submit to the Committee written explanations or statements clarifying the matter and the remedy, if any, that may have been taken by that State

(4) The Committee shall consider communications received under this Article in the light of all information made available to it by or on behalf of the individual and by the State Party concerned.

(5) The Committee shall not consider any communications from an individual under this Article unless it has ascertained that:

(a) The same matter has not been, and is not being, examined under another procedure of international investigation or settlement;

(b) The individual has exhausted all available domestic remedies; this shall not be the rule where the application of the remedies is unreasonably prolonged or is unlikely to bring effective relief to the person who is the victim of the violation of this Convention.

(6) The Committee shall hold closed meetings when examining communications under this Article.

(7) The Committee shall forward its views to the State Party concerned and to the individual.

(8) The provisions of this Article shall come into force when five States Parties to this Convention have made declarations under paragraph (1) of this Article. Such declarations shall be deposited by the States Parties with the Secretary-General of the United Nations, who shall transmit copies thereof to the other States Parties. A declaration may be withdrawn at any time by notification to the Secretary-General. Such a withdrawal shall not prejudice the consideration of any matter which is the subject of a communication already transmitted under this Article; no further communication by or on behalf of an individual shall be received under this Article after the notification of withdrawal of the declaration has been received by the Secretary-General, unless the State Party has made a new declaration.

Article 23

The members of the Committee and of the ad hoc conciliation commissions which may be appointed under Article 21, paragraph (1)(e), shall be entitled to the facilities, privileges and immunities of experts on mission for the United Nations as laid down in the relevant Sections of the Convention on the Privileges and Immunities of the United Nations.

Article 24

The Committee shall submit an annual report on its activities under this Convention to the States Parties and to the General Assembly of the United Nations.

Part III

Article 25

(1) This Convention is open for signature by all States.

(2) This Convention is subject to ratification. Instruments of ratification shall be deposited with the Secretary-General of the United Nations.

Article 26

This Convention is open to accession by all States. Accession shall be effected by the deposit of an instrument of accession with the Secretary-General of the United Nations.

Article 27

(1) This Convention shall enter into force on the thirtieth day after the date of the deposit with the Secretary-General of the United Nations of the twentieth instrument of ratification or accession.

(2) For each State ratifying this Convention or acceding to it after the deposit of the twentieth instrument of ratification or accession, the Convention shall enter into force on the thirtieth day after the date of the deposit of its own instrument of ratification or accession.

Article 28

(1) Each State may, at the time of signature or ratification of this Convention or accession thereto, declare that it does not recognize the competence of the Committee provided for in Article 20.

(2) Any State Party having made a reservation in accordance with paragraph (1) of this Article may, at any time, withdraw this reservation by notification to the Secretary-General of the United Nations.

Article 29

(1) Any State Party to this Convention may propose an amendment and file it with the Secretary-General of the United Nations. The Secretary-General shall thereupon communicate the proposed amendment to the States Parties with a request that they notify him whether they favour

a conference of States Parties for the purpose of considering and voting upon the proposal. In the event that within four months from the date of such communication at least one third of the States Parties favours such a conference, the Secretary-General shall convene the conference under the auspices of the United Nations. Any amendment adopted by a majority of the States Parties present and voting at the conference shall be submitted by the Secretary-General to all the States Parties for acceptance.

(2) An amendment adopted in accordance with paragraph (1) of this Article shall enter into force when two thirds of the States Parties to this Convention have notified the Secretary-General of the United Nations that they have accepted it in accordance with their respective constitutional processes.

(3) When amendments enter into force, they shall be binding on those States Parties which have accepted them, other States Parties still being bound by the provisions of this Convention and any earlier amendments which they have accepted.

Article 30

(1) Any dispute between two or more States Parties concerning the interpretation or application of this Convention which cannot be settled through negotiation shall, at the request of one of them, be submitted to arbitration. If within six months from the date of the request for arbitration the Parties are unable to agree on the organization of the arbitration, any one of those Parties may refer the dispute to the International Court of Justice by request in conformity with the Statute of the Court.

(2) Each State may, at the time of signature or ratification of this Convention or accession thereto, declare that it does not consider itself bound by paragraph (1) of this Article. The other States Parties shall not be bound by paragraph (1) of this Article with respect to any State Party having made such a reservation.

(3) Any State Party having made a reservation in accordance with paragraph (2) of this Article may at any time withdraw this reservation by notification to the Secretary-General of the United Nations.

Article 31

(1) A State Party may denounce this Convention by written notification to the Secretary-General of the United Nations. Denunciation becomes effective one year after the date of receipt of the notification by the Secretary-General.

(2) Such a denunciation shall not have the effect of releasing the State Party from its obligations under this Convention in regard to any act or omission which occurs prior to the date at which the denunciation becomes effective, nor shall denunciation prejudice in any way the continued consideration of any matter which is already under consideration by the Committee prior to the date at which the denunciation becomes effective.

(3) Following the date at which the denunciation of a State Party becomes effective, the Committee shall not commence consideration of any new matter regarding that State.

Article 32

The Secretary-General of the United Nations shall inform all States Members of the United Nations and all States which have signed this Convention or acceded to it of the following:

(a) Signatures, ratifications and accessions under Articles 25 and 26;

(b) The date of entry into force of this Convention under Article 27 and the date of the entry into force of any amendments under Article 29;

(c) Denunciations under Article 31.

Article 33

(1) This Convention, of which the Arabic, Chinese, English, French, Russian and Spanish texts are equally authentic, shall be deposited with the Secretary-General of the United Nations.

(2) The Secretary-General of the United Nations shall transmit certified copies of this Convention to all States.

Reservations Applicable to Hong Kong

China

On 10 June 1997, the Secretary-General received communications concerning the status of Hong Kong from the Governments of China and the United Kingdom (see also note 2 under "China" and note 2 under "United Kingdom of Great Britain and Northern Ireland" regarding Hong Kong in the "Historical Information" Section).* Upon resuming the exercise of sovereignty over Hong Kong, China notified the Secretary-General that the Convention with the reservation made by China will also apply to the Hong Kong special Administrative Region.

Reservations made upon signature and confirmed upon ratification:

(1) The Chinese Government does not recognize the competence of the Committee against Torture as provided for in Article 20 of the Convention.

(2) The Chinese Government does not consider itself bound by paragraph (l) of Article 30 of the Convention.

General Comments

(1) General Comment No. 1: Implementation of Article 3 of the Convention in the context of Article 22 (16 September 1998)

(2) General Comment No. 2: Implementation of Article 2 by States parties (24 January 2008)

(3) General Comment No. 3: Implementation of Article 14 by States parties (13 December 2012)

(4) General Comment No. 4 on the implementation of Article 3 of the Convention in the context of Article 22 (4 September 2018)

CONVENTION ON THE ELIMINATION OF ALL FORMS OF DISCRIMINATION AGAINST WOMEN

(Adopted: 18 December 1979; Entry into force: 3 September 1981, in accordance with Article 27(1))

The States Parties to the present Convention,

* These notes can be accessed at https://treaties.un.org/Pages/HistoricalInfo.aspx?clang=_en#. They have also been reproduced in the footnotes on pages 180–184 of this volume.

Noting that the Charter of the United Nations reaffirms faith in fundamental human rights, in the dignity and worth of the human person and in the equal rights of men and women,

Noting that the Universal Declaration of Human Rights affirms the principle of the inadmissibility of discrimination and proclaims that all human beings are born free and equal in dignity and rights and that everyone is entitled to all the rights and freedoms set forth therein, without distinction of any kind, including distinction based on sex,

Noting that the States Parties to the International Covenants on Human Rights have the obligation to ensure the equal rights of men and women to enjoy all economic, social, cultural, civil and political rights,

Considering the international conventions concluded under the auspices of the United Nations and the specialized agencies promoting equality of rights of men and women,

Noting also the resolutions, declarations and recommendations adopted by the United Nations and the specialized agencies promoting equality of rights of men and women,

Concerned, however, that despite these various instruments extensive discrimination against women continues to exist,

Recalling that discrimination against women violates the principles of equality of rights and respect for human dignity, is an obstacle to the participation of women, on equal terms with men, in the political, social, economic and cultural life of their countries, hampers the growth of the prosperity of society and the family and makes more difficult the full development of the potentialities of women in the service of their countries and of humanity,

Concerned that in situations of poverty women have the least access to food, health, education, training and opportunities for employment and other needs,

Convinced that the establishment of the new international economic order based on equity and justice will contribute significantly towards the promotion of equality between men and women,

Emphasizing that the eradication of apartheid, all forms of racism, racial discrimination, colonialism, neo-colonialism, aggression, foreign occupation and domination and interference in the internal affairs of States is essential to the full enjoyment of the rights of men and women,

Affirming that the strengthening of international peace and security, the relaxation of international tension, mutual co-operation among all States irrespective of their social and economic systems, general and complete disarmament, in particular nuclear disarmament under strict and effective international control, the affirmation of the principles of justice, equality and mutual benefit in relations among countries and the realization of the right of peoples under alien and colonial domination and foreign occupation to self-determination and independence, as well as respect for national sovereignty and territorial integrity, will promote social progress and development and as a consequence will contribute to the attainment of full equality between men and women,

Convinced that the full and complete development of a country, the welfare of the world and the cause of peace require the maximum participation of women on equal terms with men in all fields,

Bearing in mind the great contribution of women to the welfare of the family and to the development of society, so far not fully recognized, the social significance of maternity and the role of both parents in the family and in the upbringing of children, and aware that the role of women in procreation should not be a basis for discrimination but that the upbringing of children requires a sharing of responsibility between men and women and society as a whole,

Aware that a change in the traditional role of men as well as the role of women in society and in the family is needed to achieve full equality between men and women,

Determined to implement the principles set forth in the Declaration on the Elimination of Discrimination against Women and, for that purpose, to adopt the measures required for the elimination of such discrimination in all its forms and manifestations,

Have agreed on the following:

Part I

Article 1

For the purposes of the present Convention, the term "discrimination against women" shall mean any distinction, exclusion or restriction made on the basis of sex which has the effect or purpose of impairing or nullifying the recognition, enjoyment or exercise by women, irrespective of their marital status, on a basis of equality of men and women, of human rights and fundamental freedoms in the political, economic, social, cultural, civil or any other field.

Article 2

States Parties condemn discrimination against women in all its forms, agree to pursue by all appropriate means and without delay a policy of eliminating discrimination against women and, to this end, undertake:

(a) To embody the principle of the equality of men and women in their national constitutions or other appropriate legislation if not yet incorporated therein and to ensure, through law and other appropriate means, the practical realization of this principle;

(b) To adopt appropriate legislative and other measures, including sanctions where appropriate, prohibiting all discrimination against women;

(c) To establish legal protection of the rights of women on an equal basis with men and to ensure through competent national tribunals and other public institutions the effective protection of women against any act of discrimination;

(d) To refrain from engaging in any act or practice of discrimination against women and to ensure that public authorities and institutions shall act in conformity with this obligation;

(e) To take all appropriate measures to eliminate discrimination against women by any person, organization or enterprise;

(f) To take all appropriate measures, including legislation, to modify or abolish existing laws, regulations, customs and practices which constitute discrimination against women;

(g) To repeal all national penal provisions which constitute discrimination against women.

Article 3

States Parties shall take in all fields, in particular in the political, social, economic and cultural fields, all appropriate measures, including legislation, to ensure the full development and advancement of women, for the purpose of guaranteeing them the exercise and enjoyment of human rights and fundamental freedoms on a basis of equality with men.

Article 4

(1) Adoption by States Parties of temporary special measures aimed at accelerating de facto equality between men and women shall not be considered discrimination as defined in the present Convention, but shall in no way entail as a consequence the maintenance of unequal or separate standards; these measures shall be discontinued when the objectives of equality of opportunity and treatment have been achieved.

(2) Adoption by States Parties of special measures, including those measures contained in the present Convention, aimed at protecting maternity shall not be considered discriminatory.

Article 5

States Parties shall take all appropriate measures:

(a) To modify the social and cultural patterns of conduct of men and women, with a view to achieving the elimination of prejudices and customary and all other practices which are based on the idea of the inferiority or the superiority of either of the sexes or on stereotyped roles for men and women;

(b) To ensure that family education includes a proper understanding of maternity as a social function and the recognition of the common responsibility of men and women in the upbringing and development of their children, it being understood that the interest of the children is the primordial consideration in all cases.

Article 6

States Parties shall take all appropriate measures, including legislation, to suppress all forms of traffic in women and exploitation of prostitution of women.

Part II

Article 7

States Parties shall take all appropriate measures to eliminate discrimination against women in the political and public life of the country and, in particular, shall ensure to women, on equal terms with men, the right:

(a) To vote in all elections and public referenda and to be eligible for election to all publicly elected bodies;

(b) To participate in the formulation of government policy and the implementation thereof and to hold public office and perform all public functions at all levels of government;

(c) To participate in non-governmental organizations and associations concerned with the public and political life of the country.

Article 8

States Parties shall take all appropriate measures to ensure to women, on equal terms with men and without any discrimination, the opportunity to represent their Governments at the international level and to participate in the work of international organizations.

Article 9

(1) States Parties shall grant women equal rights with men to acquire, change or retain their nationality. They shall ensure in particular that neither marriage to an alien nor change of nationality by the husband during marriage shall automatically change the nationality of the wife, render her stateless or force upon her the nationality of the husband.

(2) States Parties shall grant women equal rights with men with respect to the nationality of their children.

Part III

Article 10

States Parties shall take all appropriate measures to eliminate discrimination against women in order to ensure to them equal rights with men in the field of education and in particular to ensure, on a basis of equality of men and women:

(a) The same conditions for career and vocational guidance, for access to studies and for the achievement of diplomas in educational establishments of all categories in rural as well as in urban areas; this equality shall be ensured in pre-school, general, technical, professional and higher technical education, as well as in all types of vocational training;

(b) Access to the same curricula, the same examinations, teaching staff with qualifications of the same standard and school premises and equipment of the same quality;

(c) The elimination of any stereotyped concept of the roles of men and women at all levels and in all forms of education by encouraging coeducation and other types of education which will help to achieve this aim and, in particular, by the revision of textbooks and school programmes and the adaptation of teaching methods;

(d) The same opportunities to benefit from scholarships and other study grants;

(e) The same opportunities for access to programmes of continuing education, including adult and functional literacy programmes, particularly those aimed at reducing, at the earliest possible time, any gap in education existing between men and women;

(f) The reduction of female student drop-out rates and the organization of programmes for girls and women who have left school prematurely;

(g) The same Opportunities to participate actively in sports and physical education;

(h) Access to specific educational information to help to ensure the health and well-being of families, including information and advice on family planning.

Article 11

(1) States Parties shall take all appropriate measures to eliminate discrimination against women in the field of employment in order to ensure, on a basis of equality of men and women, the same rights, in particular:

(a) The right to work as an inalienable right of all human beings;

(b) The right to the same employment opportunities, including the application of the same criteria for selection in matters of employment;

(c) The right to free choice of profession and employment, the right to promotion, job security and all benefits and conditions of service and the right to receive vocational training and retraining, including apprenticeships, advanced vocational training and recurrent training;

(d) The right to equal remuneration, including benefits, and to equal treatment in respect of work of equal value, as well as equality of treatment in the evaluation of the quality of work;

(e) The right to social security, particularly in cases of retirement, unemployment, sickness, invalidity and old age and other incapacity to work, as well as the right to paid leave;

(f) The right to protection of health and to safety in working conditions, including the safeguarding of the function of reproduction.

(2) In order to prevent discrimination against women on the grounds of marriage or maternity and to ensure their effective right to work, States Parties shall take appropriate measures:

(a) To prohibit, subject to the imposition of sanctions, dismissal on the grounds of pregnancy or of maternity leave and discrimination in dismissals on the basis of marital status;

(b) To introduce maternity leave with pay or with comparable social benefits without loss of former employment, seniority or social allowances;

(c) To encourage the provision of the necessary supporting social services to enable parents to combine family obligations with work responsibilities and participation in public life, in particular through promoting the establishment and development of a network of child-care facilities;

(d) To provide special protection to women during pregnancy in types of work proved to be harmful to them.

(3) Protective legislation relating to matters covered in this Article shall be reviewed periodically in the light of scientific and technological knowledge and shall be revised, repealed or extended as necessary.

Article 12

(1) States Parties shall take all appropriate measures to eliminate discrimination against women in the field of health care in order to ensure, on a basis of equality of men and women, access to health care services, including those related to family planning.

(2) Notwithstanding the provisions of paragraph (1) of this Article, States Parties shall ensure to women appropriate services in connection with pregnancy, confinement and the post-natal period, granting free services where necessary, as well as adequate nutrition during pregnancy and lactation.

Article 13

States Parties shall take all appropriate measures to eliminate discrimination against women in other areas of economic and social life in order to ensure, on a basis of equality of men and women, the same rights, in particular:

(a) The right to family benefits;

(b) The right to bank loans, mortgages and other forms of financial credit;

(c) The right to participate in recreational activities, sports and all aspects of cultural life.

Article 14

(1) States Parties shall take into account the particular problems faced by rural women and the significant roles which rural women play in the economic survival of their families, including their work in the non-monetized sectors of the economy, and shall take all appropriate measures to ensure the application of the provisions of the present Convention to women in rural areas.

(2) States Parties shall take all appropriate measures to eliminate discrimination against women in rural areas in order to ensure, on a basis of equality of men and women, that they participate in and benefit from rural development and, in particular, shall ensure to such women the right:

(a) To participate in the elaboration and implementation of development planning at all levels;

(b) To have access to adequate health care facilities, including information, counselling and services in family planning;

(c) To benefit directly from social security programmes;

(d) To obtain all types of training and education, formal and non-formal, including that relating to functional literacy, as well as, inter alia, the benefit of all community and extension services, in order to increase their technical proficiency;

(e) To organize self-help groups and co-operatives in order to obtain equal access to economic opportunities through employment or self-employment;

(f) To participate in all community activities;

(g) To have access to agricultural credit and loans, marketing facilities, appropriate technology and equal treatment in land and agrarian reform as well as in land resettlement schemes;

(h) To enjoy adequate living conditions, particularly in relation to housing, sanitation, electricity and water supply, transport and communications.

Part IV

Article 15

(1) States Parties shall accord to women equality with men before the law.

(2) States Parties shall accord to women, in civil matters, a legal capacity identical to that of men and the same opportunities to exercise that capacity. In particular, they shall give women equal

rights to conclude contracts and to administer property and shall treat them equally in all stages of procedure in courts and tribunals.

(3) States Parties agree that all contracts and all other private instruments of any kind with a legal effect which is directed at restricting the legal capacity of women shall be deemed null and void.

(4) States Parties shall accord to men and women the same rights with regard to the law relating to the movement of persons and the freedom to choose their residence and domicile.

Article 16

(1) States Parties shall take all appropriate measures to eliminate discrimination against women in all matters relating to marriage and family relations and in particular shall ensure, on a basis of equality of men and women:

(a) The same right to enter into marriage;

(b) The same right freely to choose a spouse and to enter into marriage only with their free and full consent;

(c) The same rights and responsibilities during marriage and at its dissolution;

(d) The same rights and responsibilities as parents, irrespective of their marital status, in matters relating to their children; in all cases the interests of the children shall be paramount;

(e) The same rights to decide freely and responsibly on the number and spacing of their children and to have access to the information, education and means to enable them to exercise these rights;

(f) The same rights and responsibilities with regard to guardianship, wardship, trusteeship and adoption of children, or similar institutions where these concepts exist in national legislation; in all cases the interests of the children shall be paramount;

(g) The same personal rights as husband and wife, including the right to choose a family name, a profession and an occupation;

(h) The same rights for both spouses in respect of the ownership, acquisition, management, administration, enjoyment and disposition of property, whether free of charge or for a valuable consideration.

(2) The betrothal and the marriage of a child shall have no legal effect, and all necessary action, including legislation, shall be taken to specify a minimum age for marriage and to make the registration of marriages in an official registry compulsory.

Part V

Article 17

(1) For the purpose of considering the progress made in the implementation of the present Convention, there shall be established a Committee on the Elimination of Discrimination against Women (hereinafter referred to as the Committee) consisting, at the time of entry into force of the Convention, of eighteen and, after ratification of or accession to the Convention by the thirty-fifth State Party, of twenty-three experts of high moral standing and competence in the field covered by the Convention. The experts shall be elected by States Parties from among their nationals and shall serve in their personal capacity, consideration being given to equitable geographical distribution and to the representation of the different forms of civilization as well as the principal legal systems.

(2) The members of the Committee shall be elected by secret ballot from a list of persons nominated by States Parties. Each State Party may nominate one person from among its own nationals.

(3) The initial election shall be held six months after the date of the entry into force of the present Convention. At least three months before the date of each election the Secretary-General of the United Nations shall address a letter to the States Parties inviting them to submit their nominations within two months. The Secretary-General shall prepare a list in alphabetical order of all persons thus nominated, indicating the States Parties which have nominated them, and shall submit it to the States Parties.

(4) Elections of the members of the Committee shall be held at a meeting of States Parties convened by the Secretary-General at United Nations Headquarters. At that meeting, for which two thirds of the States Parties shall constitute a quorum, the persons elected to the Committee shall be those nominees who obtain the largest number of votes and an absolute majority of the votes of the representatives of States Parties present and voting.

(5) The members of the Committee shall be elected for a term of four years. However, the terms of nine of the members elected at the first election shall expire at the end of two years; immediately after the first election the names of these nine members shall be chosen by lot by the Chairman of the Committee.

(6) The election of the five additional members of the Committee shall be held in accordance with the provisions of paragraphs (2), (3) and (4) of this Article, following the thirty-fifth ratification or accession. The terms of two of the additional members elected on this occasion shall expire at the end of two years, the names of these two members having been chosen by lot by the Chairman of the Committee.

(7) For the filling of casual vacancies, the State Party whose expert has ceased to function as a member of the Committee shall appoint another expert from among its nationals, subject to the approval of the Committee.

(8) The members of the Committee shall, with the approval of the General Assembly, receive emoluments from United Nations resources on such terms and conditions as the Assembly may decide, having regard to the importance of the Committee's responsibilities.

(9) The Secretary-General of the United Nations shall provide the necessary staff and facilities for the effective performance of the functions of the Committee under the present Convention.

Article 18

(1) States Parties undertake to submit to the Secretary-General of the United Nations, for consideration by the Committee, a report on the legislative, judicial, administrative or other measures which they have adopted to give effect to the provisions of the present Convention and on the progress made in this respect:

   (a) Within one year after the entry into force for the State concerned;

   (b) Thereafter at least every four years and further whenever the Committee so requests.

(2) Reports may indicate factors and difficulties affecting the degree of fulfilment of obligations under the present Convention.

Article 19

(1) The Committee shall adopt its own rules of procedure.

(2) The Committee shall elect its officers for a term of two years.

Article 20

(1) The Committee shall normally meet for a period of not more than two weeks annually in order to consider the reports submitted in accordance with Article 18 of the present Convention.

(2) The meetings of the Committee shall normally be held at United Nations Headquarters or at any other convenient place as determined by the Committee. (amendment, status of ratification)

Article 21

(1) The Committee shall, through the Economic and Social Council, report annually to the General Assembly of the United Nations on its activities and may make suggestions and General Recommendations based on the examination of reports and information received from the States Parties. Such suggestions and General Recommendations shall be included in the report of the Committee together with comments, if any, from States Parties.

(2) The Secretary-General of the United Nations shall transmit the reports of the Committee to the Commission on the Status of Women for its information.

Article 22

The specialized agencies shall be entitled to be represented at the consideration of the implementation of such provisions of the present Convention as fall within the scope of their activities. The Committee may invite the specialized agencies to submit reports on the implementation of the Convention in areas falling within the scope of their activities.

Part VI

Article 23

Nothing in the present Convention shall affect any provisions that are more conducive to the achievement of equality between men and women which may be contained:

(a) In the legislation of a State Party; or

(b) In any other international convention, treaty or agreement in force for that State.

Article 24

States Parties undertake to adopt all necessary measures at the national level aimed at achieving the full realization of the rights recognized in the present Convention.

Article 25

(1) The present Convention shall be open for signature by all States.

(2) The Secretary-General of the United Nations is designated as the depositary of the present Convention.

(3) The present Convention is subject to ratification. Instruments of ratification shall be deposited with the Secretary-General of the United Nations.

(4) The present Convention shall be open to accession by all States. Accession shall be effected by the deposit of an instrument of accession with the Secretary-General of the United Nations.

Article 26

(1) A request for the revision of the present Convention may be made at any time by any State Party by means of a notification in writing addressed to the Secretary-General of the United Nations.

(2) The General Assembly of the United Nations shall decide upon the steps, if any, to be taken in respect of such a request.

Article 27

(1) The present Convention shall enter into force on the thirtieth day after the date of deposit with the Secretary-General of the United Nations of the twentieth instrument of ratification or accession.

(2) For each State ratifying the present Convention or acceding to it after the deposit of the twentieth instrument of ratification or accession, the Convention shall enter into force on the thirtieth day after the date of the deposit of its own instrument of ratification or accession.

Article 28

(1) The Secretary-General of the United Nations shall receive and circulate to all States the text of reservations made by States at the time of ratification or accession.

(2) A reservation incompatible with the object and purpose of the present Convention shall not be permitted.

(3) Reservations may be withdrawn at any time by notification to this effect addressed to the Secretary-General of the United Nations, who shall then inform all States thereof. Such notification shall take effect on the date on which it is received.

Article 29

(1) Any dispute between two or more States Parties concerning the interpretation or application of the present Convention which is not settled by negotiation shall, at the request of one of them, be submitted to arbitration. If within six months from the date of the request for arbitration the parties are unable to agree on the organization of the arbitration, any one of those parties may refer the dispute to the International Court of Justice by request in conformity with the Statute of the Court.

(2) Each State Party may at the time of signature or ratification of the present Convention or accession thereto declare that it does not consider itself bound by paragraph (1) of this Article. The other States Parties shall not be bound by that paragraph with respect to any State Party which has made such a reservation.

(3) Any State Party which has made a reservation in accordance with paragraph (2) of this Article may at any time withdraw that reservation by notification to the Secretary-General of the United Nations.

Article 30

The present Convention, the Arabic, Chinese, English, French, Russian and Spanish texts of which are equally authentic, shall be deposited with the Secretary-General of the United Nations.

IN WITNESS WHEREOF the undersigned, duly authorized, have signed the present Convention.

Reservations Applicable to Hong Kong

United Kingdom of Great Britain and Northern Ireland

The instrument of ratification specifies that the said Convention is ratified in respect of the United Kingdom of Great Britain and Northern Ireland, the Isle of Man, British Virgin Islands, Falkland Islands (Malvinas), South Georgia and the South Sandwich Islands, and Turks and Caicos Islands.

[...]

Further, on 14 October 1996, the Secretary-General received from the Government of the United Kingdom a communication stating that it had decided to apply the Convention to Hong Kong, subject to the following reservations and declarations:

General

(a) The United Kingdom on behalf of Hong Kong understands the main purpose of the Convention, in the light of the definition contained in Article 1, to the reduction, in accordance with its terms, of discrimination against women, and does not therefore regard the Convention as imposing any requirement to repeal or modify any existing laws, regulations, customs or practices which provide for women to be treated more favourably than men, whether temporarily or in the longer term. Undertakings by the United Kingdom on behalf of Hong Kong under Article 4, paragraph (1), and other provisions of the Convention are to be construed accordingly.

(b) The right to continue to apply such immigration legislation governing entry into, stay in and departure from Hong Kong as may be deemed necessary from time to time is reserved by the United Kingdom on behalf of Hong Kong. Accordingly, acceptance of Article 15(4), and of the other provisions of the Convention, is subject to the provisions of any such legislation as regards persons not at the time having the right under the law of Hong Kong to enter and remain in Hong Kong.

(c) In the light of the definition contained in Article 1, the United Kingdom's extension of its ratification to Hong Kong is subject to the understanding that none of its obligations under the Convention in Hong Kong shall be treated as extending to the affairs of religious denominations or orders.

(d) Laws applicable in the New Territories which enable male indigenous villagers to exercise certain rights in respect of property and which provide for rent concessions in respect of land or property held by indigenous persons or their lawful successors through the male line will continue to be applied.

Specific Articles

Article 9

The British Nationality Act 1981, which was brought into force with effect from January 1983, is based on principles which do not allow of any discrimination against women within the meaning of Article 1 as regards acquisition, change, or retention of their nationality or as regards the nationality of their children. The United Kingdom's acceptance of Article 9 on behalf of Hong Kong shall not, however, be taken to invalidate the continuation of certain temporary or transitional provisions which will continue in force beyond that date.

Article 11

The United Kingdom on behalf of Hong Kong reserves the right to apply all Hong Kong legislation and the rules of pension schemes affecting retirement pensions, survivors' benefits and other benefits in relation to death or retirement (including retirement on grounds of redundancy) whether or not derived from a social security scheme.

This reservation will apply equally to any further legislation which may modify or replace such legislation, or the rules of pension schemes, on the understanding that the terms of such legislation will be compatible with the United Kingdom's obligations under the Convention in respect of Hong Kong.

The United Kingdom on behalf of Hong Kong reserves the right to apply any non-discriminatory requirement for a qualifying period of employment for the application of the provisions contained in Article 11(2).

Article 15

In relation to Article 15, paragraph (3), the United Kingdom on behalf of Hong Kong understands the intention of this provisions to be that only those terms or elements of a contract or other private instrument which are discriminatory in the sense described are to be deemed null and void, but not necessarily the contract or instrument as a whole.

China

On 10 June 1997, the Secretary-General received communications concerning the status of Hong Kong from the Governments of China and the United Kingdom (see also note 2 under "China" and note 2

under "United Kingdom of Great Britain and Northern Ireland" regarding Hong Kong in the "Historical Information" Section).*

Upon resuming the exercise of sovereignty over Hong Kong, China notified the Secretary-General that the Convention with the reservation made by China will also apply to the Hong Kong special Administrative Region.

In addition, the notification made by the Government of China contained the following declarations:

(1) [...]

(2) The Government of the People's Republic of China understands, on behalf of the Hong Kong Special Administrative Region, the main purpose of the Convention, in the light of the definition contained in Article 1, to be the reduction, in accordance with its terms, of discrimination against women, and does not therefore regard the Convention as imposing any requirement upon the Hong Kong Special Administrative Region to repeal or modify any of its existing laws, regulations, customs or practices which provide for women to be treated more favourably than men, whether temporarily or in the longer term. Undertakings by the Government of the People's Republic of China on behalf of the Hong Kong Special Administrative Region under Article 4, paragraph (1), and other provisions of the Convention are to be construed accordingly.

(3) The Government of the People's Republic of China reserves, for the Hong Kong Special Administrative Region, the right to continue to apply relevant immigration legislation governing the entry into, stay in and departure from the Hong Kong Special Administrative Region as may be deemed necessary from time to time. Accordingly, acceptance of Article 15, paragraph (4), and of the other provisions of the Convention is subject to the provisions of any such legislation ass not at the time having the right under the laws of the Hong Kong Special Administrative Region to enter and remain in the Hong Kong Special Administrative Region.

(4) The Government of the People's Republic of China understands, in the light of the definition contained in Article 1, that none of its obligations under the Convention shall be treated as extending to the affairs of religious denominations or orders in the Hong Kong Special Administrative Region.

(5) Laws applicable in the New Territories of the Hong Kong Special Administrative Region which enable male indigenous villagers to exercise certain rights in respect of property and which provide for rent concessions in respect of land or property held by indigenous persons or their lawful successors through the male line will continue to [be] applied.

(6) The Government of the People's Republic of China reserves, for the Hong Kong Special Administrative Region, the right to apply all its legislation and the rules of pension schemes affecting retirement pensions, survivors' benefits in relation to death or retirement (including retirement on ground of redundancy), whether or not derived from a social security scheme.

This reservation will apply to any future legislation which may modify or replace such aforesaid legislation, or the rules of pension schemes, on the understanding that the terms of such legislation will be compatible with the Government of the People's Republic of China's obligations under the Convention in respect of the Hong Kong Special Administrative Region.

The Government of the People's Republic of China reserves the right for the Hong Kong Special Administrative Region to apply any non-discriminatory requirement for a qualifying period of employment for the application of the provisions contained in Article 11, paragraph (2) of the Convention.

* These notes can be accessed at https://treaties.un.org/Pages/HistoricalInfo.aspx?clang=_en#. They have also been reproduced in the footnotes on pages 180–184 of this volume.

(7) The Government of the People's Republic of China understands, on behalf of the Hong Kong Special Administrative Region, the intention of Article 15, paragraph (3), of the Convention to be that only those terms or elements of the contract or other private instrument which are discriminatory in the sense described are to be deemed null and void, but not necessarily the contract or instrument as a whole.

China

Declaration made upon signature and confirmed upon ratification:

The People's Republic of China does not consider itself bound by paragraph (1) of Article 29 of the Convention.

General Recommendations

(1) General Recommendation No. 1: Reporting guidelines (1986)

(2) General Recommendation No. 2: Reporting guidelines (1987)

(3) General Recommendation No. 3: Education and public information programmes (1987)

(4) General Recommendation No. 4: Reservations (1987)

(5) General Recommendation No. 5: Temporary special measures (1988)

(6) General Recommendation No. 6: Effective national machinery and publicity (1988)

(7) General Recommendation No. 7: Resources (1988)

(8) General Recommendation No. 8: Article 8 (1988)

(9) General Recommendation No. 9: Statistical data (1989)

(10) General Recommendation No. 10: Tenth anniversary of the adoption of CEDAW (1989)

(11) General Recommendation No. 11: Technical advisory services for reporting (1989)

(12) General Recommendation No. 12: Violence against women (1989)

(13) General Recommendation No. 13: Equal remuneration for work of equal value (1989)

(14) General Recommendation No. 14: Female circumcision (1990)

(15) General Recommendation No. 15: Women and AIDS (1990)

(16) General Recommendation No. 16: Unpaid women workers in rural and urban family enterprises (1991)

(17) General Recommendation No. 17: Measurement and quantification of the unremunerated domestic activities of women and their recognition in the GNP (1991)

(18) General Recommendation No. 18: Disabled women (1991)

(19) General Recommendation No. 19: Violence against women (1992)

(20) General Recommendation No. 20: Reservations (1992)

(21) General Recommendation No. 21: Equality in marriage and family relations (1994)

(22) General Recommendation No. 22: Article 20 of the Convention (1995)

(23) General Recommendation No. 23: Women in political and public life (1997)

(24) General Recommendation No. 24: Article 12 (Women and health) (1999)

(25) General Recommendation No. 25: Article 4, paragraph (1) (Temporary special measures) (2004)

(26) General Recommendation No. 26: Women migrant workers (2008)

(27) General Recommendation No. 27: Older women and protection of their human rights (2010)

(28) General Recommendation No. 28: The Core Obligations of States Parties under Article 2 of the Convention on the Elimination of All Forms of Discrimination against Women (2010)

(29) General Recommendation No. 29: Article 16 (Economic consequences of marriage, family relations and their dissolution) (2012)

CONVENTION ON THE RIGHTS OF THE CHILD

(Adopted: 20 November 1989; Entry into force: 2 September 1990, in accordance with Article 49)

Preamble

The States Parties to the present Convention,

Considering that, in accordance with the principles proclaimed in the Charter of the United Nations, recognition of the inherent dignity and of the equal and inalienable rights of all members of the human family is the foundation of freedom, justice and peace in the world,

Bearing in mind that the peoples of the United Nations have, in the Charter, reaffirmed their faith in fundamental human rights and in the dignity and worth of the human person, and have determined to promote social progress and better standards of life in larger freedom,

Recognizing that the United Nations has, in the Universal Declaration of Human Rights and in the International Covenants on Human Rights, proclaimed and agreed that everyone is entitled to all the rights and freedoms set forth therein, without distinction of any kind, such as race, colour, sex, language, religion, political or other opinion, national or social origin, property, birth or other status,

Recalling that, in the Universal Declaration of Human Rights, the United Nations has proclaimed that childhood is entitled to special care and assistance,

Convinced that the family, as the fundamental group of society and the natural environment for the growth and well-being of all its members and particularly children, should be afforded the necessary protection and assistance so that it can fully assume its responsibilities within the community,

Recognizing that the child, for the full and harmonious development of his or her personality, should grow up in a family environment, in an atmosphere of happiness, love and understanding,

Considering that the child should be fully prepared to live an individual life in society, and brought up in the spirit of the ideals proclaimed in the Charter of the United Nations, and in particular in the spirit of peace, dignity, tolerance, freedom, equality and solidarity,

Bearing in mind that the need to extend particular care to the child has been stated in the Geneva Declaration of the Rights of the Child of 1924 and in the Declaration of the Rights of the Child adopted by the General Assembly on 20 November 1959 and recognized in the Universal Declaration of Human Rights, in the International Covenant on Civil and Political Rights (in particular in Articles 23 and 24), in the International Covenant on Economic, Social and Cultural Rights (in particular in Article 10) and in the statutes and relevant instruments of specialized agencies and international organizations concerned with the welfare of children,

Bearing in mind that, as indicated in the Declaration of the Rights of the Child, "the child, by reason of his physical and mental immaturity, needs special safeguards and care, including appropriate legal protection, before as well as after birth",

Recalling the provisions of the Declaration on Social and Legal Principles relating to the Protection and Welfare of Children, with Special Reference to Foster Placement and Adoption Nationally and Internationally; the United Nations Standard Minimum Rules for the Administration of Juvenile Justice (The Beijing Rules); and the Declaration on the Protection of Women and Children in Emergency and Armed Conflict, Recognizing that, in all countries in the world, there are children living in exceptionally difficult conditions, and that such children need special consideration,

Taking due account of the importance of the traditions and cultural values of each people for the protection and harmonious development of the child, Recognizing the importance of international co-operation for improving the living conditions of children in every country, in particular in the developing countries,

Have agreed as follows:

Part I

Article 1

For the purposes of the present Convention, a child means every human being below the age of eighteen years unless under the law applicable to the child, majority is attained earlier.

Article 2

(1) States Parties shall respect and ensure the rights set forth in the present Convention to each child within their jurisdiction without discrimination of any kind, irrespective of the child's or his or her parent's or legal guardian's race, colour, sex, language, religion, political or other opinion, national, ethnic or social origin, property, disability, birth or other status.

(2) States Parties shall take all appropriate measures to ensure that the child is protected against all forms of discrimination or punishment on the basis of the status, activities, expressed opinions, or beliefs of the child's parents, legal guardians, or family members.

Article 3

(1) In all actions concerning children, whether undertaken by public or private social welfare institutions, courts of law, administrative authorities or legislative bodies, the best interests of the child shall be a primary consideration.

(2) States Parties undertake to ensure the child such protection and care as is necessary for his or her well-being, taking into account the rights and duties of his or her parents, legal guardians, or other individuals legally responsible for him or her, and, to this end, shall take all appropriate legislative and administrative measures.

(3) States Parties shall ensure that the institutions, services and facilities responsible for the care or protection of children shall conform with the standards established by competent authorities, particularly in the areas of safety, health, in the number and suitability of their staff, as well as competent supervision.

Article 4

States Parties shall undertake all appropriate legislative, administrative, and other measures for the implementation of the rights recognized in the present Convention. With regard to economic, social and cultural rights, States Parties shall undertake such measures to the maximum extent of their available resources and, where needed, within the framework of international co-operation.

Article 5

States Parties shall respect the responsibilities, rights and duties of parents or, where applicable, the members of the extended family or community as provided for by local custom, legal guardians or other persons legally responsible for the child, to provide, in a manner consistent with the evolving capacities of the child, appropriate direction and guidance in the exercise by the child of the rights recognized in the present Convention.

Article 6

(1) States Parties recognize that every child has the inherent right to life.

(2) States Parties shall ensure to the maximum extent possible the survival and development of the child.

Article 7

(1) The child shall be registered immediately after birth and shall have the right from birth to a name, the right to acquire a nationality and, as far as possible, the right to know and be cared for by his or her parents.

(2) States Parties shall ensure the implementation of these rights in accordance with their national law and their obligations under the relevant international instruments in this field, in particular where the child would otherwise be stateless.

Article 8

(1) States Parties undertake to respect the right of the child to preserve his or her identity, including nationality, name and family relations as recognized by law without unlawful interference.

(2) Where a child is illegally deprived of some or all of the elements of his or her identity, States Parties shall provide appropriate assistance and protection, with a view to re-establishing speedily his or her identity.

Article 9

(1) States Parties shall ensure that a child shall not be separated from his or her parents against their will, except when competent authorities subject to judicial review determine, in accordance with applicable law and procedures, that such separation is necessary for the best interests of the child. Such determination may be necessary in a particular case such as one involving abuse or neglect of the child by the parents, or one where the parents are living separately and a decision must be made as to the child's place of residence.

(2) In any proceedings pursuant to paragraph (1) of the present Article, all interested parties shall be given an opportunity to participate in the proceedings and make their views known.

(3) States Parties shall respect the right of the child who is separated from one or both parents to maintain personal relations and direct contact with both parents on a regular basis, except if it is contrary to the child's best interests.

(4) Where such separation results from any action initiated by a State Party, such as the detention, imprisonment, exile, deportation or death (including death arising from any cause while the person is in the custody of the State) of one or both parents or of the child, that State Party shall, upon request, provide the parents, the child or, if appropriate, another member of the family with the essential information concerning the whereabouts of the absent member(s) of the family unless the provision of the information would be detrimental to the well-being of the child. States Parties shall further ensure that the submission of such a request shall of itself entail no adverse consequences for the person(s) concerned.

Article 10

(1) In accordance with the obligation of States Parties under Article 9, paragraph (1), applications by a child or his or her parents to enter or leave a State Party for the purpose of family reunification shall be dealt with by States Parties in a positive, humane and expeditious manner. States Parties shall further ensure that the submission of such a request shall entail no adverse consequences for the applicants and for the members of their family.

(2) A child whose parents reside in different States shall have the right to maintain on a regular basis, save in exceptional circumstances personal relations and direct contacts with both parents. Towards that end and in accordance with the obligation of States Parties under Article 9, paragraph (1), States Parties shall respect the right of the child and his or her parents to leave any country, including their own, and to enter their own country. The right to leave any country shall be subject only to such restrictions as are prescribed by law and which are necessary to protect the national security, public order (ordre public), public health or morals or the rights and freedoms of others and are consistent with the other rights recognized in the present Convention.

Article 11

(1) States Parties shall take measures to combat the illicit transfer and non-return of children abroad.

(2) To this end, States Parties shall promote the conclusion of bilateral or multilateral agreements or accession to existing agreements.

Article 12

(1) States Parties shall assure to the child who is capable of forming his or her own views the right to express those views freely in all matters affecting the child, the views of the child being given due weight in accordance with the age and maturity of the child.

(2) For this purpose, the child shall in particular be provided the opportunity to be heard in any judicial and administrative proceedings affecting the child, either directly, or through a representative or an appropriate body, in a manner consistent with the procedural rules of national law.

Article 13

(1) The child shall have the right to freedom of expression; this right shall include freedom to seek, receive and impart information and ideas of all kinds, regardless of frontiers, either orally, in writing or in print, in the form of art, or through any other media of the child's choice.

(2) The exercise of this right may be subject to certain restrictions, but these shall only be such as are provided by law and are necessary:

 (a) For respect of the rights or reputations of others; or

 (b) For the protection of national security or of public order (ordre public), or of public health or morals.

Article 14

(1) States Parties shall respect the right of the child to freedom of thought, conscience and religion.

(2) States Parties shall respect the rights and duties of the parents and, when applicable, legal guardians, to provide direction to the child in the exercise of his or her right in a manner consistent with the evolving capacities of the child.

(3) Freedom to manifest one's religion or beliefs may be subject only to such limitations as are prescribed by law and are necessary to protect public safety, order, health or morals, or the fundamental rights and freedoms of others.

Article 15

(1) States Parties recognize the rights of the child to freedom of association and to freedom of peaceful assembly.

(2) No restrictions may be placed on the exercise of these rights other than those imposed in conformity with the law and which are necessary in a democratic society in the interests of national security or public safety, public order (ordre public), the protection of public health or morals or the protection of the rights and freedoms of others.

Article 16

(1) No child shall be subjected to arbitrary or unlawful interference with his or her privacy, family, home or correspondence, nor to unlawful attacks on his or her honour and reputation.

(2) The child has the right to the protection of the law against such interference or attacks.

Article 17

States Parties recognize the important function performed by the mass media and shall ensure that the child has access to information and material from a diversity of national and international sources, especially those aimed at the promotion of his or her social, spiritual and moral well-being and physical and mental health.

To this end, States Parties shall:

(a) Encourage the mass media to disseminate information and material of social and cultural benefit to the child and in accordance with the spirit of Article 29;

(b) Encourage international co-operation in the production, exchange and dissemination of such information and material from a diversity of cultural, national and international sources;

(c) Encourage the production and dissemination of children's books;

(d) Encourage the mass media to have particular regard to the linguistic needs of the child who belongs to a minority group or who is indigenous;

(e) Encourage the development of appropriate guidelines for the protection of the child from information and material injurious to his or her well-being, bearing in mind the provisions of Articles 13 and 18.

Article 18

(1) States Parties shall use their best efforts to ensure recognition of the principle that both parents have common responsibilities for the upbringing and development of the child. Parents or, as the case may be, legal guardians, have the primary responsibility for the upbringing and development of the child. The best interests of the child will be their basic concern.

(2) For the purpose of guaranteeing and promoting the rights set forth in the present Convention, States Parties shall render appropriate assistance to parents and legal guardians in the performance of their child-rearing responsibilities and shall ensure the development of institutions, facilities and services for the care of children.

(3) States Parties shall take all appropriate measures to ensure that children of working parents have the right to benefit from child-care services and facilities for which they are eligible.

Article 19

(1) States Parties shall take all appropriate legislative, administrative, social and educational measures to protect the child from all forms of physical or mental violence, injury or abuse, neglect or negligent treatment, maltreatment or exploitation, including sexual abuse, while in the care of parent(s), legal guardian(s) or any other person who has the care of the child.

(2) Such protective measures should, as appropriate, include effective procedures for the establishment of social programmes to provide necessary support for the child and for those who have the care of the child, as well as for other forms of prevention and for identification, reporting, referral, investigation, treatment and follow-up of instances of child maltreatment described heretofore, and, as appropriate, for judicial involvement.

Article 20

(1) A child temporarily or permanently deprived of his or her family environment, or in whose own best interests cannot be allowed to remain in that environment, shall be entitled to special protection and assistance provided by the State.

(2) States Parties shall in accordance with their national laws ensure alternative care for such a child.

(3) Such care could include, inter alia, foster placement, kafalah of Islamic law, adoption or if necessary placement in suitable institutions for the care of children. When considering solutions, due regard shall be paid to the desirability of continuity in a child's upbringing and to the child's ethnic, religious, cultural and linguistic background.

Article 21

States Parties that recognize and/or permit the system of adoption shall ensure that the best interests of the child shall be the paramount consideration and they shall:

(a) Ensure that the adoption of a child is authorized only by competent authorities who determine, in accordance with applicable law and procedures and on the basis of all pertinent and reliable information, that the adoption is permissible in view of the child's status concerning parents, relatives and legal guardians and that, if required, the persons concerned have given their informed consent to the adoption on the basis of such counselling as may be necessary;

(b) Recognize that inter-country adoption may be considered as an alternative means of child's care, if the child cannot be placed in a foster or an adoptive family or cannot in any suitable manner be cared for in the child's country of origin;

(c) Ensure that the child concerned by inter-country adoption enjoys safeguards and standards equivalent to those existing in the case of national adoption;

(d) Take all appropriate measures to ensure that, in inter-country adoption, the placement does not result in improper financial gain for those involved in it;

(e) Promote, where appropriate, the objectives of the present Article by concluding bilateral or multilateral arrangements or agreements, and endeavour, within this framework, to ensure that the placement of the child in another country is carried out by competent authorities or organs.

Article 22

(1) States Parties shall take appropriate measures to ensure that a child who is seeking refugee status or who is considered a refugee in accordance with applicable international or domestic law and procedures shall, whether unaccompanied or accompanied by his or her parents or by any other person, receive appropriate protection and humanitarian assistance in the enjoyment of applicable rights set forth in the present Convention and in other international human rights or humanitarian instruments to which the said States are Parties.

(2) For this purpose, States Parties shall provide, as they consider appropriate, co-operation in any efforts by the United Nations and other competent intergovernmental organizations or non-governmental organizations co-operating with the United Nations to protect and assist such a child and to trace the parents or other members of the family of any refugee child in order to obtain information necessary for reunification with his or her family. In cases where no parents or other members of the family can be found, the child shall be accorded the same protection as any other child permanently or temporarily deprived of his or her family environment for any reason, as set forth in the present Convention.

Article 23

(1) States Parties recognize that a mentally or physically disabled child should enjoy a full and decent life, in conditions which ensure dignity, promote self-reliance and facilitate the child's active participation in the community.

(2) States Parties recognize the right of the disabled child to special care and shall encourage and ensure the extension, subject to available resources, to the eligible child and those responsible for his or her care, of assistance for which application is made and which is appropriate to the child's condition and to the circumstances of the parents or others caring for the child.

(3) Recognizing the special needs of a disabled child, assistance extended in accordance with paragraph (2) of the present Article shall be provided free of charge, whenever possible, taking into account the financial resources of the parents or others caring for the child, and shall be designed to ensure that the disabled child has effective access to and receives education, training, health care services, rehabilitation services, preparation for employment and recreation opportunities in a manner conducive to the child's achieving the fullest possible social integration and individual development, including his or her cultural and spiritual development

(4) States Parties shall promote, in the spirit of international cooperation, the exchange of appropriate information in the field of preventive health care and of medical, psychological and functional treatment of disabled children, including dissemination of and access to information concerning methods of rehabilitation, education and vocational services, with the aim of enabling States Parties to improve their capabilities and skills and to widen their experience in these areas. In this regard, particular account shall be taken of the needs of developing countries.

Article 24

(1) States Parties recognize the right of the child to the enjoyment of the highest attainable standard of health and to facilities for the treatment of illness and rehabilitation of health. States Parties shall strive to ensure that no child is deprived of his or her right of access to such health care services.

(2) States Parties shall pursue full implementation of this right and, in particular, shall take appropriate measures:

  (a) To diminish infant and child mortality;

  (b) To ensure the provision of necessary medical assistance and health care to all children with emphasis on the development of primary health care;

  (c) To combat disease and malnutrition, including within the framework of primary health care, through, inter alia, the application of readily available technology and through the provision of adequate nutritious foods and clean drinking-water, taking into consideration the dangers and risks of environmental pollution;

  (d) To ensure appropriate pre-natal and post-natal health care for mothers;

  (e) To ensure that all segments of society, in particular parents and children, are informed, have access to education and are supported in the use of basic knowledge of child health and nutrition, the advantages of breastfeeding, hygiene and environmental sanitation and the prevention of accidents;

  (f) To develop preventive health care, guidance for parents and family planning education and services.

(3) States Parties shall take all effective and appropriate measures with a view to abolishing traditional practices prejudicial to the health of children

(4) States Parties undertake to promote and encourage international co-operation with a view to achieving progressively the full realization of the right recognized in the present Article. In this regard, particular account shall be taken of the needs of developing countries.

Article 25

States Parties recognize the right of a child who has been placed by the competent authorities for the purposes of care, protection or treatment of his or her physical or mental health, to a periodic review of the treatment provided to the child and all other circumstances relevant to his or her placement.

Article 26

(1) States Parties shall recognize for every child the right to benefit from social security, including social insurance, and shall take the necessary measures to achieve the full realization of this right in accordance with their national law.

(2) The benefits should, where appropriate, be granted, taking into account the resources and the circumstances of the child and persons having responsibility for the maintenance of the child, as well as any other consideration relevant to an application for benefits made by or on behalf of the child.

Article 27

(1) States Parties recognize the right of every child to a standard of living adequate for the child's physical, mental, spiritual, moral and social development.

(2) The parent(s) or others responsible for the child have the primary responsibility to secure, within their abilities and financial capacities, the conditions of living necessary for the child's development.

(3) States Parties, in accordance with national conditions and within their means, shall take appropriate measures to assist parents and others responsible for the child to implement this right and shall in case of need provide material assistance and support programmes, particularly with regard to nutrition, clothing and housing.

(4) States Parties shall take all appropriate measures to secure the recovery of maintenance for the child from the parents or other persons having financial responsibility for the child, both within the State Party and from abroad. In particular, where the person having financial responsibility for the child lives in a State different from that of the child, States Parties shall promote the accession to international agreements or the conclusion of such agreements, as well as the making of other appropriate arrangements.

Article 28

(1) States Parties recognize the right of the child to education, and with a view to achieving this right progressively and on the basis of equal opportunity, they shall, in particular:

(a) Make primary education compulsory and available free to all;

(b) Encourage the development of different forms of secondary education, including general and vocational education, make them available and accessible to every child, and take appropriate measures such as the introduction of free education and offering financial assistance in case of need;

(c) Make higher education accessible to all on the basis of capacity by every appropriate means;

(d) Make educational and vocational information and guidance available and accessible to all children;

(e) Take measures to encourage regular attendance at schools and the reduction of drop-out rates.

(2) States Parties shall take all appropriate measures to ensure that school discipline is administered in a manner consistent with the child's human dignity and in conformity with the present Convention.

(3) States Parties shall promote and encourage international cooperation in matters relating to education, in particular with a view to contributing to the elimination of ignorance and illiteracy throughout the world and facilitating access to scientific and technical knowledge and modern teaching methods. In this regard, particular account shall be taken of the needs of developing countries.

Article 29

(1) States Parties agree that the education of the child shall be directed to:

(a) The development of the child's personality, talents and mental and physical abilities to their fullest potential;

(b) The development of respect for human rights and fundamental freedoms, and for the principles enshrined in the Charter of the United Nations;

(c) The development of respect for the child's parents, his or her own cultural identity, language and values, for the national values of the country in which the child is living, the country from which he or she may originate, and for civilizations different from his or her own;

(d) The preparation of the child for responsible life in a free society, in the spirit of understanding, peace, tolerance, equality of sexes, and friendship among all peoples, ethnic, national and religious groups and persons of indigenous origin;

(e) The development of respect for the natural environment.

(2) No part of the present Article or Article 28 shall be construed so as to interfere with the liberty of individuals and bodies to establish and direct educational institutions, subject always to the observance of the principle set forth in paragraph (1) of the present Article and to the requirements that the education given in such institutions shall conform to such minimum standards as may be laid down by the State.

Article 30

In those States in which ethnic, religious or linguistic minorities or persons of indigenous origin exist, a child belonging to such a minority or who is indigenous shall not be denied the right, in community with other members of his or her group, to enjoy his or her own culture, to profess and practise his or her own religion, or to use his or her own language.

Article 31

(1) States Parties recognize the right of the child to rest and leisure, to engage in play and recreational activities appropriate to the age of the child and to participate freely in cultural life and the arts.

(2) States Parties shall respect and promote the right of the child to participate fully in cultural and artistic life and shall encourage the provision of appropriate and equal opportunities for cultural, artistic, recreational and leisure activity.

Article 32

(1) States Parties recognize the right of the child to be protected from economic exploitation and from performing any work that is likely to be hazardous or to interfere with the child's education, or to be harmful to the child's health or physical, mental, spiritual, moral or social development.

(2) States Parties shall take legislative, administrative, social and educational measures to ensure the implementation of the present Article. To this end, and having regard to the relevant provisions of other international instruments, States Parties shall in particular:

(a) Provide for a minimum age or minimum ages for admission to employment;

(b) Provide for appropriate regulation of the hours and conditions of employment;

(c) Provide for appropriate penalties or other sanctions to ensure the effective enforcement of the present Article.

Article 33

States Parties shall take all appropriate measures, including legislative, administrative, social and educational measures, to protect children from the illicit use of narcotic drugs and psychotropic substances as defined in the relevant international treaties, and to prevent the use of children in the illicit production and trafficking of such substances.

Article 34

States Parties undertake to protect the child from all forms of sexual exploitation and sexual abuse. For these purposes, States Parties shall in particular take all appropriate national, bilateral and multilateral measures to prevent:

(a) The inducement or coercion of a child to engage in any unlawful sexual activity;

(b) The exploitative use of children in prostitution or other unlawful sexual practices;

(c) The exploitative use of children in pornographic performances and materials.

Article 35

States Parties shall take all appropriate national, bilateral and multilateral measures to prevent the abduction of, the sale of or traffic in children for any purpose or in any form.

Article 36

States Parties shall protect the child against all other forms of exploitation prejudicial to any aspects of the child's welfare.

Article 37

States Parties shall ensure that:

(a) No child shall be subjected to torture or other cruel, inhuman or degrading treatment or punishment. Neither capital punishment nor life imprisonment without possibility of release shall be imposed for offences committed by persons below eighteen years of age;

(b) No child shall be deprived of his or her liberty unlawfully or arbitrarily. The arrest, detention or imprisonment of a child shall be in conformity with the law and shall be used only as a measure of last resort and for the shortest appropriate period of time;

(c) Every child deprived of liberty shall be treated with humanity and respect for the inherent dignity of the human person, and in a manner which takes into account the needs of persons of his or her age. In particular, every child deprived of liberty shall be separated from adults unless it is considered in the child's best interest not to do so and shall have the right to maintain contact with his or her family through correspondence and visits, save in exceptional circumstances;

(d) Every child deprived of his or her liberty shall have the right to prompt access to legal and other appropriate assistance, as well as the right to challenge the legality of the deprivation of his or her liberty before a court or other competent, independent and impartial authority, and to a prompt decision on any such action.

Article 38

(1) States Parties undertake to respect and to ensure respect for rules of international humanitarian law applicable to them in armed conflicts which are relevant to the child.

(2) States Parties shall take all feasible measures to ensure that persons who have not attained the age of fifteen years do not take a direct part in hostilities.

(3) States Parties shall refrain from recruiting any person who has not attained the age of fifteen years into their armed forces. In recruiting among those persons who have attained the age of fifteen years but who have not attained the age of eighteen years, States Parties shall endeavour to give priority to those who are oldest.

(4) In accordance with their obligations under international humanitarian law to protect the civilian population in armed conflicts, States Parties shall take all feasible measures to ensure protection and care of children who are affected by an armed conflict.

Article 39

States Parties shall take all appropriate measures to promote physical and psychological recovery and social reintegration of a child victim of: any form of neglect, exploitation, or abuse; torture or any other form of cruel, inhuman or degrading treatment or punishment; or armed conflicts. Such recovery and reintegration shall take place in an environment which fosters the health, self-respect and dignity of the child.

Article 40

(1) States Parties recognize the right of every child alleged as, accused of, or recognized as having infringed the penal law to be treated in a manner consistent with the promotion of the child's sense of dignity and worth, which reinforces the child's respect for the human rights and fundamental freedoms of others and which takes into account the child's age and the desirability of promoting the child's reintegration and the child's assuming a constructive role in society.

(2) To this end, and having regard to the relevant provisions of international instruments, States Parties shall, in particular, ensure that:

(a) No child shall be alleged as, be accused of, or recognized as having infringed the penal law by reason of acts or omissions that were not prohibited by national or international law at the time they were committed;

(b) Every child alleged as or accused of having infringed the penal law has at least the following guarantees:

(i) To be presumed innocent until proven guilty according to law;

(ii) To be informed promptly and directly of the charges against him or her, and, if appropriate, through his or her parents or legal guardians, and to have legal or other appropriate assistance in the preparation and presentation of his or her defence;

(iii) To have the matter determined without delay by a competent, independent and impartial authority or judicial body in a fair hearing according to law, in the presence of legal or other appropriate assistance and, unless it is considered not to be in the best interest of the child, in particular, taking into account his or her age or situation, his or her parents or legal guardians;

(iv) Not to be compelled to give testimony or to confess guilt; to examine or have examined adverse witnesses and to obtain the participation and examination of witnesses on his or her behalf under conditions of equality;

(v) If considered to have infringed the penal law, to have this decision and any measures imposed in consequence thereof reviewed by a higher competent, independent and impartial authority or judicial body according to law;

(vi) To have the free assistance of an interpreter if the child cannot understand or speak the language used;

(vii) To have his or her privacy fully respected at all stages of the proceedings.

(3) States Parties shall seek to promote the establishment of laws, procedures, authorities and institutions specifically applicable to children alleged as, accused of, or recognized as having infringed the penal law, and, in particular:

(a) The establishment of a minimum age below which children shall be presumed not to have the capacity to infringe the penal law;

(b) Whenever appropriate and desirable, measures for dealing with such children without resorting to judicial proceedings, providing that human rights and legal safeguards are fully respected. 4. A variety of dispositions, such as care, guidance and supervision orders; counselling; probation; foster care; education and vocational training programmes and other alternatives to institutional care shall be available to ensure that children are dealt with in a manner appropriate to their well-being and proportionate both to their circumstances and the offence.

Article 41

Nothing in the present Convention shall affect any provisions which are more conducive to the realization of the rights of the child and which may be contained in:

(a) The law of a State party; or

(b) International law in force for that State.

Part II

Article 42

States Parties undertake to make the principles and provisions of the Convention widely known, by appropriate and active means, to adults and children alike.

Article 43

(1) For the purpose of examining the progress made by States Parties in achieving the realization of the obligations undertaken in the present Convention, there shall be established a Committee on the Rights of the Child, which shall carry out the functions hereinafter provided.

(2) The Committee shall consist of eighteen experts of high moral standing and recognized competence in the field covered by this Convention.* The members of the Committee shall be elected by States Parties from among their nationals and shall serve in their personal capacity, consideration being given to equitable geographical distribution, as well as to the principal legal systems.

(3) The members of the Committee shall be elected by secret ballot from a list of persons nominated by States Parties. Each State Party may nominate one person from among its own nationals.

(4) The initial election to the Committee shall be held no later than six months after the date of the entry into force of the present Convention and thereafter every second year. At least four months before the date of each election, the Secretary-General of the United Nations shall address a letter to States Parties inviting them to submit their nominations within two months. The Secretary-General shall subsequently prepare a list in alphabetical order of all persons thus nominated, indicating States Parties which have nominated them, and shall submit it to the States Parties to the present Convention.

(5) The elections shall be held at meetings of States Parties convened by the Secretary-General at United Nations Headquarters. At those meetings, for which two thirds of States Parties shall constitute a quorum, the persons elected to the Committee shall be those who obtain the largest number of votes and an absolute majority of the votes of the representatives of States Parties present and voting.

(6) The members of the Committee shall be elected for a term of four years. They shall be eligible for re-election if renominated. The term of five of the members elected at the first election shall expire at the end of two years; immediately after the first election, the names of these five members shall be chosen by lot by the Chairman of the meeting.

(7) If a member of the Committee dies or resigns or declares that for any other cause he or she can no longer perform the duties of the Committee, the State Party which nominated the member shall appoint another expert from among its nationals to serve for the remainder of the term, subject to the approval of the Committee.

(8) The Committee shall establish its own rules of procedure.

(9) The Committee shall elect its officers for a period of two years.

(10) The meetings of the Committee shall normally be held at United Nations Headquarters or at any other convenient place as determined by the Committee. The Committee shall normally meet annually. The duration of the meetings of the Committee shall be determined, and reviewed, if

* The General Assembly, in its Resolution 50/155 of 21 December 1995, approved the amendment to Article 43, paragraph (2), of the Convention on the Rights of the Child, replacing the word "ten" with the word "eighteen". The amendment entered into force on 18 November 2002 when it had been accepted by a two-thirds majority of the States parties (128 out of 191).

necessary, by a meeting of the States Parties to the present Convention, subject to the approval of the General Assembly.

(11) The Secretary-General of the United Nations shall provide the necessary staff and facilities for the effective performance of the functions of the Committee under the present Convention.

(12) With the approval of the General Assembly, the members of the Committee established under the present Convention shall receive emoluments from United Nations resources on such terms and conditions as the Assembly may decide.

Article 44

(1) States Parties undertake to submit to the Committee, through the Secretary-General of the United Nations, reports on the measures they have adopted which give effect to the rights recognized herein and on the progress made on the enjoyment of those rights

- (a) Within two years of the entry into force of the Convention for the State Party concerned;
- (b) Thereafter every five years.

(2) Reports made under the present Article shall indicate factors and difficulties, if any, affecting the degree of fulfilment of the obligations under the present Convention. Reports shall also contain sufficient information to provide the Committee with a comprehensive understanding of the implementation of the Convention in the country concerned.

(3) A State Party which has submitted a comprehensive initial report to the Committee need not, in its subsequent reports submitted in accordance with paragraph (1)(b) of the present Article, repeat basic information previously provided.

(4) The Committee may request from States Parties further information relevant to the implementation of the Convention.

(5) The Committee shall submit to the General Assembly, through the Economic and Social Council, every two years, reports on its activities.

(6) States Parties shall make their reports widely available to the public in their own countries.

Article 45

In order to foster the effective implementation of the Convention and to encourage international co-operation in the field covered by the Convention:

- (a) The specialized agencies, the United Nations Children's Fund, and other United Nations organs shall be entitled to be represented at the consideration of the implementation of such provisions of the present Convention as fall within the scope of their mandate. The Committee may invite the specialized agencies, the United Nations Children's Fund and other competent bodies as it may consider appropriate to provide expert advice on the implementation of the Convention in areas falling within the scope of their respective mandates. The Committee may invite the specialized agencies, the United Nations Children's Fund, and other United Nations organs to submit reports on the implementation of the Convention in areas falling within the scope of their activities;
- (b) The Committee shall transmit, as it may consider appropriate, to the specialized agencies, the United Nations Children's Fund and other competent bodies, any reports from States Parties that contain a request, or indicate a need, for technical advice or assistance, along with the Committee's observations and suggestions, if any, on these requests or indications;
- (c) The Committee may recommend to the General Assembly to request the Secretary-General to undertake on its behalf studies on specific issues relating to the rights of the child;

(d) The Committee may make suggestions and General Recommendations based on information received pursuant to Articles 44 and 45 of the present Convention. Such suggestions and General Recommendations shall be transmitted to any State Party concerned and reported to the General Assembly, together with comments, if any, from States Parties.

Part III

Article 46

The present Convention shall be open for signature by all States.

Article 47

The present Convention is subject to ratification. Instruments of ratification shall be deposited with the Secretary-General of the United Nations.

Article 48

The present Convention shall remain open for accession by any State. The instruments of accession shall be deposited with the Secretary-General of the United Nations.

Article 49

(1) The present Convention shall enter into force on the thirtieth day following the date of deposit with the Secretary-General of the United Nations of the twentieth instrument of ratification or accession.

(2) For each State ratifying or acceding to the Convention after the deposit of the twentieth instrument of ratification or accession, the Convention shall enter into force on the thirtieth day after the deposit by such State of its instrument of ratification or accession.

Article 50

(1) Any State Party may propose an amendment and file it with the Secretary-General of the United Nations. The Secretary-General shall thereupon communicate the proposed amendment to States Parties, with a request that they indicate whether they favour a conference of States Parties for the purpose of considering and voting upon the proposals. In the event that, within four months from the date of such communication, at least one third of the States Parties favour such a conference, the Secretary-General shall convene the conference under the auspices of the United Nations. Any amendment adopted by a majority of States Parties present and voting at the conference shall be submitted to the General Assembly for approval.

(2) An amendment adopted in accordance with paragraph (1) of the present Article shall enter into force when it has been approved by the General Assembly of the United Nations and accepted by a two-thirds majority of States Parties.

(3) When an amendment enters into force, it shall be binding on those States Parties which have accepted it, other States Parties still being bound by the provisions of the present Convention and any earlier amendments which they have accepted.

Article 51

(1) The Secretary-General of the United Nations shall receive and circulate to all States the text of reservations made by States at the time of ratification or accession.

(2) A reservation incompatible with the object and purpose of the present Convention shall not be permitted.

(3) Reservations may be withdrawn at any time by notification to that effect addressed to the Secretary-General of the United Nations, who shall then inform all States. Such notification shall take effect on the date on which it is received by the Secretary-General

Article 52

A State Party may denounce the present Convention by written notification to the Secretary-General of the United Nations. Denunciation becomes effective one year after the date of receipt of the notification by the Secretary-General.

Article 53

The Secretary-General of the United Nations is designated as the depositary of the present Convention.

Article 54

The original of the present Convention, of which the Arabic, Chinese, English, French, Russian and Spanish texts are equally authentic, shall be deposited with the Secretary-General of the United Nations.

IN WITNESS THEREOF the undersigned plenipotentiaries, being duly authorized thereto by their respective Governments, have signed the present Convention.

Reservations Applicable to Hong Kong

*United Kingdom of Great Britain and Northern Ireland**

Signed on 19 April 1990
Ratified on 16 December 1991

Upon signature:

The United Kingdom reserves the right to formulate, upon ratifying the Convention, any reservations or interpretative declarations which it might consider necessary.

Upon ratification:

Declarations:

(a) The United Kingdom interprets the Convention as applicable only following a live birth.

(b) The United Kingdom interprets the references in the Convention to 'parents' to mean only those persons who, as a matter of national law, are treated as parents. This includes cases where the law regards a child as having only one parent, for example where a child has been adopted by one person only and in certain cases where a child is conceived other than as a result of sexual intercourse by the woman who gives birth to it and she is treated as the only parent.

* In a communication received on 7 September 1994, the Government of the United Kingdom of Great Britain and Northern Ireland indicated that the Convention will apply to Hong Kong.

Reservations:

[...]

Declaration:

The United Kingdom reserves the right to extend the Convention at a later date to any territory for whose international relations the Government of the United Kingdom is responsible.

7 September 1994

Declarations:

The United Kingdom refers to the reservation and declarations (a), (b) and (c) which accompanied its instrument of ratification and makes a similar reservation and declarations in respect to each of its dependent territories.

The United Kingdom, in respect of each of its dependent territories except Hong Kong and Pitcairn, reserves the right to apply Article 32 subject to the laws of those territories which treat certain persons under 18 not as children but as 'young people'. In respect of Hong Kong, the United Kingdom reserves the right not to apply Article 32(b) in so far as it might require regulation of the hours of employment of young persons who have attained the age of fifteen years in respect of work in non-industrial establishments.

Where at any time there is a lack of suitable detention facilities or where the mixing of adults and children is deemed to be mutually beneficial, the United Kingdom, in respect of each of its dependent territories, reserves the right not to apply Article 37(c) in so far as those provisions require children who are detained to be accommodated separately from adults.

The United Kingdom, in respect of Hong Kong and the Cayman Islands, will seek to apply the Convention to the fullest extent to children seeking asylum in those territories except in so far as conditions and resources make full implementation impracticable. In particular, in relation to Article 22, the United Kingdom reserves the right to continue to apply any legislation in those territories governing the detention of children seeking refugee status, the determination of their status and their entry into, stay in and departure from those territories.

The Government of the United Kingdom reserves the right to extend the Convention at a later date to any other territories for whose international relations the Government of the United Kingdom is responsible.

Territorial Application

Participant	Date of receipt of the notification	Territories
China	10 April 2003	Hong Kong Special Administrative Region
United Kingdom of Great Britain and Northern Ireland	7 September 1994	Hong Kong

China *

Signed on 29 August 1990
Ratified on 2 March 1992

Reservation:

[T]he People's Republic of China shall fulfil its obligations provided by Article 6 of the Convention under the prerequisite that the Convention accords with the provisions of Article 25 concerning family planning of the Constitution of the People's Republic of China and in conformity with the provisions of Article 2 of the Law of Minor Children of the People's Republic of China.

---

* On 10 June 1997, the Secretary-General received communications concerning the status of Hong Kong from the Governments of China and the United Kingdom (see also note 2 under "China" and note 2 under "United Kingdom of Great Britain and Northern Ireland" regarding Hong Kong in the "Historical Information" Section at https://treaties.un.org/Pages/HistoricalInfo.aspx?clang=_en#, which have been reproduced in the footnotes on pages 180–184 of this volume). Upon resuming the exercise of sovereignty over Hong Kong, China notified the Secretary-General that the Convention with the reservation made by China will also apply to the Hong Kong special Administrative Region.

In addition, the notification made by the Government of China contained the following declaration:

1. The Government of the People's Republic of China, on behalf of the Hong Kong Special Administrative Region, interprets the Convention as applicable only following a live birth.
2. The Government of the People's Republic of China reserves, for the Hong Kong Special Administrative Region, the right to apply such legislation, in so far as it relates to the entry into, stay in and departure from the Hong Kong Special Administrative Region of those who do not have the right under the laws of the Hong Kong Special Administrative Region to enter and remain in the Hong Kong Special Administrative Region, and to the acquisition and possession of residentship as it may deem necessary from time to time.
3. The Government of the People's Republic of China interprets, on behalf of the Hong Kong Special Administrative Region, the references in the Convention to "parents" to mean only those persons who, under the laws of the Hong Kong Special Administrative Region, are treated as parents. This includes cases where the laws regard a child as having only one parent, for example where a child has been adopted by one person only and in certain cases where a child is conceived other than as a result of sexual intercourse by the woman who gives birth to it and she is treated as the only parent.
4. The Government of the People's Republic of China reserves, for the Hong Kong Special Administrative Region, the right not to apply Article 32(2)(b) of the Convention in so far as it might require regulation of the hours of employment of young persons who have attained the age of fifteen years in respect of work in non-industrial establishments.
5. [...]
6. Where at any time there is a lack of suitable detention facilities, or where the mixing of adults and children is deemed to be mutually beneficial, the Government of the People's Republic of China reserves, for the Hong Kong Special Administrative Region, the right not to apply Article 37(c) of the Convention in so far as those provisions require children who are detained to be accommodated separately from adults.

In regard to the above-mentioned declaration, by a notification received on 10 April 2003, the Government of the People's Republic of China informed the Secretary-General that it had decided to withdraw its declaration relating to Article 22 of the Convention. The declaration reads as follows:

The Government of the People's Republic of China, on behalf of the Hong Kong Special Administrative Region, seeks to apply the Convention to the fullest extent to children seeking asylum in the Hong Kong Special Administrative Region except in so far as conditions and resources make full implementation impracticable. In particular, in relation to Article 22 of the Convention the Government of the People's Republic of China reserves the right to continue to apply legislation in the Hong Kong Special Administrative Region governing the detention of children seeking refugee status, the determination of their status and their entry into, stay in and departure from the Hong Kong Special Administrative Region.

General Comments

(1) General Comment No. 1: The Aims of Education (17 April 2001)

(2) General Comment No. 2: The Role of Independent National Human Rights Institutions in the Promotion and Protection of the Rights of the Child (15 November 2002)

(3) General Comment No. 3: HIV/AIDS and the rights of the child (17 March 2003)

(4) General Comment No. 4: Adolescent health and development in the context of the Convention on the Rights of the Child (21 July 2003)

(5) General Comment No. 5: General Measures of Implementation of the Convention on the Rights of the Child (3 October 2003)

(6) General Comment No. 6: Treatment of Unaccompanied and Separated Children Outside Their Country of Origin (1 September 2005)

(7) General Comment No. 7: Implementing child rights in early childhood (20 September 2006)

(8) General Comment No. 8:The right of the child to protection from corporal punishment and other cruel or degrading forms of punishment (Arts. 19; 28, para. 2; and 37, inter alia) (2 March 2007)

(9) General Comment No. 9: The rights of children with disabilities (13 November 2007)

(10) General Comment No. 10: Children's rights in juvenile justice (25 April 2007)

(11) General Comments No. 11: Indigenous children and their rights under the Convention (12 February 2009)

(12) Observation générale No. 12: Le droit de l'enfant d'être entendu [General Comment No. 12: The right of the child to be heard] (20 July 2009)

(13) General Comment No. 13: The right of the child to freedom from all forms of violence (18 April 2011)

(14) General Comment No. 14 on the right of the child to have his or her best interests taken as a primary consideration (Art. 3, para. 1) (29 May 2013)

(15) General Comment No. 15 on the right of the child to the enjoyment of the highest attainable standard of health (Art. 24) (17 April 2013)

(16) General Comment No. 16 on State obligations regarding the impact of the business sector on children's rights (17 April 2013)

(17) General Comment No. 17 on the right of the child to rest, leisure, play, recreational activities, cultural life and the arts (Art. 31) (17 April 2013)

(18) Joint General Recommendation No. 31 of the Committee on the Elimination of Discrimination against Women/General Comment No. 18 of the Committee on the Rights of the Child on harmful practices (14 November 2014)

(19) Revision of Joint General Recommendation No. 31 of the Committee on the Elimination of Discrimination against Women/General Comment No. 18 of the Committee on the Rights of the Child on harmful practices (8 May 2019)

(20) General Comment No. 19 on public budgeting for the realization of children's rights (Art. 4) (21 July 2016)

(21) General Comment No. 20 on the implementation of the rights of the child during adolescence (6 December 2016)

(22) General Comment No. 21 on children in street situations (21 June 2017)

(23) Joint General Comment No. 3 of the Committee on the Protection of All Migrant Workers and Members of Their Families and No. 22 of the Committee on the Rights of the Child on the general principles regarding the human rights of children in the context of international migration (16 November 2017)

(24) Joint General Comment No. 4 of the Committee on the Protection of the Rights of All Migrant Workers and Members of Their Families and No. 23 of the Committee on the Rights of the Child on State obligations regarding the human rights of children in the context of international migration in countries of origin, transit, destination and return (16 November 2017)

(25) General Comment No. 24 on children's rights in the child justice system (18 September 2019)

(26) General Comment No. 25 on children's rights in relation to the digital environment (12 August 2020)

Optional Protocol to the Convention on the Rights of the Child on the Involvement of Children in Armed Conflict

(Adopted: 25 May 2000; Entry into force: 12 February 2002)

The States Parties to the present Protocol,

Encouraged by the overwhelming support for the Convention on the Rights of the Child, demonstrating the widespread commitment that exists to strive for the promotion and protection of the rights of the child,

Reaffirming that the rights of children require special protection, and calling for continuous improvement of the situation of children without distinction, as well as for their development and education in conditions of peace and security,

Disturbed by the harmful and widespread impact of armed conflict on children and the long-term consequences it has for durable peace, security and development,

Condemning the targeting of children in situations of armed conflict and direct attacks on objects protected under international law, including places that generally have a significant presence of children, such as schools and hospitals,

Noting the adoption of the Rome Statute of the International Criminal Court, in particular, the inclusion therein as a war crime, of conscripting or enlisting children under the age of 15 years or using them to participate actively in hostilities in both international and non-international armed conflict,

Considering therefore that to strengthen further the implementation of rights recognized in the Convention on the Rights of the Child there is a need to increase the protection of children from involvement in armed conflict,

Noting that Article 1 of the Convention on the Rights of the Child specifies that, for the purposes of that Convention, a child means every human being below the age of 18 years unless, under the law applicable to the child, majority is attained earlier,

Convinced that an Optional Protocol to the Convention that raises the age of possible recruitment of persons into armed forces and their participation in hostilities will contribute effectively to the implementation of the principle that the best interests of the child are to be a primary consideration in all actions concerning children,

Noting that the twenty-sixth International Conference of the Red Cross and Red Crescent in December 1995 recommended, inter alia, that parties to conflict take every feasible step to ensure that children below the age of 18 years do not take part in hostilities,

Welcoming the unanimous adoption, in June 1999, of International Labour Organization Convention No. 182 on the Prohibition and Immediate Action for the Elimination of the Worst Forms of Child Labour, which prohibits, inter alia, forced or compulsory recruitment of children for use in armed conflict,

Condemning with the gravest concern the recruitment, training and use within and across national borders of children in hostilities by armed groups distinct from the armed forces of a State, and recognizing the responsibility of those who recruit, train and use children in this regard,

Recalling the obligation of each party to an armed conflict to abide by the provisions of international humanitarian law,

Stressing that the present Protocol is without prejudice to the purposes and principles contained in the Charter of the United Nations, including Article 51, and relevant norms of humanitarian law,

Bearing in mind that conditions of peace and security based on full respect of the purposes and principles contained in the Charter and observance of applicable human rights instruments are indispensable for the full protection of children, in particular during armed conflict and foreign occupation,

Recognizing the special needs of those children who are particularly vulnerable to recruitment or use in hostilities contrary to the present Protocol owing to their economic or social status or gender,

Mindful of the necessity of taking into consideration the economic, social and political root causes of the involvement of children in armed conflict,

Convinced of the need to strengthen international cooperation in the implementation of the present Protocol, as well as the physical and psychosocial rehabilitation and social reintegration of children who are victims of armed conflict,

Encouraging the participation of the community and, in particular, children and child victims in the dissemination of informational and educational programmes concerning the implementation of the Protocol,

Have agreed as follows:

Article 1

States Parties shall take all feasible measures to ensure that members of their armed forces who have not attained the age of 18 years do not take a direct part in hostilities.

Article 2

States Parties shall ensure that persons who have not attained the age of 18 years are not compulsorily recruited into their armed forces.

Article 3

(1) States Parties shall raise the minimum age for the voluntary recruitment of persons into their national armed forces from that set out in Article 38, paragraph (3), of the Convention on the Rights of the Child, taking account of the principles contained in that Article and recognizing that under the Convention persons under the age of 18 years are entitled to special protection.

(2) Each State Party shall deposit a binding declaration upon ratification of or accession to the present Protocol that sets forth the minimum age at which it will permit voluntary recruitment into its national armed forces and a description of the safeguards it has adopted to ensure that such recruitment is not forced or coerced.

(3) States Parties that permit voluntary recruitment into their national armed forces under the age of 18 years shall maintain safeguards to ensure, as a minimum, that:

  (a) Such recruitment is genuinely voluntary;

  (b) Such recruitment is carried out with the informed consent of the person's parents or legal guardians;

  (c) Such persons are fully informed of the duties involved in such military service;

  (d) Such persons provide reliable proof of age prior to acceptance into national military service.

(4) Each State Party may strengthen its declaration at any time by notification to that effect addressed to the Secretary-General of the United Nations, who shall inform all States Parties. Such notification shall take effect on the date on which it is received by the Secretary-General.

(5) The requirement to raise the age in paragraph (1) of the present Article does not apply to schools operated by or under the control of the armed forces of the States Parties, in keeping with Articles 28 and 29 of the Convention on the Rights of the Child.

Article 4

(1) Armed groups that are distinct from the armed forces of a State should not, under any circumstances, recruit or use in hostilities persons under the age of 18 years.

(2) States Parties shall take all feasible measures to prevent such recruitment and use, including the adoption of legal measures necessary to prohibit and criminalize such practices.

(3) The application of the present Article shall not affect the legal status of any party to an armed conflict.

Article 5

Nothing in the present Protocol shall be construed as precluding provisions in the law of a State Party or in international instruments and international humanitarian law that are more conducive to the realization of the rights of the child.

Article 6

(1) Each State Party shall take all necessary legal, administrative and other measures to ensure the effective implementation and enforcement of the provisions of the present Protocol within its jurisdiction.

(2) States Parties undertake to make the principles and provisions of the present Protocol widely known and promoted by appropriate means, to adults and children alike.

(3) States Parties shall take all feasible measures to ensure that persons within their jurisdiction recruited or used in hostilities contrary to the present Protocol are demobilized or otherwise released from service. States Parties shall, when necessary, accord to such persons all appropriate assistance for their physical and psychological recovery and their social reintegration.

Article 7

(1) States Parties shall cooperate in the implementation of the present Protocol, including in the prevention of any activity contrary thereto and in the rehabilitation and social reintegration of persons who are victims of acts contrary thereto, including through technical cooperation and financial assistance. Such assistance and cooperation will be undertaken in consultation with the States Parties concerned and the relevant international organizations.

(2) States Parties in a position to do so shall provide such assistance through existing multilateral, bilateral or other programmes or, inter alia, through a voluntary fund established in accordance with the rules of the General Assembly.

Article 8

(1) Each State Party shall, within two years following the entry into force of the present Protocol for that State Party, submit a report to the Committee on the Rights of the Child providing comprehensive information on the measures it has taken to implement the provisions of the Protocol, including the measures taken to implement the provisions on participation and recruitment.

(2) Following the submission of the comprehensive report, each State Party shall include in the reports it submits to the Committee on the Rights of the Child, in accordance with Article 44

of the Convention, any further information with respect to the implementation of the Protocol. Other States Parties to the Protocol shall submit a report every five years.

(3) The Committee on the Rights of the Child may request from States Parties further information relevant to the implementation of the present Protocol.

Article 9

(1) The present Protocol is open for signature by any State that is a party to the Convention or has signed it.

(2) The present Protocol is subject to ratification and is open to accession by any State. Instruments of ratification or accession shall be deposited with the Secretary-General of the United Nations.

(3) The Secretary-General, in his capacity as depositary of the Convention and the Protocol, shall inform all States Parties to the Convention and all States that have signed the Convention of each instrument of declaration pursuant to Article 3.

Article 10

(1) The present Protocol shall enter into force three months after the deposit of the tenth instrument of ratification or accession.

(2) For each State ratifying the present Protocol or acceding to it after its entry into force, the Protocol shall enter into force one month after the date of the deposit of its own instrument of ratification or accession.

Article 11

(1) Any State Party may denounce the present Protocol at any time by written notification to the Secretary-General of the United Nations, who shall thereafter inform the other States Parties to the Convention and all States that have signed the Convention. The denunciation shall take effect one year after the date of receipt of the notification by the Secretary-General. If, however, on the expiry of that year the denouncing State Party is engaged in armed conflict, the denunciation shall not take effect before the end of the armed conflict.

(2) Such a denunciation shall not have the effect of releasing the State Party from its obligations under the present Protocol in regard to any act that occurs prior to the date on which the denunciation becomes effective. Nor shall such a denunciation prejudice in any way the continued consideration of any matter that is already under consideration by the Committee on the Rights of the Child prior to the date on which the denunciation becomes effective.

Article 12

(1) Any State Party may propose an amendment and file it with the Secretary-General of the United Nations. The Secretary-General shall thereupon communicate the proposed amendment to States Parties with a request that they indicate whether they favour a conference of States Parties for the purpose of considering and voting upon the proposals. In the event that, within four months from the date of such communication, at least one third of the States Parties favour such a conference, the Secretary-General shall convene the conference under the auspices of the United Nations. Any amendment adopted by a majority of States Parties present and voting at the conference shall be submitted to the General Assembly of the United Nations for approval.

(2) An amendment adopted in accordance with paragraph (1) of the present Article shall enter into force when it has been approved by the General Assembly and accepted by a two-thirds majority of States Parties.

(3) When an amendment enters into force, it shall be binding on those States Parties that have accepted it, other States Parties still being bound by the provisions of the present Protocol and any earlier amendments they have accepted.

Article 13

(1) The present Protocol, of which the Arabic, Chinese, English, French, Russian and Spanish texts are equally authentic, shall be deposited in the archives of the United Nations.

(2) The Secretary-General of the United Nations shall transmit certified copies of the present Protocol to all States Parties to the Convention and all States that have signed the Convention.

Reservations Applicable to Hong Kong

China *

Signed on 15 March 2001

Ratified on 20 February 2008

CONVENTION ON THE RIGHTS OF PERSONS WITH DISABILITIES

(Adopted: 13 December 2006; Entry into force: 3 May 2008)

Preamble

The States Parties to the present Convention,

(a) Recalling the principles proclaimed in the Charter of the United Nations which recognize the inherent dignity and worth and the equal and inalienable rights of all members of the human family as the foundation of freedom, justice and peace in the world,

(b) Recognizing that the United Nations, in the Universal Declaration of Human Rights and in the International Covenants on Human Rights, has proclaimed and agreed that everyone is entitled to all the rights and freedoms set forth therein, without distinction of any kind,

(c) Reaffirming the universality, indivisibility, interdependence and interrelatedness of all human rights and fundamental freedoms and the need for persons with disabilities to be guaranteed their full enjoyment without discrimination,

(d) Recalling the International Covenant on Economic, Social and Cultural Rights, the International Covenant on Civil and Political Rights, the International Convention on the Elimination of All Forms of Racial Discrimination, the Convention on the Elimination of All Forms of Discrimination against Women, the Convention against Torture and Other

* In a communication received on 20 February 2008, the Government of China informed the Secretary-General of the following:
In accordance with provisions of Article 153 of the Basic Law of the Hong Kong Special Administrative Region of the People's Republic of China, the Government of the People's Republic of China decides that the ratification shall apply to the Hong Kong Special Administrative Region.

Cruel, Inhuman or Degrading Treatment or Punishment, the Convention on the Rights of the Child, and the International Convention on the Protection of the Rights of All Migrant Workers and Members of Their Families,

(e) Recognizing that disability is an evolving concept and that disability results from the interaction between persons with impairments and attitudinal and environmental barriers that hinders their full and effective participation in society on an equal basis with others,

(f) Recognizing the importance of the principles and policy guidelines contained in the World Programme of Action concerning Disabled Persons and in the Standard Rules on the Equalization of Opportunities for Persons with Disabilities in influencing the promotion, formulation and evaluation of the policies, plans, programmes and actions at the national, regional and international levels to further equalize opportunities for persons with disabilities,

(g) Emphasizing the importance of mainstreaming disability issues as an integral part of relevant strategies of sustainable development,

(h) Recognizing also that discrimination against any person on the basis of disability is a violation of the inherent dignity and worth of the human person,

(i) Recognizing further the diversity of persons with disabilities,

(j) Recognizing the need to promote and protect the human rights of all persons with disabilities, including those who require more intensive support,

(k) Concerned that, despite these various instruments and undertakings, persons with disabilities continue to face barriers in their participation as equal members of society and violations of their human rights in all parts of the world,

(l) Recognizing the importance of international cooperation for improving the living conditions of persons with disabilities in every country, particularly in developing countries,

(m) Recognizing the valued existing and potential contributions made by persons with disabilities to the overall well-being and diversity of their communities, and that the promotion of the full enjoyment by persons with disabilities of their human rights and fundamental freedoms and of full participation by persons with disabilities will result in their enhanced sense of belonging and in significant advances in the human, social and economic development of society and the eradication of poverty,

(n) Recognizing the importance for persons with disabilities of their individual autonomy and independence, including the freedom to make their own choices,

(o) Considering that persons with disabilities should have the opportunity to be actively involved in decision-making processes about policies and programmes, including those directly concerning them,

(p) Concerned about the difficult conditions faced by persons with disabilities who are subject to multiple or aggravated forms of discrimination on the basis of race, colour, sex, language, religion, political or other opinion, national, ethnic, indigenous or social origin, property, birth, age or other status,

(q) Recognizing that women and girls with disabilities are often at greater risk, both within and outside the home of violence, injury or abuse, neglect or negligent treatment, maltreatment or exploitation,

(r) Recognizing that children with disabilities should have full enjoyment of all human rights and fundamental freedoms on an equal basis with other children, and recalling obligations to that end undertaken by States Parties to the Convention on the Rights of the Child,

(s) Emphasizing the need to incorporate a gender perspective in all efforts to promote the full enjoyment of human rights and fundamental freedoms by persons with disabilities,

(t) Highlighting the fact that the majority of persons with disabilities live in conditions of poverty, and in this regard recognizing the critical need to address the negative impact of poverty on persons with disabilities,

(u) Bearing in mind that conditions of peace and security based on full respect for the purposes and principles contained in the Charter of the United Nations and observance of applicable human rights instruments are indispensable for the full protection of persons with disabilities, in particular during armed conflicts and foreign occupation,

(v) Recognizing the importance of accessibility to the physical, social, economic and cultural environment, to health and education and to information and communication, in enabling persons with disabilities to fully enjoy all human rights and fundamental freedoms,

(w) Realizing that the individual, having duties to other individuals and to the community to which he or she belongs, is under a responsibility to strive for the promotion and observance of the rights recognized in the International Bill of Human Rights,

(x) Convinced that the family is the natural and fundamental group unit of society and is entitled to protection by society and the State, and that persons with disabilities and their family members should receive the necessary protection and assistance to enable families to contribute towards the full and equal enjoyment of the rights of persons with disabilities,

(y) Convinced that a comprehensive and integral international convention to promote and protect the rights and dignity of persons with disabilities will make a significant contribution to redressing the profound social disadvantage of persons with disabilities and promote their participation in the civil, political, economic, social and cultural spheres with equal opportunities, in both developing and developed countries,

Have agreed as follows:

Article 1 Purpose

The purpose of the present Convention is to promote, protect and ensure the full and equal enjoyment of all human rights and fundamental freedoms by all persons with disabilities, and to promote respect for their inherent dignity.

Persons with disabilities include those who have long-term physical, mental, intellectual or sensory impairments which in interaction with various barriers may hinder their full and effective participation in society on an equal basis with others.

Article 2 Definitions

For the purposes of the present Convention:

"Communication" includes languages, display of text, Braille, tactile communication, large print, accessible multimedia as well as written, audio, plain-language, human-reader and augmentative and alternative modes, means and formats of communication, including accessible information and communication technology;

"Language" includes spoken and signed languages and other forms of non-spoken languages;

"Discrimination on the basis of disability" means any distinction, exclusion or restriction on the basis of disability which has the purpose or effect of impairing or nullifying the recognition, enjoyment or exercise, on an equal basis with others, of all human rights and fundamental freedoms in the political, economic, social, cultural, civil or any other field. It includes all forms of discrimination, including denial of reasonable accommodation;

"Reasonable accommodation" means necessary and appropriate modification and adjustments not imposing a disproportionate or undue burden, where needed in a particular case, to ensure to persons with disabilities the enjoyment or exercise on an equal basis with others of all human rights and fundamental freedoms;

"Universal design" means the design of products, environments, programmes and services to be usable by all people, to the greatest extent possible, without the need for adaptation or specialized design. "Universal design" shall not exclude assistive devices for particular groups of persons with disabilities where this is needed.

Article 3 General Principles

The principles of the present Convention shall be:

(1) Respect for inherent dignity, individual autonomy including the freedom to make one's own choices, and independence of persons;

(2) Non-discrimination;

(3) Full and effective participation and inclusion in society;

(4) Respect for difference and acceptance of persons with disabilities as part of human diversity and humanity;

(5) Equality of opportunity;

(6) Accessibility;

(7) Equality between men and women;

(8) Respect for the evolving capacities of children with disabilities and respect for the right of children with disabilities to preserve their identities.

Article 4 General Obligations

(1) States Parties undertake to ensure and promote the full realization of all human rights and fundamental freedoms for all persons with disabilities without discrimination of any kind on the basis of disability. To this end, States Parties undertake:

(a) To adopt all appropriate legislative, administrative and other measures for the implementation of the rights recognized in the present Convention;

(b) To take all appropriate measures, including legislation, to modify or abolish existing laws, regulations, customs and practices that constitute discrimination against persons with disabilities;

(c) To take into account the protection and promotion of the human rights of persons with disabilities in all policies and programmes;

(d) To refrain from engaging in any act or practice that is inconsistent with the present Convention and to ensure that public authorities and institutions act in conformity with the present Convention;

(e) To take all appropriate measures to eliminate discrimination on the basis of disability by any person, organization or private enterprise;

(f) To undertake or promote research and development of universally designed goods, services, equipment and facilities, as defined in Article 2 of the present Convention, which should require the minimum possible adaptation and the least cost to meet the specific needs of a person with disabilities, to promote their availability and use, and to promote universal design in the development of standards and guidelines;

(g) To undertake or promote research and development of, and to promote the availability and use of new technologies, including information and communications technologies, mobility aids, devices and assistive technologies, suitable for persons with disabilities, giving priority to technologies at an affordable cost;

(h) To provide accessible information to persons with disabilities about mobility aids, devices and assistive technologies, including new technologies, as well as other forms of assistance, support services and facilities;

(i) To promote the training of professionals and staff working with persons with disabilities in the rights recognized in this Convention so as to better provide the assistance and services guaranteed by those rights.

(2) With regard to economic, social and cultural rights, each State Party undertakes to take measures to the maximum of its available resources and, where needed, within the framework of international cooperation, with a view to achieving progressively the full realization of these rights, without prejudice to those obligations contained in the present Convention that are immediately applicable according to international law.

(3) In the development and implementation of legislation and policies to implement the present Convention, and in other decision-making processes concerning issues relating to persons with disabilities, States Parties shall closely consult with and actively involve persons with disabilities, including children with disabilities, through their representative organizations.

(4) Nothing in the present Convention shall affect any provisions which are more conducive to the realization of the rights of persons with disabilities and which may be contained in the law of a State Party or international law in force for that State. There shall be no restriction upon or derogation from any of the human rights and fundamental freedoms recognized or existing in any State Party to the present Convention pursuant to law, conventions, regulation or custom on the pretext that the present Convention does not recognize such rights or freedoms or that it recognizes them to a lesser extent.

(5) The provisions of the present Convention shall extend to all parts of federal states without any limitations or exceptions.

Article 5 Equality and Non-discrimination

(1) States Parties recognize that all persons are equal before and under the law and are entitled without any discrimination to the equal protection and equal benefit of the law.

(2) States Parties shall prohibit all discrimination on the basis of disability and guarantee to persons with disabilities equal and effective legal protection against discrimination on all grounds.

(3) In order to promote equality and eliminate discrimination, States Parties shall take all appropriate steps to ensure that reasonable accommodation is provided.

(4) Specific measures which are necessary to accelerate or achieve de facto equality of persons with disabilities shall not be considered discrimination under the terms of the present Convention.

Article 6 Women with Disabilities

(1) States Parties recognize that women and girls with disabilities are subject to multiple discrimination, and in this regard shall take measures to ensure the full and equal enjoyment by them of all human rights and fundamental freedoms.

(2) States Parties shall take all appropriate measures to ensure the full development, advancement and empowerment of women, for the purpose of guaranteeing them the exercise and enjoyment of the human rights and fundamental freedoms set out in the present Convention.

Article 7 Children with Disabilities

(1) States Parties shall take all necessary measures to ensure the full enjoyment by children with disabilities of all human rights and fundamental freedoms on an equal basis with other children.

(2) In all actions concerning children with disabilities, the best interests of the child shall be a primary consideration.

(3) States Parties shall ensure that children with disabilities have the right to express their views freely on all matters affecting them, their views being given due weight in accordance with their age and maturity, on an equal basis with other children, and to be provided with disability and age-appropriate assistance to realize that right.

Article 8 Awareness-raising

(1) States Parties undertake to adopt immediate, effective and appropriate measures:

(a) To raise awareness throughout society, including at the family level, regarding persons with disabilities, and to foster respect for the rights and dignity of persons with disabilities;

(b) To combat stereotypes, prejudices and harmful practices relating to persons with disabilities, including those based on sex and age, in all areas of life;

(c) To promote awareness of the capabilities and contributions of persons with disabilities.

(2) Measures to this end include:

(a) Initiating and maintaining effective public awareness campaigns designed:

(i) To nurture receptiveness to the rights of persons with disabilities;

(ii) To promote positive perceptions and greater social awareness towards persons with disabilities;

(iii) To promote recognition of the skills, merits and abilities of persons with disabilities, and of their contributions to the workplace and the labour market;

(b) Fostering at all levels of the education system, including in all children from an early age, an attitude of respect for the rights of persons with disabilities;

(c) Encouraging all organs of the media to portray persons with disabilities in a manner consistent with the purpose of the present Convention;

(d) Promoting awareness-training programmes regarding persons with disabilities and the rights of persons with disabilities.

Article 9 Accessibility

(1) To enable persons with disabilities to live independently and participate fully in all aspects of life, States Parties shall take appropriate measures to ensure to persons with disabilities access, on an equal basis with others, to the physical environment, to transportation, to information and communications, including information and communications technologies and systems, and to other facilities and services open or provided to the public, both in urban and in rural areas. These measures, which shall include the identification and elimination of obstacles and barriers to accessibility, shall apply to, inter alia:

(a) Buildings, roads, transportation and other indoor and outdoor facilities, including schools, housing, medical facilities and workplaces;

(b) Information, communications and other services, including electronic services and emergency services.

(2) States Parties shall also take appropriate measures:

(a) To develop, promulgate and monitor the implementation of minimum standards and guidelines for the accessibility of facilities and services open or provided to the public;

(b) To ensure that private entities that offer facilities and services which are open or provided to the public take into account all aspects of accessibility for persons with disabilities;

(c) To provide training for stakeholders on accessibility issues facing persons with disabilities;

(d) To provide in buildings and other facilities open to the public signage in Braille and in easy to read and understand forms;

(e) To provide forms of live assistance and intermediaries, including guides, readers and professional sign language interpreters, to facilitate accessibility to buildings and other facilities open to the public;

(f) To promote other appropriate forms of assistance and support to persons with disabilities to ensure their access to information;

(g) To promote access for persons with disabilities to new information and communications technologies and systems, including the Internet;

(h) To promote the design, development, production and distribution of accessible information and communications technologies and systems at an early stage, so that these technologies and systems become accessible at minimum cost.

Article 10 Right to Life

States Parties reaffirm that every human being has the inherent right to life and shall take all necessary measures to ensure its effective enjoyment by persons with disabilities on an equal basis with others.

Article 11 Situations of Risk and Humanitarian Emergencies

States Parties shall take, in accordance with their obligations under international law, including international humanitarian law and international human rights law, all necessary measures to ensure the protection and safety of persons with disabilities in situations of risk, including situations of armed conflict, humanitarian emergencies and the occurrence of natural disasters.

Article 12 Equal Recognition before the Law

(1) States Parties reaffirm that persons with disabilities have the right to recognition everywhere as persons before the law.

(2) States Parties shall recognize that persons with disabilities enjoy legal capacity on an equal basis with others in all aspects of life.

(3) States Parties shall take appropriate measures to provide access by persons with disabilities to the support they may require in exercising their legal capacity.

(4) States Parties shall ensure that all measures that relate to the exercise of legal capacity provide for appropriate and effective safeguards to prevent abuse in accordance with international human rights law. Such safeguards shall ensure that measures relating to the exercise of legal capacity respect the rights, will and preferences of the person, are free of conflict of interest and undue influence, are proportional and tailored to the person's circumstances, apply for the shortest time possible and are subject to regular review by a competent, independent and impartial authority or judicial body. The safeguards shall be proportional to the degree to which such measures affect the person's rights and interests.

(5) Subject to the provisions of this Article, States Parties shall take all appropriate and effective measures to ensure the equal right of persons with disabilities to own or inherit property, to control their own financial affairs and to have equal access to bank loans, mortgages and other forms of financial credit, and shall ensure that persons with disabilities are not arbitrarily deprived of their property.

Article 13 Access to Justice

(1) States Parties shall ensure effective access to justice for persons with disabilities on an equal basis with others, including through the provision of procedural and age-appropriate accommodations, in order to facilitate their effective role as direct and indirect participants, including as witnesses, in all legal proceedings, including at investigative and other preliminary stages.

(2) In order to help to ensure effective access to justice for persons with disabilities, States Parties shall promote appropriate training for those working in the field of administration of justice, including police and prison staff.

Article 14 Liberty and Security of the Person

(1) States Parties shall ensure that persons with disabilities, on an equal basis with others:

(a) Enjoy the right to liberty and security of person;

(b) Are not deprived of their liberty unlawfully or arbitrarily, and that any deprivation of liberty is in conformity with the law, and that the existence of a disability shall in no case justify a deprivation of liberty.

(2) States Parties shall ensure that if persons with disabilities are deprived of their liberty through any process, they are, on an equal basis with others, entitled to guarantees in accordance with international human rights law and shall be treated in compliance with the objectives and principles of this Convention, including by provision of reasonable accommodation.

Article 15 Freedom from Torture or Cruel, Inhuman or Degrading Treatment or Punishment

(1) No one shall be subjected to torture or to cruel, inhuman or degrading treatment or punishment. In particular, no one shall be subjected without his or her free consent to medical or scientific experimentation.

(2) States Parties shall take all effective legislative, administrative, judicial or other measures to prevent persons with disabilities, on an equal basis with others, from being subjected to torture or cruel, inhuman or degrading treatment or punishment.

Article 16 Freedom from Exploitation, Violence and Abuse

(1) States Parties shall take all appropriate legislative, administrative, social, educational and other measures to protect persons with disabilities, both within and outside the home, from all forms of exploitation, violence and abuse, including their gender-based aspects.

(2) States Parties shall also take all appropriate measures to prevent all forms of exploitation, violence and abuse by ensuring, inter alia, appropriate forms of gender- and age-sensitive assistance and support for persons with disabilities and their families and caregivers, including through the provision of information and education on how to avoid, recognize and report instances of exploitation, violence and abuse. States Parties shall ensure that protection services are age-, gender- and disability-sensitive.

(3) In order to prevent the occurrence of all forms of exploitation, violence and abuse, States Parties shall ensure that all facilities and programmes designed to serve persons with disabilities are effectively monitored by independent authorities.

(4) States Parties shall take all appropriate measures to promote the physical, cognitive and psychological recovery, rehabilitation and social reintegration of persons with disabilities who become victims of any form of exploitation, violence or abuse, including through the provision of protection services. Such recovery and reintegration shall take place in an environment that fosters the health, welfare, self-respect, dignity and autonomy of the person and takes into account gender- and age-specific needs.

(5) States Parties shall put in place effective legislation and policies, including women- and child-focused legislation and policies, to ensure that instances of exploitation, violence and abuse against persons with disabilities are identified, investigated and, where appropriate, prosecuted.

Article 17 Protecting the Integrity of the Person

Every person with disabilities has a right to respect for his or her physical and mental integrity on an equal basis with others.

Article 18 Liberty of Movement and Nationality

(1) States Parties shall recognize the rights of persons with disabilities to liberty of movement, to freedom to choose their residence and to a nationality, on an equal basis with others, including by ensuring that persons with disabilities:

(a) Have the right to acquire and change a nationality and are not deprived of their nationality arbitrarily or on the basis of disability;

(b) Are not deprived, on the basis of disability, of their ability to obtain, possess and utilize documentation of their nationality or other documentation of identification, or to utilize relevant processes such as immigration proceedings, that may be needed to facilitate exercise of the right to liberty of movement;

(c) Are free to leave any country, including their own;

(d) Are not deprived, arbitrarily or on the basis of disability, of the right to enter their own country.

(2) Children with disabilities shall be registered immediately after birth and shall have the right from birth to a name, the right to acquire a nationality and, as far as possible, the right to know and be cared for by their parents.

Article 19 Living Independently and Being Included in the Community

States Parties to this Convention recognize the equal right of all persons with disabilities to live in the community, with choices equal to others, and shall take effective and appropriate measures to facilitate full enjoyment by persons with disabilities of this right and their full inclusion and participation in the community, including by ensuring that:

(a) Persons with disabilities have the opportunity to choose their place of residence and where and with whom they live on an equal basis with others and are not obliged to live in a particular living arrangement;

(b) Persons with disabilities have access to a range of in-home, residential and other community support services, including personal assistance necessary to support living and inclusion in the community, and to prevent isolation or segregation from the community;

(c) Community services and facilities for the general population are available on an equal basis to persons with disabilities and are responsive to their needs.

Article 20 Personal Mobility

States Parties shall take effective measures to ensure personal mobility with the greatest possible independence for persons with disabilities, including by:

(a) Facilitating the personal mobility of persons with disabilities in the manner and at the time of their choice, and at affordable cost;

(b) Facilitating access by persons with disabilities to quality mobility aids, devices, assistive technologies and forms of live assistance and intermediaries, including by making them available at affordable cost;

(c) Providing training in mobility skills to persons with disabilities and to specialist staff working with persons with disabilities;

(d) Encouraging entities that produce mobility aids, devices and assistive technologies to take into account all aspects of mobility for persons with disabilities.

Article 21 Freedom of Expression and Opinion, and Access to Information

States Parties shall take all appropriate measures to ensure that persons with disabilities can exercise the right to freedom of expression and opinion, including the freedom to seek, receive and impart information and ideas on an equal basis with others and through all forms of communication of their choice, as defined in Article 2 of the present Convention, including by:

(a) Providing information intended for the general public to persons with disabilities in accessible formats and technologies appropriate to different kinds of disabilities in a timely manner and without additional cost;

(b) Accepting and facilitating the use of sign languages, Braille, augmentative and alternative communication, and all other accessible means, modes and formats of communication of their choice by persons with disabilities in official interactions;

(c) Urging private entities that provide services to the general public, including through the Internet, to provide information and services in accessible and usable formats for persons with disabilities;

(d) Encouraging the mass media, including providers of information through the Internet, to make their services accessible to persons with disabilities;

(e) Recognizing and promoting the use of sign languages.

Article 22 Respect for Privacy

(1) No person with disabilities, regardless of place of residence or living arrangements, shall be subjected to arbitrary or unlawful interference with his or her privacy, family, home or correspondence or other types of communication or to unlawful attacks on his or her honour and reputation. Persons with disabilities have the right to the protection of the law against such interference or attacks.

(2) States Parties shall protect the privacy of personal, health and rehabilitation information of persons with disabilities on an equal basis with others.

Article 23 Respect for Home and the Family

(1) States Parties shall take effective and appropriate measures to eliminate discrimination against persons with disabilities in all matters relating to marriage, family, parenthood and relationships, on an equal basis with others, so as to ensure that:

(a) The right of all persons with disabilities who are of marriageable age to marry and to found a family on the basis of free and full consent of the intending spouses is recognized;

(b) The rights of persons with disabilities to decide freely and responsibly on the number and spacing of their children and to have access to age-appropriate information, reproductive and family planning education are recognized, and the means necessary to enable them to exercise these rights are provided;

(c) Persons with disabilities, including children, retain their fertility on an equal basis with others.

(2) States Parties shall ensure the rights and responsibilities of persons with disabilities, with regard to guardianship, wardship, trusteeship, adoption of children or similar institutions, where these concepts exist in national legislation; in all cases the best interests of the child shall be paramount. States Parties shall render appropriate assistance to persons with disabilities in the performance of their child-rearing responsibilities.

(3) States Parties shall ensure that children with disabilities have equal rights with respect to family life. With a view to realizing these rights, and to prevent concealment, abandonment, neglect and segregation of children with disabilities, States Parties shall undertake to provide early and comprehensive information, services and support to children with disabilities and their families.

(4) States Parties shall ensure that a child shall not be separated from his or her parents against their will, except when competent authorities subject to judicial review determine, in accordance with applicable law and procedures, that such separation is necessary for the best interests of the child. In no case shall a child be separated from parents on the basis of a disability of either the child or one or both of the parents.

(5) States Parties shall, where the immediate family is unable to care for a child with disabilities, undertake every effort to provide alternative care within the wider family, and failing that, within the community in a family setting.

Article 24 Education

(1) States Parties recognize the right of persons with disabilities to education. With a view to realizing this right without discrimination and on the basis of equal opportunity, States Parties shall ensure an inclusive education system at all levels and life-long learning directed to:

(a) The full development of human potential and sense of dignity and self-worth, and the strengthening of respect for human rights, fundamental freedoms and human diversity;

(b) The development by persons with disabilities of their personality, talents and creativity, as well as their mental and physical abilities, to their fullest potential;

(c) Enabling persons with disabilities to participate effectively in a free society.

(2) In realizing this right, States Parties shall ensure that:

(a) Persons with disabilities are not excluded from the general education system on the basis of disability, and that children with disabilities are not excluded from free and compulsory primary education, or from secondary education, on the basis of disability;

(b) Persons with disabilities can access an inclusive, quality and free primary education and secondary education on an equal basis with others in the communities in which they live;

(c) Reasonable accommodation of the individual's requirements is provided;

(d) Persons with disabilities receive the support required, within the general education system, to facilitate their effective education;

(e) Effective individualized support measures are provided in environments that maximize academic and social development, consistent with the goal of full inclusion.

(3) States Parties shall enable persons with disabilities to learn life and social development skills to facilitate their full and equal participation in education and as members of the community. To this end, States Parties shall take appropriate measures, including:

(a) Facilitating the learning of Braille, alternative script, augmentative and alternative modes, means and formats of communication and orientation and mobility skills, and facilitating peer support and mentoring;

(b) Facilitating the learning of sign language and the promotion of the linguistic identity of the deaf community;

(c) Ensuring that the education of persons, and in particular children, who are blind, deaf or deafblind, is delivered in the most appropriate languages and modes and means of communication for the individual, and in environments which maximize academic and social development.

(4) In order to help ensure the realization of this right, States Parties shall take appropriate measures to employ teachers, including teachers with disabilities, who are qualified in sign language and/or Braille, and to train professionals and staff who work at all levels of education. Such training shall incorporate disability awareness and the use of appropriate augmentative and alternative modes, means and formats of communication, educational techniques and materials to support persons with disabilities.

(5) States Parties shall ensure that persons with disabilities are able to access general tertiary education, vocational training, adult education and lifelong learning without discrimination and on an equal basis with others. To this end, States Parties shall ensure that reasonable accommodation is provided to persons with disabilities.

Article 25 Health

States Parties recognize that persons with disabilities have the right to the enjoyment of the highest attainable standard of health without discrimination on the basis of disability. States Parties shall take all appropriate measures to ensure access for persons with disabilities to health services that are gender-sensitive, including health-related rehabilitation. In particular, States Parties shall:

(a) Provide persons with disabilities with the same range, quality and standard of free or affordable health care and programmes as provided to other persons, including in the area of sexual and reproductive health and population-based public health programmes;

(b) Provide those health services needed by persons with disabilities specifically because of their disabilities, including early identification and intervention as appropriate, and services designed to minimize and prevent further disabilities, including among children and older persons;

(c) Provide these health services as close as possible to people's own communities, including in rural areas;

(d) Require health professionals to provide care of the same quality to persons with disabilities as to others, including on the basis of free and informed consent by, inter alia, raising awareness of the human rights, dignity, autonomy and needs of persons with disabilities through training and the promulgation of ethical standards for public and private health care;

(e) Prohibit discrimination against persons with disabilities in the provision of health insurance, and life insurance where such insurance is permitted by national law, which shall be provided in a fair and reasonable manner;

(f) Prevent discriminatory denial of health care or health services or food and fluids on the basis of disability.

Article 26 Habilitation and Rehabilitation

(1) States Parties shall take effective and appropriate measures, including through peer support, to enable persons with disabilities to attain and maintain maximum independence, full physical, mental, social and vocational ability, and full inclusion and participation in all aspects of life. To that end, States Parties shall organize, strengthen and extend comprehensive habilitation and rehabilitation services and programmes, particularly in the areas of health, employment, education and social services, in such a way that these services and programmes:

(a) Begin at the earliest possible stage, and are based on the multidisciplinary assessment of individual needs and strengths;

(b) Support participation and inclusion in the community and all aspects of society, are voluntary, and are available to persons with disabilities as close as possible to their own communities, including in rural areas.

(2) States Parties shall promote the development of initial and continuing training for professionals and staff working in habilitation and rehabilitation services.

(3) States Parties shall promote the availability, knowledge and use of assistive devices and technologies, designed for persons with disabilities, as they relate to habilitation and rehabilitation.

Article 27 Work and Employment

(1) States Parties recognize the right of persons with disabilities to work, on an equal basis with others; this includes the right to the opportunity to gain a living by work freely chosen or accepted in a labour market and work environment that is open, inclusive and accessible to persons with disabilities. States Parties shall safeguard and promote the realization of the right to work, including for those who acquire a disability during the course of employment, by taking appropriate steps, including through legislation, to, inter alia:

(a) Prohibit discrimination on the basis of disability with regard to all matters concerning all forms of employment, including conditions of recruitment, hiring and employment, continuance of employment, career advancement and safe and healthy working conditions;

(b) Protect the rights of persons with disabilities, on an equal basis with others, to just and favourable conditions of work, including equal opportunities and equal remuneration for work of equal value, safe and healthy working conditions, including protection from harassment, and the redress of grievances;

(c) Ensure that persons with disabilities are able to exercise their labour and trade union rights on an equal basis with others;

(d) Enable persons with disabilities to have effective access to general technical and vocational guidance programmes, placement services and vocational and continuing training;

(e) Promote employment opportunities and career advancement for persons with disabilities in the labour market, as well as assistance in finding, obtaining, maintaining and returning to employment;

(f) Promote opportunities for self-employment, entrepreneurship, the development of cooperatives and starting one's own business;

(g) Employ persons with disabilities in the public sector;

(h) Promote the employment of persons with disabilities in the private sector through appropriate policies and measures, which may include affirmative action programmes, incentives and other measures;

(i) Ensure that reasonable accommodation is provided to persons with disabilities in the workplace;

(j) Promote the acquisition by persons with disabilities of work experience in the open labour market;

(k) Promote vocational and professional rehabilitation, job retention and return-to-work programmes for persons with disabilities.

(2) States Parties shall ensure that persons with disabilities are not held in slavery or in servitude, and are protected, on an equal basis with others, from forced or compulsory labour.

Article 28 Adequate Standard of Living and Social Protection

(1) States Parties recognize the right of persons with disabilities to an adequate standard of living for themselves and their families, including adequate food, clothing and housing, and to the continuous improvement of living conditions, and shall take appropriate steps to safeguard and promote the realization of this right without discrimination on the basis of disability.

(2) States Parties recognize the right of persons with disabilities to social protection and to the enjoyment of that right without discrimination on the basis of disability, and shall take appropriate steps to safeguard and promote the realization of this right, including measures:

(a) To ensure equal access by persons with disabilities to clean water services, and to ensure access to appropriate and affordable services, devices and other assistance for disability-related needs;

(b) To ensure access by persons with disabilities, in particular women and girls with disabilities and older persons with disabilities, to social protection programmes and poverty reduction programmes;

(c) To ensure access by persons with disabilities and their families living in situations of poverty to assistance from the State with disability-related expenses, including adequate training, counselling, financial assistance and respite care;

(d) To ensure access by persons with disabilities to public housing programmes;

(e) To ensure equal access by persons with disabilities to retirement benefits and programmes.

Article 29 Participation in Political and Public Life

States Parties shall guarantee to persons with disabilities political rights and the opportunity to enjoy them on an equal basis with others, and shall undertake to:

(a) Ensure that persons with disabilities can effectively and fully participate in political and public life on an equal basis with others, directly or through freely chosen representatives, including the right and opportunity for persons with disabilities to vote and be elected, inter alia, by:

(i) Ensuring that voting procedures, facilities and materials are appropriate, accessible and easy to understand and use;

(ii) Protecting the right of persons with disabilities to vote by secret ballot in elections and public referendums without intimidation, and to stand for elections, to effectively hold office and perform all public functions at all levels of government, facilitating the use of assistive and new technologies where appropriate;

(iii) Guaranteeing the free expression of the will of persons with disabilities as electors and to this end, where necessary, at their request, allowing assistance in voting by a person of their own choice;

(b) Promote actively an environment in which persons with disabilities can effectively and fully participate in the conduct of public affairs, without discrimination and on an equal basis with others, and encourage their participation in public affairs, including:

(i) Participation in non-governmental organizations and associations concerned with the public and political life of the country, and in the activities and administration of political parties;

(ii) Forming and joining organizations of persons with disabilities to represent persons with disabilities at international, national, regional and local levels.

Article 30 Participation in Cultural Life, Recreation, Leisure and Sport

(1) States Parties recognize the right of persons with disabilities to take part on an equal basis with others in cultural life, and shall take all appropriate measures to ensure that persons with disabilities:

(a) Enjoy access to cultural materials in accessible formats;

(b) Enjoy access to television programmes, films, theatre and other cultural activities, in accessible formats;

(c) Enjoy access to places for cultural performances or services, such as theatres, museums, cinemas, libraries and tourism services, and, as far as possible, enjoy access to monuments and sites of national cultural importance.

(2) States Parties shall take appropriate measures to enable persons with disabilities to have the opportunity to develop and utilize their creative, artistic and intellectual potential, not only for their own benefit, but also for the enrichment of society.

(3) States Parties shall take all appropriate steps, in accordance with international law, to ensure that laws protecting intellectual property rights do not constitute an unreasonable or discriminatory barrier to access by persons with disabilities to cultural materials.

(4) Persons with disabilities shall be entitled, on an equal basis with others, to recognition and support of their specific cultural and linguistic identity, including sign languages and deaf culture.

(5) With a view to enabling persons with disabilities to participate on an equal basis with others in recreational, leisure and sporting activities, States Parties shall take appropriate measures:

(a) To encourage and promote the participation, to the fullest extent possible, of persons with disabilities in mainstream sporting activities at all levels;

(b) To ensure that persons with disabilities have an opportunity to organize, develop and participate in disability-specific sporting and recreational activities and, to this end, encourage the provision, on an equal basis with others, of appropriate instruction, training and resources;

(c) To ensure that persons with disabilities have access to sporting, recreational and tourism venues;

(d) To ensure that children with disabilities have equal access with other children to participation in play, recreation and leisure and sporting activities, including those activities in the school system;

(e) To ensure that persons with disabilities have access to services from those involved in the organization of recreational, tourism, leisure and sporting activities.

Article 31 Statistics and Data Collection

(1) States Parties undertake to collect appropriate information, including statistical and research data, to enable them to formulate and implement policies to give effect to the present Convention. The process of collecting and maintaining this information shall:

(a) Comply with legally established safeguards, including legislation on data protection, to ensure confidentiality and respect for the privacy of persons with disabilities;

(b) Comply with internationally accepted norms to protect human rights and fundamental freedoms and ethical principles in the collection and use of statistics.

(2) The information collected in accordance with this Article shall be disaggregated, as appropriate, and used to help assess the implementation of States Parties' obligations under the present Convention and to identify and address the barriers faced by persons with disabilities in exercising their rights.

(3) States Parties shall assume responsibility for the dissemination of these statistics and ensure their accessibility to persons with disabilities and others.

Article 32 International Cooperation

(1) States Parties recognize the importance of international cooperation and its promotion, in support of national efforts for the realization of the purpose and objectives of the present Convention, and will undertake appropriate and effective measures in this regard, between and among States and, as appropriate, in partnership with relevant international and regional organizations and civil society, in particular organizations of persons with disabilities. Such measures could include, inter alia:

(a) Ensuring that international cooperation, including international development programmes, is inclusive of and accessible to persons with disabilities;

(b) Facilitating and supporting capacity-building, including through the exchange and sharing of information, experiences, training programmes and best practices;

(c) Facilitating cooperation in research and access to scientific and technical knowledge;

(d) Providing, as appropriate, technical and economic assistance, including by facilitating access to and sharing of accessible and assistive technologies, and through the transfer of technologies.

(2) The provisions of this Article are without prejudice to the obligations of each State Party to fulfil its obligations under the present Convention.

Article 33 National Implementation and Monitoring

(1) States Parties, in accordance with their system of organization, shall designate one or more focal points within government for matters relating to the implementation of the present Convention, and shall give due consideration to the establishment or designation of a coordination mechanism within government to facilitate related action in different sectors and at different levels.

(2) States Parties shall, in accordance with their legal and administrative systems, maintain, strengthen, designate or establish within the State Party, a framework, including one or more independent mechanisms, as appropriate, to promote, protect and monitor implementation of the present Convention. When designating or establishing such a mechanism, States Parties shall take into account the principles relating to the status and functioning of national institutions for protection and promotion of human rights.

(3) Civil society, in particular persons with disabilities and their representative organizations, shall be involved and participate fully in the monitoring process.

Article 34 Committee on the Rights of Persons with Disabilities

(1) There shall be established a Committee on the Rights of Persons with Disabilities (hereafter referred to as "the Committee"), which shall carry out the functions hereinafter provided.

(2) The Committee shall consist, at the time of entry into force of the present Convention, of twelve experts. After an additional sixty ratifications or accessions to the Convention, the membership of the Committee shall increase by six members, attaining a maximum number of eighteen members.

(3) The members of the Committee shall serve in their personal capacity and shall be of high moral standing and recognized competence and experience in the field covered by the present Convention. When nominating their candidates, States Parties are invited to give due consideration to the provision set out in Article 4, paragraph (3) of the present Convention.

(4) The members of the Committee shall be elected by States Parties, consideration being given to equitable geographical distribution, representation of the different forms of civilization and of the principal legal systems, balanced gender representation and participation of experts with disabilities.

(5) The members of the Committee shall be elected by secret ballot from a list of persons nominated by the States Parties from among their nationals at meetings of the Conference of States Parties. At those meetings, for which two thirds of States Parties shall constitute a quorum, the persons elected to the Committee shall be those who obtain the largest number of votes and an absolute majority of the votes of the representatives of States Parties present and voting.

(6) The initial election shall be held no later than six months after the date of entry into force of the present Convention. At least four months before the date of each election, the Secretary-General of the United Nations shall address a letter to the States Parties inviting them to submit the nominations within two months. The Secretary-General shall subsequently prepare a list in alphabetical order of all persons thus nominated, indicating the State Parties which have nominated them, and shall submit it to the States Parties to the present Convention.

(7) The members of the Committee shall be elected for a term of four years. They shall be eligible for re-election once. However, the term of six of the members elected at the first election shall expire at the end of two years; immediately after the first election, the names of these six members shall be chosen by lot by the chairperson of the meeting referred to in paragraph (5) of this Article.

(8) The election of the six additional members of the Committee shall be held on the occasion of regular elections, in accordance with the relevant provisions of this Article.

(9) If a member of the Committee dies or resigns or declares that for any other cause she or he can no longer perform her or his duties, the State Party which nominated the member shall appoint another expert possessing the qualifications and meeting the requirements set out in the relevant provisions of this Article, to serve for the remainder of the term.

(10) The Committee shall establish its own rules of procedure.

(11) The Secretary-General of the United Nations shall provide the necessary staff and facilities for the effective performance of the functions of the Committee under the present Convention, and shall convene its initial meeting.

(12) With the approval of the General Assembly, the members of the Committee established under the present Convention shall receive emoluments from United Nations resources on such terms and conditions as the Assembly may decide, having regard to the importance of the Committee's responsibilities.

(13) The members of the Committee shall be entitled to the facilities, privileges and immunities of experts on mission for the United Nations as laid down in the relevant Sections of the Convention on the Privileges and Immunities of the United Nations.

Article 35 Reports by States Parties

(1) Each State Party shall submit to the Committee, through the Secretary-General of the United Nations, a comprehensive report on measures taken to give effect to its obligations under the

present Convention and on the progress made in that regard, within two years after the entry into force of the present Convention for the State Party concerned.

(2) Thereafter, States Parties shall submit subsequent reports at least every four years and further whenever the Committee so requests.

(3) The Committee shall decide any guidelines applicable to the content of the reports.

(4) A State Party which has submitted a comprehensive initial report to the Committee need not, in its subsequent reports, repeat information previously provided. When preparing reports to the Committee, States Parties are invited to consider doing so in an open and transparent process and to give due consideration to the provision set out in Article 4, paragraph (3) of the present Convention.

(5) Reports may indicate factors and difficulties affecting the degree of fulfilment of obligations under the present Convention.

Article 36 Consideration of Reports

(1) Each report shall be considered by the Committee, which shall make such suggestions and General Recommendations on the report as it may consider appropriate and shall forward these to the State Party concerned. The State Party may respond with any information it chooses to the Committee. The Committee may request further information from States Parties relevant to the implementation of the present Convention.

(2) If a State Party is significantly overdue in the submission of a report, the Committee may notify the State Party concerned of the need to examine the implementation of the present Convention in that State Party, on the basis of reliable information available to the Committee, if the relevant report is not submitted within three months following the notification. The Committee shall invite the State Party concerned to participate in such examination. Should the State Party respond by submitting the relevant report, the provisions of paragraph (1) of this Article will apply.

(3) The Secretary-General of the United Nations shall make available the reports to all States Parties.

(4) States Parties shall make their reports widely available to the public in their own countries and facilitate access to the suggestions and General Recommendations relating to these reports.

(5) The Committee shall transmit, as it may consider appropriate, to the specialized agencies, funds and programmes of the United Nations, and other competent bodies, reports from States Parties in order to address a request or indication of a need for technical advice or assistance contained therein, along with the Committee's observations and recommendations, if any, on these requests or indications.

Article 37 Cooperation between States Parties and the Committee

(1) Each State Party shall cooperate with the Committee and assist its members in the fulfilment of their mandate.

(2) In its relationship with States Parties, the Committee shall give due consideration to ways and means of enhancing national capacities for the implementation of the present Convention, including through international cooperation.

Article 38 Relationship of the Committee with Other Bodies

In order to foster the effective implementation of the present Convention and to encourage international cooperation in the field covered by the present Convention:

(a) The specialized agencies and other United Nations organs shall be entitled to be represented at the consideration of the implementation of such provisions of the present Convention as fall within the scope of their mandate. The Committee may invite the specialized agencies and other competent bodies as it may consider appropriate to provide expert advice on the implementation of the Convention in areas falling within the scope of their respective mandates. The Committee may invite specialized agencies and other

United Nations organs to submit reports on the implementation of the Convention in areas falling within the scope of their activities;

(b) The Committee, as it discharges its mandate, shall consult, as appropriate, other relevant bodies instituted by international human rights treaties, with a view to ensuring the consistency of their respective reporting guidelines, suggestions and General Recommendations, and avoiding duplication and overlap in the performance of their functions.

Article 39 Report of the Committee

The Committee shall report every two years to the General Assembly and to the Economic and Social Council on its activities, and may make suggestions and General Recommendations based on the examination of reports and information received from the States Parties. Such suggestions and General Recommendations shall be included in the report of the Committee together with comments, if any, from States Parties.

Article 40 Conference of States Parties

(1) The States Parties shall meet regularly in a Conference of States Parties in order to consider any matter with regard to the implementation of the present Convention.

(2) No later than six months after the entry into force of the present Convention, the Conference of the States Parties shall be convened by the Secretary-General of the United Nations. The subsequent meetings shall be convened by the Secretary-General of the United Nations biennially or upon the decision of the Conference of States Parties.

Article 41 Depositary

The Secretary-General of the United Nations shall be the depositary of the present Convention.

Article 42 Signature

The present Convention shall be open for signature by all States and by regional integration organizations at United Nations Headquarters in New York as of 30 March 2007.

Article 43 Consent to be Bound

The present Convention shall be subject to ratification by signatory States and to formal confirmation by signatory regional integration organizations. It shall be open for accession by any State or regional integration organization which has not signed the Convention.

Article 44 Regional Integration Organizations

(1) "Regional integration organization" shall mean an organization constituted by sovereign States of a given region, to which its member States have transferred competence in respect of matters governed by this Convention. Such organizations shall declare, in their instruments of formal confirmation or accession, the extent of their competence with respect to matters governed by this Convention. Subsequently, they shall inform the depositary of any substantial modification in the extent of their competence.

(2) References to "States Parties" in the present Convention shall apply to such organizations within the limits of their competence.

(3) the purposes of Article 45, paragraph (1), and Article 47, paragraphs (2) and (3), any instrument deposited by a regional integration organization shall not be counted.

(4) Regional integration organizations, in matters within their competence, may exercise their right to vote in the Conference of States Parties, with a number of votes equal to the number of their member States that are Parties to this Convention. Such an organization shall not exercise its right to vote if any of its member States exercises its right, and vice versa.

Article 45 Entry into Force

(1) The present Convention shall enter into force on the thirtieth day after the deposit of the twentieth instrument of ratification or accession.

(2) For each State or regional integration organization ratifying, formally confirming or acceding to the Convention after the deposit of the twentieth such instrument, the Convention shall enter into force on the thirtieth day after the deposit of its own such instrument.

Article 46 Reservations

(1) Reservations incompatible with the object and purpose of the present Convention shall not be permitted.

(2) Reservations may be withdrawn at any time.

Article 47 Amendments

(1) Any State Party may propose an amendment to the present Convention and submit it to the Secretary-General of the United Nations. The Secretary-General shall communicate any proposed amendments to States Parties, with a request to be notified whether they favour a conference of States Parties for the purpose of considering and deciding upon the proposals. In the event that, within four months from the date of such communication, at least one third of the States Parties favour such a conference, the Secretary-General shall convene the conference under the auspices of the United Nations. Any amendment adopted by a majority of two thirds of the States Parties present and voting shall be submitted by the Secretary-General to the General Assembly for approval and thereafter to all States Parties for acceptance.

(2) An amendment adopted and approved in accordance with paragraph (1) of this Article shall enter into force on the thirtieth day after the number of instruments of acceptance deposited reaches two thirds of the number of States Parties at the date of adoption of the amendment. Thereafter, the amendment shall enter into force for any State Party on the thirtieth day following the deposit of its own instrument of acceptance. An amendment shall be binding only on those States Parties which have accepted it.

(3) If so decided by the Conference of States Parties by consensus, an amendment adopted and approved in accordance with paragraph (1) of this Article which relates exclusively to Articles 34, 38, 39 and 40 shall enter into force for all States Parties on the thirtieth day after the number of instruments of acceptance deposited reaches two thirds of the number of States Parties at the date of adoption of the amendment.

Article 48 Denunciation

A State Party may denounce the present Convention by written notification to the Secretary-General of the United Nations. The denunciation shall become effective one year after the date of receipt of the notification by the Secretary-General.

Article 49 Accessible Format

The text of the present Convention shall be made available in accessible formats.

Article 50 Authentic Texts

The Arabic, Chinese, English, French, Russian and Spanish texts of the present Convention shall be equally authentic.

IN WITNESS THEREOF the undersigned plenipotentiaries, being duly authorized thereto by their respective Governments, have signed the present Convention.

Reservations Applicable to Hong Kong

China *

Signed on 30 March 2007
Ratified on 1 August 2008

General Comments

(1) General Comment No. 1: Article 12 (Equal recognition before the law) (11 April 2014)
(2) General Comment No. 2: Article 9 (Accessibility) (11 April 2014)
(3) General Comment No. 3: Article 6 (Women and girls with disabilities) (26 August 2016)
(4) General Comment No. 4: Article 24 (Right to inclusive education) (26 August 2016)
(5) General Comment No. 5: Article 19 (Right to independent living) (31 August 2017)
(6) General Comment No. 6: Article 5 (Equality and non-discrimination) (9 March 2018)
(7) General Comment No. 7: Articles 4.3 and 33.3 (Participation with persons with disabilities in the implementation and monitoring of the Convention) (21 September 2018)

* On 1 August 2008, the Secretary-General received from the Government of China the following declarations in respect of Hong Kong Special Administrative Region and Macao Special Administrative Region:

In accordance with the Basic Law of the Hong Kong Special Administrative Region of the People's Republic of China and the Basic Law of the Macao Special Administrative Region of the People's Republic of China, the Government of the People's Republic of China decides that the Convention shall apply to the Hong Kong Special Administrative Region and the Macao Special Administrative Region of the People's Republic of China.

The application of the provisions regarding Liberty of movement and nationality of the Convention on the Rights of Persons with Disabilities to the Hong Kong Special Administrative Region of the People's Republic of China, shall not change the validity of relevant laws on immigration control and nationality application of the Hong Kong Special Administrative Region of the People's Republic of China.

SECTION II
CRIMINAL LAW

This Section includes three international instruments related to criminal law as applied in Hong Kong. They are:

(1) The Convention on the Prevention and Punishment of the Crime of Genocide

(2) The United Nations Convention against Transnational Organized Crime

(3) The International Convention for the Suppression of the Financing of Terrorism

CONVENTION ON THE PREVENTION AND PUNISHMENT OF THE CRIME OF GENOCIDE

(Approved: 9 December 1948; Entry into force: 12 January 1951, in accordance with Article XIII)

The Contracting Parties,

Having considered the declaration made by the General Assembly of the United Nations in its Resolution 96(I) dated 11 December 1946 that genocide is a crime under international law, contrary to the spirit and aims of the United Nations and condemned by the civilized world,

Recognizing that at all periods of history genocide has inflicted great losses on humanity, and

Being convinced that, in order to liberate mankind from such an odious scourge, international co-operation is required,

Hereby agree as hereinafter provided:

Article I

The Contracting Parties confirm that genocide, whether committed in time of peace or in time of war, is a crime under international law which they undertake to prevent and to punish.

Article II

In the present Convention, genocide means any of the following acts committed with intent to destroy, in whole or in part, a national, ethnical, racial or religious group, as such:

(a) Killing members of the group;

(b) Causing serious bodily or mental harm to members of the group;

(c) Deliberately inflicting on the group conditions of life calculated to bring about its physical destruction in whole or in part;

(d) Imposing measures intended to prevent births within the group;

(e) Forcibly transferring children of the group to another group.

Article III

The following acts shall be punishable:

(a) Genocide;

(b) Conspiracy to commit genocide;

(c) Direct and public incitement to commit genocide;

(d) Attempt to commit genocide;

(e) Complicity in genocide.

Article IV

Persons committing genocide or any of the other acts enumerated in Article III shall be punished, whether they are constitutionally responsible rulers, public officials or private individuals.

Article V

The Contracting Parties undertake to enact, in accordance with their respective Constitutions, the necessary legislation to give effect to the provisions of the present Convention, and, in particular, to provide effective penalties for persons guilty of genocide or any of the other acts enumerated in Article III.

Article VI

Persons charged with genocide or any of the other acts enumerated in Article III shall be tried by a competent tribunal of the State in the territory of which the act was committed, or by such international penal tribunal as may have jurisdiction with respect to those Contracting Parties which shall have accepted its jurisdiction.

Article VII

Genocide and the other acts enumerated in Article III shall not be considered as political crimes for the purpose of extradition.

The Contracting Parties pledge themselves in such cases to grant extradition in accordance with their laws and treaties in force.

Article VIII

Any Contracting Party may call upon the competent organs of the United Nations to take such action under the Charter of the United Nations as they consider appropriate for the prevention and suppression of acts of genocide or any of the other acts enumerated in Article III.

Article IX

Disputes between the Contracting Parties relating to the interpretation, application or fulfilment of the present Convention, including those relating to the responsibility of a State for genocide or for any of the other acts enumerated in Article III, shall be submitted to the International Court of Justice at the request of any of the parties to the dispute.

Article X

The present Convention, of which the Chinese, English, French, Russian and Spanish texts are equally authentic, shall bear the date of 9 December 1948.

Article XI

The present Convention shall be open until 31 December 1949 for signature on behalf of any Member of the United Nations and of any non-member State to which an invitation to sign has been addressed by the General Assembly.

The present Convention shall be ratified, and the instruments of ratification shall be deposited with the Secretary-General of the United Nations.

After 1 January 1950, the present Convention may be acceded to on behalf of any Member of the United Nations and of any non-member State which has received an invitation as aforesaid.

Instruments of accession shall be deposited with the Secretary-General of the United Nations.

Article XII

Any Contracting Party may at any time, by notification addressed to the Secretary-General of the United Nations, extend the application of the present Convention to all or any of the territories for the conduct of whose foreign relations that Contracting Party is responsible.

Article XIII

On the day when the first twenty instruments of ratification or accession have been deposited, the Secretary-General shall draw up a procès-verbal and transmit a copy thereof to each Member of the United Nations and to each of the non-member States contemplated in Article XI.

The present Convention shall come into force on the ninetieth day following the date of deposit of the twentieth instrument of ratification or accession.

Any ratification or accession effected subsequent to the latter date shall become effective on the ninetieth day following the deposit of the instrument of ratification or accession.

Article XIV

The present Convention shall remain in effect for a period of ten years as from the date of its coming into force.

It shall thereafter remain in force for successive periods of five years for such Contracting Parties as have not denounced it at least six months before the expiration of the current period.

Denunciation shall be effected by a written notification addressed to the Secretary-General of the United Nations.

Article XV

If, as a result of denunciations, the number of Parties to the present Convention should become less than sixteen, the Convention shall cease to be in force as from the date on which the last of these denunciations shall become effective.

Article XVI

A request for the revision of the present Convention may be made at any time by any Contracting Party by means of a notification in writing addressed to the Secretary-General.

The General Assembly shall decide upon the steps, if any, to be taken in respect of such request.

Article XVII

The Secretary-General of the United Nations shall notify all Members of the United Nations and the non-member States contemplated in Article XI of the following:

(a) Signatures, ratifications and accessions received in accordance with Article XI;

(b) Notifications received in accordance with Article XII;

(c) The date upon which the present Convention comes into force in accordance with Article XIII;

(d) Denunciations received in accordance with Article XIV;

(e) The abrogation of the Convention in accordance with Article XV;

(f) Notifications received in accordance with Article XVI.

Article XVIII

The original of the present Convention shall be deposited in the archives of the United Nations.

A certified copy of the Convention shall be transmitted to each Member of the United Nations and to each of the non-member States contemplated in Article XI.

Article XIX

The present Convention shall be registered by the Secretary-General of the United Nations on the date of its coming into force.

Reservations Applicable to Hong Kong

United Kingdom of Great Britain and Northern Ireland

Ratified on 30 January 1970

Territorial Application

Participant	Date of receipt of the notification	Territories
United Kingdom of Great Britain and Northern Ireland	2 June 1970	Hong Kong

China *

Signed on 20 July 1949

Ratified on 18 April 1983

* On 6 and 10 June 1997, the Secretary-General received communications concerning the status of Hong Kong from the Governments of the United Kingdom and China (see also note 2 under "China" and note 2 under "United Kingdom of Great Britain and Northern Ireland" regarding Hong Kong in the "Historical Information" Section at https://treaties.un.org/Pages/HistoricalInfo.aspx?clang=_en#, which have also been reproduced in the footnotes on pages 180–184 of this volume.). Upon resuming the exercise of sovereignty over Hong Kong, China notified the Secretary-General that the Convention with the reservation made by China will also apply to the Hong Kong Special Administrative Region.

UNITED NATIONS CONVENTION AGAINST TRANSNATIONAL ORGANIZED CRIME

(Adopted: 15 November 2000)

Article 1 Statement of Purpose

The purpose of this Convention is to promote cooperation to prevent and combat transnational organized crime more effectively.

Article 2 Use of Terms

For the purposes of this Convention:

(a) "Organized criminal group" shall mean a structured group of three or more persons, existing for a period of time and acting in concert with the aim of committing one or more serious crimes or offences established in accordance with this Convention, in order to obtain, directly or indirectly, a financial or other material benefit;

(b) "Serious crime" shall mean conduct constituting an offence punishable by a maximum deprivation of liberty of at least four years or a more serious penalty;

(c) "Structured group" shall mean a group that is not randomly formed for the immediate commission of an offence and that does not need to have formally defined roles for its members, continuity of its membership or a developed structure;

(d) "Property" shall mean assets of every kind, whether corporeal or incorporeal, movable or immovable, tangible or intangible, and legal documents or instruments evidencing title to, or interest in, such assets;

(e) "Proceeds of crime" shall mean any property derived from or obtained, directly or indirectly, through the commission of an offence;

(f) "Freezing" or "seizure" shall mean temporarily prohibiting the transfer, conversion, disposition or movement of property or temporarily assuming custody or control of property on the basis of an order issued by a court or other competent authority;

(g) "Confiscation", which includes forfeiture where applicable, shall mean the permanent deprivation of property by order of a court or other competent authority;

(h) "Predicate offence" shall mean any offence as a result of which proceeds have been generated that may become the subject of an offence as defined in Article 6 of this Convention;

(i) "Controlled delivery" shall mean the technique of allowing illicit or suspect consignments to pass out of, through or into the territory of one or more States, with the knowledge and under the supervision of their competent authorities, with a view to the investigation of an offence and the identification of persons involved in the commission of the offence;

(j) "Regional economic integration organization" shall mean an organization constituted by sovereign States of a given region, to which its member States have transferred competence in respect of matters governed by this Convention and which has been duly authorized, in accordance with its internal procedures, to sign, ratify, accept, approve or accede to it; references to "States Parties" under this Convention shall apply to such organizations within the limits of their competence.

Article 3 Scope of Application

(1) This Convention shall apply, except as otherwise stated herein, to the prevention, investigation and prosecution of:

(a) The offences established in accordance with Articles 5, 6, 8 and 23 of this Convention; and

(b) Serious crime as defined in Article 2 of this Convention;

where the offence is transnational in nature and involves an organized criminal group.

(2) For the purpose of paragraph (1) of this Article, an offence is transnational in nature if:

(a) It is committed in more than one State;

(b) It is committed in one State but a substantial part of its preparation, planning, direction or control takes place in another State;

(c) It is committed in one State but involves an organized criminal group that engages in criminal activities in more than one State; or

(d) It is committed in one State but has substantial effects in another State.

Article 4 Protection of Sovereignty

(1) States Parties shall carry out their obligations under this Convention in a manner consistent with the principles of sovereign equality and territorial integrity of States and that of non-intervention in the domestic affairs of other States.

(2) Nothing in this Convention entitles a State Party to undertake in the territory of another State the exercise of jurisdiction and performance of functions that are reserved exclusively for the authorities of that other State by its domestic law.

Article 5 Criminalization of Participation in an Organized Criminal Group

(1) Each State Party shall adopt such legislative and other measures as may be necessary to establish as criminal offences, when committed intentionally:

(a) Either or both of the following as criminal offences distinct from those involving the attempt or completion of the criminal activity:

(i) Agreeing with one or more other persons to commit a serious crime for a purpose relating directly or indirectly to the obtaining of a financial or other material benefit and, where required by domestic law, involving an act undertaken by one of the participants in furtherance of the agreement or involving an organized criminal group;

(ii) Conduct by a person who, with knowledge of either the aim and general criminal activity of an organized criminal group or its intention to commit the crimes in question, takes an active part in:

a. Criminal activities of the organized criminal group;

b. Other activities of the organized criminal group in the knowledge that his or her participation will contribute to the achievement of the above-described criminal aim;

(b) Organizing, directing, aiding, abetting, facilitating or counselling the commission of serious crime involving an organized criminal group.

(2) The knowledge, intent, aim, purpose or agreement referred to in paragraph (1) of this Article may be inferred from objective factual circumstances.

(3) States Parties whose domestic law requires involvement of an organized criminal group for purposes of the offences established in accordance with paragraph (1)(a)(i) of this Article shall ensure that their domestic law covers all serious crimes involving organized criminal groups. Such States Parties, as well as States Parties whose domestic law requires an act in furtherance of the agreement for purposes of the offences established in accordance with paragraph (1)(a)(i) of this Article, shall so inform the Secretary-General of the United Nations at the time of their signature or of deposit of their instrument of ratification, acceptance or approval of or accession to this Convention.

Article 6 Criminalization of the Laundering of Proceeds of Crime

(1) Each State Party shall adopt, in accordance with fundamental principles of its domestic law, such legislative and other measures as may be necessary to establish as criminal offences, when committed intentionally:

(a)

(i) The conversion or transfer of property, knowing that such property is the proceeds of crime, for the purpose of concealing or disguising the illicit origin of the property or of helping any person who is involved in the commission of the predicate offence to evade the legal consequences of his or her action;

(ii) The concealment or disguise of the true nature, source, location, disposition, movement or ownership of or rights with respect to property, knowing that such property is the proceeds of crime;

(b) Subject to the basic concepts of its legal system:

(i) The acquisition, possession or use of property, knowing, at the time of receipt, that such property is the proceeds of crime;

(ii) Participation in, association with or conspiracy to commit, attempts to commit and aiding, abetting, facilitating and counselling the commission of any of the offences established in accordance with this Article.

(2) For purposes of implementing or applying paragraph (1) of this Article:

(a) Each State Party shall seek to apply paragraph (1) of this Article to the widest range of predicate offences;

(b) Each State Party shall include as predicate offences all serious crime as defined in Article 2 of this Convention and the offences established in accordance with Articles 5, 8 and 23 of this Convention. In the case of States Parties whose legislation sets out a list of specific predicate offences, they shall, at a minimum, include in such list a comprehensive range of offences associated with organized criminal groups;

(c) For the purposes of subparagraph (b), predicate offences shall include offences committed both within and outside the jurisdiction of the State Party in question. However, offences committed outside the jurisdiction of a State Party shall constitute predicate offences only when the relevant conduct is a criminal offence under the domestic law of the State where it is committed and would be a criminal offence under the domestic law of the State Party implementing or applying this Article had it been committed there;

(d) Each State Party shall furnish copies of its laws that give effect to this Article and of any subsequent changes to such laws or a description thereof to the Secretary-General of the United Nations;

(e) If required by fundamental principles of the domestic law of a State Party, it may be provided that the offences set forth in paragraph (1) of this Article do not apply to the persons who committed the predicate offence;

(f) Knowledge, intent or purpose required as an element of an offence set forth in paragraph (1) of this Article may be inferred from objective factual circumstances.

Article 7 Measures to Combat Money-laundering

(1) Each State Party:

(a) Shall institute a comprehensive domestic regulatory and supervisory regime for banks and non-bank financial institutions and, where appropriate, other bodies particularly susceptible to money-laundering, within its competence, in order to deter and detect all forms of money-laundering, which regime shall emphasize requirements for customer identification, record-keeping and the reporting of suspicious transactions;

(b) Shall, without prejudice to Articles 18 and 27 of this Convention, ensure that administrative, regulatory, law enforcement and other authorities dedicated to combating money-laundering (including, where appropriate under domestic law, judicial authorities) have the ability to cooperate and exchange information at the national and international levels within the conditions prescribed by its domestic law and, to that end, shall consider the establishment of a financial intelligence unit to serve as a national centre for the collection, analysis and dissemination of information regarding potential money-laundering.

(2) States Parties shall consider implementing feasible measures to detect and monitor the movement of cash and appropriate negotiable instruments across their borders, subject to safeguards to ensure proper use of information and without impeding in any way the movement of legitimate capital. Such measures may include a requirement that individuals and businesses report the cross-border transfer of substantial quantities of cash and appropriate negotiable instruments.

(3) In establishing a domestic regulatory and supervisory regime under the terms of this Article, and without prejudice to any other Article of this Convention, States Parties are called upon to use as a guideline the relevant initiatives of regional, interregional and multilateral organizations against money-laundering.

(4) States Parties shall endeavour to develop and promote global, regional, subregional and bilateral cooperation among judicial, law enforcement and financial regulatory authorities in order to combat money-laundering.

Article 8 Criminalization of Corruption

(1) Each State Party shall adopt such legislative and other measures as may be necessary to establish as criminal offences, when committed intentionally:

(a) The promise, offering or giving to a public official, directly or indirectly, of an undue advantage, for the official himself or herself or another person or entity, in order that the official act or refrain from acting in the exercise of his or her official duties;

(b) The solicitation or acceptance by a public official, directly or indirectly, of an undue advantage, for the official himself or herself or another person or entity, in order that the official act or refrain from acting in the exercise of his or her official duties.

(2) Each State Party shall consider adopting such legislative and other measures as may be necessary to establish as criminal offences conduct referred to in paragraph (1) of this Article involving a foreign public official or international civil servant. Likewise, each State Party shall consider establishing as criminal offences other forms of corruption.

(3) Each State Party shall also adopt such measures as may be necessary to establish as a criminal offence participation as an accomplice in an offence established in accordance with this Article.

(4) For the purposes of paragraph (1) of this Article and Article 9 of this Convention, "public official" shall mean a public official or a person who provides a public service as defined in the domestic law and as applied in the criminal law of the State Party in which the person in question performs that function.

Article 9 Measures against Corruption

(1) In addition to the measures set forth in Article 8 of this Convention, each State Party shall, to the extent appropriate and consistent with its legal system, adopt legislative, administrative or other effective measures to promote integrity and to prevent, detect and punish the corruption of public officials.

(2) Each State Party shall take measures to ensure effective action by its authorities in the prevention, detection and punishment of the corruption of public officials, including providing such authorities with adequate independence to deter the exertion of inappropriate influence on their actions.

Article 10 Liability of Legal Persons

(1) Each State Party shall adopt such measures as may be necessary, consistent with its legal principles, to establish the liability of legal persons for participation in serious crimes involving an organized criminal group and for the offences established in accordance with Articles 5, 6, 8 and 23 of this Convention.

(2) Subject to the legal principles of the State Party, the liability of legal persons may be criminal, civil or administrative.

(3) Such liability shall be without prejudice to the criminal liability of the natural persons who have committed the offences.

(4) Each State Party shall, in particular, ensure that legal persons held liable in accordance with this Article are subject to effective, proportionate and dissuasive criminal or non-criminal sanctions, including monetary sanctions.

Article 11 Prosecution, Adjudication and Sanctions

(1) Each State Party shall make the commission of an offence established in accordance with Articles 5, 6, 8 and 23 of this Convention liable to sanctions that take into account the gravity of that offence.

(2) Each State Party shall endeavour to ensure that any discretionary legal powers under its domestic law relating to the prosecution of persons for offences covered by this Convention are exercised to maximize the effectiveness of law enforcement measures in respect of those offences and with due regard to the need to deter the commission of such offences.

(3) In the case of offences established in accordance with Articles 5, 6, 8 and 23 of this Convention, each State Party shall take appropriate measures, in accordance with its domestic law and with due regard to the rights of the defence, to seek to ensure that conditions imposed in connection with decisions on release pending trial or appeal take into consideration the need to ensure the presence of the defendant at subsequent criminal proceedings.

(4) Each State Party shall ensure that its courts or other competent authorities bear in mind the grave nature of the offences covered by this Convention when considering the eventuality of early release or parole of persons convicted of such offences.

(5) Each State Party shall, where appropriate, establish under its domestic law a long statute of limitations period in which to commence proceedings for any offence covered by this Convention and a longer period where the alleged offender has evaded the administration of justice.

(6) Nothing contained in this Convention shall affect the principle that the description of the offences established in accordance with this Convention and of the applicable legal defences or other legal principles controlling the lawfulness of conduct is reserved to the domestic law of a State Party and that such offences shall be prosecuted and punished in accordance with that law.

Article 12 Confiscation and Seizure

(1) States Parties shall adopt, to the greatest extent possible within their domestic legal systems, such measures as may be necessary to enable confiscation of:

   (a) Proceeds of crime derived from offences covered by this Convention or property the value of which corresponds to that of such proceeds;

   (b) Property, equipment or other instrumentalities used in or destined for use in offences covered by this Convention.

(2) States Parties shall adopt such measures as may be necessary to enable the identification, tracing, freezing or seizure of any item referred to in paragraph (1) of this Article for the purpose of eventual confiscation.

(3) If proceeds of crime have been transformed or converted, in part or in full, into other property, such property shall be liable to the measures referred to in this Article instead of the proceeds.

(4) If proceeds of crime have been intermingled with property acquired from legitimate sources, such property shall, without prejudice to any powers relating to freezing or seizure, be liable to confiscation up to the assessed value of the intermingled proceeds.

(5) Income or other benefits derived from proceeds of crime, from property into which proceeds of crime have been transformed or converted or from property with which proceeds of crime have been intermingled shall also be liable to the measures referred to in this Article, in the same manner and to the same extent as proceeds of crime.

(6) For the purposes of this Article and Article 13 of this Convention, each State Party shall empower its courts or other competent authorities to order that bank, financial or commercial records be made available or be seized. States Parties shall not decline to act under the provisions of this paragraph on the ground of bank secrecy.

(7) States Parties may consider the possibility of requiring that an offender demonstrate the lawful origin of alleged proceeds of crime or other property liable to confiscation, to the extent that such a requirement is consistent with the principles of their domestic law and with the nature of the judicial and other proceedings.

(8) The provisions of this Article shall not be construed to prejudice the rights of bona fide third parties.

(9) Nothing contained in this Article shall affect the principle that the measures to which it refers shall be defined and implemented in accordance with and subject to the provisions of the domestic law of a State Party.

Article 13 International Cooperation for Purposes of Confiscation

(1) A State Party that has received a request from another State Party having jurisdiction over an offence covered by this Convention for confiscation of proceeds of crime, property, equipment or other instrumentalities referred to in Article 12, paragraph (1), of this Convention situated in its territory shall, to the greatest extent possible within its domestic legal system:

(a) Submit the request to its competent authorities for the purpose of obtaining an order of confiscation and, if such an order is granted, give effect to it; or

(b) Submit to its competent authorities, with a view to giving effect to it to the extent requested, an order of confiscation issued by a court in the territory of the requesting State Party in accordance with Article 12, paragraph (1), of this Convention insofar as it relates to proceeds of crime, property, equipment or other instrumentalities referred to in Article 12, paragraph (1), situated in the territory of the requested State Party.

(2) Following a request made by another State Party having jurisdiction over an offence covered by this Convention, the requested State Party shall take measures to identify, trace and freeze or seize proceeds of crime, property, equipment or other instrumentalities referred to in Article 12, paragraph (1), of this Convention for the purpose of eventual confiscation to be ordered either by the requesting State Party or, pursuant to a request under paragraph (1) of this Article, by the requested State Party.

(3) The provisions of Article 18 of this Convention are applicable, *mutatis mutandis*, to this Article. In addition to the information specified in Article 18, paragraph (15), requests made pursuant to this Article shall contain:

(a) In the case of a request pertaining to paragraph (1)(a) of this Article, a description of the property to be confiscated and a statement of the facts relied upon by the requesting State Party sufficient to enable the requested State Party to seek the order under its domestic law;

(b) In the case of a request pertaining to paragraph (1)(b) of this Article, a legally admissible copy of an order of confiscation upon which the request is based issued by the requesting State Party, a statement of the facts and information as to the extent to which execution of the order is requested;

(c) In the case of a request pertaining to paragraph (2) of this Article, a statement of the facts relied upon by the requesting State Party and a description of the actions requested.

(4) The decisions or actions provided for in paragraphs (1) and (2) of this Article shall be taken by the requested State Party in accordance with and subject to the provisions of its domestic law and its procedural rules or any bilateral or multilateral treaty, agreement or arrangement to which it may be bound in relation to the requesting State Party.

(5) Each State Party shall furnish copies of its laws and regulations that give effect to this Article and of any subsequent changes to such laws and regulations or a description thereof to the Secretary-General of the United Nations.

(6) If a State Party elects to make the taking of the measures referred to in paragraphs (1) and (2) of this Article conditional on the existence of a relevant treaty, that State Party shall consider this Convention the necessary and sufficient treaty basis.

(7) Cooperation under this Article may be refused by a State Party if the offence to which the request relates is not an offence covered by this Convention.

(8) The provisions of this Article shall not be construed to prejudice the rights of bona fide third parties.

(9) States Parties shall consider concluding bilateral or multilateral treaties, agreements or arrangements to enhance the effectiveness of international cooperation undertaken pursuant to this Article.

Article 14 Disposal of Confiscated Proceeds of Crime or Property

(1) Proceeds of crime or property confiscated by a State Party pursuant to Articles 12 or 13, paragraph (1), of this Convention shall be disposed of by that State Party in accordance with its domestic law and administrative procedures.

(2) When acting on the request made by another State Party in accordance with Article 13 of this Convention, States Parties shall, to the extent permitted by domestic law and if so requested, give priority consideration to returning the confiscated proceeds of crime or property to the requesting State Party so that it can give compensation to the victims of the crime or return such proceeds of crime or property to their legitimate owners.

(3) When acting on the request made by another State Party in accordance with Articles 12 and 13 of this Convention, a State Party may give special consideration to concluding agreements or arrangements on:

   (a) Contributing the value of such proceeds of crime or property or funds derived from the sale of such proceeds of crime or property or a part thereof to the account designated in accordance with Article 30, paragraph (2)(c), of this Convention and to intergovernmental bodies specializing in the fight against organized crime;

   (b) Sharing with other States Parties, on a regular or case-by-case basis, such proceeds of crime or property, or funds derived from the sale of such proceeds of crime or property, in accordance with its domestic law or administrative procedures.

Article 15 Jurisdiction

(1) Each State Party shall adopt such measures as may be necessary to establish its jurisdiction over the offences established in accordance with Articles 5, 6, 8 and 23 of this Convention when:

   (a) The offence is committed in the territory of that State Party; or

   (b) The offence is committed on board a vessel that is flying the flag of that State Party or an aircraft that is registered under the laws of that State Party at the time that the offence is committed.

(2) Subject to Article 4 of this Convention, a State Party may also establish its jurisdiction over any such offence when:

   (a) The offence is committed against a national of that State Party;

   (b) The offence is committed by a national of that State Party or a stateless person who has his or her habitual residence in its territory; or

(c) The offence is:

(i) One of those established in accordance with Article 5, paragraph (1), of this Convention and is committed outside its territory with a view to the commission of a serious crime within its territory;

(ii) One of those established in accordance with Article 6, paragraph (1)(b)(ii), of this Convention and is committed outside its territory with a view to the commission of an offence established in accordance with Article 6, paragraph (1)(a)(i) or (ii) or (b)(i), of this Convention within its territory.

(3) For the purposes of Article 16, paragraph (10), of this Convention, each State Party shall adopt such measures as may be necessary to establish its jurisdiction over the offences covered by this Convention when the alleged offender is present in its territory and it does not extradite such person solely on the ground that he or she is one of its nationals.

(4) Each State Party may also adopt such measures as may be necessary to establish its jurisdiction over the offences covered by this Convention when the alleged offender is present in its territory and it does not extradite him or her.

(5) If a State Party exercising its jurisdiction under paragraph (1) or (2) of this Article has been notified, or has otherwise learned, that one or more other States Parties are conducting an investigation, prosecution or judicial proceeding in respect of the same conduct, the competent authorities of those States Parties shall, as appropriate, consult one another with a view to coordinating their actions.

(6) Without prejudice to norms of general international law, this Convention does not exclude the exercise of any criminal jurisdiction established by a State Party in accordance with its domestic law.

Article 16 Extradition

(1) This Article shall apply to the offences covered by this Convention or in cases where an offence referred to in Article 3, paragraph (1)(a) or (b), involves an organized criminal group and the person who is the subject of the request for extradition is located in the territory of the requested State Party, provided that the offence for which extradition is sought is punishable under the domestic law of both the requesting State Party and the requested State Party.

(2) If the request for extradition includes several separate serious crimes, some of which are not covered by this Article, the requested State Party may apply this Article also in respect of the latter offences.

(3) Each of the offences to which this Article applies shall be deemed to be included as an extraditable offence in any extradition treaty existing between States Parties. States Parties undertake to include such offences as extraditable offences in every extradition treaty to be concluded between them.

(4) If a State Party that makes extradition conditional on the existence of a treaty receives a request for extradition from another State Party with which it has no extradition treaty, it may consider this Convention the legal basis for extradition in respect of any offence to which this Article applies.

(5) States Parties that make extradition conditional on the existence of a treaty shall:

(a) At the time of deposit of their instrument of ratification, acceptance, approval of or accession to this Convention, inform the Secretary-General of the United Nations whether they will take this Convention as the legal basis for cooperation on extradition with other States Parties to this Convention; and

(b) If they do not take this Convention as the legal basis for cooperation on extradition, seek, where appropriate, to conclude treaties on extradition with other States Parties to this Convention in order to implement this Article.

(6) States Parties that do not make extradition conditional on the existence of a treaty shall recognize offences to which this Article applies as extraditable offences between themselves.

(7) Extradition shall be subject to the conditions provided for by the domestic law of the requested State Party or by applicable extradition treaties, including, inter alia, conditions in relation to the minimum penalty requirement for extradition and the grounds upon which the requested State Party may refuse extradition.

(8) States Parties shall, subject to their domestic law, endeavour to expedite extradition procedures and to simplify evidentiary requirements relating thereto in respect of any offence to which this Article applies.

(9) Subject to the provisions of its domestic law and its extradition treaties, the requested State Party may, upon being satisfied that the circumstances so warrant and are urgent and at the request of the requesting State Party, take a person whose extradition is sought and who is present in its territory into custody or take other appropriate measures to ensure his or her presence at extradition proceedings.

(10) A State Party in whose territory an alleged offender is found, if it does not extradite such person in respect of an offence to which this Article applies solely on the ground that he or she is one of its nationals, shall, at the request of the State Party seeking extradition, be obliged to submit the case without undue delay to its competent authorities for the purpose of prosecution. Those authorities shall take their decision and conduct their proceedings in the same manner as in the case of any other offence of a grave nature under the domestic law of that State Party. The States Parties concerned shall cooperate with each other, in particular on procedural and evidentiary aspects, to ensure the efficiency of such prosecution.

(11) Whenever a State Party is permitted under its domestic law to extradite or otherwise surrender one of its nationals only upon the condition that the person will be returned to that State Party to serve the sentence imposed as a result of the trial or proceedings for which the extradition or surrender of the person was sought and that State Party and the State Party seeking the extradition of the person agree with this option and other terms that they may deem appropriate, such conditional extradition or surrender shall be sufficient to discharge the obligation set forth in paragraph (10) of this Article.

(12) If extradition, sought for purposes of enforcing a sentence, is refused because the person sought is a national of the requested State Party, the requested Party shall, if its domestic law so permits and in conformity with the requirements of such law, upon application of the requesting Party, consider the enforcement of the sentence that has been imposed under the domestic law of the requesting Party or the remainder thereof.

(13) Any person regarding whom proceedings are being carried out in connection with any of the offences to which this Article applies shall be guaranteed fair treatment at all stages of the proceedings, including enjoyment of all the rights and guarantees provided by the domestic law of the State Party in the territory of which that person is present.

(14) Nothing in this Convention shall be interpreted as imposing an obligation to extradite if the requested State Party has substantial grounds for believing that the request has been made for the purpose of prosecuting or punishing a person on account of that person's sex, race, religion, nationality, ethnic origin or political opinions or that compliance with the request would cause prejudice to that person's position for any one of these reasons.

(15) States Parties may not refuse a request for extradition on the sole ground that the offence is also considered to involve fiscal matters.

(16) Before refusing extradition, the requested State Party shall, where appropriate, consult with the requesting State Party to provide it with ample opportunity to present its opinions and to provide information relevant to its allegation.

(17) States Parties shall seek to conclude bilateral and multilateral agreements or arrangements to carry out or to enhance the effectiveness of extradition.

Article 17 Transfer of Sentenced Persons

States Parties may consider entering into bilateral or multilateral agreements or arrangements on the transfer to their territory of persons sentenced to imprisonment or other forms of deprivation of liberty for offences covered by this Convention, in order that they may complete their sentences there.

Article 18 Mutual Legal Assistance

(1) States Parties shall afford one another the widest measure of mutual legal assistance in investigations, prosecutions and judicial proceedings in relation to the offences covered by this Convention as provided for in Article 3 and shall reciprocally extend to one another similar assistance where the requesting State Party has reasonable grounds to suspect that the offence referred to in Article 3, paragraph (1)(a) or (b), is transnational in nature, including that victims, witnesses, proceeds, instrumentalities or evidence of such offences are located in the requested State Party and that the offence involves an organized criminal group.

(2) Mutual legal assistance shall be afforded to the fullest extent possible under relevant laws, treaties, agreements and arrangements of the requested State Party with respect to investigations, prosecutions and judicial proceedings in relation to the offences for which a legal person may be held liable in accordance with Article 10 of this Convention in the requesting State Party.

(3) Mutual legal assistance to be afforded in accordance with this Article may be requested for any of the following purposes:

  (a) Taking evidence or statements from persons;

  (b) Effecting service of judicial documents;

  (c) Executing searches and seizures, and freezing;

  (d) Examining objects and sites;

  (e) Providing information, evidentiary items and expert evaluations;

  (f) Providing originals or certified copies of relevant documents and records, including government, bank, financial, corporate or business records;

  (g) Identifying or tracing proceeds of crime, property, instrumentalities or other things for evidentiary purposes;

  (h) Facilitating the voluntary appearance of persons in the requesting State Party;

  (i) Any other type of assistance that is not contrary to the domestic law of the requested State Party.

(4) Without prejudice to domestic law, the competent authorities of a State Party may, without prior request, transmit information relating to criminal matters to a competent authority in another State Party where they believe that such information could assist the authority in undertaking or successfully concluding inquiries and criminal proceedings or could result in a request formulated by the latter State Party pursuant to this Convention.

(5) The transmission of information pursuant to paragraph (4) of this Article shall be without prejudice to inquiries and criminal proceedings in the State of the competent authorities providing the information. The competent authorities receiving the information shall comply with a request that said information remain confidential, even temporarily, or with restrictions on its use. However, this shall not prevent the receiving State Party from disclosing in its proceedings information that is exculpatory to an accused person. In such a case, the receiving State Party shall notify the transmitting State Party prior to the disclosure and, if so requested, consult with the transmitting State Party. If, in an exceptional case, advance notice is not possible, the receiving State Party shall inform the transmitting State Party of the disclosure without delay.

(6) The provisions of this Article shall not affect the obligations under any other treaty, bilateral or multilateral, that governs or will govern, in whole or in part, mutual legal assistance.

(7) Paragraphs (9) to (29) of this Article shall apply to requests made pursuant to this Article if the States Parties in question are not bound by a treaty of mutual legal assistance. If those States Parties are bound by such a treaty, the corresponding provisions of that treaty shall apply unless the States Parties agree to apply paragraphs (9) to (29) of this Article in lieu thereof. States Parties are strongly encouraged to apply these paragraphs if they facilitate cooperation.

(8) States Parties shall not decline to render mutual legal assistance pursuant to this Article on the ground of bank secrecy.

(9) States Parties may decline to render mutual legal assistance pursuant to this Article on the ground of absence of dual criminality. However, the requested State Party may, when it deems appropriate, provide assistance, to the extent it decides at its discretion, irrespective of whether the conduct would constitute an offence under the domestic law of the requested State Party.

(10) A person who is being detained or is serving a sentence in the territory of one State Party whose presence in another State Party is requested for purposes of identification, testimony or otherwise providing assistance in obtaining evidence for investigations, prosecutions or judicial proceedings in relation to offences covered by this Convention may be transferred if the following conditions are met:

(a) The person freely gives his or her informed consent;

(b) The competent authorities of both States Parties agree, subject to such conditions as those States Parties may deem appropriate.

(11) For the purposes of paragraph (10) of this Article:

(a) The State Party to which the person is transferred shall have the authority and obligation to keep the person transferred in custody, unless otherwise requested or authorized by the State Party from which the person was transferred;

(b) The State Party to which the person is transferred shall without delay implement its obligation to return the person to the custody of the State Party from which the person was transferred as agreed beforehand, or as otherwise agreed, by the competent authorities of both States Parties;

(c) The State Party to which the person is transferred shall not require the State Party from which the person was transferred to initiate extradition proceedings for the return of the person;

(d) The person transferred shall receive credit for service of the sentence being served in the State from which he or she was transferred for time spent in the custody of the State Party to which he or she was transferred.

(12) Unless the State Party from which a person is to be transferred in accordance with paragraphs (10) and (11) of this Article so agrees, that person, whatever his or her nationality, shall not be prosecuted, detained, punished or subjected to any other restriction of his or her personal liberty in the territory of the State to which that person is transferred in respect of acts, omissions or convictions prior to his or her departure from the territory of the State from which he or she was transferred.

(13) Each State Party shall designate a central authority that shall have the responsibility and power to receive requests for mutual legal assistance and either to execute them or to transmit them to the competent authorities for execution. Where a State Party has a special region or territory with a separate system of mutual legal assistance, it may designate a distinct central authority that shall have the same function for that region or territory. Central authorities shall ensure the speedy and proper execution or transmission of the requests received. Where the central authority transmits the request to a competent authority for execution, it shall encourage the speedy and proper execution of the request by the competent authority. The Secretary-General of the United Nations shall be notified of the central authority designated for this purpose at the time each State Party deposits its instrument of ratification, acceptance or approval of or accession to this

Convention. Requests for mutual legal assistance and any communication related thereto shall be transmitted to the central authorities designated by the States Parties. This requirement shall be without prejudice to the right of a State Party to require that such requests and communications be addressed to it through diplomatic channels and, in urgent circumstances, where the States Parties agree, through the International Criminal Police Organization, if possible.

(14) Requests shall be made in writing or, where possible, by any means capable of producing a written record, in a language acceptable to the requested State Party, under conditions allowing that State Party to establish authenticity. The Secretary-General of the United Nations shall be notified of the language or languages acceptable to each State Party at the time it deposits its instrument of ratification, acceptance or approval of or accession to this Convention. In urgent circumstances and where agreed by the States Parties, requests may be made orally, but shall be confirmed in writing forthwith.

(15) A request for mutual legal assistance shall contain:

(a) The identity of the authority making the request;

(b) The subject matter and nature of the investigation, prosecution or judicial proceeding to which the request relates and the name and functions of the authority conducting the investigation, prosecution or judicial proceeding;

(c) A summary of the relevant facts, except in relation to requests for the purpose of service of judicial documents;

(d) A description of the assistance sought and details of any particular procedure that the requesting State Party wishes to be followed;

(e) Where possible, the identity, location and nationality of any person concerned; and

(f) The purpose for which the evidence, information or action is sought.

(16) The requested State Party may request additional information when it appears necessary for the execution of the request in accordance with its domestic law or when it can facilitate such execution.

(17) A request shall be executed in accordance with the domestic law of the requested State Party and, to the extent not contrary to the domestic law of the requested State Party and where possible, in accordance with the procedures specified in the request.

(18) Wherever possible and consistent with fundamental principles of domestic law, when an individual is in the territory of a State Party and has to be heard as a witness or expert by the judicial authorities of another State Party, the first State Party may, at the request of the other, permit the hearing to take place by video conference if it is not possible or desirable for the individual in question to appear in person in the territory of the requesting State Party. States Parties may agree that the hearing shall be conducted by a judicial authority of the requesting State Party and attended by a judicial authority of the requested State Party.

(19) The requesting State Party shall not transmit or use information or evidence furnished by the requested State Party for investigations, prosecutions or judicial proceedings other than those stated in the request without the prior consent of the requested State Party. Nothing in this paragraph shall prevent the requesting State Party from disclosing in its proceedings information or evidence that is exculpatory to an accused person. In the latter case, the requesting State Party shall notify the requested State Party prior to the disclosure and, if so requested, consult with the requested State Party. If, in an exceptional case, advance notice is not possible, the requesting State Party shall inform the requested State Party of the disclosure without delay.

(20) The requesting State Party may require that the requested State Party keep confidential the fact and substance of the request, except to the extent necessary to execute the request. If the requested State Party cannot comply with the requirement of confidentiality, it shall promptly inform the requesting State Party.

(21) Mutual legal assistance may be refused:

(a) If the request is not made in conformity with the provisions of this Article;

(b) If the requested State Party considers that execution of the request is likely to prejudice its sovereignty, security, ordre public or other essential interests;

(c) If the authorities of the requested State Party would be prohibited by its domestic law from carrying out the action requested with regard to any similar offence, had it been subject to investigation, prosecution or judicial proceedings under their own jurisdiction;

(d) If it would be contrary to the legal system of the requested State Party relating to mutual legal assistance for the request to be granted.

(22) States Parties may not refuse a request for mutual legal assistance on the sole ground that the offence is also considered to involve fiscal matters.

(23) Reasons shall be given for any refusal of mutual legal assistance.

(24) The requested State Party shall execute the request for mutual legal assistance as soon as possible and shall take as full account as possible of any deadlines suggested by the requesting State Party and for which reasons are given, preferably in the request. The requested State Party shall respond to reasonable requests by the requesting State Party on progress of its handling of the request. The requesting State Party shall promptly inform the requested State Party when the assistance sought is no longer required.

(25) Mutual legal assistance may be postponed by the requested State Party on the ground that it interferes with an ongoing investigation, prosecution or judicial proceeding.

(26) Before refusing a request pursuant to paragraph (21) of this Article or postponing its execution pursuant to paragraph (25) of this Article, the requested State Party shall consult with the requesting State Party to consider whether assistance may be granted subject to such terms and conditions as it deems necessary. If the requesting State Party accepts assistance subject to those conditions, it shall comply with the conditions.

(27) Without prejudice to the application of paragraph (12) of this Article, a witness, expert or other person who, at the request of the requesting State Party, consents to give evidence in a proceeding or to assist in an investigation, prosecution or judicial proceeding in the territory of the requesting State Party shall not be prosecuted, detained, punished or subjected to any other restriction of his or her personal liberty in that territory in respect of acts, omissions or convictions prior to his or her departure from the territory of the requested State Party. Such safe conduct shall cease when the witness, expert or other person having had, for a period of fifteen consecutive days or for any period agreed upon by the States Parties from the date on which he or she has been officially informed that his or her presence is no longer required by the judicial authorities, an opportunity of leaving, has nevertheless remained voluntarily in the territory of the requesting State Party or, having left it, has returned of his or her own free will.

(28) The ordinary costs of executing a request shall be borne by the requested State Party, unless otherwise agreed by the States Parties concerned. If expenses of a substantial or extraordinary nature are or will be required to fulfil the request, the States Parties shall consult to determine the terms and conditions under which the request will be executed, as well as the manner in which the costs shall be borne.

(29) The requested State Party:

(a) Shall provide to the requesting State Party copies of government records, documents or information in its possession that under its domestic law are available to the general public;

(b) May, at its discretion, provide to the requesting State Party in whole, in part or subject to such conditions as it deems appropriate, copies of any government records, documents or information in its possession that under its domestic law are not available to the general public.

(30) States Parties shall consider, as may be necessary, the possibility of concluding bilateral or multilateral agreements or arrangements that would serve the purposes of, give practical effect to or enhance the provisions of this Article.

Article 19 Joint Investigations

States Parties shall consider concluding bilateral or multilateral agreements or arrangements whereby, in relation to matters that are the subject of investigations, prosecutions or judicial proceedings in one or more States, the competent authorities concerned may establish joint investigative bodies. In the absence of such agreements or arrangements, joint investigations may be undertaken by agreement on a case-by-case basis. The States Parties involved shall ensure that the sovereignty of the State Party in whose territory such investigation is to take place is fully respected.

Article 20 Special Investigative Techniques

(1) If permitted by the basic principles of its domestic legal system, each State Party shall, within its possibilities and under the conditions prescribed by its domestic law, take the necessary measures to allow for the appropriate use of controlled delivery and, where it deems appropriate, for the use of other special investigative techniques, such as electronic or other forms of surveillance and undercover operations, by its competent authorities in its territory for the purpose of effectively combating organized crime.

(2) For the purpose of investigating the offences covered by this Convention, States Parties are encouraged to conclude, when necessary, appropriate bilateral or multilateral agreements or arrangements for using such special investigative techniques in the context of cooperation at the international level. Such agreements or arrangements shall be concluded and implemented in full compliance with the principle of sovereign equality of States and shall be carried out strictly in accordance with the terms of those agreements or arrangements.

(3) In the absence of an agreement or arrangement as set forth in paragraph (2) of this Article, decisions to use such special investigative techniques at the international level shall be made on a case-by-case basis and may, when necessary, take into consideration financial arrangements and understandings with respect to the exercise of jurisdiction by the States Parties concerned.

(4) Decisions to use controlled delivery at the international level may, with the consent of the States Parties concerned, include methods such as intercepting and allowing the goods to continue intact or be removed or replaced in whole or in part.

Article 21 Transfer of Criminal Proceedings

States Parties shall consider the possibility of transferring to one another proceedings for the prosecution of an offence covered by this Convention in cases where such transfer is considered to be in the interests of the proper administration of justice, in particular in cases where several jurisdictions are involved, with a view to concentrating the prosecution.

Article 22 Establishment of Criminal Record

Each State Party may adopt such legislative or other measures as may be necessary to take into consideration, under such terms as and for the purpose that it deems appropriate, any previous conviction in another State of an alleged offender for the purpose of using such information in criminal proceedings relating to an offence covered by this Convention.

Article 23 Criminalization of Obstruction of Justice

Each State Party shall adopt such legislative and other measures as may be necessary to establish as criminal offences, when committed intentionally:

(a) The use of physical force, threats or intimidation or the promise, offering or giving of an undue advantage to induce false testimony or to interfere in the giving of testimony or the production of evidence in a proceeding in relation to the commission of offences covered by this Convention;

(b) The use of physical force, threats or intimidation to interfere with the exercise of official duties by a justice or law enforcement official in relation to the commission of offences covered by this Convention. Nothing in this subparagraph shall prejudice the right of States Parties to have legislation that protects other categories of public officials.

Article 24 Protection of Witnesses

(1) Each State Party shall take appropriate measures within its means to provide effective protection from potential retaliation or intimidation for witnesses in criminal proceedings who give testimony concerning offences covered by this Convention and, as appropriate, for their relatives and other persons close to them.

(2) The measures envisaged in paragraph (1) of this Article may include, inter alia, without prejudice to the rights of the defendant, including the right to due process:

(a) Establishing procedures for the physical protection of such persons, such as, to the extent necessary and feasible, relocating them and permitting, where appropriate, non-disclosure or limitations on the disclosure of information concerning the identity and whereabouts of such persons;

(b) Providing evidentiary rules to permit witness testimony to be given in a manner that ensures the safety of the witness, such as permitting testimony to be given through the use of communications technology such as video links or other adequate means.

(3) States Parties shall consider entering into agreements or arrangements with other States for the relocation of persons referred to in paragraph (1) of this Article.

(4) The provisions of this Article shall also apply to victims insofar as they are witnesses.

Article 25 Assistance to and Protection of Victims

(1) Each State Party shall take appropriate measures within its means to provide assistance and protection to victims of offences covered by this Convention, in particular in cases of threat of retaliation or intimidation.

(2) Each State Party shall establish appropriate procedures to provide access to compensation and restitution for victims of offences covered by this Convention.

(3) Each State Party shall, subject to its domestic law, enable views and concerns of victims to be presented and considered at appropriate stages of criminal proceedings against offenders in a manner not prejudicial to the rights of the defence.

Article 26 Measures to Enhance Cooperation with Law Enforcement Authorities

(1) Each State Party shall take appropriate measures to encourage persons who participate or who have participated in organized criminal groups:

(a) To supply information useful to competent authorities for investigative and evidentiary purposes on such matters as:

(i) The identity, nature, composition, structure, location or activities of organized criminal groups;

(ii) Links, including international links, with other organized criminal groups;

(iii) Offences that organized criminal groups have committed or may commit;

(b) To provide factual, concrete help to competent authorities that may contribute to depriving organized criminal groups of their resources or of the proceeds of crime.

(2) Each State Party shall consider providing for the possibility, in appropriate cases, of mitigating punishment of an accused person who provides substantial cooperation in the investigation or prosecution of an offence covered by this Convention.

(3) Each State Party shall consider providing for the possibility, in accordance with fundamental principles of its domestic law, of granting immunity from prosecution to a person who provides substantial cooperation in the investigation or prosecution of an offence covered by this Convention.

(4) Protection of such persons shall be as provided for in Article 24 of this Convention.

(5) Where a person referred to in paragraph (1) of this Article located in one State Party can provide substantial cooperation to the competent authorities of another State Party, the States Parties concerned may consider entering into agreements or arrangements, in accordance with their domestic law, concerning the potential provision by the other State Party of the treatment set forth in paragraphs (2) and (3) of this Article.

Article 27 Law Enforcement Cooperation

(1) States Parties shall cooperate closely with one another, consistent with their respective domestic legal and administrative systems, to enhance the effectiveness of law enforcement action to combat the offences covered by this Convention. Each State Party shall, in particular, adopt effective measures:

(a) To enhance and, where necessary, to establish channels of communication between their competent authorities, agencies and services in order to facilitate the secure and rapid exchange of information concerning all aspects of the offences covered by this Convention, including, if the States Parties concerned deem it appropriate, links with other criminal activities;

(b) To cooperate with other States Parties in conducting inquiries with respect to offences covered by this Convention concerning:

(i) The identity, whereabouts and activities of persons suspected of involvement in such offences or the location of other persons concerned;

(ii) The movement of proceeds of crime or property derived from the commission of such offences;

(iii) The movement of property, equipment or other instrumentalities used or intended for use in the commission of such offences;

(c) To provide, when appropriate, necessary items or quantities of substances for analytical or investigative purposes;

(d) To facilitate effective coordination between their competent authorities, agencies and services and to promote the exchange of personnel and other experts, including, subject to bilateral agreements or arrangements between the States Parties concerned, the posting of liaison officers;

(e) To exchange information with other States Parties on specific means and methods used by organized criminal groups, including, where applicable, routes and conveyances and the use of false identities, altered or false documents or other means of concealing their activities;

(f) To exchange information and coordinate administrative and other measures taken as appropriate for the purpose of early identification of the offences covered by this Convention.

(2) With a view to giving effect to this Convention, States Parties shall consider entering into bilateral or multilateral agreements or arrangements on direct cooperation between their law enforcement agencies and, where such agreements or arrangements already exist, amending them. In the absence of such agreements or arrangements between the States Parties concerned, the Parties may consider this Convention as the basis for mutual law enforcement cooperation in respect of the offences covered by this Convention. Whenever appropriate, States Parties shall make full use of agreements or arrangements, including international or regional organizations, to enhance the cooperation between their law enforcement agencies.

(3) States Parties shall endeavour to cooperate within their means to respond to transnational organized crime committed through the use of modern technology.

Article 28 Collection, Exchange and Analysis of Information on the Nature of Organized Crime

(1) Each State Party shall consider analysing, in consultation with the scientific and academic communities, trends in organized crime in its territory, the circumstances in which organized crime operates, as well as the professional groups and technologies involved.

(2) States Parties shall consider developing and sharing analytical expertise concerning organized criminal activities with each other and through international and regional organizations. For that purpose, common definitions, standards and methodologies should be developed and applied as appropriate.

(3) Each State Party shall consider monitoring its policies and actual measures to combat organized crime and making assessments of their effectiveness and efficiency.

Article 29 Training and Technical Assistance

(1) Each State Party shall, to the extent necessary, initiate, develop or improve specific training programmes for its law enforcement personnel, including prosecutors, investigating magistrates and customs personnel, and other personnel charged with the prevention, detection and control of the offences covered by this Convention. Such programmes may include secondments and exchanges of staff. Such programmes shall deal, in particular and to the extent permitted by domestic law, with the following:

  (a) Methods used in the prevention, detection and control of the offences covered by this Convention;

  (b) Routes and techniques used by persons suspected of involvement in offences covered by this Convention, including in transit States, and appropriate countermeasures;

  (c) Monitoring of the movement of contraband;

  (d) Detection and monitoring of the movements of proceeds of crime, property, equipment or other instrumentalities and methods used for the transfer, concealment or disguise of such proceeds, property, equipment or other instrumentalities, as well as methods used in combating money-laundering and other financial crimes;

  (e) Collection of evidence;

  (f) Control techniques in free trade zones and free ports;

  (g) Modern law enforcement equipment and techniques, including electronic surveillance, controlled deliveries and undercover operations;

  (h) Methods used in combating transnational organized crime committed through the use of computers, telecommunications networks or other forms of modern technology; and

  (i) Methods used in the protection of victims and witnesses.

(2) States Parties shall assist one another in planning and implementing research and training programmes designed to share expertise in the areas referred to in paragraph (1) of this Article and to that end shall also, when appropriate, use regional and international conferences and seminars to promote cooperation and to stimulate discussion on problems of mutual concern, including the special problems and needs of transit States.

(3) States Parties shall promote training and technical assistance that will facilitate extradition and mutual legal assistance. Such training and technical assistance may include language training, secondments and exchanges between personnel in central authorities or agencies with relevant responsibilities.

(4) In the case of existing bilateral and multilateral agreements or arrangements, States Parties shall strengthen, to the extent necessary, efforts to maximize operational and training activities within

international and regional organizations and within other relevant bilateral and multilateral agreements or arrangements.

Article 30 Other Measures: Implementation of the Convention through Economic Development and Technical Assistance

(1) States Parties shall take measures conducive to the optimal implementation of this Convention to the extent possible, through international cooperation, taking into account the negative effects of organized crime on society in general, in particular on sustainable development.

(2) States Parties shall make concrete efforts to the extent possible and in coordination with each other, as well as with international and regional organizations:

(a) To enhance their cooperation at various levels with developing countries, with a view to strengthening the capacity of the latter to prevent and combat transnational organized crime;

(b) To enhance financial and material assistance to support the efforts of developing countries to fight transnational organized crime effectively and to help them implement this Convention successfully;

(c) To provide technical assistance to developing countries and countries with economies in transition to assist them in meeting their needs for the implementation of this Convention. To that end, States Parties shall endeavour to make adequate and regular voluntary contributions to an account specifically designated for that purpose in a United Nations funding mechanism. States Parties may also give special consideration, in accordance with their domestic law and the provisions of this Convention, to contributing to the aforementioned account a percentage of the money or of the corresponding value of proceeds of crime or property confiscated in accordance with the provisions of this Convention;

(d) To encourage and persuade other States and financial institutions as appropriate to join them in efforts in accordance with this Article, in particular by providing more training programmes and modern equipment to developing countries in order to assist them in achieving the objectives of this Convention.

(3) To the extent possible, these measures shall be without prejudice to existing foreign assistance commitments or to other financial cooperation arrangements at the bilateral, regional or international level.

(4) States Parties may conclude bilateral or multilateral agreements or arrangements on material and logistical assistance, taking into consideration the financial arrangements necessary for the means of international cooperation provided for by this Convention to be effective and for the prevention, detection and control of transnational organized crime.

Article 31 Prevention

(1) States Parties shall endeavour to develop and evaluate national projects and to establish and promote best practices and policies aimed at the prevention of transnational organized crime.

(2) States Parties shall endeavour, in accordance with fundamental principles of their domestic law, to reduce existing or future opportunities for organized criminal groups to participate in lawful markets with proceeds of crime, through appropriate legislative, administrative or other measures. These measures should focus on:

(a) The strengthening of cooperation between law enforcement agencies or prosecutors and relevant private entities, including industry;

(b) The promotion of the development of standards and procedures designed to safeguard the integrity of public and relevant private entities, as well as codes of conduct for relevant professions, in particular lawyers, notaries public, tax consultants and accountants;

(c) The prevention of the misuse by organized criminal groups of tender procedures conducted by public authorities and of subsidies and licences granted by public authorities for commercial activity;

(d) The prevention of the misuse of legal persons by organized criminal groups; such measures could include:

(i) The establishment of public records on legal and natural persons involved in the establishment, management and funding of legal persons;

(ii) The introduction of the possibility of disqualifying by court order or any appropriate means for a reasonable period of time persons convicted of offences covered by this Convention from acting as directors of legal persons incorporated within their jurisdiction;

(iii) The establishment of national records of persons disqualified from acting as directors of legal persons; and

(iv) The exchange of information contained in the records referred to in subparagraphs (d)(i) and (iii) of this paragraph with the competent authorities of other States Parties.

(3) States Parties shall endeavour to promote the reintegration into society of persons convicted of offences covered by this Convention.

(4) States Parties shall endeavour to evaluate periodically existing relevant legal instruments and administrative practices with a view to detecting their vulnerability to misuse by organized criminal groups.

(5) States Parties shall endeavour to promote public awareness regarding the existence, causes and gravity of and the threat posed by transnational organized crime. Information may be disseminated where appropriate through the mass media and shall include measures to promote public participation in preventing and combating such crime.

(6) Each State Party shall inform the Secretary-General of the United Nations of the name and address of the authority or authorities that can assist other States Parties in developing measures to prevent transnational organized crime.

(7) States Parties shall, as appropriate, collaborate with each other and relevant international and regional organizations in promoting and developing the measures referred to in this Article. This includes participation in international projects aimed at the prevention of transnational organized crime, for example by alleviating the circumstances that render socially marginalized groups vulnerable to the action of transnational organized crime.

Article 32 Conference of the Parties to the Convention

(1) A Conference of the Parties to the Convention is hereby established to improve the capacity of States Parties to combat transnational organized crime and to promote and review the implementation of this Convention.

(2) The Secretary-General of the United Nations shall convene the Conference of the Parties not later than one year following the entry into force of this Convention. The Conference of the Parties shall adopt rules of procedure and rules governing the activities set forth in paragraphs (3) and (4) of this Article (including rules concerning payment of expenses incurred in carrying out those activities).

(3) The Conference of the Parties shall agree upon mechanisms for achieving the objectives mentioned in paragraph (1) of this Article, including:

(a) Facilitating activities by States Parties under Articles 29, 30 and 31 of this Convention, including by encouraging the mobilization of voluntary contributions;

(b) Facilitating the exchange of information among States Parties on patterns and trends in transnational organized crime and on successful practices for combating it;

(c) Cooperating with relevant international and regional organizations and non-governmental organizations;

(d) Reviewing periodically the implementation of this Convention;

(e) Making recommendations to improve this Convention and its implementation.

(4) For the purpose of paragraphs (3)(d) and (e) of this Article, the Conference of the Parties shall acquire the necessary knowledge of the measures taken by States Parties in implementing this Convention and the difficulties encountered by them in doing so through information provided by them and through such supplemental review mechanisms as may be established by the Conference of the Parties.

(5) Each State Party shall provide the Conference of the Parties with information on its programmes, plans and practices, as well as legislative and administrative measures to implement this Convention, as required by the Conference of the Parties.

Article 33 Secretariat

(1) The Secretary-General of the United Nations shall provide the necessary secretariat services to the Conference of the Parties to the Convention.

(2) The secretariat shall:

(a) Assist the Conference of the Parties in carrying out the activities set forth in Article 32 of this Convention and make arrangements and provide the necessary services for the sessions of the Conference of the Parties;

(b) Upon request, assist States Parties in providing information to the Conference of the Parties as envisaged in Article 32, paragraph (5), of this Convention; and

(c) Ensure the necessary coordination with the secretariats of relevant international and regional organizations.

Article 34 Implementation of the Convention

(1) Each State Party shall take the necessary measures, including legislative and administrative measures, in accordance with fundamental principles of its domestic law, to ensure the implementation of its obligations under this Convention.

(2) The offences established in accordance with Articles 5, 6, 8 and 23 of this Convention shall be established in the domestic law of each State Party independently of the transnational nature or the involvement of an organized criminal group as described in Article 3, paragraph (1), of this Convention, except to the extent that Article 5 of this Convention would require the involvement of an organized criminal group.

(3) Each State Party may adopt more strict or severe measures than those provided for by this Convention for preventing and combating transnational organized crime.

Article 35 Settlement of Disputes

(1) States Parties shall endeavour to settle disputes concerning the interpretation or application of this Convention through negotiation.

(2) Any dispute between two or more States Parties concerning the interpretation or application of this Convention that cannot be settled through negotiation within a reasonable time shall, at the request of one of those States Parties, be submitted to arbitration. If, six months after the date of the request for arbitration, those States Parties are unable to agree on the organization of the arbitration, any one of those States Parties may refer the dispute to the International Court of Justice by request in accordance with the Statute of the Court.

(3) Each State Party may, at the time of signature, ratification, acceptance or approval of or accession to this Convention, declare that it does not consider itself bound by paragraph (2) of this Article. The other States Parties shall not be bound by paragraph (2) of this Article with respect to any State Party that has made such a reservation.

(4) Any State Party that has made a reservation in accordance with paragraph (3) of this Article may at any time withdraw that reservation by notification to the Secretary-General of the United Nations.

Article 36 Signature, Ratification, Acceptance, Approval and Accession

(1) This Convention shall be open to all States for signature from 12 to 15 December 2000 in Palermo, Italy, and thereafter at United Nations Headquarters in New York until 12 December 2002.

(2) This Convention shall also be open for signature by regional economic integration organizations provided that at least one member State of such organization has signed this Convention in accordance with paragraph (1) of this Article.

(3) This Convention is subject to ratification, acceptance or approval. Instruments of ratification, acceptance or approval shall be deposited with the Secretary-General of the United Nations. A regional economic integration organization may deposit its instrument of ratification, acceptance or approval if at least one of its member States has done likewise. In that instrument of ratification, acceptance or approval, such organization shall declare the extent of its competence with respect to the matters governed by this Convention. Such organization shall also inform the depositary of any relevant modification in the extent of its competence.

(4) This Convention is open for accession by any State or any regional economic integration organization of which at least one member State is a Party to this Convention. Instruments of accession shall be deposited with the Secretary-General of the United Nations. At the time of its accession, a regional economic integration organization shall declare the extent of its competence with respect to matters governed by this Convention. Such organization shall also inform the depositary of any relevant modification in the extent of its competence.

Article 37 Relation with Protocols

(1) This Convention may be supplemented by one or more Protocols.

(2) In order to become a Party to a Protocol, a State or a regional economic integration organization must also be a Party to this Convention.

(3) A State Party to this Convention is not bound by a Protocol unless it becomes a Party to the Protocol in accordance with the provisions thereof.

(4) Any Protocol to this Convention shall be interpreted together with this Convention, taking into account the purpose of that Protocol.

Article 38 Entry into Force

(1) This Convention shall enter into force on the ninetieth day after the date of deposit of the fortieth instrument of ratification, acceptance, approval or accession. For the purpose of this paragraph, any instrument deposited by a regional economic integration organization shall not be counted as additional to those deposited by member States of such organization.

(2) For each State or regional economic integration organization ratifying, accepting, approving or acceding to this Convention after the deposit of the fortieth instrument of such action, this Convention shall enter into force on the thirtieth day after the date of deposit by such State or organization of the relevant instrument.

Article 39 Amendment

(1) After the expiry of five years from the entry into force of this Convention, a State Party may propose an amendment and file it with the Secretary-General of the United Nations, who shall thereupon communicate the proposed amendment to the States Parties and to the Conference of the Parties to the Convention for the purpose of considering and deciding on the proposal. The Conference of the Parties shall make every effort to achieve consensus on each amendment. If all efforts at consensus have been exhausted and no agreement has been reached, the amendment shall, as a last resort, require for its adoption a two-thirds majority vote of the States Parties present and voting at the meeting of the Conference of the Parties.

(2) Regional economic integration organizations, in matters within their competence, shall exercise their right to vote under this Article with a number of votes equal to the number of their member

States that are Parties to this Convention. Such organizations shall not exercise their right to vote if their member States exercise theirs and vice versa.

(3) An amendment adopted in accordance with paragraph (1) of this Article is subject to ratification, acceptance or approval by States Parties.

(4) An amendment adopted in accordance with paragraph (1) of this Article shall enter into force in respect of a State Party ninety days after the date of the deposit with the Secretary-General of the United Nations of an instrument of ratification, acceptance or approval of such amendment.

(5) When an amendment enters into force, it shall be binding on those States Parties which have expressed their consent to be bound by it. Other States Parties shall still be bound by the provisions of this Convention and any earlier amendments that they have ratified, accepted or approved.

Article 40 Denunciation

(1) A State Party may denounce this Convention by written notification to the Secretary-General of the United Nations. Such denunciation shall become effective one year after the date of receipt of the notification by the Secretary-General.

(2) A regional economic integration organization shall cease to be a Party to this Convention when all of its member States have denounced it.

(3) Denunciation of this Convention in accordance with paragraph (1) of this Article shall entail the denunciation of any Protocols thereto.

Article 41 Depositary and Languages

(1) The Secretary-General of the United Nations is designated depositary of this Convention.

(2) The original of this Convention, of which the Arabic, Chinese, English, French, Russian and Spanish texts are equally authentic, shall be deposited with the Secretary-General of the United Nations.

IN WITNESS WHEREOF, the undersigned plenipotentiaries, being duly authorized thereto by their respective Governments, have signed this Convention.

Reservations Applicable to Hong Kong

*China**

30 November 2012

* With the following declaration in respect of Hong Kong:

In accordance with the Basic Law of the Hong Kong Special Administrative Region of the People's Republic of China and after consultation with the Government of the Hong Kong Special Administrative Region (hereinafter as HKSAR), the application of the Convention to the HKSAR requires prior enactment of domestic legislation by the HKSAR. To this end, the Convention shall not apply to the HKSAR until the Government of the People's Republic of China notifies otherwise.

Further, in a communication received on 27 September 2006, the Government of China declared the following:

In accordance with the provisions of Article 153 of the Basic Law of the Hong Kong Special Administrative Region of the People's Republic of China, the Government of the People's Republic of China decides that the Convention shall apply to the Hong Kong Special Administrative Region of the People's Republic of China (hereafter referred to as HKSAR).

In accordance with the provisions of paragraph (13) of Article 18 of the Convention and for the application of the Convention to the HKSAR, the HKSAR designates the Secretary for Justice of the Department of Justice of the HKSAR as the Central Authority. (Address: 47/F High Block, Queensway Government Offices, 66 Queensway, Hong Kong). In accordance with the provisions of paragraph (14) of Article 18 of the Convention, Chinese or English is the only language acceptable to the HKSAR for the written requests for legal assistance.

[...]

2 With regard to Hong Kong Special Administrative Region, the Secretary for Justice of the Department of Justice of Hong Kong Special Administrative Region is designated as the competent authority for cooperation on surrender of fugitive offenders for the purpose of Article 16 of the Convention.

Address: 47/F High Block, Queensway Government Offices, 66 Queensway, Hong Kong.

INTERNATIONAL CONVENTION FOR THE SUPPRESSION OF THE FINANCING OF TERRORISM

(Adopted: 9 December 1999)

Preamble

The States Parties to this Convention,

Bearing in mind the purposes and principles of the Charter of the United Nations concerning the maintenance of international peace and security and the promotion of good-neighbourliness and friendly relations and cooperation among States,

Deeply concerned about the worldwide escalation of acts of terrorism in all its forms and manifestations,

Recalling the Declaration on the Occasion of the Fiftieth Anniversary of the United Nations, contained in General Assembly Resolution 50/6 of 24 October 1995,

Recalling also all the relevant General Assembly Resolutions on the matter, including Resolution 49/60 of 9 December 1994 and its Annex on the Declaration on Measures to Eliminate International Terrorism, in which the States Members of the United Nations solemnly reaffirmed their unequivocal condemnation of all acts, methods and practices of terrorism as criminal and unjustifiable, wherever and by whomever committed, including those which jeopardize the friendly relations among States and peoples and threaten the territorial integrity and security of States,

Noting that the Declaration on Measures to Eliminate International Terrorism also encouraged States to review urgently the scope of the existing international legal provisions on the prevention, repression and elimination of terrorism in all its forms and manifestations, with the aim of ensuring that there is a comprehensive legal framework covering all aspects of the matter,

Recalling General Assembly Resolution 51/210 of 17 December 1996, paragraph (3), subparagraph (f), in which the Assembly called upon all States to take steps to prevent and counteract, through appropriate domestic measures, the financing of terrorists and terrorist organizations, whether such financing is direct or indirect through organizations which also have or claim to have charitable, social or cultural goals or which are also engaged in unlawful activities such as illicit arms trafficking, drug dealing and racketeering, including the exploitation of persons for purposes of funding terrorist activities, and in particular to consider, where appropriate, adopting regulatory measures to prevent and counteract movements of funds suspected to be intended for terrorist purposes without impeding in any way the freedom of legitimate capital movements and to intensify the exchange of information concerning international movements of such funds,

Recalling also General Assembly Resolution 52/165 of 15 December 1997, in which the Assembly called upon States to consider, in particular, the implementation of the measures set out in paragraphs (3)(a) to (f) of its Resolution 51/210 of 17 December 1996,

Recalling further General Assembly Resolution 53/108 of 8 December 1998, in which the Assembly decided that the Ad Hoc Committee established by General Assembly Resolution 51/210 of 17 December 1996 should elaborate a draft international convention for the suppression of terrorist financing to supplement related existing international instruments,

Considering that the financing of terrorism is a matter of grave concern to the international community as a whole,

Noting that the number and seriousness of acts of international terrorism depend on the financing that terrorists may obtain,

Noting also that existing multilateral legal instruments do not expressly address such financing,

Being convinced of the urgent need to enhance international cooperation among States in devising and adopting effective measures for the prevention of the financing of terrorism, as well as for its suppression through the prosecution and punishment of its perpetrators,

Have agreed as follows:

Article 1

For the purposes of this Convention:

(1) AFunds@ means assets of every kind, whether tangible or intangible, movable or immovable, however acquired, and legal documents or instruments in any form, including electronic or digital, evidencing title to, or interest in, such assets, including, but not limited to, bank credits, travellers cheques, bank cheques, money orders, shares, securities, bonds, drafts, letters of credit.

(2) AA State or governmental facility@ means any permanent or temporary facility or conveyance that is used or occupied by representatives of a State, members of Government, the legislature or the judiciary or by officials or employees of a State or any other public authority or entity or by employees or officials of an intergovernmental organization in connection with their official duties.

(3) AProceeds@ means any funds derived from or obtained, directly or indirectly, through the commission of an offence set forth in Article 2.

Article 2

(1) Any person commits an offence within the meaning of this Convention if that person by any means, directly or indirectly, unlawfully and wilfully, provides or collects funds with the intention that they should be used or in the knowledge that they are to be used, in full or in part, in order to carry out:

(a) An act which constitutes an offence within the scope of and as defined in one of the treaties listed in the Annex; or

(b) Any other act intended to cause death or serious bodily injury to a civilian, or to any other person not taking an active part in the hostilities in a situation of armed conflict, when the purpose of such act, by its nature or context, is to intimidate a population, or to compel a government or an international organization to do or to abstain from doing any act.

(2)

(a) On depositing its instrument of ratification, acceptance, approval or accession, a State Party which is not a party to a treaty listed in the Annex may declare that, in the application of this Convention to the State Party, the treaty shall be deemed not to be included in the Annex referred to in paragraph (1), subparagraph (a). The declaration shall cease to have effect as soon as the treaty enters into force for the State Party, which shall notify the depositary of this fact;

(b) When a State Party ceases to be a party to a treaty listed in the Annex, it may make a declaration as provided for in this Article, with respect to that treaty.

(3) For an act to constitute an offence set forth in paragraph (1), it shall not be necessary that the funds were actually used to carry out an offence referred to in paragraph (1), subparagraphs (a) or (b).

(4) Any person also commits an offence if that person attempts to commit an offence as set forth in paragraph (1) of this Article.

(5) Any person also commits an offence if that person:

(a) Participates as an accomplice in an offence as set forth in paragraph (1) or (4) of this Article;

(b) Organizes or directs others to commit an offence as set forth in paragraph (1) or (4) of this Article;

(c) Contributes to the commission of one or more offences as set forth in paragraphs (1) or (4) of this Article by a group of persons acting with a common purpose. Such contribution shall be intentional and shall either:

(i) Be made with the aim of furthering the criminal activity or criminal purpose of the group, where such activity or purpose involves the commission of an offence as set forth in paragraph (1) of this Article; or

(ii) Be made in the knowledge of the intention of the group to commit an offence as set forth in paragraph (1) of this Article.

Article 3

This Convention shall not apply where the offence is committed within a single State, the alleged offender is a national of that State and is present in the territory of that State and no other State has a basis under Article 7, paragraph (1), or Article 7, paragraph (2), to exercise jurisdiction, except that the provisions of Articles 12 to 18 shall, as appropriate, apply in those cases.

Article 4

Each State Party shall adopt such measures as may be necessary:

(a) To establish as criminal offences under its domestic law the offences set forth in Article 2;

(b) To make those offences punishable by appropriate penalties which take into account the grave nature of the offences.

Article 5

(1) Each State Party, in accordance with its domestic legal principles, shall take the necessary measures to enable a legal entity located in its territory or organized under its laws to be held liable when a person responsible for the management or control of that legal entity has, in that capacity, committed an offence set forth in Article 2. Such liability may be criminal, civil or administrative.

(2) Such liability is incurred without prejudice to the criminal liability of individuals having committed the offences.

(3) Each State Party shall ensure, in particular, that legal entities liable in accordance with paragraph (1) above are subject to effective, proportionate and dissuasive criminal, civil or administrative sanctions. Such sanctions may include monetary sanctions.

Article 6

Each State Party shall adopt such measures as may be necessary, including, where appropriate, domestic legislation, to ensure that criminal acts within the scope of this Convention are under no circumstances justifiable by considerations of a political, philosophical, ideological, racial, ethnic, religious or other similar nature.

Article 7

(1) Each State Party shall take such measures as may be necessary to establish its jurisdiction over the offences set forth in Article 2 when:

(a) The offence is committed in the territory of that State;

(b) The offence is committed on board a vessel flying the flag of that State or an aircraft registered under the laws of that State at the time the offence is committed;

(c) The offence is committed by a national of that State.

(2) A State Party may also establish its jurisdiction over any such offence when:

(a) The offence was directed towards or resulted in the carrying out of an offence referred to in Article 2, paragraph (1), subparagraph (a) or (b), in the territory of or against a national of that State;

(b) The offence was directed towards or resulted in the carrying out of an offence referred to in Article 2, paragraph (1), subparagraph (a) or (b), against a State or government facility of that State abroad, including diplomatic or consular premises of that State;

(c) The offence was directed towards or resulted in an offence referred to in Article 2, paragraph (1), subparagraph (a) or (b), committed in an attempt to compel that State to do or abstain from doing any act;

(d) The offence is committed by a stateless person who has his or her habitual residence in the territory of that State;

(e) The offence is committed on board an aircraft which is operated by the Government of that State.

(3) Upon ratifying, accepting, approving or acceding to this Convention, each State Party shall notify the Secretary-General of the United Nations of the jurisdiction it has established in accordance with paragraph (2). Should any change take place, the State Party concerned shall immediately notify the Secretary-General.

(4) Each State Party shall likewise take such measures as may be necessary to establish its jurisdiction over the offences set forth in Article 2 in cases where the alleged offender is present in its territory and it does not extradite that person to any of the States Parties that have established their jurisdiction in accordance with paragraphs (1) or (2).

(5) When more than one State Party claims jurisdiction over the offences set forth in Article 2, the relevant States Parties shall strive to coordinate their actions appropriately, in particular concerning the conditions for prosecution and the modalities for mutual legal assistance.

(6) Without prejudice to the norms of general international law, this Convention does not exclude the exercise of any criminal jurisdiction established by a State Party in accordance with its domestic law.

Article 8

(1) Each State Party shall take appropriate measures, in accordance with its domestic legal principles, for the identification, detection and freezing or seizure of any funds used or allocated for the purpose of committing the offences set forth in Article 2 as well as the proceeds derived from such offences, for purposes of possible forfeiture.

(2) Each State Party shall take appropriate measures, in accordance with its domestic legal principles, for the forfeiture of funds used or allocated for the purpose of committing the offences set forth in Article 2 and the proceeds derived from such offences.

(3) Each State Party concerned may give consideration to concluding agreements on the sharing with other States Parties, on a regular or case-by-case basis, of the funds derived from the forfeitures referred to in this Article.

(4) Each State Party shall consider establishing mechanisms whereby the funds derived from the forfeitures referred to in this Article are utilized to compensate the victims of offences referred to in Article 2, paragraph (1), subparagraph (a) or (b), or their families.

(5) The provisions of this Article shall be implemented without prejudice to the rights of third parties acting in good faith.

Article 9

(1) Upon receiving information that a person who has committed or who is alleged to have committed an offence set forth in Article 2 may be present in its territory, the State Party concerned shall take such measures as may be necessary under its domestic law to investigate the facts contained in the information.

(2) Upon being satisfied that the circumstances so warrant, the State Party in whose territory the offender or alleged offender is present shall take the appropriate measures under its domestic law so as to ensure that person's presence for the purpose of prosecution or extradition.

(3) Any person regarding whom the measures referred to in paragraph (2) are being taken shall be entitled to:

  (a) Communicate without delay with the nearest appropriate representative of the State of which that person is a national or which is otherwise entitled to protect that person's rights or, if that person is a stateless person, the State in the territory of which that person habitually resides;

  (b) Be visited by a representative of that State;

  (c) Be informed of that person's rights under subparagraphs (a) and (b).

(4) The rights referred to in paragraph (3) shall be exercised in conformity with the laws and regulations of the State in the territory of which the offender or alleged offender is present, subject to the provision that the said laws and regulations must enable full effect to be given to the purposes for which the rights accorded under paragraph (3) are intended.

(5) The provisions of paragraphs (3) and (4) shall be without prejudice to the right of any State Party having a claim to jurisdiction in accordance with Article 7, paragraph (1), subparagraph (b), or paragraph (2), subparagraph (b), to invite the International Committee of the Red Cross to communicate with and visit the alleged offender.

(6) When a State Party, pursuant to the present Article, has taken a person into custody, it shall immediately notify, directly or through the Secretary-General of the United Nations, the States Parties which have established jurisdiction in accordance with Article 7, paragraph (1) or (2), and, if it considers it advisable, any other interested States Parties, of the fact that such person is in custody and of the circumstances which warrant that persons detention. The State which makes the investigation contemplated in paragraph (1) shall promptly inform the said States Parties of its findings and shall indicate whether it intends to exercise jurisdiction.

Article 10

(1) The State Party in the territory of which the alleged offender is present shall, in cases to which Article 7 applies, if it does not extradite that person, be obliged, without exception whatsoever and whether or not the offence was committed in its territory, to submit the case without undue delay to its competent authorities for the purpose of prosecution, through proceedings in accordance with the laws of that State. Those authorities shall take their decision in the same manner as in the case of any other offence of a grave nature under the law of that State.

(2) Whenever a State Party is permitted under its domestic law to extradite or otherwise surrender one of its nationals only upon the condition that the person will be returned to that State to serve the sentence imposed as a result of the trial or proceeding for which the extradition or surrender of the person was sought, and this State and the State seeking the extradition of the person agree with this

option and other terms they may deem appropriate, such a conditional extradition or surrender shall be sufficient to discharge the obligation set forth in paragraph (1).

Article 11

(1) The offences set forth in Article 2 shall be deemed to be included as extraditable offences in any extradition treaty existing between any of the States Parties before the entry into force of this Convention. States Parties undertake to include such offences as extraditable offences in every extradition treaty to be subsequently concluded between them.

(2) When a State Party which makes extradition conditional on the existence of a treaty receives a request for extradition from another State Party with which it has no extradition treaty, the requested State Party may, at its option, consider this Convention as a legal basis for extradition in respect of the offences set forth in Article 2. Extradition shall be subject to the other conditions provided by the law of the requested State.

(3) States Parties which do not make extradition conditional on the existence of a treaty shall recognize the offences set forth in Article 2 as extraditable offences between themselves, subject to the conditions provided by the law of the requested State.

(4) If necessary, the offences set forth in Article 2 shall be treated, for the purposes of extradition between States Parties, as if they had been committed not only in the place in which they occurred but also in the territory of the States that have established jurisdiction in accordance with Article 7, paragraphs (1) and (2).

(5) The provisions of all extradition treaties and arrangements between States Parties with regard to offences set forth in Article 2 shall be deemed to be modified as between States Parties to the extent that they are incompatible with this Convention.

Article 12

(1) States Parties shall afford one another the greatest measure of assistance in connection with criminal investigations or criminal or extradition proceedings in respect of the offences set forth in Article 2, including assistance in obtaining evidence in their possession necessary for the proceedings.

(2) States Parties may not refuse a request for mutual legal assistance on the ground of bank secrecy.

(3) The requesting Party shall not transmit nor use information or evidence furnished by the requested Party for investigations, prosecutions or proceedings other than those stated in the request without the prior consent of the requested Party.

(4) Each State Party may give consideration to establishing mechanisms to share with other States Parties information or evidence needed to establish criminal, civil or administrative liability pursuant to Article 5.

(5) States Parties shall carry out their obligations under paragraphs (1) and (2) in conformity with any treaties or other arrangements on mutual legal assistance or information exchange that may exist between them. In the absence of such treaties or arrangements, States Parties shall afford one another assistance in accordance with their domestic law.

Article 13

None of the offences set forth in Article 2 shall be regarded, for the purposes of extradition or mutual legal assistance, as a fiscal offence. Accordingly, States Parties may not refuse a request for extradition or for mutual legal assistance on the sole ground that it concerns a fiscal offence.

Article 14

None of the offences set forth in Article 2 shall be regarded for the purposes of extradition or mutual legal assistance as a political offence or as an offence connected with a political offence or as an offence inspired by political motives. Accordingly, a request for extradition or for mutual legal assistance based on such an offence may not be refused on the sole ground that it concerns a political offence or an offence connected with a political offence or an offence inspired by political motives.

Article 15

Nothing in this Convention shall be interpreted as imposing an obligation to extradite or to afford mutual legal assistance, if the requested State Party has substantial grounds for believing that the request for extradition for offences set forth in Article 2 or for mutual legal assistance with respect to such offences has been made for the purpose of prosecuting or punishing a person on account of that person's race, religion, nationality, ethnic origin or political opinion or that compliance with the request would cause prejudice to that person's position for any of these reasons.

Article 16

(1) A person who is being detained or is serving a sentence in the territory of one State Party whose presence in another State Party is requested for purposes of identification, testimony or otherwise providing assistance in obtaining evidence for the investigation or prosecution of offences set forth in Article 2 may be transferred if the following conditions are met:

(a) The person freely gives his or her informed consent;

(b) The competent authorities of both States agree, subject to such conditions as those States may deem appropriate.

(2) For the purposes of the present Article:

(a) The State to which the person is transferred shall have the authority and obligation to keep the person transferred in custody, unless otherwise requested or authorized by the State from which the person was transferred;

(b) The State to which the person is transferred shall without delay implement its obligation to return the person to the custody of the State from which the person was transferred as agreed beforehand, or as otherwise agreed, by the competent authorities of both States;

(c) The State to which the person is transferred shall not require the State from which the person was transferred to initiate extradition proceedings for the return of the person;

(d) The person transferred shall receive credit for service of the sentence being served in the State from which he or she was transferred for time spent in the custody of the State to which he or she was transferred.

(3) Unless the State Party from which a person is to be transferred in accordance with the present Article so agrees, that person, whatever his or her nationality, shall not be prosecuted or detained or subjected to any other restriction of his or her personal liberty in the territory of the State to which that person is transferred in respect of acts or convictions anterior to his or her departure from the territory of the State from which such person was transferred.

Article 17

Any person who is taken into custody or regarding whom any other measures are taken or proceedings are carried out pursuant to this Convention shall be guaranteed fair treatment, including enjoyment of all rights and guarantees in conformity with the law of the State in the territory of which that person is present and applicable provisions of international law, including international human rights law.

Article 18

(1) States Parties shall cooperate in the prevention of the offences set forth in Article 2 by taking all practicable measures, inter alia, by adapting their domestic legislation, if necessary, to prevent and counter preparations in their respective territories for the commission of those offences within or outside their territories, including:

(a) Measures to prohibit in their territories illegal activities of persons and organizations that knowingly encourage, instigate, organize or engage in the commission of offences set forth in Article 2;

(b) Measures requiring financial institutions and other professions involved in financial transactions to utilize the most efficient measures available for the identification of their usual or occasional customers, as well as customers in whose interest accounts are opened, and to pay special attention to unusual or suspicious transactions and report transactions suspected of stemming from a criminal activity. For this purpose, States Parties shall consider:

(i) Adopting regulations prohibiting the opening of accounts the holders or beneficiaries of which are unidentified or unidentifiable, and measures to ensure that such institutions verify the identity of the real owners of such transactions;

(ii) With respect to the identification of legal entities, requiring financial institutions, when necessary, to take measures to verify the legal existence and the structure of the customer by obtaining, either from a public register or from the customer or both, proof of incorporation, including information concerning the customer's name, legal form, address, directors and provisions regulating the power to bind the entity;

(iii) Adopting regulations imposing on financial institutions the obligation to report promptly to the competent authorities all complex, unusual large transactions and unusual patterns of transactions, which have no apparent economic or obviously lawful purpose, without fear of assuming criminal or civil liability for breach of any restriction on disclosure of information if they report their suspicions in good faith;

(iv) Requiring financial institutions to maintain, for at least five years, all necessary records on transactions, both domestic or international.

(2) States Parties shall further cooperate in the prevention of offences set forth in Article 2 by considering:

(a) Measures for the supervision, including, for exampl18e, the licensing, of all money-transmission agencies;

(b) Feasible measures to detect or monitor the physical cross-border transportation of cash and bearer negotiable instruments, subject to strict safeguards to ensure proper use of information and without impeding in any way the freedom of capital movements.

(3) States Parties shall further cooperate in the prevention of the offences set forth in Article 2 by exchanging accurate and verified information in accordance with their domestic law and coordinating administrative and other measures taken, as appropriate, to prevent the commission of offences set forth in Article 2, in particular by:

(a) Establishing and maintaining channels of communication between their competent agencies and services to facilitate the secure and rapid exchange of information concerning all aspects of offences set forth in Article 2;

(b) Cooperating with one another in conducting inquiries, with respect to the offences set forth in Article 2, concerning:

(i) The identity, whereabouts and activities of persons in respect of whom reasonable suspicion exists that they are involved in such offences;

(ii) The movement of funds relating to the commission of such offences.

(4) States Parties may exchange information through the International Criminal Police Organization (Interpol).

Article 19

The State Party where the alleged offender is prosecuted shall, in accordance with its domestic law or applicable procedures, communicate the final outcome of the proceedings to the Secretary-General of the United Nations, who shall transmit the information to the other States Parties.

Article 20

The States Parties shall carry out their obligations under this Convention in a manner consistent with the principles of sovereign equality and territorial integrity of States and that of non-intervention in the domestic affairs of other States.

Article 21

Nothing in this Convention shall affect other rights, obligations and responsibilities of States and individuals under international law, in particular the purposes of the Charter of the United Nations, international humanitarian law and other relevant conventions.

Article 22

Nothing in this Convention entitles a State Party to undertake in the territory of another State Party the exercise of jurisdiction or performance of functions which are exclusively reserved for the authorities of that other State Party by its domestic law.

Article 23

(1) The Annex may be amended by the addition of relevant treaties that:

   (a) Are open to the participation of all States;

   (b) Have entered into force;

   (c) Have been ratified, accepted, approved or acceded to by at least twenty-two States Parties to the present Convention.

(2) After the entry into force of this Convention, any State Party may propose such an amendment. Any proposal for an amendment shall be communicated to the depositary in written form. The depositary shall notify proposals that meet the requirements of paragraph (1) to all States Parties and seek their views on whether the proposed amendment should be adopted.

(3) The proposed amendment shall be deemed adopted unless one third of the States Parties object to it by a written notification not later than 180 days after its circulation.

(4) The adopted amendment to the Annex shall enter into force 30 days after the deposit of the twenty-second instrument of ratification, acceptance or approval of such amendment for all those States Parties having deposited such an instrument. For each State Party ratifying, accepting or approving the amendment after the deposit of the twenty-second instrument, the amendment shall enter into force on the thirtieth day after deposit by such State Party of its instrument of ratification, acceptance or approval.

Article 24

(1) Any dispute between two or more States Parties concerning the interpretation or application of this Convention which cannot be settled through negotiation within a reasonable time shall, at the request of one of them, be submitted to arbitration. If, within six months from the date of the request for arbitration, the parties are unable to agree on the organization of the arbitration, any one of those parties may refer the dispute to the International Court of Justice, by application, in conformity with the Statute of the Court.

(2) Each State may at the time of signature, ratification, acceptance or approval of this Convention or accession thereto declare that it does not consider itself bound by paragraph (1). The other States Parties shall not be bound by paragraph (1) with respect to any State Party which has made such a reservation.

(3) Any State which has made a reservation in accordance with paragraph (2) may at any time withdraw that reservation by notification to the Secretary-General of the United Nations.

Article 25

(1) This Convention shall be open for signature by all States from 10 January 2000 to 31 December 2001 at United Nations Headquarters in New York.

(2) This Convention is subject to ratification, acceptance or approval. The instruments of ratification, acceptance or approval shall be deposited with the Secretary-General of the United Nations.

(3) This Convention shall be open to accession by any State. The instruments of accession shall be deposited with the Secretary-General of the United Nations.

Article 26

(1) This Convention shall enter into force on the thirtieth day following the date of the deposit of the twenty-second instrument of ratification, acceptance, approval or accession with the Secretary-General of the United Nations.

(2) For each State ratifying, accepting, approving or acceding to the Convention after the deposit of the twenty-second instrument of ratification, acceptance, approval or accession, the Convention shall enter into force on the thirtieth day after deposit by such State of its instrument of ratification, acceptance, approval or accession.

Article 27

(1) Any State Party may denounce this Convention by written notification to the Secretary-General of the United Nations.

(2) Denunciation shall take effect one year following the date on which notification is received by the Secretary-General of the United Nations.

Article 28

The original of this Convention, of which the Arabic, Chinese, English, French, Russian and Spanish texts are equally authentic, shall be deposited with the Secretary-General of the United Nations who shall send certified copies thereof to all States.

IN WITNESS WHEREOF, the undersigned, being duly authorized thereto by their respective Governments, have signed this Convention, opened for signature at United Nations Headquarters in New York on 10 January 2000.

Annex

(1) Convention for the Suppression of Unlawful Seizure of Aircraft, done at The Hague on 16 December 1970.

(2) Convention for the Suppression of Unlawful Acts against the Safety of Civil Aviation, done at Montreal on 23 September 1971.

(3) Convention on the Prevention and Punishment of Crimes against Internationally Protected Persons, including Diplomatic Agents, adopted by the General Assembly of the United Nations on 14 December 1973.

(4) International Convention against the Taking of Hostages, adopted by the General Assembly of the United Nations on 17 December 1979.

(5) Convention on the Physical Protection of Nuclear Material, adopted at Vienna on 3 March 1980.

(6) Protocol for the Suppression of Unlawful Acts of Violence at Airports Serving International Civil Aviation, supplementary to the Convention for the Suppression of Unlawful Acts against the Safety of Civil Aviation, done at Montreal on 24 February 1988.

(7) Convention for the Suppression of Unlawful Acts against the Safety of Maritime Navigation, done at Rome on 10 March 1988.

(8) Protocol for the Suppression of Unlawful Acts against the Safety of Fixed Platforms located on the Continental Shelf, done at Rome on 10 March 1988.

(9) International Convention for the Suppression of Terrorist Bombings, adopted by the General Assembly of the United Nations on 15 December 1997.

Reservations Applicable to Hong Kong

China *

Signed on 13 November 2001

Ratified on 19 April 2006

In accordance with paragraph (3) of Article 7 of the Convention, the People's Republic of China has established the jurisdiction over five offences stipulated in paragraph (2) of Article 7 of the Convention, but this jurisdiction shall not apply to the Hong Kong Special Administrative Region of the People's Republic of China.

* With a communication with respect to Hong Kong:

1. In accordance with the provisions of Article 153 of the Basic Law of the Hong Kong Special Administrative Region of the People's Republic of China, the Government of the People's Republic of China decides that the Convention shall apply to the Hong Kong Special Administrative Region of the People's Republic of China.
2. The reservation made by the People's Republic of China on paragraph (1) of Article 24 of the Convention shall apply to the Hong Kong Special Administrative Region of the People's Republic of China.
3. The jurisdiction over five offences established by the People's Republic of China in accordance with paragraph (2) of Article 7 of the Convention shall not apply to the Hong Kong Special Administrative Region of the People's Republic of China.

SECTION III
LABOUR RIGHTS

This Section includes eight international instruments related to labour rights as applied in Hong Kong. They are:

(1) The Maternity Protection Convention

(2) The Forced Labour Convention

(3) The Freedom of Association and Protection of the Right to Organize Convention

(4) The Right to Organize and Collective Bargaining Convention

(5) The Abolition of Forced Labour Convention

(6) The Minimum Age Convention

(7) The Worst Forms of Child Labour Convention

(8) The ILO Declaration of Fundamental Principles and Rights at Work

MATERNITY PROTECTION CONVENTION, 1919 (No. 3)

(Adopted: 29 November 1919; Entry into force: 13 June 1921; Applied to Hong Kong: 1 July 1997)

Preamble

The General Conference of the International Labour Organization,

Having been convened at Washington by the Government of the United States of America on the 29th day of October 1919, and

Having decided upon the adoption of certain proposals with regard to "women's employment, before and after childbirth, including the question of maternity benefit", which is part of the third item in the agenda for the Washington meeting of the Conference, and

Having determined that these proposals shall take the form of an international Convention,

adopts the following Convention, which may be cited as the Maternity Protection Convention, 1919, for ratification by the Members of the International Labour Organization in accordance with the provisions of the Constitution of the International Labour Organization:

Article 1

(1) For the purpose of this Convention, the term *industrial undertaking* includes particularly —

(a) mines, quarries, and other works for the extraction of minerals from the earth;

(b) industries in which articles are manufactured, altered, cleaned, repaired, ornamented, finished, adapted for sale, broken up or demolished, or in which materials are transformed; including shipbuilding and the generation, transformation, and transmission of electricity or motive power of any kind;

(c) construction, reconstruction, maintenance, repair, alteration, or demolition of any building, railway, tramway, harbour, dock, pier, canal, inland waterway, road, tunnel, bridge, viaduct, sewer, drain, well, telegraphic or telephonic installation, electrical undertaking, gas work, water work, or other work of construction, as well as the preparation for or laying the foundation of any such work or structure;

(d) transport of passengers or goods by road, rail, sea, or inland waterway, including the handling of goods at docks, quays, wharves, and warehouses, but excluding transport by hand.

(2) For the purpose of this Convention, the term *commercial undertaking* includes any place where articles are sold or where commerce is carried on.

(3) The competent authority in each country shall define the line of division which separates industry and commerce from agriculture.

Article 2

For the purpose of this Convention, the term *woman* signifies any female person, irrespective of age or nationality, whether married or unmarried, and the term *child* signifies any child whether legitimate or illegitimate.

Article 3

In any public or private industrial or commercial undertaking, or in any branch thereof, other than an undertaking in which only members of the same family are employed, a woman —

(a) shall not be permitted to work during the six weeks following her confinement;

(b) shall have the right to leave her work if she produces a medical certificate stating that her confinement will probably take place within six weeks;

(c) shall, while she is absent from her work in pursuance of paragraphs (a) and (b), be paid benefits sufficient for the full and healthy maintenance of herself and her child, provided either out of public funds or by means of a system of insurance, the exact amount of which shall be determined by the competent authority in each country, and as an additional benefit shall be entitled to free attendance by a doctor or certified midwife; no mistake of the medical adviser in estimating the date of confinement shall preclude a woman from receiving these benefits from the date of the medical certificate up to the date on which the confinement actually takes place;

(d) shall in any case, if she is nursing her child, be allowed half an hour twice a day during her working hours for this purpose.

Article 4

Where a woman is absent from her work in accordance with paragraph (a) or (b) of Article 3 of this Convention, or remains absent from her work for a longer period as a result of illness medically certified to arise out of pregnancy or confinement and rendering her unfit for work, it shall not be lawful, until her absence shall have exceeded a maximum period to be fixed by the competent authority in each country, for her employer to give her notice of dismissal during such absence, nor to give her notice of dismissal at such a time that the notice would expire during such absence.

Article 5

The formal ratifications of this Convention, under the conditions set forth in the Constitution of the International Labour Organization, shall be communicated to the Director-General of the International Labour Office for registration.

Article 6

(1) Each Member of the International Labour Organization which ratifies this Convention engages to apply it to its colonies, protectorates and possessions which are not fully self-governing —

(a) except where owing to the local conditions its provisions are inapplicable; or

(b) subject to such modifications as may be necessary to adapt its provisions to local conditions.

(2) Each Member shall notify to the International Labour Office the action taken in respect of each of its colonies, protectorates, and possessions which are not fully self-governing.

Article 7

As soon as the ratifications of two Members of the International Labour Organization have been registered with the International Labour Office, the Director-General of the International Labour Office shall so notify all the Members of the International Labour Organization.

Article 8

This Convention shall come into force at the date on which such notification is issued by the Director-General of the International Labour Office, but it shall then be binding only upon those Members which have registered their ratifications with the International Labour Office. Thereafter this Convention will come into force for any other Member at the date on which its ratification is registered with the International Labour Office.

Article 9

Each Member which ratifies this Convention agrees to bring its provisions into operation not later than 1 July 1922, and to take such action as may be necessary to make these provisions effective.

Article 10

A Member which has ratified this Convention may denounce it after the expiration of ten years from the date on which the Convention first comes into force, by an act communicated to the Director-General of the International Labour Office for registration. Such denunciation shall not take effect until one year after the date on which it is registered with the International Labour Office.

Article 11

At such times as it may consider necessary the Governing Body of the International Labour Office shall present to the General Conference a report on the working of this Convention and shall examine the desirability of placing on the agenda of the Conference the question of its revision in whole or in part.

Article 12

The French and English texts of this Convention shall both be authentic.

FORCED LABOUR CONVENTION, 1930 (No. 29)

Adopted: 28 June 1930; Entry into force: 1 May 1932; Applied to Hong Kong: 1 July 1997)

Preamble

The General Conference of the International Labour Organization,

Having been convened at Geneva by the Governing Body of the International Labour Office, and having met in its Fourteenth Session on 10 June 1930, and

Having decided upon the adoption of certain proposals with regard to forced or compulsory labour, which is included in the first item on the agenda of the Session, and

Having determined that these proposals shall take the form of an international Convention,

adopts this twenty-eighth day of June of the year one thousand nine hundred and thirty the following Convention, which may be cited as the Forced Labour Convention, 1930, for ratification by the Members of the International Labour Organization in accordance with the provisions of the Constitution of the International Labour Organization:

Article 1

(1) Each Member of the International Labour Organization which ratifies this Convention undertakes to suppress the use of forced or compulsory labour in all its forms within the shortest possible period.

(2) [deleted pursuant to Article 7 of the Protocol of 2014 to the Forced Labour Convention, 1930]

(3) [deleted pursuant to Article 7 of the Protocol of 2014 to the Forced Labour Convention, 1930]

Article 2

(1) For the purposes of this Convention the term *forced or compulsory labour* shall mean all work or service which is exacted from any person under the menace of any penalty and for which the said person has not offered himself voluntarily.

(2) Nevertheless, for the purposes of this Convention, the term *forced or compulsory labour* shall not include—

(a) any work or service exacted in virtue of compulsory military service laws for work of a purely military character;

(b) any work or service which forms part of the normal civic obligations of the citizens of a fully self-governing country;

(c) any work or service exacted from any person as a consequence of a conviction in a court of law, provided that the said work or service is carried out under the supervision and control of a public authority and that the said person is not hired to or placed at the disposal of private individuals, companies or associations;

(d) any work or service exacted in cases of emergency, that is to say, in the event of war or of a calamity or threatened calamity, such as fire, flood, famine, earthquake, violent epidemic or epizootic diseases, invasion by animal, insect or vegetable pests, and in general any circumstance that would endanger the existence or the well-being of the whole or part of the population;

(e) minor communal services of a kind which, being performed by the members of the community in the direct interest of the said community, can therefore be considered as normal civic obligations incumbent upon the members of the community, provided that the members of the community or their direct representatives shall have the right to be consulted in regard to the need for such services.

Articles 3 to 24

[deleted pursuant to Article 7 of the Protocol of 2014 to the Forced Labour Convention, 1930]

Article 25

The illegal exaction of forced or compulsory labour shall be punishable as a penal offence, and it shall be an obligation on any Member ratifying this Convention to ensure that the penalties imposed by law are really adequate and are strictly enforced.

Article 26*

1 Each Member of the International Labour Organization which ratifies this Convention undertakes to apply it to the territories placed under its sovereignty, jurisdiction, protection, suzerainty,

* To avoid confusion, the original numbering scheme used in this Article has been retained.

tutelage or authority, so far as it has the right to accept obligations affecting matters of internal jurisdiction; provided that, if such Member may desire to take advantage of the provisions of Article 35 of the Constitution of the International Labour Organization, it shall append to its ratification a declaration stating —

(1) the territories to which it intends to apply the provisions of this Convention without modification;

(2) the territories to which it intends to apply the provisions of this Convention with modifications, together with details of the said modifications;

(3) the territories in respect of which it reserves its decision.

2 The aforesaid declaration shall be deemed to be an integral part of the ratification and shall have the force of ratification. It shall be open to any Member, by a subsequent declaration, to cancel in whole or in part the reservations made, in pursuance of the provisions of subparagraphs (2) and (3) of this Article, in the original declaration.

Article 27

The formal ratifications of this Convention under the conditions set forth in the Constitution of the International Labour Organization shall be communicated to the Director-General of the International Labour Office for registration.

Article 28

(1) This Convention shall be binding only upon those Members whose ratifications have been registered with the International Labour Office.

(2) It shall come into force twelve months after the date on which the ratifications of two Members of the International Labour Organization have been registered with the Director-General.

(3) Thereafter, this Convention shall come into force for any Member twelve months after the date on which the ratification has been registered.

Article 29

As soon as the ratifications of two Members of the International Labour Organization have been registered with the International Labour Office, the Director-General of the International Labour Office shall so notify all the Members of the International Labour Organization. He shall likewise notify them of the registration of ratifications which may be communicated subsequently by other Members of the Organization.

Article 30

(1) A Member which has ratified this Convention may denounce it after the expiration of ten years from the date on which the Convention first comes into force, by an act communicated to the Director-General of the International Labour Office for registration. Such denunciation shall not take effect until one year after the date on which it is registered with the International Labour Office.

(2) Each Member which has ratified this Convention and which does not, within the year following the expiration of the period of ten years mentioned in the preceding paragraph, exercise the right of denunciation provided for in this Article, will be bound for another period of five years and, thereafter, may denounce this Convention at the expiration of each period of five years under the terms provided for in this Article.

Article 31

At such times as it may consider necessary the Governing Body of the International Labour Office shall present to the General Conference a report on the working of this Convention and shall examine the desirability of placing on the agenda of the Conference the question of its revision in whole or in part.

Article 32

(1) Should the Conference adopt a new Convention revising this Convention in whole or in part, the ratification by a Member of the new revising Convention shall ipso jure involve denunciation of this Convention without any requirement of delay, notwithstanding the provisions of Article 30 above, if and when the new revising Convention shall have come into force.

(2) As from the date of the coming into force of the new revising Convention, the present Convention shall cease to be open to ratification by the Members.

(3) Nevertheless, this Convention shall remain in force in its actual form and content for those Members which have ratified it but have not ratified the revising Convention.

Article 33

The French and English texts of this Convention shall both be authentic.

Protocol of 2014 to the Forced Labour Convention, 1930

(Adopted: 11 June 2014; Entry into force: 9 November 2016)

Preamble

The General Conference of the International Labour Organization,

Having been convened at Geneva by the Governing Body of the International Labour Office, and having met in its 103rd Session on 28 May 2014, and

Recognizing that the prohibition of forced or compulsory labour forms part of the body of fundamental rights, and that forced or compulsory labour violates the human rights and dignity of millions of women and men, girls and boys, contributes to the perpetuation of poverty and stands in the way of the achievement of decent work for all, and

Recognizing the vital role played by the Forced Labour Convention, 1930 (No. 29), hereinafter referred to as "the Convention", and the Abolition of Forced Labour Convention, 1957 (No. 105), in combating all forms of forced or compulsory labour, but that gaps in their implementation call for additional measures, and

Recalling that the definition of forced or compulsory labour under Article 2 of the Convention covers forced or compulsory labour in all its forms and manifestations and is applicable to all human beings without distinction, and

Emphasizing the urgency of eliminating forced and compulsory labour in all its forms and manifestations, and

Recalling the obligation of Members that have ratified the Convention to make forced or compulsory labour punishable as a penal offence, and to ensure that the penalties imposed by law are really adequate and are strictly enforced, and

Noting that the transitional period provided for in the Convention has expired, and the provisions of Article 1, paragraphs (2) and (3), and Articles 3 to 24 are no longer applicable, and

Recognizing that the context and forms of forced or compulsory labour have changed and trafficking in persons for the purposes of forced or compulsory labour, which may involve sexual exploitation, is the subject of growing international concern and requires urgent action for its effective elimination, and

Noting that there is an increased number of workers who are in forced or compulsory labour in the private economy, that certain sectors of the economy are particularly vulnerable, and that certain groups of workers have a higher risk of becoming victims of forced or compulsory labour, especially migrants, and

Noting that the effective and sustained suppression of forced or compulsory labour contributes to ensuring fair competition among employers as well as protection for workers, and

Recalling the relevant international labour standards, including, in particular, the Freedom of Association and Protection of the Right to Organize Convention, 1948 (No. 87), the Right to Organize and Collective Bargaining Convention, 1949 (No. 98), the Equal Remuneration Convention, 1951 (No. 100), the Discrimination (Employment and Occupation) Convention, 1958 (No. 111), the Minimum Age Convention, 1973 (No. 138), the Worst Forms of Child Labour Convention, 1999 (No. 182), the Migration for Employment Convention (Revised), 1949 (No. 97), the Migrant Workers (Supplementary Provisions) Convention, 1975 (No. 143), the Domestic Workers Convention, 2011 (No. 189), the Private Employment Agencies Convention, 1997 (No. 181), the Labour Inspection Convention, 1947 (No. 81), the Labour Inspection (Agriculture) Convention, 1969 (No. 129), as well as the ILO Declaration on Fundamental Principles and Rights at Work (1998), and the ILO Declaration on Social Justice for a Fair Globalization (2008), and

Noting other relevant international instruments, in particular the Universal Declaration of Human Rights (1948), the International Covenant on Civil and Political Rights (1966), the International Covenant on Economic, Social and Cultural Rights (1966), the Slavery Convention (1926), the Supplementary Convention on the Abolition of Slavery, the Slave Trade, and Institutions and Practices Similar to Slavery (1956), the United Nations Convention against Transnational Organized Crime (2000), the Protocol to Prevent, Suppress and Punish Trafficking in Persons, especially Women and Children (2000), the Protocol against the Smuggling of Migrants by Land, Sea and Air (2000), the International Convention on the Protection of the Rights of All Migrant Workers and Members of Their Families (1990), the Convention against Torture and Other Cruel, Inhuman or Degrading Treatment or Punishment (1984), the Convention on the Elimination of All Forms of Discrimination against Women (1979), and the Convention on the Rights of Persons with Disabilities (2006), and

Having decided upon the adoption of certain proposals to address gaps in implementation of the Convention, and reaffirmed that measures of prevention, protection, and remedies, such as compensation and rehabilitation, are necessary to achieve the effective and sustained suppression of forced or compulsory labour, pursuant to the fourth item on the agenda of the session, and

Having determined that these proposals shall take the form of a Protocol to the Convention;

adopts this eleventh day of June two thousand and fourteen the following Protocol, which may be cited as the Protocol of 2014 to the Forced Labour Convention, 1930.

Article 1

(1) In giving effect to its obligations under the Convention to suppress forced or compulsory labour, each Member shall take effective measures to prevent and eliminate its use, to provide to victims protection and access to appropriate and effective remedies, such as compensation, and to sanction the perpetrators of forced or compulsory labour.

(2) Each Member shall develop a national policy and plan of action for the effective and sustained suppression of forced or compulsory labour in consultation with employers' and workers' organizations, which shall involve systematic action by the competent authorities and, as appropriate, in coordination with employers' and workers' organizations, as well as with other groups concerned.

(3) The definition of forced or compulsory labour contained in the Convention is reaffirmed, and therefore the measures referred to in this Protocol shall include specific action against trafficking in persons for the purposes of forced or compulsory labour.

Article 2

The measures to be taken for the prevention of forced or compulsory labour shall include:

(a) educating and informing people, especially those considered to be particularly vulnerable, in order to prevent their becoming victims of forced or compulsory labour;

(b) educating and informing employers, in order to prevent their becoming involved in forced or compulsory labour practices;

(c) undertaking efforts to ensure that:

 (i) the coverage and enforcement of legislation relevant to the prevention of forced or compulsory labour, including labour law as appropriate, apply to all workers and all sectors of the economy; and

 (ii) labour inspection services and other services responsible for the implementation of this legislation are strengthened;

(d) protecting persons, particularly migrant workers, from possible abusive and fraudulent practices during the recruitment and placement process;

(e) supporting due diligence by both the public and private sectors to prevent and respond to risks of forced or compulsory labour; and

(f) addressing the root causes and factors that heighten the risks of forced or compulsory labour.

Article 3

Each Member shall take effective measures for the identification, release, protection, recovery and rehabilitation of all victims of forced or compulsory labour, as well as the provision of other forms of assistance and support.

Article 4

(1) Each Member shall ensure that all victims of forced or compulsory labour, irrespective of their presence or legal status in the national territory, have access to appropriate and effective remedies, such as compensation.

(2) Each Member shall, in accordance with the basic principles of its legal system, take the necessary measures to ensure that competent authorities are entitled not to prosecute or impose penalties on victims of forced or compulsory labour for their involvement in unlawful activities which they have been compelled to commit as a direct consequence of being subjected to forced or compulsory labour.

Article 5

Members shall cooperate with each other to ensure the prevention and elimination of all forms of forced or compulsory labour.

Article 6

The measures taken to apply the provisions of this Protocol and of the Convention shall be determined by national laws or regulations or by the competent authority, after consultation with the organizations of employers and workers concerned.

Article 7

The transitional provisions of Article 1, paragraphs (2) and (3), and Articles 3 to 24 of the Convention shall be deleted.

Article 8

(1) A Member may ratify this Protocol at the same time as or at any time after its ratification of the Convention, by communicating its formal ratification to the Director-General of the International Labour Office for registration.

(2) The Protocol shall come into force twelve months after the date on which ratifications of two Members have been registered by the Director-General. Thereafter, this Protocol shall come into force for a Member twelve months after the date on which its ratification is registered and the

Convention shall be binding on the Member concerned with the addition of Articles 1 to 7 of this Protocol.

Article 9

(1) A Member which has ratified this Protocol may denounce it whenever the Convention is open to denunciation in accordance with its Article 30, by an act communicated to the Director-General of the International Labour Office for registration.

(2) Denunciation of the Convention in accordance with its Articles 30 or 32 shall ipso jure involve the denunciation of this Protocol.

(3) Any denunciation in accordance with paragraphs (1) or (2) of this Article shall not take effect until one year after the date on which it is registered.

Article 10

(1) The Director-General of the International Labour Office shall notify all Members of the International Labour Organization of the registration of all ratifications, declarations and denunciations communicated by the Members of the Organization.

(2) When notifying the Members of the Organization of the registration of the second ratification, the Director-General shall draw the attention of the Members of the Organization to the date upon which the Protocol shall come into force.

Article 11

The Director-General of the International Labour Office shall communicate to the Secretary-General of the United Nations, for registration in accordance with Article 102 of the Charter of the United Nations, full particulars of all ratifications, declarations and denunciations registered by the Director-General.

Article 12

The English and French versions of the text of this Protocol are equally authoritative.

FREEDOM OF ASSOCIATION AND PROTECTION OF THE RIGHT TO ORGANIZE CONVENTION, 1948 (No. 87)

(Adopted: 9 July 1948; Entry into force: 4 July 1950; Applied to Hong Kong: 1 July 1997)

Preamble

The General Conference of the International Labour Organization,

Having been convened at San Francisco by the Governing Body of the International Labour Office, and having met in its Thirty-first Session on 17 June 1948;

Having decided to adopt, in the form of a Convention, certain proposals concerning freedom of association and protection of the right to organize, which is the seventh item on the agenda of the session;

Considering that the Preamble to the Constitution of the International Labour Organization declares "recognition of the principle of freedom of association" to be a means of improving conditions of labour and of establishing peace;

Considering that the Declaration of Philadelphia reaffirms that "freedom of expression and of association are essential to sustained progress";

Considering that the International Labour Conference, at its Thirtieth Session, unanimously adopted the principles which should form the basis for international regulation;

Considering that the General Assembly of the United Nations, at its Second Session, endorsed these principles and requested the International Labour Organization to continue every effort in order that it may be possible to adopt one or several international Conventions;

adopts this ninth day of July of the year one thousand nine hundred and forty-eight the following Convention, which may be cited as the Freedom of Association and Protection of the Right to Organize Convention, 1948:

Part I Freedom of Association

Article 1

Each Member of the International Labour Organization for which this Convention is in force undertakes to give effect to the following provisions.

Article 2

Workers and employers, without distinction whatsoever, shall have the right to establish and, subject only to the rules of the organization concerned, to join organizations of their own choosing without previous authorization.

Article 3

(1) Workers' and employers' organizations shall have the right to draw up their constitutions and rules, to elect their representatives in full freedom, to organize their administration and activities and to formulate their programmes.

(2) The public authorities shall refrain from any interference which would restrict this right or impede the lawful exercise thereof.

Article 4

Workers' and employers' organizations shall not be liable to be dissolved or suspended by administrative authority.

Article 5

Workers' and employers' organizations shall have the right to establish and join federations and confederations and any such organization, federation or confederation shall have the right to affiliate with international organizations of workers and employers.

Article 6

The provisions of Articles 2, 3 and 4 hereof apply to federations and confederations of workers' and employers' organizations.

Article 7

The acquisition of legal personality by workers' and employers' organizations, federations and confederations shall not be made subject to conditions of such a character as to restrict the application of the provisions of Articles 2, 3 and 4 hereof.

Article 8

(1) In exercising the rights provided for in this Convention workers and employers and their respective organizations, like other persons or organized collectivities, shall respect the law of the land.

(2) The law of the land shall not be such as to impair, nor shall it be so applied as to impair, the guarantees provided for in this Convention.

Article 9

(1) The extent to which the guarantees provided for in this Convention shall apply to the armed forces and the police shall be determined by national laws or regulations.

(2) In accordance with the principle set forth in paragraph (8) of Article 19 of the Constitution of the International Labour Organization the ratification of this Convention by any Member shall not be deemed to affect any existing law, award, custom or agreement in virtue of which members of the armed forces or the police enjoy any right guaranteed by this Convention.

Article 10

In this Convention the term *organization* means any organization of workers or of employers for furthering and defending the interests of workers or of employers.

Part II Protection of the Right to Organize

Article 11

Each Member of the International Labour Organization for which this Convention is in force undertakes to take all necessary and appropriate measures to ensure that workers and employers may exercise freely the right to organize.

Part III Miscellaneous Provisions

Article 12

(1) In respect of the territories referred to in Article 35 of the Constitution of the International Labour Organization as amended by the Constitution of the International Labour Organization Instrument of Amendment 1946, other than the territories referred to in paragraphs (4) and (5) of the said Article as so amended, each Member of the Organization which ratifies this Convention shall communicate to the Director-General of the International Labour Office with or as soon as possible after its ratification a declaration stating:

  (a) the territories in respect of which it undertakes that the provisions of the Convention shall be applied without modification;

  (b) the territories in respect of which it undertakes that the provisions of the Convention shall be applied subject to modifications, together with details of the said modifications;

  (c) the territories in respect of which the Convention is inapplicable and in such cases the grounds on which it is inapplicable;

  (d) the territories in respect of which it reserves its decision.

(2) The undertakings referred to in subparagraphs (a) and (b) of paragraph (1) of this Article shall be deemed to be an integral part of the ratification and shall have the force of ratification.

(3) Any Member may at any time by a subsequent declaration cancel in whole or in part any reservations made in its original declaration in virtue of subparagraphs (b), (c) or (d) of paragraph (1) of this Article.

(4) Any Member may, at any time at which the Convention is subject to denunciation in accordance with the provisions of Article 16, communicate to the Director-General a declaration modifying in any other respect the terms of any former declaration and stating the present position in respect of such territories as it may specify.

Article 13

(1) Where the subject-matter of this Convention is within the self-governing powers of any non-metropolitan territory, the Member responsible for the international relations of that territory may, in agreement with the government of the territory, communicate to the Director-General of the International Labour Office a declaration accepting on behalf of the territory the obligations of this Convention.

(2) A declaration accepting the obligations of this Convention may be communicated to the Director-General of the International Labour Office:

(a) by two or more Members of the Organization in respect of any territory which is under their joint authority; or

(b) by any international authority responsible for the administration of any territory, in virtue of the Charter of the United Nations or otherwise, in respect of any such territory.

(3) Declarations communicated to the Director-General of the International Labour Office in accordance with the preceding paragraphs of this Article shall indicate whether the provisions of the Convention will be applied in the territory concerned without modification or subject to modifications; when the declaration indicates that the provisions of the Convention will be applied subject to modifications it shall give details of the said modifications.

(4) The Member, Members or international authority concerned may at any time by a subsequent declaration renounce in whole or in part the right to have recourse to any modification indicated in any former declaration.

(5) The Member, Members or international authority concerned may, at any time at which this Convention is subject to denunciation in accordance with the provisions of Article 16, communicate to the Director-General a declaration modifying in any other respect the terms of any former declaration and stating the present position in respect of the application of the Convention.

Part IV Final Provisions

Article 14

The formal ratifications of this Convention shall be communicated to the Director-General of the International Labour Office for registration.

Article 15

(1) This Convention shall be binding only upon those Members of the International Labour Organization whose ratifications have been registered with the Director-General.

(2) It shall come into force twelve months after the date on which the ratifications of two Members have been registered with the Director-General.

(3) Thereafter, this Convention shall come into force for any Member twelve months after the date on which its ratifications has been registered.

Article 16

(1) A Member which has ratified this Convention may denounce it after the expiration of ten years from the date on which the Convention first comes into force, by an act communicated to the Director-General of the International Labour Office for registration. Such denunciation shall not take effect until one year after the date on which it is registered.

(2) Each Member which has ratified this Convention and which does not, within the year following the expiration of the period of ten years mentioned in the preceding paragraph, exercise the right of denunciation provided for in this Article, will be bound for another period of ten years and,

thereafter, may denounce this Convention at the expiration of each period of ten years under the terms provided for in this Article.

Article 17

(1) The Director-General of the International Labour Office shall notify all Members of the International Labour Organization of the registration of all ratifications, declarations and denunciations communicated to him by the Members of the Organization.

(2) When notifying the Members of the Organization of the registration of the second ratification communicated to him, the Director-General shall draw the attention of the Members of the Organization to the date upon which the Convention will come into force.

Article 18

The Director-General of the International Labour Office shall communicate to the Secretary-General of the United Nations for registration in accordance with Article 102 of the Charter of the United Nations full particulars of all ratifications, declarations and acts of denunciation registered by him in accordance with the provisions of the preceding Articles.

Article 19

At such times as it may consider necessary the Governing Body of the International Labour Office shall present to the General Conference a report on the working of this Convention and shall examine the desirability of placing on the agenda of the Conference the question of its revision in whole or in part.

Article 20

(1) Should the Conference adopt a new Convention revising this Convention in whole or in part, then, unless the new Convention otherwise provides:

  (a) the ratification by a Member of the new revising Convention shall ipso jure involve the immediate denunciation of this Convention, notwithstanding the provisions of Article 16 above, if and when the new revising Convention shall have come into force;

  (b) as from the date when the new revising Convention comes into force this Convention shall cease to be open to ratification by the Members.

(2) This Convention shall in any case remain in force in its actual form and content for those Members which have ratified it but have not ratified the revising Convention.

Article 21

The English and French versions of the text of this Convention are equally authoritative.

RIGHT TO ORGANIZE AND COLLECTIVE BARGAINING CONVENTION, 1949 (No. 98)

(Adopted: 1 July 1949; Entry into force: 18 July 1951; Applied to Hong Kong: 1 July 1997)

Preamble

The General Conference of the International Labour Organization,

Having been convened at Geneva by the Governing Body of the International Labour Office, and having met in its Thirty-second Session on 8 June 1949, and

Having decided upon the adoption of certain proposals concerning the application of the principles of the right to organize and to bargain collectively, which is the fourth item on the agenda of the session, and

Having determined that these proposals shall take the form of an international Convention,

adopts this first day of July of the year one thousand nine hundred and forty-nine the following Convention, which may be cited as the Right to Organize and Collective Bargaining Convention, 1949:

Article 1

(1) Workers shall enjoy adequate protection against acts of anti-union discrimination in respect of their employment.

(2) Such protection shall apply more particularly in respect of acts calculated to —

- (a) make the employment of a worker subject to the condition that he shall not join a union or shall relinquish trade union membership;
- (b) cause the dismissal of or otherwise prejudice a worker by reason of union membership or because of participation in union activities outside working hours or, with the consent of the employer, within working hours.

Article 2

(1) Workers' and employers' organizations shall enjoy adequate protection against any acts of interference by each other or each other's agents or members in their establishment, functioning or administration.

(2) In particular, acts which are designed to promote the establishment of workers' organizations under the domination of employers or employers' organizations, or to support workers' organizations by financial or other means, with the object of placing such organizations under the control of employers or employers' organizations, shall be deemed to constitute acts of interference within the meaning of this Article.

Article 3

Machinery appropriate to national conditions shall be established, where necessary, for the purpose of ensuring respect for the right to organize as defined in the preceding Articles.

Article 4

Measures appropriate to national conditions shall be taken, where necessary, to encourage and promote the full development and utilization of machinery for voluntary negotiation between employers or employers' organizations and workers' organizations, with a view to the regulation of terms and conditions of employment by means of collective agreements.

Article 5

(1) The extent to which the guarantees provided for in this Convention shall apply to the armed forces and the police shall be determined by national laws or regulations.

(2) In accordance with the principle set forth in paragraph (8) of Article 19 of the Constitution of the International Labour Organization the ratification of this Convention by any Member shall not be deemed to affect any existing law, award, custom or agreement in virtue of which members of the armed forces or the police enjoy any right guaranteed by this Convention.

Article 6

This Convention does not deal with the position of public servants engaged in the administration of the State, nor shall it be construed as prejudicing their rights or status in any way.

Article 7

The formal ratifications of this Convention shall be communicated to the Director-General of the International Labour Office for registration.

Article 8

(1) This Convention shall be binding only upon those Members of the International Labour Organization whose ratifications have been registered with the Director-General.

(2) It shall come into force twelve months after the date on which the ratifications of two Members have been registered with the Director-General.

(3) Thereafter, this Convention shall come into force for any Member twelve months after the date on which its ratification has been registered.

Article 9

(1) Declarations communicated to the Director-General of the International Labour Office in accordance with paragraph (2) of Article 35 of the Constitution of the International Labour Organization shall indicate –

(a) the territories in respect of which the Member concerned undertakes that the provisions of the Convention shall be applied without modification;

(b) the territories in respect of which it undertakes that the provisions of the Convention shall be applied subject to modifications, together with details of the said modifications;

(c) the territories in respect of which the Convention is inapplicable and in such cases the grounds on which it is inapplicable;

(d) the territories in respect of which it reserves its decision pending further consideration of the position.

(2) The undertakings referred to in subparagraphs (a) and (b) of paragraph (1) of this Article shall be deemed to be an integral part of the ratification and shall have the force of ratification.

(3) Any Member may at any time by a subsequent declaration cancel in whole or in part any reservation made in its original declaration in virtue of subparagraph (b), (c) or (d) of paragraph (1) of this Article.

(4) Any Member may, at any time at which the Convention is subject to denunciation in accordance with the provisions of Article 11, communicate to the Director-General a declaration modifying in any other respect the terms of any former declaration and stating the present position in respect of such territories as it may specify.

Article 10

(1) Declarations communicated to the Director-General of the International Labour Office in accordance with paragraph (4) or (5) of Article 35 of the Constitution of the International Labour Organization shall indicate whether the provisions of the Convention will be applied in the territory concerned without modification or subject to modifications; when the declaration indicates that the provisions of the Convention will be applied subject to modifications, it shall give details of the said modifications.

(2) The Member, Members or international authority concerned may at any time by a subsequent declaration renounce in whole or in part the right to have recourse to any modification indicated in any former declaration.

(3) The Member, Members or international authority concerned may, at any time at which this Convention is subject to denunciation in accordance with the provisions of Article 11, communicate to the Director-General a declaration modifying in any other respect the terms of any former declaration and stating the present position in respect of the application of the Convention.

Article 11

(1) A Member which has ratified this Convention may denounce it after the expiration of ten years from the date on which the Convention first comes into force, by an act communicated to the Director-General of the International Labour Office for registration. Such denunciation shall not take effect until one year after the date on which it is registered.

(2) Each Member which has ratified this Convention and which does not, within the year following the expiration of the period of ten years mentioned in the preceding paragraph, exercise the right of denunciation provided for in this Article, will be bound for another period of ten years and, thereafter, may denounce this Convention at the expiration of each period of ten years under the terms provided for in this Article.

Article 12

(1) The Director-General of the International Labour Office shall notify all Members of the International Labour Organization of the registration of all ratifications, declarations and denunciations communicated to him by the Members of the Organization.

(2) When notifying the Members of the Organization of the registration of the second ratification communicated to him, the Director-General shall draw the attention of the Members of the Organization to the date upon which the Convention will come into force.

Article 13

The Director-General of the International Labour Office shall communicate to the Secretary-General of the United Nations for registration in accordance with Article 102 of the Charter of the United Nations full particulars of all ratifications, declarations and acts of denunciation registered by him in accordance with the provisions of the preceding Articles.

Article 14

At such times as it may consider necessary the Governing Body of the International Labour Office shall present to the General Conference a report on the working of this Convention and shall examine the desirability of placing on the agenda of the Conference the question of its revision in whole or in part.

Article 15

(1) Should the Conference adopt a new Convention revising this Convention in whole or in part, then, unless the new Convention otherwise provides,

  (a) the ratification by a Member of the new revising Convention shall ipso jure involve the immediate denunciation of this Convention, notwithstanding the provisions of Article 11 above, if and when the new revising Convention shall have come into force;

  (b) as from the date when the new revising Convention comes into force, this Convention shall cease to be open to ratification by the Members.

(2) This Convention shall in any case remain in force in its actual form and content for those Members which have ratified it but have not ratified the revising Convention.

Article 16

The English and French versions of the text of this Convention are equally authoritative.

ABOLITION OF FORCED LABOUR CONVENTION, 1957 (No. 105)

(Adopted: 25 June 1957; Entry into force: 17 January 1959; Applied to Hong Kong: 1 July 1997)

Preamble

The General Conference of the International Labour Organization,

Having been convened at Geneva by the Governing Body of the International Labour Office, and having met in its Fortieth Session on 5 June 1957, and

Having considered the question of forced labour, which is the fourth item on the agenda of the session, and

Having noted the provisions of the Forced Labour Convention, 1930, and

Having noted that the Slavery Convention, 1926, provides that all necessary measures shall be taken to prevent compulsory or forced labour from developing into conditions analogous to slavery and that the Supplementary Convention on the Abolition of Slavery, the Slave Trade and Institutions and Practices Similar to Slavery, 1956, provides for the complete abolition of debt bondage and serfdom, and

Having noted that the Protection of Wages Convention, 1949, provides that wages shall be paid regularly and prohibits methods of payment which deprive the worker of a genuine possibility of terminating his employment, and

Having decided upon the adoption of further proposals with regard to the abolition of certain forms of forced or compulsory labour constituting a violation of the rights of man referred to in the Charter of the United Nations and enunciated by the Universal Declaration of Human Rights, and

Having determined that these proposals shall take the form of an international Convention,

adopts this twenty-fifth day of June of the year one thousand nine hundred and fifty-seven the following Convention, which may be cited as the Abolition of Forced Labour Convention, 1957:

Article 1

Each Member of the International Labour Organization which ratifies this Convention undertakes to suppress and not to make use of any form of forced or compulsory labour —

(a) as a means of political coercion or education or as a punishment for holding or expressing political views or views ideologically opposed to the established political, social or economic system;

(b) as a method of mobilizing and using labour for purposes of economic development;

(c) as a means of labour discipline;

(d) as a punishment for having participated in strikes;

(e) as a means of racial, social, national or religious discrimination.

Article 2

Each Member of the International Labour Organization which ratifies this Convention undertakes to take effective measures to secure the immediate and complete abolition of forced or compulsory labour as specified in Article 1 of this Convention.

Article 3

The formal ratifications of this Convention shall be communicated to the Director-General of the International Labour Office for registration.

Article 4

(1) This Convention shall be binding only upon those Members of the International Labour Organization whose ratifications have been registered with the Director-General.

(2) It shall come into force twelve months after the date on which the ratifications of two Members have been registered with the Director-General.

(3) Thereafter, this Convention shall come into force for any Member twelve months after the date on which its ratification has been registered.

Article 5

(1) A Member which has ratified this Convention may denounce it after the expiration of ten years from the date on which the Convention first comes into force, by an act communicated to the Director-General of the International Labour Office for registration. Such denunciation shall not take effect until one year after the date on which it is registered.

(2) Each Member which has ratified this Convention and which does not, within the year following the expiration of the period of ten years mentioned in the preceding paragraph, exercise the right of denunciation provided for in this Article, will be bound for another period of ten years and, thereafter, may denounce this Convention at the expiration of each period of ten years under the terms provided for in this Article.

Article 6

(1) The Director-General of the International Labour Office shall notify all Members of the International Labour Organization of the registration of all ratifications and denunciations communicated to him by the Members of the Organization.

(2) When notifying the Members of the Organization of the registration of the second ratification communicated to him, the Director-General shall draw the attention of the Members of the Organization to the date upon which the Convention will come into force.

Article 7

The Director-General of the International Labour Office shall communicate to the Secretary-General of the United Nations for registration in accordance with Article 102 of the Charter of the United Nations full particulars of all ratifications and acts of denunciation registered by him in accordance with the provisions of the preceding Articles.

Article 8

At such times as it may consider necessary the Governing Body of the International Labour Office shall present to the General Conference a report on the working of this Convention and shall examine the desirability of placing on the agenda of the Conference the question of its revision in whole or in part.

Article 9

(1) Should the Conference adopt a new Convention revising this Convention in whole or in part, then, unless the new Convention otherwise provides:

   (a) the ratification by a Member of the new revising Convention shall ipso jure involve the immediate denunciation of this Convention, notwithstanding the provisions of Article 5 above, if and when the new revising Convention shall have come into force;

   (b) as from the date when the new revising Convention comes into force this Convention shall cease to be open to ratification by the Members.

(2) This Convention shall in any case remain in force in its actual form and content for those Members which have ratified it but have not ratified the revising Convention.

Article 10

The English and French versions of the text of this Convention are equally authoritative.

MINIUMUM AGE CONVENTION, 1973 (No. 138)

(Adopted: 26 June 1973; Entry into force: 19 June 1976; Applied to Hong Kong: 28 April 1999)

Preamble

The General Conference of the International Labour Organization,

Having been convened at Geneva by the Governing Body of the International Labour Office, and having met in its Fifty-eighth Session on 6 June 1973, and

Having decided upon the adoption of certain proposals with regard to minimum age for admission to employment, which is the fourth item on the agenda of the session, and

Noting the terms of the Minimum Age (Industry) Convention, 1919, the Minimum Age (Sea) Convention, 1920, the Minimum Age (Agriculture) Convention, 1921, the Minimum Age (Trimmers and Stokers) Convention, 1921, the Minimum Age (Non-Industrial Employment) Convention, 1932, the Minimum Age (Sea) Convention (Revised), 1936, the Minimum Age (Industry) Convention (Revised), 1937, the Minimum Age (Non-Industrial Employment) Convention (Revised), 1937, the Minimum Age (Fishermen) Convention, 1959, and the Minimum Age (Underground Work) Convention, 1965, and

Considering that the time has come to establish a general instrument on the subject, which would gradually replace the existing ones applicable to limited economic sectors, with a view to achieving the total abolition of child labour, and

Having determined that these proposals shall take the form of an international Convention,

adopts this twenty-sixth day of June of the year one thousand nine hundred and seventy-three the following Convention, which may be cited as the Minimum Age Convention, 1973:

Article 1

Each Member for which this Convention is in force undertakes to pursue a national policy designed to ensure the effective abolition of child labour and to raise progressively the minimum age for admission to employment or work to a level consistent with the fullest physical and mental development of young persons.

Article 2

(1) Each Member which ratifies this Convention shall specify, in a declaration appended to its ratification, a minimum age for admission to employment or work within its territory and on means of transport registered in its territory; subject to Articles 4 to 8 of this Convention, no one under that age shall be admitted to employment or work in any occupation.

(2) Each Member which has ratified this Convention may subsequently notify the Director-General of the International Labour Office, by further declarations, that it specifies a minimum age higher than that previously specified.

(3) The minimum age specified in pursuance of paragraph (1) of this Article shall not be less than the age of completion of compulsory schooling and, in any case, shall not be less than 15 years.

(4) Notwithstanding the provisions of paragraph (3) of this Article, a Member whose economy and educational facilities are insufficiently developed may, after consultation with the organizations of employers and workers concerned, where such exist, initially specify a minimum age of 14 years.

(5) Each Member which has specified a minimum age of 14 years in pursuance of the provisions of the preceding paragraph shall include in its reports on the application of this Convention

submitted under Article 22 of the Constitution of the International Labour Organization a statement —

(a) that its reason for doing so subsists; or

(b) that it renounces its right to avail itself of the provisions in question as from a stated date.

Article 3

(1) The minimum age for admission to any type of employment or work which by its nature or the circumstances in which it is carried out is likely to jeopardize the health, safety or morals of young persons shall not be less than 18 years.

(2) The types of employment or work to which paragraph (1) of this Article applies shall be determined by national laws or regulations or by the competent authority, after consultation with the organizations of employers and workers concerned, where such exist.

(3) Notwithstanding the provisions of paragraph (1) of this Article, national laws or regulations or the competent authority may, after consultation with the organizations of employers and workers concerned, where such exist, authorize employment or work as from the age of 16 years on condition that the health, safety and morals of the young persons concerned are fully protected and that the young persons have received adequate specific instruction or vocational training in the relevant branch of activity.

Article 4

(1) In so far as necessary, the competent authority, after consultation with the organizations of employers and workers concerned, where such exist, may exclude from the application of this Convention limited categories of employment or work in respect of which special and substantial problems of application arise.

(2) Each Member which ratifies this Convention shall list in its first report on the application of the Convention submitted under Article 22 of the Constitution of the International Labour Organization any categories which may have been excluded in pursuance of paragraph (1) of this Article, giving the reasons for such exclusion, and shall state in subsequent reports the position of its law and practice in respect of the categories excluded and the extent to which effect has been given or is proposed to be given to the Convention in respect of such categories.

(3) Employment or work covered by Article 3 of this Convention shall not be excluded from the application of the Convention in pursuance of this Article.

Article 5

(1) A Member whose economy and administrative facilities are insufficiently developed may, after consultation with the organizations of employers and workers concerned, where such exist, initially limit the scope of application of this Convention.

(2) Each Member which avails itself of the provisions of paragraph (1) of this Article shall specify, in a declaration appended to its ratification, the branches of economic activity or types of undertakings to which it will apply the provisions of the Convention.

(3) The provisions of the Convention shall be applicable as a minimum to the following: mining and quarrying; manufacturing; construction; electricity, gas and water; sanitary services; transport, storage and communication; and plantations and other agricultural undertakings mainly producing for commercial purposes, but excluding family and small-scale holdings producing for local consumption and not regularly employing hired workers.

(4) Any Member which has limited the scope of application of this Convention in pursuance of this Article —

(a) shall indicate in its reports under Article 22 of the Constitution of the International Labour Organization the general position as regards the employment or work of young persons and children in the branches of activity which are excluded from the scope of application of this Convention and any progress which may have been made towards wider application of the provisions of the Convention;

(b) may at any time formally extend the scope of application by a declaration addressed to the Director-General of the International Labour Office.

Article 6

This Convention does not apply to work done by children and young persons in schools for general, vocational or technical education or in other training institutions, or to work done by persons at least 14 years of age in undertakings, where such work is carried out in accordance with conditions prescribed by the competent authority, after consultation with the organizations of employers and workers concerned, where such exist, and is an integral part of —

(a) a course of education or training for which a school or training institution is primarily responsible;

(b) a programme of training mainly or entirely in an undertaking, which programme has been approved by the competent authority; or

(c) a programme of guidance or orientation designed to facilitate the choice of an occupation or of a line of training.

Article 7

(1) National laws or regulations may permit the employment or work of persons 13 to 15 years of age on light work which is —

(a) not likely to be harmful to their health or development; and

(b) not such as to prejudice their attendance at school, their participation in vocational orientation or training programmes approved by the competent authority or their capacity to benefit from the instruction received.

(2) National laws or regulations may also permit the employment or work of persons who are at least 15 years of age but have not yet completed their compulsory schooling on work which meets the requirements set forth in subparagraphs (a) and (b) of paragraph (1) of this Article.

(3) The competent authority shall determine the activities in which employment or work may be permitted under paragraphs (1) and (2) of this Article and shall prescribe the number of hours during which and the conditions in which such employment or work may be undertaken.

(4) Notwithstanding the provisions of paragraphs (1) and (2) of this Article, a Member which has availed itself of the provisions of paragraph (4) of Article 2 may, for as long as it continues to do so, substitute the ages 12 and 14 for the ages 13 and 15 in paragraph (1) and the age 14 for the age 15 in paragraph (2) of this Article.

Article 8

(1) After consultation with the organizations of employers and workers concerned, where such exist, the competent authority may, by permits granted in individual cases, allow exceptions to the prohibition of employment or work provided for in Article 2 of this Convention, for such purposes as participation in artistic performances.

(2) Permits so granted shall limit the number of hours during which and prescribe the conditions in which employment or work is allowed.

Article 9

(1) All necessary measures, including the provision of appropriate penalties, shall be taken by the competent authority to ensure the effective enforcement of the provisions of this Convention.

(2) National laws or regulations or the competent authority shall define the persons responsible for compliance with the provisions giving effect to the Convention.

(3) National laws or regulations or the competent authority shall prescribe the registers or other documents which shall be kept and made available by the employer; such registers or documents shall contain the names and ages or dates of birth, duly certified wherever possible, of persons whom he employs or who work for him and who are less than 18 years of age.

Article 10

(1) This Convention revises, on the terms set forth in this Article, the Minimum Age (Industry) Convention, 1919, the Minimum Age (Sea) Convention, 1920, the Minimum Age (Agriculture) Convention, 1921, the Minimum Age (Trimmers and Stokers) Convention, 1921, the Minimum Age (Non-Industrial Employment) Convention, 1932, the Minimum Age (Sea) Convention (Revised), 1936, the Minimum Age (Industry) Convention (Revised), 1937, the Minimum Age (Non-Industrial Employment) Convention (Revised), 1937, the Minimum Age (Fishermen) Convention, 1959, and the Minimum Age (Underground Work) Convention, 1965.

(2) The coming into force of this Convention shall not close the Minimum Age (Sea) Convention (Revised), 1936, the Minimum Age (Industry) Convention (Revised), 1937, the Minimum Age (Non-Industrial Employment) Convention (Revised), 1937, the Minimum Age (Fishermen) Convention, 1959, or the Minimum Age (Underground Work) Convention, 1965, to further ratification.

(3) The Minimum Age (Industry) Convention, 1919, the Minimum Age (Sea) Convention, 1920, the Minimum Age (Agriculture) Convention, 1921, and the Minimum Age (Trimmers and Stokers) Convention, 1921, shall be closed to further ratification when all the parties thereto have consented to such closing by ratification of this Convention or by a declaration communicated to the Director-General of the International Labour Office.

(4) When the obligations of this Convention are accepted —

(a) by a Member which is a party to the Minimum Age (Industry) Convention (Revised), 1937, and a minimum age of not less than 15 years is specified in pursuance of Article 2 of this Convention, this shall ipso jure involve the immediate denunciation of that Convention,

(b) in respect of non-industrial employment as defined in the Minimum Age (Non-Industrial Employment) Convention, 1932, by a Member which is a party to that Convention, this shall ipso jure involve the immediate denunciation of that Convention,

(c) in respect of non-industrial employment as defined in the Minimum Age (Non-Industrial Employment) Convention (Revised), 1937, by a Member which is a party to that Convention, and a minimum age of not less than 15 years is specified in pursuance of Article 2 of this Convention, this shall ipso jure involve the immediate denunciation of that Convention,

(d) in respect of maritime employment, by a Member which is a party to the Minimum Age (Sea) Convention (Revised), 1936, and a minimum age of not less than 15 years is specified in pursuance of Article 2 of this Convention or the Member specifies that Article 3 of this Convention applies to maritime employment, this shall ipso jure involve the immediate denunciation of that Convention,

(e) in respect of employment in maritime fishing, by a Member which is a party to the Minimum Age (Fishermen) Convention, 1959, and a minimum age of not less than 15 years is specified in pursuance of Article 2 of this Convention or the Member specifies that Article 3 of this Convention applies to employment in maritime fishing, this shall ipso jure involve the immediate denunciation of that Convention,

(f) by a Member which is a party to the Minimum Age (Underground Work) Convention, 1965, and a minimum age of not less than the age specified in pursuance of that Convention is specified in pursuance of Article 2 of this Convention or the Member specifies that such an age applies to employment underground in mines in virtue of Article 3 of this Convention, this shall ipso jure involve the immediate denunciation of that Convention,

if and when this Convention shall have come into force.

(5) Acceptance of the obligations of this Convention –

(a) shall involve the denunciation of the Minimum Age (Industry) Convention, 1919, in accordance with Article 12 thereof,

(b) in respect of agriculture shall involve the denunciation of the Minimum Age (Agriculture) Convention, 1921, in accordance with Article 9 thereof,

(c) in respect of maritime employment shall involve the denunciation of the Minimum Age (Sea) Convention, 1920, in accordance with Article 10 thereof, and of the Minimum Age (Trimmers and Stokers) Convention, 1921, in accordance with Article 12 thereof,

if and when this Convention shall have come into force.

Article 11

The formal ratifications of this Convention shall be communicated to the Director-General of the International Labour Office for registration.

Article 12

(1) This Convention shall be binding only upon those Members of the International Labour Organization whose ratifications have been registered with the Director-General.

(2) It shall come into force twelve months after the date on which the ratifications of two Members have been registered with the Director-General.

(3) Thereafter, this Convention shall come into force for any Member twelve months after the date on which its ratifications has been registered.

Article 13

(1) A Member which has ratified this Convention may denounce it after the expiration of ten years from the date on which the Convention first comes into force, by an act communicated to the Director-General of the International Labour Office for registration. Such denunciation shall not take effect until one year after the date on which it is registered.

(2) Each Member which has ratified this Convention and which does not, within the year following the expiration of the period of ten years mentioned in the preceding paragraph, exercise the right of denunciation provided for in this Article, will be bound for another period of ten years and, thereafter, may denounce this Convention at the expiration of each period of ten years under the terms provided for in this Article.

Article 14

(1) The Director-General of the International Labour Office shall notify all Members of the International Labour Organization of the registration of all ratifications and denunciations communicated to him by the Members of the Organization.

(2) When notifying the Members of the Organization of the registration of the second ratification communicated to him, the Director-General shall draw the attention of the Members of the Organization to the date upon which the Convention will come into force.

Article 15

The Director-General of the International Labour Office shall communicate to the Secretary-General of the United Nations for registration in accordance with Article 102 of the Charter of the United Nations full particulars of all ratifications and acts of denunciation registered by him in accordance with the provisions of the preceding Articles.

Article 16

At such times as it may consider necessary the Governing Body of the International Labour Office shall present to the General Conference a report on the working of this Convention and shall examine the desirability of placing on the agenda of the Conference the question of its revision in whole or in part.

Article 17

(1) Should the Conference adopt a new Convention revising this Convention in whole or in part, then, unless the new Convention otherwise provides:

 (a) the ratification by a Member of the new revising Convention shall ipso jure involve the immediate denunciation of this Convention, notwithstanding the provisions of Article 13 above, if and when the new revising Convention shall have come into force;

 (b) as from the date when the new revising Convention comes into force this Convention shall cease to be open to ratification by the Members.

(2) This Convention shall in any case remain in force in its actual form and content for those Members which have ratified it but have not ratified the revising Convention.

Article 18

The English and French versions of the text of this Convention are equally authoritative.

WORST FORMS OF CHILD LABOUR CONVENTION, 1999 (No. 182)

(Adopted: 17 June 1999; Entry into force: 19 November 2000; Applied to Hong Kong: 8 August 2002)

Preamble

The General Conference of the International Labour Organization,

Having been convened at Geneva by the Governing Body of the International Labour Office, and having met in its 87th Session on 1 June 1999, and

Considering the need to adopt new instruments for the prohibition and elimination of the worst forms of child labour, as the main priority for national and international action, including international cooperation and assistance, to complement the Convention and the Recommendation concerning Minimum Age for Admission to Employment, 1973, which remain fundamental instruments on child labour, and

Considering that the effective elimination of the worst forms of child labour requires immediate and comprehensive action, taking into account the importance of free basic education and the need to remove the children concerned from all such work and to provide for their rehabilitation and social integration while addressing the needs of their families, and

Recalling the Resolution concerning the elimination of child labour adopted by the International Labour Conference at its 83rd Session in 1996, and

Recognizing that child labour is to a great extent caused by poverty and that the long-term solution lies in sustained economic growth leading to social progress, in particular poverty alleviation and universal education, and

Recalling the Convention on the Rights of the Child adopted by the United Nations General Assembly on 20 November 1989, and

Recalling the ILO Declaration on Fundamental Principles and Rights at Work and its Follow-up, adopted by the International Labour Conference at its 86th Session in 1998, and

Recalling that some of the worst forms of child labour are covered by other international instruments, in particular the Forced Labour Convention, 1930, and the United Nations Supplementary Convention on the Abolition of Slavery, the Slave Trade, and Institutions and Practices Similar to Slavery, 1956, and

Having decided upon the adoption of certain proposals with regard to child labour, which is the fourth item on the agenda of the session, and

Having determined that these proposals shall take the form of an international Convention;

adopts this seventeenth day of June of the year one thousand nine hundred and ninety-nine the following Convention, which may be cited as the Worst Forms of Child Labour Convention, 1999.

Article 1

Each Member which ratifies this Convention shall take immediate and effective measures to secure the prohibition and elimination of the worst forms of child labour as a matter of urgency.

Article 2

For the purposes of this Convention, the term *child* shall apply to all persons under the age of 18.

Article 3

For the purposes of this Convention, the term *the worst forms of child labour* comprises:

(a) all forms of slavery or practices similar to slavery, such as the sale and trafficking of children, debt bondage and serfdom and forced or compulsory labour, including forced or compulsory recruitment of children for use in armed conflict;

(b) the use, procuring or offering of a child for prostitution, for the production of pornography or for pornographic performances;

(c) the use, procuring or offering of a child for illicit activities, in particular for the production and trafficking of drugs as defined in the relevant international treaties;

(d) work which, by its nature or the circumstances in which it is carried out, is likely to harm the health, safety or morals of children.

Article 4

(1) The types of work referred to under Article 3(d) shall be determined by national laws or regulations or by the competent authority, after consultation with the organizations of employers and workers concerned, taking into consideration relevant international standards, in particular paragraphs (3) and (4) of the Worst Forms of Child Labour Recommendation, 1999.

(2) The competent authority, after consultation with the organizations of employers and workers concerned, shall identify where the types of work so determined exist.

(3) The list of the types of work determined under paragraph (1) of this Article shall be periodically examined and revised as necessary, in consultation with the organizations of employers and workers concerned.

Article 5

Each Member shall, after consultation with employers' and workers' organizations, establish or designate appropriate mechanisms to monitor the implementation of the provisions giving effect to this Convention.

Article 6

(1) Each Member shall design and implement programmes of action to eliminate as a priority the worst forms of child labour.

(2) Such programmes of action shall be designed and implemented in consultation with relevant government institutions and employers' and workers' organizations, taking into consideration the views of other concerned groups as appropriate.

Article 7

(1) Each Member shall take all necessary measures to ensure the effective implementation and enforcement of the provisions giving effect to this Convention including the provision and application of penal sanctions or, as appropriate, other sanctions.

(2) Each Member shall, taking into account the importance of education in eliminating child labour, take effective and time-bound measures to:

(a) prevent the engagement of children in the worst forms of child labour;

(b) provide the necessary and appropriate direct assistance for the removal of children from the worst forms of child labour and for their rehabilitation and social integration;

(c) ensure access to free basic education, and, wherever possible and appropriate, vocational training, for all children removed from the worst forms of child labour;

(d) identify and reach out to children at special risk; and

(e) take account of the special situation of girls.

(3) Each Member shall designate the competent authority responsible for the implementation of the provisions giving effect to this Convention.

Article 8

Members shall take appropriate steps to assist one another in giving effect to the provisions of this Convention through enhanced international cooperation and/or assistance including support for social and economic development, poverty eradication programmes and universal education.

Article 9

The formal ratifications of this Convention shall be communicated to the Director-General of the International Labour Office for registration.

Article 10

(1) This Convention shall be binding only upon those Members of the International Labour Organization whose ratifications have been registered with the Director-General of the International Labour Office.

(2) It shall come into force 12 months after the date on which the ratifications of two Members have been registered with the Director-General.

(3) Thereafter, this Convention shall come into force for any Member 12 months after the date on which its ratification has been registered.

Article 11

(1) A Member which has ratified this Convention may denounce it after the expiration of ten years from the date on which the Convention first comes into force, by an act communicated to the Director-General of the International Labour Office for registration. Such denunciation shall not take effect until one year after the date on which it is registered.

(2) Each Member which has ratified this Convention and which does not, within the year following the expiration of the period of ten years mentioned in the preceding paragraph, exercise the right of denunciation provided for in this Article, will be bound for another period of ten years and,

thereafter, may denounce this Convention at the expiration of each period of ten years under the terms provided for in this Article.

Article 12

(1) The Director-General of the International Labour Office shall notify all Members of the International Labour Organization of the registration of all ratifications and acts of denunciation communicated by the Members of the Organization.

(2) When notifying the Members of the Organization of the registration of the second ratification, the Director-General shall draw the attention of the Members of the Organization to the date upon which the Convention shall come into force.

Article 13

The Director-General of the International Labour Office shall communicate to the Secretary-General of the United Nations, for registration in accordance with Article 102 of the Charter of the United Nations, full particulars of all ratifications and acts of denunciation registered by the Director-General in accordance with the provisions of the preceding Articles.

Article 14

At such times as it may consider necessary, the Governing Body of the International Labour Office shall present to the General Conference a report on the working of this Convention and shall examine the desirability of placing on the agenda of the Conference the question of its revision in whole or in part.

Article 15

(1) Should the Conference adopt a new Convention revising this Convention in whole or in part, then, unless the new Convention otherwise provides —

    (a) the ratification by a Member of the new revising Convention shall ipso jure involve the immediate denunciation of this Convention, notwithstanding the provisions of Article 11 above, if and when the new revising Convention shall have come into force;

    (b) as from the date when the new revising Convention comes into force, this Convention shall cease to be open to ratification by the Members.

(2) This Convention shall in any case remain in force in its actual form and content for those Members which have ratified it but have not ratified the revising Convention.

Article 16

The English and French versions of the text of this Convention are equally authoritative.

ILO DECLARATION ON FUNDAMENTAL PRINCIPLES AND RIGHTS AT WORK

(Adopted: 18 June 1998; Annex revised: 15 June 2010)

Whereas the ILO was founded in the conviction that social justice is essential to universal and lasting peace;

Whereas economic growth is essential but not sufficient to ensure equity, social progress and the eradication of poverty, confirming the need for the ILO to promote strong social policies, justice and democratic institutions;

Whereas the ILO should, now more than ever, draw upon all its standard-setting, technical cooperation and research resources in all its areas of competence, in particular employment, vocational training and working conditions, to ensure that, in the context of a global strategy for economic and social development, economic and social policies are mutually reinforcing components in order to create broad-based sustainable development;

Whereas the ILO should give special attention to the problems of persons with special social needs, particularly the unemployed and migrant workers, and mobilize and encourage international, regional and national efforts aimed at resolving their problems, and promote effective policies aimed at job creation;

Whereas, in seeking to maintain the link between social progress and economic growth, the guarantee of fundamental principles and rights at work is of particular significance in that it enables the persons concerned, to claim freely and on the basis of equality of opportunity, their fair share of the wealth which they have helped to generate, and to achieve fully their human potential;

Whereas the ILO is the constitutionally mandated international organization and the competent body to set and deal with international labour standards, and enjoys universal support and acknowledgement in promoting fundamental rights at work as the expression of its constitutional principles;

Whereas it is urgent, in a situation of growing economic interdependence, to reaffirm the immutable nature of the fundamental principles and rights embodied in the Constitution of the Organization and to promote their universal application;

The International Labour Conference

(1) Recalls:

  (a) that in freely joining the ILO, all Members have endorsed the principles and rights set out in its Constitution and in the Declaration of Philadelphia, and have undertaken to work towards attaining the overall objectives of the Organization to the best of their resources and fully in line with their specific circumstances;

  (b) that these principles and rights have been expressed and developed in the form of specific rights and obligations in Conventions recognized as fundamental both inside and outside the Organization.

(2) Declares that all Members, even if they have not ratified the Conventions in question, have an obligation arising from the very fact of membership in the Organization to respect, to promote and to realize, in good faith and in accordance with the Constitution, the principles concerning the fundamental rights which are the subject of those Conventions, namely:

  (a) freedom of association and the effective recognition of the right to collective bargaining;

  (b) the elimination of all forms of forced or compulsory labour;

  (c) the effective abolition of child labour; and

  (d) the elimination of discrimination in respect of employment and occupation.

(3) Recognizes the obligation on the Organization to assist its Members, in response to their established and expressed needs, in order to attain these objectives by making full use of its constitutional, operational and budgetary resources, including, by the mobilization of external resources and support, as well as by encouraging other international organizations with which the ILO has established relations, pursuant to Article 12 of its Constitution, to support these efforts:

  (a) by offering technical cooperation and advisory services to promote the ratification and implementation of the fundamental Conventions;

  (b) by assisting those Members not yet in a position to ratify some or all of these Conventions in their efforts to respect, to promote and to realize the principles concerning fundamental rights which are the subject of these Conventions; and

(c) by helping the Members in their efforts to create a climate for economic and social development.

(4) Decides that, to give full effect to this Declaration, a promotional follow-up, which is meaningful and effective, shall be implemented in accordance with the measures specified in the Annex hereto, which shall be considered as an integral part of this Declaration.

(5) Stresses that labour standards should not be used for protectionist trade purposes, and that nothing in this Declaration and its follow-up shall be invoked or otherwise used for such purposes; in addition, the comparative advantage of any country should in no way be called into question by this Declaration and its follow-up.

Annex (Revised)
Follow-up to the Declaration

Overall Purpose

(1) The aim of the follow-up described below is to encourage the efforts made by the Members of the Organization to promote the fundamental principles and rights enshrined in the Constitution of the ILO and the Declaration of Philadelphia and reaffirmed in this Declaration.

(2) In line with this objective, which is of a strictly promotional nature, this follow-up will allow the identification of areas in which the assistance of the Organization through its technical cooperation activities may prove useful to its Members to help them implement these fundamental principles and rights. It is not a substitute for the established supervisory mechanisms, nor shall it impede their functioning; consequently, specific situations within the purview of those mechanisms shall not be examined or re-examined within the framework of this follow-up.

(3) The two aspects of this follow-up, described below, are based on existing procedures: the annual follow-up concerning non-ratified fundamental Conventions will entail merely some adaptation of the present modalities of application of Article 19, paragraph (5)(e), of the Constitution; and the Global Report on the effect given to the promotion of the fundamental principles and rights at work that will serve to inform the recurrent discussion at the Conference on the needs of the Members, the ILO action undertaken, and the results achieved in the promotion of the fundamental principles and rights at work.

Annual Follow-up Concerning Non-ratified Fundamental Conventions

Purpose and Scope

(1) The purpose is to provide an opportunity to review each year, by means of simplified procedures, the efforts made in accordance with the Declaration by Members which have not yet ratified all the fundamental Conventions.

(2) The follow-up will cover the four categories of fundamental principles and rights specified in the Declaration.

Modalities

(1) The follow-up will be based on reports requested from Members under Article 19, paragraph (5)(e), of the Constitution. The report forms will be drawn up so as to obtain information from governments which have not ratified one or more of the fundamental Conventions, on any changes which may have taken place in their law and practice, taking due account of Article 23 of the Constitution and established practice.

(2) These reports, as compiled by the Office, will be reviewed by the Governing Body.

(3) Adjustments to the Governing Body's existing procedures should be examined to allow Members which are not represented on the Governing Body to provide, in the most appropriate way, clarifications which might prove necessary or useful during Governing Body discussions to supplement the information contained in their reports.

Global Report on Fundamental Principles and Rights at Work

Purpose and Scope

(1) The purpose of the Global Report is to provide a dynamic global picture relating to the four categories of fundamental principles and rights at work noted during the preceding period, and to serve as a basis for assessing the effectiveness of the assistance provided by the Organization, and for determining priorities for the following period, including in the form of action plans for technical cooperation designed in particular to mobilize the internal and external resources necessary to carry them out.

Modalities

(1) The report will be drawn up under the responsibility of the Director-General on the basis of official information, or information gathered and assessed in accordance with established procedures. In the case of States which have not ratified the fundamental Conventions, it will be based in particular on the findings of the aforementioned annual follow-up. In the case of Members which have ratified the Conventions concerned, the report will be based in particular on reports as dealt with pursuant to Article 22 of the Constitution. It will also refer to the experience gained from technical cooperation and other relevant activities of the ILO.

(2) This report will be submitted to the Conference for a recurrent discussion on the strategic objective of fundamental principles and rights at work based on the modalities agreed by the Governing Body. It will then be for the Conference to draw conclusions from this discussion on all available ILO means of action, including the priorities and plans of action for technical cooperation to be implemented for the following period, and to guide the Governing Body and the Office in their responsibilities.

It is understood that:

(1) The Conference shall, in due course, review the operation of this follow-up in the light of the experience acquired to assess whether it has adequately fulfilled the overall purpose articulated in Part I.

SECTION IV
ENVIRONMENT AND CLIMATE

This Section includes six international instruments related to the environment and climate as applied in Hong Kong. They are:

(1) The Basel Convention on the Control of Transboundary Movement of Hazardous Wastes and Their Disposal

(2) The United Nations Framework Convention on Climate Change

(3) The Kyoto Protocol to the United Nations Framework Convention on Climate Change

(4) The Paris Agreement under the United Nations Framework Convention on Climate Change

(5) The International Convention for the Prevention of Pollution from Ships

(6) The Convention on International Trade in Endangered Species of Wild Fauna and Flora

BASEL CONVENTION ON THE CONTROL OF TRANSBOUNDARY MOVEMENTS OF HAZARDOUS WASTES AND THEIR DISPOSAL

(Adopted: 22 March 1989, Entry into force: 5 May 1992; Applied to Hong Kong: 1 July 1997)

Preamble

The Parties to this Convention,

Aware of the risk of damage to human health and the environment caused by hazardous wastes and other wastes and the transboundary movement thereof,

Mindful of the growing threat to human health and the environment posed by the increased generation and complexity, and transboundary movement of hazardous wastes and other wastes,

Mindful also that the most effective way of protecting human health and the environment from the dangers posed by such wastes is the reduction of their generation to a minimum in terms of quantity and/or hazard potential,

Convinced that States should take necessary measures to ensure that the management of hazardous wastes and other wastes including their transboundary movement and disposal is consistent with the protection of human health and the environment whatever the place of disposal,

Noting that States should ensure that the generator should carry out duties with regard to the transport and disposal of hazardous wastes and other wastes in a manner that is consistent with the protection of the environment, whatever the place of disposal,

Fully recognizing that any State has the sovereign right to ban the entry or disposal of foreign hazardous wastes and other wastes in its territory,

Recognizing also the increasing desire for the prohibition of transboundary movements of hazardous wastes and their disposal in other States, especially developing countries,

Recognizing that transboundary movements of hazardous wastes, especially to developing countries, have a high risk of not constituting an environmentally sound management of hazardous wastes as required by this Convention,

Convinced that hazardous wastes and other wastes should, as far as is compatible with environmentally sound and efficient management, be disposed of in the State where they were generated,

Aware also that transboundary movements of such wastes from the State of their generation to any other State should be permitted only when conducted under conditions which do not endanger human health and the environment, and under conditions in conformity with the provisions of this Convention,*

Considering that enhanced control of transboundary movement of hazardous wastes and other wastes will act as an incentive for their environmentally sound management and for the reduction of the volume of such transboundary movement,

Convinced that States should take measures for the proper exchange of information on and control of the transboundary movement of hazardous wastes and other wastes from and to those States,

Noting that a number of international and regional agreements have addressed the issue of protection and preservation of the environment with regard to the transit of dangerous goods,

Taking into account the Declaration of the United Nations Conference on the Human Environment (Stockholm, 1972), the Cairo Guidelines and Principles for the Environmentally Sound Management of Hazardous Wastes adopted by the Governing Council of the United Nations Environment Programme (UNEP) by decision 14/30 of 17 June 1987, the Recommendations of the United Nations Committee of Experts on the Transport of Dangerous Goods (formulated in 1957 and updated biennially), relevant recommendations, declarations, instruments and regulations adopted within the United Nations system and the work and studies done within other international and regional organizations,

Mindful of the spirit, principles, aims and functions of the World Charter for Nature adopted by the General Assembly of the United Nations at its thirty-seventh session (1982) as the rule of ethics in respect of the protection of the human environment and the conservation of natural resources,

Affirming that States are responsible for the fulfilment of their international obligations concerning the protection of human health and protection and preservation of the environment, and are liable in accordance with international law,

Recognizing that in the case of a material breach of the provisions of this Convention or any Protocol thereto the relevant international law of treaties shall apply,

Aware of the need to continue the development and implementation of environmentally sound low-waste technologies, recycling options, good house-keeping and management systems with a view to reducing to a minimum the generation of hazardous wastes and other wastes,

Aware also of the growing international concern about the need for stringent control of transboundary movement of hazardous wastes and other wastes, and of the need as far as possible to reduce such movement to a minimum,

Concerned about the problem of illegal transboundary traffic in hazardous wastes and other wastes,

Taking into account also the limited capabilities of the developing countries to manage hazardous wastes and other wastes,

Recognizing the need to promote the transfer of technology for the sound management of hazardous wastes and other wastes produced locally, particularly to the developing countries in accordance with the

* The Conference of the Parties adopted decision III/1 at its third meeting to amend the Convention by adding, inter alia, a new preambular paragraph (7) bis. This amendment entered into force on 5 December 2019 (depositary notification C.N.420.2019).

spirit of the Cairo Guidelines and decision 14/16 of the Governing Council of UNEP on Promotion of the transfer of environmental protection technology,

Recognizing also that hazardous wastes and other wastes should be transported in accordance with relevant international conventions and recommendations,

Convinced also that the transboundary movement of hazardous wastes and other wastes should be permitted only when the transport and the ultimate disposal of such wastes is environmentally sound, and

Determined to protect, by strict control, human health and the environment against the adverse effects which may result from the generation and management of hazardous wastes and other wastes,

Have agreed as follows:

Article 1 Scope of the Convention

(1) The following wastes that are subject to transboundary movement shall be "hazardous wastes" for the purposes of this Convention:

  (a) Wastes that belong to any category contained in Annex I, unless they do not possess any of the characteristics contained in Annex III; and

  (b) Wastes that are not covered under paragraph (a) but are defined as, or are considered to be, hazardous wastes by the domestic legislation of the Party of export, import or transit.

(2) Wastes that belong to any category contained in Annex II that are subject to transboundary movement shall be "other wastes" for the purposes of this Convention.

(3) Wastes which, as a result of being radioactive, are subject to other international control systems, including international instruments, applying specifically to radioactive materials, are excluded from the scope of this Convention.

(4) Wastes which derive from the normal operations of a ship, the discharge of which is covered by another international instrument, are excluded from the scope of this Convention.

Article 2 Definitions

For the purposes of this Convention:

(1) "Wastes" are substances or objects which are disposed of or are intended to be disposed of or are required to be disposed of by the provisions of national law;

(2) "Management" means the collection, transport and disposal of hazardous wastes or other wastes, including after-care of disposal sites;

(3) "Transboundary movement" means any movement of hazardous wastes or other wastes from an area under the national jurisdiction of one State to or through an area under the national jurisdiction of another State or to or through an area not under the national jurisdiction of any State, provided at least two States are involved in the movement;

(4) "Disposal" means any operation specified in Annex IV to this Convention;

(5) "Approved site or facility" means a site or facility for the disposal of hazardous wastes or other wastes which is authorized or permitted to operate for this purpose by a relevant authority of the State where the site or facility is located;

(6) "Competent authority" means one governmental authority designated by a Party to be responsible, within such geographical areas as the Party may think fit, for receiving the notification of a transboundary movement of hazardous wastes or other wastes, and any information related to it, and for responding to such a notification, as provided in Article 6;

(7) "Focal point" means the entity of a Party referred to in Article 5 responsible for receiving and submitting information as provided for in Articles 13 and 16;

(8) "Environmentally sound management of hazardous wastes or other wastes" means taking all practicable steps to ensure that hazardous wastes or other wastes are managed in a manner

which will protect human health and the environment against the adverse effects which may result from such wastes;

(9) "Area under the national jurisdiction of a State" means any land, marine area or airspace within which a State exercises administrative and regulatory responsibility in accordance with international law in regard to the protection of human health or the environment;

(10) "State of export" means a Party from which a transboundary movement of hazardous wastes or other wastes is planned to be initiated or is initiated;

(11) "State of import" means a Party to which a transboundary movement of hazardous wastes or other wastes is planned or takes place for the purpose of disposal therein or for the purpose of loading prior to disposal in an area not under the national jurisdiction of any State;

(12) "State of transit" means any State, other than the State of export or import, through which a movement of hazardous wastes or other wastes is planned or takes place;

(13) "States concerned" means Parties which are States of export or import, or transit States, whether or not Parties;

(14) "Person" means any natural or legal person;

(15) "Exporter" means any person under the jurisdiction of the State of export who arranges for hazardous wastes or other wastes to be exported;

(16) "Importer" means any person under the jurisdiction of the State of import who arranges for hazardous wastes or other wastes to be imported;

(17) "Carrier" means any person who carries out the transport of hazardous wastes or other wastes;

(18) "Generator" means any person whose activity produces hazardous wastes or other wastes or, if that person is not known, the person who is in possession and/or control of those wastes;

(19) "Disposer" means any person to whom hazardous wastes or other wastes are shipped and who carries out the disposal of such wastes;

(20) "Political and/or economic integration organization" means an organization constituted by sovereign States to which its member States have transferred competence in respect of matters governed by this Convention and which has been duly authorized, in accordance with its internal procedures, to sign, ratify, accept, approve, formally confirm or accede to it;

(21) "Illegal traffic" means any transboundary movement of hazardous wastes or other wastes as specified in Article 9.

Article 3 National Definitions of Hazardous Wastes

(1) Each Party shall, within six months of becoming a Party to this Convention, inform the Secretariat of the Convention of the wastes, other than those listed in Annexes I and II, considered or defined as hazardous under its national legislation and of any requirements concerning transboundary movement procedures applicable to such wastes.

(2) Each Party shall subsequently inform the Secretariat of any significant changes to the information it has provided pursuant to paragraph (1).

(3) The Secretariat shall forthwith inform all Parties of the information it has received pursuant to paragraphs (1) and (2).

(4) Parties shall be responsible for making the information transmitted to them by the Secretariat under paragraph (3) available to their exporters.

Article 4 General Obligations

(1)

(a) Parties exercising their right to prohibit the import of hazardous wastes or other wastes for disposal shall inform the other Parties of their decision pursuant to Article 13.

(b) Parties shall prohibit or shall not permit the export of hazardous wastes and other wastes to the Parties which have prohibited the import of such wastes, when notified pursuant to subparagraph (a) above.

(c) Parties shall prohibit or shall not permit the export of hazardous wastes and other wastes if the State of import does not consent in writing to the specific import, in the case where that State of import has not prohibited the import of such wastes.

(2) Each Party shall take the appropriate measures to:

(a) Ensure that the generation of hazardous wastes and other wastes within it is reduced to a minimum, taking into account social, technological and economic aspects;

(b) Ensure the availability of adequate disposal facilities, for the environmentally sound management of hazardous wastes and other wastes, that shall be located, to the extent possible, within it, whatever the place of their disposal;

(c) Ensure that persons involved in the management of hazardous wastes or other wastes within it take such steps as are necessary to prevent pollution due to hazardous wastes and other wastes arising from such management and, if such pollution occurs, to minimize the consequences thereof for human health and the environment;

(d) Ensure that the transboundary movement of hazardous wastes and other wastes is reduced to the minimum consistent with the environmentally sound and efficient management of such wastes, and is conducted in a manner which will protect human health and the environment against the adverse effects which may result from such movement;

(e) Not allow the export of hazardous wastes or other wastes to a State or group of States belonging to an economic and/or political integration organization that are Parties, particularly developing countries, which have prohibited by their legislation all imports, or if it has reason to believe that the wastes in question will not be managed in an environmentally sound manner, according to criteria to be decided on by the Parties at their first meeting;

(f) Require that information about a proposed transboundary movement of hazardous wastes and other wastes be provided to the States concerned, according to Annex V.A, to state clearly the effects of the proposed movement on human health and the environment;

(g) Prevent the import of hazardous wastes and other wastes if it has reason to believe that the wastes in question will not be managed in an environmentally sound manner;

(h) Co-operate in activities with other Parties and interested organizations, directly and through the Secretariat, including the dissemination of information on the transboundary movement of hazardous wastes and other wastes, in order to improve the environmentally sound management of such wastes and to achieve the prevention of illegal traffic.

(3) The Parties consider that illegal traffic in hazardous wastes or other wastes is criminal.

(4) Each Party shall take appropriate legal, administrative and other measures to implement and enforce the provisions of this Convention, including measures to prevent and punish conduct in contravention of the Convention.

(5) A Party shall not permit hazardous wastes or other wastes to be exported to a non-Party or to be imported from a non-Party.

(6) The Parties agree not to allow the export of hazardous wastes or other wastes for disposal within the area south of 60° South latitude, whether or not such wastes are subject to transboundary movement.

(7) Furthermore, each Party shall:

(a) Prohibit all persons under its national jurisdiction from transporting or disposing of hazardous wastes or other wastes unless such persons are authorized or allowed to perform such types of operations;

(b) Require that hazardous wastes and other wastes that are to be the subject of a transboundary movement be packaged, labelled, and transported in conformity with generally accepted and recognized international rules and standards in the field of packaging, labelling, and transport, and that due account is taken of relevant internationally recognized practices;

(c) Require that hazardous wastes and other wastes be accompanied by a movement document from the point at which a transboundary movement commences to the point of disposal.

(8) Each Party shall require that hazardous wastes or other wastes, to be exported, are managed in an environmentally sound manner in the State of import or elsewhere. Technical guidelines for the environmentally sound management of wastes subject to this Convention shall be decided by the Parties at their first meeting.

(9) Parties shall take the appropriate measures to ensure that the transboundary movement of hazardous wastes and other wastes only be allowed if:

(a) The State of export does not have the technical capacity and the necessary facilities, capacity or suitable disposal sites in order to dispose of the wastes in question in an environmentally sound and efficient manner; or

(b) The wastes in question are required as a raw material for recycling or recovery industries in the State of import; or

(c) The transboundary movement in question is in accordance with other criteria to be decided by the Parties, provided those criteria do not differ from the objectives of this Convention.

(10) The obligation under this Convention of States in which hazardous wastes and other wastes are generated to require that those wastes are managed in an environmentally sound manner may not under any circumstances be transferred to the States of import or transit.

(11) Nothing in this Convention shall prevent a Party from imposing additional requirements that are consistent with the provisions of this Convention, and are in accordance with the rules of international law, in order better to protect human health and the environment.

(12) Nothing in this Convention shall affect in any way the sovereignty of States over their territorial sea established in accordance with international law, and the sovereign rights and the jurisdiction which States have in their exclusive economic zones and their continental shelves in accordance with international law, and the exercise by ships and aircraft of all States of navigational rights and freedoms as provided for in international law and as reflected in relevant international instruments.

(13) Parties shall undertake to review periodically the possibilities for the reduction of the amount and/or the pollution potential of hazardous wastes and other wastes which are exported to other States, in particular to developing countries.

Article 4A General Obligations *

(1) Each Party listed in Annex VII shall prohibit all transboundary movements of hazardous wastes which are destined for operations according to Annex IV A to States not listed in Annex VII.

(2) Each Party listed in Annex VII shall phase out by 31 December 1997, and prohibit as of that date, all transboundary movements of hazardous wastes under Article 1(1)(a) of the Convention which are destined for operations according to Annex IV B to States not listed in Annex VII. Such transboundary movement shall not be prohibited unless the wastes in question are characterized as hazardous under the Convention.

* The Conference of the Parties adopted decision III/1 at its third meeting to amend the Convention by adding, inter alia, a new Article 4A. This amendment entered into force on 5 December 2019 (depositary notification C.N.420.2019). For information on the status of individual Parties in relation to the amendment/s, please see the Status of Ratifications page on the Basel Convention website.

Article 5 Designation of Competent Authorities and Focal Point

To facilitate the implementation of this Convention, the Parties shall:

(1) Designate or establish one or more competent authorities and one focal point. One competent authority shall be designated to receive the notification in case of a State of transit;

(2) Inform the Secretariat, within three months of the date of the entry into force of this Convention for them, which agencies they have designated as their focal point and their competent authorities;

(3) Inform the Secretariat, within one month of the date of decision, of any changes regarding the designation made by them under paragraph (2) above.

Article 6 Transboundary Movement between Parties

(1) The State of export shall notify, or shall require the generator or exporter to notify, in writing, through the channel of the competent authority of the State of export, the competent authority of the States concerned of any proposed transboundary movement of hazardous wastes or other wastes. Such notification shall contain the declarations and information specified in Annex V.A, written in a language acceptable to the State of import. Only one notification needs to be sent to each State concerned.

(2) The State of import shall respond to the notifier in writing, consenting to the movement with or without conditions, denying permission for the movement, or requesting additional information. A copy of the final response of the State of import shall be sent to the competent authorities of the States concerned which are Parties.

(3) The State of export shall not allow the generator or exporter to commence the transboundary movement until it has received written confirmation that:

(a) The notifier has received the written consent of the State of import; and

(b) The notifier has received from the State of import confirmation of the existence of a contract between the exporter and the disposer specifying environmentally sound management of the wastes in question.

(4) Each State of transit which is a Party shall promptly acknowledge to the notifier receipt of the notification. It may subsequently respond to the notifier in writing, within 60 days, consenting to the movement with or without conditions, denying permission for the movement, or requesting additional information. The State of export shall not allow the transboundary movement to commence until it has received the written consent of the State of transit. However, if at any time a Party decides not to require prior written consent, either generally or under specific conditions, for transit transboundary movements of hazardous wastes or other wastes, or modifies its requirements in this respect, it shall forthwith inform the other Parties of its decision pursuant to Article 13. In this latter case, if no response is received by the State of export within 60 days of the receipt of a given notification by the State of transit, the State of export may allow the export to proceed through the State of transit.

(5) In the case of a transboundary movement of wastes where the wastes are legally defined as or considered to be hazardous wastes only:

(a) By the State of export, the requirements of paragraph (9) of this Article that apply to the importer or disposer and the State of import shall apply *mutatis mutandis* to the exporter and State of export, respectively;

(b) By the State of import, or by the States of import and transit which are Parties, the requirements of paragraphs (1), (3), (4) and (6) of this Article that apply to the exporter and State of export shall apply *mutatis mutandis* to the importer or disposer and State of import, respectively; or

(c) By any State of transit which is a Party, the provisions of paragraph (4) shall apply to such State.

(6) The State of export may, subject to the written consent of the States concerned, allow the generator or the exporter to use a general notification where hazardous wastes or other wastes having the same physical and chemical characteristics are shipped regularly to the same disposer via the same customs office of exit of the State of export via the same customs office of entry of the State of import, and, in the case of transit, via the same customs office of entry and exit of the State or States of transit.

(7) The States concerned may make their written consent to the use of the general notification referred to in paragraph (6) subject to the supply of certain information, such as the exact quantities or periodical lists of hazardous wastes or other wastes to be shipped.

(8) The general notification and written consent referred to in paragraphs (6) and (7) may cover multiple shipments of hazardous wastes or other wastes during a maximum period of 12 months.

(9) The Parties shall require that each person who takes charge of a transboundary movement of hazardous wastes or other wastes sign the movement document either upon delivery or receipt of the wastes in question. They shall also require that the disposer inform both the exporter and the competent authority of the State of export of receipt by the disposer of the wastes in question and, in due course, of the completion of disposal as specified in the notification. If no such information is received within the State of export, the competent authority of the State of export or the exporter shall so notify the State of import.

(10) The notification and response required by this Article shall be transmitted to the competent authority of the Parties concerned or to such governmental authority as may be appropriate in the case of non-Parties.

(11) Any transboundary movement of hazardous wastes or other wastes shall be covered by insurance, bond or other guarantee as may be required by the State of import or any State of transit which is a Party.

Article 7 Transboundary Movement from a Party through States which are not Parties

Paragraph (1) of Article 6 of the Convention shall apply *mutatis mutandis* to transboundary movement of hazardous wastes or other wastes from a Party through a State or States which are not Parties.

Article 8 Duty to Re-import

When a transboundary movement of hazardous wastes or other wastes to which the consent of the States concerned has been given, subject to the provisions of this Convention, cannot be completed in accordance with the terms of the contract, the State of export shall ensure that the wastes in question are taken back into the State of export, by the exporter, if alternative arrangements cannot be made for their disposal in an environmentally sound manner, within 90 days from the time that the importing State informed the State of export and the Secretariat, or such other period of time as the States concerned agree. To this end, the State of export and any Party of transit shall not oppose, hinder or prevent the return of those wastes to the State of export.

Article 9 Illegal Traffic

(1) For the purpose of this Convention, any transboundary movement of hazardous wastes or other wastes:

(a) without notification pursuant to the provisions of this Convention to all States concerned; or

(b) without the consent pursuant to the provisions of this Convention of a State concerned; or

(c) with consent obtained from States concerned through falsification, misrepresentation or fraud; or

(d) that does not conform in a material way with the documents; or

(e) that results in deliberate disposal (e.g., dumping) of hazardous wastes or other wastes in contravention of this Convention and of general principles of international law,

shall be deemed to be illegal traffic.

(2) In case of a transboundary movement of hazardous wastes or other wastes deemed to be illegal traffic as the result of conduct on the part of the exporter or generator, the State of export shall ensure that the wastes in question are:

(a) taken back by the exporter or the generator or, if necessary, by itself into the State of export, or, if impracticable,

(b) are otherwise disposed of in accordance with the provisions of this Convention,

within 30 days from the time the State of export has been informed about the illegal traffic or such other period of time as States concerned may agree. To this end the Parties concerned shall not oppose, hinder or prevent the return of those wastes to the State of export.

(3) In the case of a transboundary movement of hazardous wastes or other wastes deemed to be illegal traffic as the result of conduct on the part of the importer or disposer, the State of import shall ensure that the wastes in question are disposed of in an environmentally sound manner by the importer or disposer or, if necessary, by itself within 30 days from the time the illegal traffic has come to the attention of the State of import or such other period of time as the States concerned may agree. To this end, the Parties concerned shall co-operate, as necessary, in the disposal of the wastes in an environmentally sound manner.

(4) In cases where the responsibility for the illegal traffic cannot be assigned either to the exporter or generator or to the importer or disposer, the Parties concerned or other Parties, as appropriate, shall ensure, through co-operation, that the wastes in question are disposed of as soon as possible in an environmentally sound manner either in the State of export or the State of import or elsewhere as appropriate.

(5) Each Party shall introduce appropriate national/domestic legislation to prevent and punish illegal traffic. The Parties shall co-operate with a view to achieving the objects of this Article.

Article 10 International Co-operation

(1) The Parties shall co-operate with each other in order to improve and achieve environmentally sound management of hazardous wastes and other wastes.

(2) To this end, the Parties shall:

(a) Upon request, make available information, whether on a bilateral or multilateral basis, with a view to promoting the environmentally sound management of hazardous wastes and other wastes, including harmonization of technical standards and practices for the adequate management of hazardous wastes and other wastes;

(b) Co-operate in monitoring the effects of the management of hazardous wastes on human health and the environment;

(c) Co-operate, subject to their national laws, regulations and policies, in the development and implementation of new environmentally sound low-waste technologies and the improvement of existing technologies with a view to eliminating, as far as practicable, the generation of hazardous wastes and other wastes and achieving more effective and efficient methods of ensuring their management in an environmentally sound manner, including the study of the economic, social and environmental effects of the adoption of such new or improved technologies;

(d) Co-operate actively, subject to their national laws, regulations and policies, in the transfer of technology and management systems related to the environmentally sound management of hazardous wastes and other wastes. They shall also co-operate in developing the technical capacity among Parties, especially those which may need and request technical assistance in this field;

(e) Co-operate in developing appropriate technical guidelines and/or codes of practice.

(3) The Parties shall employ appropriate means to co-operate in order to assist developing countries in the implementation of subparagraphs (a), (b), (c) and (d) of paragraph (2) of Article 4.

(4) Taking into account the needs of developing countries, co-operation between Parties and the competent international organizations is encouraged to promote, inter alia, public awareness, the development of sound management of hazardous wastes and other wastes and the adoption of new low-waste technologies.

Article 11 Bilateral, Multilateral and Regional Agreements

(1) Notwithstanding the provisions of Article 4 paragraph (5), Parties may enter into bilateral, multilateral, or regional agreements or arrangements regarding transboundary movement of hazardous wastes or other wastes with Parties or non-Parties provided that such agreements or arrangements do not derogate from the environmentally sound management of hazardous wastes and other wastes as required by this Convention. These agreements or arrangements shall stipulate provisions which are not less environmentally sound than those provided for by this Convention in particular taking into account the interests of developing countries.

(2) Parties shall notify the Secretariat of any bilateral, multilateral or regional agreements or arrangements referred to in paragraph (1) and those which they have entered into prior to the entry into force of this Convention for them, for the purpose of controlling transboundary movements of hazardous wastes and other wastes which take place entirely among the Parties to such agreements. The provisions of this Convention shall not affect transboundary movements which take place pursuant to such agreements provided that such agreements are compatible with the environmentally sound management of hazardous wastes and other wastes as required by this Convention.

Article 12 Consultations on Liability

The Parties shall co-operate with a view to adopting, as soon as practicable, a Protocol setting out appropriate rules and procedures in the field of liability and compensation for damage resulting from the transboundary movement and disposal of hazardous wastes and other wastes.

Article 13 Transmission of Information

(1) The Parties shall, whenever it comes to their knowledge, ensure that, in the case of an accident occurring during the transboundary movement of hazardous wastes or other wastes or their disposal, which are likely to present risks to human health and the environment in other States, those States are immediately informed.

(2) The Parties shall inform each other, through the Secretariat, of:

(a) Changes regarding the designation of competent authorities and/or focal points, pursuant to Article 5;

(b) Changes in their national definition of hazardous wastes, pursuant to Article 3;

and, as soon as possible,

(c) Decisions made by them not to consent totally or partially to the import of hazardous wastes or other wastes for disposal within the area under their national jurisdiction;

(d) Decisions taken by them to limit or ban the export of hazardous wastes or other wastes;

(e) Any other information required pursuant to paragraph (4) of this Article.

(3) The Parties, consistent with national laws and regulations, shall transmit, through the Secretariat, to the Conference of the Parties established under Article 15, before the end of each calendar year, a report on the previous calendar year, containing the following information:

(a) Competent authorities and focal points that have been designated by them pursuant to Article 5;

(b) Information regarding transboundary movements of hazardous wastes or other wastes in which they have been involved, including:

(i) The amount of hazardous wastes and other wastes exported, their category, characteristics, destination, any transit country and disposal method as stated on the response to notification;

(ii) The amount of hazardous wastes and other wastes imported, their category, characteristics, origin, and disposal methods;

(iii) Disposals which did not proceed as intended;

(iv) Efforts to achieve a reduction of the amount of hazardous wastes or other wastes subject to transboundary movement;

(c) Information on the measures adopted by them in implementation of this Convention;

(d) Information on available qualified statistics which have been compiled by them on the effects on human health and the environment of the generation, transportation and disposal of hazardous wastes or other wastes;

(e) Information concerning bilateral, multilateral and regional agreements and arrangements entered into pursuant to Article 11 of this Convention;

(f) Information on accidents occurring during the transboundary movement and disposal of hazardous wastes and other wastes and on the measures undertaken to deal with them;

(g) Information on disposal options operated within the area of their national jurisdiction;

(h) Information on measures undertaken for development of technologies for the reduction and/or elimination of production of hazardous wastes and other wastes; and

(i) Such other matters as the Conference of the Parties shall deem relevant.

(4) The Parties, consistent with national laws and regulations, shall ensure that copies of each notification concerning any given transboundary movement of hazardous wastes or other wastes, and the response to it, are sent to the Secretariat when a Party considers that its environment may be affected by that transboundary movement has requested that this should be done.

Article 14 Financial Aspects

(1) The Parties agree that, according to the specific needs of different regions and subregions, regional or subregional centres for training and technology transfers regarding the management of hazardous wastes and other wastes and the minimization of their generation should be established. The Parties shall decide on the establishment of appropriate funding mechanisms of a voluntary nature.

(2) The Parties shall consider the establishment of a revolving fund to assist on an interim basis in case of emergency situations to minimize damage from accidents arising from transboundary movements of hazardous wastes and other wastes or during the disposal of those wastes.

Article 15 Conference of the Parties

(1) A Conference of the Parties is hereby established. The first meeting of the Conference of the Parties shall be convened by the Executive Director of UNEP not later than one year after the entry into force of this Convention. Thereafter, ordinary meetings of the Conference of the Parties shall be held at regular intervals to be determined by the Conference at its first meeting.

(2) Extraordinary meetings of the Conference of the Parties shall be held at such other times as may be deemed necessary by the Conference, or at the written request of any Party, provided that, within six months of the request being communicated to them by the Secretariat, it is supported by at least one third of the Parties.

(3) The Conference of the Parties shall by consensus agree upon and adopt rules of procedure for itself and for any subsidiary body it may establish, as well as financial rules to determine in particular the financial participation of the Parties under this Convention.

(4) The Parties at their first meeting shall consider any additional measures needed to assist them in fulfilling their responsibilities with respect to the protection and the preservation of the marine environment in the context of this Convention.

(5) The Conference of the Parties shall keep under continuous review and evaluation the effective implementation of this Convention, and, in addition, shall:

(a) Promote the harmonization of appropriate policies, strategies and measures for minimizing harm to human health and the environment by hazardous wastes and other wastes;

(b) Consider and adopt, as required, amendments to this Convention and its Annexes, taking into consideration, inter alia, available scientific, technical, economic and environmental information;

(c) Consider and undertake any additional action that may be required for the achievement of the purposes of this Convention in the light of experience gained in its operation and in the operation of the agreements and arrangements envisaged in Article 11;

(d) Consider and adopt Protocols as required; and

(e) Establish such subsidiary bodies as are deemed necessary for the implementation of this Convention.

(6) The United Nations, its specialized agencies, as well as any State not Party to this Convention, may be represented as observers at meetings of the Conference of the Parties. Any other body or agency, whether national or international, governmental or non-governmental, qualified in fields relating to hazardous wastes or other wastes which has informed the Secretariat of its wish to be represented as an observer at a meeting of the Conference of the Parties, may be admitted unless at least one third of the Parties present object. The admission and participation of observers shall be subject to the rules of procedure adopted by the Conference of the Parties.

(7) The Conference of the Parties shall undertake three years after the entry into force of this Convention, and at least every six years thereafter, an evaluation of its effectiveness and, if deemed necessary, to consider the adoption of a complete or partial ban of transboundary movements of hazardous wastes and other wastes in light of the latest scientific, environmental, technical and economic information.

Article 16 Secretariat

(1) The functions of the Secretariat shall be:

(a) To arrange for and service meetings provided for in Articles 15 and 17;

(b) To prepare and transmit reports based upon information received in accordance with Articles 3, 4, 6, 11 and 13 as well as upon information derived from meetings of subsidiary bodies established under Article 15 as well as upon, as appropriate, information provided by relevant intergovernmental and non-governmental entities;

(c) To prepare reports on its activities carried out in implementation of its functions under this Convention and present them to the Conference of the Parties;

(d) To ensure the necessary coordination with relevant international bodies, and in particular to enter into such administrative and contractual arrangements as may be required for the effective discharge of its function;

(e) To communicate with focal points and competent authorities established by the Parties in accordance with Article 5 of this Convention;

(f) To compile information concerning authorized national sites and facilities of Parties available for the disposal of their hazardous wastes and other wastes and to circulate this information among Parties;

(g) To receive and convey information from and to Parties on:
   - sources of technical assistance and training;
   - available technical and scientific know-how;
   - sources of advice and expertise; and
   - availability of resources

   with a view to assisting them, upon request, in such areas as:
   - the handling of the notification system of this Convention;
   - the management of hazardous wastes and other wastes;
   - environmentally sound technologies relating to hazardous wastes and other wastes, such as low- and non-waste technology;
   - the assessment of disposal capabilities and sites;
   - the monitoring of hazardous wastes and other wastes; and
   - emergency responses;

(h) To provide Parties, upon request, with information on consultants or consulting firms having the necessary technical competence in the field, which can assist them to examine a notification for a transboundary movement, the concurrence of a shipment of hazardous wastes or other wastes with the relevant notification, and/or the fact that the proposed disposal facilities for hazardous wastes or other wastes are environmentally sound, when they have reason to believe that the wastes in question will not be managed in an environmentally sound manner. Any such examination would not be at the expense of the Secretariat;

(i) To assist Parties upon request in their identification of cases of illegal traffic and to circulate immediately to the Parties concerned any information it has received regarding illegal traffic;

(j) To co-operate with Parties and with relevant and competent international organizations and agencies in the provision of experts and equipment for the purpose of rapid assistance to States in the event of an emergency situation; and

(k) To perform such other functions relevant to the purposes of this Convention as may be determined by the Conference of the Parties.

(2) The secretariat functions will be carried out on an interim basis by UNEP until the completion of the first meeting of the Conference of the Parties held pursuant to Article 15.

(3) At its first meeting, the Conference of the Parties shall designate the Secretariat from among those existing competent intergovernmental organizations which have signified their willingness to carry out the secretariat functions under this Convention. At this meeting, the Conference of the Parties shall also evaluate the implementation by the interim Secretariat of the functions assigned to it, in particular under paragraph (1) above, and decide upon the structures appropriate for those functions.

Article 17 Amendment of the Convention

(1) Any Party may propose amendments to this Convention and any Party to a Protocol may propose amendments to that Protocol. Such amendments shall take due account, inter alia, of relevant scientific and technical considerations.

(2) Amendments to this Convention shall be adopted at a meeting of the Conference of the Parties. Amendments to any Protocol shall be adopted at a meeting of the Parties to the Protocol in question. The text of any proposed amendment to this Convention or to any Protocol, except as may otherwise be provided in such Protocol, shall be communicated to the Parties by the Secretariat at least six months before the meeting at which it is proposed for adoption. The Secretariat shall also communicate proposed amendments to the Signatories to this Convention for information.

(3) The Parties shall make every effort to reach agreement on any proposed amendment to this Convention by consensus. If all efforts at consensus have been exhausted, and no agreement

reached, the amendment shall as a last resort be adopted by a three-fourths majority vote of the Parties present and voting at the meeting, and shall be submitted by the Depositary to all Parties for ratification, approval, formal confirmation or acceptance.

(4) The procedure mentioned in paragraph (3) above shall apply to amendments to any Protocol, except that a two-thirds majority of the Parties to that Protocol present and voting at the meeting shall suffice for their adoption.

(5) Instruments of ratification, approval, formal confirmation or acceptance of amendments shall be deposited with the Depositary. Amendments adopted in accordance with paragraphs (3) or (4) above shall enter into force between Parties having accepted them on the ninetieth day after the receipt by the Depositary of their instrument of ratification, approval, formal confirmation or acceptance by at least three-fourths of the Parties who accepted them or by at least two thirds of the Parties to the Protocol concerned who accepted them, except as may otherwise be provided in such Protocol. The amendments shall enter into force for any other Party on the ninetieth day after that Party deposits its instrument of ratification, approval, formal confirmation or acceptance of the amendments.

(6) For the purpose of this Article, "Parties present and voting" means Parties present and casting an affirmative or negative vote.

Article 18 Adoption and Amendment of Annexes

(1) The Annexes to this Convention or to any Protocol shall form an integral part of this Convention or of such Protocol, as the case may be and, unless expressly provided otherwise, a reference to this Convention or its Protocols constitutes at the same time a reference to any Annexes thereto. Such Annexes shall be restricted to scientific, technical and administrative matters.

(2) Except as may be otherwise provided in any Protocol with respect to its Annexes, the following procedure shall apply to the proposal, adoption and entry into force of additional Annexes to this Convention or of Annexes to a Protocol:

  (a) Annexes to this Convention and its Protocols shall be proposed and adopted according to the procedure laid down in Article 17, paragraphs (2), (3) and (4);

  (b) Any Party that is unable to accept an additional Annex to this Convention or an Annex to any Protocol to which it is party shall so notify the Depositary, in writing, within six months from the date of the communication of the adoption by the Depositary. The Depositary shall without delay notify all Parties of any such notification received. A Party may at any time substitute an acceptance for a previous declaration of objection and the Annexes shall thereupon enter into force for that Party;

  (c) On the expiry of six months from the date of the circulation of the communication by the Depositary, the Annex shall become effective for all Parties to this Convention or to any Protocol concerned, which have not submitted a notification in accordance with the provision of subparagraph (b) above.

(3) The proposal, adoption and entry into force of amendments to Annexes to this Convention or to any Protocol shall be subject to the same procedure as for the proposal, adoption and entry into force of Annexes to the Convention or Annexes to a Protocol. Annexes and amendments thereto shall take due account, inter alia, of relevant scientific and technical considerations.

(4) If an additional Annex or an amendment to an Annex involves an amendment to this Convention or to any Protocol, the additional Annex or amended Annex shall not enter into force until such time the amendment to this Convention or to the Protocol enters into force.

Article 19 Verification

Any Party which has reason to believe that another Party is acting or has acted in breach of its obligations under this Convention may inform the Secretariat thereof, and in such an event, shall simultaneously and immediately inform, directly or through the Secretariat, the Party against whom the allegations are made. All relevant information should be submitted by the Secretariat to the Parties.

Article 20 Settlement of Disputes

(1) In case of a dispute between Parties as to the interpretation or application of, or compliance with, this Convention or any Protocol thereto, they shall seek a settlement of the dispute through negotiation or any other peaceful means of their own choice.

(2) If the Parties concerned cannot settle their dispute through the means mentioned in the preceding paragraph, the dispute, if the Parties to the dispute agree, shall be submitted to the International Court of Justice or to arbitration under the conditions set out in Annex VI on Arbitration. However, failure to reach common agreement on submission of the dispute to the International Court of Justice or to arbitration shall not absolve the Parties from the responsibility of continuing to seek to resolve it by the means referred to in paragraph (1).

(3) When ratifying, accepting, approving, formally confirming or acceding to this Convention, or at any time thereafter, a State or political and/or economic integration organization may declare that it recognizes as compulsory ipso facto and without special agreement, in relation to any Party accepting the same obligation:

(a) submission of the dispute to the International Court of Justice; and/or

(b) arbitration in accordance with the procedures set out in Annex VI.

Such declaration shall be notified in writing to the Secretariat which shall communicate it to the Parties.

Article 21 Signature

This Convention shall be open for signature by States, by Namibia, represented by the United Nations Council for Namibia, and by political and/or economic integration organizations, in Basel on 22 March 1989, at the Federal Department of Foreign Affairs of Switzerland in Berne from 23 March 1989 to 30 June 1989 and at United Nations Headquarters in New York from 1 July 1989 to 22 March 1990.

Article 22 Ratification, Acceptance, Formal Confirmation or Approval

(1) This Convention shall be subject to ratification, acceptance or approval by States and by Namibia, represented by the United Nations Council for Namibia, and to formal confirmation or approval by political and/or economic integration organizations. Instruments of ratification, acceptance, formal confirmation, or approval shall be deposited with the Depositary.

(2) Any organization referred to in paragraph (1) above which becomes a Party to this Convention without any of its member States being a Party shall be bound by all the obligations under the Convention. In the case of such organizations, one or more of whose member States is a Party to the Convention, the organization and its member States shall decide on their respective responsibilities for the performance of their obligations under the Convention. In such cases, the organization and the member States shall not be entitled to exercise rights under the Convention concurrently.

(3) In their instruments of formal confirmation or approval, the organizations referred to in paragraph (1) above shall declare the extent of their competence with respect to the matters governed by the Convention. These organizations shall also inform the Depositary, who will inform the Parties of any substantial modification in the extent of their competence.

Article 23 Accession

(1) This Convention shall be open for accession by States, by Namibia, represented by the United Nations Council for Namibia, and by political and/or economic integration organizations from the

day after the date on which the Convention is closed for signature. The instruments of accession shall be deposited with the Depositary.

(2) In their instruments of accession, the organizations referred to in paragraph (1) above shall declare the extent of their competence with respect to the matters governed by the Convention. These organizations shall also inform the Depositary of any substantial modification in the extent of their competence.

(3) The provisions of Article 22, paragraph (2), shall apply to political and/or economic integration organizations which accede to this Convention.

Article 24 Right to Vote

(1) Except as provided for in paragraph (2) below, each Contracting Party to this Convention shall have one vote.

(2) Political and/or economic integration organizations, in matters within their competence, in accordance with Article 22, paragraph (3), and Article 23, paragraph (2), shall exercise their right to vote with a number of votes equal to the number of their member States which are Parties to the Convention or the relevant Protocol. Such organizations shall not exercise their right to vote if their member States exercise theirs, and vice versa.

Article 25 Entry into Force

(1) This Convention shall enter into force on the ninetieth day after the date of deposit of the twentieth instrument of ratification, acceptance, formal confirmation, approval or accession.

(2) For each State or political and/or economic integration organization which ratifies, accepts, approves or formally confirms this Convention or accedes thereto after the date of the deposit of the twentieth instrument of ratification, acceptance, approval, formal confirmation or accession, it shall enter into force on the ninetieth day after the date of deposit by such State or political and/or economic integration organization of its instrument of ratification, acceptance, approval, formal confirmation or accession.

(3) For the purpose of paragraphs (1) and (2) above, any instrument deposited by a political and/or economic integration organization shall not be counted as additional to those deposited by member States of such organization.

Article 26 Reservations and Declarations

(1) No reservation or exception may be made to this Convention.

(2) Paragraph (1) of this Article does not preclude a State or political and/or economic integration organization, when signing, ratifying, accepting, approving, formally confirming or acceding to this Convention, from making declarations or statements, however phrased or named, with a view, inter alia, to the harmonization of its laws and regulations with the provisions of this Convention, provided that such declarations or statements do not purport to exclude or to modify the legal effects of the provisions of the Convention in their application to that State.

Article 27 Withdrawal

(1) At any time after three years from the date on which this Convention has entered into force for a Party, that Party may withdraw from the Convention by giving written notification to the Depositary.

(2) Withdrawal shall be effective one year from receipt of notification by the Depositary, or on such later date as may be specified in the notification.

Article 28 Depository

The Secretary-General of the United Nations shall be the Depository of this Convention and of any Protocol thereto.

Article 29 Authentic texts

The original Arabic, Chinese, English, French, Russian and Spanish texts of this Convention are equally authentic.

IN WITNESS WHEREOF the undersigned, being duly authorized to that effect, have signed this Convention.

DONE at Basel on the 22 day of March 1989.

Annex I
Categories of Wastes to be Controlled

Waste Streams

Y1	Clinical wastes from medical care in hospitals, medical centres and clinics
Y2	Wastes from the production and preparation of pharmaceutical products
Y3	Waste pharmaceuticals, drugs and medicines
Y4	Wastes from the production, formulation and use of biocides and phytopharmaceuticals
Y5	Wastes from the manufacture, formulation and use of wood preserving chemicals
Y6	Wastes from the production, formulation and use of organic solvents
Y7	Wastes from heat treatment and tempering operations containing cyanides
Y8	Waste mineral oils unfit for their originally intended use
Y9	Waste oils/water, hydrocarbons/water mixtures, emulsions
Y10	Waste substances and articles containing or contaminated with polychlorinated biphenyls (PCBs) and/or polychlorinated terphenyls (PCTs) and/or polybrominated biphenyls (PBBs)
Y11	Waste tarry residues arising from refining, distillation and any pyrolytic treatment
Y12	Wastes from production, formulation and use of inks, dyes, pigments, paints, lacquers, varnish
Y13	Wastes from production, formulation and use of resins, latex, plasticizers, glues/adhesives
Y14	Waste chemical substances arising from research and development or teaching activities which are not identified and/or are new and whose effects on man and/or the environment are not known
Y15	Wastes of an explosive nature not subject to other legislation
Y16	Wastes from production, formulation and use of photographic chemicals and processing materials
Y17	Wastes resulting from surface treatment of metals and plastics
Y18	Residues arising from industrial waste disposal operations

Wastes Having as Constituents

Y19	Metal carbonyls
Y20	Beryllium; beryllium compounds

Y21	Hexavalent chromium compounds
Y22	Copper compounds
Y23	Zinc compounds
Y24	Arsenic; arsenic compounds
Y25	Selenium; selenium compounds
Y26	Cadmium; cadmium compounds
Y27	Antimony; antimony compounds
Y28	Tellurium; tellurium compounds
Y29	Mercury; mercury compounds
Y30	Thallium; thallium compounds
Y31	Lead; lead compounds
Y32	Inorganic fluorine compounds excluding calcium fluoride
Y33	Inorganic cyanides
Y34	Acidic solutions or acids in solid form
Y35	Basic solutions or bases in solid form
Y36	Asbestos (dust and fibres)
Y37	Organic phosphorus compounds
Y38	Organic cyanides
Y39	Phenols; phenol compounds including chlorophenols
Y40	Ethers
Y41	Halogenated organic solvents
Y42	Organic solvents excluding halogenated solvents
Y43	Any congenor of polychlorinated dibenzo-furan
Y44	Any congenor of polychlorinated dibenzo-p-dioxin
Y45	Organohalogen compounds other than substances referred to in this Annex (e.g., Y39, Y41, Y42, Y43, Y44)

(a) To facilitate the application of this Convention, and subject to paragraphs (b), (c) and (d), wastes listed in Annex VIII are characterized as hazardous pursuant to Article 1, paragraph (1)(a), of this Convention, and wastes listed in Annex IX are not covered by Article 1, paragraph (1)(a), of this Convention.

(b) Designation of a waste on Annex VIII does not preclude, in a particular case, the use of Annex III to demonstrate that a waste is not hazardous pursuant to Article 1, paragraph (1)(a), of this Convention.

(c) Designation of a waste on Annex IX does not preclude, in a particular case, characterization of such a waste as hazardous pursuant to Article 1, paragraph (1)(a), of this Convention if it contains Annex I material to an extent causing it to exhibit an Annex III characteristic.

(d) Annexes VIII and IX do not affect the application of Article 1, paragraph (1)(a), of this Convention for the purpose of characterization of wastes.*

* The amendment whereby paragraphs (a), (b), (c) and (d) were added to the end of Annex I entered into force on 6 November 1998, six months following the issuance of depositary notification C.N.77.1998 of 6 May 1998 (reflecting decision IV/9, adopted by the Conference of the Parties at its fourth meeting).

Annex II*

Categories of Wastes Requiring Special Consideration

Y46	Wastes collected from households
Y47	Residues arising from the incineration of household wastes
Y48[†]	Plastic waste, including mixtures of such waste, with the exception of the following: • Plastic waste that is hazardous waste pursuant to paragraph (1)(a) of Article 1[‡] • Plastic waste listed below, provided it is destined for recycling[§] in an environmentally sound manner and almost free from contamination and other types of wastes:[¶] – Plastic waste almost exclusively[**] consisting of one non-halogenated polymer, including but not limited to the following polymers: Polyethylene (PE) Polypropylene (PP) Polystyrene (PS) Acrylonitrile butadiene styrene (ABS) Polyethylene terephthalate (PET) Polycarbonates (PC) Polyethers – Plastic waste almost exclusively consisting of one cured resin or condensation product, including but not limited to the following resins: Urea formaldehyde resins Phenol formaldehyde resins Melamine formaldehyde resins Epoxy resins Alkyd resins – Plastic waste almost exclusively consisting of one of the following fluorinated polymers:[††] Perfluoroethylene/propylene (FEP) Perfluoroalkoxy alkanes: - Tetrafluoroethylene/perfluoroalkyl vinyl ether (PFA) - Tetrafluoroethylene/perfluoromethyl vinyl ether (MFA)

* This amendment to Annex II whereby one new entry was added entered into force on 24 March 2020 (depositary notification C.N. 432.2019), reflecting decision BC-14/12 adopted by the Conference of the Parties at its fourteenth meeting. For information on the status of individual Parties in relation to the amendment/s, please see the Status of Ratifications page on the Basel Convention website.

† Parties can impose stricter requirements in relation to this entry.

‡ Note the related entry on list A A3210 in Annex VIII.

§ Recycling/reclamation of organic substances that are not used as solvents (R3 in Annex IV, Section B) or, if needed, temporary storage limited to one instance, provided that it is followed by operation R3 and evidenced by contractual or relevant official documentation.

¶ In relation to "almost free from contamination and other types of wastes", international and national specifications may offer a point of reference.

** In relation to "almost exclusively", international and national specifications may offer a point of reference.

†† Post-consumer wastes are excluded.

Polyvinylfluoride (PVF)

Polyvinylidenefluoride (PVDF)

- Mixtures of plastic waste, consisting of polyethylene (PE), polypropylene (PP) and/or polyethylene terephthalate (PET), provided they are destined for separate recycling* of each material and in an environmentally sound manner and almost free from contamination and other types of wastes.

Annex III
List of Hazardous Characteristics

UN Class†	Code	Characteristics
1	H1	Explosive
		An explosive substance or waste is a solid or liquid substance or waste (or mixture of substances or wastes) which is in itself capable by chemical reaction of producing gas at such a temperature and pressure and at such a speed as to cause damage to the surroundings.
3	H3	Flammable liquids
		The word "flammable" has the same meaning as "inflammable". Flammable liquids are liquids, or mixtures of liquids, or liquids containing solids in solution or suspension (for example, paints, varnishes, lacquers, etc., but not including substances or wastes otherwise classified on account of their dangerous characteristics) which give off a flammable vapour at temperatures of not more than 60.5°C, closed-cup test, or not more than 65.6°C, open-cup test. (Since the results of open-cup tests and of closed-cup tests are not strictly comparable and even individual results by the same test are often variable, regulations varying from the above figures to make allowance for such differences would be within the spirit of this definition.)
4.1	H4.1	Flammable solids
		Solids, or waste solids, other than those classed as explosives, which under conditions encountered in transport are readily combustible, or may cause or contribute to fire through friction.
4.2	H4.2	Substances or wastes liable to spontaneous combustion
		Substances or wastes which are liable to spontaneous heating under normal conditions encountered in transport, or to heating up on contact with air, and being then liable to catch fire.

* Recycling/reclamation of organic substances that are not used as solvents (R3 in Annex IV, Section B), with prior sorting and, if needed, temporary storage limited to one instance, provided that it is followed by operation R3 and evidenced by contractual or relevant official documentation.

† Corresponds to the hazard classification system included in the United Nations Recommendations on the Transport of Dangerous Goods (ST/SG/AC.10/1Rev.5, United Nations, New York, 1988).

4.3	H4.3	Substances or wastes which, in contact with water emit flammable gases
		Substances or wastes which, by interaction with water, are liable to become spontaneously flammable or to give off flammable gases in dangerous quantities.
5.1	H5.1	Oxidizing
		Substances or wastes which, while in themselves not necessarily combustible, may, generally by yielding oxygen cause, or contribute to, the combustion of other materials.
5.2	H5.2	Organic Peroxides
		Organic substances or wastes which contain the bivalent-o-o-structure are thermally unstable substances which may undergo exothermic self-accelerating decomposition.
6.1	H6.1	Poisonous (Acute)
		Substances or wastes liable either to cause death or serious injury or to harm human health if swallowed or inhaled or by skin contact.
6.2	H6.2	Infectious substances
		Substances or wastes containing viable microorganisms or their toxins which are known or suspected to cause disease in animals or humans.
8	H8	Corrosives
		Substances or wastes which, by chemical action, will cause severe damage when in contact with living tissue, or, in the case of leakage, will materially damage, or even destroy, other goods or the means of transport; they may also cause other hazards.
9	H10	Liberation of toxic gases in contact with air or water
		Substances or wastes which, by interaction with air or water, are liable to give off toxic gases in dangerous quantities.
9	H11	Toxic (Delayed or chronic)
		Substances or wastes which, if they are inhaled or ingested or if they penetrate the skin, may involve delayed or chronic effects, including carcinogenicity.
9	H12	Ecotoxic
		Substances or wastes which if released present or may present immediate or delayed adverse impacts to the environment by means of bioaccumulation and/or toxic effects upon biotic systems.
9	H13	Capable, by any means, after disposal, of yielding another material (e.g., leachate), which possesses any of the characteristics listed above.

Tests

The potential hazards posed by certain types of wastes are not yet fully documented; tests to define quantitatively these hazards do not exist. Further research is necessary in order to develop means to characterize potential hazards posed to man and/or the environment by these wastes. Standardized tests have been derived with respect to pure substances and materials. Many countries have developed national tests which can be applied to materials listed in Annex I, in order to decide if these materials exhibit any of the characteristics listed in this Annex.

Annex IV
Disposal Operations

A. *Operations Which Do Not Lead to the Possibility of Resource Recovery, Recycling, Reclamation, Direct Re-use or Alternative Uses*

Section A encompasses all such disposal operations which occur in practice.

D1	Deposit into or onto land, (e.g., landfill, etc.)
D2	Land treatment, (e.g., biodegradation of liquid or sludgy discards in soils, etc.)
D3	Deep injection, (e.g., injection of pumpable discards into wells, salt domes of naturally occurring repositories, etc.)
D4	Surface impoundment, (e.g., placement of liquid or sludge discards into pits, ponds or lagoons, etc.)
D5	Specially engineered landfill, (e.g., placement into lined discrete cells which are capped and isolated from one another and the environment, etc.)
D6	Release into a water body except seas/oceans
D7	Release into seas/oceans including sea-bed insertion
D8	Biological treatment not specified elsewhere in this Annex which results in final compounds or mixtures which are discarded by means of any of the operations in Section A
D9	Physico-chemical treatment not specified elsewhere in this Annex which results in final compounds or mixtures which are discarded by means of any of the operations in Section A, (e.g., evaporation, drying, calcination, neutralization, precipitation, etc.)
D10	Incineration on land
D11	Incineration at sea
D12	Permanent storage (e.g., emplacement of containers in a mine, etc.)
D13	Blending or mixing prior to submission to any of the operations in Section A
D14	Repackaging prior to submission to any of the operations in Section A
D15	Storage pending any of the operations in Section A

B. *Operations Which May Lead to Resource Recovery, Recycling Reclamation, Direct Re-use or Alternative Uses*

Section B encompasses all such operations with respect to materials legally defined as or considered to be hazardous wastes and which otherwise would have been destined for operations included in Section A

R1	Use as a fuel (other than in direct incineration) or other means to generate energy
R2	Solvent reclamation/regeneration
R3	Recycling/reclamation of organic substances which are not used as solvents
R4	Recycling/reclamation of metals and metal compounds
R5	Recycling/reclamation of other inorganic materials
R6	Regeneration of acids or bases
R7	Recovery of components used for pollution abatement

R8	Recovery of components from catalysts
R9	Used oil re-refining or other reuses of previously used oil
R10	Land treatment resulting in benefit to agriculture or ecological improvement
R11	Uses of residual materials obtained from any of the operations numbered R1–R10
R12	Exchange of wastes for submission to any of the operations numbered R1–R11
R13	Accumulation of material intended for any operation in Section B

Annex V.A
Information to be Provided on Notification

(1) Reason for waste export

(2) Exporter of the waste *

(3) Generator(s) of the waste and site of generation *

(4) Disposer of the waste and actual site of disposal *

(5) Intended carrier(s) of the waste or their agents, if known *

(6) Country of export of the waste
Competent authority †

(7) Expected countries of transit
Competent authority †

(8) Country of import of the waste
Competent authority †

(9) General or single notification

(10) Projected date(s) of shipment(s) and period of time over which waste is to be exported and proposed itinerary (including point of entry and exit) ‡

(11) Means of transport envisaged (road, rail, sea, air, inland waters)

(12) Information relating to insurance §

(13) Designation and physical description of the waste including Y number and UN number and its composition ¶ and information on any special handling requirements including emergency provisions in case of accidents

(14) Type of packaging envisaged (e.g., bulk, drummed, tanker)

(15) Estimated quantity in weight/volume **

* Full name and address, telephone, telex or telefax number and the name, address, telephone, telex or telefax number of the person to be contacted.

† Full name and address, telephone, telex or telefax number.

‡ In the case of a general notification covering several shipments, either the expected dates of each shipment or, if this is not known, the expected frequency of the shipments will be required.

§ Information to be provided on relevant insurance requirements and how they are met by exporter, carrier and disposer.

¶ The nature and the concentration of the most hazardous components, in terms of toxicity and other dangers presented by the waste both in handling and in relation to the proposed disposal method.

** In the case of a general notification covering several shipments, both the estimated total quantity and the estimated quantities for each individual shipment will be required.

(16) Process by which the waste is generated *

(17) For wastes listed in Annex I, classifications from Annex III: hazardous characteristic, H number, and UN class

(18) Method of disposal as per Annex IV

(19) Declaration by the generator and exporter that the information is correct

(20) Information transmitted (including technical description of the plant) to the exporter or generator from the disposer of the waste upon which the latter has based his assessment that there was no reason to believe that the wastes will not be managed in an environmentally sound manner in accordance with the laws and regulations of the country of import

(21) Information concerning the contract between the exporter and disposer.

Annex V.B
Information to be Provided on the Movement Document

(1) Exporter of the waste †

(2) Generator(s) of the waste and site of generation †

(3) Disposer of the waste and actual site of disposal †

(4) Carrier(s) of the waste † or his agent(s)

(5) Subject of general or single notification

(6) The date the transboundary movement started and date(s) and signature on receipt by each person who takes charge of the waste

(7) Means of transport (road, rail, inland waterway, sea, air) including countries of export, transit and import, also point of entry and exit where these have been designated

(8) General description of the waste (physical state, proper UN shipping name and class, UN number, Y number and H number as applicable)

(9) Information on special handling requirements including emergency provision in case of accidents

(10) Type and number of packages

(11) Quantity in weight/volume

(12) Declaration by the generator or exporter that the information is correct

(13) Declaration by the generator or exporter indicating no objection from the competent authorities of all States concerned which are Parties

(14) Certification by disposer of receipt at designated disposal facility and indication of method of disposal and of the approximate date of disposal.

Notes

The information required on the movement document shall where possible be integrated in one document with that required under transport rules. Where this is not possible the information should complement rather than duplicate that required under the transport rules. The movement document shall carry instructions as to who is to provide information and fill-out any form.

---

* Insofar as this is necessary to assess the hazard and determine the appropriateness of the proposed disposal operation.

† Full name and address, telephone, telex or telefax number and the name, address, telephone, telex or telefax number of the person to be contacted in case of emergency.

Annex VI
Arbitration

Article 1

Unless the agreement referred to in Article 20 of the Convention provides otherwise, the arbitration procedure shall be conducted in accordance with Articles 2 to 10 below.

Article 2

The claimant Party shall notify the Secretariat that the Parties have agreed to submit the dispute to arbitration pursuant to paragraph (2) or paragraph (3) of Article 20 and include, in particular, the Articles of the Convention the interpretation or application of which are at issue. The Secretariat shall forward the information thus received to all Parties to the Convention.

Article 3

The arbitral tribunal shall consist of three members. Each of the Parties to the dispute shall appoint an arbitrator, and the two arbitrators so appointed shall designate by common agreement the third arbitrator, who shall be the chairman of the tribunal. The latter shall not be a national of one of the Parties to the dispute, nor have his usual place of residence in the territory of one of these Parties, nor be employed by any of them, nor have dealt with the case in any other capacity.

Article 4

(1) If the chairman of the arbitral tribunal has not been designated within two months of the appointment of the second arbitrator, the Secretary-General of the United Nations shall, at the request of either Party, designate him within a further two months period.

(2) If one of the Parties to the dispute does not appoint an arbitrator within two months of the receipt of the request, the other Party may inform the Secretary-General of the United Nations who shall designate the chairman of the arbitral tribunal within a further two months' period. Upon designation, the chairman of the arbitral tribunal shall request the Party which has not appointed an arbitrator to do so within two months. After such period, he shall inform the Secretary-General of the United Nations, who shall make this appointment within a further two months' period.

Article 5

(1) The arbitral tribunal shall render its decision in accordance with international law and in accordance with the provisions of this Convention.

(2) Any arbitral tribunal constituted under the provisions of this Annex shall draw up its own rules of procedure.

Article 6

(1) The decisions of the arbitral tribunal both on procedure and on substance, shall be taken by majority vote of its members.

(2) The tribunal may take all appropriate measures in order to establish the facts. It may, at the request of one of the Parties, recommend essential interim measures of protection.

(3) The Parties to the dispute shall provide all facilities necessary for the effective conduct of the proceedings.

(4) The absence or default of a Party in the dispute shall not constitute an impediment to the proceedings.

Article 7

The tribunal may hear and determine counter-claims arising directly out of the subject-matter of the dispute.

Article 8

Unless the arbitral tribunal determines otherwise because of the particular circumstances of the case, the expenses of the tribunal, including the remuneration of its members, shall be borne by the Parties to the dispute in equal shares. The tribunal shall keep a record of all its expenses, and shall furnish a final statement thereof to the Parties.

Article 9

Any Party that has an interest of a legal nature in the subject-matter of the dispute which may be affected by the decision in the case, may intervene in the proceedings with the consent of the tribunal.

Article 10

(1) The tribunal shall render its award within five months of the date on which it is established unless it finds it necessary to extend the time-limit for a period which should not exceed five months.

(2) The award of the arbitral tribunal shall be accompanied by a statement of reasons. It shall be final and binding upon the Parties to the dispute.

(3) Any dispute which may arise between the Parties concerning the interpretation or execution of the award may be submitted by either Party to the arbitral tribunal which made the award or, if the latter cannot be seized thereof, to another tribunal constituted for this purpose in the same manner as the first.

Annex VII *

Parties and other States which are members of OECD, EC, Liechtenstein

Annex VIII †
List A

Wastes contained in this Annex are characterized as hazardous under Article 1, paragraph (1)(a), of this Convention, and their designation on this Annex does not preclude the use of Annex III to demonstrate that a waste is not hazardous.

* The amendment whereby Annex VII was added to the Convention entered into force on 5 December 2019, in accordance with Article 17(5) of the Convention (depositary notification C.N.420.2019), reflecting decision III/1 adopted by the Conference of the Parties at its third meeting

† The amendment whereby Annex VIII was added to the Convention entered into force on 6 November 1998, six months following the issuance of depositary notification C.N.77.1998 of 6 May 1998 (reflecting decision IV/9 adopted by the Conference of the Parties at its fourth meeting). The amendment to Annex VIII whereby new entries were added entered into force on 20 November 2003 (depositary notification C.N.1314.2003), six months following the issuance of depositary notification C.N.399.2003 of 20 May 2003 (reflecting decision VI/35 adopted by the Conference of the Parties at its sixth meeting). The amendment to Annex VIII whereby one new entry was added entered into force on 8 October 2005 (depositary notification C.N.1044.2005), six months following the issuance of depositary notification C.N.263.2005 of 8 April 2005 (re-issued on 13 June 2005, reflecting decision VII/19 adopted by the Conference of the Parties at its seventh meeting). The amendment to Annex VIII whereby one new entry was added entered into force on 24 March 2020, six months following the issuance of depositary notification C.N.432.2019 of 24 September 2019 (reflecting decision BC-14/12 adopted by the Conference of the Parties at its fourteenth meeting). The present text includes all amendments. For information on the status of individual Parties in relation to the amendment/s, please see the Status of Ratifications page on the Basel Convention website.

A1 *Metal and Metal-bearing Wastes*

A1010	Metal wastes and waste consisting of alloys of any of the following: • Antimony • Arsenic • Beryllium • Cadmium • Lead • Mercury • Selenium • Tellurium • Thallium but excluding such wastes specifically listed on list B.
A1020	Waste having as constituents or contaminants, excluding metal waste in massive form, any of the following: • Antimony; antimony compounds • Beryllium; beryllium compounds • Cadmium; cadmium compounds • Lead; lead compounds • Selenium; selenium compounds • Tellurium; tellurium compounds
A1030	Wastes having as constituents or contaminants any of the following: • Arsenic; arsenic compounds • Mercury; mercury compounds • Thallium; thallium compounds
A1040	Wastes having as constituents any of the following: • Metal carbonyls • Hexavalent chromium compounds
A1050	Galvanic sludges
A1060	Waste liquors from the pickling of metals
A1070	Leaching residues from zinc processing, dust and sludges such as jarosite, hematite, etc.
A1080	Waste zinc residues not included on list B, containing lead and cadmium in concentrations sufficient to exhibit Annex III characteristics
A1090	Ashes from the incineration of insulated copper wire
A1100	Dusts and residues from gas cleaning systems of copper smelters
A1110	Spent electrolytic solutions from copper electrorefining and electrowinning operations
A1120	Waste sludges, excluding anode slimes, from electrolyte purification systems in copper electrorefining and electrowinning operations
A1130	Spent etching solutions containing dissolved copper
A1140	Waste cupric chloride and copper cyanide catalysts

A1150	Precious metal ash from incineration of printed circuit boards not included on list B*
A1160	Waste lead-acid batteries, whole or crushed
A1170	Unsorted waste batteries excluding mixtures of only list B batteries. Waste batteries not specified on list B containing Annex I constituents to an extent to render them hazardous
A1180	Waste electrical and electronic assemblies or scrap† containing components such as accumulators and other batteries included on list A, mercury-switches, glass from cathode-ray tubes and other activated glass and PCB-capacitors, or contaminated with Annex I constituents (e.g., cadmium, mercury, lead, polychlorinated biphenyl) to an extent that they possess any of the characteristics contained in Annex III (note the related entry on list B B1110)‡
A1190	Waste metal cables coated or insulated with plastics containing or contaminated with coal tar, PCB,§ lead, cadmium, other organohalogen compounds or other Annex I constituents to an extent that they exhibit Annex III characteristics.

A2 *Wastes Containing Principally Inorganic Constituents, Which May Contain Metals and Organic Materials*

A2010	Glass waste from cathode-ray tubes and other activated glasses
A2020	Waste inorganic fluorine compounds in the form of liquids or sludges but excluding such wastes specified on list B
A2030	Waste catalysts but excluding such wastes specified on list B
A2040	Waste gypsum arising from chemical industry processes, when containing Annex I constituents to the extent that it exhibits an Annex III hazardous characteristic (note the related entry on list B B2080)
A2050	Waste asbestos (dusts and fibres)
A2060	Coal-fired power plant fly-ash containing Annex I substances in concentrations sufficient to exhibit Annex III characteristics (note the related entry on list B B2050)

A3 *Wastes Containing Principally Organic Constituents, Which May Contain Metals and Inorganic Materials*

A3010	Waste from the production or processing of petroleum coke and bitumen
A3020	Waste mineral oils unfit for their originally intended use
A3030	Wastes that contain, consist of or are contaminated with leaded anti-knock compound sludges
A3040	Waste thermal (heat transfer) fluids

* Note that mirror entry on list B (B1160) does not specify exceptions.

† This entry does not include scrap assemblies from electric power generation.

‡ PCBs are at a concentration level of 50 mg/kg or more.

§ PCBs are at a concentration level of 50 mg/kg or more.

A3050	Wastes from production, formulation and use of resins, latex, plasticizers, glues/adhesives excluding such wastes specified on list B (note the related entry on list B B4020)
A3060	Waste nitrocellulose
A3070	Waste phenols, phenol compounds including chlorophenol in the form of liquids or sludges
A3080	Waste ethers not including those specified on list B
A3090	Waste leather dust, ash, sludges and flours when containing hexavalent chromium compounds or biocides (note the related entry on list B B3100)
A3100	Waste paring and other waste of leather or of composition leather not suitable for the manufacture of leather articles containing hexavalent chromium compounds or biocides (note the related entry on list B B3090)
A3110	Fellmongery wastes containing hexavalent chromium compounds or biocides or infectious substances (note the related entry on list B B3110)
A3120	Fluff-light fraction from shredding
A3130	Waste organic phosphorous compounds
A3140	Waste non-halogenated organic solvents but excluding such wastes specified on list B
A3150	Waste halogenated organic solvents
A3160	Waste halogenated or unhalogenated non-aqueous distillation residues arising from organic solvent recovery operations
A3170	Wastes arising from the production of aliphatic halogenated hydrocarbons (such as chloromethane, dichloro-ethane, vinyl chloride, vinylidene chloride, allyl chloride and epichlorhydrin)
A3180	Wastes, substances and articles containing, consisting of or contaminated with polychlorinated biphenyl (PCB), polychlorinated terphenyl (PCT), polychlorinated naphthalene (PCN) or polybrominated biphenyl (PBB), or any other polybrominated analogues of these compounds, at a concentration level of 50 mg/kg or more *
A3190	Waste tarry residues (excluding asphalt cements) arising from refining, distillation and any pyrolitic treatment of organic materials
A3200	Bituminous material (asphalt waste) from road construction and maintenance, containing tar (note the related entry on list B B2130)
A3210	Plastic waste, including mixtures of such waste, containing or contaminated with Annex I constituents, to an extent that it exhibits an Annex III characteristic (note the related entries Y48 in Annex II and on list B B3011).

A4 Wastes Which May Contain Either Inorganic or Organic Constituents

A4010	Wastes from the production, preparation and use of pharmaceutical products but excluding such wastes specified on list B

* The 50 mg/kg level is considered to be an internationally practical level for all wastes. However, many individual countries have established lower regulatory levels (e.g., 20 mg/kg) for specific wastes.

A4020	Clinical and related wastes; that is wastes arising from medical, nursing, dental, veterinary, or similar practices, and wastes generated in hospitals or other facilities during the investigation or treatment of patients, or research projects
A4030	Wastes from the production, formulation and use of biocides and phytopharmaceuticals, including waste pesticides and herbicides which are off-specification, outdated,* or unfit for their originally intended use
A4040	Wastes from the manufacture, formulation and use of wood-preserving chemicals†
A4050	Wastes that contain, consist of or are contaminated with any of the following: • Inorganic cyanides, excepting precious-metal-bearing residues in solid form containing traces of inorganic cyanides • Organic cyanides
A4060	Waste oils/water, hydrocarbons/water mixtures, emulsions
A4070	Wastes from the production, formulation and use of inks, dyes, pigments, paints, lacquers, varnish excluding any such waste specified on list B (note the related entry on list B B4010)
A4080	Wastes of an explosive nature (but excluding such wastes specified on list B)
A4090	Waste acidic or basic solutions, other than those specified in the corresponding entry on list B (note the related entry on list B B2120)
A4100	Wastes from industrial pollution control devices for cleaning of industrial off-gases but excluding such wastes specified on list B
A4110	Wastes that contain, consist of or are contaminated with any of the following: • Any congenor of polychlorinated dibenzo-furan • Any congenor of polychlorinated dibenzo-p-dioxin
A4120	Wastes that contain, consist of or are contaminated with peroxides
A4130	Waste packages and containers containing Annex I substances in concentrations sufficient to exhibit Annex III hazard characteristics
A4140	Waste consisting of or containing off specification or outdated‡ chemicals corresponding to Annex I categories and exhibiting Annex III hazard characteristics
A4150	Waste chemical substances arising from research and development or teaching activities which are not identified and/or are new and whose effects on human health and/or the environment are not known
A4160	Spent activated carbon not included on list B (note the related entry on list B B2060)

* "Outdated" means unused within the period recommended by the manufacturer.

† This entry does not include wood treated with wood preserving chemicals.

‡ "Outdated" means unused within the period recommended by the manufacturer.

Annex IX*

List B

Wastes contained in the Annex will not be wastes covered by Article 1, paragraph (1)(a), of this Convention unless they contain Annex I material to an extent causing them to exhibit an Annex III characteristic.

B1 Metal and metal-bearing wastes

B1010	Metal and metal-alloy wastes in metallic, non-dispersible form: • Precious metals (gold, silver, the platinum group, but not mercury) • Iron and steel scrap • Copper scrap • Nickel scrap • Aluminium scrap • Zinc scrap • Tin scrap • Tungsten scrap • Molybdenum scrap • Tantalum scrap • Magnesium scrap • Cobalt scrap • Bismuth scrap • Titanium scrap • Zirconium scrap • Manganese scrap • Germanium scrap

* The amendment whereby Annex IX was added to the Convention entered into force on 6 November 1998, six months following the issuance of depositary notification C.N.77.1998 (reflecting decision IV/9 adopted by the Conference of the Parties at its fourth meeting). The amendment to Annex IX whereby new entries were added entered into force on 20 November 2003 (depositary notification C.N.1314.2003), six months following the issuance of depositary notification C.N.399.2003 of 20 May 2003 (reflecting decision VI/35 adopted by the Conference of the Parties at its sixth meeting). The amendment to Annex IX whereby one entry was added entered into force on 8 October 2005 (depositary notification C.N.1044.2005) six months following the issuance of depositary notification C.N.263.2005 of 8 April 2005 (re-issued on 13 June 2005, reflecting decision VII/19 adopted by the Conference of the Parties at its seventh meeting). The amendment to Annex IX whereby new entries where added entered into force on 27 May 2014 (depositary notification C.N. 304.2014) six months following the issuance of depositary notification C.N. 965.2013 of 26 November 2013 (reflecting decision BC-11/6 adopted by the Conference of the Parties at its eleventh meeting). Amendments to Annex IX entered into force on 24 March 2020, six months following the issuance of depositary notification C.N.432.2019 of 24 September 2019 (reflecting decision BC-14/12 adopted by the Conference of the Parties at its fourteenth meeting). The present text includes all amendments. For information on the status of individual Parties in relation to the amendment/s, please see the Status of Ratifications page on the Basel Convention website.

	• Vanadium scrap • Scrap of hafnium, indium, niobium, rhenium and gallium • Thorium scrap • Rare earths scrap • Chromium scrap
B1020	Clean, uncontaminated metal scrap, including alloys, in bulk finished form (sheet, plate, beams, rods, etc.), of: • Antimony scrap • Beryllium scrap • Cadmium scrap • Lead scrap (but excluding lead-acid batteries) • Selenium scrap • Tellurium scrap
B1030	Refractory metals containing residues
B1031	Molybdenum, tungsten, titanium, tantalum, niobium and rhenium metal and metal alloy wastes in metallic dispersible form (metal powder), excluding such wastes as specified in list A under entry A1050, Galvanic sludges
B1040	Scrap assemblies from electrical power generation not contaminated with lubricating oil, PCB or PCT to an extent to render them hazardous
B1050	Mixed non-ferrous metal, heavy fraction scrap, not containing Annex I materials in concentrations sufficient to exhibit Annex III characteristics *
B1060	Waste selenium and tellurium in metallic elemental form including powder
B1070	Waste of copper and copper alloys in dispersible form, unless they contain Annex I constituents to an extent that they exhibit Annex III characteristics
B1080	Zinc ash and residues including zinc alloys residues in dispersible form unless containing Annex I constituents in concentration such as to exhibit Annex III characteristics †
B1090	Waste batteries conforming to a specification, excluding those made with lead, cadmium or mercury
B1100	Metal-bearing wastes arising from melting, smelting and refining of metals: • Hard zinc spelter • Zinc-containing drosses: – Galvanizing slab zinc top dross (>90% Zn) – Galvanizing slab zinc bottom dross (>92% Zn) – Zinc die casting dross (>85% Zn) – Hot dip galvanizers slab zinc dross (batch) (>92% Zn) – Zinc skimmings • Aluminium skimmings (or skims) excluding salt slag

* Note that even where low level contamination with Annex I materials initially exists, subsequent processes, including recycling processes, may result in separated fractions containing significantly enhanced concentrations of those Annex I materials.

† The status of zinc ash is currently under review and there is a recommendation with the United Nations Conference on Trade and Development (UNCTAD) that zinc ashes should not be dangerous goods.

	• Slags from copper processing for further processing or refining not containing arsenic, lead or cadmium to an extent that they exhibit Annex III hazard characteristics • Wastes of refractory linings, including crucibles, originating from copper smelting • Slags from precious metals processing for further refining • Tantalum-bearing tin slags with less than 0.5% tin
B1110	Electrical and electronic assemblies: • Electronic assemblies consisting only of metals or alloys • Waste electrical and electronic assemblies or scrap* (including printed circuit boards) not containing components such as accumulators and other batteries included on list A, mercury-switches, glass from cathode-ray tubes and other activated glass and PCB-capacitors, or not contaminated with Annex I constituents (e.g., cadmium, mercury, lead, polychlorinated biphenyl) or from which these have been removed, to an extent that they do not possess any of the characteristics contained in Annex III (note the related entry on list A A1180) • Electrical and electronic assemblies (including printed circuit boards, electronic components and wires) destined for direct reuse,† and not for recycling or final disposal‡
B1115	Waste metal cables coated or insulated with plastics, not included in list A A1190, excluding those destined for Annex IVA operations or any other disposal operations involving, at any stage, uncontrolled thermal processes, such as open-burning.
B1120	Spent catalysts excluding liquids used as catalysts, containing any of:
	Transition metals, excluding waste catalysts (spent catalysts, liquid used catalysts or other catalysts) on list A: • Scandium • Vanadium • Manganese • Cobalt • Copper • Yttrium • Niobium • Hafnium • Tungsten • Titanium • Chromium • Iron • Nickel • Zinc • Zirconium • Molybdenum • Tantalum • Rhenium Lanthanides (rare earth metals): • Lanthanum • Praseodymium • Samarium • Gadolinium • Dysprosium • Erbium • Ytterbium • Cerium • Neodymium • Europium • Terbium • Holmium • Thulium • Lutetium
B1130	Cleaned spent precious-metal-bearing catalysts
B1140	Precious-metal-bearing residues in solid form which contain traces of inorganic cyanides
B1150	Precious metals and alloy wastes (gold, silver, the platinum group, but not mercury) in a dispersible, non-liquid form with appropriate packaging and labelling
B1160	Precious-metal ash from the incineration of printed circuit boards (note the related entry on list A A1150)
B1170	Precious-metal ash from the incineration of photographic film
B1180	Waste photographic film containing silver halides and metallic silver

* This entry does not include scrap from electrical power generation.

† Reuse can include repair, refurbishment or upgrading, but not major reassembly.

‡ In some countries these materials destined for direct re-use are not considered wastes.

B1190	Waste photographic paper containing silver halides and metallic silver
B1200	Granulated slag arising from the manufacture of iron and steel
B1210	Slag arising from the manufacture of iron and steel including slags as a source of TiO_2 and vanadium
B1220	Slag from zinc production, chemically stabilized, having a high iron content (above 20%) and processed according to industrial specifications (e.g., DIN 4301) mainly for construction
B1230	Mill scaling arising from the manufacture of iron and steel
B1240	Copper oxide mill-scale
B1250	Waste end-of-life motor vehicles, containing neither liquids nor other hazardous components

B2 *Wastes Containing Principally Inorganic Constituents, Which May Contain Metals and Organic Materials*

B2010	Wastes from mining operations in non-dispersible form: • Natural graphite waste • Slate waste, whether or not roughly trimmed or merely cut, by sawing or otherwise • Mica waste • Leucite, nepheline and nepheline syenite waste • Feldspar waste • Fluorspar waste • Silica wastes in solid form excluding those used in foundry operations
B2020	Glass waste in non-dispersible form: • Cullet and other waste and scrap of glass except for glass from cathode-ray tubes and other activated glasses
B2030	Ceramic wastes in non-dispersible form: • Cermet wastes and scrap (metal ceramic composites) • Ceramic based fibres not elsewhere specified or included
B2040	Other wastes containing principally inorganic constituents: • Partially refined calcium sulphate produced from flue-gas desulphurization (FGD) • Waste gypsum wallboard or plasterboard arising from the demolition of buildings • Slag from copper production, chemically stabilized, having a high iron content (above 20%) and processed according to industrial specifications (e.g., DIN 4301 and DIN 8201) mainly for construction and abrasive applications • Sulphur in solid form • Limestone from the production of calcium cyanamide (having a pH less than 9) • Sodium, potassium, calcium chlorides • Carborundum (silicon carbide) • Broken concrete • Lithium-tantalum and lithium-niobium containing glass scraps
B2050	Coal-fired power plant fly-ash, not included on list A (note the related entry on list A A2060)

B2060	Spent activated carbon not containing any Annex I constituents to an extent they exhibit Annex III characteristics, for example, carbon resulting from the treatment of potable water and processes of the food industry and vitamin production (note the related entry on list A A4160)
B2070	Calcium fluoride sludge
B2080	Waste gypsum arising from chemical industry processes not included on List A (note the related entry on list A A2040)
B2090	Waste anode butts from steel or aluminium production made of petroleum coke or bitumen and cleaned to normal industry specifications (excluding anode butts from chlor alkali electrolyses and from metallurgical industry)
B2100	Waste hydrates of aluminium and waste alumina and residues from alumina production excluding such materials used for gas cleaning, flocculation or filtration processes
B2110	Bauxite residue ("red mud") (pH moderated to less than 11.5)
B2120	Waste acidic or basic solutions with a pH greater than 2 and less than 11.5, which are not corrosive or otherwise hazardous (note the related entry on list A A4090)
B2130	Bituminous material (asphalt waste) from road construction and maintenance, not containing tar* (note the related entry on list A A3200)

B3 *Wastes Containing Principally Organic Constituents, Which May Contain Metals and Inorganic Materials*

B3010	*[no longer effective as of 1 January 2021]*
B3011	Plastic waste (note the related entries Y48 in Annex II and on list A A3210): • Plastic waste listed below, provided it is destined for recycling† in an environmentally sound manner and almost free from contamination and other types of wastes:‡ – Plastic waste almost exclusively§ consisting of one non-halogenated polymer, including but not limited to the following polymers: Polyethylene (PE) Polypropylene (PP) Polystyrene (PS) Acrylonitrile butadiene styrene (ABS) Polyethylene terephthalate (PET) Polycarbonates (PC) Polyethers

* The concentration level of Benzol (a) pyrene should not be 50mg/kg or more.

† Recycling/reclamation of organic substances that are not used as solvents (R3 in Annex IV, Section B) or, if needed, temporary storage limited to one instance, provided that it is followed by operation R3 and evidenced by contractual or relevant official documentation.

‡ In relation to "almost free from contamination and other types of wastes", international and national specifications may offer a point of reference.

§ In relation to "almost exclusively", international and national specifications may offer a point of reference.

	– Plastic waste almost exclusively consisting of one cured resin or condensation product, including but not limited to the following resins: Urea formaldehyde resins Phenol formaldehyde resins Melamine formaldehyde resins Epoxy resins Alkyd resins – Plastic waste almost exclusively consisting of one of the following fluorinated polymers:* Perfluoroethylene/propylene (FEP) Perfluoroalkoxy alkanes: Tetrafluoroethylene/perfluoroalkyl vinyl ether (PFA) Tetrafluoroethylene/perfluoromethyl vinyl ether (MFA) Polyvinylfluoride (PVF) Polyvinylidenefluoride (PVDF) • Mixtures of plastic waste, consisting of polyethylene (PE), polypropylene (PP) and/or polyethylene terephthalate (PET), provided they are destined for separate recycling† of each material and in an environmentally sound manner, and almost free from contamination and other types of wastes.
B3020	Paper, paperboard and paper product wastes The following materials, provided they are not mixed with hazardous wastes: Waste and scrap of paper or paperboard of: • unbleached paper or paperboard or of corrugated paper or paperboard • other paper or paperboard, made mainly of bleached chemical pulp, not coloured in the mass • paper or paperboard made mainly of mechanical pulp (for example, newspapers, journals and similar printed matter) • other, including but not limited to 1) laminated paperboard 2) unsorted scrap
B3026	The following waste from the pre-treatment of composite packaging for liquids, not containing Annex I materials in concentrations sufficient to exhibit Annex III characteristics: • Non-separable plastic fraction • Non-separable plastic-aluminium fraction
B3027	Self-adhesive label laminate waste containing raw materials used in label material production
B3030	Textile wastes The following materials, provided they are not mixed with other wastes and are prepared to a specification: • Silk waste (including cocoons unsuitable for reeling, yarn waste and garnetted stock) – not carded or combed

* Post-consumer wastes are excluded.

† Recycling/reclamation of organic substances that are not used as solvents (R3 in Annex IV, Section B), with prior sorting and, if needed, temporary storage limited to one instance, provided that it is followed by operation R3 and evidenced by contractual or relevant official documentation.

	– other • Waste of wool or of fine or coarse animal hair, including yarn waste but excluding garnetted stock – noils of wool or of fine animal hair – other waste of wool or of fine animal hair – waste of coarse animal hair • Cotton waste (including yarn waste and garnetted stock) – yarn waste (including thread waste) – garnetted stock – other • Flax tow and waste • Tow and waste (including yarn waste and garnetted stock) of true hemp (*Cannabis sativa L.*) • Tow and waste (including yarn waste and garnetted stock) of jute and other textile bast fibres (excluding flax, true hemp and ramie) • Tow and waste (including yarn waste and garnetted stock) of sisal and other textile fibres of the genus Agave • Tow, noils and waste (including yarn waste and garnetted stock) of coconut • Tow, noils and waste (including yarn waste and garnetted stock) of abaca (Manila hemp or *Musa textilis Nee*) • Tow, noils and waste (including yarn waste and garnetted stock) of ramie and other vegetable textile fibres, not elsewhere specified or included • Waste (including noils, yarn waste and garnetted stock) of man-made fibres – of synthetic fibres – of artificial fibres • Worn clothing and other worn textile articles • Used rags, scrap twine, cordage, rope and cables and worn out articles of twine, cordage, rope or cables of textile materials – sorted – other
B3035	Waste textile floor coverings, carpets
B3040	Rubber wastes The following materials, provided they are not mixed with other wastes: • Waste and scrap of hard rubber (e.g., ebonite) • Other rubber wastes (excluding such wastes specified elsewhere)
B3050	Untreated cork and wood waste: • Wood waste and scrap, whether or not agglomerated in logs, briquettes, pellets or similar forms • Cork waste: crushed, granulated or ground cork
B3060	Wastes arising from agro-food industries provided it is not infectious: • Wine lees • Dried and sterilized vegetable waste, residues and byproducts, whether or not in the form of pellets, of a kind used in animal feeding, not elsewhere specified or included

	• Degras: residues resulting from the treatment of fatty substances or animal or vegetable waxes • Waste of bones and horn-cores, unworked, defatted, simply prepared (but not cut to shape), treated with acid or degelatinised • Fish waste • Cocoa shells, husks, skins and other cocoa waste • Other wastes from the agro-food industry excluding by-products which meet national and international requirements and standards for human or animal consumption
B3065	Waste edible fats and oils of animal or vegetable origin (e.g., frying oils), provided they do not exhibit an Annex III characteristic
B3070	The following wastes: • Waste of human hair • Waste straw • Deactivated fungus mycelium from penicillin production to be used as animal feed
B3080	Waste parings and scrap of rubber
B3090	Paring and other wastes of leather or of composition leather not suitable for the manufacture of leather articles, excluding leather sludges, not containing hexavalent chromium compounds and biocides (note the related entry on list A A3100)
B3100	Leather dust, ash, sludges or flours not containing hexavalent chromium compounds or biocides (note the related entry on list A A3090)
B3110	Fellmongery wastes not containing hexavalent chromium compounds or biocides or infectious substances (note the related entry on list A A3110)
B3120	Wastes consisting of food dyes
B3130	Waste polymer ethers and waste non-hazardous monomer ethers incapable of forming peroxides
B3140	Waste pneumatic tyres, excluding those destined for Annex IVA operations

B4 Wastes Which May Contain Either Inorganic or Organic Constituents

B4010	Wastes consisting mainly of water-based/latex paints, inks and hardened varnishes not containing organic solvents, heavy metals or biocides to an extent to render them hazardous (note the related entry on list A A4070)
B4020	Wastes from production, formulation and use of resins, latex, plasticizers, glues/adhesives, not listed on list A, free of solvents and other contaminants to an extent that they do not exhibit Annex III characteristics (e.g., water-based, or glues based on casein, starch, dextrin, cellulose ethers, polyvinyl alcohols) (note the related entry on list A A3050)
B4030	Used single-use cameras, with batteries not included on list A

UNITED NATIONS FRAMEWORK CONVENTION ON CLIMATE CHANGE

(Adopted: 9 May 1992; Entry into force: 21 March 1994; Applied to Hong Kong: 8 April 2003)

The Parties to this Convention,

Acknowledging that change in the Earth's climate and its adverse effects are a common concern of humankind,

Concerned that human activities have been substantially increasing the atmospheric concentrations of greenhouse gases, that these increases enhance the natural greenhouse effect, and that this will result on average in an additional warming of the Earth's surface and atmosphere and may adversely affect natural ecosystems and humankind,

Noting that the largest share of historical and current global emissions of greenhouse gases has originated in developed countries, that per capita emissions in developing countries are still relatively low and that the share of global emissions originating in developing countries will grow to meet their social and development needs,

Aware of the role and importance in terrestrial and marine ecosystems of sinks and reservoirs of greenhouse gases,

Noting that there are many uncertainties in predictions of climate change, particularly with regard to the timing, magnitude and regional patterns thereof,

Acknowledging that the global nature of climate change calls for the widest possible cooperation by all countries and their participation in an effective and appropriate international response, in accordance with their common but differentiated responsibilities and respective capabilities and their social and economic conditions,

Recalling the pertinent provisions of the Declaration of the United Nations Conference on the Human Environment, adopted at Stockholm on 16 June 1972,

Recalling also that States have, in accordance with the Charter of the United Nations and the principles of international law, the sovereign right to exploit their own resources pursuant to their own environmental and developmental policies, and the responsibility to ensure that activities within their jurisdiction or control do not cause damage to the environment of other States or of areas beyond the limits of national jurisdiction,

Reaffirming the principle of sovereignty of States in international cooperation to address climate change,

Recognizing that States should enact effective environmental legislation, that environmental standards, management objectives and priorities should reflect the environmental and developmental context to which they apply, and that standards applied by some countries may be inappropriate and of unwarranted economic and social cost to other countries, in particular developing countries,

Recalling the provisions of General Assembly Resolution 44/228 of 22 December 1989 on the United Nations Conference on Environment and Development, and Resolutions 43/53 of 6 December 1988, 44/207 of 22 December 1989, 45/212 of 21 December 1990 and 46/169 of 19 December 1991 on protection of global climate for present and future generations of mankind,

Recalling also the provisions of General Assembly Resolution 44/206 of 22 December 1989 on the possible adverse effects of sea-level rise on islands and coastal areas, particularly low-lying coastal areas and the pertinent provisions of General Assembly Resolution 44/172 of 19 December 1989 on the implementation of the Plan of Action to Combat Desertification,

Recalling further the Vienna Convention for the Protection of the Ozone Layer, 1985, and the Montreal Protocol on Substances that Deplete the Ozone Layer, 1987, as adjusted and amended on 29 June 1990,

Noting the Ministerial Declaration of the Second World Climate Conference adopted on 7 November 1990,

Conscious of the valuable analytical work being conducted by many States on climate change and of the important contributions of the World Meteorological Organization, the United Nations Environment Programme and other organs, organizations and bodies of the United Nations system, as well as other international and intergovernmental bodies, to the exchange of results of scientific research and the coordination of research,

Recognizing that steps required to understand and address climate change will be environmentally, socially and economically most effective if they are based on relevant scientific, technical and economic considerations and continually re-evaluated in the light of new findings in these areas,

Recognizing that various actions to address climate change can be justified economically in their own right and can also help in solving other environmental problems,

Recognizing also the need for developed countries to take immediate action in a flexible manner on the basis of clear priorities, as a first step towards comprehensive response strategies at the global, national and, where agreed, regional levels that take into account all greenhouse gases, with due consideration of their relative contributions to the enhancement of the greenhouse effect,

Recognizing further that low-lying and other small island countries, countries with low-lying coastal, arid and semi-arid areas or areas liable to floods, drought and desertification, and developing countries with fragile mountainous ecosystems are particularly vulnerable to the adverse effects of climate change,

Recognizing the special difficulties of those countries, especially developing countries, whose economies are particularly dependent on fossil fuel production, use and exportation, as a consequence of action taken on limiting greenhouse gas emissions,

Affirming that responses to climate change should be coordinated with social and economic development in an integrated manner with a view to avoiding adverse impacts on the latter, taking into full account the legitimate priority needs of developing countries for the achievement of sustained economic growth and the eradication of poverty,

Recognizing that all countries, especially developing countries, need access to resources required to achieve sustainable social and economic development and that, in order for developing countries to progress towards that goal, their energy consumption will need to grow taking into account the possibilities for achieving greater energy efficiency and for controlling greenhouse gas emissions in general, including through the application of new technologies on terms which make such an application economically and socially beneficial,

Determined to protect the climate system for present and future generations,

Have agreed as follows:

Article 1 Definitions

For the purposes of this Convention:

(1) "Adverse effects of climate change" means changes in the physical environment or biota resulting from climate change which have significant deleterious effects on the composition, resilience or productivity of natural and managed ecosystems or on the operation of socio-economic systems or on human health and welfare.

(2) "Climate change" means a change of climate which is attributed directly or indirectly to human activity that alters the composition of the global atmosphere and which is in addition to natural climate variability observed over comparable time periods.

(3) "Climate system" means the totality of the atmosphere, hydrosphere, biosphere and geosphere and their interactions.

(4) "Emissions" means the release of greenhouse gases and/or their precursors into the atmosphere over a specified area and period of time.

(5) "Greenhouse gases" means those gaseous constituents of the atmosphere, both natural and anthropogenic, that absorb and re-emit infrared radiation.

(6) "Regional economic integration organization" means an organization constituted by sovereign States of a given region which has competence in respect of matters governed by this Convention or its Protocols and has been duly authorized, in accordance with its internal procedures, to sign, ratify, accept, approve or accede to the instruments concerned.

(7) "Reservoir" means a component or components of the climate system where a greenhouse gas or a precursor of a greenhouse gas is stored.

(8) "Sink" means any process, activity or mechanism which removes a greenhouse gas, an aerosol or a precursor of a greenhouse gas from the atmosphere.

(9) "Source" means any process or activity which releases a greenhouse gas, an aerosol or a precursor of a greenhouse gas into the atmosphere.

Article 2 Objective

The ultimate objective of this Convention and any related legal instruments that the Conference of the Parties may adopt is to achieve, in accordance with the relevant provisions of the Convention, stabilization of greenhouse gas concentrations in the atmosphere at a level that would prevent dangerous anthropogenic interference with the climate system. Such a level should be achieved within a time frame sufficient to allow ecosystems to adapt naturally to climate change, to ensure that food production is not threatened and to enable economic development to proceed in a sustainable manner.

Article 3 Principles

In their actions to achieve the objective of the Convention and to implement its provisions, the Parties shall be guided, inter alia, by the following:

(1) The Parties should protect the climate system for the benefit of present and future generations of humankind, on the basis of equity and in accordance with their common but differentiated responsibilities and respective capabilities. Accordingly, the developed country Parties should take the lead in combating climate change and the adverse effects thereof.

(2) The specific needs and special circumstances of developing country Parties, especially those that are particularly vulnerable to the adverse effects of climate change, and of those Parties, especially developing country Parties, that would have to bear a disproportionate or abnormal burden under the Convention, should be given full consideration.

(3) The Parties should take precautionary measures to anticipate, prevent or minimize the causes of climate change and mitigate its adverse effects. Where there are threats of serious or irreversible damage, lack of full scientific certainty should not be used as a reason for postponing such measures, taking into account that policies and measures to deal with climate change should be cost-effective so as to ensure global benefits at the lowest possible cost. To achieve this, such policies and measures should take into account different socio-economic contexts, be comprehensive, cover all relevant sources, sinks and reservoirs of greenhouse gases and adaptation, and comprise all economic sectors. Efforts to address climate change may be carried out cooperatively by interested Parties.

(4) The Parties have a right to, and should, promote sustainable development. Policies and measures to protect the climate system against human-induced change should be appropriate for the specific conditions of each Party and should be integrated with national

development programmes, taking into account that economic development is essential for adopting measures to address climate change.

(5) The Parties should cooperate to promote a supportive and open international economic system that would lead to sustainable economic growth and development in all Parties, particularly developing country Parties, thus enabling them better to address the problems of climate change. Measures taken to combat climate change, including unilateral ones, should not constitute a means of arbitrary or unjustifiable discrimination or a disguised restriction on international trade.

Article 4 Commitments

(1) All Parties, taking into account their common but differentiated responsibilities and their specific national and regional development priorities, objectives and circumstances, shall:

(a) Develop, periodically update, publish and make available to the Conference of the Parties, in accordance with Article 12, national inventories of anthropogenic emissions by sources and removals by sinks of all greenhouse gases not controlled by the Montreal Protocol, using comparable methodologies to be agreed upon by the Conference of the Parties;

(b) Formulate, implement, publish and regularly update national and, where appropriate, regional programmes containing measures to mitigate climate change by addressing anthropogenic emissions by sources and removals by sinks of all greenhouse gases not controlled by the Montreal Protocol, and measures to facilitate adequate adaptation to climate change;

(c) Promote and cooperate in the development, application and diffusion, including transfer, of technologies, practices and processes that control, reduce or prevent anthropogenic emissions of greenhouse gases not controlled by the Montreal Protocol in all relevant sectors, including the energy, transport, industry, agriculture, forestry and waste management sectors;

(d) Promote sustainable management, and promote and cooperate in the conservation and enhancement, as appropriate, of sinks and reservoirs of all greenhouse gases not controlled by the Montreal Protocol, including biomass, forests and oceans as well as other terrestrial, coastal and marine ecosystems;

(e) Cooperate in preparing for adaptation to the impacts of climate change; develop and elaborate appropriate and integrated plans for coastal zone management, water resources and agriculture, and for the protection and rehabilitation of areas, particularly in Africa, affected by drought and desertification, as well as floods;

(f) Take climate change considerations into account, to the extent feasible, in their relevant social, economic and environmental policies and actions, and employ appropriate methods, for example impact assessments, formulated and determined nationally, with a view to minimizing adverse effects on the economy, on public health and on the quality of the environment, of projects or measures undertaken by them to mitigate or adapt to climate change;

(g) Promote and cooperate in scientific, technological, technical, socio-economic and other research, systematic observation and development of data archives related to the climate system and intended to further the understanding and to reduce or eliminate the remaining uncertainties regarding the causes, effects, magnitude and timing of climate change and the economic and social consequences of various response strategies;

(h) Promote and cooperate in the full, open and prompt exchange of relevant scientific, technological, technical, socio-economic and legal information related to the climate system and climate change, and to the economic and social consequences of various response strategies;

(i) Promote and cooperate in education, training and public awareness related to climate change and encourage the widest participation in this process, including that of non-governmental organizations; and

(j) Communicate to the Conference of the Parties information related to implementation, in accordance with Article 12.

(2) The developed country Parties and other Parties included in Annex I commit themselves specifically as provided for in the following:

(a) Each of these Parties shall adopt national* policies and take corresponding measures on the mitigation of climate change, by limiting its anthropogenic emissions of greenhouse gases and protecting and enhancing its greenhouse gas sinks and reservoirs. These policies and measures will demonstrate that developed countries are taking the lead in modifying longer-term trends in anthropogenic emissions consistent with the objective of the Convention, recognizing that the return by the end of the present decade to earlier levels of anthropogenic emissions of carbon dioxide and other greenhouse gases not controlled by the Montreal Protocol would contribute to such modification, and taking into account the differences in these Parties' starting points and approaches, economic structures and resource bases, the need to maintain strong and sustainable economic growth, available technologies and other individual circumstances, as well as the need for equitable and appropriate contributions by each of these Parties to the global effort regarding that objective. These Parties may implement such policies and measures jointly with other Parties and may assist other Parties in contributing to the achievement of the objective of the Convention and, in particular, that of this subparagraph;

(b) In order to promote progress to this end, each of these Parties shall communicate, within six months of the entry into force of the Convention for it and periodically thereafter, and in accordance with Article 12, detailed information on its policies and measures referred to in subparagraph (a) above, as well as on its resulting projected anthropogenic emissions by sources and removals by sinks of greenhouse gases not controlled by the Montreal Protocol for the period referred to in subparagraph (a), with the aim of returning individually or jointly to their 1990 levels these anthropogenic emissions of carbon dioxide and other greenhouse gases not controlled by the Montreal Protocol. This information will be reviewed by the Conference of the Parties, at its first session and periodically thereafter, in accordance with Article 7;

(c) Calculations of emissions by sources and removals by sinks of greenhouse gases for the purposes of subparagraph (b) above should take into account the best available scientific knowledge, including of the effective capacity of sinks and the respective contributions of such gases to climate change. The Conference of the Parties shall consider and agree on methodologies for these calculations at its first session and review them regularly thereafter;

(d) The Conference of the Parties shall, at its first session, review the adequacy of subparagraphs (a) and (b) above. Such review shall be carried out in the light of the best available scientific information and assessment on climate change and its impacts, as well as relevant technical, social and economic information. Based on this review, the Conference of the Parties shall take appropriate action, which may include the adoption of amendments to the commitments in subparagraphs (a) and (b) above. The Conference of the Parties, at its first session, shall also take decisions regarding criteria for joint implementation as indicated in subparagraph (a) above. A second review of subparagraphs (a) and (b) shall take place not later than 31 December 1998, and thereafter at regular intervals determined by the Conference of the Parties, until the objective of the Convention is met;

* This includes policies and measures adopted by regional economic integration organizations.

(e) Each of these Parties shall:

(i) Coordinate as appropriate with other such Parties, relevant economic and administrative instruments developed to achieve the objective of the Convention; and

(ii) Identify and periodically review its own policies and practices which encourage activities that lead to greater levels of anthropogenic emissions of greenhouse gases not controlled by the Montreal Protocol than would otherwise occur;

(f) The Conference of the Parties shall review, not later than 31 December 1998, available information with a view to taking decisions regarding such amendments to the lists in Annexes I and II as may be appropriate, with the approval of the Party concerned;

(g) Any Party not included in Annex I may, in its instrument of ratification, acceptance, approval or accession, or at any time thereafter, notify the Depositary that it intends to be bound by subparagraphs (a) and (b) above. The Depositary shall inform the other signatories and Parties of any such notification.

(3) The developed country Parties and other developed Parties included in Annex II shall provide new and additional financial resources to meet the agreed full costs incurred by developing country Parties in complying with their obligations under Article 12, paragraph (1). They shall also provide such financial resources, including for the transfer of technology, needed by the developing country Parties to meet the agreed full incremental costs of implementing measures that are covered by paragraph (1) of this Article and that are agreed between a developing country Party and the international entity or entities referred to in Article 11, in accordance with that Article. The implementation of these commitments shall take into account the need for adequacy and predictability in the flow of funds and the importance of appropriate burden sharing among the developed country Parties.

(4) The developed country Parties and other developed Parties included in Annex II shall also assist the developing country Parties that are particularly vulnerable to the adverse effects of climate change in meeting costs of adaptation to those adverse effects.

(5) The developed country Parties and other developed Parties included in Annex II shall take all practicable steps to promote, facilitate and finance, as appropriate, the transfer of, or access to, environmentally sound technologies and know-how to other Parties, particularly developing country Parties, to enable them to implement the provisions of the Convention. In this process, the developed country Parties shall support the development and enhancement of endogenous capacities and technologies of developing country Parties. Other Parties and organizations in a position to do so may also assist in facilitating the transfer of such technologies.

(6) In the implementation of their commitments under paragraph (2) above, a certain degree of flexibility shall be allowed by the Conference of the Parties to the Parties included in Annex I undergoing the process of transition to a market economy, in order to enhance the ability of these Parties to address climate change, including with regard to the historical level of anthropogenic emissions of greenhouse gases not controlled by the Montreal Protocol chosen as a reference.

(7) The extent to which developing country Parties will effectively implement their commitments under the Convention will depend on the effective implementation by developed country Parties of their commitments under the Convention related to financial resources and transfer of technology and will take fully into account that economic and social development and poverty eradication are the first and overriding priorities of the developing country Parties.

(8) In the implementation of the commitments in this Article, the Parties shall give full consideration to what actions are necessary under the Convention, including actions related to funding, insurance and the transfer of technology, to meet the specific needs and concerns of developing country Parties arising from the adverse effects of climate change and/or the impact of the implementation of response measures, especially on:

(a) Small island countries;

(b) Countries with low-lying coastal areas;

(c) Countries with arid and semi-arid areas, forested areas and areas liable to forest decay;

(d) Countries with areas prone to natural disasters;

(e) Countries with areas liable to drought and desertification;

(f) Countries with areas of high urban atmospheric pollution;

(g) Countries with areas with fragile ecosystems, including mountainous ecosystems;

(h) Countries whose economies are highly dependent on income generated from the production, processing and export, and/or on consumption of fossil fuels and associated energy-intensive products; and

(i) Landlocked and transit countries.

Further, the Conference of the Parties may take actions, as appropriate, with respect to this paragraph.

(9) The Parties shall take full account of the specific needs and special situations of the least developed countries in their actions with regard to funding and transfer of technology.

(10) The Parties shall, in accordance with Article 10, take into consideration in the implementation of the commitments of the Convention the situation of Parties, particularly developing country Parties, with economies that are vulnerable to the adverse effects of the implementation of measures to respond to climate change. This applies notably to Parties with economies that are highly dependent on income generated from the production, processing and export, and/or consumption of fossil fuels and associated energy-intensive products and/or the use of fossil fuels for which such Parties have serious difficulties in switching to alternatives.

Article 5 Research and Systematic Observation

In carrying out their commitments under Article 4, paragraph (1)(g), the Parties shall:

(a) Support and further develop, as appropriate, international and intergovernmental programmes and networks or organizations aimed at defining, conducting, assessing and financing research, data collection and systematic observation, taking into account the need to minimize duplication of effort;

(b) Support international and intergovernmental efforts to strengthen systematic observation and national scientific and technical research capacities and capabilities, particularly in developing countries, and to promote access to, and the exchange of, data and analyses thereof obtained from areas beyond national jurisdiction; and

(c) Take into account the particular concerns and needs of developing countries and cooperate in improving their endogenous capacities and capabilities to participate in the efforts referred to in subparagraphs (a) and (b) above.

Article 6 Education, Training and Public Awareness

In carrying out their commitments under Article 4, paragraph (1)(i), the Parties shall:

(a) Promote and facilitate at the national and, as appropriate, subregional and regional levels, and in accordance with national laws and regulations, and within their respective capacities:

(i) The development and implementation of educational and public awareness programmes on climate change and its effects;

(ii) Public access to information on climate change and its effects;

(iii) Public participation in addressing climate change and its effects and developing adequate responses; and

(iv) Training of scientific, technical and managerial personnel;

(b) Cooperate in and promote, at the international level, and, where appropriate, using existing bodies:

(i) The development and exchange of educational and public awareness material on climate change and its effects; and

(ii) The development and implementation of education and training programmes, including the strengthening of national institutions and the exchange or secondment of personnel to train experts in this field, in particular for developing countries.

Article 7 Conference of the Parties

(1) A Conference of the Parties is hereby established.

(2) The Conference of the Parties, as the supreme body of this Convention, shall keep under regular review the implementation of the Convention and any related legal instruments that the Conference of the Parties may adopt, and shall make, within its mandate, the decisions necessary to promote the effective implementation of the Convention. To this end, it shall:

(a) Periodically examine the obligations of the Parties and the institutional arrangements under the Convention, in the light of the objective of the Convention, the experience gained in its implementation and the evolution of scientific and technological knowledge;

(b) Promote and facilitate the exchange of information on measures adopted by the Parties to address climate change and its effects, taking into account the differing circumstances, responsibilities and capabilities of the Parties and their respective commitments under the Convention;

(c) Facilitate, at the request of two or more Parties, the coordination of measures adopted by them to address climate change and its effects, taking into account the differing circumstances, responsibilities and capabilities of the Parties and their respective commitments under the Convention;

(d) Promote and guide, in accordance with the objective and provisions of the Convention, the development and periodic refinement of comparable methodologies, to be agreed on by the Conference of the Parties, inter alia, for preparing inventories of greenhouse gas emissions by sources and removals by sinks, and for evaluating the effectiveness of measures to limit the emissions and enhance the removals of these gases;

(e) Assess, on the basis of all information made available to it in accordance with the provisions of the Convention, the implementation of the Convention by the Parties, the overall effects of the measures taken pursuant to the Convention, in particular environmental, economic and social effects as well as their cumulative impacts and the extent to which progress towards the objective of the Convention is being achieved;

(f) Consider and adopt regular reports on the implementation of the Convention and ensure their publication;

(g) Make recommendations on any matters necessary for the implementation of the Convention;

(h) Seek to mobilize financial resources in accordance with Article 4, paragraphs (3), (4) and (5), and Article 11;

(i) Establish such subsidiary bodies as are deemed necessary for the implementation of the Convention;

(j) Review reports submitted by its subsidiary bodies and provide guidance to them;

(k) Agree upon and adopt, by consensus, rules of procedure and financial rules for itself and for any subsidiary bodies;

(l) Seek and utilize, where appropriate, the services and cooperation of, and information provided by, competent international organizations and intergovernmental and non-governmental bodies; and

(m) Exercise such other functions as are required for the achievement of the objective of the Convention as well as all other functions assigned to it under the Convention.

(3) The Conference of the Parties shall, at its first session, adopt its own rules of procedure as well as those of the subsidiary bodies established by the Convention, which shall include decision-making procedures for matters not already covered by decision-making procedures stipulated in the Convention. Such procedures may include specified majorities required for the adoption of particular decisions.

(4) The first session of the Conference of the Parties shall be convened by the interim secretariat referred to in Article 21 and shall take place not later than one year after the date of entry into force of the Convention. Thereafter, ordinary sessions of the Conference of the Parties shall be held every year unless otherwise decided by the Conference of the Parties.

(5) Extraordinary sessions of the Conference of the Parties shall be held at such other times as may be deemed necessary by the Conference, or at the written request of any Party, provided that, within six months of the request being communicated to the Parties by the secretariat, it is supported by at least one third of the Parties.

(6) The United Nations, its specialized agencies and the International Atomic Energy Agency, as well as any State member thereof or observers thereto not Party to the Convention, may be represented at sessions of the Conference of the Parties as observers. Anybody or agency, whether national or international, governmental or non-governmental, which is qualified in matters covered by the Convention, and which has informed the secretariat of its wish to be represented at a session of the Conference of the Parties as an observer, may be so admitted unless at least one third of the Parties present object. The admission and participation of observers shall be subject to the rules of procedure adopted by the Conference of the Parties.

Article 8 Secretariat

(1) A secretariat is hereby established.

(2) The functions of the secretariat shall be:

(a) To make arrangements for sessions of the Conference of the Parties and its subsidiary bodies established under the Convention and to provide them with services as required;

(b) To compile and transmit reports submitted to it;

(c) To facilitate assistance to the Parties, particularly developing country Parties, on request, in the compilation and communication of information required in accordance with the provisions of the Convention;

(d) To prepare reports on its activities and present them to the Conference of the Parties;

(e) To ensure the necessary coordination with the secretariats of other relevant international bodies;

(f) To enter, under the overall guidance of the Conference of the Parties, into such administrative and contractual arrangements as may be required for the effective discharge of its functions; and

(g) To perform the other secretariat functions specified in the Convention and in any of its Protocols and such other functions as may be determined by the Conference of the Parties.

(3) The Conference of the Parties, at its first session, shall designate a permanent secretariat and make arrangements for its functioning.

Article 9 Subsidiary Body for Scientific and Technological Advice

(1) A subsidiary body for scientific and technological advice is hereby established to provide the Conference of the Parties and, as appropriate, its other subsidiary bodies with timely information and advice on scientific and technological matters relating to the Convention. This body shall be

open to participation by all Parties and shall be multidisciplinary. It shall comprise government representatives competent in the relevant field of expertise. It shall report regularly to the Conference of the Parties on all aspects of its work.

(2) Under the guidance of the Conference of the Parties, and drawing upon existing competent international bodies, this body shall:

(a) Provide assessments of the state of scientific knowledge relating to climate change and its effects;

(b) Prepare scientific assessments on the effects of measures taken in the implementation of the Convention;

(c) Identify innovative, efficient and state-of-the-art technologies and know-how and advise on the ways and means of promoting development and/or transferring such technologies;

(d) Provide advice on scientific programmes, international cooperation in research and development related to climate change, as well as on ways and means of supporting endogenous capacity-building in developing countries; and

(e) Respond to scientific, technological and methodological questions that the Conference of the Parties and its subsidiary bodies may put to the body.

(3) The functions and terms of reference of this body may be further elaborated by the Conference of the Parties.

Article 10 Subsidiary Body for Implementation

(1) A subsidiary body for implementation is hereby established to assist the Conference of the Parties in the assessment and review of the effective implementation of the Convention. This body shall be open to participation by all Parties and comprise government representatives who are experts on matters related to climate change. It shall report regularly to the Conference of the Parties on all aspects of its work.

(2) Under the guidance of the Conference of the Parties, this body shall:

(a) Consider the information communicated in accordance with Article 12, paragraph (1), to assess the overall aggregated effect of the steps taken by the Parties in the light of the latest scientific assessments concerning climate change;

(b) Consider the information communicated in accordance with Article 12, paragraph (2), in order to assist the Conference of the Parties in carrying out the reviews required by Article 4, paragraph (2)(d); and

(c) Assist the Conference of the Parties, as appropriate, in the preparation and implementation of its decisions.

Article 11 Financial Mechanism

(1) A mechanism for the provision of financial resources on a grant or concessional basis, including for the transfer of technology, is hereby defined. It shall function under the guidance of and be accountable to the Conference of the Parties, which shall decide on its policies, programme priorities and eligibility criteria related to this Convention. Its operation shall be entrusted to one or more existing international entities.

(2) The financial mechanism shall have an equitable and balanced representation of all Parties within a transparent system of governance.

(3) The Conference of the Parties and the entity or entities entrusted with the operation of the financial mechanism shall agree upon arrangements to give effect to the above paragraphs, which shall include the following:

(a) Modalities to ensure that the funded projects to address climate change are in conformity with the policies, programme priorities and eligibility criteria established by the Conference of the Parties;

(b) Modalities by which a particular funding decision may be reconsidered in light of these policies, programme priorities and eligibility criteria;

(c) Provision by the entity or entities of regular reports to the Conference of the Parties on its funding operations, which is consistent with the requirement for accountability set out in paragraph (1) above; and

(d) Determination in a predictable and identifiable manner of the amount of funding necessary and available for the implementation of this Convention and the conditions under which that amount shall be periodically reviewed.

(4) The Conference of the Parties shall make arrangements to implement the abovementioned provisions at its first session, reviewing and taking into account the interim arrangements referred to in Article 21, paragraph (3), and shall decide whether these interim arrangements shall be maintained. Within four years thereafter, the Conference of the Parties shall review the financial mechanism and take appropriate measures.

(5) The developed country Parties may also provide and developing country Parties avail themselves of, financial resources related to the implementation of the Convention through bilateral, regional and other multilateral channels.

Article 12 Communication of Information Related to Implementation

(1) In accordance with Article 4, paragraph (1), each Party shall communicate to the Conference of the Parties, through the secretariat, the following elements of information:

(a) A national inventory of anthropogenic emissions by sources and removals by sinks of all greenhouse gases not controlled by the Montreal Protocol, to the extent its capacities permit, using comparable methodologies to be promoted and agreed upon by the Conference of the Parties;

(b) A general description of steps taken or envisaged by the Party to implement the Convention; and

(c) Any other information that the Party considers relevant to the achievement of the objective of the Convention and suitable for inclusion in its communication, including, if feasible, material relevant for calculations of global emission trends.

(2) Each developed country Party and each other Party included in Annex I shall incorporate in its communication the following elements of information:

(a) A detailed description of the policies and measures that it has adopted to implement its commitment under Article 4, paragraphs (2)(a) and (b); and

(b) A specific estimate of the effects that the policies and measures referred to in subparagraph (a) immediately above will have on anthropogenic emissions by its sources and removals by its sinks of greenhouse gases during the period referred to in Article 4, paragraph (2)(a).

(3) In addition, each developed country Party and each other developed Party included in Annex II shall incorporate details of measures taken in accordance with Article 4, paragraphs (3), (4) and (5).

(4) Developing country Parties may, on a voluntary basis, propose projects for financing, including specific technologies, materials, equipment, techniques or practices that would be needed to implement such projects, along with, if possible, an estimate of all incremental costs, of the reductions of emissions and increments of removals of greenhouse gases, as well as an estimate of the consequent benefits.

(5) Each developed country Party and each other Party included in Annex I shall make its initial communication within six months of the entry into force of the Convention for that Party. Each Party not so listed shall make its initial communication within three years of the entry into force of the Convention for that Party, or of the availability of financial resources in accordance

with Article 4, paragraph (3). Parties that are least developed countries may make their initial communication at their discretion. The frequency of subsequent communications by all Parties shall be determined by the Conference of the Parties, taking into account the differentiated timetable set by this paragraph.

(6) Information communicated by Parties under this Article shall be transmitted by the secretariat as soon as possible to the Conference of the Parties and to any subsidiary bodies concerned. If necessary, the procedures for the communication of information may be further considered by the Conference of the Parties.

(7) From its first session, the Conference of the Parties shall arrange for the provision to developing country Parties of technical and financial support, on request, in compiling and communicating information under this Article, as well as in identifying the technical and financial needs associated with proposed projects and response measures under Article 4. Such support may be provided by other Parties, by competent international organizations and by the secretariat, as appropriate.

(8) Any group of Parties may, subject to guidelines adopted by the Conference of the Parties, and to prior notification to the Conference of the Parties, make a joint communication in fulfilment of their obligations under this Article, provided that such a communication includes information on the fulfilment by each of these Parties of its individual obligations under the Convention.

(9) Information received by the secretariat that is designated by a Party as confidential, in accordance with criteria to be established by the Conference of the Parties, shall be aggregated by the secretariat to protect its confidentiality before being made available to any of the bodies involved in the communication and review of information.

(10) Subject to paragraph (9) above, and without prejudice to the ability of any Party to make public its communication at any time, the secretariat shall make communications by Parties under this Article publicly available at the time they are submitted to the Conference of the Parties.

Article 13 Resolution of Questions Regarding Implementation

The Conference of the Parties shall, at its first session, consider the establishment of a multilateral consultative process, available to Parties on their request, for the resolution of questions regarding the implementation of the Convention.

Article 14 Settlement of Disputes

(1) In the event of a dispute between any two or more Parties concerning the interpretation or application of the Convention, the Parties concerned shall seek a settlement of the dispute through negotiation or any other peaceful means of their own choice.

(2) When ratifying, accepting, approving or acceding to the Convention, or at any time thereafter, a Party which is not a regional economic integration organization may declare in a written instrument submitted to the Depositary that, in respect of any dispute concerning the interpretation or application of the Convention, it recognizes as compulsory ipso facto and without special agreement, in relation to any Party accepting the same obligation:

(a) Submission of the dispute to the International Court of Justice; and/or

(b) Arbitration in accordance with procedures to be adopted by the Conference of the Parties as soon as practicable, in an Annex on arbitration.

A Party which is a regional economic integration organization may make a declaration with like effect in relation to arbitration in accordance with the procedures referred to in subparagraph (b) above.

(3) A declaration made under paragraph (2) above shall remain in force until it expires in accordance with its terms or until three months after written notice of its revocation has been deposited with the Depositary.

(4) A new declaration, a notice of revocation or the expiry of a declaration shall not in any way affect proceedings pending before the International Court of Justice or the arbitral tribunal, unless the parties to the dispute otherwise agree.

(5) Subject to the operation of paragraph (2) above, if after twelve months following notification by one Party to another that a dispute exists between them, the Parties concerned have not been able to settle their dispute through the means mentioned in paragraph (1) above, the dispute shall be submitted, at the request of any of the parties to the dispute, to conciliation.

(6) A conciliation commission shall be created upon the request of one of the parties to the dispute. The commission shall be composed of an equal number of members appointed by each party concerned and a chairman chosen jointly by the members appointed by each party. The commission shall render a recommendatory award, which the parties shall consider in good faith.

(7) Additional procedures relating to conciliation shall be adopted by the Conference of the Parties, as soon as practicable, in an Annex on conciliation.

(8) The provisions of this Article shall apply to any related legal instrument which the Conference of the Parties may adopt, unless the instrument provides otherwise.

Article 15 Amendments to the Convention

(1) Any Party may propose amendments to the Convention.

(2) Amendments to the Convention shall be adopted at an ordinary session of the Conference of the Parties. The text of any proposed amendment to the Convention shall be communicated to the Parties by the secretariat at least six months before the meeting at which it is proposed for adoption. The secretariat shall also communicate proposed amendments to the signatories to the Convention and, for information, to the Depositary.

(3) The Parties shall make every effort to reach agreement on any proposed amendment to the Convention by consensus. If all efforts at consensus have been exhausted, and no agreement reached, the amendment shall as a last resort be adopted by a three-fourths majority vote of the Parties present and voting at the meeting. The adopted amendment shall be communicated by the secretariat to the Depositary, who shall circulate it to all Parties for their acceptance.

(4) Instruments of acceptance in respect of an amendment shall be deposited with the Depositary. An amendment adopted in accordance with paragraph (3) above shall enter into force for those Parties having accepted it on the ninetieth day after the date of receipt by the Depositary of an instrument of acceptance by at least three fourths of the Parties to the Convention.

(5) The amendment shall enter into force for any other Party on the ninetieth day after the date on which that Party deposits with the Depositary its instrument of acceptance of the said amendment.

(6) For the purposes of this Article, "Parties present and voting" means Parties present and casting an affirmative or negative vote.

Article 16 Adoption and Amendment of Annexes to the Convention

(1) Annexes to the Convention shall form an integral part thereof and, unless otherwise expressly provided, a reference to the Convention constitutes at the same time a reference to any Annexes thereto. Without prejudice to the provisions of Article 14, paragraphs (2)(b) and (7), such Annexes shall be restricted to lists, forms and any other material of a descriptive nature that is of a scientific, technical, procedural or administrative character.

(2) Annexes to the Convention shall be proposed and adopted in accordance with the procedure set forth in Article 15, paragraphs (2), (3) and (4).

(3) An Annex that has been adopted in accordance with paragraph (2) above shall enter into force for all Parties to the Convention six months after the date of the communication by the Depositary to such Parties of the adoption of the Annex, except for those Parties that have notified the

Depositary, in writing, within that period of their non-acceptance of the Annex. The Annex shall enter into force for Parties which withdraw their notification of non-acceptance on the ninetieth day after the date on which withdrawal of such notification has been received by the Depositary.

(4) The proposal, adoption and entry into force of amendments to Annexes to the Convention shall be subject to the same procedure as that for the proposal, adoption and entry into force of Annexes to the Convention in accordance with paragraphs (2) and (3) above.

(5) If the adoption of an Annex or an amendment to an Annex involves an amendment to the Convention, that Annex or amendment to an Annex shall not enter into force until such time as the amendment to the Convention enters into force.

Article 17 Protocols

(1) The Conference of the Parties may, at any ordinary session, adopt Protocols to the Convention.

(2) The text of any proposed Protocol shall be communicated to the Parties by the secretariat at least six months before such a session.

(3) The requirements for the entry into force of any Protocol shall be established by that instrument.

(4) Only Parties to the Convention may be Parties to a Protocol.

(5) Decisions under any Protocol shall be taken only by the Parties to the Protocol concerned.

Article 18 Right to Vote

(1) Each Party to the Convention shall have one vote, except as provided for in paragraph (2) below.

(2) Regional economic integration organizations, in matters within their competence, shall exercise their right to vote with a number of votes equal to the number of their member States that are Parties to the Convention. Such an organization shall not exercise its right to vote if any of its member States exercises its right, and vice versa.

Article 19 Depositary

The Secretary-General of the United Nations shall be the Depositary of the Convention and of Protocols adopted in accordance with Article 17.

Article 20 Signature

This Convention shall be open for signature by States Members of the United Nations or of any of its specialized agencies or that are Parties to the Statute of the International Court of Justice and by regional economic integration organizations at Rio de Janeiro, during the United Nations Conference on Environment and Development, and thereafter at United Nations Headquarters in New York from 20 June 1992 to 19 June 1993.

Article 21 Interim Arrangements

(1) The secretariat functions referred to in Article 8 will be carried out on an interim basis by the secretariat established by the General Assembly of the United Nations in its Resolution 45/212 of 21 December 1990, until the completion of the first session of the Conference of the Parties.

(2) The head of the interim secretariat referred to in paragraph (1) above will cooperate closely with the Intergovernmental Panel on Climate Change to ensure that the Panel can respond to the need for objective scientific and technical advice. Other relevant scientific bodies could also be consulted.

(3) The Global Environment Facility of the United Nations Development Programme, the United Nations Environment Programme and the International Bank for Reconstruction and Development shall be the international entity entrusted with the operation of the financial mechanism referred to in Article 11 on an interim basis. In this connection, the Global Environment Facility should be appropriately restructured and its membership made universal to enable it to fulfil the requirements of Article 11.

Article 22 Ratification, Acceptance, Approval or Accession

(1) The Convention shall be subject to ratification, acceptance, approval or accession by States and by regional economic integration organizations. It shall be open for accession from the day after the date on which the Convention is closed for signature. Instruments of ratification, acceptance, approval or accession shall be deposited with the Depositary.

(2) Any regional economic integration organization which becomes a Party to the Convention without any of its member States being a Party shall be bound by all the obligations under the Convention. In the case of such organizations, one or more of whose member States is a Party to the Convention, the organization and its member States shall decide on their respective responsibilities for the performance of their obligations under the Convention. In such cases, the organization and the member States shall not be entitled to exercise rights under the Convention concurrently.

(3) In their instruments of ratification, acceptance, approval or accession, regional economic integration organizations shall declare the extent of their competence with respect to the matters governed by the Convention. These organizations shall also inform the Depositary, who shall in turn inform the Parties, of any substantial modification in the extent of their competence.

Article 23 Entry into Force

(1) The Convention shall enter into force on the ninetieth day after the date of deposit of the fiftieth instrument of ratification, acceptance, approval or accession.

(2) For each State or regional economic integration organization that ratifies, accepts or approves the Convention or accedes thereto after the deposit of the fiftieth instrument of ratification, acceptance, approval or accession, the Convention shall enter into force on the ninetieth day after the date of deposit by such State or regional economic integration organization of its instrument of ratification, acceptance, approval or accession.

(3) For the purposes of paragraphs (1) and (2) above, any instrument deposited by a regional economic integration organization shall not be counted as additional to those deposited by States members of the organization.

Article 24 Reservations

No reservations may be made to the Convention.

Article 25 Withdrawal

(1) At any time after three years from the date on which the Convention has entered into force for a Party, that Party may withdraw from the Convention by giving written notification to the Depositary.

(2) Any such withdrawal shall take effect upon expiry of one year from the date of receipt by the Depositary of the notification of withdrawal, or on such later date as may be specified in the notification of withdrawal.

(3) Any Party that withdraws from the Convention shall be considered as also having withdrawn from any Protocol to which it is a Party.

Article 26 Authentic Texts

The original of this Convention, of which the Arabic, Chinese, English, French, Russian and Spanish texts are equally authentic, shall be deposited with the Secretary-General of the United Nations.

IN WITNESS WHEREOF the undersigned, being duly authorized to that effect, have signed this Convention.

DONE at New York this ninth day of May one thousand nine hundred and ninety-two.

Annex I

Australia
Austria
Belarus *
Belgium
Bulgaria *
Canada
Croatia *†
Cyprus §
Czech Republic *†
Denmark
European Economic Community
Estonia *
Finland
France
Germany
Greece
Hungary *
Iceland
Ireland
Italy
Japan
Latvia *
Liechtenstein †
Lithuania *
Luxembourg
Malta ‡
Monaco †
Netherlands
New Zealand
Norway
Poland *
Portugal
Romania *
Russian Federation *
Slovakia *†
Slovenia *†
Spain
Sweden
Switzerland
Turkey
Ukraine *
United Kingdom of Great Britain and Northern Ireland
United States of America

* Countries that are undergoing the process of transition to a market economy.

† *Publisher's note*: Countries added to Annex I by an amendment that entered into force on 13 August 1998, pursuant to decision 4/CP.3 adopted at COP 3.

‡ *Publisher's note*: Country added to Annex I by an amendment that entered into force on 26 October 2010, pursuant to decision 3/CP.15 adopted at COP 15.

§ *Publisher's note*: Country added to Annex I by an amendment that entered into force on 9 January 2013, pursuant to decision 10/CP.17 adopted at COP 17.

Annex II*

Australia
Austria
Belgium
Canada
Denmark
European Economic Community
Finland
France
Germany
Greece
Iceland
Ireland
Italy
Japan
Luxembourg
Netherlands
New Zealand
Norway
Portugal
Spain
Sweden
Switzerland
United States of America
United Kingdom of Great Britain and Northern Ireland

* Turkey was deleted from Annex II by an amendment that entered into force 28 June 2002, pursuant to decision 26/CP.7 adopted at COP7.

KYOTO PROTOCOL TO THE UNITED NATIONS FRAMEWORK CONVENTION ON CLIMATE CHANGE

(Adopted: 11 December 1997; Entry into force: 16 February 2005; Applied to Hong Kong: 8 April 2003)

The Parties to this Protocol,

Being Parties to the United Nations Framework Convention on Climate Change, hereinafter referred to as "the Convention",

In pursuit of the ultimate objective of the Convention as stated in its Article 2,

Recalling the provisions of the Convention,

Being guided by Article 3 of the Convention,

Pursuant to the Berlin Mandate adopted by decision 1/CP.1 of the

Conference of the Parties to the Convention at its first session,

Have agreed as follows:

Article 1

For the purposes of this Protocol, the definitions contained in Article 1 of the Convention shall apply. In addition:

(1) "Conference of the Parties" means the Conference of the Parties to the Convention.

(2) "Convention" means the United Nations Framework Convention on Climate Change, adopted in New York on 9 May 1992.

(3) "Intergovernmental Panel on Climate Change" means the Intergovernmental Panel on Climate Change established in 1988 jointly by the World Meteorological Organization and the United Nations Environment Programme.

(4) "Montreal Protocol" means the Montreal Protocol on Substances that Deplete the Ozone Layer, adopted in Montreal on 16 September 1987 and as subsequently adjusted and amended.

(5) "Parties present and voting" means Parties present and casting an affirmative or negative vote.

(6) "Party" means, unless the context otherwise indicates, a Party to this Protocol.

(7) "Party included in Annex I" means a Party included in Annex I to the Convention, as may be amended, or a Party which has made a notification under Article 4, paragraph (2)(g), of the Convention.

Article 2

(1) Each Party included in Annex I, in achieving its quantified emission limitation and reduction commitments under Article 3, in order to promote sustainable development, shall:

(a) Implement and/or further elaborate policies and measures in accordance with its national circumstances, such as:

(i) Enhancement of energy efficiency in relevant sectors of the national economy;

(ii) Protection and enhancement of sinks and reservoirs of greenhouse gases not controlled by the Montreal Protocol, taking into account its commitments under relevant international environmental agreements; promotion of sustainable forest management practices, afforestation and reforestation;

(iii) Promotion of sustainable forms of agriculture in light of climate change considerations;

(iv) Research on, and promotion, development and increased use of, new and renewable forms of energy, of carbon dioxide sequestration technologies and of advanced and innovative environmentally sound technologies;

(v) Progressive reduction or phasing out of market imperfections, fiscal incentives, tax and duty exemptions and subsidies in all greenhouse gas emitting sectors that run counter to the objective of the Convention and application of market instruments;

(vi) Encouragement of appropriate reforms in relevant sectors aimed at promoting policies and measures which limit or reduce emissions of greenhouse gases not controlled by the Montreal Protocol;

(vii) Measures to limit and/or reduce emissions of greenhouse gases not controlled by the Montreal Protocol in the transport sector;

(viii) Limitation and/or reduction of methane emissions through recovery and use in waste management, as well as in the production, transport and distribution of energy;

(b) Cooperate with other such Parties to enhance the individual and combined effectiveness of their policies and measures adopted under this Article, pursuant to Article 4, paragraph (2)(e)(i), of the Convention. To this end, these Parties shall take steps to share their experience and exchange information on such policies and measures, including developing ways of improving their comparability, transparency and effectiveness. The Conference of the Parties serving as the meeting of the Parties to this Protocol shall, at its first session or as soon as practicable thereafter, consider ways to facilitate such cooperation, taking into account all relevant information.

(2) The Parties included in Annex I shall pursue limitation or reduction of emissions of greenhouse gases not controlled by the Montreal Protocol from aviation and marine bunker fuels, working through the International Civil Aviation Organization and the International Maritime Organization, respectively.

(3) The Parties included in Annex I shall strive to implement policies and measures under this Article in such a way as to minimize adverse effects, including the adverse effects of climate change, effects on international trade, and social, environmental and economic impacts on other Parties, especially developing country Parties and in particular those identified in Article 4, paragraphs (8) and (9), of the Convention, taking into account Article 3 of the Convention. The Conference of the Parties serving as the meeting of the Parties to this Protocol may take further action, as appropriate, to promote the implementation of the provisions of this paragraph.

(4) The Conference of the Parties serving as the meeting of the Parties to this Protocol, if it decides that it would be beneficial to coordinate any of the policies and measures in paragraph (1)(a) above, taking into account different national circumstances and potential effects, shall consider ways and means to elaborate the coordination of such policies and measures.

Article 3

(1) The Parties included in Annex I shall, individually or jointly, ensure that their aggregate anthropogenic carbon dioxide equivalent emissions of the greenhouse gases listed in Annex A do not exceed their assigned amounts, calculated pursuant to their quantified emission limitation and reduction commitments inscribed in Annex B and in accordance with the provisions of this Article, with a view to reducing their overall emissions of such gases by at least 5 percent below 1990 levels in the commitment period 2008 to 2012.

(2) Each Party included in Annex I shall, by 2005, have made demonstrable progress in achieving its commitments under this Protocol.

(3) The net changes in greenhouse gas emissions by sources and removals by sinks resulting from direct human-induced land-use change and forestry activities, limited to afforestation, reforestation and deforestation since 1990, measured as verifiable changes in carbon stocks in

each commitment period, shall be used to meet the commitments under this Article of each Party included in Annex I. The greenhouse gas emissions by sources and removals by sinks associated with those activities shall be reported in a transparent and verifiable manner and reviewed in accordance with Articles 7 and 8.

(4) Prior to the first session of the Conference of the Parties serving as the meeting of the Parties to this Protocol, each Party included in Annex I shall provide, for consideration by the Subsidiary Body for Scientific and Technological Advice, data to establish its level of carbon stocks in 1990 and to enable an estimate to be made of its changes in carbon stocks in subsequent years. The Conference of the Parties serving as the meeting of the Parties to this Protocol shall, at its first session or as soon as practicable thereafter, decide upon modalities, rules and guidelines as to how, and which, additional human-induced activities related to changes in greenhouse gas emissions by sources and removals by sinks in the agricultural soils and the land-use change and forestry categories shall be added to, or subtracted from, the assigned amounts for Parties included in Annex I, taking into account uncertainties, transparency in reporting, verifiability, the methodological work of the Intergovernmental Panel on Climate Change, the advice provided by the Subsidiary Body for Scientific and Technological Advice in accordance with Article 5 and the decisions of the Conference of the Parties. Such a decision shall apply in the second and subsequent commitment periods. A Party may choose to apply such a decision on these additional human-induced activities for its first commitment period, provided that these activities have taken place since 1990.

(5) The Parties included in Annex I undergoing the process of transition to a market economy whose base year or period was established pursuant to decision 9/CP.2 of the Conference of the Parties at its second session shall use that base year or period for the implementation of their commitments under this Article. Any other Party included in Annex I undergoing the process of transition to a market economy which has not yet submitted its first national communication under Article 12 of the Convention may also notify the Conference of the Parties serving as the meeting of the Parties to this Protocol that it intends to use an historical base year or period other than 1990 for the implementation of its commitments under this Article. The Conference of the Parties serving as the meeting of the Parties to this Protocol shall decide on the acceptance of such notification.

(6) Taking into account Article 4, paragraph (6), of the Convention, in the implementation of their commitments under this Protocol other than those under this Article, a certain degree of flexibility shall be allowed by the Conference of the Parties serving as the meeting of the Parties to this Protocol to the Parties included in Annex I undergoing the process of transition to a market economy.

(7) In the first quantified emission limitation and reduction commitment period, from 2008 to 2012, the assigned amount for each Party included in Annex I shall be equal to the percentage inscribed for it in Annex B of its aggregate anthropogenic carbon dioxide equivalent emissions of the greenhouse gases listed in Annex A in 1990, or the base year or period determined in accordance with paragraph (5) above, multiplied by five. Those Parties included in Annex I for whom land-use change and forestry constituted a net source of greenhouse gas emissions in 1990 shall include in their 1990 emissions base year or period the aggregate anthropogenic carbon dioxide equivalent emissions by sources minus removals by sinks in 1990 from land-use change for the purposes of calculating their assigned amount.

(8) Any Party included in Annex I may use 1995 as its base year for hydrofluorocarbons, perfluorocarbons and sulphur hexafluoride, for the purposes of the calculation referred to in paragraph (7) above.

(9) Commitments for subsequent periods for Parties included in Annex I shall be established in amendments to Annex B to this Protocol, which shall be adopted in accordance with the provisions of Article 21, paragraph (7). The Conference of the Parties serving as the meeting of the Parties to this Protocol shall initiate the consideration of such commitments at least seven years before the end of the first commitment period referred to in paragraph (1) above.

(10) Any emission reduction units, or any part of an assigned amount, which a Party acquires from another Party in accordance with the provisions of Article 6 or of Article 17 shall be added to the assigned amount for the acquiring Party.

(11) Any emission reduction units, or any part of an assigned amount, which a Party transfers to another Party in accordance with the provisions of Article 6 or of Article 17 shall be subtracted from the assigned amount for the transferring Party.

(12) Any certified emission reductions which a Party acquires from another Party in accordance with the provisions of Article 12 shall be added to the assigned amount for the acquiring Party.

(13) If the emissions of a Party included in Annex I in a commitment period are less than its assigned amount under this Article, this difference shall, on request of that Party, be added to the assigned amount for that Party for subsequent commitment periods.

(14) Each Party included in Annex I shall strive to implement the commitments mentioned in paragraph (1) above in such a way as to minimize adverse social, environmental and economic impacts on developing country Parties, particularly those identified in Article 4, paragraphs (8) and (9), of the Convention. In line with relevant decisions of the Conference of the Parties on the implementation of those paragraphs, the Conference of the Parties serving as the meeting of the Parties to this Protocol shall, at its first session, consider what actions are necessary to minimize the adverse effects of climate change and/or the impacts of response measures on Parties referred to in those paragraphs. Among the issues to be considered shall be the establishment of funding, insurance and transfer of technology.

Article 4

(1) Any Parties included in Annex I that have reached an agreement to fulfil their commitments under Article 3 jointly, shall be deemed to have met those commitments provided that their total combined aggregate anthropogenic carbon dioxide equivalent emissions of the greenhouse gases listed in Annex A do not exceed their assigned amounts calculated pursuant to their quantified emission limitation and reduction commitments inscribed in Annex B and in accordance with the provisions of Article 3. The respective emission level allocated to each of the Parties to the agreement shall be set out in that agreement.

(2) The Parties to any such agreement shall notify the secretariat of the terms of the agreement on the date of deposit of their instruments of ratification, acceptance or approval of this Protocol, or accession thereto. The secretariat shall in turn inform the Parties and signatories to the Convention of the terms of the agreement.

(3) Any such agreement shall remain in operation for the duration of the commitment period specified in Article 3, paragraph (7).

(4) If Parties acting jointly do so in the framework of, and together with, a regional economic integration organization, any alteration in the composition of the organization after adoption of this Protocol shall not affect existing commitments under this Protocol. Any alteration in the composition of the organization shall only apply for the purposes of those commitments under Article 3 that are adopted subsequent to that alteration.

(5) In the event of failure by the Parties to such an agreement to achieve their total combined level of emission reductions, each Party to that agreement shall be responsible for its own level of emissions set out in the agreement.

(6) If Parties acting jointly do so in the framework of, and together with, a regional economic integration organization which is itself a Party to this Protocol, each member State of that regional economic integration organization individually, and together with the regional economic integration organization acting in accordance with Article 24, shall, in the event of failure to achieve the total combined level of emission reductions, be responsible for its level of emissions as notified in accordance with this Article.

Article 5

(1) Each Party included in Annex I shall have in place, no later than one year prior to the start of the first commitment period, a national system for the estimation of anthropogenic emissions by sources and removals by sinks of all greenhouse gases not controlled by the Montreal Protocol. Guidelines for such national systems, which shall incorporate the methodologies specified in paragraph (2) below, shall be decided upon by the Conference of the Parties serving as the meeting of the Parties to this Protocol at its first session.

(2) Methodologies for estimating anthropogenic emissions by sources and removals by sinks of all greenhouse gases not controlled by the Montreal Protocol shall be those accepted by the Intergovernmental Panel on Climate Change and agreed upon by the Conference of the Parties at its third session. Where such methodologies are not used, appropriate adjustments shall be applied according to methodologies agreed upon by the Conference of the Parties serving as the meeting of the Parties to this Protocol at its first session. Based on the work of, inter alia, the Intergovernmental Panel on Climate Change and advice provided by the Subsidiary Body for Scientific and Technological Advice, the Conference of the Parties serving as the meeting of the Parties to this Protocol shall regularly review and, as appropriate, revise such methodologies and adjustments, taking fully into account any relevant decisions by the Conference of the Parties. Any revision to methodologies or adjustments shall be used only for the purposes of ascertaining compliance with commitments under Article 3 in respect of any commitment period adopted subsequent to that revision.

(3) The global warming potentials used to calculate the carbon dioxide equivalence of anthropogenic emissions by sources and removals by sinks of greenhouse gases listed in Annex A shall be those accepted by the Intergovernmental Panel on Climate Change and agreed upon by the Conference of the Parties at its third session. Based on the work of, inter alia, the Intergovernmental Panel on Climate Change and advice provided by the Subsidiary Body for Scientific and Technological Advice, the Conference of the Parties serving as the meeting of the Parties to this Protocol shall regularly review and, as appropriate, revise the global warming potential of each such greenhouse gas, taking fully into account any relevant decisions by the Conference of the Parties. Any revision to a global warming potential shall apply only to commitments under Article 3 in respect of any commitment period adopted subsequent to that revision.

Article 6

(1) For the purpose of meeting its commitments under Article 3, any Party included in Annex I may transfer to, or acquire from, any other such Party emission reduction units resulting from projects aimed at reducing anthropogenic emissions by sources or enhancing anthropogenic removals by sinks of greenhouse gases in any sector of the economy, provided that:

  (a) Any such project has the approval of the Parties involved;

  (b) Any such project provides a reduction in emissions by sources, or an enhancement of removals by sinks, that is additional to any that would otherwise occur;

  (c) It does not acquire any emission reduction units if it is not in compliance with its obligations under Articles 5 and 7; and

  (d) The acquisition of emission reduction units shall be supplemental to domestic actions for the purposes of meeting commitments under Article 3.

(2) The Conference of the Parties serving as the meeting of the Parties to this Protocol may, at its first session or as soon as practicable thereafter, further elaborate guidelines for the implementation of this Article, including for verification and reporting.

(3) A Party included in Annex I may authorize legal entities to participate, under its responsibility, in actions leading to the generation, transfer or acquisition under this Article of emission reduction units.

(4) If a question of implementation by a Party included in Annex I of the requirements referred to in this Article is identified in accordance with the relevant provisions of Article 8, transfers and acquisitions of emission reduction units may continue to be made after the question has been identified, provided that any such units may not be used by a Party to meet its commitments under Article 3 until any issue of compliance is resolved.

Article 7

(1) Each Party included in Annex I shall incorporate in its annual inventory of anthropogenic emissions by sources and removals by sinks of greenhouse gases not controlled by the Montreal Protocol, submitted in accordance with the relevant decisions of the Conference of the Parties, the necessary supplementary information for the purposes of ensuring compliance with Article 3, to be determined in accordance with paragraph (4) below.

(2) Each Party included in Annex I shall incorporate in its national communication, submitted under Article 12 of the Convention, the supplementary information necessary to demonstrate compliance with its commitments under this Protocol, to be determined in accordance with paragraph (4) below.

(3) Each Party included in Annex I shall submit the information required under paragraph (1) above annually, beginning with the first inventory due under the Convention for the first year of the commitment period after this Protocol has entered into force for that Party. Each such Party shall submit the information required under paragraph (2) above as part of the first national communication due under the Convention after this Protocol has entered into force for it and after the adoption of guidelines as provided for in paragraph (4) below. The frequency of subsequent submission of information required under this Article shall be determined by the Conference of the Parties serving as the meeting of the Parties to this Protocol, taking into account any timetable for the submission of national communications decided upon by the Conference of the Parties.

(4) The Conference of the Parties serving as the meeting of the Parties to this Protocol shall adopt at its first session, and review periodically thereafter, guidelines for the preparation of the information required under this Article, taking into account guidelines for the preparation of national communications by Parties included in Annex I adopted by the Conference of the Parties. The Conference of the Parties serving as the meeting of the Parties to this Protocol shall also, prior to the first commitment period, decide upon modalities for the accounting of assigned amounts.

Article 8

(1) The information submitted under Article 7 by each Party included in Annex I shall be reviewed by expert review teams pursuant to the relevant decisions of the Conference of the Parties and in accordance with guidelines adopted for this purpose by the Conference of the Parties serving as the meeting of the Parties to this Protocol under paragraph (4) below. The information submitted under Article 7, paragraph (1), by each Party included in Annex I shall be reviewed as part of the annual compilation and accounting of emissions inventories and assigned amounts. Additionally, the information submitted under Article 7, paragraph (2), by each Party included in Annex I shall be reviewed as part of the review of communications.

(2) Expert review teams shall be coordinated by the secretariat and shall be composed of experts selected from those nominated by Parties to the Convention and, as appropriate, by intergovernmental organizations, in accordance with guidance provided for this purpose by the Conference of the Parties.

(3) The review process shall provide a thorough and comprehensive technical assessment of all aspects of the implementation by a Party of this Protocol. The expert review teams shall prepare a report to the Conference of the Parties serving as the meeting of the Parties to this Protocol, assessing the implementation of the commitments of the Party and identifying any potential problems in, and factors influencing, the fulfilment of commitments. Such reports shall be circulated

by the secretariat to all Parties to the Convention. The secretariat shall list those questions of implementation indicated in such reports for further consideration by the Conference of the Parties serving as the meeting of the Parties to this Protocol.

(4) The Conference of the Parties serving as the meeting of the Parties to this Protocol shall adopt at its first session, and review periodically thereafter, guidelines for the review of implementation of this Protocol by expert review teams taking into account the relevant decisions of the Conference of the Parties.

(5) The Conference of the Parties serving as the meeting of the Parties to this Protocol shall, with the assistance of the Subsidiary Body for Implementation and, as appropriate, the Subsidiary Body for Scientific and Technological Advice, consider:

(a) The information submitted by Parties under Article 7 and the reports of the expert reviews thereon conducted under this Article; and

(b) Those questions of implementation listed by the secretariat under paragraph (3) above, as well as any questions raised by Parties.

(6) Pursuant to its consideration of the information referred to in paragraph (5) above, the Conference of the Parties serving as the meeting of the Parties to this Protocol shall take decisions on any matter required for the implementation of this Protocol.

Article 9

(1) The Conference of the Parties serving as the meeting of the Parties to this Protocol shall periodically review this Protocol in the light of the best available scientific information and assessments on climate change and its impacts, as well as relevant technical, social and economic information. Such reviews shall be coordinated with pertinent reviews under the Convention, in particular those required by Article 4, paragraph (2)(d), and Article 7, paragraph (2)(a), of the Convention. Based on these reviews, the Conference of the Parties serving as the meeting of the Parties to this Protocol shall take appropriate action.

(2) The first review shall take place at the second session of the Conference of the Parties serving as the meeting of the Parties to this Protocol. Further reviews shall take place at regular intervals and in a timely manner.

Article 10

All Parties, taking into account their common but differentiated responsibilities and their specific national and regional development priorities, objectives and circumstances, without introducing any new commitments for Parties not included in Annex I, but reaffirming existing commitments under Article 4, paragraph (1), of the Convention, and continuing to advance the implementation of these commitments in order to achieve sustainable development, taking into account Article 4, paragraphs (3), (5) and (7), of the Convention, shall:

(a) Formulate, where relevant and to the extent possible, cost-effective national and, where appropriate, regional programmes to improve the quality of local emission factors, activity data and/or models which reflect the socio-economic conditions of each Party for the preparation and periodic updating of national inventories of anthropogenic emissions by sources and removals by sinks of all greenhouse gases not controlled by the Montreal Protocol, using comparable methodologies to be agreed upon by the Conference of the Parties, and consistent with the guidelines for the preparation of national communications adopted by the Conference of the Parties;

(b) Formulate, implement, publish and regularly update national and, where appropriate, regional programmes containing measures to mitigate climate change and measures to facilitate adequate adaptation to climate change:

(i) Such programmes would, inter alia, concern the energy, transport and industry sectors as well as agriculture, forestry and waste management. Furthermore, adaptation technologies and methods for improving spatial planning would improve adaptation to climate change; and

(ii) Parties included in Annex I shall submit information on action under this Protocol, including national programmes, in accordance with Article 7; and other Parties shall seek to include in their national communications, as appropriate, information on programmes which contain measures that the Party believes contribute to addressing climate change and its adverse impacts, including the abatement of increases in greenhouse gas emissions, and enhancement of and removals by sinks, capacity building and adaptation measures;

(c) Cooperate in the promotion of effective modalities for the development, application and diffusion of, and take all practicable steps to promote, facilitate and finance, as appropriate, the transfer of, or access to, environmentally sound technologies, know-how, practices and processes pertinent to climate change, in particular to developing countries, including the formulation of policies and programmes for the effective transfer of environmentally sound technologies that are publicly owned or in the public domain and the creation of an enabling environment for the private sector, to promote and enhance the transfer of, and access to, environmentally sound technologies;

(d) Cooperate in scientific and technical research and promote the maintenance and the development of systematic observation systems and development of data archives to reduce uncertainties related to the climate system, the adverse impacts of climate change and the economic and social consequences of various response strategies, and promote the development and strengthening of endogenous capacities and capabilities to participate in international and intergovernmental efforts, programmes and networks on research and systematic observation, taking into account Article 5 of the Convention;

(e) Cooperate in and promote at the international level, and, where appropriate, using existing bodies, the development and implementation of education and training programmes, including the strengthening of national capacity building, in particular human and institutional capacities and the exchange or secondment of personnel to train experts in this field, in particular for developing countries, and facilitate at the national level public awareness of, and public access to information on, climate change. Suitable modalities should be developed to implement these activities through the relevant bodies of the Convention, taking into account Article 6 of the Convention;

(f) Include in their national communications information on programmes and activities undertaken pursuant to this Article in accordance with relevant decisions of the Conference of the Parties; and

(g) Give full consideration, in implementing the commitments under this Article, to Article 4, paragraph (8), of the Convention.

Article 11

(1) In the implementation of Article 10, Parties shall take into account the provisions of Article 4, paragraphs (4), (5), (7), (8) and (9), of the Convention.

(2) In the context of the implementation of Article 4, paragraph (1), of the Convention, in accordance with the provisions of Article 4, paragraph (3), and Article 11 of the Convention, and through the entity or entities entrusted with the operation of the financial mechanism of the Convention, the developed country Parties and other developed Parties included in Annex II to the Convention shall:

(a) Provide new and additional financial resources to meet the agreed full costs incurred by developing country Parties in advancing the implementation of existing commitments under Article 4, paragraph (1)(a), of the Convention that are covered in Article 10, subparagraph (a); and

(b) Also provide such financial resources, including for the transfer of technology, needed by the developing country Parties to meet the agreed full incremental costs of advancing the implementation of existing commitments under Article 4, paragraph (1), of the Convention that are covered by Article 10 and that are agreed between a developing country Party and the international entity or entities referred to in Article 11 of the Convention, in accordance with that Article.

The implementation of these existing commitments shall take into account the need for adequacy and predictability in the flow of funds and the importance of appropriate burden sharing among developed country Parties. The guidance to the entity or entities entrusted with the operation of the financial mechanism of the Convention in relevant decisions of the Conference of the Parties, including those agreed before the adoption of this Protocol, shall apply *mutatis mutandis* to the provisions of this paragraph.

(3) The developed country Parties and other developed Parties in Annex II to the Convention may also provide, and developing country Parties avail themselves of, financial resources for the implementation of Article 10, through bilateral, regional and other multilateral channels.

Article 12

(1) A clean development mechanism is hereby defined.

(2) The purpose of the clean development mechanism shall be to assist Parties not included in Annex I in achieving sustainable development and in contributing to the ultimate objective of the Convention, and to assist Parties included in Annex I in achieving compliance with their quantified emission limitation and reduction commitments under Article 3.

(3) Under the clean development mechanism:

(a) Parties not included in Annex I will benefit from project activities resulting in certified emission reductions; and

(b) Parties included in Annex I may use the certified emission reductions accruing from such project activities to contribute to compliance with part of their quantified emission limitation and reduction commitments under Article 3, as determined by the Conference of the Parties serving as the meeting of the Parties to this Protocol.

(4) The clean development mechanism shall be subject to the authority and guidance of the Conference of the Parties serving as the meeting of the Parties to this Protocol and be supervised by an executive board of the clean development mechanism.

(5) Emission reductions resulting from each project activity shall be certified by operational entities to be designated by the Conference of the Parties serving as the meeting of the Parties to this Protocol, on the basis of:

(a) Voluntary participation approved by each Party involved;

(b) Real, measurable, and long-term benefits related to the mitigation of climate change; and

(c) Reductions in emissions that are additional to any that would occur in the absence of the certified project activity.

(6) The clean development mechanism shall assist in arranging funding of certified project activities as necessary.

(7) The Conference of the Parties serving as the meeting of the Parties to this Protocol shall, at its first session, elaborate modalities and procedures with the objective of ensuring transparency, efficiency and accountability through independent auditing and verification of project activities.

(8) The Conference of the Parties serving as the meeting of the Parties to this Protocol shall ensure that a share of the proceeds from certified project activities is used to cover administrative expenses as well as to assist developing country Parties that are particularly vulnerable to the adverse effects of climate change to meet the costs of adaptation.

(9) Participation under the clean development mechanism, including in activities mentioned in paragraph (3)(a) above and in the acquisition of certified emission reductions, may involve private and/or public entities, and is to be subject to whatever guidance may be provided by the executive board of the clean development mechanism.

(10) Certified emission reductions obtained during the period from the year 2000 up to the beginning of the first commitment period can be used to assist in achieving compliance in the first commitment period.

Article 13

(1) The Conference of the Parties, the supreme body of the Convention, shall serve as the meeting of the Parties to this Protocol.

(2) Parties to the Convention that are not Parties to this Protocol may participate as observers in the proceedings of any session of the Conference of the Parties serving as the meeting of the Parties to this Protocol. When the Conference of the Parties serves as the meeting of the Parties to this Protocol, decisions under this Protocol shall be taken only by those that are Parties to this Protocol.

(3) When the Conference of the Parties serves as the meeting of the Parties to this Protocol, any member of the Bureau of the Conference of the Parties representing a Party to the Convention but, at that time, not a Party to this Protocol, shall be replaced by an additional member to be elected by and from amongst the Parties to this Protocol.

(4) The Conference of the Parties serving as the meeting of the Parties to this Protocol shall keep under regular review the implementation of this Protocol and shall make, within its mandate, the decisions necessary to promote its effective implementation. It shall perform the functions assigned to it by this Protocol and shall:

(a) Assess, on the basis of all information made available to it in accordance with the provisions of this Protocol, the implementation of this Protocol by the Parties, the overall effects of the measures taken pursuant to this Protocol, in particular environmental, economic and social effects as well as their cumulative impacts and the extent to which progress towards the objective of the Convention is being achieved;

(b) Periodically examine the obligations of the Parties under this Protocol, giving due consideration to any reviews required by Article 4, paragraph (2)(d), and Article 7, paragraph (2), of the Convention, in the light of the objective of the Convention, the experience gained in its implementation and the evolution of scientific and technological knowledge, and in this respect consider and adopt regular reports on the implementation of this Protocol;

(c) Promote and facilitate the exchange of information on measures adopted by the Parties to address climate change and its effects, taking into account the differing circumstances, responsibilities and capabilities of the Parties and their respective commitments under this Protocol;

(d) Facilitate, at the request of two or more Parties, the coordination of measures adopted by them to address climate change and its effects, taking into account the differing circumstances, responsibilities and capabilities of the Parties and their respective commitments under this Protocol;

(e) Promote and guide, in accordance with the objective of the Convention and the provisions of this Protocol, and taking fully into account the relevant decisions by the Conference of the Parties, the development and periodic refinement of comparable methodologies for the effective implementation of this Protocol, to be agreed on by the Conference of the Parties serving as the meeting of the Parties to this Protocol;

(f) Make recommendations on any matters necessary for the implementation of this Protocol;

(g) Seek to mobilize additional financial resources in accordance with Article 11, paragraph (2);

(h) Establish such subsidiary bodies as are deemed necessary for the implementation of this Protocol;

(i) Seek and utilize, where appropriate, the services and cooperation of, and information provided by, competent international organizations and intergovernmental and non-governmental bodies; and

(j) Exercise such other functions as may be required for the implementation of this Protocol, and consider any assignment resulting from a decision by the Conference of the Parties.

(5) The rules of procedure of the Conference of the Parties and financial procedures applied under the Convention shall be applied *mutatis mutandis* under this Protocol, except as may be otherwise decided by consensus by the Conference of the Parties serving as the meeting of the Parties to this Protocol.

(6) The first session of the Conference of the Parties serving as the meeting of the Parties to this Protocol shall be convened by the secretariat in conjunction with the first session of the Conference of the Parties that is scheduled after the date of the entry into force of this Protocol. Subsequent ordinary sessions of the Conference of the Parties serving as the meeting of the Parties to this Protocol shall be held every year and in conjunction with ordinary sessions of the Conference of the Parties, unless otherwise decided by the Conference of the Parties serving as the meeting of the Parties to this Protocol.

(7) Extraordinary sessions of the Conference of the Parties serving as the meeting of the Parties to this Protocol shall be held at such other times as may be deemed necessary by the Conference of the Parties serving as the meeting of the Parties to this Protocol, or at the written request of any Party, provided that, within six months of the request being communicated to the Parties by the secretariat, it is supported by at least one third of the Parties.

(8) The United Nations, its specialized agencies and the International Atomic Energy Agency, as well as any State member thereof or observers thereto not party to the Convention, may be represented at sessions of the Conference of the Parties serving as the meeting of the Parties to this Protocol as observers. Any body or agency, whether national or international, governmental or non-governmental, which is qualified in matters covered by this Protocol and which has informed the secretariat of its wish to be represented at a session of the Conference of the Parties serving as the meeting of the Parties to this Protocol as an observer, may be so admitted unless at least one third of the Parties present object. The admission and participation of observers shall be subject to the rules of procedure, as referred to in paragraph (5) above.

Article 14

(1) The secretariat established by Article 8 of the Convention shall serve as the secretariat of this Protocol.

(2) Article 8, paragraph (2), of the Convention on the functions of the secretariat, and Article 8, paragraph (3), of the Convention on arrangements made for the functioning of the secretariat, shall apply *mutatis mutandis* to this Protocol. The secretariat shall, in addition, exercise the functions assigned to it under this Protocol.

Article 15

(1) The Subsidiary Body for Scientific and Technological Advice and the Subsidiary Body for Implementation established by Articles 9 and 10 of the Convention shall serve as, respectively, the Subsidiary Body for Scientific and Technological Advice and the Subsidiary Body for Implementation of this Protocol. The provisions relating to the functioning of these two bodies under the Convention shall apply *mutatis mutandis* to this Protocol. Sessions of the meetings of the Subsidiary Body for Scientific and Technological Advice and the Subsidiary Body for Implementation of this Protocol shall be held in conjunction with the meetings of, respectively, the Subsidiary Body for Scientific and Technological Advice and the Subsidiary Body for Implementation of the Convention.

(2) Parties to the Convention that are not Parties to this Protocol may participate as observers in the proceedings of any session of the subsidiary bodies. When the subsidiary bodies serve as the subsidiary bodies of this Protocol, decisions under this Protocol shall be taken only by those that are Parties to this Protocol.

(3) When the subsidiary bodies established by Articles 9 and 10 of the Convention exercise their functions with regard to matters concerning this Protocol, any member of the Bureaux of those subsidiary bodies representing a Party to the Convention but, at that time, not a party to this Protocol, shall be replaced by an additional member to be elected by and from amongst the Parties to this Protocol.

Article 16

The Conference of the Parties serving as the meeting of the Parties to this Protocol shall, as soon as practicable, consider the application to this Protocol of, and modify as appropriate, the multilateral consultative process referred to in Article 13 of the Convention, in the light of any relevant decisions that may be taken by the Conference of the Parties. Any multilateral consultative process that may be applied to this Protocol shall operate without prejudice to the procedures and mechanisms established in accordance with Article 18.

Article 17

The Conference of the Parties shall define the relevant principles, modalities, rules and guidelines, in particular for verification, reporting and accountability for emissions trading. The Parties included in Annex B may participate in emissions trading for the purposes of fulfilling their commitments under Article 3. Any such trading shall be supplemental to domestic actions for the purpose of meeting quantified emission limitation and reduction commitments under that Article.

Article 18

The Conference of the Parties serving as the meeting of the Parties to this Protocol shall, at its first session, approve appropriate and effective procedures and mechanisms to determine and to address cases of non-compliance with the provisions of this Protocol, including through the development of an indicative list of consequences, taking into account the cause, type, degree and frequency of non-compliance. Any procedures and mechanisms under this Article entailing binding consequences shall be adopted by means of an amendment to this Protocol.

Article 19

The provisions of Article 14 of the Convention on settlement of disputes shall apply *mutatis mutandis* to this Protocol.

Article 20

(1) Any Party may propose amendments to this Protocol.

(2) Amendments to this Protocol shall be adopted at an ordinary session of the Conference of the Parties serving as the meeting of the Parties to this Protocol. The text of any proposed amendment to this Protocol shall be communicated to the Parties by the secretariat at least six months before the meeting at which it is proposed for adoption. The secretariat shall also communicate the text of any proposed amendments to the Parties and signatories to the Convention and, for information, to the Depositary.

(3) The Parties shall make every effort to reach agreement on any proposed amendment to this Protocol by consensus. If all efforts at consensus have been exhausted, and no agreement reached, the amendment shall as a last resort be adopted by a three-fourths majority vote of the Parties present and voting at the meeting. The adopted amendment shall be communicated by the secretariat to the Depositary, who shall circulate it to all Parties for their acceptance.

(4) Instruments of acceptance in respect of an amendment shall be deposited with the Depositary. An amendment adopted in accordance with paragraph (3) above shall enter into force for those Parties having accepted it on the ninetieth day after the date of receipt by the Depositary of an instrument of acceptance by at least three fourths of the Parties to this Protocol.

(5) The amendment shall enter into force for any other Party on the ninetieth day after the date on which that Party deposits with the Depositary its instrument of acceptance of the said amendment.

Article 21

(1) Annexes to this Protocol shall form an integral part thereof and, unless otherwise expressly provided, a reference to this Protocol constitutes at the same time a reference to any Annexes thereto. Any Annexes adopted after the entry into force of this Protocol shall be restricted to lists, forms and any other material of a descriptive nature that is of a scientific, technical, procedural or administrative character.

(2) Any Party may make proposals for an Annex to this Protocol and may propose amendments to Annexes to this Protocol.

(3) Annexes to this Protocol and amendments to Annexes to this Protocol shall be adopted at an ordinary session of the Conference of the Parties serving as the meeting of the Parties to this Protocol. The text of any proposed Annex or amendment to an Annex shall be communicated to the Parties by the secretariat at least six months before the meeting at which it is proposed for adoption. The secretariat shall also communicate the text of any proposed Annex or amendment to an Annex to the Parties and signatories to the Convention and, for information, to the Depositary.

(4) The Parties shall make every effort to reach agreement on any proposed Annex or amendment to an Annex by consensus. If all efforts at consensus have been exhausted, and no agreement reached, the Annex or amendment to an Annex shall as a last resort be adopted by a three-fourths majority vote of the Parties present and voting at the meeting. The adopted Annex or amendment to an Annex shall be communicated by the secretariat to the Depositary, who shall circulate it to all Parties for their acceptance.

(5) An Annex, or amendment to an Annex other than Annex A or B, that has been adopted in accordance with paragraphs (3) and (4) above shall enter into force for all Parties to this Protocol six months after the date of the communication by the Depositary to such Parties of the adoption of the Annex or adoption of the amendment to the Annex, except for those Parties that have notified the Depositary, in writing, within that period of their non-acceptance of the Annex or amendment to the Annex. The Annex or amendment to an Annex shall enter into force for Parties which withdraw their notification of non-acceptance on the ninetieth day after the date on which withdrawal of such notification has been received by the Depositary.

(6) If the adoption of an Annex or an amendment to an Annex involves an amendment to this Protocol, that Annex or amendment to an Annex shall not enter into force until such time as the amendment to this Protocol enters into force.

(7) Amendments to Annexes A and B to this Protocol shall be adopted and enter into force in accordance with the procedure set out in Article 20, provided that any amendment to Annex B shall be adopted only with the written consent of the Party concerned.

Article 22

(1) Each Party shall have one vote, except as provided for in paragraph (2) below.

(2) Regional economic integration organizations, in matters within their competence, shall exercise their right to vote with a number of votes equal to the number of their member States that are Parties to this Protocol. Such an organization shall not exercise its right to vote if any of its member States exercises its right, and vice versa.

Article 23

The Secretary-General of the United Nations shall be the Depositary of this Protocol.

Article 24

(1) This Protocol shall be open for signature and subject to ratification, acceptance or approval by States and regional economic integration organizations which are Parties to the Convention. It shall be open for signature at United Nations Headquarters in New York from 16 March 1998 to 15 March 1999. This Protocol shall be open for accession from the day after the date on which it is closed for signature. Instruments of ratification, acceptance, approval or accession shall be deposited with the Depositary.

(2) Any regional economic integration organization which becomes a Party to this Protocol without any of its member States being a Party shall be bound by all the obligations under this Protocol. In the case of such organizations, one or more of whose member States is a Party to this Protocol, the organization and its member States shall decide on their respective responsibilities for the performance of their obligations under this Protocol. In such cases, the organization and the member States shall not be entitled to exercise rights under this Protocol concurrently.

(3) In their instruments of ratification, acceptance, approval or accession, regional economic integration organizations shall declare the extent of their competence with respect to the matters governed by this Protocol. These organizations shall also inform the Depositary, who shall in turn inform the Parties, of any substantial modification in the extent of their competence.

Article 25

(1) This Protocol shall enter into force on the ninetieth day after the date on which not less than 55 Parties to the Convention, incorporating Parties included in Annex I which accounted in total for at least 55 percent of the total carbon dioxide emissions for 1990 of the Parties included in Annex I, have deposited their instruments of ratification, acceptance, approval or accession.

(2) For the purposes of this Article, "the total carbon dioxide emissions for 1990 of the Parties included in Annex I" means the amount communicated on or before the date of adoption of this Protocol by the Parties included in Annex I in their first national communications submitted in accordance with Article 12 of the Convention.

(3) For each State or regional economic integration organization that ratifies, accepts or approves this Protocol or accedes thereto after the conditions set out in paragraph (1) above for entry into force have been fulfilled, this Protocol shall enter into force on the ninetieth day following the date of deposit of its instrument of ratification, acceptance, approval or accession.

(4) For the purposes of this Article, any instrument deposited by a regional economic integration organization shall not be counted as additional to those deposited by States members of the organization.

Article 26

No reservations may be made to this Protocol.

Article 27

(1) At any time after three years from the date on which this Protocol has entered into force for a Party, that Party may withdraw from this Protocol by giving written notification to the Depositary.

(2) Any such withdrawal shall take effect upon expiry of one year from the date of receipt by the Depositary of the notification of withdrawal, or on such later date as may be specified in the notification of withdrawal.

(3) Any Party that withdraws from the Convention shall be considered as also having withdrawn from this Protocol.

Article 28

The original of this Protocol, of which the Arabic, Chinese, English, French, Russian and Spanish texts are equally authentic, shall be deposited with the Secretary-General of the United Nations.

DONE at Kyoto this eleventh day of December one thousand nine hundred and ninety-seven.

IN WITNESS WHEREOF the undersigned, being duly authorized to that effect, have affixed their signatures to this Protocol on the dates indicated.

Annex A

Greenhouse Gases

Carbon dioxide (CO_2)

Methane (CH_4)

Nitrous oxide (N_2O)

Hydrofluorocarbons (HFCs)

Perfluorocarbons (PFCs)

Sulphur hexafluoride (SF_6)

Sectors/Source Categories

- Energy
  - Fuel combustion
    - Energy industries
    - Manufacturing industries and construction
    - Transport
    - Other sectors
    - Other
  - Fugitive emissions from fuels
    - Solid fuels
    - Oil and natural gas
    - Other
- Industrial processes
  - Mineral products
  - Chemical industry
  - Metal production
  - Other production
  - Production of halocarbons and sulphur hexafluoride
  - Consumption of halocarbons and sulphur hexafluoride
  - Other
- Solvent and other product use
- Agriculture
  - Enteric fermentation

Manure management

Rice cultivation

Agricultural soils

Prescribed burning of savannas

Field burning of agricultural residues

Other

Waste

Solid waste disposal on land

Wastewater handling

Waste incineration

Other

Annex B

Party	Quantified emission limitation or reduction commitment (percentage of base year or period)
Australia	108
Austria	92
Belgium	92
Bulgaria *	92
Canada	94
Croatia *	95
Czech Republic *	92
Denmark	92
Estonia *	92
European Community	92
Finland	92
France	92
Germany	92
Greece	92
Hungary *	94
Iceland	110
Ireland	92
Italy	92
Japan	94
Latvia *	92
Liechtenstein	92
Lithuania *	92
Luxembourg	92
Monaco	92
Netherlands	92
New Zealand	100
Norway	101
Poland *	94
Portugal	92

Romania *	92
Russian Federation *	100
Slovakia *	92
Slovenia *	92
Spain	92
Sweden	92
Switzerland	92
Ukraine *	100
United Kingdom of Great Britain and Northern Ireland	92
United States of America	93

* Countries that are undergoing the process of transition to a market economy.

PARIS AGREEMENT UNDER THE UNITED NATIONS FRAMEWORK CONVENTION ON CLIMATE CHANGE

(Adopted: 22 April 2016; Entry into force: 4 November 2016; Applied to Hong Kong: 3 September 2016)

The Parties to this Agreement,

Being Parties to the United Nations Framework Convention on Climate Change, hereinafter referred to as "the Convention",

Pursuant to the Durban Platform for Enhanced Action established by decision 1/CP.17 of the Conference of the Parties to the Convention at its seventeenth session,

In pursuit of the objective of the Convention, and being guided by its principles, including the principle of equity and common but differentiated responsibilities and respective capabilities, in the light of different national circumstances,

Recognizing the need for an effective and progressive response to the urgent threat of climate change on the basis of the best available scientific knowledge,

Also recognizing the specific needs and special circumstances of developing country Parties, especially those that are particularly vulnerable to the adverse effects of climate change, as provided for in the Convention,

Taking full account of the specific needs and special situations of the least developed countries with regard to funding and transfer of technology,

Recognizing that Parties may be affected not only by climate change, but also by the impacts of the measures taken in response to it,

Emphasizing the intrinsic relationship that climate change actions, responses and impacts have with equitable access to sustainable development and eradication of poverty,

Recognizing the fundamental priority of safeguarding food security and ending hunger, and the particular vulnerabilities of food production systems to the adverse impacts of climate change,

Taking into account the imperatives of a just transition of the workforce and the creation of decent work and quality jobs in accordance with nationally defined development priorities,

Acknowledging that climate change is a common concern of humankind, Parties should, when taking action to address climate change, respect, promote and consider their respective obligations on human rights, the right to health, the rights of indigenous peoples, local communities, migrants, children, persons with disabilities and people in vulnerable situations and the right to development, as well as gender equality, empowerment of women and intergenerational equity,

Recognizing the importance of the conservation and enhancement, as appropriate, of sinks and reservoirs of the greenhouse gases referred to in the Convention,

Noting the importance of ensuring the integrity of all ecosystems, including oceans, and the protection of biodiversity, recognized by some cultures as Mother Earth, and noting the importance for some of the concept of "climate justice", when taking action to address climate change,

Affirming the importance of education, training, public awareness, public participation, public access to information and cooperation at all levels on the matters addressed in this Agreement,

Recognizing the importance of the engagements of all levels of government and various actors, in accordance with respective national legislations of Parties, in addressing climate change,

Also recognizing that sustainable lifestyles and sustainable patterns of consumption and production, with developed country Parties taking the lead, play an important role in addressing climate change,

Have agreed as follows:

Article 1

For the purpose of this Agreement, the definitions contained in Article 1 of the Convention shall apply. In addition:

(a) "Convention" means the United Nations Framework Convention on Climate Change, adopted in New York on 9 May 1992;

(b) "Conference of the Parties" means the Conference of the Parties to the Convention;

(c) "Party" means a Party to this Agreement.

Article 2

(1) This Agreement, in enhancing the implementation of the Convention, including its objective, aims to strengthen the global response to the threat of climate change, in the context of sustainable development and efforts to eradicate poverty, including by:

(a) Holding the increase in the global average temperature to well below 2°C above pre-industrial levels and pursuing efforts to limit the temperature increase to 1.5°C above pre-industrial levels, recognizing that this would significantly reduce the risks and impacts of climate change;

(b) Increasing the ability to adapt to the adverse impacts of climate change and foster climate resilience and low greenhouse gas emissions development, in a manner that does not threaten food production; and

(c) Making finance flows consistent with a pathway towards low greenhouse gas emissions and climate-resilient development.

(2) This Agreement will be implemented to reflect equity and the principle of common but differentiated responsibilities and respective capabilities, in the light of different national circumstances.

Article 3

As nationally determined contributions to the global response to climate change, all Parties are to undertake and communicate ambitious efforts as defined in Articles 4, 7, 9, 10, 11 and 13 with the view to achieving the purpose of this Agreement as set out in Article 2. The efforts of all Parties will represent a progression over time, while recognizing the need to support developing country Parties for the effective implementation of this Agreement.

Article 4

(1) In order to achieve the long-term temperature goal set out in Article 2, Parties aim to reach global peaking of greenhouse gas emissions as soon as possible, recognizing that peaking will take longer for developing country Parties, and to undertake rapid reductions thereafter in accordance with best available science, so as to achieve a balance between anthropogenic emissions by sources and removals by sinks of greenhouse gases in the second half of this century, on the basis of equity, and in the context of sustainable development and efforts to eradicate poverty.

(2) Each Party shall prepare, communicate and maintain successive nationally determined contributions that it intends to achieve. Parties shall pursue domestic mitigation measures, with the aim of achieving the objectives of such contributions.

(3) Each Party's successive nationally determined contribution will represent a progression beyond the Party's then current nationally determined contribution and reflect its highest possible ambition, reflecting its common but differentiated responsibilities and respective capabilities, in the light of different national circumstances.

(4) Developed country Parties should continue taking the lead by undertaking economy-wide absolute emission reduction targets. Developing country Parties should continue enhancing their mitigation efforts, and are encouraged to move over time towards economy-wide emission reduction or limitation targets in the light of different national circumstances.

(5) Support shall be provided to developing country Parties for the implementation of this Article, in accordance with Articles 9, 10 and 11, recognizing that enhanced support for developing country Parties will allow for higher ambition in their actions.

(6) The least developed countries and small island developing States may prepare and communicate strategies, plans and actions for low greenhouse gas emissions development reflecting their special circumstances.

(7) Mitigation co-benefits resulting from Parties' adaptation actions and/or economic diversification plans can contribute to mitigation outcomes under this Article.

(8) In communicating their nationally determined contributions, all Parties shall provide the information necessary for clarity, transparency and understanding in accordance with decision 1/CP.21 and any relevant decisions of the Conference of the Parties serving as the meeting of the Parties to this Agreement.

(9) Each Party shall communicate a nationally determined contribution every five years in accordance with decision 1/CP.21 and any relevant decisions of the Conference of the Parties serving as the meeting of the Parties to this Agreement and be informed by the outcomes of the global stocktake referred to in Article 14.

(10) The Conference of the Parties serving as the meeting of the Parties to this Agreement shall consider common time frames for nationally determined contributions at its first session.

(11) A Party may at any time adjust its existing nationally determined contribution with a view to enhancing its level of ambition, in accordance with guidance adopted by the Conference of the Parties serving as the meeting of the Parties to this Agreement.

(12) Nationally determined contributions communicated by Parties shall be recorded in a public registry maintained by the secretariat.

(13) Parties shall account for their nationally determined contributions. In accounting for anthropogenic emissions and removals corresponding to their nationally determined contributions, Parties shall promote environmental integrity, transparency, accuracy, completeness, comparability and consistency, and ensure the avoidance of double counting, in accordance with guidance adopted by the Conference of the Parties serving as the meeting of the Parties to this Agreement.

(14) In the context of their nationally determined contributions, when recognizing and implementing mitigation actions with respect to anthropogenic emissions and removals, Parties should take into

account, as appropriate, existing methods and guidance under the Convention, in the light of the provisions of paragraph (13) of this Article.

(15) Parties shall take into consideration in the implementation of this Agreement the concerns of Parties with economies most affected by the impacts of response measures, particularly developing country Parties.

(16) Parties, including regional economic integration organizations and their member States, that have reached an agreement to act jointly under paragraph (2) of this Article shall notify the secretariat of the terms of that agreement, including the emission level allocated to each Party within the relevant time period, when they communicate their nationally determined contributions. The secretariat shall in turn inform the Parties and signatories to the Convention of the terms of that agreement.

(17) Each party to such an agreement shall be responsible for its emission level as set out in the agreement referred to in paragraph (16) of this Article in accordance with paragraphs (13) and (14) of this Article and Articles 13 and 15.

(18) If Parties acting jointly do so in the framework of, and together with, a regional economic integration organization which is itself a Party to this Agreement, each member State of that regional economic integration organization individually, and together with the regional economic integration organization, shall be responsible for its emission level as set out in the agreement communicated under paragraph (16) of this Article in accordance with paragraphs (13) and (14) of this Article and Articles 13 and 15.

(19) All Parties should strive to formulate and communicate long-term low greenhouse gas emission development strategies, mindful of Article 2 taking into account their common but differentiated responsibilities and respective capabilities, in the light of different national circumstances.

Article 5

(1) Parties should take action to conserve and enhance, as appropriate, sinks and reservoirs of greenhouse gases as referred to in Article 4, paragraph (1)(d), of the Convention, including forests.

(2) Parties are encouraged to take action to implement and support, including through results-based payments, the existing framework as set out in related guidance and decisions already agreed under the Convention for: policy approaches and positive incentives for activities relating to reducing emissions from deforestation and forest degradation, and the role of conservation, sustainable management of forests and enhancement of forest carbon stocks in developing countries; and alternative policy approaches, such as joint mitigation and adaptation approaches for the integral and sustainable management of forests, while reaffirming the importance of incentivizing, as appropriate, non-carbon benefits associated with such approaches.

Article 6

(1) Parties recognize that some Parties choose to pursue voluntary cooperation in the implementation of their nationally determined contributions to allow for higher ambition in their mitigation and adaptation actions and to promote sustainable development and environmental integrity.

(2) Parties shall, where engaging on a voluntary basis in cooperative approaches that involve the use of internationally transferred mitigation outcomes towards nationally determined contributions, promote sustainable development and ensure environmental integrity and transparency, including in governance, and shall apply robust accounting to ensure, inter alia, the avoidance of double counting, consistent with guidance adopted by the Conference of the Parties serving as the meeting of the Parties to this Agreement.

(3) The use of internationally transferred mitigation outcomes to achieve nationally determined contributions under this Agreement shall be voluntary and authorized by participating Parties.

(4) A mechanism to contribute to the mitigation of greenhouse gas emissions and support sustainable development is hereby established under the authority and guidance of the Conference of the

Parties serving as the meeting of the Parties to this Agreement for use by Parties on a voluntary basis. It shall be supervised by a body designated by the Conference of the Parties serving as the meeting of the Parties to this Agreement, and shall aim:

(a) To promote the mitigation of greenhouse gas emissions while fostering sustainable development;

(b) To incentivize and facilitate participation in the mitigation of greenhouse gas emissions by public and private entities authorized by a Party;

(c) To contribute to the reduction of emission levels in the host Party, which will benefit from mitigation activities resulting in emission reductions that can also be used by another Party to fulfil its nationally determined contribution; and

(d) To deliver an overall mitigation in global emissions.

(5) Emission reductions resulting from the mechanism referred to in paragraph (4) of this Article shall not be used to demonstrate achievement of the host Party's nationally determined contribution if used by another Party to demonstrate achievement of its nationally determined contribution.

(6) The Conference of the Parties serving as the meeting of the Parties to this Agreement shall ensure that a share of the proceeds from activities under the mechanism referred to in paragraph (4) of this Article is used to cover administrative expenses as well as to assist developing country Parties that are particularly vulnerable to the adverse effects of climate change to meet the costs of adaptation.

(7) The Conference of the Parties serving as the meeting of the Parties to this Agreement shall adopt rules, modalities and procedures for the mechanism referred to in paragraph (4) of this Article at its first session.

(8) Parties recognize the importance of integrated, holistic and balanced non-market approaches being available to Parties to assist in the implementation of their nationally determined contributions, in the context of sustainable development and poverty eradication, in a coordinated and effective manner, including through, inter alia, mitigation, adaptation, finance, technology transfer and capacity-building, as appropriate. These approaches shall aim to:

(a) Promote mitigation and adaptation ambition;

(b) Enhance public and private sector participation in the implementation of nationally determined contributions; and

(c) Enable opportunities for coordination across instruments and relevant institutional arrangements.

(9) A framework for non-market approaches to sustainable development is hereby defined to promote the non-market approaches referred to in paragraph (8) of this Article.

Article 7

(1) Parties hereby establish the global goal on adaptation of enhancing adaptive capacity, strengthening resilience and reducing vulnerability to climate change, with a view to contributing to sustainable development and ensuring an adequate adaptation response in the context of the temperature goal referred to in Article 2.

(2) Parties recognize that adaptation is a global challenge faced by all with local, subnational, national, regional and international dimensions, and that it is a key component of and makes a contribution to the long-term global response to climate change to protect people, livelihoods and ecosystems, taking into account the urgent and immediate needs of those developing country Parties that are particularly vulnerable to the adverse effects of climate change.

(3) The adaptation efforts of developing country Parties shall be recognized, in accordance with the modalities to be adopted by the Conference of the Parties serving as the meeting of the Parties to this Agreement at its first session.

(4) Parties recognize that the current need for adaptation is significant and that greater levels of mitigation can reduce the need for additional adaptation efforts, and that greater adaptation needs can involve greater adaptation costs.

(5) Parties acknowledge that adaptation action should follow a country-driven, gender-responsive, participatory and fully transparent approach, taking into consideration vulnerable groups, communities and ecosystems, and should be based on and guided by the best available science and, as appropriate, traditional knowledge, knowledge of indigenous peoples and local knowledge systems, with a view to integrating adaptation into relevant socioeconomic and environmental policies and actions, where appropriate.

(6) Parties recognize the importance of support for and international cooperation on adaptation efforts and the importance of taking into account the needs of developing country Parties, especially those that are particularly vulnerable to the adverse effects of climate change.

(7) Parties should strengthen their cooperation on enhancing action on adaptation, taking into account the Cancun Adaptation Framework, including with regard to:

(a) Sharing information, good practices, experiences and lessons learned, including, as appropriate, as these relate to science, planning, policies and implementation in relation to adaptation actions;

(b) Strengthening institutional arrangements, including those under the Convention that serve this Agreement, to support the synthesis of relevant information and knowledge, and the provision of technical support and guidance to Parties;

(c) Strengthening scientific knowledge on climate, including research, systematic observation of the climate system and early warning systems, in a manner that informs climate services and supports decision-making;

(d) Assisting developing country Parties in identifying effective adaptation practices, adaptation needs, priorities, support provided and received for adaptation actions and efforts, and challenges and gaps, in a manner consistent with encouraging good practices; and

(e) Improving the effectiveness and durability of adaptation actions.

(8) United Nations specialized organizations and agencies are encouraged to support the efforts of Parties to implement the actions referred to in paragraph (7) of this Article, taking into account the provisions of paragraph (5) of this Article.

(9) Each Party shall, as appropriate, engage in adaptation planning processes and the implementation of actions, including the development or enhancement of relevant plans, policies and/or contributions, which may include:

(a) The implementation of adaptation actions, undertakings and/or efforts;

(b) The process to formulate and implement national adaptation plans;

(c) The assessment of climate change impacts and vulnerability, with a view to formulating nationally determined prioritized actions, taking into account vulnerable people, places and ecosystems;

(d) Monitoring and evaluating and learning from adaptation plans, policies, programmes and actions; and

(e) Building the resilience of socioeconomic and ecological systems, including through economic diversification and sustainable management of natural resources.

(10) Each Party should, as appropriate, submit and update periodically an adaptation communication, which may include its priorities, implementation and support needs, plans and actions, without creating any additional burden for developing country Parties.

(11) The adaptation communication referred to in paragraph (10) of this Article shall be, as appropriate, submitted and updated periodically, as a component of or in conjunction with other

communications or documents, including a national adaptation plan, a nationally determined contribution as referred to in Article 4, paragraph (2), and/or a national communication.

(12) The adaptation communications referred to in paragraph (10) of this Article shall be recorded in a public registry maintained by the secretariat.

(13) Continuous and enhanced international support shall be provided to developing country Parties for the implementation of paragraphs (7), (9), (10) and (11) of this Article, in accordance with the provisions of Articles 9, 10 and 11.

(14) The global stocktake referred to in Article 14 shall, inter alia:

(a) Recognize adaptation efforts of developing country Parties;

(b) Enhance the implementation of adaptation action taking into account the adaptation communication referred to in paragraph (10) of this Article;

(c) Review the adequacy and effectiveness of adaptation and support provided for adaptation; and

(d) Review the overall progress made in achieving the global goal on adaptation referred to in paragraph (1) of this Article.

Article 8

(1) Parties recognize the importance of averting, minimizing and addressing loss and damage associated with the adverse effects of climate change, including extreme weather events and slow onset events, and the role of sustainable development in reducing the risk of loss and damage.

(2) The Warsaw International Mechanism for Loss and Damage associated with Climate Change Impacts shall be subject to the authority and guidance of the Conference of the Parties serving as the meeting of the Parties to this Agreement and may be enhanced and strengthened, as determined by the Conference of the Parties serving as the meeting of the Parties to this Agreement.

(3) Parties should enhance understanding, action and support, including through the Warsaw International Mechanism, as appropriate, on a cooperative and facilitative basis with respect to loss and damage associated with the adverse effects of climate change.

(4) Accordingly, areas of cooperation and facilitation to enhance understanding, action and support may include:

(a) Early warning systems;

(b) Emergency preparedness;

(c) Slow onset events;

(d) Events that may involve irreversible and permanent loss and damage;

(e) Comprehensive risk assessment and management;

(f) Risk insurance facilities, climate risk pooling and other insurance solutions;

(g) Non-economic losses; and

(h) Resilience of communities, livelihoods and ecosystems.

(5) The Warsaw International Mechanism shall collaborate with existing bodies and expert groups under the Agreement, as well as relevant organizations and expert bodies outside the Agreement.

Article 9

(1) Developed country Parties shall provide financial resources to assist developing country Parties with respect to both mitigation and adaptation in continuation of their existing obligations under the Convention.

(2) Other Parties are encouraged to provide or continue to provide such support voluntarily.

(3) As part of a global effort, developed country Parties should continue to take the lead in mobilizing climate finance from a wide variety of sources, instruments and channels, noting the significant role of public funds, through a variety of actions, including supporting country-driven strategies, and taking into account the needs and priorities of developing country Parties. Such mobilization of climate finance should represent a progression beyond previous efforts.

(4) The provision of scaled-up financial resources should aim to achieve a balance between adaptation and mitigation, taking into account country-driven strategies, and the priorities and needs of developing country Parties, especially those that are particularly vulnerable to the adverse effects of climate change and have significant capacity constraints, such as the least developed countries and small island developing States, considering the need for public and grant-based resources for adaptation.

(5) Developed country Parties shall biennially communicate indicative quantitative and qualitative information related to paragraphs (1) and (3) of this Article, as applicable, including, as available, projected levels of public financial resources to be provided to developing country Parties. Other Parties providing resources are encouraged to communicate biennially such information on a voluntary basis.

(6) The global stocktake referred to in Article 14 shall take into account the relevant information provided by developed country Parties and/or Agreement bodies on efforts related to climate finance.

(7) Developed country Parties shall provide transparent and consistent information on support for developing country Parties provided and mobilized through public interventions biennially in accordance with the modalities, procedures and guidelines to be adopted by the Conference of the Parties serving as the meeting of the Parties to this Agreement, at its first session, as stipulated in Article 13, paragraph (13). Other Parties are encouraged to do so.

(8) The Financial Mechanism of the Convention, including its operating entities, shall serve as the financial mechanism of this Agreement.

(9) The institutions serving this Agreement, including the operating entities of the Financial Mechanism of the Convention, shall aim to ensure efficient access to financial resources through simplified approval procedures and enhanced readiness support for developing country Parties, in particular for the least developed countries and small island developing States, in the context of their national climate strategies and plans.

Article 10

(1) Parties share a long-term vision on the importance of fully realizing technology development and transfer in order to improve resilience to climate change and to reduce greenhouse gas emissions.

(2) Parties, noting the importance of technology for the implementation of mitigation and adaptation actions under this Agreement and recognizing existing technology deployment and dissemination efforts, shall strengthen cooperative action on technology development and transfer.

(3) The Technology Mechanism established under the Convention shall serve this Agreement.

(4) A technology framework is hereby established to provide overarching guidance to the work of the Technology Mechanism in promoting and facilitating enhanced action on technology development and transfer in order to support the implementation of this Agreement, in pursuit of the long-term vision referred to in paragraph (1) of this Article.

(5) Accelerating, encouraging and enabling innovation is critical for an effective, long-term global response to climate change and promoting economic growth and sustainable development. Such effort shall be, as appropriate, supported, including by the Technology Mechanism and, through financial means, by the Financial Mechanism of the Convention, for collaborative approaches to research and development, and facilitating access to technology, in particular for early stages of the technology cycle, to developing country Parties.

(6) Support, including financial support, shall be provided to developing country Parties for the implementation of this Article, including for strengthening cooperative action on technology development and transfer at different stages of the technology cycle, with a view to achieving a balance between support for mitigation and adaptation. The global stocktake referred to in Article 14 shall take into account available information on efforts related to support on technology development and transfer for developing country Parties.

Article 11

(1) Capacity-building under this Agreement should enhance the capacity and ability of developing country Parties, in particular countries with the least capacity, such as the least developed countries, and those that are particularly vulnerable to the adverse effects of climate change, such as small island developing States, to take effective climate change action, including, inter alia, to implement adaptation and mitigation actions, and should facilitate technology development, dissemination and deployment, access to climate finance, relevant aspects of education, training and public awareness, and the transparent, timely and accurate communication of information.

(2) Capacity-building should be country-driven, based on and responsive to national needs, and foster country ownership of Parties, in particular, for developing country Parties, including at the national, subnational and local levels. Capacity-building should be guided by lessons learned, including those from capacity-building activities under the Convention, and should be an effective, iterative process that is participatory, cross-cutting and gender-responsive.

(3) All Parties should cooperate to enhance the capacity of developing country Parties to implement this Agreement. Developed country Parties should enhance support for capacity-building actions in developing country Parties.

(4) All Parties enhancing the capacity of developing country Parties to implement this Agreement, including through regional, bilateral and multilateral approaches, shall regularly communicate on these actions or measures on capacity-building. Developing country Parties should regularly communicate progress made on implementing capacity building plans, policies, actions or measures to implement this Agreement.

(5) Capacity-building activities shall be enhanced through appropriate institutional arrangements to support the implementation of this Agreement, including the appropriate institutional arrangements established under the Convention that serve this Agreement. The Conference of the Parties serving as the meeting of the Parties to this Agreement shall, at its first session, consider and adopt a decision on the initial institutional arrangements for capacity-building.

Article 12

Parties shall cooperate in taking measures, as appropriate, to enhance climate change education, training, public awareness, public participation and public access to information, recognizing the importance of these steps with respect to enhancing actions under this Agreement.

Article 13

(1) In order to build mutual trust and confidence and to promote effective implementation, an enhanced transparency framework for action and support, with built-in flexibility which takes into account Parties' different capacities and builds upon collective experience is hereby established.

(2) The transparency framework shall provide flexibility in the implementation of the provisions of this Article to those developing country Parties that need it in the light of their capacities. The modalities, procedures and guidelines referred to in paragraph (13) of this Article shall reflect such flexibility.

(3) The transparency framework shall build on and enhance the transparency arrangements under the Convention, recognizing the special circumstances of the least developed countries and

small island developing States, and be implemented in a facilitative, non-intrusive, non-punitive manner, respectful of national sovereignty, and avoid placing undue burden on Parties.

(4) The transparency arrangements under the Convention, including national communications, biennial reports and biennial update reports, international assessment and review and international consultation and analysis, shall form part of the experience drawn upon for the development of the modalities, procedures and guidelines under paragraph (13) of this Article.

(5) The purpose of the framework for transparency of action is to provide a clear understanding of climate change action in the light of the objective of the Convention as set out in its Article 2, including clarity and tracking of progress towards achieving Parties' individual nationally determined contributions under Article 4, and Parties' adaptation actions under Article 7, including good practices, priorities, needs and gaps, to inform the global stocktake under Article 14.

(6) The purpose of the framework for transparency of support is to provide clarity on support provided and received by relevant individual Parties in the context of climate change actions under Articles 4, 7, 9, 10 and 11, and, to the extent possible, to provide a full overview of aggregate financial support provided, to inform the global stocktake under Article 14.

(7) Each Party shall regularly provide the following information:

- (a) A national inventory report of anthropogenic emissions by sources and removals by sinks of greenhouse gases, prepared using good practice methodologies accepted by the Intergovernmental Panel on Climate Change and agreed upon by the Conference of the Parties serving as the meeting of the Parties to this Agreement; and
- (b) Information necessary to track progress made in implementing and achieving its nationally determined contribution under Article 4.

(8) Each Party should also provide information related to climate change impacts and adaptation under Article 7, as appropriate.

(9) Developed country Parties shall, and other Parties that provide support should, provide information on financial, technology transfer and capacity-building support provided to developing country Parties under Articles 9, 10 and 11.

(10) Developing country Parties should provide information on financial, technology transfer and capacity-building support needed and received under Articles 9, 10 and 11.

(11) Information submitted by each Party under paragraphs (7) and (9) of this Article shall undergo a technical expert review, in accordance with decision 1/CP.21. For those developing country Parties that need it in the light of their capacities, the review process shall include assistance in identifying capacity-building needs. In addition, each Party shall participate in a facilitative, multilateral consideration of progress with respect to efforts under Article 9, and its respective implementation and achievement of its nationally determined contribution.

(12) The technical expert review under this paragraph shall consist of a consideration of the Party's support provided, as relevant, and its implementation and achievement of its nationally determined contribution. The review shall also identify areas of improvement for the Party, and include a review of the consistency of the information with the modalities, procedures and guidelines referred to in paragraph (13) of this Article, taking into account the flexibility accorded to the Party under paragraph (2) of this Article. The review shall pay particular attention to the respective national capabilities and circumstances of developing country Parties.

(13) The Conference of the Parties serving as the meeting of the Parties to this Agreement shall, at its first session, building on experience from the arrangements related to transparency under the Convention, and elaborating on the provisions in this Article, adopt common modalities, procedures and guidelines, as appropriate, for the transparency of action and support.

(14) Support shall be provided to developing countries for the implementation of this Article.

(15) Support shall also be provided for the building of transparency-related capacity of developing country Parties on a continuous basis.

Article 14

(1) The Conference of the Parties serving as the meeting of the Parties to this Agreement shall periodically take stock of the implementation of this Agreement to assess the collective progress towards achieving the purpose of this Agreement and its long-term goals (referred to as the "global stocktake"). It shall do so in a comprehensive and facilitative manner, considering mitigation, adaptation and the means of implementation and support, and in the light of equity and the best available science.

(2) The Conference of the Parties serving as the meeting of the Parties to this Agreement shall undertake its first global stocktake in 2023 and every five years thereafter unless otherwise decided by the Conference of the Parties serving as the meeting of the Parties to this Agreement.

(3) The outcome of the global stocktake shall inform Parties in updating and enhancing, in a nationally determined manner, their actions and support in accordance with the relevant provisions of this Agreement, as well as in enhancing international cooperation for climate action.

Article 15

(1) A mechanism to facilitate implementation of and promote compliance with the provisions of this Agreement is hereby established.

(2) The mechanism referred to in paragraph (1) of this Article shall consist of a committee that shall be expert-based and facilitative in nature and function in a manner that is transparent, non-adversarial and non-punitive. The committee shall pay particular attention to the respective national capabilities and circumstances of Parties.

(3) The committee shall operate under the modalities and procedures adopted by the Conference of the Parties serving as the meeting of the Parties to this Agreement at its first session and report annually to the Conference of the Parties serving as the meeting of the Parties to this Agreement.

Article 16

(1) The Conference of the Parties, the supreme body of the Convention, shall serve as the meeting of the Parties to this Agreement.

(2) Parties to the Convention that are not Parties to this Agreement may participate as observers in the proceedings of any session of the Conference of the Parties serving as the meeting of the Parties to this Agreement. When the Conference of the Parties serves as the meeting of the Parties to this Agreement, decisions under this Agreement shall be taken only by those that are Parties to this Agreement.

(3) When the Conference of the Parties serves as the meeting of the Parties to this Agreement, any member of the Bureau of the Conference of the Parties representing a Party to the Convention but, at that time, not a Party to this Agreement, shall be replaced by an additional member to be elected by and from amongst the Parties to this Agreement.

(4) The Conference of the Parties serving as the meeting of the Parties to this Agreement shall keep under regular review the implementation of this Agreement and shall make, within its mandate, the decisions necessary to promote its effective implementation. It shall perform the functions assigned to it by this Agreement and shall:

  (a) Establish such subsidiary bodies as deemed necessary for the implementation of this Agreement; and

  (b) Exercise such other functions as may be required for the implementation of this Agreement.

(5) The rules of procedure of the Conference of the Parties and the financial procedures applied under the Convention shall be applied *mutatis mutandis* under this Agreement, except as may be otherwise decided by consensus by the Conference of the Parties serving as the meeting of the Parties to this Agreement.

(6) The first session of the Conference of the Parties serving as the meeting of the Parties to this Agreement shall be convened by the secretariat in conjunction with the first session of the Conference of the Parties that is scheduled after the date of entry into force of this Agreement. Subsequent ordinary sessions of the Conference of the Parties serving as the meeting of the Parties to this Agreement shall be held in conjunction with ordinary sessions of the Conference of the Parties, unless otherwise decided by the Conference of the Parties serving as the meeting of the Parties to this Agreement.

(7) Extraordinary sessions of the Conference of the Parties serving as the meeting of the Parties to this Agreement shall be held at such other times as may be deemed necessary by the Conference of the Parties serving as the meeting of the Parties to this Agreement or at the written request of any Party, provided that, within six months of the request being communicated to the Parties by the secretariat, it is supported by at least one third of the Parties.

(8) The United Nations and its specialized agencies and the International Atomic Energy Agency, as well as any State member thereof or observers thereto not party to the Convention, may be represented at sessions of the Conference of the Parties serving as the meeting of the Parties to this Agreement as observers. Any body or agency, whether national or international, governmental or non-governmental, which is qualified in matters covered by this Agreement and which has informed the secretariat of its wish to be represented at a session of the Conference of the Parties serving as the meeting of the Parties to this Agreement as an observer, may be so admitted unless at least one third of the Parties present object. The admission and participation of observers shall be subject to the rules of procedure referred to in paragraph (5) of this Article.

Article 17

(1) The secretariat established by Article 8 of the Convention shall serve as the secretariat of this Agreement.

(2) Article 8, paragraph (2), of the Convention on the functions of the secretariat, and Article 8, paragraph (3), of the Convention, on the arrangements made for the functioning of the secretariat, shall apply *mutatis mutandis* to this Agreement. The secretariat shall, in addition, exercise the functions assigned to it under this Agreement and by the Conference of the Parties serving as the meeting of the Parties to this Agreement.

Article 18

(1) The Subsidiary Body for Scientific and Technological Advice and the Subsidiary Body for Implementation established by Articles 9 and 10 of the Convention shall serve, respectively, as the Subsidiary Body for Scientific and Technological Advice and the Subsidiary Body for Implementation of this Agreement. The provisions of the Convention relating to the functioning of these two bodies shall apply *mutatis mutandis* to this Agreement. Sessions of the meetings of the Subsidiary Body for Scientific and Technological Advice and the Subsidiary Body for Implementation of this Agreement shall be held in conjunction with the meetings of, respectively, the Subsidiary Body for Scientific and Technological Advice and the Subsidiary Body for Implementation of the Convention.

(2) Parties to the Convention that are not Parties to this Agreement may participate as observers in the proceedings of any session of the subsidiary bodies. When the subsidiary bodies serve as the subsidiary bodies of this Agreement, decisions under this Agreement shall be taken only by those that are Parties to this Agreement.

(3) When the subsidiary bodies established by Articles 9 and 10 of the Convention exercise their functions with regard to matters concerning this Agreement, any member of the bureaux of those subsidiary bodies representing a Party to the Convention but, at that time, not a Party to this

Agreement, shall be replaced by an additional member to be elected by and from amongst the Parties to this Agreement.

Article 19

(1) Subsidiary bodies or other institutional arrangements established by or under the Convention, other than those referred to in this Agreement, shall serve this Agreement upon a decision of the Conference of the Parties serving as the meeting of the Parties to this Agreement. The Conference of the Parties serving as the meeting of the Parties to this Agreement shall specify the functions to be exercised by such subsidiary bodies or arrangements.

(2) The Conference of the Parties serving as the meeting of the Parties to this Agreement may provide further guidance to such subsidiary bodies and institutional arrangements.

Article 20

(1) This Agreement shall be open for signature and subject to ratification, acceptance or approval by States and regional economic integration organizations that are Parties to the Convention. It shall be open for signature at the United Nations Headquarters in New York from 22 April 2016 to 21 April 2017. Thereafter, this Agreement shall be open for accession from the day following the date on which it is closed for signature. Instruments of ratification, acceptance, approval or accession shall be deposited with the Depositary.

(2) Any regional economic integration organization that becomes a Party to this Agreement without any of its member States being a Party shall be bound by all the obligations under this Agreement. In the case of regional economic integration organizations with one or more member States that are Parties to this Agreement, the organization and its member States shall decide on their respective responsibilities for the performance of their obligations under this Agreement. In such cases, the organization and the member States shall not be entitled to exercise rights under this Agreement concurrently.

(3) In their instruments of ratification, acceptance, approval or accession, regional economic integration organizations shall declare the extent of their competence with respect to the matters governed by this Agreement. These organizations shall also inform the Depositary, who shall in turn inform the Parties, of any substantial modification in the extent of their competence.

Article 21

(1) This Agreement shall enter into force on the thirtieth day after the date on which at least 55 Parties to the Convention accounting in total for at least an estimated 55 percent of the total global greenhouse gas emissions have deposited their instruments of ratification, acceptance, approval or accession.

(2) Solely for the limited purpose of paragraph (1) of this Article, "total global greenhouse gas emissions" means the most up-to-date amount communicated on or before the date of adoption of this Agreement by the Parties to the Convention.

(3) For each State or regional economic integration organization that ratifies, accepts or approves this Agreement or accedes thereto after the conditions set out in paragraph (1) of this Article for entry into force have been fulfilled, this Agreement shall enter into force on the thirtieth day after the date of deposit by such State or regional economic integration organization of its instrument of ratification, acceptance, approval or accession.

(4) For the purposes of paragraph (1) of this Article, any instrument deposited by a regional economic integration organization shall not be counted as additional to those deposited by its member States.

Article 22

The provisions of Article 15 of the Convention on the adoption of amendments to the Convention shall apply *mutatis mutandis* to this Agreement.

Article 23

(1) The provisions of Article 16 of the Convention on the adoption and amendment of Annexes to the Convention shall apply *mutatis mutandis* to this Agreement.

(2) Annexes to this Agreement shall form an integral part thereof and, unless otherwise expressly provided for, a reference to this Agreement constitutes at the same time a reference to any Annexes thereto. Such Annexes shall be restricted to lists, forms and any other material of a descriptive nature that is of a scientific, technical, procedural or administrative character.

Article 24

The provisions of Article 14 of the Convention on settlement of disputes shall apply *mutatis mutandis* to this Agreement.

Article 25

(1) Each Party shall have one vote, except as provided for in paragraph (2) of this Article.

(2) Regional economic integration organizations, in matters within their competence, shall exercise their right to vote with a number of votes equal to the number of their member States that are Parties to this Agreement. Such an organization shall not exercise its right to vote if any of its member States exercises its right, and vice versa.

Article 26

The Secretary-General of the United Nations shall be the Depositary of this Agreement.

Article 27

No reservations may be made to this Agreement.

Article 28

(1) At any time after three years from the date on which this Agreement has entered into force for a Party, that Party may withdraw from this Agreement by giving written notification to the Depositary.

(2) Any such withdrawal shall take effect upon expiry of one year from the date of receipt by the Depositary of the notification of withdrawal, or on such later date as may be specified in the notification of withdrawal.

(3) Any Party that withdraws from the Convention shall be considered as also having withdrawn from this Agreement.

Article 29

The original of this Agreement, of which the Arabic, Chinese, English, French, Russian and Spanish texts are equally authentic, shall be deposited with the Secretary-General of the United Nations.

DONE at Paris this twelfth day of December two thousand and fifteen.

IN WITNESS WHEREOF, the undersigned, being duly authorized to that effect, have signed this Agreement.

INTERNATIONAL CONVENTION FOR THE PREVENTION OF POLLUTION FROM SHIPS

(Adopted: 2 November 1973; Entry into force: 2 October 1983; Applied to Hong Kong: 1 July 1997)

The Parties to the Convention,

Being conscious of the need to preserve the human environment in general and the marine environment in particular,

Recognizing that deliberate, negligent or accidental release of oil and other harmful substances from ships constitutes a serious source of pollution,

Recognizing also the importance of the International Convention for the Prevention of Pollution of the Sea by Oil, 1954, as being the first multilateral instrument to be concluded with the prime objective of protecting the environment, and appreciating the significant contribution which that Convention has made in preserving the seas and coastal environment from pollution,

Desiring to achieve the complete elimination of intentional pollution of the marine environment by oil and other harmful substances and the minimization of accidental discharge of such substances,

Considering that this object may best be achieved by establishing rules not limited to oil pollution having a universal purport,

Have agreed as follows:

Article 1 General Obligations under the Convention

(1) The Parties to the Convention undertake to give effect to the provisions of the present Convention and those Annexes thereto by which they are bound, in order to prevent the pollution of the marine environment by the discharge of harmful substances or effluents containing such substances in contravention of the Convention.

(2) Unless expressly provided otherwise, a reference to the present Convention constitutes at the same time a reference to its Protocols and to the Annexes.

Article 2 Definitions

For the purposes of the present Convention, unless expressly provided otherwise:

(1) "Regulation" means the regulations contained in the Annexes to the present Convention

(2) "Harmful substance" means any substance which, if introduced into the sea, is liable to create hazards to human health, to harm living resources and marine life, to damage amenities or to interfere with other legitimate uses of the sea, and includes any substance subject to control by the present Convention.

(3)

(a) "Discharge", in relation to harmful substances or effluents containing such substances, means any release howsoever caused from a ship and includes any escape, disposal, spilling, leaking, pumping, emitting or emptying;

(b) "Discharge" does not include:

(i) dumping within the meaning of the Convention on the Prevention of Marine Pollution by Dumping of Wastes and Other Matter, done at London on 13 November 1972; or

(ii) release of harmful substances directly arising from the exploration, exploitation and associated off-shore processing of sea-bed mineral resources; or

(iii) release of harmful substances for purposes of legitimate scientific research into pollution abatement or control.

(4) "Ship" means a vessel of any type whatsoever operating in the marine environment and includes hydrofoil boats, air-cushion vehicles, submersibles, floating craft and fixed or floating platforms.

(5) "Administration" means the Government of the State under whose authority the ship is operating. With respect to a ship entitled to fly a flag of any State, the Administration is the Government of that State. With respect to fixed or floating platforms engaged in exploration and exploitation of the sea-bed and subsoil thereof adjacent to the coast over which the coastal State exercises sovereign rights for the purposes of exploration and exploitation of their natural resources, the Administration is the Government of the coastal State concerned.

(6) "Incident" means an event involving the actual or probable discharge into the sea of a harmful substance, or effluents containing such a substance.

(7) "Organization" means the Inter-Governmental Maritime Consultative Organization.*

Article 3 Application

(1) The present Convention shall apply to:

(a) ships entitled to fly the flag of a Party to the Convention; and

(b) ships not entitled to fly the flag of a Party but which operate under the authority of a Party.

(2) Nothing in the present Article shall be construed as derogating from or extending the sovereign rights of the Parties under international law over the sea-bed and subsoil thereof adjacent to their coasts for the purposes of exploration and exploitation of their natural resources.

(3) The present Convention shall not apply to any warship, naval auxiliary or other ship owned or operated by a State and used, for the time being, only on government non-commercial service. However, each Party shall ensure by the adoption of appropriate measures not impairing the operations or operational capabilities of such ships owned or operated by it, that such ships act in a manner consistent, so far as is reasonable and practicable, with the present Convention.

Article 4 Violation

(1) Any violation of the requirements of the present Convention shall be prohibited and sanctions shall be established therefor under the law of the Administration of the ship concerned wherever the violation occurs. If the Administration is informed of such a violation and is satisfied that sufficient evidence is available to enable proceedings to be brought in respect of the alleged violation, it shall cause such proceedings to be taken as soon as possible, in accordance with its law.

(2) Any violation of the requirements of the present Convention within the jurisdiction of any Party to the Convention shall be prohibited and sanctions shall be established therefore under the law of that Party. Whenever such violation occurs, the Party shall either:

(a) cause proceedings to be taken in accordance with its law; or

(b) furnish to the Administration of the ship such information and evidence as may be in its possession that a violation has occurred.

(3) Where information or evidence with respect to any violation of the present Convention by a ship is furnished to the Administration of that ship, the Administration shall promptly inform the Party which has furnished the information or evidence, and the Organization, of the action taken.

* The name of the Organization was changed to "International Maritime Organization" by virtue of amendments to the Organization's Convention which entered into force on 22 May 1982.

(4) The penalties specified under the law of a Party pursuant to the present Article shall be adequate in severity to discourage violations of the present Convention and shall be equally severe irrespective of where the violations occur.

Article 5 Certificates and Special Rules on Inspection of Ships

(1) Subject to the provisions of paragraph (2) of the present Article a certificate issued under the authority of a Party to the Convention in accordance with the provisions of the regulations shall be accepted by the other Parties and regarded for all purposes covered by the present Convention as having the same validity as a certificate issued by them.

(2) A ship required to hold a certificate in accordance with the provisions of the regulations is subject, while in the ports or off-shore terminals under the jurisdiction of a Party, to inspection by officers duly authorized by that Party. Any such inspection shall be limited to verifying that there is on board a valid certificate, unless there are clear grounds for believing that the condition of the ship or its equipment does not correspond substantially with the particulars of that certificate. In that case, or if the ship does not carry a valid certificate the Party carrying out the inspection shall take such steps as will ensure that the ship shall not sail until it can proceed to sea without presenting an unreasonable threat of harm to the marine environment. That Party may, however, grant such a ship permission to leave the port or off-shore terminal for the purpose of proceeding to the nearest appropriate repair yard available.

(3) If a Party denies a foreign ship entry to the ports or off-shore terminals under its jurisdiction or takes any action against such a ship for the reason that the ship does not comply with the provisions of the present Convention, the Party shall immediately inform the consul or diplomatic representative of the Party whose flag the ship is entitled to fly, or if this is not possible, the Administration of the ship concerned. Before denying entry or taking such action the Party may request consultation with the Administration of the ship concerned. Information shall also be given to the Administration when a ship does not carry a valid certificate in accordance with the provisions of the regulations.

(4) With respect to the ships of non-Parties to the Convention, Parties shall apply the requirements of the present Convention as may be necessary to ensure that no more favourable treatment is given to such ships.

Article 6 Detection of Violations and Enforcement of the Convention

(1) Parties to the Convention shall co-operate in the detection of violations and the enforcement of the provisions of the present Convention, using all appropriate and practicable measures of detection and environmental monitoring, adequate procedures for reporting and accumulation of evidence.

(2) A ship to which the present Convention applies may, in any port or off-shore terminal of a Party, be subject to inspection by officers appointed or authorized by that Party for the purpose of verifying whether the ship has discharged any harmful substances in violation of the provisions of the regulations. If an inspection indicates a violation of the Convention, a report shall be forwarded to the Administration for any appropriate action.

(3) Any Party shall furnish to the Administration evidence, if any, that the ship has discharged harmful substances or effluents containing such substances in violation of the provisions of the regulations. If it is practicable to do so, the competent authority of the former Party shall notify the Master of the ship of the alleged violation.

(4) Upon receiving such evidence, the Administration so informed shall investigate the matter, and may request the other Party to furnish further or better evidence of the alleged contravention. If the Administration is satisfied that sufficient evidence is available to enable proceedings to be brought in respect of the alleged violation, it shall cause such proceedings to be taken in accordance with its law as soon as possible. The Administration shall promptly inform the Party which has reported the alleged violation, as well as the Organization, of the action taken.

(5) A Party may also inspect a ship to which the present Convention applies when it enters the ports or off-shore terminals under its jurisdiction, if a request for an investigation is received from any Party together with sufficient evidence that the ship has discharged harmful substances or effluents containing such substances in any place. The report of such investigation shall be sent to the Party requesting it and to the Administration so that the appropriate action may be taken under the present Convention.

Article 7 Undue Delay to Ships

(1) All possible efforts shall be made to avoid a ship being unduly detained or delayed under Articles 4, 5, or 6 of the present Convention.

(2) When a ship is unduly detained or delayed under Articles 4, 5, 6 of the present Convention, it shall be entitled to compensation for any loss or damage suffered.

Article 8 Reports on Incidents Involving Harmful Substances

(1) A report of an incident shall be made without delay to the fullest extent possible in accordance with the provisions of Protocol I to the present Convention.

(2) Each Party to the Convention shall:

(a) make all arrangements necessary for an appropriate officer or agency to receive and process all reports on incidents; and

(b) notify the Organization with complete details of such arrangements for circulation to other Parties and Member States of the Organization.

(3) Whenever a Party receives a report under the provisions of the present Article, that Party shall relay the report without delay to:

(a) the Administration of the ship involved; and

(b) any other State which may be affected.

(4) Each Party to the Convention undertakes to issue instructions to its maritime inspection vessels and aircraft and to other appropriate services, to report to its authorities any incident referred to in Protocol I to the present Convention. That Party shall, if it considers it appropriate, report accordingly to the Organization and to any other Party concerned.

Article 9 Other Treaties and Interpretation

(1) Upon its entry into force, the present Convention supersedes the International Convention for the Prevention of Pollution of the Sea by Oil, 1954, as amended, as between Parties to that Convention.

(2) Nothing in the present Convention shall prejudice the codification and development of the law of the sea by the United Nations Conference on the Law of the Sea convened pursuant to Resolution 2750 C (XXV) of the General Assembly of the United Nations nor the present or future claims and legal views of any State concerning the law of the sea and the nature and extent of coastal and flag State jurisdiction.

(3) The term "jurisdiction" in the present Convention shall be construed in the light of international law in force at the time of application or interpretation of the present Convention.

Article 10 Settlement of Disputes

Any dispute between two or more Parties to the Convention concerning the interpretation or application of the present Convention shall, if settlement by negotiation between the Parties involved has not been possible, and if these Parties do not otherwise agree, be submitted upon request of any of them to arbitration as set out in Protocol II to the present Convention.

Article 11 Communication of Information

(1) The Parties to the Convention undertake to communicate to the Organization:

(a) the text of laws, orders, decrees and regulations and other instruments which have been promulgated on the various matters within the scope of the present Convention;

(b) a list of non-governmental agencies which are authorized to act on their behalf in matters relating to the design, construction and equipment of ships carrying harmful substances in accordance with the provisions of the regulations;*

(c) a sufficient number of specimens of their certificates issued under the provisions of the regulations;

(d) a list of reception facilities including their location, capacity and available facilities and other characteristics;

(e) official reports or summaries of official reports in so far as they show the results of the application of the present Convention; and

(f) an annual statistical report, in a form standardized by the Organization, of penalties actually imposed for infringement of the present Convention.

(2) The Organization shall notify Parties of the receipt of any communications under the present Article and circulate to all Parties any information communicated to it under subparagraphs (1)(b) to (f) of the present Article.

Article 12 Casualties to Ships

(1) Each Administration undertakes to conduct an investigation of any casualty occurring to any of its ships subject to the provisions of the regulations if such casualty has produced a major deleterious effect upon the marine environment.

(2) Each Party to the Convention undertakes to supply the Organization with information concerning the findings of such investigation, when it judges that such information may assist in determining what changes in the present Convention might be desirable.

Article 13 Signatures, Ratification, Acceptance, Approval and Accession

(1) The present Convention shall remain open for signature at the Headquarters of the Organization from 15 January 1974 until 31 December 1974 and shall thereafter remain open for accession. States may become Parties to the present Convention by:

a) signature without reservation as to ratification, acceptance or approval; or

b) signature subject to ratification, acceptance or approval, followed by ratification, acceptance or approval; or

c) accession.

(2) Ratification, acceptance, approval or accession shall be effected by the deposit of an instrument to that effect with the Secretary-General of the Organization.

(3) The Secretary-General of the Organization shall inform all States which have signed the present Convention or acceded to it of any signature or of the deposit of any new instrument of ratification, acceptance, approval or accession and the date of its deposit.

Article 14 Optional Annexes

(1) A State may at the time of signing, ratifying, accepting, approving or acceding to the present Convention declare that it does not accept any one or all of Annexes III, IV, and V (hereinafter

* The text of this subparagraph is replaced by that contained in Article III of the 1978 Protocol.

referred to as "Optional Annexes") of the present Convention. Subject to the above, Parties to the Convention shall be bound by any Annex in its entirety.

(2) A State which has declared that it is not bound by an Optional Annex may at any time accept such Annex by depositing with the Organization an instrument of the kind referred to in Article 13(2).

(3) A State which makes a declaration under paragraph (1) of the present Article in respect of an Optional Annex and which has not subsequently accepted that Annex in accordance with paragraph (2) of the present Article shall not be under any obligation nor entitled to claim any privileges under the present Convention in respect of matters related to such Annex and all references to Parties in the present Convention shall not include that State in so far as matters related to such Annex are concerned.

(4) The Organization shall inform the States which have signed or acceded to the present Convention of any declaration under the present Article as well as the receipt of any instrument deposited in accordance with the provisions of paragraph (2) of the present Article.

Article 15 Entry into Force

(1) The Convention shall enter into force twelve months after the date on which not less than 15 States, the combined merchant fleets of which constitute not less than 50 percent of the gross tonnage of the world's merchant shipping, have become parties to it in accordance with Article 13.

(2) An Optional Annex shall enter into force twelve months after the date on which the conditions stipulated in paragraph (1) of the present Article have been satisfied in relation to that Annex.

(3) The Organization shall inform the States which have signed the present Convention or acceded to it of the date on which it enters into force and of the date on which an Optional Annex enters into force in accordance with paragraph (2) of the present Article.

(4) For States which have deposited an instrument of ratification, acceptance, approval or accession in respect of the present Convention or any Optional Annex after the requirements for entry into force thereof have been met but prior to the date of entry into force, the ratification, acceptance, approval or accession shall take effect on the date of entry into force of the Convention or such Annex or three months after the date of deposit of the instrument whichever is the later date.

(5) For States which have deposited an instrument of ratification, acceptance, approval or accession after the date on which the Convention or an Optional Annex entered into force, the Convention or the Optional Annex shall become effective three months after the date of deposit of the instrument.

(6) After the date on which all the conditions required under Article 16 to bring an amendment to the present Convention or an Optional Annex into force have been fulfilled, any instrument of ratification, acceptance, approval or accession deposited shall apply to the Convention or Annex as amended.

Article 16 Amendments

(1) The present Convention may be amended by any of the procedures specified in the following paragraphs.

(2) Amendments after consideration by the Organization:

(a) any amendment proposed by a Party to the Convention shall be submitted to the Organization and circulated by its Secretary-General to all Members of the Organization and all Parties at least six months prior to its consideration;

(b) any amendment proposed and circulated as above shall be submitted to an appropriate body by the Organization for consideration;

(c) Parties to the Convention, whether or not Members of the Organization, shall be entitled to participate in the proceedings of the appropriate body;

(d) amendments shall be adopted by a two-thirds majority of only the Parties to the Convention present and voting;

(e) if adopted in accordance with subparagraph (d) above, amendments shall be communicated by the Secretary-General of the Organization to all the Parties to the Convention for acceptance;

(f) an amendment shall be deemed to have been accepted in the following circumstances:

(i) an amendment to an Article of the Convention shall be deemed to have been accepted on the date on which it is accepted by two-thirds of the Parties, the combined merchant fleets of which constitute not less than 50 percent of the gross tonnage of the world's merchant fleet;

(ii) an amendment to an Annex to the Convention shall be deemed to have been accepted in accordance with the procedure specified in subparagraph (f)(iii) unless the appropriate body, at the time of its adoption, determines that the amendment shall be deemed to have been accepted on the date on which it is accepted by two-thirds of the Parties, the combined merchant fleets of which constitute not less than 50 percent of the gross tonnage of the world's merchant fleet. Nevertheless, at any time before the entry into force of an amendment to an Annex to the Convention, a Party may notify the Secretary-General of the Organization that its express approval will be necessary before the amendment enters into force for it. The latter shall bring such notification and the date of its receipt to the notice of Parties;

(iii) an amendment to an Appendix to an Annex to the Convention shall be deemed to have been accepted at the end of a period to be determined by the appropriate body at the time of its adoption, which period shall be not less than ten months, unless within that period an objection is communicated to the Organization by not less than one-third of the Parties or by the Parties the combined merchant fleets of which constitute not less than 50 percent of the gross tonnage of the world's merchant fleet whichever condition is fulfilled;

(iv) an amendment to Protocol I to the Convention shall be subject to the same procedures as for the amendments to the Annexes to the Convention, as provided for in subparagraphs (f)(ii) or (iii) above;

(v) an amendment to Protocol II to the Convention shall be subject to the same procedures as for the amendments to an Article of the Convention, as provided for in subparagraph (f)(i) above;

(g) the amendment shall enter into force under the following conditions:

(i) in the case of an amendment to an Article of the Convention, to Protocol II, or to Protocol I or to an Annex to the Convention not under the procedure specified in subparagraph (f)(iii), the amendment accepted in conformity with the foregoing provisions shall enter into force six months after the date of its acceptance with respect to the Parties which have declared that they have accepted it;

(ii) in the case of an amendment to Protocol I, to an Appendix to an Annex or to an Annex to the Convention under the procedure specified in subparagraph (f)(iii), the amendment deemed to have been accepted in accordance with the foregoing conditions shall enter into force six months after its acceptance for all the Parties with the exception of those which, before that date, have made a declaration that they do not accept it or a declaration under subparagraph (f)(ii), that their express approval is necessary.

(3) Amendment by a Conference;

(a) Upon the request of a Party, concurred in by at least one-third of the Parties, the Organization shall convene a Conference of Parties to the Convention to consider amendments to the present Convention.

(b) Every amendment adopted by such a Conference by a two-thirds majority of those present and voting of the Parties shall be communicated by the Secretary-General of the Organization to all Contracting Parties for their acceptance.

(c) Unless the Conference decides otherwise, the amendment shall be deemed to have been accepted and to have entered into force in accordance with the procedures specified for that purpose in paragraph (2)(f) and (g) above.

(4)

(a) In the case of an amendment to an Optional Annex, a reference in the present Article to a "Party to the Convention" shall be deemed to mean a reference to a Party bound by that Annex.

(b) Any Party which has declined to accept an amendment to an Annex shall be treated as a non-Party only for the purpose of application of that Amendment.

(5) The adoption and entry into force of a new Annex shall be subject to the same procedures as for the adoption and entry into force of an amendment to an Article of the Convention.

(6) Unless expressly provided otherwise, any amendment to the present Convention made under this Article, which relates to the structure of a ship, shall apply only to ships for which the building contract is placed, or in the absence of a building contract, the keel of which is laid, on or after the date on which the amendment comes into force.

(7) Any amendment to a Protocol or to an Annex shall relate to the substance of that Protocol or Annex and shall be consistent with the Articles of the present Convention.

(8) The Secretary-General of the Organization shall inform all Parties of any amendments which enter into force under the present Article, together with the date on which each such amendment enters into force.

(9) Any declaration of acceptance or of objection to an amendment under the present Article shall be notified in writing to the Secretary-General of the Organization. The latter shall bring such notification and the date of its receipt to the notice of the Parties to the Convention.

Article 17 Promotion of Technical Co-operation

The Parties to the Convention shall promote, in consultation with the Organization and other international bodies, with assistance and coordination by the Executive Director of the United Nations Environment Programme, support for those Parties which request technical assistance for:

(a) the training of scientific and technical personnel;

(b) the supply of necessary equipment and facilities for reception and monitoring;

(c) the facilitation of other measures and arrangements to prevent or mitigate pollution of the marine environment by ships; and

(d) the encouragement of research;

preferably within the countries concerned, so furthering the aims and purposes of the present Convention.

Article 18 Denunciation

(1) The present Convention or any Optional Annex may be denounced by any Parties to the Convention at any time after the expiry of five years from the date on which the Convention or such Annex enters into force for that Party.

(2) Denunciation shall be effected by notification in writing to the Secretary-General of the Organization who shall inform all the other Parties of any such notification received and of the date of its receipt as well as the date on which such denunciation takes effect.

(3) A denunciation shall take effect twelve months after receipt of the notification of denunciation by the Secretary-General of the Organization or after the expiry of any other longer period which may be indicated in the notification.

Article 19 Deposit and Registration

(1) The present Convention shall be deposited with the Secretary-General of the Organization who shall transmit certified true copies thereof to all States which have signed the present Convention or acceded to it.

(2) As soon as the present Convention enters into force, the text shall be transmitted by the Secretary-General of the Organization to the Secretary-General of the United Nations for registration and publication, in accordance with Article 102 of the Charter of the United Nations.

Article 20 Languages

The present Convention is established in a single copy in the English, French, Russian and Spanish languages, each text being equally authentic. Official translations in the Arabic, German, Italian and Japanese languages shall be prepared and deposited with the signed original.

IN WITNESS WHEREOF the undersigned * being duly authorized by their respective Governments for that purpose have signed the present Convention.

DONE at London this second day of November, one thousand nine hundred and seventy-three.

CONVENTION ON INTERNATIONAL TRADE IN ENDANGERED SPECIES OF WILD FAUNA AND FLORA

(Adopted: 3 March 1973; Entry into force: 1 July 1975; Applied in Hong Kong: 6 August 1976, via the now-repealed Animals and Plants (Protection of Endangered Species) Ordinance (Cap. 187))

The Contracting States,

Recognizing that wild fauna and flora in their many beautiful and varied forms are an irreplaceable part of the natural systems of the earth which must be protected for this and the generations to come;

Conscious of the ever-growing value of wild fauna and flora from aesthetic, scientific, cultural, recreational and economic points of view;

Recognizing that peoples and States are and should be the best protectors of their own wild fauna and flora;

Recognizing, in addition, that international co-operation is essential for the protection of certain species of wild fauna and flora against over-exploitation through international trade;

Convinced of the urgency of taking appropriate measures to this end;

Have agreed as follows:

Article I Definitions

For the purpose of the present Convention, unless the context otherwise requires:

(a) "Species" means any species, subspecies, or geographically separate population thereof;

---

* Signatures omitted.

(b) "Specimen" means:

(i) any animal or plant, whether alive or dead;

(ii) in the case of an animal: for species included in Appendices I and II, any readily recognizable part or derivative thereof; and for species included in Appendix III, any readily recognizable part or derivative thereof specified in Appendix III in relation to the species; and

(iii) in the case of a plant: for species included in Appendix I, any readily recognizable part or derivative thereof; and for species included in Appendices II and III, any readily recognizable part or derivative thereof specified in Appendices II and III in relation to the species;

(c) "Trade" means export, re-export, import and introduction from the sea;

(d) "Re-export" means export of any specimen that has previously been imported;

(e) "Introduction from the sea" means transportation into a State of specimens of any species which were taken in the marine environment not under the jurisdiction of any State;

(f) "Scientific Authority" means a national scientific authority designated in accordance with Article IX;

(g) "Management Authority" means a national management authority designated in accordance with Article IX;

(h) "Party" means a State for which the present Convention has entered into force.

Article II Fundamental Principles

(1) Appendix I shall include all species threatened with extinction which are or may be affected by trade. Trade in specimens of these species must be subject to particularly strict regulation in order not to endanger further their survival and must only be authorized in exceptional circumstances.

(2) Appendix II shall include:

(a) all species which although not necessarily now threatened with extinction may become so unless trade in specimens of such species is subject to strict regulation in order to avoid utilization incompatible with their survival; and

(b) other species which must be subject to regulation in order that trade in specimens of certain species referred to in subparagraph (a) of this paragraph may be brought under effective control.

(3) Appendix III shall include all species which any Party identifies as being subject to regulation within its jurisdiction for the purpose of preventing or restricting exploitation, and as needing the co-operation of other Parties in the control of trade.

(4) The Parties shall not allow trade in specimens of species included in Appendices I, II and III except in accordance with the provisions of the present Convention.

Article III Regulation of Trade in Specimens of Species Included in Appendix I

(1) All trade in specimens of species included in Appendix I shall be in accordance with the provisions of this Article.

(2) The export of any specimen of a species included in Appendix I shall require the prior grant and presentation of an export permit. An export permit shall only be granted when the following conditions have been met:

(a) a Scientific Authority of the State of export has advised that such export will not be detrimental to the survival of that species;

(b) a Management Authority of the State of export is satisfied that the specimen was not obtained in contravention of the laws of that State for the protection of fauna and flora;

(c) a Management Authority of the State of export is satisfied that any living specimen will be so prepared and shipped as to minimize the risk of injury, damage to health or cruel treatment; and

(d) a Management Authority of the State of export is satisfied that an import permit has been granted for the specimen.

(3) The import of any specimen of a species included in Appendix I shall require the prior grant and presentation of an import permit and either an export permit or a re-export certificate. An import permit shall only be granted when the following conditions have been met:

(a) a Scientific Authority of the State of import has advised that the import will be for purposes which are not detrimental to the survival of the species involved;

(b) a Scientific Authority of the State of import is satisfied that the proposed recipient of a living specimen is suitably equipped to house and care for it; and

(c) a Management Authority of the State of import is satisfied that the specimen is not to be used for primarily commercial purposes.

(4) The re-export of any specimen of a species included in Appendix I shall require the prior grant and presentation of a re-export certificate. A re-export certificate shall only be granted when the following conditions have been met:

(a) a Management Authority of the State of re-export is satisfied that the specimen was imported into that State in accordance with the provisions of the present Convention;

(b) a Management Authority of the State of re-export is satisfied that any living specimen will be so prepared and shipped as to minimize the risk of injury, damage to health or cruel treatment; and

(c) a Management Authority of the State of re-export is satisfied that an import permit has been granted for any living specimen.

(5) The introduction from the sea of any specimen of a species included in Appendix I shall require the prior grant of a certificate from a Management Authority of the State of introduction. A certificate shall only be granted when the following conditions have been met:

(a) a Scientific Authority of the State of introduction advises that the introduction will not be detrimental to the survival of the species involved;

(b) a Management Authority of the State of introduction is satisfied that the proposed recipient of a living specimen is suitably equipped to house and care for it; and

(c) a Management Authority of the State of introduction is satisfied that the specimen is not to be used for primarily commercial purposes.

Article IV Regulation of Trade in Specimens of Species Included in Appendix II

(1) All trade in specimens of species included in Appendix II shall be in accordance with the provisions of this Article.

(2) The export of any specimen of a species included in Appendix II shall require the prior grant and presentation of an export permit. An export permit shall only be granted when the following conditions have been met:

(a) a Scientific Authority of the State of export has advised that such export will not be detrimental to the survival of that species;

(b) a Management Authority of the State of export is satisfied that the specimen was not obtained in contravention of the laws of that State for the protection of fauna and flora; and

(c) a Management Authority of the State of export is satisfied that any living specimen will be so prepared and shipped as to minimize the risk of injury, damage to health or cruel treatment.

(3) A Scientific Authority in each Party shall monitor both the export permits granted by that State for specimens of species included in Appendix II and the actual exports of such specimens. Whenever a Scientific Authority determines that the export of specimens of any such species should be limited in order to maintain that species throughout its range at a level consistent with its role in the ecosystems in which it occurs and well above the level at which that species might become eligible for inclusion in Appendix I, the Scientific Authority shall advise the appropriate Management Authority of suitable measures to be taken to limit the grant of export permits for specimens of that species.

(4) The import of any specimen of a species included in Appendix II shall require the prior presentation of either an export permit or a re-export certificate.

(5) The re-export of any specimen of a species included in Appendix II shall require the prior grant and presentation of a re-export certificate. A re-export certificate shall only be granted when the following conditions have been met:

(a) a Management Authority of the State of re-export is satisfied that the specimen was imported into that State in accordance with the provisions of the present Convention; and

(b) a Management Authority of the State of re-export is satisfied that any living specimen will be so prepared and shipped as to minimize the risk of injury, damage to health or cruel treatment.

(6) The introduction from the sea of any specimen of a species included in Appendix II shall require the prior grant of a certificate from a Management Authority of the State of introduction. A certificate shall only be granted when the following conditions have been met:

(a) a Scientific Authority of the State of introduction advises that the introduction will not be detrimental to the survival of the species involved; and

(b) a Management Authority of the State of introduction is satisfied that any living specimen will be so handled as to minimize the risk of injury, damage to health or cruel treatment.

(7) Certificates referred to in paragraph (6) of this Article may be granted on the advice of a Scientific Authority, in consultation with other national scientific authorities or, when appropriate, international scientific authorities, in respect of periods not exceeding one year for total numbers of specimens to be introduced in such periods.

Article V Regulation of Trade in Specimens of Species Included in Appendix III

(1) All trade in specimens of species included in Appendix III shall be in accordance with the provisions of this Article.

(2) The export of any specimen of a species included in Appendix III from any State which has included that species in Appendix III shall require the prior grant and presentation of an export permit. An export permit shall only be granted when the following conditions have been met:

(a) a Management Authority of the State of export is satisfied that the specimen was not obtained in contravention of the laws of that State for the protection of fauna and flora; and

(b) a Management Authority of the State of export is satisfied that any living specimen will be so prepared and shipped as to minimize the risk of injury, damage to health or cruel treatment.

(3) The import of any specimen of a species included in Appendix III shall require, except in circumstances to which paragraph (4) of this Article applies, the prior presentation of a certificate of origin and, where the import is from a State which has included that species in Appendix III, an export permit.

(4) In the case of re-export, a certificate granted by the Management Authority of the State of re-export that the specimen was processed in that State or is being re-exported shall be accepted by the State of import as evidence that the provisions of the present Convention have been complied with in respect of the specimen concerned.

Article VI Permits and Certificates

(1) Permits and certificates granted under the provisions of Articles III, IV, and V shall be in accordance with the provisions of this Article.

(2) An export permit shall contain the information specified in the model set forth in Appendix IV, and may only be used for export within a period of six months from the date on which it was granted.

(3) Each permit or certificate shall contain the title of the present Convention, the name and any identifying stamp of the Management Authority granting it and a control number assigned by the Management Authority.

(4) Any copies of a permit or certificate issued by a Management Authority shall be clearly marked as copies only and no such copy may be used in place of the original, except to the extent endorsed thereon.

(5) A separate permit or certificate shall be required for each consignment of specimens.

(6) A Management Authority of the State of import of any specimen shall cancel and retain the export permit or re-export certificate and any corresponding import permit presented in respect of the import of that specimen.

(7) Where appropriate and feasible a Management Authority may affix a mark upon any specimen to assist in identifying the specimen. For these purposes "mark" means any indelible imprint, lead seal or other suitable means of identifying a specimen, designed in such a way as to render its imitation by unauthorized persons as difficult as possible.

Article VII Exemptions and Other Special Provisions Relating to Trade

(1) The provisions of Articles III, IV and V shall not apply to the transit or transhipment of specimens through or in the territory of a Party while the specimens remain in Customs control.

(2) Where a Management Authority of the State of export or re-export is satisfied that a specimen was acquired before the provisions of the present Convention applied to that specimen, the provisions of Articles III, IV and V shall not apply to that specimen where the Management Authority issues a certificate to that effect.

(3) The provisions of Articles III, IV and V shall not apply to specimens that are personal or household effects. This exemption shall not apply where:

  (a) in the case of specimens of a species included in Appendix I, they were acquired by the owner outside his State of usual residence, and are being imported into that State; or

  (b) in the case of specimens of species included in Appendix II:

    (i) they were acquired by the owner outside his State of usual residence and in a State where removal from the wild occurred;

    (ii) they are being imported into the owner's State of usual residence; and

    (iii) the State where removal from the wild occurred requires the prior grant of export permits before any export of such specimens;

  unless a Management Authority is satisfied that the specimens were acquired before the provisions of the present Convention applied to such specimens.

(4) Specimens of an animal species included in Appendix I bred in captivity for commercial purposes, or of a plant species included in Appendix I artificially propagated for commercial purposes, shall be deemed to be specimens of species included in Appendix II.

(5) Where a Management Authority of the State of export is satisfied that any specimen of an animal species was bred in captivity or any specimen of a plant species was artificially propagated, or is a part of such an animal or plant or was derived therefrom, a certificate by that Management Authority to that effect shall be accepted in lieu of any of the permits or certificates required under the provisions of Article III, IV or V.

(6) The provisions of Articles III, IV and V shall not apply to the non-commercial loan, donation or exchange between scientists or scientific institutions registered by a Management Authority of their State, of herbarium specimens, other preserved, dried or embedded museum specimens, and live plant material which carry a label issued or approved by a Management Authority.

(7) A Management Authority of any State may waive the requirements of Articles III, IV and V and allow the movement without permits or certificates of specimens which form part of a travelling zoo, circus, menagerie, plant exhibition or other travelling exhibition provided that:

(a) the exporter or importer registers full details of such specimens with that Management Authority;

(b) the specimens are in either of the categories specified in paragraph (2) or (5) of this Article; and

(c) the Management Authority is satisfied that any living specimen will be so transported and cared for as to minimize the risk of injury, damage to health or cruel treatment.

Article VIII Measures to Be Taken by the Parties

(1) The Parties shall take appropriate measures to enforce the provisions of the present Convention and to prohibit trade in specimens in violation thereof. These shall include measures:

(a) to penalize trade in, or possession of, such specimens, or both; and

(b) to provide for the confiscation or return to the State of export of such specimens.

(2) In addition to the measures taken under paragraph (1) of this Article, a Party may, when it deems it necessary, provide for any method of internal reimbursement for expenses incurred as a result of the confiscation of a specimen traded in violation of the measures taken in the application of the provisions of the present Convention.

(3) As far as possible, the Parties shall ensure that specimens shall pass through any formalities required for trade with a minimum of delay. To facilitate such passage, a Party may designate ports of exit and ports of entry at which specimens must be presented for clearance. The Parties shall ensure further that all living specimens, during any period of transit, holding or shipment, are properly cared for so as to minimize the risk of injury, damage to health or cruel treatment.

(4) Where a living specimen is confiscated as a result of measures referred to in paragraph (1) of this Article:

(a) the specimen shall be entrusted to a Management Authority of the State of confiscation;

(b) the Management Authority shall, after consultation with the State of export, return the specimen to that State at the expense of that State, or to a rescue centre or such other place as the Management Authority deems appropriate and consistent with the purposes of the present Convention; and

(c) the Management Authority may obtain the advice of a Scientific Authority, or may, whenever it considers it desirable, consult the Secretariat in order to facilitate the decision under subparagraph (b) of this paragraph, including the choice of a rescue centre or other place.

(5) A rescue centre as referred to in paragraph (4) of this Article means an institution designated by a Management Authority to look after the welfare of living specimens, particularly those that have been confiscated.

(6) Each Party shall maintain records of trade in specimens of species included in Appendices I, II and III which shall cover:

(a) the names and addresses of exporters and importers; and

(b) the number and type of permits and certificates granted; the States with which such trade occurred; the numbers or quantities and types of specimens, names of species as included in Appendices I, II and III and, where applicable, the size and sex of the specimens in question.

(7) Each Party shall prepare periodic reports on its implementation of the present Convention and shall transmit to the Secretariat:

(a) an annual report containing a summary of the information specified in subparagraph (b) of paragraph (6) of this Article; and

(b) a biennial report on legislative, regulatory and administrative measures taken to enforce the provisions of the present Convention.

(8) The information referred to in paragraph (7) of this Article shall be available to the public where this is not inconsistent with the law of the Party concerned.

Article IX Management and Scientific Authorities

(1) Each Party shall designate for the purposes of the present Convention:

(a) one or more Management Authorities competent to grant permits or certificates on behalf of that Party; and

(b) one or more Scientific Authorities.

(2) A State depositing an instrument of ratification, acceptance, approval or accession shall at that time inform the Depositary Government of the name and address of the Management Authority authorized to communicate with other Parties and with the Secretariat.

(3) Any changes in the designations or authorizations under the provisions of this Article shall be communicated by the Party concerned to the Secretariat for transmission to all other Parties.

(4) Any Management Authority referred to in paragraph (2) of this Article shall, if so requested by the Secretariat or the Management Authority of another Party, communicate to it impression of stamps, seals or other devices used to authenticate permits or certificates.

Article X Trade with States not Party to the Convention

Where export or re-export is to, or import is from, a State not a Party to the present Convention, comparable documentation issued by the competent authorities in that State which substantially conforms with the requirements of the present Convention for permits and certificates may be accepted in lieu thereof by any Party.

Article XI Conference of the Parties

(1) The Secretariat shall call a meeting of the Conference of the Parties not later than two years after the entry into force of the present Convention.

(2) Thereafter the Secretariat shall convene regular meetings at least once every two years, unless the Conference decides otherwise, and extraordinary meetings at any time on the written request of at least one-third of the Parties.

(3) At meetings, whether regular or extraordinary, the Parties shall review the implementation of the present Convention and may:

(a) make such provision as may be necessary to enable the Secretariat to carry out its duties, and adopt financial provisions;

(b) consider and adopt amendments to Appendices I and II in accordance with Article XV;

(c) review the progress made towards the restoration and conservation of the species included in Appendices I, II and III;

(d) receive and consider any reports presented by the Secretariat or by any Party; and

(e) where appropriate, make recommendations for improving the effectiveness of the present Convention.

(4) At each regular meeting, the Parties may determine the time and venue of the next regular meeting to be held in accordance with the provisions of paragraph (2) of this Article.

(5) At any meeting, the Parties may determine and adopt rules of procedure for the meeting.

(6) The United Nations, its Specialized Agencies and the International Atomic Energy Agency, as well as any State not a Party to the present Convention, may be represented at meetings of the Conference by observers, who shall have the right to participate but not to vote.

(7) Any body or agency technically qualified in protection, conservation or management of wild fauna and flora, in the following categories, which has informed the Secretariat of its desire to be represented at meetings of the Conference by observers, shall be admitted unless at least one-third of the Parties present object:

(a) international agencies or bodies, either governmental or non-governmental, and national governmental agencies and bodies; and

(b) national non-governmental agencies or bodies which have been approved for this purpose by the State in which they are located.

Once admitted, these observers shall have the right to participate but not to vote.

Article XII The Secretariat

(1) Upon entry into force of the present Convention, a Secretariat shall be provided by the Executive Director of the United Nations Environment Programme. To the extent and in the manner he considers appropriate, he may be assisted by suitable inter-governmental or non-governmental international or national agencies and bodies technically qualified in protection, conservation and management of wild fauna and flora.

(2) The functions of the Secretariat shall be:

(a) to arrange for and service meetings of the Parties;

(b) to perform the functions entrusted to it under the provisions of Articles XV and XVI of the present Convention;

(c) to undertake scientific and technical studies in accordance with programmes authorized by the Conference of the Parties as will contribute to the implementation of the present Convention, including studies concerning standards for appropriate preparation and shipment of living specimens and the means of identifying specimens;

(d) to study the reports of Parties and to request from Parties such further information with respect thereto as it deems necessary to ensure implementation of the present Convention;

(e) to invite the attention of the Parties to any matter pertaining to the aims of the present Convention;

(f) to publish periodically and distribute to the Parties current editions of Appendices I, II and III together with any information which will facilitate identification of specimens of species included in those Appendices;

(g) to prepare annual reports to the Parties on its work and on the implementation of the present Convention and such other reports as meetings of the Parties may request;

(h) to make recommendations for the implementation of the aims and provisions of the present Convention, including the exchange of information of a scientific or technical nature;

(i) to perform any other function as may be entrusted to it by the Parties.

Article XIII International Measures

(1) When the Secretariat in the light of information received is satisfied that any species included in Appendix I or II is being affected adversely by trade in specimens of that species or that the provisions of the present Convention are not being effectively implemented, it shall communicate such information to the authorized Management Authority of the Party or Parties concerned.

(2) When any Party receives a communication as indicated in paragraph (1) of this Article, it shall, as soon as possible, inform the Secretariat of any relevant facts insofar as its laws permit and, where

appropriate, propose remedial action. Where the Party considers that an inquiry is desirable, such inquiry may be carried out by one or more persons expressly authorized by the Party.

(3) The information provided by the Party or resulting from any inquiry as specified in paragraph (2) of this Article shall be reviewed by the next Conference of the Parties which may make whatever recommendations it deems appropriate.

Article XIV Effect on Domestic Legislation and International Conventions

(1) The provisions of the present Convention shall in no way affect the right of Parties to adopt:

(a) stricter domestic measures regarding the conditions for trade, taking, possession or transport of specimens of species included in Appendices I, II and III, or the complete prohibition thereof; or

(b) domestic measures restricting or prohibiting trade, taking, possession or transport of species not included in Appendix I, II or III.

(2) The provisions of the present Convention shall in no way affect the provisions of any domestic measures or the obligations of Parties deriving from any treaty, convention, or international agreement relating to other aspects of trade, taking, possession or transport of specimens which is in force or subsequently may enter into force for any Party including any measure pertaining to the Customs, public health, veterinary or plant quarantine fields.

(3) The provisions of the present Convention shall in no way affect the provisions of, or the obligations deriving from, any treaty, convention or international agreement concluded or which may be concluded between States creating a union or regional trade agreement establishing or maintaining a common external Customs control and removing Customs control between the parties thereto insofar as they relate to trade among the States members of that union or agreement.

(4) A State party to the present Convention, which is also a party to any other treaty, convention or international agreement which is in force at the time of the coming into force of the present Convention and under the provisions of which protection is afforded to marine species included in Appendix II, shall be relieved of the obligations imposed on it under the provisions of the present Convention with respect to trade in specimens of species included in Appendix II that are taken by ships registered in that State and in accordance with the provisions of such other treaty, convention or international agreement.

(5) Notwithstanding the provisions of Articles III, IV and V, any export of a specimen taken in accordance with paragraph (4) of this Article shall only require a certificate from a Management Authority of the State of introduction to the effect that the specimen was taken in accordance with the provisions of the other treaty, convention or international agreement in question.

(6) Nothing in the present Convention shall prejudice the codification and development of the law of the sea by the United Nations Conference on the Law of the Sea convened pursuant to Resolution 2750 C (XXV) of the General Assembly of the United Nations nor the present or future claims and legal views of any State concerning the law of the sea and the nature and extent of coastal and flag State jurisdiction.

Article XV Amendments to Appendices I and II

(1) The following provisions shall apply in relation to amendments to Appendices I and II at meetings of the Conference of the Parties:

(a) Any Party may propose an amendment to Appendix I or II for consideration at the next meeting. The text of the proposed amendment shall be communicated to the Secretariat at least 150 days before the meeting. The Secretariat shall consult the other Parties and interested bodies on the amendment in accordance with the provisions of subparagraphs (b) and (c) of paragraph (2) of this Article and shall communicate the response to all Parties not later than 30 days before the meeting.

(b) Amendments shall be adopted by a two-thirds majority of Parties present and voting. For these purposes "Parties present and voting" means Parties present and casting an affirmative or negative vote. Parties abstaining from voting shall not be counted among the two-thirds required for adopting an amendment.

(c) Amendments adopted at a meeting shall enter into force 90 days after that meeting for all Parties except those which make a reservation in accordance with paragraph (3) of this Article.

(2) The following provisions shall apply in relation to amendments to Appendices I and II between meetings of the Conference of the Parties:

(a) Any Party may propose an amendment to Appendix I or II for consideration between meetings by the postal procedures set forth in this paragraph.

(b) For marine species, the Secretariat shall, upon receiving the text of the proposed amendment, immediately communicate it to the Parties. It shall also consult inter-governmental bodies having a function in relation to those species especially with a view to obtaining scientific data these bodies may be able to provide and to ensuring co-ordination with any conservation measures enforced by such bodies. The Secretariat shall communicate the views expressed and data provided by these bodies and its own findings and recommendations to the Parties as soon as possible.

(c) For species other than marine species, the Secretariat shall, upon receiving the text of the proposed amendment, immediately communicate it to the Parties, and, as soon as possible thereafter, its own recommendations.

(d) Any Party may, within 60 days of the date on which the Secretariat communicated its recommendations to the Parties under subparagraph (b) or (c) of this paragraph, transmit to the Secretariat any comments on the proposed amendment together with any relevant scientific data and information.

(e) The Secretariat shall communicate the replies received together with its own recommendations to the Parties as soon as possible.

(f) If no objection to the proposed amendment is received by the Secretariat within 30 days of the date the replies and recommendations were communicated under the provisions of subparagraph (e) of this paragraph, the amendment shall enter into force 90 days later for all Parties except those which make a reservation in accordance with paragraph (3) of this Article.

(g) If an objection by any Party is received by the Secretariat, the proposed amendment shall be submitted to a postal vote in accordance with the provisions of subparagraphs (h), (i) and (j) of this paragraph.

(h) The Secretariat shall notify the Parties that notification of objection has been received.

(i) Unless the Secretariat receives the votes for, against or in abstention from at least one-half of the Parties within 60 days of the date of notification under subparagraph (h) of this paragraph, the proposed amendment shall be referred to the next meeting of the Conference for further consideration.

(j) Provided that votes are received from one-half of the Parties, the amendment shall be adopted by a two-thirds majority of Parties casting an affirmative or negative vote.

(k) The Secretariat shall notify all Parties of the result of the vote.

(l) If the proposed amendment is adopted it shall enter into force 90 days after the date of the notification by the Secretariat of its acceptance for all Parties except those which make a reservation in accordance with paragraph (3) of this Article.

(3) During the period of 90 days provided for by subparagraph (c) of paragraph (1) or subparagraph (l) of paragraph (2) of this Article any Party may by notification in writing to the Depositary Government make a reservation with respect to the amendment.

Until such reservation is withdrawn the Party shall be treated as a State not a Party to the present Convention with respect to trade in the species concerned.

Article XVI Appendix III and Amendments thereto

(1) Any Party may at any time submit to the Secretariat a list of species which it identifies as being subject to regulation within its jurisdiction for the purpose mentioned in paragraph (3) of Article II. Appendix III shall include the names of the Parties submitting the species for inclusion therein, the scientific names of the species so submitted, and any parts or derivatives of the animals or plants concerned that are specified in relation to the species for the purposes of subparagraph (b) of Article I.

(2) Each list submitted under the provisions of paragraph (1) of this Article shall be communicated to the Parties by the Secretariat as soon as possible after receiving it. The list shall take effect as part of Appendix III 90 days after the date of such communication. At any time after the communication of such list, any Party may by notification in writing to the Depositary Government enter a reservation with respect to any species or any parts or derivatives, and until such reservation is withdrawn, the State shall be treated as a State not a Party to the present Convention with respect to trade in the species or part or derivative concerned.

(3) A Party which has submitted a species for inclusion in Appendix III may withdraw it at any time by notification to the Secretariat which shall communicate the withdrawal to all Parties. The withdrawal shall take effect 30 days after the date of such communication.

(4) Any Party submitting a list under the provisions of paragraph (1) of this Article shall submit to the Secretariat a copy of all domestic laws and regulations applicable to the protection of such species, together with any interpretations which the Party may deem appropriate or the Secretariat may request. The Party shall, for as long as the species in question is included in Appendix III, submit any amendments of such laws and regulations or any interpretations as they are adopted.

Article XVII Amendment of the Convention

(1) An extraordinary meeting of the Conference of the Parties shall be convened by the Secretariat on the written request of at least one-third of the Parties to consider and adopt amendments to the present Convention. Such amendments shall be adopted by a two-thirds majority of Parties present and voting. For these purposes "Parties present and voting" means Parties present and casting an affirmative or negative vote. Parties abstaining from voting shall not be counted among the two-thirds required for adopting an amendment.

(2) The text of any proposed amendment shall be communicated by the Secretariat to all Parties at least 90 days before the meeting.

(3) An amendment shall enter into force for the Parties which have accepted it 60 days after two-thirds of the Parties have deposited an instrument of acceptance of the amendment with the Depositary Government. Thereafter, the amendment shall enter into force for any other Party 60 days after that Party deposits its instrument of acceptance of the amendment.

Article XVIII Resolution of Disputes

(1) Any dispute which may arise between two or more Parties with respect to the interpretation or application of the provisions of the present Convention shall be subject to negotiation between the Parties involved in the dispute.

(2) If the dispute cannot be resolved in accordance with paragraph (1) of this Article, the Parties may, by mutual consent, submit the dispute to arbitration, in particular that of the Permanent Court of Arbitration at The Hague, and the Parties submitting the dispute shall be bound by the arbitral decision.

Article XIX Signature

The present Convention shall be open for signature at Washington until 30 April 1973 and thereafter at Berne until 31 December 1974.

Article XX Ratification, Acceptance, Approval

The present Convention shall be subject to ratification, acceptance or approval. Instruments of ratification, acceptance or approval shall be deposited with the Government of the Swiss Confederation which shall be the Depositary Government.

Article XXI Accession

(1) The present Convention shall be open indefinitely for accession. Instruments of accession shall be deposited with the Depositary Government.

(2) This Convention shall be open for accession by regional economic integration organizations constituted by sovereign States which have competence in respect of the negotiation, conclusion and implementation of international agreements in matters transferred to them by their Member States and covered by this Convention.

(3) In their instruments of accession, such organizations shall declare the extent of their competence with respect to the matters governed by the Convention. These organizations shall also inform the Depositary Government of any substantial modification in the extent of their competence. Notifications by regional economic integration organizations concerning their competence with respect to matters governed by this Convention and modifications thereto shall be distributed to the Parties by the Depositary Government.

(4) In matters within their competence, such regional economic integration organizations shall exercise the rights and fulfil the obligations which this Convention attributes to their Member States, which are Parties to the Convention. In such cases the Member States of the organizations shall not be entitled to exercise such rights individually.

(5) In the fields of their competence, regional economic integration organizations shall exercise their right to vote with a number of votes equal to the number of their Member States which are Parties to the Convention. Such organizations shall not exercise their right to vote if their Member States exercise theirs, and vice versa.

(6) Any reference to "Party" in the sense used in Article I (h) of this Convention to "State"/"States" or to "State Party"/"State Parties" to the Convention shall be construed as including a reference to any regional economic integration organization having competence in respect of the negotiation, conclusion and application of international agreements in matters covered by this Convention.

Article XXII Entry into Force

(1) The present Convention shall enter into force 90 days after the date of deposit of the tenth instrument of ratification, acceptance, approval or accession, with the Depositary Government.

(2) For each State which ratifies, accepts or approves the present Convention or accedes thereto after the deposit of the tenth instrument of ratification, acceptance, approval or accession, the present Convention shall enter into force 90 days after the deposit by such State of its instrument of ratification, acceptance, approval or accession.

Article XXIII Reservations

(1) The provisions of the present Convention shall not be subject to general reservations. Specific reservations may be entered in accordance with the provisions of this Article and Articles XV and XVI.

(2) Any State may, on depositing its instrument of ratification, acceptance, approval or accession, enter a specific reservation with regard to:

(a) any species included in Appendix I, II or III; or

(b) any parts or derivatives specified in relation to a species included in Appendix III.

(3) Until a Party withdraws its reservation entered under the provisions of this Article, it shall be treated as a State not a Party to the present Convention with respect to trade in the particular species or parts or derivatives specified in such reservation.

Article XXIV Denunciation

Any Party may denounce the present Convention by written notification to the Depositary Government at any time. The denunciation shall take effect twelve months after the Depositary Government has received the notification.

Article XXV Depositary

(1) The original of the present Convention, in the Chinese, English, French, Russian and Spanish languages, each version being equally authentic, shall be deposited with the Depositary Government, which shall transmit certified copies thereof to all States that have signed it or deposited instruments of accession to it.

(2) The Depositary Government shall inform all signatory and acceding States and the Secretariat of signatures, deposit of instruments of ratification, acceptance, approval or accession, entry into force of the present Convention, amendments thereto, entry and withdrawal of reservations and notifications of denunciation.

(3) As soon as the present Convention enters into force, a certified copy thereof shall be transmitted by the Depositary Government to the Secretariat of the United Nations for registration and publication in accordance with Article 102 of the Charter of the United Nations.

IN WITNESS WHEREOF the undersigned Plenipotentiaries, being duly authorized to that effect, have signed the present Convention.

DONE at Washington this third day of March, One Thousand Nine Hundred and Seventy-three.

SECTION V
BUSINESS AND HUMAN RIGHTS

This Section includes two international instruments related to business and human rights as applied in Hong Kong. They are:

(1) The Guiding Principles on Business and Human Rights: Implementing the United Nations "Protect, Respect and Remedy" Framework

(2) The ILO Tripartite Declaration of Principles Concerning Multinational Enterprises and Social Policy

GUIDING PRINCIPLES ON BUSINESS AND HUMAND RIGHTS: IMPLEMENTING THE UNITED NATIONS "PROTECT, RESPECT AND REMEDY" FRAMEWORK, A/HRC/17/31 (21 March 2011)

(Endorsed: 16 June 2011)

General Principles

These Guiding Principles are grounded in recognition of:

(a) States' existing obligations to respect, protect and fulfil human rights and fundamental freedoms;

(b) The role of business enterprises as specialized organs of society performing specialized functions, required to comply with all applicable laws and to respect human rights;

(c) The need for rights and obligations to be matched to appropriate and effective remedies when breached.

These Guiding Principles apply to all States and to all business enterprises, both transnational and others, regardless of their size, sector, location, ownership and structure.

These Guiding Principles should be understood as a coherent whole and should be read, individually and collectively, in terms of their objective of enhancing standards and practices with regard to business and human rights so as to achieve tangible results for affected individuals and communities, and thereby also contributing to a socially sustainable globalization.

Nothing in these Guiding Principles should be read as creating new international law obligations, or as limiting or undermining any legal obligations a State may have undertaken or be subject to under international law with regard to human rights.

These Guiding Principles should be implemented in a non-discriminatory manner, with particular attention to the rights and needs of, as well as the challenges faced by, individuals from groups or populations that may be at heightened risk of becoming vulnerable or marginalized, and with due regard to the different risks that may be faced by women and men.

I The State Duty to Protect Human Rights

A *Foundational Principles*

(1) States must protect against human rights abuse within their territory and/or jurisdiction by third parties, including business enterprises. This requires taking appropriate steps to prevent, investigate, punish and redress such abuse through effective policies, legislation, regulations and adjudication.

Commentary

States' international human rights law obligations require that they respect, protect and fulfil the human rights of individuals within their territory and/or jurisdiction. This includes the duty to protect against human rights abuse by third parties, including business enterprises.

The State duty to protect is a standard of conduct. Therefore, States are not per se responsible for human rights abuse by private actors. However, States may breach their international human rights law obligations where such abuse can be attributed to them, or where they fail to take appropriate steps to prevent, investigate, punish and redress private actors' abuse. While States generally have discretion in deciding upon these steps, they should consider the full range of permissible preventative and remedial measures, including policies, legislation, regulations and adjudication. States also have the duty to protect and promote the rule of law, including by taking measures to ensure equality before the law, fairness in its application, and by providing for adequate accountability, legal certainty, and procedural and legal transparency.

This Chapter focuses on preventative measures while Chapter III outlines remedial measures.

(2) States should set out clearly the expectation that all business enterprises domiciled in their territory and/or jurisdiction respect human rights throughout their operations.

Commentary

At present States are not generally required under international human rights law to regulate the extraterritorial activities of businesses domiciled in their territory and/or jurisdiction. Nor are they generally prohibited from doing so, provided there is a recognized jurisdictional basis. Within these parameters some human rights treaty bodies recommend that home States take steps to prevent abuse abroad by business enterprises within their jurisdiction.

There are strong policy reasons for home States to set out clearly the expectation that businesses respect human rights abroad, especially where the State itself is involved in or supports those businesses. The reasons include ensuring predictability for business enterprises by providing coherent and consistent messages, and preserving the State's own reputation.

States have adopted a range of approaches in this regard. Some are domestic measures with extraterritorial implications. Examples include requirements on "parent" companies to report on the global operations of the entire enterprise; multilateral soft-law instruments such as the Guidelines for Multinational Enterprises of the Organization for Economic Cooperation and Development; and performance standards required by institutions that support overseas investments. Other approaches amount to direct extraterritorial legislation and enforcement. This includes criminal regimes that allow for prosecutions based on the nationality of the perpetrator no matter where the offence occurs. Various factors may contribute to the perceived and actual reasonableness of States' actions, for example whether they are grounded in multilateral agreement.

B *Operational Principles*

General State Regulatory and Policy Functions

(3) In meeting their duty to protect, States should:

(a) Enforce laws that are aimed at, or have the effect of, requiring business enterprises to respect human rights, and periodically to assess the adequacy of such laws and address any gaps;

(b) Ensure that other laws and policies governing the creation and ongoing operation of business enterprises, such as corporate law, do not constrain but enable business respect for human rights;

(c) Provide effective guidance to business enterprises on how to respect human rights throughout their operations;

(d) Encourage, and where appropriate require, business enterprises to communicate how they address their human rights impacts.

Commentary

States should not assume that businesses invariably prefer, or benefit from, State inaction, and they should consider a smart mix of measures — national and international, mandatory and voluntary — to foster business respect for human rights.

The failure to enforce existing laws that directly or indirectly regulate business respect for human rights is often a significant legal gap in State practice. Such laws might range from non-discrimination and labour laws to environmental, property, privacy and anti-bribery laws. Therefore, it is important for States to consider whether such laws are currently being enforced effectively, and if not, why this is the case and what measures may reasonably correct the situation.

It is equally important for States to review whether these laws provide the necessary coverage in light of evolving circumstances and whether, together with relevant policies, they provide an environment conducive to business respect for human rights. For example, greater clarity in some areas of law and policy, such as those governing access to land, including entitlements in relation to ownership or use of land, is often necessary to protect both rights-holders and business enterprises.

Laws and policies that govern the creation and ongoing operation of business enterprises, such as corporate and securities laws, directly shape business behaviour. Yet their implications for human rights remain poorly understood. For example, there is a lack of clarity in corporate and securities law regarding what companies and their officers are permitted, let alone required, to do regarding human rights. Laws and policies in this area should provide sufficient guidance to enable enterprises to respect human rights, with due regard to the role of existing governance structures such as corporate boards.

Guidance to business enterprises on respecting human rights should indicate expected outcomes and help share best practices. It should advise on appropriate methods, including human rights due diligence, and how to consider effectively issues of gender, vulnerability and/or marginalization, recognizing the specific challenges that may be faced by indigenous peoples, women, national or ethnic minorities, religious and linguistic minorities, children, persons with disabilities, and migrant workers and their families.

National human rights institutions that comply with the Paris Principles have an important role to play in helping States identify whether relevant laws are aligned with their human rights obligations and are being effectively enforced, and in providing guidance on human rights also to business enterprises and other non-State actors.

Communication by business enterprises on how they address their human rights impacts can range from informal engagement with affected stakeholders to formal public reporting. State encouragement of, or where appropriate requirements for, such communication are important in fostering respect for human rights by business enterprises. Incentives to communicate adequate information could include provisions to give weight to such self-reporting in the event of any judicial or administrative proceeding. A requirement to communicate can be particularly appropriate where the nature of business operations or operating contexts pose a significant risk to human rights. Policies or laws in this area can usefully clarify what and how businesses should communicate, helping to ensure both the accessibility and accuracy of communications.

Any stipulation of what would constitute adequate communication should take into account risks that it may pose to the safety and security of individuals and facilities; legitimate requirements of commercial confidentiality; and variations in companies' size and structures.

Financial reporting requirements should clarify that human rights impacts in some instances may be "material" or "significant" to the economic performance of the business enterprise.

The State-Business Nexus

(4) States should take additional steps to protect against human rights abuses by business enterprises that are owned or controlled by the State, or that receive substantial support and services from State agencies such as export credit agencies and official investment insurance or guarantee agencies, including, where appropriate, by requiring human rights due diligence.

Commentary

States individually are the primary duty-bearers under international human rights law, and collectively they are the trustees of the international human rights regime. Where a business enterprise is controlled by the State or where its acts can be attributed otherwise to the State, an abuse of human rights by the business enterprise may entail a violation of the State's own international law obligations. Moreover, the closer a business enterprise is to the State, or the more it relies on statutory authority or taxpayer support, the stronger the State's policy rationale becomes for ensuring that the enterprise respects human rights.

Where States own or control business enterprises, they have greatest means within their powers to ensure that relevant policies, legislation and regulations regarding respect for human rights are implemented. Senior management typically reports to State agencies, and associated government departments have greater scope for scrutiny and oversight, including ensuring that effective human rights due diligence is implemented. (These enterprises are also subject to the corporate responsibility to respect human rights, addressed in Chapter II.)

A range of agencies linked formally or informally to the State may provide support and services to business activities. These include export credit agencies, official investment insurance or guarantee agencies, development agencies and development finance institutions. Where these agencies do not explicitly consider the actual and potential adverse impacts on human rights of beneficiary enterprises, they put themselves at risk — in reputational, financial, political and potentially legal terms — for supporting any such harm, and they may add to the human rights challenges faced by the recipient State.

Given these risks, States should encourage and, where appropriate, require human rights due diligence by the agencies themselves and by those business enterprises or projects receiving their support. A requirement for human rights due diligence is most likely to be appropriate where the nature of business operations or operating contexts pose significant risk to human rights.

(5) States should exercise adequate oversight in order to meet their international human rights obligations when they contract with, or legislate for, business enterprises to provide services that may impact upon the enjoyment of human rights.

Commentary

States do not relinquish their international human rights law obligations when they privatize the delivery of services that may impact upon the enjoyment of human rights. Failure by States to ensure that business enterprises performing such services operate in a manner consistent with the State's human rights obligations may entail both reputational and legal consequences for the State itself. As a necessary step, the relevant service contracts or enabling legislation should clarify the State's expectations that these enterprises respect human rights. States should ensure that they can effectively oversee the enterprises' activities, including through the provision of adequate independent monitoring and accountability mechanisms.

(6) States should promote respect for human rights by business enterprises with which they conduct commercial transactions.

Commentary

States conduct a variety of commercial transactions with business enterprises, not least through their procurement activities. This provides States — individually and collectively — with unique opportunities to promote awareness of and respect for human rights by those enterprises, including through the terms of contracts, with due regard to States' relevant obligations under national and international law.

Supporting Business Respect for Human Rights in Conflict-affected Areas

(7) Because the risk of gross human rights abuses is heightened in conflict-affected areas, States should help ensure that business enterprises operating in those contexts are not involved with such abuses, including by:

(a) Engaging at the earliest stage possible with business enterprises to help them identify, prevent and mitigate the human rights-related risks of their activities and business relationships;

(b) Providing adequate assistance to business enterprises to assess and address the heightened risks of abuses, paying special attention to both gender-based and sexual violence;

(c) Denying access to public support and services for a business enterprise that is involved with gross human rights abuses and refuses to cooperate in addressing the situation;

(d) Ensuring that their current policies, legislation, regulations and enforcement measures are effective in addressing the risk of business involvement in gross human rights abuses.

Commentary

Some of the worst human rights abuses involving business occur amid conflict over the control of territory, resources or a Government itself — where the human rights regime cannot be expected to function as intended. Responsible businesses increasingly seek guidance from States about how to avoid contributing to human rights harm in these difficult contexts. Innovative and practical approaches are needed. In particular, it is important to pay attention to the risk of sexual and gender-based violence, which is especially prevalent during times of conflict.

It is important for all States to address issues early before situations on the ground deteriorate. In conflict-affected areas, the "host" State may be unable to protect human rights adequately due to a lack of effective control. Where transnational corporations are involved, their "home" States therefore have roles to play in assisting both those corporations and host States to ensure that businesses are not involved with human rights abuse, while neighbouring States can provide important additional support.

To achieve greater policy coherence and assist business enterprises adequately in such situations, home States should foster closer cooperation among their development assistance agencies, foreign and trade ministries, and export finance institutions in their capitals and within their embassies, as well as between these agencies and host Government actors; develop early-warning indicators to alert Government agencies and business enterprises to problems; and attach appropriate consequences to any failure by enterprises to cooperate in these contexts, including by denying or withdrawing existing public support or services, or where that is not possible, denying their future provision.

States should warn business enterprises of the heightened risk of being involved with gross abuses of human rights in conflict-affected areas. They should review whether their policies, legislation, regulations and enforcement measures effectively address this heightened risk, including through provisions for human rights due diligence by business. Where they identify gaps, States should take appropriate steps to address them. This may include exploring civil, administrative or criminal liability for enterprises domiciled or operating in their territory and/or jurisdiction that commit or contribute to gross human rights abuses. Moreover, States should consider multilateral approaches to prevent and address such acts, as well as support effective collective initiatives.

All these measures are in addition to States' obligations under international humanitarian law in situations of armed conflict, and under international criminal law.

Ensuring Policy Coherence

(8) States should ensure that governmental departments, agencies and other State-based institutions that shape business practices are aware of and observe the State's human rights obligations when fulfilling their respective mandates, including by providing them with relevant information, training and support.

Commentary

There is no inevitable tension between States' human rights obligations and the laws and policies they put in place that shape business practices. However, at times, States have to make difficult balancing decisions to reconcile different societal needs. To achieve the appropriate balance, States need to take a broad approach to managing the business and human rights agenda, aimed at ensuring both vertical and horizontal domestic policy coherence.

Vertical policy coherence entails States having the necessary policies, laws and processes to implement their international human rights law obligations. Horizontal policy coherence means supporting and equipping departments and agencies, at both the national and sub-national levels, that shape business practices — including those responsible for corporate law and securities regulation, investment, export credit and insurance, trade and labour — to be informed of and act in a manner compatible with the Governments' human rights obligations.

(9) States should maintain adequate domestic policy space to meet their human rights obligations when pursuing business-related policy objectives with other States or business enterprises, for instance through investment treaties or contracts.

Commentary

Economic agreements concluded by States, either with other States or with business enterprises — such as bilateral investment treaties, free-trade agreements or contracts for investment projects — create economic opportunities for States. But they can also affect the domestic policy space of governments. For example, the terms of international investment agreements may constrain States from fully implementing new human rights legislation, or put them at risk of binding international arbitration if they do so. Therefore, States should ensure that they retain adequate policy and regulatory ability to protect human rights under the terms of such agreements, while providing the necessary investor protection.

(10) States, when acting as members of multilateral institutions that deal with business-related issues, should:

(a) Seek to ensure that those institutions neither restrain the ability of their member States to meet their duty to protect nor hinder business enterprises from respecting human rights;

(b) Encourage those institutions, within their respective mandates and capacities, to promote business respect for human rights and, where requested, to help States meet their duty to protect against human rights abuse by business enterprises, including through technical assistance, capacity-building and awareness-raising;

(c) Draw on these Guiding Principles to promote shared understanding and advance international cooperation in the management of business and human rights challenges.

Commentary

Greater policy coherence is also needed at the international level, including where States participate in multilateral institutions that deal with business-related issues, such as international trade and financial institutions. States retain their international human rights law obligations when they participate in such institutions.

Capacity-building and awareness-raising through such institutions can play a vital role in helping all States to fulfil their duty to protect, including by enabling the sharing of information about challenges and best practices, thus promoting more consistent approaches.

Collective action through multilateral institutions can help States level the playing field with regard to business respect for human rights, but it should do so by raising the performance of laggards. Cooperation between States, multilateral institutions and other stakeholders can also play an important role.

These Guiding Principles provide a common reference point in this regard, and could serve as a useful basis for building a cumulative positive effect that takes into account the respective roles and responsibilities of all relevant stakeholders.

II The Corporate Responsibility to Respect Human Rights

A Foundational Principles

(11) Business enterprises should respect human rights. This means that they should avoid infringing on the human rights of others and should address adverse human rights impacts with which they are involved.

Commentary

The responsibility to respect human rights is a global standard of expected conduct for all business enterprises wherever they operate. It exists independently of States' abilities and/or willingness to fulfil their own human rights obligations, and does not diminish those obligations. And it exists over and above compliance with national laws and regulations protecting human rights.

Addressing adverse human rights impacts requires taking adequate measures for their prevention, mitigation and, where appropriate, remediation.

Business enterprises may undertake other commitments or activities to support and promote human rights, which may contribute to the enjoyment of rights. But this does not offset a failure to respect human rights throughout their operations.

Business enterprises should not undermine States' abilities to meet their own human rights obligations, including by actions that might weaken the integrity of judicial processes.

(12) The responsibility of business enterprises to respect human rights refers to internationally recognized human rights — understood, at a minimum, as those expressed in the International Bill of Human Rights and the principles concerning fundamental rights set out in the International Labour Organization's Declaration on Fundamental Principles and Rights at Work.

Commentary

Because business enterprises can have an impact on virtually the entire spectrum of internationally recognized human rights, their responsibility to respect applies to all such rights. In practice, some human rights may be at greater risk than others in particular industries or contexts, and therefore will be the focus of heightened attention. However, situations may change, so all human rights should be the subject of periodic review.

An authoritative list of the core internationally recognized human rights is contained in the International Bill of Human Rights (consisting of the Universal Declaration of Human Rights and the main instruments through which it has been codified: the International Covenant on Civil and Political Rights and the International Covenant on Economic, Social and Cultural Rights), coupled with the principles concerning fundamental rights in the eight ILO core conventions as set out in the Declaration on Fundamental Principles and Rights at Work. These are the benchmarks against which other social actors assess the human rights impacts of business enterprises. The responsibility of business enterprises to respect human rights is distinct from issues of legal liability and enforcement, which remain defined largely by national law provisions in relevant jurisdictions.

Depending on circumstances, business enterprises may need to consider additional standards. For instance, enterprises should respect the human rights of individuals belonging to specific groups or populations that require particular attention, where they may have adverse human rights impacts on them. In this connection, United Nations instruments have elaborated further on the rights of indigenous peoples; women; national or ethnic, religious and linguistic minorities; children; persons with disabilities; and migrant workers and their families. Moreover, in situations of armed conflict enterprises should respect the standards of international humanitarian law.

(13) The responsibility to respect human rights requires that business enterprises:

(a) Avoid causing or contributing to adverse human rights impacts through their own activities, and address such impacts when they occur;

(b) Seek to prevent or mitigate adverse human rights impacts that are directly linked to their operations, products or services by their business relationships, even if they have not contributed to those impacts.

Commentary

Business enterprises may be involved with adverse human rights impacts either through their own activities or as a result of their business relationships with other parties. Guiding Principle 19 elaborates further on the implications for how business enterprises should address these situations. For the purpose of these Guiding Principles a business enterprise's "activities" are understood to include both actions and omissions; and its "business relationships" are understood to include relationships with business partners, entities in its value chain, and any other non-State or State entity directly linked to its business operations, products or services.

(14) The responsibility of business enterprises to respect human rights applies to all enterprises regardless of their size, sector, operational context, ownership and structure. Nevertheless, the scale and complexity of the means through which enterprises meet that responsibility may vary according to these factors and with the severity of the enterprise's adverse human rights impacts.

Commentary

The means through which a business enterprise meets its responsibility to respect human rights will be proportional to, among other factors, its size. Small and medium-sized enterprises may have less capacity as well as more informal processes and management structures than larger companies, so their respective policies and processes will take on different forms. But some small and medium-sized enterprises can have severe human rights impacts, which will require corresponding measures regardless of their size. Severity of impacts will be judged by their scale, scope and irremediable character. The means through which a business enterprise meets its responsibility to respect human rights may also vary depending on whether, and the extent to which, it conducts business through a corporate group or individually. However, the responsibility to respect human rights applies fully and equally to all business enterprises.

(15) In order to meet their responsibility to respect human rights, business enterprises should have in place policies and processes appropriate to their size and circumstances, including:

(a) A policy commitment to meet their responsibility to respect human rights;

(b) A human rights due-diligence process to identify, prevent, mitigate and account for how they address their impacts on human rights;

(c) Processes to enable the remediation of any adverse human rights impacts they cause or to which they contribute.

Commentary

Business enterprises need to know and show that they respect human rights. They cannot do so unless they have certain policies and processes in place. Principles 16 to 24 elaborate further on these.

B Operational Principles

Policy Commitment

(16) As the basis for embedding their responsibility to respect human rights, business enterprises should express their commitment to meet this responsibility through a statement of policy that:

(a) Is approved at the most senior level of the business enterprise;

(b) Is informed by relevant internal and/or external expertise;

(c) Stipulates the enterprise's human rights expectations of personnel, business partners and other parties directly linked to its operations, products or services;

(d) Is publicly available and communicated internally and externally to all personnel, business partners and other relevant parties;

(e) Is reflected in operational policies and procedures necessary to embed it throughout the business enterprise.

Commentary

The term "statement" is used generically, to describe whatever means an enterprise employs to set out publicly its responsibilities, commitments, and expectations.

The level of expertise required to ensure that the policy statement is adequately informed will vary according to the complexity of the business enterprise's operations. Expertise can be drawn from various sources, ranging from credible online or written resources to consultation with recognized experts.

The statement of commitment should be publicly available. It should be communicated actively to entities with which the enterprise has contractual relationships; others directly linked to its operations, which may include State security forces; investors; and, in the case of operations with significant human rights risks, to the potentially affected stakeholders.

Internal communication of the statement and of related policies and procedures should make clear what the lines and systems of accountability will be, and should be supported by any necessary training for personnel in relevant business functions.

Just as States should work towards policy coherence, so business enterprises need to strive for coherence between their responsibility to respect human rights and policies and procedures that govern their wider business activities and relationships. This should include, for example, policies and procedures that set financial and other performance incentives for personnel; procurement practices; and lobbying activities where human rights are at stake.

Through these and any other appropriate means, the policy statement should be embedded from the top of the business enterprise through all its functions, which otherwise may act without awareness or regard for human rights.

Human Rights Due Diligence

(17) In order to identify, prevent, mitigate and account for how they address their adverse human rights impacts, business enterprises should carry out human rights due diligence. The process should include assessing actual and potential human rights impacts, integrating and acting upon

the findings, tracking responses, and communicating how impacts are addressed. Human rights due diligence:

(a) Should cover adverse human rights impacts that the business enterprise may cause or contribute to through its own activities, or which may be directly linked to its operations, products or services by its business relationships;

(b) Will vary in complexity with the size of the business enterprise, the risk of severe human rights impacts, and the nature and context of its operations;

(c) Should be ongoing, recognizing that the human rights risks may change over time as the business enterprise's operations and operating context evolve.

Commentary

This principle defines the parameters for human rights due diligence, while Principles 18 through 21 elaborate its essential components.

Human rights risks are understood to be the business enterprise's potential adverse human rights impacts. Potential impacts should be addressed through prevention or mitigation, while actual impacts — those that have already occurred — should be a subject for remediation (Principle 22).

Human rights due diligence can be included within broader enterprise risk-management systems, provided that it goes beyond simply identifying and managing material risks to the company itself, to include risks to rights-holders.

Human rights due diligence should be initiated as early as possible in the development of a new activity or relationship, given that human rights risks can be increased or mitigated already at the stage of structuring contracts or other agreements, and may be inherited through mergers or acquisitions.

Where business enterprises have large numbers of entities in their value chains it may be unreasonably difficult to conduct due diligence for adverse human rights impacts across them all. If so, business enterprises should identify general areas where the risk of adverse human rights impacts is most significant, whether due to certain suppliers' or clients' operating context, the particular operations, products or services involved, or other relevant considerations, and prioritize these for human rights due diligence.

Questions of complicity may arise when a business enterprise contributes to, or is seen as contributing to, adverse human rights impacts caused by other parties. Complicity has both non-legal and legal meanings. As a non-legal matter, business enterprises may be perceived as being "complicit" in the acts of another party where, for example, they are seen to benefit from an abuse committed by that party.

As a legal matter, most national jurisdictions prohibit complicity in the commission of a crime, and a number allow for criminal liability of business enterprises in such cases. Typically, civil actions can also be based on an enterprise's alleged contribution to a harm, although these may not be framed in human rights terms. The weight of international criminal law jurisprudence indicates that the relevant standard for aiding and abetting is knowingly providing practical assistance or encouragement that has a substantial effect on the commission of a crime.

Conducting appropriate human rights due diligence should help business enterprises address the risk of legal claims against them by showing that they took every reasonable step to avoid involvement with an alleged human rights abuse. However, business enterprises conducting such due diligence should not assume that, by itself, this will automatically and fully absolve them from liability for causing or contributing to human rights abuses.

(18) In order to gauge human rights risks, business enterprises should identify and assess any actual or potential adverse human rights impacts with which they may be involved either through their own activities or as a result of their business relationships. This process should:

(a) Draw on internal and/or independent external human rights expertise;

(b) Involve meaningful consultation with potentially affected groups and other relevant stakeholders, as appropriate to the size of the business enterprise and the nature and context of the operation.

Commentary

The initial step in conducting human rights due diligence is to identify and assess the nature of the actual and potential adverse human rights impacts with which a business enterprise may be involved. The purpose is to understand the specific impacts on specific people, given a specific context of operations. Typically this includes assessing the human rights context prior to a proposed business activity, where possible; identifying who may be affected; cataloguing the relevant human rights standards and issues; and projecting how the proposed activity and associated business relationships could have adverse human rights impacts on those identified. In this process, business enterprises should pay special attention to any particular human rights impacts on individuals from groups or populations that may be at heightened risk of vulnerability or marginalization, and bear in mind the different risks that may be faced by women and men.

While processes for assessing human rights impacts can be incorporated within other processes such as risk assessments or environmental and social impact assessments, they should include all internationally recognized human rights as a reference point, since enterprises may potentially impact virtually any of these rights.

Because human rights situations are dynamic, assessments of human rights impacts should be undertaken at regular intervals: prior to a new activity or relationship; prior to major decisions or changes in the operation (e.g., market entry, product launch, policy change, or wider changes to the business); in response to or anticipation of changes in the operating environment (e.g., rising social tensions); and periodically throughout the life of an activity or relationship.

To enable business enterprises to assess their human rights impacts accurately, they should seek to understand the concerns of potentially affected stakeholders by consulting them directly in a manner that takes into account language and other potential barriers to effective engagement. In situations where such consultation is not possible, business enterprises should consider reasonable alternatives such as consulting credible, independent expert resources, including human rights defenders and others from civil society.

The assessment of human rights impacts informs subsequent steps in the human rights due diligence process.

(19) In order to prevent and mitigate adverse human rights impacts, business enterprises should integrate the findings from their impact assessments across relevant internal functions and processes, and take appropriate action.

(a) Effective integration requires that:

(i) Responsibility for addressing such impacts is assigned to the appropriate level and function within the business enterprise;

(ii) Internal decision-making, budget allocations and oversight processes enable effective responses to such impacts.

(b) Appropriate action will vary according to:

(i) Whether the business enterprise causes or contributes to an adverse impact, or whether it is involved solely because the impact is directly linked to its operations, products or services by a business relationship;

(ii) The extent of its leverage in addressing the adverse impact.

Commentary

The horizontal integration across the business enterprise of specific findings from assessing human rights impacts can only be effective if its human rights policy commitment has been embedded into all relevant business functions. This is required to ensure that the assessment findings are properly understood, given due weight, and acted upon.

In assessing human rights impacts, business enterprises will have looked for both actual and potential adverse impacts. Potential impacts should be prevented or mitigated through the horizontal integration of findings across the business enterprise, while actual impacts — those that have already occurred — should be a subject for remediation (Principle 22).

Where a business enterprise causes or may cause an adverse human rights impact, it should take the necessary steps to cease or prevent the impact.

Where a business enterprise contributes or may contribute to an adverse human rights impact, it should take the necessary steps to cease or prevent its contribution and use its leverage to mitigate any remaining impact to the greatest extent possible. Leverage is considered to exist where the enterprise has the ability to effect change in the wrongful practices of an entity that causes a harm.

Where a business enterprise has not contributed to an adverse human rights impact, but that impact is nevertheless directly linked to its operations, products or services by its business relationship with another entity, the situation is more complex. Among the factors that will enter into the determination of the appropriate action in such situations are the enterprise's leverage over the entity concerned, how crucial the relationship is to the enterprise, the severity of the abuse, and whether terminating the relationship with the entity itself would have adverse human rights consequences.

The more complex the situation and its implications for human rights, the stronger is the case for the enterprise to draw on independent expert advice in deciding how to respond.

If the business enterprise has leverage to prevent or mitigate the adverse impact, it should exercise it. And if it lacks leverage there may be ways for the enterprise to increase it. Leverage may be increased by, for example, offering capacity-building or other incentives to the related entity, or collaborating with other actors.

There are situations in which the enterprise lacks the leverage to prevent or mitigate adverse impacts and is unable to increase its leverage. Here, the enterprise should consider ending the relationship, taking into account credible assessments of potential adverse human rights impacts of doing so.

Where the relationship is "crucial" to the enterprise, ending it raises further challenges. A relationship could be deemed as crucial if it provides a product or service that is essential to the enterprise's business, and for which no reasonable alternative source exists. Here the severity of the adverse human rights impact must also be considered: the more severe the abuse, the more quickly the enterprise will need to see change before it takes a decision on whether it should end the relationship. In any case, for as long as the abuse continues and the enterprise remains in the relationship, it should be able to demonstrate its own ongoing efforts to mitigate the impact and be prepared to accept any consequences — reputational, financial or legal — of the continuing connection.

(20) In order to verify whether adverse human rights impacts are being addressed, business enterprises should track the effectiveness of their response. Tracking should:

(a) Be based on appropriate qualitative and quantitative indicators;

(b) Draw on feedback from both internal and external sources, including affected stakeholders.

Commentary

Tracking is necessary in order for a business enterprise to know if its human rights policies are being implemented optimally, whether it has responded effectively to the identified human rights impacts, and to drive continuous improvement.

Business enterprises should make particular efforts to track the effectiveness of their responses to impacts on individuals from groups or populations that may be at heightened risk of vulnerability or marginalization.

Tracking should be integrated into relevant internal reporting processes. Business enterprises might employ tools they already use in relation to other issues. This could include performance contracts and reviews as well as surveys and audits, using gender-disaggregated data where relevant. Operational-level grievance mechanisms can also provide important feedback on the effectiveness of the business enterprise's human rights due diligence from those directly affected (see Principle 29).

(21) In order to account for how they address their human rights impacts, business enterprises should be prepared to communicate this externally, particularly when concerns are raised by or on behalf of affected stakeholders. Business enterprises whose operations or operating contexts pose risks of severe human rights impacts should report formally on how they address them. In all instances, communications should:

(a) Be of a form and frequency that reflect an enterprise's human rights impacts and that are accessible to its intended audiences;

(b) Provide information that is sufficient to evaluate the adequacy of an enterprise's response to the particular human rights impact involved;

(c) In turn not pose risks to affected stakeholders, personnel or to legitimate requirements of commercial confidentiality.

Commentary

The responsibility to respect human rights requires that business enterprises have in place policies and processes through which they can both know and show that they respect human rights in practice. Showing involves communication, providing a measure of transparency and accountability to individuals or groups who may be impacted and to other relevant stakeholders, including investors.

Communication can take a variety of forms, including in-person meetings, online dialogues, consultation with affected stakeholders, and formal public reports. Formal reporting is itself evolving, from traditional annual reports and corporate responsibility/sustainability reports, to include on-line updates and integrated financial and non-financial reports.

Formal reporting by enterprises is expected where risks of severe human rights impacts exist, whether this is due to the nature of the business operations or operating contexts. The reporting should cover topics and indicators concerning how enterprises identify and address adverse impacts on human rights. Independent verification of human rights reporting can strengthen its content and credibility. Sector-specific indicators can provide helpful additional detail.

Remediation

(22) Where business enterprises identify that they have caused or contributed to adverse impacts, they should provide for or cooperate in their remediation through legitimate processes.

Commentary

Even with the best policies and practices, a business enterprise may cause or contribute to an adverse human rights impact that it has not foreseen or been able to prevent.

Where a business enterprise identifies such a situation, whether through its human rights due diligence process or other means, its responsibility to respect human rights requires active engagement in remediation, by itself or in cooperation with other actors. Operational-level grievance mechanisms for those potentially impacted by the business enterprise's activities can be one effective means of enabling remediation when they meet certain core criteria, as set out in Principle 31.

Where adverse impacts have occurred that the business enterprise has not caused or contributed to, but which are directly linked to its operations, products or services by a business relationship, the responsibility to respect human rights does not require that the enterprise itself provide for remediation, though it may take a role in doing so.

Some situations, in particular where crimes are alleged, typically will require cooperation with judicial mechanisms.

Further guidance on mechanisms through which remediation may be sought, including where allegations of adverse human rights impacts are contested, is included in Chapter III on access to remedy.

Issues of Context

(23) In all contexts, business enterprises should:

(a) Comply with all applicable laws and respect internationally recognized human rights, wherever they operate;

(b) Seek ways to honour the principles of internationally recognized human rights when faced with conflicting requirements;

(c) Treat the risk of causing or contributing to gross human rights abuses as a legal compliance issue wherever they operate.

Commentary

Although particular country and local contexts may affect the human rights risks of an enterprise's activities and business relationships, all business enterprises have the same responsibility to respect human rights wherever they operate. Where the domestic context renders it impossible to meet this responsibility fully, business enterprises are expected to respect the principles of internationally recognized human rights to the greatest extent possible in the circumstances, and to be able to demonstrate their efforts in this regard.

Some operating environments, such as conflict-affected areas, may increase the risks of enterprises being complicit in gross human rights abuses committed by other actors (security forces, for example). Business enterprises should treat this risk as a legal compliance issue, given the expanding web of potential corporate legal liability arising from extraterritorial civil claims, and from the incorporation of the provisions of the Rome Statute of the International Criminal Court in jurisdictions that provide for corporate criminal responsibility. In addition, corporate directors, officers and employees may be subject to individual liability for acts that amount to gross human rights abuses.

In complex contexts such as these, business enterprises should ensure that they do not exacerbate the situation. In assessing how best to respond, they will often be well advised to draw on not only expertise and cross-functional consultation within the enterprise, but also to consult externally with credible, independent experts, including from governments, civil society, national human rights institutions and relevant multi-stakeholder initiatives.

(24) Where it is necessary to prioritize actions to address actual and potential adverse human rights impacts, business enterprises should first seek to prevent and mitigate those that are most severe or where delayed response would make them irremediable.

Commentary

While business enterprises should address all their adverse human rights impacts, it may not always be possible to address them simultaneously. In the absence of specific legal guidance, if prioritization is necessary business enterprises should begin with those human rights impacts that would be most severe, recognizing that a delayed response may affect remediability. Severity is not an absolute concept in this context, but is relative to the other human rights impacts the business enterprise has identified.

III Access to Remedy

A Foundational Principle

(25) As part of their duty to protect against business-related human rights abuse, States must take appropriate steps to ensure, through judicial, administrative, legislative or other appropriate means, that when such abuses occur within their territory and/or jurisdiction those affected have access to effective remedy.

Commentary

Unless States take appropriate steps to investigate, punish and redress business-related human rights abuses when they do occur, the State duty to protect can be rendered weak or even meaningless.

Access to effective remedy has both procedural and substantive aspects. The remedies provided by the grievance mechanisms discussed in this Section may take a range of substantive forms the aim of which, generally speaking, will be to counteract or make good any human rights harms that have occurred. Remedy may include apologies, restitution, rehabilitation, financial or non-financial compensation and punitive sanctions (whether criminal or administrative, such as fines), as well as the prevention of harm through, for example, injunctions or guarantees of non-repetition. Procedures for the provision of remedy should be impartial, protected from corruption and free from political or other attempts to influence the outcome.

For the purpose of these Guiding Principles, a grievance is understood to be a perceived injustice evoking an individual's or a group's sense of entitlement, which may be based on law, contract, explicit or implicit promises, customary practice, or general notions of fairness of aggrieved communities. The term grievance mechanism is used to indicate any routinized, State-based or non-State-based, judicial or non-judicial process through which grievances concerning business-related human rights abuse can be raised and remedy can be sought.

State-based grievance mechanisms may be administered by a branch or agency of the State, or by an independent body on a statutory or constitutional basis. They may be judicial or non-judicial. In some mechanisms, those affected are directly involved in seeking remedy; in others, an intermediary seeks remedy on their behalf. Examples include the courts (for both criminal and civil actions), labour tribunals, National Human Rights Institutions, National Contact Points under the Guidelines for Multinational Enterprises of the Organization for Economic Cooperation and Development, many ombudsperson offices, and Government-run complaints offices.

Ensuring access to remedy for business-related human rights abuses requires also that States facilitate public awareness and understanding of these mechanisms, how they can be accessed, and any support (financial or expert) for doing so.

State-based judicial and non-judicial grievance mechanisms should form the foundation of a wider system of remedy. Within such a system, operational-level grievance mechanisms can provide early-stage recourse and resolution. State-based and operational-level mechanisms, in turn, can be supplemented or enhanced by the remedial functions of collaborative initiatives as well as those of international and regional human rights mechanisms. Further guidance with regard to these mechanisms is provided in Guiding Principles 26 to 31.

B Operational Principles

State-based Judicial Mechanisms

(26) States should take appropriate steps to ensure the effectiveness of domestic judicial mechanisms when addressing business-related human rights abuses, including considering ways to reduce legal, practical and other relevant barriers that could lead to a denial of access to remedy.

Commentary

Effective judicial mechanisms are at the core of ensuring access to remedy. Their ability to address business-related human rights abuses depends on their impartiality, integrity and ability to accord due process.

States should ensure that they do not erect barriers to prevent legitimate cases from being brought before the courts in situations where judicial recourse is an essential part of accessing remedy or alternative sources of effective remedy are unavailable. They should also ensure that the provision of justice is not prevented by corruption of the judicial process, that courts are independent of economic or political pressures from other State agents and from business actors, and that the legitimate and peaceful activities of human rights defenders are not obstructed.

Legal barriers that can prevent legitimate cases involving business-related human rights abuse from being addressed can arise where, for example:

- The way in which legal responsibility is attributed among members of a corporate group under domestic criminal and civil laws facilitates the avoidance of appropriate accountability;
- Where claimants face a denial of justice in a host State and cannot access home State courts regardless of the merits of the claim;
- Where certain groups, such as indigenous peoples and migrants, are excluded from the same level of legal protection of their human rights that applies to the wider population.

Practical and procedural barriers to accessing judicial remedy can arise where, for example:

- The costs of bringing claims go beyond being an appropriate deterrent to unmeritorious cases and/or cannot be reduced to reasonable levels through government support, "market-based" mechanisms (such as litigation insurance and legal fee structures), or other means;
- Claimants experience difficulty in securing legal representation, due to a lack of resources or of other incentives for lawyers to advise claimants in this area;
- There are inadequate options for aggregating claims or enabling representative proceedings (such as class actions and other collective action procedures), and this prevents effective remedy for individual claimants;
- State prosecutors lack adequate resources, expertise and support to meet the State's own obligations to investigate individual and business involvement in human rights-related crimes.

Many of these barriers are the result of, or compounded by, the frequent imbalances between the parties to business-related human rights claims, such as in their financial resources, access to information and expertise. Moreover, whether through active discrimination or as the unintended consequences of the way judicial mechanisms are designed and operate, individuals from groups or populations at heightened risk of vulnerability or marginalization often face additional cultural, social, physical and financial impediments to accessing, using and benefiting from these mechanisms. Particular attention should be given to the rights and specific needs of such groups or populations at each stage of the remedial process: access, procedures and outcome.

State-based Non-judicial Grievance Mechanisms

(27) States should provide effective and appropriate non-judicial grievance mechanisms, alongside judicial mechanisms, as part of a comprehensive State-based system for the remedy of business-related human rights abuse.

Commentary

Administrative, legislative and other non-judicial mechanisms play an essential role in complementing and supplementing judicial mechanisms. Even where judicial systems are effective and well-resourced, they cannot carry the burden of addressing all alleged abuses; judicial remedy is not always required; nor is it always the favoured approach for all claimants.

Gaps in the provision of remedy for business-related human rights abuses could be filled, where appropriate, by expanding the mandates of existing non-judicial mechanisms and/or by adding new mechanisms. These may be mediation-based, adjudicative or follow other culturally-appropriate and rights-compatible processes — or involve some combination of these — depending on the issues concerned, any public interest involved, and the potential needs of the parties. To ensure their effectiveness, they should meet the criteria set out in Principle 31.

National human rights institutions have a particularly important role to play in this regard.

As with judicial mechanisms, States should consider ways to address any imbalances between the parties to business-related human rights claims and any additional barriers to access faced by individuals from groups or populations at heightened risk of vulnerability or marginalization.

Non-State-based Grievance Mechanisms

(28) States should consider ways to facilitate access to effective non-State-based grievance mechanisms dealing with business-related human rights harms.

Commentary

One category of non-State-based grievance mechanisms encompasses those administered by a business enterprise alone or with stakeholders, by an industry association or a multi-stakeholder group. They are non-judicial, but may use adjudicative, dialogue-based or other culturally appropriate and rights-compatible processes. These mechanisms may offer particular benefits such as speed of access and remediation, reduced costs and/or transnational reach.

Another category comprises regional and international human rights bodies. These have dealt most often with alleged violations by States of their obligations to respect human rights. However, some have also dealt with the failure of a State to meet its duty to protect against human rights abuse by business enterprises.

States can play a helpful role in raising awareness of, or otherwise facilitating access to, such options, alongside the mechanisms provided by States themselves.

(29) To make it possible for grievances to be addressed early and remediated directly, business enterprises should establish or participate in effective operational-level grievance mechanisms for individuals and communities who may be adversely impacted.

Commentary

Operational-level grievance mechanisms are accessible directly to individuals and communities who may be adversely impacted by a business enterprise. They are typically administered by enterprises, alone or in collaboration with others, including relevant stakeholders. They may also be provided through recourse to a mutually acceptable external expert or body. They do not require that those bringing a complaint first access other means of recourse. They can engage the business enterprise directly in assessing the issues and seeking remediation of any harm.

Operational-level grievance mechanisms perform two key functions regarding the responsibility of business enterprises to respect human rights.

- First, they support the identification of adverse human rights impacts as a part of an enterprise's on-going human rights due diligence. They do so by providing a channel for those directly impacted by the enterprise's operations to raise concerns when they believe they are being or will be adversely impacted. By analysing trends and patterns in complaints, business enterprises can also identify systemic problems and adapt their practices accordingly
- Second, these mechanisms make it possible for grievances, once identified, to be addressed and for adverse impacts to be remediated early and directly by the business enterprise, thereby preventing harms from compounding and grievances from escalating.

Such mechanisms need not require that a complaint or grievance amount to an alleged human rights abuse before it can be raised, but specifically aim to identify any legitimate concerns of those who may be adversely impacted. If those concerns are not identified and addressed, they may over time escalate into more major disputes and human rights abuses.

Operational-level grievance mechanisms should reflect certain criteria to ensure their effectiveness in practice (Principle 31). These criteria can be met through many different forms of grievance mechanism according to the demands of scale, resource, sector, culture and other parameters.

Operational-level grievance mechanisms can be important complements to wider stakeholder engagement and collective bargaining processes, but cannot substitute for either. They should not be used to undermine the role of legitimate trade unions in addressing labour-related disputes, nor to preclude access to judicial or other non-judicial grievance mechanisms.

(30) Industry, multi-stakeholder and other collaborative initiatives that are based on respect for human rights-related standards should ensure that effective grievance mechanisms are available.

Commentary

Human rights-related standards are increasingly reflected in commitments undertaken by industry bodies, multi-stakeholder and other collaborative initiatives, through codes of conduct, performance standards, global framework agreements between trade unions and transnational corporations, and similar undertakings.

Such collaborative initiatives should ensure the availability of effective mechanisms through which affected parties or their legitimate representatives can raise concerns when they believe the commitments in question have not been met. The legitimacy of such initiatives may be put at risk if they do not provide for such mechanisms. The mechanisms could be at the level of individual members, of the collaborative initiative, or both. These mechanisms should provide for accountability and help enable the remediation of adverse human rights impacts.

Effectiveness Criteria for Non-judicial Grievance Mechanisms

(31) In order to ensure their effectiveness, non-judicial grievance mechanisms, both State-based and non-State-based, should be:

(a) Legitimate: enabling trust from the stakeholder groups for whose use they are intended, and being accountable for the fair conduct of grievance processes;

(b) Accessible: being known to all stakeholder groups for whose use they are intended, and providing adequate assistance for those who may face particular barriers to access;

(c) Predictable: providing a clear and known procedure with an indicative timeframe for each stage, and clarity on the types of process and outcome available and means of monitoring implementation;

(d) Equitable: seeking to ensure that aggrieved parties have reasonable access to sources of information, advice and expertise necessary to engage in a grievance process on fair, informed and respectful terms;

(e) Transparent: keeping parties to a grievance informed about its progress, and providing sufficient information about the mechanism's performance to build confidence in its effectiveness and meet any public interest at stake;

(f) Rights-compatible: ensuring that outcomes and remedies accord with internationally recognized human rights;

(g) A source of continuous learning: drawing on relevant measures to identify lessons for improving the mechanism and preventing future grievances and harms;

Operational-level mechanisms should also be:

(h) Based on engagement and dialogue: consulting the stakeholder groups for whose use they are intended on their design and performance, and focusing on dialogue as the means to address and resolve grievances.

Commentary

A grievance mechanism can only serve its purpose if the people it is intended to serve know about it, trust it and are able to use it. These criteria provide a benchmark for designing, revising or assessing a non-judicial grievance mechanism to help ensure that it is effective in practice. Poorly designed or implemented grievance mechanisms can risk compounding a sense of grievance amongst affected stakeholders by heightening their sense of disempowerment and disrespect by the process.

The first seven criteria apply to any State-based or non-State-based, adjudicative or dialogue-based mechanism. The eighth criterion is specific to operational-level mechanisms that business enterprises help administer.

The term "grievance mechanism" is used here as a term of art. The term itself may not always be appropriate or helpful when applied to a specific mechanism, but the criteria for effectiveness remain the same. Commentary on the specific criteria follows:

(a) Stakeholders for whose use a mechanism is intended must trust it if they are to choose to use it. Accountability for ensuring that the parties to a grievance process cannot interfere with its fair conduct is typically one important factor in building stakeholder trust;

(b) Barriers to access may include a lack of awareness of the mechanism, language, literacy, costs, physical location and fears of reprisal;

(c) In order for a mechanism to be trusted and used, it should provide public information about the procedure it offers. Timeframes for each stage should be respected wherever possible, while allowing that flexibility may sometimes be needed;

(d) In grievances or disputes between business enterprises and affected stakeholders, the latter frequently have much less access to information and expert resources, and often lack the financial resources to pay for them. Where this imbalance is not redressed, it can reduce both the achievement and perception of a fair process and make it harder to arrive at durable solutions;

(e) Communicating regularly with parties about the progress of individual grievances can be essential to retaining confidence in the process. Providing transparency about the mechanism's performance to wider stakeholders, through statistics, case studies or more detailed information about the handling of certain cases, can be important to demonstrate its legitimacy and retain broad trust. At the same time, confidentiality of the dialogue between parties and of individuals' identities should be provided where necessary;

(f) Grievances are frequently not framed in terms of human rights and many do not initially raise human rights concerns. Regardless, where outcomes have implications for human rights, care should be taken to ensure that they are in line with internationally recognized human rights;

(g) Regular analysis of the frequency, patterns and causes of grievances can enable the institution administering the mechanism to identify and influence policies, procedures or practices that should be altered to prevent future harm;

(h) For an operational-level grievance mechanism, engaging with affected stakeholder groups about its design and performance can help to ensure that it meets their needs, that they will use it in practice, and that there is a shared interest in ensuring its success. Since a business enterprise cannot, with legitimacy, both be the subject of complaints and unilaterally determine their outcome, these mechanisms should focus on reaching agreed solutions through dialogue. Where adjudication is needed, this should be provided by a legitimate, independent third-party mechanism.

ILO TRIPARTITE DECLARATION OF PRINCIPLES CONCERNING MULTINATIONAL ENTERPRISES AND SOCIAL POLICY

(Adopted: November 1977; Amended: November 2000, March 2006, and March 2017)

The International Labour Organization (ILO), with its unique tripartite structure, its competence, and its long-standing experience in the social field, has an essential role to play in evolving principles for the guidance of governments, employers' and workers' organizations, and multinational enterprises themselves.

The Governing Body of the International Labour Office approved the Tripartite Declaration of Principles concerning Multinational Enterprises and Social Policy at its 204th Session (November 1977) and subsequently amended it at its 279th Session (November 2000) and 295th Session (March 2006). The Governing Body decides at its 329th Session (March 2017) to further amend the Declaration taking account of developments since the previous update in 2006 within the ILO such as the ILO Declaration on Social Justice for a Fair Globalization, adopted by the International Labour Conference (ILC) in 2008, new international labour standards, the ILC Conclusions concerning the promotion of sustainable enterprises (2007) and the ILC Conclusions concerning decent work in global supply chains (2016); as well as the Guiding Principles on Business and Human Rights: Implementing the United Nations "Protect,

Respect and Remedy" Framework (2011) and the goals and targets of the 2030 Agenda for Sustainable Development (2015) that are particularly relevant to the Declaration; and noting the Addis Ababa Action Agenda (2015) on financing for development, the Paris Agreement (2015) concerning climate change, and the OECD Guidelines for Multinational Enterprises (as revised in 2011). The Governing Body approves the following revised Tripartite Declaration of Principles concerning Multinational Enterprises and Social Policy, which may be cited as the MNE Declaration, and invites governments of States Members of the ILO, the employers' and workers' organizations concerned and the multinational enterprises operating in their territories to observe the principles embodied therein.

Aim and Scope

(1) Multinational enterprises play an important part in the economies of most countries and in international economic relations. This is of increasing interest to governments as well as to employers and workers and their respective organizations. Through international direct investment, trade and other means, such enterprises can bring substantial benefits to home and host countries by contributing to the more efficient utilization of capital, technology and labour. Within the framework of sustainable development policies established by governments, they can also make an important contribution to the promotion of economic and social welfare; to the improvement of living standards and the satisfaction of basic needs; to the creation of employment opportunities, both directly and indirectly; and to the enjoyment of human rights, including freedom of association, throughout the world. On the other hand, the advances made by multinational enterprises in organizing their operations beyond the national framework may lead to abuse of concentrations of economic power and to conflicts with national policy objectives and with the interest of the workers. In addition, the complexity of multinational enterprises and the difficulty of clearly perceiving their diverse structures, operations and policies sometimes give rise to concern either in the home or in the host countries, or in both.

(2) The aim of this Declaration is to encourage the positive contribution which multinational enterprises can make to economic and social progress and the realization of decent work for all; and to minimize and resolve the difficulties to which their various operations may give rise.

(3) This aim will be furthered by appropriate laws and policies, measures and actions adopted by the governments, including in the fields of labour administration and public labour inspection, and by cooperation among the governments and the employers' and workers' organizations of all countries.

(4) The principles of this Declaration are intended to guide governments, employers' and workers' organizations of home and host countries and multinational enterprises in taking measures and actions and adopting social policies, including those based on the principles laid down in the Constitution and the relevant Conventions and Recommendations of the ILO, to further social progress and decent work.

(5) These principles do not aim at introducing or maintaining inequalities of treatment between multinational and national enterprises. They reflect good practice for all. Multinational and national enterprises, wherever the principles of the MNE Declaration are relevant to both, should be subject to the same expectations in respect of their conduct in general and their social practices in particular.

(6) To serve its purpose the MNE Declaration does not require a precise legal definition of multinational enterprises; this paragraph is designed to facilitate the understanding of the Declaration and not to provide such a definition. Multinational enterprises include enterprises — whether fully or partially state-owned or privately owned — which own or control production, distribution, services or other facilities outside the country in which they are based. They may be large or small; and can have their headquarters in any part of the world. The degree of autonomy of entities within multinational enterprises in relation to each other varies widely from one such enterprise to another, depending on the nature of the links between such entities and their fields of activity and having regard to the great diversity in the form of ownership, in the size, in the nature and location of the operations of the enterprises concerned. Unless otherwise specified, the term "multinational enterprise" is used in this Declaration to designate the various entities (parent companies or local entities or both or the organization as a whole) according to the distribution of responsibilities among them, in the expectation that they will cooperate and provide assistance to one another as necessary to facilitate observance of the principles laid down in this Declaration. In that regard, it also recognizes that multinational enterprises often operate through relationships with other enterprises as part of their overall production process and, as such, can contribute to further the aim of this Declaration.

(7) This Declaration sets out principles in the fields of employment, training, conditions of work and life, and industrial relations which governments, employers' and workers' organizations and multinational enterprises are recommended to observe on a voluntary basis; its principles shall not limit or otherwise affect obligations arising out of ratification of any ILO Convention.

General Policies

(8) All the parties concerned by the MNE Declaration should respect the sovereign rights of States, obey the national laws and regulations, give due consideration to local practices and respect relevant international standards. They should also honour commitments which they have freely entered into, in conformity with the national law and accepted international obligations. They should respect the Universal Declaration of Human Rights (1948) and the corresponding International Covenants (1966) adopted by the General Assembly of the United Nations as well as the Constitution of the International Labour Organization and its principles according to which freedom of expression and association are essential to sustained progress.

(9) All parties should contribute to the realization of the ILO Declaration on Fundamental Principles and Rights at Work and its Follow-up, adopted in 1998. All Members, even if they have not ratified the fundamental Conventions in question, have an obligation, arising from the very fact

of membership in the Organization, to respect, to promote and to realize, in good faith and in accordance with the Constitution, the principles concerning the fundamental rights which are the subject of those Conventions, namely: (a) freedom of association and the effective recognition of the right to collective bargaining; (b) the elimination of all forms of forced or compulsory labour; (c) the effective abolition of child labour; and (d) the elimination of discrimination in respect of employment and occupation. Governments of States which have not yet ratified the Conventions concerning fundamental principles and rights at work recognized in the 1998 Declaration are urged to do so. Multinational enterprises, through their operations, can contribute significantly to the attainment of its objectives.

(10) The principles set out in the MNE Declaration are commended to governments, employers' and workers' organizations of home and host countries and to multinational enterprises themselves. The principles thereby reflect the fact that different actors have a specific role to play. In this regard for the purpose of this Declaration:

(a) The Guiding Principles on Business and Human Rights: Implementing the United Nations "Protect, Respect and Remedy" Framework (2011) outline the respective duties and responsibilities of States and enterprises on human rights. These principles are grounded in recognition of: (i) States' existing obligations to respect, protect and fulfil human rights and fundamental freedoms ("the State duty to protect human rights"); (ii) the role of enterprises as specialized organs of society performing specialized functions, required to comply with all applicable laws and to respect human rights ("the corporate responsibility to respect human rights"); and (iii) the need for rights and obligations to be matched to appropriate and effective remedies when breached ("Access to remedy").

(b) The Guiding Principles apply to all States and to all enterprises, both multinational and others, regardless of their size, sector, operational context, ownership and structure.

(c) The corporate responsibility to respect human rights requires that enterprises, including multinational enterprises wherever they operate: (i) avoid causing or contributing to adverse impacts through their own activities, and address such impacts when they occur; and (ii) seek to prevent or mitigate adverse human rights impacts that are directly linked to their operations, products or services by their business relationships, even if they have not contributed to those impacts.

(d) Enterprises, including multinational enterprises, should carry out due diligence to identify, prevent, mitigate and account for how they address their actual and potential adverse impacts that relate to internationally recognized human rights, understood, at a minimum, as those expressed in the International Bill of Human Rights and the principles concerning fundamental rights set out in the ILO Declaration on Fundamental Principles and Rights at Work.

(e) In order to gauge human rights risks, enterprises — including multinational enterprises — should identify and assess any actual or potential adverse human rights impacts with which they may be involved either through their own activities or as a result of their business relationships. This process should involve meaningful consultation with potentially affected groups and other relevant stakeholders including workers' organizations, as appropriate to the size of the enterprise and the nature and context of the operation. For the purpose of achieving the aim of the MNE Declaration, this process should take account of the central role of freedom of association and collective bargaining as well as industrial relations and social dialogue as an ongoing process.

(11) Multinational enterprises should take fully into account established general policy objectives of the countries in which they operate. Their activities should be consistent with national law and in harmony with the development priorities and social aims and structure of the country in which they operate. To this effect, consultations should be held between multinational enterprises, the government and, wherever appropriate, the national employers' and workers' organizations concerned.

(12) Governments of host countries should promote good social practice in accordance with this Declaration among multinational enterprises operating in their territories. Governments of home countries should promote good social practice in accordance with this Declaration among their multinational enterprises operating abroad, having regard to the social and labour law, regulations and practices in host countries as well as to relevant international standards. Both host and home country governments should be prepared to have consultations with each other, whenever the need arises, on the initiative of either.

Employment

Employment Promotion

(13) With a view to stimulating sustainable economic growth and development, raising living standards, meeting employment requirements and overcoming unemployment and underemployment, governments should declare and pursue, as a major goal, an active policy designed to promote full, productive and freely chosen employment, and decent work.

(14) This is particularly important in the case of host country governments where the problems of unemployment and underemployment are most serious, and in particular in developing areas of the world. In this connection, the Global Employment Agenda (2003), the ILC Conclusions concerning the promotion of sustainable enterprises (2007), the Global Jobs Pact (2009) and Goal 8 of the Sustainable Development Goals should be kept in mind.

(15) Paragraphs (13) and (14) above establish the framework within which due attention should be paid, in both home and host countries, to the employment impact of multinational enterprises.

(16) Multinational enterprises, particularly when operating in developing countries, should endeavour to increase employment opportunities and standards, taking into account the employment policies and objectives of the governments, as well as security of employment and the long-term development of the enterprise.

(17) Before starting operations, multinational enterprises should, wherever appropriate, consult the competent authorities and the national employers' and workers' organizations in order to keep their employment plans, as far as practicable, in harmony with national social development policies. Such consultation, as in the case of national enterprises, should continue between the multinational enterprises and all parties concerned, including the workers' organizations.

(18) Multinational enterprises should give priority to the employment, occupational development, promotion and advancement of nationals of the host country at all levels in cooperation, as appropriate, with representatives of the workers employed by them or of the organizations of these workers and governmental authorities.

(19) Multinational enterprises, when investing in developing countries, should have regard to the importance of using technologies which generate employment, both directly and indirectly. To the extent permitted by the nature of the process and the conditions prevailing in the economic sector concerned, they should adapt technologies to the needs and characteristics of the host countries. They should also, where possible, take part in the development of appropriate technology in host countries.

(20) To promote employment in developing countries, in the context of an expanding world economy, multinational enterprises, wherever practicable, should give consideration to the conclusion of contracts with national enterprises for the manufacture of parts and equipment, to the use of local raw materials and to the progressive promotion of the local processing of raw materials. Such arrangements should not be used by multinational enterprises to avoid the responsibilities embodied in the principles of this Declaration.

(21) Governments should develop and implement an integrated policy framework to facilitate the transition to the formal economy, recognizing that decent work deficits are most pronounced in the informal economy. Multinational and other enterprises should also contribute to this aim.

Social Security

(22) Governments should establish and maintain, as applicable, social protection floors as a fundamental element of their national social security systems; and implement social protection floors within strategies for the extension of social security that progressively ensure higher levels of social security to as many people as possible, guided by ILO social security standards. Social partners could play a role in promoting these policies. Multinational and other enterprises could complement public social security systems and help to stimulate further their development, including through their own employer-sponsored programmes.

Elimination of Forced or Compulsory Labour

(23) Governments should take effective measures to prevent and eliminate forced labour, to provide to victims protection and access to appropriate and effective remedies, such as compensation and rehabilitation, and to sanction the perpetrators of forced or compulsory labour. Governments should develop a national policy and plan of action, in consultation with employers' and workers' organizations. This shall involve systematic action by the competent authorities and, as appropriate, in coordination with employers' and workers' organizations, as well as with other groups concerned.

(24) In order to suppress forced or compulsory labour, governments should provide guidance and support to employers and enterprises to take effective measures to identify, prevent, mitigate and account for how they address the risks of forced and compulsory labour in their operations or in products, services or operations in which they may be directly linked.

(25) Multinational as well as national enterprises should take immediate and effective measures within their own competence to secure the prohibition and elimination of forced or compulsory labour in their operations.

Effective Abolition of Child Labour: Minimum Age and Worst Forms

(26) Governments should develop a national policy designed to ensure the effective abolition of child labour; take immediate and effective measures to secure the prohibition and elimination of the worst forms of child labour as a matter of urgency; and progressively raise the minimum age for admission to employment or work to a level consistent with the fullest physical and mental development of young persons.

(27) Multinational enterprises, as well as national enterprises, should respect the minimum age for admission to employment or work in order to secure the effective abolition of child labour in their operations and should take immediate and effective measures within their own competence to secure the prohibition and elimination of the worst forms of child labour as a matter of urgency.

Equality of Opportunity and Treatment

(28) Governments should pursue policies designed to promote equality of opportunity and treatment in employment, with a view to eliminating any discrimination based on race, colour, sex, religion, political opinion, national extraction or social origin.

(29) Governments should promote equal remuneration for men and women workers for work of equal value.

(30) Multinational enterprises should be guided by the principle of non-discrimination throughout their operations without prejudice to the measures envisaged in paragraph (18) or to government policies designed to correct historical patterns of discrimination and thereby to extend equality of opportunity and treatment in employment. Multinational enterprises should accordingly make qualifications, skill and experience the basis for the recruitment, placement, training and advancement of their staff at all levels.

(31) Governments should never require or encourage multinational enterprises to discriminate on any of the grounds mentioned in paragraph (28), and continuing guidance from governments, where appropriate, on the avoidance of such discrimination in employment is encouraged.

Security of Employment

(32) Governments should carefully study the impact of multinational enterprises on employment in different industrial sectors. Governments, as well as multinational enterprises themselves, in all countries should take suitable measures to deal with the employment and labour market impacts of the operations of multinational enterprises.

(33) Multinational enterprises as well as national enterprises, through active employment planning, should endeavour to provide stable employment for workers employed by each enterprise and should observe freely negotiated obligations concerning employment stability and social security. In view of the flexibility which multinational enterprises may have, they should strive to assume a leading role in promoting security of employment, particularly in countries where the discontinuation of operations is likely to accentuate long-term unemployment.

(34) In considering changes in operations (including those resulting from mergers, takeovers or transfers of production) which would have major employment effects, multinational enterprises should provide reasonable notice of such changes to the appropriate government authorities and representatives of the workers in their employment and their organizations so that the implications may be examined jointly in order to mitigate adverse effects to the greatest possible extent. This is particularly important in the case of the closure of an entity involving collective lay-offs or dismissals.

(35) Arbitrary dismissal procedures should be avoided.

(36) Governments, in cooperation with multinational as well as national enterprises, should provide some form of income protection for workers whose employment has been terminated.

Training

(37) Governments, in cooperation with all the parties concerned, should develop national policies for vocational training and guidance, closely linked with employment. This is the framework within which multinational enterprises should pursue their training policies.

(38) In their operations, multinational enterprises should ensure that relevant training is provided for all levels of workers employed by them in the host country, as appropriate, to meet the needs of the enterprise as well as the development policies of the country. Such training should, to the extent possible, develop generally useful skills and promote career opportunities and lifelong learning. This responsibility should be carried out, where appropriate, in cooperation with the authorities of the country, employers' and workers' organizations and the competent local, national or international institutions.

(39) Multinational enterprises operating in developing countries should participate, along with national enterprises, in programmes, including special funds, encouraged by host governments and supported by employers' and workers' organizations. These programmes should have the aim

of encouraging skill formation, lifelong learning and development as well as providing vocational guidance, and should be jointly administered by the parties which support them. Wherever practicable, multinational enterprises should make the services of skilled resource personnel available to help in training programmes organized by governments as part of a contribution to national development.

(40) Multinational enterprises, with the cooperation of governments and to the extent consistent with the efficient operation of the enterprise, should afford opportunities within the enterprise as a whole to broaden the experience of local management in suitable fields such as industrial relations.

Conditions of Work and Life

Wages, Benefits and Conditions of Work

(41) Wages, benefits and conditions of work offered by multinational enterprises across their operations should be not less favourable to the workers than those offered by comparable employers in the host country. Where comparable employers do not exist, they should provide the best possible wages, benefits and conditions of work. The elements to be taken into consideration should include: (a) the needs of workers and their families, taking into account the general level of wages in the country, the cost of living, social security benefits, and the relative living standards of other social groups; and (b) economic factors, including the requirements of economic development, levels of productivity and the desirability of attaining and maintaining a high level of employment. Where the employer provides workers with basic amenities such as housing, medical care or food, these amenities should be of a good standard.

(42) Governments, especially in developing countries, should endeavour to adopt suitable measures to ensure that lower income groups and less developed areas benefit as much as possible from the activities of multinational enterprises.

Safety and Health

(43) Governments should ensure that both multinational and national enterprises provide adequate safety and health standards and contribute to a preventative safety and health culture in enterprises progressively achieving a safe and healthy working environment. This would include steps to combat workplace violence against women and men and attention to building safety. The relevant international labour standards, including the list of occupational diseases, and the ILO codes of practice and guidelines in the current list of ILO publications on occupational safety and health, should also be taken into account. Compensation should be provided to workers who have been victims of occupational accidents or diseases.

(44) Multinational enterprises should maintain the highest standards of safety and health, in conformity with national requirements, bearing in mind their relevant experience within the enterprise as a whole, including any knowledge of special hazards. They should also make available to the representatives of the workers, and upon request, to the competent authorities and the workers' and employers' organizations in all countries in which they operate, information on the safety and health standards relevant to their local operations, which they observe in other countries. In particular, they should make known to those concerned any special hazards and related protective measures associated with new products and processes. They, like comparable domestic enterprises, should be expected to play a leading role in the examination of causes of industrial safety and health hazards and in the application of resulting improvements within the enterprise as a whole.

(45) Multinational enterprises should cooperate in the work of international organizations concerned with the preparation and adoption of international safety and health standards.

(46) In accordance with national practice, multinational enterprises should cooperate fully with the competent safety and health authorities, the representatives of the workers and their organizations, and established safety and health organizations. Where appropriate, matters relating to safety and health should be incorporated in agreements with the representatives of the workers and their organizations.

Industrial Relations

(47) Multinational enterprises should observe standards of industrial relations throughout their operations.

Freedom of Association and the Right to Organize

(48) Workers employed by multinational enterprises as well as those employed by national enterprises should, without distinction whatsoever, have the right to establish and, subject only to the rules of the organization concerned, to join organizations of their own choosing without previous authorization. They should also enjoy adequate protection against acts of anti-union discrimination in respect of their employment.

(49) Organizations representing multinational enterprises or the workers in their employment should enjoy adequate protection against any acts of interference by each other or each other's agents or members in their establishment, functioning or administration.

(50) Where appropriate, in the local circumstances, multinational enterprises should support representative employers' organizations.

(51) Governments, where they do not already do so, are urged to apply the principles of Convention No. 87, Article 5, in view of the importance, in relation to multinational enterprises, of permitting organizations representing such enterprises or the workers in their employment to affiliate with international organizations of employers and workers of their own choosing.

(52) Where governments of host countries offer special incentives to attract foreign investment, these incentives should not include any limitation of the workers' freedom of association or the right to organize and bargain collectively.

(53) Representatives of the workers in multinational and national enterprises should not be hindered from meeting for consultation and exchange of views among themselves, provided that the functioning of the operations of the enterprise and the normal procedures which govern relationships with representatives of the workers and their organizations are not thereby prejudiced.

(54) Governments should not restrict the entry of representatives of employers' and workers' organizations who come from other countries at the invitation of the local or national organizations concerned for the purpose of consultation on matters of mutual concern, solely on the grounds that they seek entry in that capacity.

Collective Bargaining

(55) Workers employed by multinational enterprises should have the right, in accordance with national law and practice, to have representative organizations of their own choosing recognized for the purpose of collective bargaining.

(56) Measures appropriate to national conditions should be taken to encourage and promote the full development and utilization of machinery for voluntary negotiation between employers or employers' organizations and workers' organizations, with a view to the regulation of terms and conditions of employment by means of collective agreements.

(57) Multinational enterprises, as well as national enterprises, should provide workers' representatives with such facilities as may be necessary to assist in the development of effective collective agreements.

(58) Multinational enterprises should enable duly authorized representatives of the workers in their employment in each of the countries in which they operate to conduct negotiations with representatives of management who are authorized to take decisions on the matters under negotiation.

(59) Multinational enterprises, in the context of bona fide negotiations with the workers' representatives on conditions of employment, or while workers are exercising the right to organize, should not threaten to utilize a capacity to transfer the whole or part of an operating unit from the country concerned in order to influence unfairly those negotiations or to hinder the exercise of the right to organize; nor should they transfer workers from affiliates in foreign countries with a view to undermining bona fide negotiations with the workers' representatives or the workers' exercise of their right to organize.

(60) Collective agreements should include provisions for the settlement of disputes arising over their interpretation and application and for ensuring mutually respected rights and responsibilities.

(61) Multinational enterprises should provide workers' representatives with information required for meaningful negotiations with the entity involved and, where this accords with local law and practices, should also provide information to enable them to obtain a true and fair view of the performance of the entity or, where appropriate, of the enterprise as a whole.

(62) Governments should supply to the representatives of workers' organizations on request, where law and practice so permit, information on the industries in which the enterprise operates, which would help in laying down objective criteria in the collective bargaining process. In this context, multinational as well as national enterprises should respond constructively to requests by governments for relevant information on their operations.

Consultation

(63) In multinational as well as in national enterprises, systems devised by mutual agreement between employers and workers and their representatives should provide, in accordance with national law and practice, for regular consultation on matters of mutual concern. Such consultation should not be a substitute for collective bargaining.

Access to Remedy and Examination of Grievances

(64) As part of their duty to protect against business-related human rights abuses, governments should take appropriate steps to ensure, through judicial, administrative, legislative or other appropriate means, that when such abuses occur within their territory and/or jurisdiction any affected worker or workers have access to effective remedy.

(65) Multinational enterprises should use their leverage to encourage their business partners to provide effective means of enabling remediation for abuses of internationally recognized human rights.

(66) Multinational as well as national enterprises should respect the right of the workers whom they employ to have all their grievances processed in a manner consistent with the following provision: any worker who, acting individually or jointly with other workers, considers that he or she has grounds for a grievance should have the right to submit such grievance without suffering any prejudice whatsoever as a result, and to have such grievance examined pursuant to an appropriate procedure. This is particularly important whenever the multinational enterprises operate in countries which do not abide by the principles of ILO Conventions pertaining to freedom of association, to the right to organize and bargain collectively, to discrimination, to child labour and to forced labour.

Settlement of Industrial Disputes

(67) Governments should ensure that voluntary conciliation and arbitration machinery, appropriate to national conditions, is made available to assist in the prevention and settlement of industrial disputes between employers and workers. The procedure should be free of charge and expeditious.

(68) Multinational as well as national enterprises jointly with the representatives and organizations of the workers whom they employ should seek to establish voluntary conciliation machinery, appropriate to national conditions, which may include provisions for voluntary arbitration, to assist in the prevention and settlement of industrial disputes between employers and workers. The voluntary conciliation machinery should include equal representation of employers and workers.

PART III

SELECTED HONG KONG HUMAN RIGHTS ORDINANCES

Introduction

Part III contains a selection of Hong Kong ordinances that are relevant to the protection of human rights and civil liberties of local residents. Each of these ordinance is outlined in a separate Section.

Section I The Hong Kong Bill of Rights

Section I comprises the Hong Kong Bill of Rights Ordinance (Cap. 383), which was enacted in 1991. For the first time, most of the provisions of the International Covenant on Civil and Political Rights (ICCPR) were implemented in Hong Kong and could be directly enforced in local courts. While the effect of the ordinance was later weakened by the NPCSC Decision to abolish certain Sections of the ordinance (see Part I, Section II, Instrument 6), the Hong Kong courts have stated that the Bill of Rights is now "entrenched" by Article 39 of the Basic Law.*

Section II Anti-discrimination Ordinances

Section II includes the four major ordinances in Hong Kong that serve to materialize the general principles of anti-discrimination contained in the Hong Kong Bill of Rights Ordinance. These ordinances are: the Sex Discrimination Ordinance (Cap. 480), the Disability Discrimination Ordinance (Cap. 487), the Family Status Discrimination Ordinance (Cap. 527), and the Race Discrimination Ordinance (Cap. 602).

1 *Swire Properties Ltd and others v The Secretary for Justice* [2003] HKCFA 48, para. 53

SECTION I
HONG KONG BILL OF RIGHTS ORDINANCE
(CAP. 383)

An Ordinance to provide for the incorporation into the law of Hong Kong of provisions of the International Covenant on Civil and Political Rights as applied to Hong Kong; and for ancillary and connected matters.

[8 June 1991]

(Format changes — E.R. 1 of 2017)

(Enacting provision omitted — E.R. 1 of 2017)

Part I Preliminary

Section 1 Short Title

(Amended E.R. 1 of 2017)

(1) This Ordinance may be cited as the Hong Kong Bill of Rights Ordinance.

(2) *(Omitted as spent — E.R. 1 of 2017)*

Section 2 Interpretation

(1) In this Ordinance, unless the context otherwise requires —

Article means an Article of the Bill of Rights;

Bill of Rights (人權法案) means the Hong Kong Bill of Rights set out in Part II;

commencement date (生效日期) means the date on which this Ordinance comes into operation;

legislation (法例) means legislation that can be amended by an Ordinance;

pre-existing legislation (先前法例) means legislation enacted before the commencement date.

(2) The Bill of Rights is subject to Part III.

(3) *(Not adopted as the Laws of the HKSAR)**

(4) Nothing in this Ordinance shall be interpreted as implying for the Government or any authority, group or person any right to engage in any activity or perform any act aimed at the destruction of any of the rights and freedoms recognized in the Bill of Rights or at their limitation to a greater extent than is provided for in the Bill. *[cf. ICCPR Art. 5.1]*

(5) There shall be no restriction upon or derogation from any of the fundamental human rights recognized or existing in Hong Kong pursuant to law, conventions, regulations or custom on the pretext that the Bill of Rights does not recognize such rights or that it recognizes them to a lesser extent. *[cf. ICCPR Art. 5.2]*

* See Decision of the Standing Committee of the National People's Congress on Treatment of the Laws Previously in Force in Hong Kong in accordance with Article 160 of the Basic Law of the Hong Kong Special Administrative Region of the People's Republic of China (Instrument A206 in Hong Kong e-legislation (www.elegislation.gov.hk)).

(6) A heading to any Article does not have any legislative effect and does not in any way vary, limit or extend the meaning of the Article.

Section 3 Effect on Pre-existing Legislation

(1)–(2) *(Not adopted as the Laws of the HKSAR)**

(3)–(4) *(Repealed 2 of 1998 s. 2)*

Section 4

(Not adopted as the Laws of the HKSAR)†

Section 5 Public Emergencies

(1) In time of public emergency which threatens the life of the nation and the existence of which is officially proclaimed, measures may be taken derogating from the Bill of Rights to the extent strictly required by the exigencies of the situation, but these measures shall be taken in accordance with law.

(2) No measure shall be taken under subsection (1) that—

(a) is inconsistent with any obligation under international law that applies to Hong Kong (other than an obligation under the International Covenant on Civil and Political Rights);

(b) involves discrimination solely on the ground of race, colour, sex, language, religion or social origin; or

(c) derogates from Articles 2, 3, 4(1) and (2), 7, 12, 13 and 15.

[cf. ICCPR Art. 4]

Section 6 Remedies for Contravention of Bill of Rights

(1) A court or tribunal—

(a) in proceedings within its jurisdiction in an action for breach of this Ordinance; and

(b) in other proceedings within its jurisdiction in which a violation or threatened violation of the Bill of Rights is relevant,

may grant such remedy or relief, or make such order, in respect of such a breach, violation or threatened violation as it has power to grant or make in those proceedings and as it considers appropriate and just in the circumstances.

(2) No proceedings shall be held to be outside the jurisdiction of any court or tribunal on the ground that they relate to the Bill of Rights.

Section 7 Binding Effect of Ordinance

(1) This Ordinance binds only—

(a) the Government and all public authorities; and

---

* See Decision of the Standing Committee of the National People's Congress on Treatment of the Laws Previously In Force in Hong Kong in accordance with Article 160 of the Basic Law of the Hong Kong Special Administrative Region of the People's Republic of China (Instrument A206 in Hong Kong e-legislation (www.elegislation.gov.hk)).

† See Decision of the Standing Committee of the National People's Congress on Treatment of the Laws Previously In Force in Hong Kong in accordance with Article 160 of the Basic Law of the Hong Kong Special Administrative Region of the People's Republic of China (Instrument A206 in Hong Kong e-legislation (www.elegislation.gov.hk)).

(b) any person acting on behalf of the Government or a public authority.

(2) In this Section —

person (人) includes any body of persons, corporate or unincorporate.

Part II The Hong Kong Bill of Rights

Section 8 Hong Kong Bill of Rights

The Hong Kong Bill of Rights is as follows.

Article 1 Entitlement to Rights Without Distinction

(1) The rights recognized in this Bill of Rights shall be enjoyed without distinction of any kind, such as race, colour, sex, language, religion, political or other opinion, national or social origin, property, birth or other status.

(2) Men and women shall have an equal right to the enjoyment of all civil and political rights set forth in this Bill of Rights.

[cf. ICCPR Arts. 2 and 3]

Article 2 Right to Life

(1) Every human being has the inherent right to life. This right shall be protected by law. No one shall be arbitrarily deprived of his life.

(2) Sentence of death may be imposed only for the most serious crimes in accordance with the law in force at the time of the commission of the crime and not contrary to the provisions of this Bill of Rights and to the Convention on the Prevention and Punishment of the Crime of Genocide. This penalty can only be carried out pursuant to a final judgment rendered by a competent court.

(3) When deprivation of life constitutes the crime of genocide, nothing in this Article shall authorize the derogation in any way from any obligation assumed under the provisions of the Convention on the Prevention and Punishment of the Crime of Genocide.

(4) Anyone sentenced to death shall have the right to seek pardon or commutation of the sentence. Amnesty, pardon or commutation of the sentence of death may be granted in all cases.

(5) Sentence of death shall not be imposed for crimes committed by persons below 18 years of age and shall not be carried out on pregnant women.

(6) Nothing in this Article shall be invoked to delay or to prevent the abolition of capital punishment in Hong Kong.

[cf. ICCPR Art. 6]

Article 3 No Torture or Inhuman Treatment and No Experimentation Without Consent

No one shall be subjected to torture or to cruel, inhuman or degrading treatment or punishment. In particular, no one shall be subjected without his free consent to medical or scientific experimentation.

[cf. ICCPR Art. 7]

Article 4 No Slavery or Servitude

(1) No one shall be held in slavery; slavery and the slave-trade in all their forms shall be prohibited.

(2) No one shall be held in servitude.

(3)

(a) No one shall be required to perform forced or compulsory labour.

(b) For the purpose of this paragraph the term "forced or compulsory labour" shall not include —

(i) any work or service normally required of a person who is under detention in consequence of a lawful order of a court, or of a person during conditional release from such detention;

(ii) any service of a military character and, where conscientious objection is recognized, any national service required by law of conscientious objectors;

(iii) any service exacted in cases of emergency or calamity threatening the life or well-being of the community;

(iv) any work or service which forms part of normal civil obligations.

[cf. ICCPR Art. 8]

Article 5 Liberty and Security of Person

(1) Everyone has the right to liberty and security of person. No one shall be subjected to arbitrary arrest or detention. No one shall be deprived of his liberty except on such grounds and in accordance with such procedure as are established by law.

(2) Anyone who is arrested shall be informed, at the time of arrest, of the reasons for his arrest and shall be promptly informed of any charges against him.

(3) Anyone arrested or detained on a criminal charge shall be brought promptly before a judge or other officer authorized by law to exercise judicial power and shall be entitled to trial within a reasonable time or to release. It shall not be the general rule that persons awaiting trial shall be detained in custody, but release may be subject to guarantees to appear for trial, at any other stage of the judicial proceedings, and, should occasion arise, for execution of the judgment.

(4) Anyone who is deprived of his liberty by arrest or detention shall be entitled to take proceedings before a court, in order that that court may decide without delay on the lawfulness of his detention and order his release if the detention is not lawful.

(5) Anyone who has been the victim of unlawful arrest or detention shall have an enforceable right to compensation.

[cf. ICCPR Art. 9]

Article 6 Rights of Persons Deprived of Their Liberty

(1) All persons deprived of their liberty shall be treated with humanity and with respect for the inherent dignity of the human person.

(2)

(a) Accused persons shall, save in exceptional circumstances, be segregated from convicted persons and shall be subject to separate treatment appropriate to their status as unconvicted persons.

(b) Accused juvenile persons shall be separated from adults and brought as speedily as possible for adjudication.

(3) The penitentiary system shall comprise treatment of prisoners the essential aim of which shall be their reformation and social rehabilitation. Juvenile offenders shall be segregated from adults and be accorded treatment appropriate to their age and legal status.

[cf. ICCPR Art. 10]

Article 7 No Imprisonment for Breach of Contract

No one shall be imprisoned merely on the ground of inability to fulfil a contractual obligation.

[cf. ICCPR Art. 11]

Article 8 Liberty of Movement

(1) Everyone lawfully within Hong Kong shall, within Hong Kong, have the right to liberty of movement and freedom to choose his residence.

(2) Everyone shall be free to leave Hong Kong.

(3) The above-mentioned rights shall not be subject to any restrictions except those which are provided by law, are necessary to protect national security, public order (ordre public), public health or morals or the rights and freedoms of others, and are consistent with the other rights recognized in this Bill of Rights.

(4) No one who has the right of abode in Hong Kong shall be arbitrarily deprived of the right to enter Hong Kong.

[cf. ICCPR Art. 12]

Article 9 Restrictions on Expulsion from Hong Kong

A person who does not have the right of abode in Hong Kong but who is lawfully in Hong Kong may be expelled therefrom only in pursuance of a decision reached in accordance with law and shall, except where compelling reasons of national security otherwise require, be allowed to submit the reasons against his expulsion and to have his case reviewed by, and be represented for the purpose before, the competent authority or a person or persons especially designated by the competent authority.

[cf. ICCPR Art. 13]

Article 10 Equality before Courts and Right to Fair and Public Hearing

All persons shall be equal before the courts and tribunals. In the determination of any criminal charge against him, or of his rights and obligations in a suit at law, everyone shall be entitled to a fair and public hearing by a competent, independent and impartial tribunal established by law. The press and the public may be excluded from all or part of a trial for reasons of morals, public order (ordre public) or national security in a democratic society, or when the interest of the private lives of the parties so requires, or to the extent strictly necessary in the opinion of the court in special circumstances where publicity would prejudice the interests of justice; but any judgment rendered in a criminal case or in a suit at law shall be made public except where the interest of juvenile persons otherwise requires or the proceedings concern matrimonial disputes or the guardianship of children.

[cf. ICCPR Art. 14.1]

Article 11 Rights of Persons Charged with or Convicted of Criminal Offence

(1) Everyone charged with a criminal offence shall have the right to be presumed innocent until proved guilty according to law.

(2) In the determination of any criminal charge against him, everyone shall be entitled to the following minimum guarantees, in full equality —

  (a) to be informed promptly and in detail in a language which he understands of the nature and cause of the charge against him;

  (b) to have adequate time and facilities for the preparation of his defence and to communicate with counsel of his own choosing;

  (c) to be tried without undue delay;

  (d) to be tried in his presence, and to defend himself in person or through legal assistance of his own choosing; to be informed, if he does not have legal assistance, of this right; and to have legal assistance assigned to him, in any case where the interests of justice so require, and without payment by him in any such case if he does not have sufficient means to pay for it;

  (e) to examine, or have examined, the witnesses against him and to obtain the attendance and examination of witnesses on his behalf under the same conditions as witnesses against him;

(f) to have the free assistance of an interpreter if he cannot understand or speak the language used in court;

(g) not to be compelled to testify against himself or to confess guilt.

(3) In the case of juvenile persons, the procedure shall be such as will take account of their age and the desirability of promoting their rehabilitation.

(4) Everyone convicted of a crime shall have the right to his conviction and sentence being reviewed by a higher tribunal according to law.

(5) When a person has by a final decision been convicted of a criminal offence and when subsequently his conviction has been reversed or he has been pardoned on the ground that a new or newly discovered fact shows conclusively that there has been a miscarriage of justice, the person who has suffered punishment as a result of such conviction shall be compensated according to law, unless it is proved that the non-disclosure of the unknown fact in time is wholly or partly attributable to him.

(6) No one shall be liable to be tried or punished again for an offence for which he has already been finally convicted or acquitted in accordance with the law and penal procedure of Hong Kong.

[cf. ICCPR Art. 14.2 to 7]

Article 12 No Retrospective Criminal Offences or Penalties

(1) No one shall be held guilty of any criminal offence on account of any act or omission which did not constitute a criminal offence, under Hong Kong or international law, at the time when it was committed. Nor shall a heavier penalty be imposed than the one that was applicable at the time when the criminal offence was committed. If, subsequent to the commission of the offence, provision is made by law for the imposition of a lighter penalty, the offender shall benefit thereby.

(2) Nothing in this Article shall prejudice the trial and punishment of any person for any act or omission which, at the time when it was committed, was criminal according to the general principles of law recognized by the community of nations.

[cf. ICCPR Art. 15]

Article 13 Right to Recognition as Person before Law

Everyone shall have the right to recognition everywhere as a person before the law.

[cf. ICCPR Art. 16]

Article 14 Protection of Privacy, Family, Home, Correspondence, Honour and Reputation

(1) No one shall be subjected to arbitrary or unlawful interference with his privacy, family, home or correspondence, nor to unlawful attacks on his honour and reputation.

(2) Everyone has the right to the protection of the law against such interference or attacks.

[cf. ICCPR Art. 17]

Article 15 Freedom of Thought, Conscience and Religion

(1) Everyone shall have the right to freedom of thought, conscience and religion. This right shall include freedom to have or to adopt a religion or belief of his choice, and freedom, either individually or in community with others and in public or private, to manifest his religion or belief in worship, observance, practice and teaching.

(2) No one shall be subject to coercion which would impair his freedom to have or to adopt a religion or belief of his choice.

(3) Freedom to manifest one's religion or beliefs may be subject only to such limitations as are prescribed by law and are necessary to protect public safety, order, health, or morals or the fundamental rights and freedoms of others.

(4) The liberty of parents and, when applicable, legal guardians to ensure the religious and moral education of their children in conformity with their own convictions shall be respected.

[cf. ICCPR Art. 18]

Article 16 Freedom of Opinion and Expression

(1) Everyone shall have the right to hold opinions without interference.

(2) Everyone shall have the right to freedom of expression; this right shall include freedom to seek, receive and impart information and ideas of all kinds, regardless of frontiers, either orally, in writing or in print, in the form of art, or through any other media of his choice.

(3) The exercise of the rights provided for in paragraph (2) of this Article carries with it special duties and responsibilities. It may therefore be subject to certain restrictions, but these shall only be such as are provided by law and are necessary —

(a) for respect of the rights or reputations of others; or

(b) for the protection of national security or of public order (ordre public), or of public health or morals.

[cf. ICCPR Art. 19]

Article 17 Right of Peaceful Assembly

The right of peaceful assembly shall be recognized. No restrictions may be placed on the exercise of this right other than those imposed in conformity with the law and which are necessary in a democratic society in the interests of national security or public safety, public order (ordre public), the protection of public health or morals or the protection of the rights and freedoms of others.

[cf. ICCPR Art. 21]

Article 18 Freedom of Association

(1) Everyone shall have the right to freedom of association with others, including the right to form and join trade unions for the protection of his interests.

(2) No restrictions may be placed on the exercise of this right other than those which are prescribed by law and which are necessary in a democratic society in the interests of national security or public safety, public order (ordre public), the protection of public health or morals or the protection of the rights and freedoms of others. This Article shall not prevent the imposition of lawful restrictions on members of the armed forces and of the police in their exercise of this right.

(3) Nothing in this Article authorizes legislative measures to be taken which would prejudice, or the law to be applied in such a manner as to prejudice, the guarantees provided for in the International Labour Organization Convention of 1948 concerning Freedom of Association and Protection of the Right to Organize as it applies to Hong Kong.

[cf. ICCPR Art. 22]

Article 19 Rights in Respect of Marriage and Family

(1) The family is the natural and fundamental group unit of society and is entitled to protection by society and the State.

(2) The right of men and women of marriageable age to marry and to found a family shall be recognized.

(3) No marriage shall be entered into without the free and full consent of the intending spouses.

(4) Spouses shall have equal rights and responsibilities as to marriage, during marriage and at its dissolution. In the case of dissolution, provision shall be made for the necessary protection of any children.

[cf. ICCPR Art. 23]

Article 20 Rights of Children

(1) Every child shall have, without any discrimination as to race, colour, sex, language, religion, national or social origin, property or birth, the right to such measures of protection as are required by his status as a minor, on the part of his family, society and the State.

(2) Every child shall be registered immediately after birth and shall have a name.

[cf. ICCPR Art. 24]

Article 21 Right to Participate in Public Life

Every permanent resident shall have the right and the opportunity, without any of the distinctions mentioned in Article 1(1) and without unreasonable restrictions —

(a) to take part in the conduct of public affairs, directly or through freely chosen representatives;

(b) to vote and to be elected at genuine periodic elections which shall be by universal and equal suffrage and shall be held by secret ballot, guaranteeing the free expression of the will of the electors;

(c) to have access, on general terms of equality, to public service in Hong Kong.

[cf. ICCPR Art. 25]

Article 22 Equality before and Equal Protection of Law

All persons are equal before the law and are entitled without any discrimination to the equal protection of the law. In this respect, the law shall prohibit any discrimination and guarantee to all persons equal and effective protection against discrimination on any ground such as race, colour, sex, language, religion, political or other opinion, national or social origin, property, birth or other status.

[cf. ICCPR Art. 26]

Article 23 Rights of Minorities

Persons belonging to ethnic, religious or linguistic minorities shall not be denied the right, in community with the other members of their group, to enjoy their own culture, to profess and practise their own religion, or to use their own language.

[cf. ICCPR Art. 27]

Part III Exceptions and Savings

Section 9 Armed Forces and Persons Detained in Penal Establishments

Members of and persons serving with the armed forces of the government responsible for the foreign affairs of Hong Kong and persons lawfully detained in penal establishments of whatever character are subject to such restrictions as may from time to time be authorized by law for the preservation of service and custodial discipline.

Section 10 Juveniles under Detention

Where at any time there is a lack of suitable prison facilities or where the mixing of adults and juveniles is mutually beneficial, Article 6(2)(b) and (3) does not require juveniles who are detained to be accommodated separately from adults.

Section 11 Immigration Legislation

As regards persons not having the right to enter and remain in Hong Kong, this Ordinance does not affect any immigration legislation governing entry into, stay in and departure from Hong Kong, or the application of any such legislation.

Section 12 Persons Not Having the Right of Abode

Article 9 does not confer a right of review in respect of a decision to deport a person not having the right of abode in Hong Kong or a right to be represented for this purpose before the competent authority.

Section 13 Executive and Legislative Councils

Article 21 does not require the establishment of an elected Executive or Legislative Council in Hong Kong.

Section 14 Temporary Savings

(1) For a period of 1 year beginning on the commencement date, this Ordinance is subject to the Ordinances listed in the Schedule.

(2) This Ordinance does not affect —

 (a) any act done (including any act done in the exercise of a discretion); or

 (b) any omission authorized or required, or occurring in the exercise of a discretion,

 before the first anniversary of the commencement date, under or by any Ordinance listed in the Schedule.

(3) The Legislative Council may before the first anniversary of the commencement date by Resolution amend this Section for all or any of the following purposes —

 (a) to provide that, for a period of 1 year beginning on the first anniversary of the commencement date, this Ordinance is subject to such of the Ordinances listed in the Schedule as are specified in the amendment;

 (b) to provide that this Ordinance does not affect —

  (i) any act done (including any act done in the exercise of a discretion); or

  (ii) any omission authorized or required, or occurring in the exercise of a discretion,

  before the second anniversary of the commencement date, under or by any Ordinance listed in the Schedule that is specified in the amendment; and

 (c) to repeal this subsection.

(4) In this Section, a reference to an Ordinance includes a reference to any subsidiary legislation made under that Ordinance.

(5) This Section operates notwithstanding Section 3.

Schedule

[s. 14]

Provisions to Which Section 14(1) and (2) Applies

Immigration Ordinance (Cap. 115)

Societies Ordinance (Cap. 151)

Crimes Ordinance (Cap. 200)

Prevention of Bribery Ordinance (Cap. 201)

Independent Commission Against Corruption Ordinance (Cap. 204)

Police Force Ordinance (Cap. 232)

SECTION II
ANTI-DISCRIMINATION ORDINANCES IN HONG KONG

This Section includes four anti-discrimination ordinances as applied in Hong Kong. They are:

(1) The Sex Discrimination Ordinance (Cap. 480)

(2) The Disability Discrimination Ordinance (Cap. 487)

(3) The Family Status Discrimination Ordinance (Cap. 527)

(4) The Race Discrimination Ordinance (Cap. 602)

SEX DISCRIMINATION ORDINANCE (CAP. 480)

An Ordinance to render unlawful certain kinds of sex discrimination, discrimination on the ground of marital status or pregnancy, and sexual harassment; to provide for the establishment of a Commission with the functions of working towards the elimination of such discrimination and harassment and promoting equality of opportunity between men and women generally; and to provide for matters incidental thereto or connected therewith.

[20 May 1996]

(Format changes — E.R. 1 of 2013)

(Enacting provision omitted — E.R. 1 of 2013)

Part 1 Preliminary

Section 1 Short Title

(1) This Ordinance may be cited as the Sex Discrimination Ordinance.

(2) *(Omitted as spent — E.R. 1 of 2013)*

Section 2 Interpretation

(1) In this Ordinance, unless the context otherwise requires —

access (獲得、享用) means access as construed in accordance with Section 56;

act (作為) includes a deliberate omission;

advertisement (廣告) includes every form of advertisement, whether to the public or not, and whether —

(a) in a newspaper or other publication;

(b) by television or radio;

(c) by display of notices, signs, labels, showcards or goods;

(d) by distribution of samples, circulars, catalogues, price lists or other material;

(e) by exhibition of pictures, models or films; or

(f) in any other way,

and references to the publishing of advertisements shall be construed accordingly;

Chairperson (主席) means the Chairperson of the Commission appointed under Section 63(3)(a);

club (會社) means an association, incorporate or unincorporate, of not less than 30 persons associated together for social, literary, cultural, political, sporting, athletic or other lawful purposes and which provides and maintains its facilities, in whole or in part, from the funds of the association; *(Amended 29 of 2008 s. 91)*

Commission (委員會) means the Equal Opportunities Commission established under Section 63(1);

commission agent (佣金經紀人) means commission agent as construed in accordance with Section 20;

committee (小組委員會) means a committee established under Section 64(2)(a);

committee of management (管理委員會), in relation to a club, means the group or body of persons (howsoever described) that manages the affairs of that club;

conciliator (調停人) means any person engaged by the Commission under Section 64(2)(e); *(Amended 15 of 2012 s. 11)*

contract worker (合約工作者) means contract worker as construed in accordance with Section 13;

discrimination (歧視) means any discrimination falling within Section 5, 6, 7, 8 or 9, and related expressions shall be construed accordingly;

dispose (處置), in relation to premises, includes granting a right to occupy the premises, and any reference to acquiring premises shall be construed accordingly;

dynamically supported craft (藉動力而獲得支承的航行器) has the same meaning as in the Shipping and Port Control Ordinance (Cap. 313); *(Amended L.N. 315 of 1998)*

education (教育) includes any form of training or instruction;

educational establishment (教育機構) means an educational establishment specified in column 1 of Schedule 1;

employment (僱用) means employment under —

(a) a contract of service or of apprenticeship; or

(b) a contract personally to execute any work or labour,

and related expressions shall be construed accordingly;

employment agency (職業介紹所) means a person who, for profit or not, provides services for the purpose of finding employment for workers or supplying employers with workers;

enforcement notice (執行通知) means a notice under Section 77(2);

estate agent (地產代理) has the same meaning as in the Estate Agents Ordinance (Cap. 511); *(Replaced 29 of 2008 s. 91)*

firm (商號) means firm within the meaning of the Partnership Ordinance (Cap. 38);

formal investigation (正式調查) means an investigation under Section 70;

general notice (一般通告), in relation to any person, means a notice published by him at a time and in a manner appearing to him suitable for securing that the notice is seen within a reasonable time by persons likely to be affected by it;

genuine occupational qualification (真正的職業資格) means genuine occupational qualification as construed in accordance with Section 12(2);

intern (實習人員) — see Section 23A(2); *(Added 8 of 2020 s. 19)*

internship (實習) — see Section 23A(2); *(Added 8 of 2020 s. 19)*

man (男性) includes a male of any age;

marital status (婚姻狀況) means the state or condition of being —

(a) single;

(b) married;

(c) married but living separately and apart from one's spouse;

(d) divorced; or

(e) widowed;

near relative (近親), in relation to a person, means —

(a) the person's spouse;

(b) a parent of the person or of the spouse;

(c) a child of the person or the spouse of such a child;

(d) a brother or sister (whether of full blood or half blood) of the person or of the spouse or the spouse of such a brother or sister;

(e) a grandparent of the person or of the spouse; or

(f) a grandchild of the person or the spouse of such a grandchild,

and, in determining the above relationships, children born out of wedlock are to be included, an adopted child is to be regarded as a child of both the natural parents and the adoptive parent or parents and a step child as the child of both the natural parents and any step parent; *(Added 29 of 2008 s. 91)*

notice (通告、通知) means a notice in writing;

prescribed (訂明) means prescribed in rules made under Section 88;

profession (專業) includes any vocation or occupation;

pupillage (見習職位) — see Section 36(4); *(Added 8 of 2020 s. 19)*

responsible body (負責組織), in relation to an educational establishment, means the body specified in column 2 of Schedule 1 opposite that establishment;

retirement (退休) includes retirement (whether voluntary or not) on grounds of age, length of service or incapacity;

sex discrimination (性別歧視) means any discrimination falling within Section 5 or 6;

single-sex establishment (單性別機構) means single-sex establishment as construed in accordance with Section 26;

trade (行業) includes any business;

training (訓練) includes any form of education or instruction;

volunteer (義工) — see Section 23A(2); *(Added 8 of 2020 s. 19)*

woman (女性) includes a female of any age.

(2) References in this Ordinance to the dismissal of a person from employment or to the expulsion of a person from a position as partner include references —

(a) to the termination of that person's employment or partnership by the expiration of any period (including a period expiring by reference to an event or circumstance), not being a termination immediately after which the employment or partnership is renewed on the same terms;

(b) to the termination of that person's employment or partnership by any act of his (including the giving of notice) in circumstances such that he is entitled to terminate it without notice by reason of the conduct of the employer, or the other partners, as the case may be.

(3) For the purposes of this Ordinance, an enforcement notice or a finding by the District Court becomes final when an appeal against the notice or finding is dismissed, withdrawn or abandoned or when the time for appealing expires without an appeal having been brought; and for this purpose an appeal against an enforcement notice shall be taken to be dismissed if, notwithstanding that a requirement of the notice is quashed on appeal, a direction is given in respect of it under Section 78(3).

(4) *(Repealed 29 of 2008 s. 91)*

(5) For the purposes of this Ordinance, a person (howsoever described) sexually harasses a woman if—

(a) the person—

(i) makes an unwelcome sexual advance, or an unwelcome request for sexual favours, to her; or

(ii) engages in other unwelcome conduct of a sexual nature in relation to her,

in circumstances in which a reasonable person, having regard to all the circumstances, would have anticipated that she would be offended, humiliated or intimidated; or

(b) the person, alone or together with other persons, engages in conduct of a sexual nature which creates a hostile or intimidating environment for her. *(Amended 29 of 2008 s. 91)*

(6) *(Repealed 29 of 2008 s. 91)*

(7) In subsection (5)—

conduct of a sexual nature (涉及性的行徑) includes making a statement of a sexual nature to a woman, or in her presence, whether the statement is made orally or in writing.

(8) A provision of Part 3 or 4 framed with reference to sexual harassment of women shall be treated as applying equally to the treatment of men and for that purpose that provision, and subsections (5) and (7), shall have effect with such modifications as are necessary.

(9) Subject to subsection (10), in this Ordinance ***existing statutory provision*** (現有法例條文) means any provision of—

(a) any Ordinance enacted before this Ordinance was enacted;

(b) any subsidiary legislation made—

(i) under an Ordinance enacted before this Ordinance was enacted; and

(ii) before, on or after this Ordinance was enacted.

(10) Where an Ordinance enacted after this Ordinance was enacted re-enacts (with or without modifications) a provision of an Ordinance enacted before this Ordinance was enacted, then that provision as re-enacted shall be treated for the purposes of subsection (9) as if it continued to be contained in an Ordinance enacted before this Ordinance was enacted.

(Amended E.R. 1 of 2013)

Section 3 Application

This Ordinance binds the Government.

Section 4 Act Done Because of Sex, etc. and for Other Reason

If—

(a) an act is done for 2 or more reasons; and

(b) one of the reasons is the sex, marital status or pregnancy of a person (whether or not it is the dominant or a substantial reason for doing the act),

then, for the purpose of this Ordinance, the act shall be taken to be done for the reason specified in paragraph (b).

Part 2 Discrimination to Which Ordinance Applies

Section 5 Sex Discrimination against Women

(1) A person discriminates against a woman in any circumstances relevant for the purposes of any provision of this Ordinance if—

(a) on the ground of her sex he treats her less favourably than he treats or would treat a man; or

(b) he applies to her a requirement or condition which he applies or would apply equally to a man but—

(i) which is such that the proportion of women who can comply with it is considerably smaller than the proportion of men who can comply with it;

(ii) which he cannot show to be justifiable irrespective of the sex of the person to whom it is applied; and

(iii) which is to her detriment because she cannot comply with it.

(2) If a person treats or would treat a man differently according to the man's marital status, his treatment of a woman is for the purposes of subsection (1)(a) to be compared to his treatment of a man having the like marital status.

Section 6 Sex Discrimination against Men

(1) Section 5, and the provisions of Parts 3 and 4 relating to sex discrimination against women, shall be read as applying equally to the treatment of men, and for that purpose shall have effect with such modifications as are necessary.

(2) In the application of subsection (1) no account shall be taken of special treatment afforded to women in connection with pregnancy or childbirth.

(Amended E.R. 1 of 2013)

Section 7 Discrimination against Married, etc. Persons

(Amended L.N. 28 of 2013)

(1) A person discriminates against a person of either sex in any circumstances relevant for the purposes of any provision of Part 3 or 4 if—

(a) on the ground of his or her marital status (***the relevant marital status***) he treats that person less favourably than he treats or would treat a person of the same sex with a different marital status; or

(b) he applies to that person a requirement or condition which he applies or would apply equally to a person with a different marital status but—

(i) which is such that the proportion of persons with the relevant marital status who can comply with it is considerably smaller than the proportion of persons of the same sex with a different marital status who can comply with it;

(ii) which he cannot show to be justifiable irrespective of the marital status of the person to whom it is applied; and

(iii) which is to that person's detriment because he or she cannot comply with it.

(2) For the purposes of subsection (1), a provision of Part 3 or 4 framed with reference to discrimination against women shall be treated as applying equally to the treatment of men, and for that purpose shall have effect with such modifications as are necessary.

(Amended E.R. 1 of 2013)

Section 8 Discrimination against Pregnant Women

(Amended L.N. 28 of 2013)

A person discriminates against a woman in any circumstances relevant for the purposes of any provision of Part 3 or 4 if—

(a) on the ground of her pregnancy he treats her less favourably than he treats or would treat a person who is not pregnant; or

(b) he applies to her a requirement or condition which he applies or would apply to a person who is not pregnant but—

(i) which is such that the proportion of persons who are pregnant who can comply with it is considerably smaller than the proportion of persons who are not pregnant who can comply with it;

(ii) which he cannot show to be justifiable irrespective of whether or not the person to whom it is applied is pregnant; and

(iii) which is to her detriment because she cannot comply with it.

(Amended E.R. 1 of 2013)

Section 9 Discrimination by Way of Victimization

(1) A person (***the discriminator***) discriminates against another person (***the person victimized***) in any circumstances relevant for the purposes of any provision of this Ordinance if he treats the person victimized less favourably than in those circumstances he treats or would treat other persons, and does so by reason that the person victimized or any other person (***the third person***) has—

(a) brought proceedings against the discriminator or any other person under this Ordinance;

(b) given evidence or information in connection with proceedings brought by any person against the discriminator or any other person under this Ordinance;

(c) otherwise done anything under or by reference to this Ordinance in relation to the discriminator or any other person; or

(d) alleged that the discriminator or any other person has committed an act which (whether or not the allegation so states) would amount to a contravention of this Ordinance,

or by reason that the discriminator knows the person victimized or the third person, as the case may be, intends to do any of those things, or suspects the person victimized or the third person, as the case may be, has done, or intends to do, any of them.

(2) Subsection (1) shall not apply to treatment of a person by reason of any allegation made by him if the allegation was false and not made in good faith.

(3) For the purposes of subsection (1), a provision of Part 3 or 4 framed with reference to discrimination against, or sexual harassment of, women shall be treated as applying equally to the treatment of men and for that purpose shall have effect with such modifications as are necessary.

(Amended E.R. 1 of 2013)

Section 10 Comparison of Cases under Sections 5(1), 7(1) and 8

A comparison of the cases of persons –

(a) of different sex under Section 5(1);

(b) of different marital status under Section 7(1);

(c) who are pregnant and not pregnant under Section 8,

shall be such that the relevant circumstances in the one case are the same, or not materially different, in the other.

Part 3 Discrimination and Sexual Harassment in Employment Field

Discrimination by Employers

Section 11 Discrimination against Applicants and Employees

(1) It is unlawful for a person, in relation to employment by him at an establishment in Hong Kong, to discriminate against a woman –

(a) in the arrangements he makes for the purpose of determining who should be offered that employment;

(b) in the terms on which he offers her that employment; or

(c) by refusing or deliberately omitting to offer her that employment.

(2) It is unlawful for a person, in the case of a woman employed by him at an establishment in Hong Kong, to discriminate against her –

(a) in the way he affords her access to opportunities for promotion, transfer or training, or to any other benefits, facilities or services, or by refusing or deliberately omitting to afford her access to them;

(b) in the terms of employment he affords her; or

(c) by dismissing her, or subjecting her to any other detriment.

(3) Except in relation to discrimination falling within Section 9, subsections (1) and (2) shall not apply to employment where the number of persons employed by the employer, added to the number employed by any associated employers of his, does not exceed 5 (disregarding any persons employed for the purposes of a private home).

(4) Subject to subsection (5), subsections (1)(b) and (2) shall not apply to provision in relation to death or retirement made for a woman before 15 October 1997 in so far as any such provision continues for that woman on and after that date. *(Replaced 71 of 1997 s. 2. Amended 136 of 1997 s. 2)**

* Prior to its amendment by 136 of 1997, this subsection disapplies certain provisions of this Ordinance to certain death or retirement provision made before "the commencement of this Section" in so far as that death or retirement provision continues "on and after that commencement". According to s. 5 of 136 of 1997, "the commencement of this Section" meant, and always meant, for all purposes, the commencement of ss. 2, 3 and 4 of 71 of 1997 (i.e., 15 October 1997).

(5) Subsections (1)(b) and (2) shall apply to provision in relation to death or retirement of the kind mentioned in subsection (4) in so far as, in their application to such provision in relation to retirement, they render it unlawful for a person to discriminate against a woman —

(a) in such of the terms on which he offers her employment as make provision in relation to the way in which he will afford her access to opportunities for promotion, transfer or training or as provide for her dismissal or demotion;

(b) in the way he affords her opportunities for promotion, transfer or training or by refusing or deliberately omitting to afford her access to any such opportunities; or

(c) by dismissing her or subjecting her to any detriment which results in her dismissal or consists in or involves her demotion. *(Replaced 71 of 1997 s. 2)*

(6) Subsection (2) shall not apply to benefits, facilities or services of any description if the employer is concerned with the provision (for payment or not) of benefits, facilities or services of that description to the public, or to a section of the public comprising the woman concerned, unless —

(a) that provision differs in a material respect from the provision of the benefits, facilities or services by the employer to his employees; or

(b) the benefits, facilities or services relate to training.

(7) Subsection (3) shall expire on the 3rd anniversary of the day on which this Ordinance is enacted.

(8) For the purposes of subsection (3), 2 employers are to be treated as associated if one is a company of which the other (directly or indirectly) has control or if both are companies of which a third person (directly or indirectly) has control.

(9) The Chief Executive in Council may, by notice in the Gazette — *(Amended 66 of 1999 s. 3)*

(a) amend subsection (3) by substituting another number for the last number appearing in that subsection;

(b) amend subsection (7) by substituting another anniversary for the anniversary appearing in that subsection.

Section 12 Exception Where Sex Is Genuine Occupational Qualification

(1) In relation to sex discrimination —

(a) Section 11(1)(a) or (c) shall not apply to any employment where being a man is a genuine occupational qualification for the job;

(b) Section 11(2)(a) shall not apply to opportunities for promotion or transfer to, or training for, such employment.

(2) Being a man is a genuine occupational qualification for a job only where —

(a) the essential nature of the job calls for a man for reasons of physiology (excluding physical strength or stamina) or, in dramatic performances or other entertainment, for reasons of authenticity, so that the essential nature of the job would be materially different if carried out by a woman;

(b) the job needs to be held by a man to preserve decency or privacy because —

(i) it is likely to involve physical contact with men in circumstances where they might reasonably object to its being carried out by a woman; or

(ii) the holder of the job is likely to do his work in circumstances where men might reasonably object to the presence of a woman because they are in a state of undress or are using sanitary facilities;

(c) the job is likely to involve the holder of the job doing his work, or living, in a private home and needs to be held by a man because objection might reasonably be taken to allowing to a woman —

(i) the degree of physical or social contact with a person living in the home; or

(ii) the knowledge of intimate details of such a person's life,

which is likely, because of the nature or circumstances of the job or of the home, to be allowed to, or available to, the holder of the job;

(d) the nature or location of the establishment makes it impracticable for the holder of the job to live elsewhere than in premises provided by the employer, and —

(i) the only such premises which are available for persons holding that kind of job are lived in, or normally lived in, by men and are not equipped with separate sleeping accommodation for women and sanitary facilities which could be used by women in privacy from men; and

(ii) it is not reasonable to expect the employer to equip those premises with such accommodation and facilities or to provide other premises for women;

(e) the nature of the establishment, or of the part of it within which the work is done, requires the job to be held by a man because —

(i) it is, or is part of, a hospital, prison or other establishment for persons requiring special care, supervision or attention;

(ii) those persons are all men (disregarding any woman whose presence is exceptional); and

(iii) it is reasonable, having regard to the essential character of the establishment or that part, that the job should not be held by a woman;

(f) the holder of the job provides individuals with personal services promoting their welfare or education, or similar personal services, and those services can most effectively be provided by a man;

(g) *(Repealed 18 of 2014 s. 14)*

(h) the job needs to be held by a man because it is likely to involve the performance of duties outside Hong Kong in a place the laws or customs of which are such that the duties could not, or could not effectively, be performed by a woman, or

(i) the job is one of 2 to be held by a married couple.

(3) Subsection (2) applies where some only of the duties of the job fall within any paragraph of that subsection (except paragraph (i)) as well as where all of them do.

(4) Paragraph (a), (b), (d), (e), (f) or (h) of subsection (2) shall not apply in relation to the filling of a vacancy at a time when the employer already has male employees — *(Amended 18 of 2014 s. 14)*

(a) who are capable of carrying out the duties falling within that paragraph;

(b) whom it would be reasonable to employ on those duties; and

(c) whose numbers are sufficient to meet the employer's likely requirements in respect of those duties without undue inconvenience. *(Amended 18 of 2014 s. 14)*

Section 13 Discrimination against Contract Workers

(1) This Section applies to any work for a person (***the principal***) which is available for doing by individuals (***contract workers***) who are employed not by the principal himself but by a contractor or sub-contractor of the principal. *(Amended 29 of 2008 s. 92)*

(2) It is unlawful for the principal, in relation to work to which this Section applies, to discriminate against a woman who is a contract worker —

(a) in the terms on which he allows her to do that work;

(b) by not allowing her to do it or continue to do it;

(c) in the way he affords her access to any benefits, facilities or services or by refusing or deliberately omitting to afford her access to them; or

(d) by subjecting her to any other detriment.

(3) The principal does not contravene subsection (2)(b) by doing any act in relation to a woman at a time when if the work were to be done by a person taken into his employment being a man would be a genuine occupational qualification for the job.

(4) Subsection (2)(c) shall not apply to benefits, facilities or services of any description if the principal is concerned with the provision (for payment or not) of benefits, facilities or services of that description to the public, or to a section of the public to which the woman belongs, unless that provision differs in a material respect from the provision of the benefits, facilities or services by the principal to his contract workers.

(5) In this Section —

contractor (承判商) means a person who undertakes any work for the principal under a contract that is entered into by the person directly with the principal;

sub-contractor (次承判商) means a person who enters into a contract with another person (whether or not a contractor of the principal) to undertake all or any part of the work that a contractor of the principal has undertaken. *(Added 29 of 2008 s. 92)*

Section 14 Meaning of Employment at Establishment in Hong Kong

(1) For the purposes of this Ordinance (***the relevant purposes***), employment is to be regarded as being at an establishment in Hong Kong unless the employee does his work wholly or mainly outside Hong Kong.

(2) Subsection (1) shall not apply to —

(a) employment on board a ship registered in Hong Kong; or

(b) employment on aircraft or dynamically supported craft registered in Hong Kong and operated by a person who has his principal place of business, or is ordinarily resident, in Hong Kong,

but for the relevant purposes such employment is to be regarded as being at an establishment in Hong Kong unless the employee does his work wholly outside Hong Kong.

(3) In the case of employment on board a ship registered in Hong Kong (except where the employee does his work wholly outside Hong Kong) the ship shall for the relevant purposes be deemed to be the establishment.

(4) Where work is not done at an establishment it shall be treated for the relevant purposes as done at the establishment from which it is done or (where it is not done from any establishment) at the establishment with which it has the closest connection.

Discrimination by Other Bodies

Section 15 Partnerships

(1) It is unlawful for a firm consisting of not less than 6 partners, in relation to a position as partner in the firm, to discriminate against a woman —

(a) in the arrangements the firm makes for the purpose of determining who should be offered that position;

(b) in the terms on which the firm offers her that position;

(c) by refusing or deliberately omitting to offer her that position; or

(d) in a case where the woman already holds that position —

(i) in the way the firm affords her access to any benefits, facilities or services, or by refusing or deliberately omitting to afford her access to them; or

(ii) by expelling her from that position or subjecting her to any other detriment.

(2) Subsection (1) shall apply in relation to persons proposing to form themselves into a partnership as it applies in relation to a firm.

(3) Subsection (1)(a) and (c) shall not apply to a position as partner where, if it were employment, being a man would be a genuine occupational qualification for the job.

(4) Subject to subsection (5), subsection (1)(b) and (d) shall not apply to provision in relation to death or retirement made for a woman before 15 October 1997 in so far as any such provision continues for that woman on and after that date. *(Replaced 71 of 1997 s. 3. Amended 136 of 1997 s. 3)**

(5) Subsection (1)(b) and (d) shall apply to provision made in relation to death or retirement of the kind mentioned in subsection (4) in so far as, in their application to such provision made in relation to retirement, they render it unlawful for a firm to discriminate against a woman —

(a) in such of the terms on which the firm offers her a position as partner as provide for her expulsion from that position; or

(b) by expelling her from a position as partner or subjecting her to any detriment which results in her expulsion from such a position. *(Replaced 71 of 1997 s. 3)*

(6) In the case of a limited partnership references in subsection (1) to a partner shall be construed as references to a general partner within the meaning of Section 2 of the Limited Partnerships Ordinance (Cap. 37).

(7) The Chief Executive in Council may, by notice in the Gazette, amend subsection (1) by — *(Amended 66 of 1999 s. 3)*

(a) substituting another number for the number appearing in that subsection; or

(b) repealing the words and number appearing after "for a firm" and before ", in relation to".

Section 16 Trade Unions, etc.

(1) This Section applies to an organization of workers, an organization of employers, or any other organization whose members carry on a particular profession or trade for the purposes of which the organization exists.

(2) It is unlawful for an organization to which this Section applies, in the case of a woman who is not a member of the organization, to discriminate against her —

(a) in the terms on which it is prepared to admit her to membership; or

(b) by refusing, or deliberately omitting to accept, her application for membership.

(3) It is unlawful for an organization to which this Section applies, in the case of a woman who is a member of the organization, to discriminate against her —

(a) in the way it affords her access to any benefits, facilities or services, or by refusing or deliberately omitting to afford her access to them;

(b) by depriving her of membership, or varying the terms on which she is a member; or

(c) by subjecting her to any other detriment.

* Prior to its amendment by 136 of 1997, this subsection disapplies certain provisions of this Ordinance to certain death or retirement provision made before "the commencement of this Section" in so far as that death or retirement provision continues "on and after that commencement". According to s. 5 of 136 of 1997, "the commencement of this Section" meant, and always meant, for all purposes, the commencement of ss. 2, 3 and 4 of 71 of 1997 (i.e., 15 October 1997).

(4) This Section shall not apply to provision in relation to the death or retirement from work of a member made before 15 October 1997 in so far as any such provision continues for that member on and after that date. *(Replaced 71 of 1997 s. 4. Amended 136 of 1997 s. 4)**

(5) *(Repealed 71 of 1997 s. 4)*

Section 17 Qualifying Bodies

(1) It is unlawful for an authority or body which can confer an authorization or qualification which is needed for, or facilitates, engagement in a particular profession or trade to discriminate against a woman —

(a) in the terms on which it is prepared to confer on her that authorization or qualification;

(b) by refusing or deliberately omitting to grant her application for it; or

(c) by withdrawing it from her or varying the terms on which she holds it.

(2) Where an authority or body is required by law to satisfy itself as to his good character before conferring on a person an authorization or qualification which is needed for, or facilitates, his engagement in any profession or trade then, without prejudice to any other duty to which it is subject, that requirement shall be taken to impose on the authority or body a duty to have regard to any evidence tending to show that he, or any of his employees or agents (whether past or present), has —

(a) practised unlawful discrimination; or

(b) engaged in unlawful sexual harassment,

in, or in connection with, the carrying on of any profession or trade.

(3) Subsection (1) shall not apply to discrimination which is rendered unlawful by Section 25.

(4) In this Section —

authorization or qualification (授權或資格) includes recognition, licensing, registration, enrolment, approval and certification;

confer (授予) includes renew or extend.

Section 18 Persons Concerned with Provision of Vocational Training

(1) It is unlawful, in the case of a woman seeking or undergoing training which would help fit her for any employment, for any person who provides, or makes arrangements for the provision of, facilities for such training to discriminate against her —

(a) in the terms on which that person affords her access to any training course or other facilities concerned with such training;

(b) by refusing or deliberately omitting to afford her such access;

(c) by terminating her training; or

(d) by subjecting her to any other detriment during the course of her training.

---

* Prior to its amendment by 136 of 1997, this subsection disapplies certain provisions of this Ordinance to certain death or retirement provision made before "the commencement of this Section" in so far as that death or retirement provision continues "on and after that commencement". According to s. 5 of 136 of 1997, "the commencement of this Section" meant, and always meant, for all purposes, the commencement of ss. 2, 3 and 4 of 71 of 1997 (i.e., 15 October 1997).

(2) Subsection (1) shall not apply to —

(a) discrimination which is rendered unlawful by any of the provisions of Section 11(1) or (2) or 25; or

(b) discrimination which would be rendered unlawful by any of those provisions but for the operation of any other provision of this Ordinance.

Section 19 Employment Agencies

(1) It is unlawful for an employment agency to discriminate against a woman —

(a) in the terms on which the agency offers to provide any of its services;

(b) by refusing or deliberately omitting to provide any of its services; or

(c) in the way it provides any of its services.

(2) References in subsection (1) to the services of an employment agency include guidance on careers and any other services related to employment.

(3) This Section shall not apply if the discrimination only concerns employment which the employer could lawfully refuse to offer the woman.

(4) An employment agency shall not be subject to any liability under this Section if it proves —

(a) that it acted in reliance on a statement made to it by the employer to the effect that, by reason of the operation of subsection (3), its action would not be unlawful; and

(b) that it was reasonable for it to rely on the statement.

(5) A person who knowingly or recklessly makes a statement of the kind referred to in subsection (4)(a) which in a material respect is false or misleading commits an offence and is liable on conviction to a fine at level 4.

Section 20 Discrimination against Commission Agents

(1) This Section applies to any work for a person (***the principal***) which is available for doing by individuals (***commission agents***) as the agents of the principal and who are remunerated, whether in whole or in part, by commission.

(2) It is unlawful for the principal, in relation to work to which this Section applies, to discriminate against a woman who is a commission agent —

(a) in the terms on which he allows her to do that work;

(b) by not allowing her to do it or continue to do it;

(c) in the way he affords her access to any benefits, facilities or services or by refusing or deliberately omitting to afford her access to them; or

(d) by subjecting her to any other detriment.

(3) The principal does not contravene subsection (2)(b) by doing any act in relation to a woman at a time when if the work were to be done by a person taken into his employment being a man would be a genuine occupational qualification for the job.

(4) Subsection (2)(c) shall not apply to benefits, facilities or services of any description if the principal is concerned with the provision (for payment or not) of benefits, facilities or services of that description to the public, or to a section of the public to which the woman belongs, unless that provision differs in a material respect from the provision of the benefits, facilities or services by the principal to his commission agents.

Government

Section 21 Government

(1) Subject to subsection (2), without prejudice to the operation of the other provisions of this Part in relation to the Government, it is unlawful for the Government to discriminate against a woman in the performance of its functions or the exercise of its powers.

(2) Subsection (1) shall not render unlawful —

(a) as regards a woman not having the right to enter and remain in Hong Kong, any act done under any immigration legislation governing entry into, stay in and departure from Hong Kong; or

(b) any act done in relation to a woman if it was necessary for that act to be done in order to comply with a requirement of an existing statutory provision.

Special Cases

Section 22 Ministers of Religion, etc.

(1) Nothing in this Part applies to employment for the purposes of an organized religion where the employment is limited to one sex so as to comply with the doctrines of the religion or to avoid offending the religious susceptibilities common to its followers.

(2) Nothing in Section 17 applies to an authorization or qualification (within the meaning of that Section) for the purposes of an organized religion where the authorization or qualification is limited to one sex so as to comply with the doctrines of the religion or to avoid offending the religious susceptibilities common to its followers.

Sexual Harassment

Section 23 Employees, etc.

(1) It is unlawful for a person, in relation to employment by him at an establishment in Hong Kong, to sexually harass a woman who is seeking to be employed by the person.

(2) It is unlawful for a person, in the case of a woman employed by him at an establishment in Hong Kong, to sexually harass her.

(3) It is unlawful for a person who is employed by another person at an establishment in Hong Kong to sexually harass a woman who is seeking to be, or who is, employed by that second-mentioned person.

(4) It is unlawful for the principal, in relation to work to which Section 13 applies, to sexually harass a woman who is a contract worker.

(5) It is unlawful for a contract worker to sexually harass a woman who is a fellow contract worker.

(6) It is unlawful for a partner in a firm to sexually harass a woman who is seeking to be, or who is, a partner in the firm.

(7) Subsection (6) shall apply in relation to persons proposing to form themselves into a partnership as it applies in relation to a firm.

(8) Section 15(6) shall apply to subsection (6) as it applies to Section 15(1).

(9) It is unlawful for the principal, in relation to work to which Section 20 applies, to sexually harass a woman who is a commission agent.

(10) It is unlawful for a commission agent to sexually harass a woman who is a fellow commission agent.

(11) It is unlawful for a person who is seeking to be, or who is, employed by a woman at an establishment in Hong Kong to sexually harass her.

(12) It is unlawful for a person residing in any premises to sexually harass a woman —

(a) employed by another person at an establishment in Hong Kong (and whether or not that other person also resides in those premises or those premises are that establishment); and

(b) carrying out in those premises all or part of her work in relation to her employment (and whether or not she also resides in those premises).

Section 23A Sexual Harassment at Workplace

(1) It is unlawful for a person who is a workplace participant to sexually harass a woman who is also a workplace participant at a workplace of them both.

(2) In this Section —

intern (實習人員) means a person who is engaged by another person for an internship but is not an employee of that other person;

internship (實習) means —

(a) a period of work the completion of which is required for attaining a professional or academic qualification and includes a pupillage; or

(b) any other work that is usually described as an internship;

volunteer (義工) means a person who performs volunteer work other than in the capacity of an employer or employee;

workplace (工作場所), in relation to a person, means a place —

(a) at which the person works as a workplace participant; or

(b) that the person attends as a workplace participant;

workplace participant (場所使用者) means —

(a) an employee;

(b) an employer;

(c) a contract worker;

(d) the principal, within the meaning of Section 13(1), of a contract worker;

(e) a commission agent;

(f) the principal, within the meaning of Section 20(1), of a commission agent;

(g) a partner in a firm;

(h) an intern; or

(i) a volunteer.

(Added 8 of 2020 s. 20)

Section 24 Other Sexual Harassment

(1) It is unlawful for a member of an organization to which Section 16 applies to sexually harass a woman who is seeking to be, or who is, a member of the organization.

(2) It is unlawful for a member of an authority or body referred to in Section 17 to sexually harass a woman seeking an authorization or qualification (within the meaning of that Section) which can be conferred by the authority or body, as the case may be.

(3) It is unlawful for a person to sexually harass a woman seeking or undergoing training which would help fit her for any employment if that person provides, or makes arrangements for the provision of, facilities for such training.

(4) It is unlawful for a person who —

(a) operates an employment agency; or

(b) is a member of the staff of an employment agency,

to sexually harass a woman in the course of offering to provide, or providing, any of the agency's services to her.

Part 4 Discrimination and Sexual Harassment in Other Fields

(Amended L.N. 391 of 1996)

Education

Section 25 Discrimination by Responsible Bodies for Educational Establishments

It is unlawful for the responsible body for an educational establishment to discriminate against a woman —

(a) in the terms on which it offers to admit her to the establishment as a student;

(b) by refusing or deliberately omitting to accept an application for her admission to the establishment as a student; or

(c) where she is a student of the establishment —

(i) in the way it affords her access to any benefits, facilities or services, or by refusing or deliberately omitting to afford her access to them; or

(ii) by excluding her from the establishment or subjecting her to any other detriment.

Section 26 Exceptions for Single-Sex Establishments

(1) Section 25(a) and (b) shall not apply to the admission of students to any educational establishment (***single-sex establishment***) which admits students of one sex only, or which would be taken to admit students of one sex only if there were disregarded students of the opposite sex —

(a) whose admission is exceptional; or

(b) whose numbers are comparatively small and whose admission is confined to particular courses of instruction or teaching classes.

(2) Where an educational establishment which is not a single-sex establishment has some students as boarders and others as non-boarders, and admits as boarders students of one sex only (or would be taken to admit as boarders students of one sex only if there were disregarded boarders of the opposite sex whose numbers are comparatively small), Section 25(a) and (b) shall not apply to the admission of boarders and Section 25(c)(i) shall not apply to boarding facilities.

(3) Where an educational establishment is a single-sex establishment by reason of its inclusion in subsection (1)(b), the fact that students of one sex are confined to particular courses of instruction or teaching classes shall not be taken to contravene Section 25(c)(i).

Section 27 Exceptions for Single-Sex Establishments Turning Co-educational

(1) Where at any time —

(a) the responsible body for an educational establishment which is a single-sex establishment determines to alter its admissions arrangements so that the establishment will cease to be a single-sex establishment; or

(b) Section 26(2) applies to the admission of boarders to an educational establishment but the responsible body for the establishment determines to alter its admissions arrangements so that that Section will cease so to apply,

then the responsible body may, by notice served on the Commission, specify the date on which that determination is to take effect.

(2) Where the responsible body for an educational establishment has served a notice referred to in subsection (1), then if the responsible body, at any time during the period of 3 years beginning on the date specified in that notice as the date on which the determination concerned referred to in that subsection is to take effect (or such longer period not exceeding 3 years as the Commission may allow in any particular case), refuses or deliberately omits to accept an application for the admission of a person to the establishment as a student, that refusal or omission, as the case may be, shall not be taken to contravene any provision of this Ordinance.

(3) This Section shall not operate to afford any exemption from liability under this Ordinance except as provided for in subsection (2).

Goods, Facilities, Services and Premises

Section 28 Discrimination in Provision of Goods, Facilities or Services

(1) It is unlawful for any person concerned with the provision (for payment or not) of goods, facilities or services to the public or a section of the public to discriminate against a woman who seeks to obtain or use those goods, facilities or services —

(a) by refusing or deliberately omitting to provide her with any of them; or

(b) by refusing or deliberately omitting to provide her with goods, facilities or services of the like quality, in the like manner and on the like terms as are normal in his case in relation to male members of the public or (where she belongs to a section of the public) to male members of that section.

(2) The following are examples of the facilities and services referred to in subsection (1) —

(a) access to and use of any place which members of the public or a section of the public are permitted to enter;

(b) accommodation in a hotel, guesthouse or other similar establishment;

(c) facilities by way of banking or insurance or for grants, loans, credit or finance;

(d) facilities for education;

(e) facilities for entertainment, recreation or refreshment;

(f) facilities for transport or travel;

(g) the services of any profession or trade;

(h) the services of —

(i)–(ii)(*Repealed* 78 *of* 1999 s. 7)

(iii) any department of the Government; or

(iv) any undertaking by or of the Government.

(3) For the avoidance of doubt, it is hereby declared that where a particular skill is commonly exercised in a different way for men and for women it shall not be a contravention of subsection (1) for a person who does not normally exercise it for women to insist on exercising it for a woman only in accordance with his normal practice or, if he reasonably considers it impracticable to do that in her case, to refuse or deliberately omit to exercise it.

Section 29 Discrimination in Disposal or Management of Premises

(1) It is unlawful for a person, in relation to premises in Hong Kong of which he has power to dispose, to discriminate against a woman —

(a) in the terms on which he offers her those premises;

(b) by refusing her application for those premises; or

(c) in his treatment of her in relation to any list of persons in need of premises of that description.

(2) It is unlawful for a person, in relation to premises managed by him, to discriminate against a woman occupying the premises —

(a) in the way he affords her access to any benefits or facilities, or by refusing or deliberately omitting to afford her access to them; or

(b) by evicting her, or subjecting her to any other detriment.

(3) Subsection (1) shall not apply to a person who owns an estate or interest in the premises and wholly occupies them unless he uses the services of an estate agent for the purposes of the disposal of the premises, or publishes or causes to be published an advertisement in connection with the disposal.

(4) In this Section, in relation to premises, ***power to dispose*** (有權處置) includes the power to sell, rent, let, sub-let or otherwise part with possession of those premises.

Section 30 Discrimination: Consent for Assignment or Sub-letting

(1) Where the licence or consent of the landlord or of any other person is required for the disposal to any person of premises in Hong Kong comprised in a tenancy, it is unlawful for the landlord or other person to discriminate against a woman by withholding the licence or consent for disposal of the premises to her.

(2) Subsection (1) shall not apply if —

(a) the person withholding a licence or consent, or a near relative of his (***the relevant occupier***) resides, and intends to continue to reside, on the premises;

(b) there is on the premises, in addition to the accommodation occupied by the relevant occupier, accommodation (not being storage accommodation or means of access) shared by the relevant occupier with other persons residing on the premises who are not members of his household; and

(c) the premises are small premises as construed in accordance with Section 31(2).

(3) For the avoidance of doubt, it is hereby declared that this Section applies to tenancies created before the enactment of this Ordinance as well as to tenancies created on or after the enactment of this Ordinance.

(4) In this Section —

disposal (處置), in relation to premises comprised in a tenancy, includes assignment of the tenancy and sub-letting or parting with possession of the premises or any part of the premises;

tenancy (租賃) means a tenancy created —

(a) by a lease or sub-lease;

(b) by an agreement for a lease or sub-lease;

(c) by a tenancy agreement; or

(d) pursuant to any enactment.

Section 31 Exceptions for Small Dwellings

(1) Sections 28(1) and 29 shall not apply to the provision by a person of accommodation in any premises, or the disposal of premises by him, if—

(a) that person or a near relative of his (***the relevant occupier***) resides, and intends to continue to reside, on the premises;

(b) there is on the premises, in addition to the accommodation occupied by the relevant occupier, accommodation (not being storage accommodation or means of access) shared by the relevant occupier with other persons residing on the premises who are not members of his household; and

(c) the premises are small premises.

(2) Premises shall be treated for the purposes of subsection (1) as small premises if —

(a) in the case of premises comprising residential accommodation for one or more households (under separate letting or similar agreements) in addition to the accommodation occupied by the relevant occupier, there is not normally residential accommodation for more than 2 such households and only the relevant occupier and any member of his household reside in the accommodation occupied by him;

(b) in the case of premises not falling within paragraph (a), there is not normally residential accommodation on the premises for more than 6 persons in addition to the relevant occupier and any members of his household.

(3) The Chief Executive in Council may, by notice in the Gazette, amend subsection (2)(b) by substituting another number for the number appearing in that subsection. *(Amended 66 of 1999 s. 3)*

Section 32 Exceptions from Section 28(1) for Health and Safety Considerations

Section 28(1) shall not be construed as rendering unlawful discrimination falling within Section 8 if the discrimination is imposed in order to comply with health and safety considerations which are reasonable in the circumstances.

Section 33 Exceptions for Voluntary Bodies

(1) This Section applies to a body the activities of which are carried on otherwise than for profit.

(2) Sections 28(1) and 29 shall not be construed as rendering unlawful —

(a) the restriction of membership of any body to which this Section applies to persons of one sex (disregarding any minor exceptions); or

(b) the provision of benefits, facilities or services to members of any body to which this Section applies where the membership is so restricted,

even though membership of the body is open to the public, or to a section of the public.

(3) Nothing in Section 28 or 29 shall —

(a) be construed as affecting a provision to which this subsection applies; or

(b) render unlawful an act which is done in order to give effect to such a provision.

(4) Subsection (3) applies to a provision for conferring benefits on persons of one sex only (disregarding any benefits to persons of the opposite sex which are exceptional or are relatively insignificant), being a provision which constitutes the main object of a body to which this Section applies.

Section 34 Further Exceptions from Sections 28(1) and 29

(1) A person who provides at any place facilities or services restricted to men does not for that reason contravene Section 28(1) if—

(a) the place is, or is part of, a hospital, reception centre or other establishment for persons requiring special care, supervision or attention;

(b) the place is (permanently or for the time being) occupied or used for the purposes of an organized religion, and the facilities or services are restricted to men so as to comply with the doctrines of that religion or to avoid offending the religious susceptibilities common to its followers; or

(c) the facilities or services are provided for, or are likely to be used by, 2 or more persons at the same time, and—

(i) the facilities or services are such, or those persons are such, that male users are likely to suffer serious embarrassment at the presence of a woman; or

(ii) the facilities or services are such that a user is likely to be in a state of undress and a male user might reasonably object to the presence of a female user.

(2) A person who provides facilities or services restricted to men shall not for that reason contravene Section 28(1) if the services or facilities are such that physical contact between the user and any other person is likely, and that other person might reasonably object if the user were a woman.

(3) Sections 28(1) and 29 shall not apply—

(a) to discrimination which is rendered unlawful by any provision or Part of this Ordinance specified in column 1 of Schedule 4; or

(b) to discrimination which would be so unlawful but for any provision or Part of this Ordinance specified in column 2 of that Schedule.

Advisory Bodies

Section 35 Discrimination in Eligibility to Vote for and to be Elected or Appointed to Advisory Bodies

(1) In this Section, a reference to a relevant body means a public body, a public authority, a statutory advisory body, or a prescribed body.

(2) In this Section, a reference to a relevant position includes membership of a public body, a public authority, and a prescribed position, and the positions of Rural Representative or member or office-holder of a Rural Committee within the meaning of the Heung Yee Kuk Ordinance (Cap. 1097). (*Amended 5 of 2014 s. 2*)

(3) It is unlawful for a person to discriminate against another person in—

(a) determining the eligibility of a person to stand for election to a relevant body or relevant position, or to be selected for a relevant position;

(b) the terms or conditions on which a person is considered eligible to stand for election to a relevant body or relevant position, or to be selected for a relevant position;

(c) determining the eligibility of a person to vote in elections of members of a relevant body or the holder of a relevant position, or to take part in the selection of the holder of a relevant position;

(d) the terms or conditions on which a person is considered eligible to vote in elections of members of a relevant body or the holder of a relevant position, or to take part in the selection of the holder of a relevant position;

(e) considering whether a person should be appointed as a member of a relevant body, where some or all of the members of that body are appointed; or

(f) considering whether a person should be appointed to a relevant position, approved as a member of a relevant body or recognized as holding a relevant position.

(4) This Section shall have effect, notwithstanding the provisions of any Ordinance which provide that a person of a particular sex or marital status is not eligible to stand for election, or to be selected for, a relevant body or position, or to vote in elections for or to take part in the selection of members of a relevant body or the holder of a relevant position.

(5) Notwithstanding anything in the Heung Yee Kuk Ordinance (Cap. 1097) or in any other Ordinance, the Secretary for Home Affairs shall not —

(a) *(Repealed 2 of 2003 s. 68)*

(b) issue a certificate recognizing a body as a Rural Committee;

(c) approve a person as a Special or Co-opted Councillor,

where that person or body (or any of its members) has been elected or otherwise chosen by a procedure in which women have not been able to participate on equal terms with men, whether as candidates, nominees, electors or in some other relevant capacity.

Barristers

Section 36 Discrimination by, or in Relation to, Barristers

(1) It is unlawful for a barrister or barrister's clerk, in relation to any offer of a pupillage or tenancy, to discriminate against a woman —

(a) in the arrangements which are made for the purpose of determining to whom it should be offered;

(b) in respect of any terms on which it is offered; or

(c) by refusing, or deliberately omitting, to offer it to her.

(2) It is unlawful for a barrister or barrister's clerk, in relation to a woman who is a pupil or tenant in the chambers concerned, to discriminate against her —

(a) in respect of any terms applicable to her as a pupil or tenant;

(b) in the opportunities for training, or gaining experience, which are afforded or denied to her;

(c) in the benefits, facilities or services which are afforded or denied to her; or

(d) by terminating her pupillage or by subjecting her to any pressure to leave the chambers or other detriment.

(3) It is unlawful for any person, in relation to the giving, withholding or acceptance of instructions to a barrister, to discriminate against a woman.

(4) In this Section —

barrister's clerk (大律師書記) includes any person carrying out any of the functions of a barrister's clerk;

pupil (見習大律師), ***pupillage*** (見習職位), ***tenancy*** (租賃) and ***tenant*** (承租人) have the meanings commonly associated with their use in the context of a set of barristers' chambers.

Clubs

Section 37 Discrimination by Clubs

(1) It is unlawful for a club, the committee of management of a club or a member of the committee of management of a club to discriminate against a woman who is not a member of the club —

(a) by refusing or failing to accept her application for membership; or

(b) in the terms or conditions on which the club is prepared to admit her to membership.

(2) It is unlawful for a club, the committee of management of a club or a member of the committee of management of a club to discriminate against a woman who is a member of the club —

(a) in the terms or conditions of membership that are afforded to her;

(b) by refusing or failing to accept her application for a particular class or type of membership;

(c) by denying her access, or limiting her access, to any benefit, service or facility provided by the club;

(d) by depriving her of membership or varying the terms of membership; or

(e) by subjecting her to any other detriment.

(3) Nothing in subsection (1)(b) or (2) renders it unlawful to discriminate against a woman if the discrimination occurs in relation to the use or enjoyment of any benefit provided by the club where —

(a) it is not practicable for the benefit to be used or enjoyed —

(i) simultaneously; or

(ii) to the same extent,

by both men and women; and

(b) either —

(i) the same, or an equivalent, benefit is provided for the use of men and women separately from each other; or

(ii) men and women are each entitled to a fair and reasonable proportion of use and enjoyment of the benefit.

Government

Section 38 Government

(1) Subject to subsection (2), without prejudice to the operation of the other provisions of this Part in relation to the Government, it is unlawful for the Government to discriminate against a woman in the performance of its functions or the exercise of its powers.

(2) Subsection (1) shall not render unlawful —

(a) as regards a woman not having the right to enter and remain in Hong Kong, any act done under any immigration legislation governing entry into, stay in and departure from Hong Kong; or

(b) any act done in relation to a woman if it was necessary for that act to be done in order to comply with a requirement of an existing statutory provision.

Sexual Harassment

Section 39 Educational Establishments

(1) It is unlawful for a person who is, or is a member of, the responsible body for an educational establishment to sexually harass a woman who is seeking to be, or who is, a student of the establishment.

(2) It is unlawful for a person who is a member of the staff of an educational establishment to sexually harass a woman who is seeking to be, or who is, a student of the establishment.

(3) It is unlawful for a person who is a student of an educational establishment to sexually harass a woman who is seeking to be, or who is, a student of the establishment.

(4) It is unlawful for a person who is seeking to be, or who is, a student of an educational establishment to sexually harass a woman —

- (a) who is, or is a member of, the responsible body for; or
- (b) who is a member of the staff of,

the establishment.

Section 39A Sexual Harassment by Clubs

It is unlawful for a club, the committee of management of a club or a member of the committee of management of a club to sexually harass a woman who is, or has applied to be, a member of the club.

(Added 8 of 2020 s. 39)

Section 40 Other Sexual Harassment

(1) It is unlawful for a person to sexually harass a woman in the course of offering to provide, or providing, goods, facilities or services to her.

(1A) It is unlawful for a person to sexually harass a woman in the course of —

- (a) seeking to be provided with goods, facilities or services by her; or
- (b) being provided with goods, facilities or services by her. *(Added 19 of 2014 s. 3)*

(2) It is unlawful for a person, in relation to premises in Hong Kong of which he has power to dispose, to sexually harass a woman in the course of offering to provide, or providing, those premises to her.

(3) It is unlawful for a person, in relation to premises managed by him, to sexually harass a woman occupying the premises.

(4) Where the licence or consent of the landlord or of any other person is required for the disposal to any person of premises in Hong Kong comprised in a tenancy, it is unlawful for the landlord or other person to sexually harass a woman seeking the licence or consent for disposal of the premises to her.

(5) Section 30(4) shall apply to subsection (4) as it applies to Section 30.

(6) It is unlawful for a barrister or barrister's clerk, in relation to any chambers, to sexually harass a woman —

- (a) in the course of offering to provide to her pupillage or tenancy in the chambers; or
- (b) who is a pupil or tenant in the chambers.

(7) It is unlawful for any person, in the course of the giving, withholding or acceptance of instructions to a barrister, to sexually harass a woman who is a barrister.

(8) Section 36(4) shall apply to subsections (6) and (7) as it applies to Section 36.

Extent

Section 41 Extent of Part 4

(1) Section 28(1) –

(a) shall not apply to goods, facilities or services outside Hong Kong except as provided in subsections (2) and (3); and

(b) shall not apply to facilities by way of banking or insurance or for grants, loans, credit or finance, where the facilities are for a purpose to be carried out, or in connection with risks wholly or mainly arising, outside Hong Kong.

(2) Section 28(1) applies to the provision of facilities for travel outside Hong Kong where the refusal or omission occurs in Hong Kong or on a ship, aircraft or dynamically supported craft referred to in subsection (3).

(3) Section 28(1) applies on and in relation to –

(a) any ship registered in Hong Kong;

(b) any aircraft or dynamically supported craft registered in Hong Kong and operated by a person who has his principal place of business, or is ordinarily resident, in Hong Kong;

(c) any ship, aircraft or dynamically supported craft belonging to or possessed by the Government,

even if the ship, aircraft or dynamically supported craft is outside Hong Kong.

(4) This Section shall not render unlawful an act done in or over a place outside Hong Kong, or in or over that place's territorial waters, if any, for the purpose of complying with the laws of that place.

(5) Section 25 shall not apply to benefits, facilities or services outside Hong Kong except –

(a) travel on a ship registered in Hong Kong;

(b) benefits, facilities or services provided on a ship so registered.

(6) Section 40(1) and (1A) does not apply to sexual harassment that occurs outside Hong Kong except as provided in subsection (7). *(Added 19 of 2014 s. 4)*

(7) Section 40(1) and (1A) applies to sexual harassment that occurs on a ship, aircraft or dynamically supported craft referred to in subsection (3) even if it is outside Hong Kong. *(Added 19 of 2014 s. 4)*

(Amended E.R. 1 of 2013)

Part 5 Other Unlawful Acts

Section 42 Discriminatory Practices

(1) In this Section, ***discriminatory practice*** (歧視性的做法) means the application of a requirement or condition which results in an act of discrimination which is unlawful by virtue of any provision of Part 3 or 4 as read with Section 5(1)(b), 7(1)(b) or 8(b) or which would be likely to result in such an act of discrimination if the persons to whom it is applied were not all of one sex.

(2) A person acts in contravention of this Section if and so long as –

(a) he applies a discriminatory practice; or

(b) he operates practices or other arrangements which in any circumstances would call for the application by him of a discriminatory practice.

(3) Proceedings in respect of a contravention of this Section shall be brought only by the Commission in accordance with the provisions of Sections 77, 78, 79, 80 and 81.

(Amended E.R. 1 of 2013)

Section 43 Discriminatory Advertisements

(1) It is unlawful to publish or cause to be published an advertisement which indicates, or might reasonably be understood as indicating, an intention by a person to do any act which is or might be unlawful by virtue of Part 3 or 4.

(2) Subsection (1) shall not apply to an advertisement if the intended act would not in fact be unlawful.

(3) For the purposes of subsection (1), use of a job description which is sex specific shall be taken to indicate an intention to discriminate, unless the advertisement contains an indication to the contrary.

(4) The publisher of an advertisement made unlawful by subsection (1) shall not be subject to any liability under that subsection in respect of the publication of the advertisement if he proves —

(a) that the advertisement was published in reliance on a statement made to him by the person who caused it to be published to the effect that, by reason of the operation of subsection (2), the publication would not be unlawful; and

(b) that it was reasonable for him to rely on the statement.

(5) A person who knowingly or recklessly makes a statement of the kind referred to in subsection (4) which in a material respect is false or misleading commits an offence and is liable on conviction to a fine at level 4.

(Amended E.R. 1 of 2013)

Section 44 Instructions to Discriminate

It is unlawful for a person —

(a) who has authority over another person; or

(b) in accordance with whose wishes that other person is accustomed to act,

to instruct him to do any act which is unlawful by virtue of Part 3 or 4, or procure or attempt to procure the doing by him of any such act.

(Amended E.R. 1 of 2013)

Section 45 Pressure to Discriminate

(1) It is unlawful to induce, or attempt to induce, a person to do any act which contravenes Part 3 or 4 by —

(a) providing or offering to provide him with any benefit; or

(b) subjecting or threatening to subject him to any detriment.

(2) An offer or threat is not prevented from falling within subsection (1) because it is not made directly to the person concerned, if it is made in such a way that he is likely to hear of it.

(Amended E.R. 1 of 2013)

Section 46 Liability of Employers and Principals

(1) Anything done by a person in the course of his employment shall be treated for the purposes of this Ordinance as done by his employer as well as by him, whether or not it was done with the employer's knowledge or approval.

(2) Anything done by a person as agent for another person with the authority (whether express or implied, and whether precedent or subsequent) of that other person shall be treated for the purposes of this Ordinance as done by that other person as well as by him.

(3) In proceedings brought under this Ordinance against any person in respect of an act alleged to have been done by an employee of his it shall be a defence for that person to prove that he took such steps as were reasonably practicable to prevent the employee from doing that act, or from doing in the course of his employment acts of that description.

(4) For the avoidance of doubt, it is hereby declared that this Section shall not apply for the purposes of any criminal proceedings.

Section 46A Liability of Persons Engaging Interns and Volunteers

(1) This Section applies for the purposes of Section 23A.

(2) For the avoidance of doubt, this Section does not apply for the purposes of any criminal proceedings.

(3) An act done by an intern in the course of an internship is to be treated as an act done —

(a) by the intern; and

(b) by the person who engaged the intern for the internship, whether or not the act was done with the knowledge or approval of that person.

(4) In proceedings brought under this Ordinance against a person in respect of an act alleged to have been done by an intern engaged by the person, it is a defence for the person to prove that the person took reasonably practicable steps to prevent the intern —

(a) from doing that act; or

(b) from doing acts of that description in the course of the internship.

(5) Subsections (6) and (7) apply if a volunteer is engaged by another person to perform volunteer work.

(6) An act done by a volunteer in the course of performing volunteer work is to be treated as an act done —

(a) by the volunteer; and

(b) by the person who engaged the volunteer to perform the work, whether or not the act was done with the knowledge or approval of that person.

(7) In proceedings brought under this Ordinance against a person in respect of an act alleged to have been done by a volunteer engaged by the person, it is a defence for the person to prove that the person took reasonably practicable steps to prevent the volunteer —

(a) from doing that act; or

(b) from doing acts of that description in the course of performing volunteer work.

(Added 8 of 2020 s. 21)

Section 47 Aiding Unlawful Acts

(1) A person who knowingly aids another person to do an act made unlawful by this Ordinance shall be treated for the purposes of this Ordinance as himself doing an unlawful act of the like description.

(2) For the purposes of subsection (1), an employee or agent for whose act the employer or principal is liable under Section 46 (or would be so liable but for Section 46(3)) shall be deemed to aid the doing of the act by the employer or principal.

(2A) For the purposes of subsection (1), if a person who engaged an intern —

(a) is liable under Section 46A for an act done by the intern; or

(b) would be liable under Section 46A for the act but for Section 46A(4),

the intern is deemed to aid the doing of the act by that person. *(Added 8 of 2020 s. 22)*

(2B) For the purposes of subsection (1), if a person who engaged a volunteer —

(a) is liable under Section 46A for an act done by the volunteer; or

(b) would be liable under Section 46A for the act but for Section 46A(7),

the volunteer is deemed to aid the doing of the act by that person. *(Added 8 of 2020 s. 22)*

(3) A person does not under this Section knowingly aid another to do an unlawful act if —

(a) he acts in reliance on a statement made to him by that other person that, by reason of any provision of this Ordinance, the act which he aids would not be unlawful; and

(b) it is reasonable for him to rely on the statement.

(4) A person who knowingly or recklessly makes a statement of the kind referred to in subsection (3)(a) which in a material respect is false or misleading commits an offence and is liable on conviction to a fine at level 4.

Part 6 General Exceptions from Parts 3 to 5

(Amended E.R. 1 of 2013)

Section 48 Special Measures

Nothing in Part 3, 4 or 5 shall render unlawful an act that is reasonably intended to —

(a) ensure that persons of a particular sex or marital status, or who are pregnant, have equal opportunities with other persons in circumstances in relation to which a provision is made by this Ordinance.

(b) afford persons of a particular sex or marital status, or who are pregnant, goods or access to services, facilities or opportunities to meet their special needs in relation to —

(i) employment, education, clubs or sport; or

(ii) the provision of premises, goods, services or facilities;

(c) afford persons of a particular sex or marital status, or who are pregnant, grants, benefits or programmes, whether direct or indirect, to meet their special needs in relation to —

(i) employment, education, clubs or sport; or

(ii) the provision of premises, goods, services or facilities.

(Amended E.R. 1 of 2013)

Section 49 Charities

(1) Nothing in Part 3, 4 or 5 shall —

(a) be construed as affecting a provision to which this subsection applies; or

(b) render unlawful an act which is done in order to give effect to such a provision.

(2) Subsection (1) applies to a provision for conferring benefits on persons of one sex only (disregarding any benefits to persons of the opposite sex which are exceptional or are relatively insignificant), being a provision which is contained in a charitable instrument.

(3) In applying this Section, account shall be taken of Section 88 of the Inland Revenue Ordinance (Cap. 112).

(4) In this Section —

charitable instrument (慈善文書) means an enactment or other instrument so far as it relates to charitable purposes;

charitable purposes (慈善目的) means purposes which are exclusively charitable according to any enactment or rule of law.

(Amended E.R. 1 of 2013)

Section 50 Sport, etc.

Nothing in Part 3, 4 or 5 shall, in relation to any sport, game or other activity of a competitive nature where the physical strength, stamina or physique of the average woman puts her at a disadvantage to the average man, render unlawful any act related to the participation of a person as a competitor in events involving that activity which are confined to competitors of one sex.

(Amended E.R. 1 of 2013)

Section 51 Insurance, etc.

Nothing in Part 3, 4 or 5 shall render unlawful the treatment of a person in relation to any class of insurance business, or similar matter involving the assessment of risk, where the treatment —

(a) was effected by reference to actuarial or other data from a source on which it was reasonable to rely; and

(b) was reasonable having regard to the data and any other relevant factors.

(Amended E.R. 1 of 2013)

Section 52 Communal Accommodation

(1) In this Section, ***communal accommodation*** (共用住宿地方) means residential accommodation which includes dormitories or other shared sleeping accommodation which for reasons of privacy or decency should be used by men only, or by women only (but which may include some shared sleeping accommodation for men, and some for women, or some ordinary sleeping accommodation).

(2) In this Section, ***communal accommodation*** (共用住宿地方) also includes residential accommodation all or part of which should be used by men only, or by women only, because of the nature of the sanitary facilities serving the accommodation.

(3) Nothing in Part 3 or 4 shall render unlawful sex discrimination in the admission of persons to communal accommodation if the accommodation is managed in a way which, given the exigencies of the situation, comes as near as may be to fair and equitable treatment of men and women.

(4) In applying subsection (3) account shall be taken of —

(a) whether and how far it is reasonable to expect that the accommodation should be altered or extended, or that further alternative accommodation should be provided; and

(b) the frequency of the demand or need for use of the accommodation by men as compared with women.

(5) Nothing in Part 3 or 4 shall render unlawful sex discrimination against a woman, or against a man, in respect of the provision of any benefit, facility or service if —

(a) the benefit, facility or service cannot properly and effectively be provided except for those using communal accommodation; and

(b) in the relevant circumstances the woman or the man, as the case may be, could lawfully be refused the use of the accommodation by virtue of subsection (3).

(6) Neither subsection (3) nor subsection (5) is a defence to an act of sex discrimination under Part 3 unless such arrangements as are reasonably practicable are made to compensate for the detriment caused by the discrimination; but in considering under subsection (5)(b) whether the use of

communal accommodation could lawfully be refused (in a case based on Part 3), it shall be assumed that the requirements of this subsection have been complied with in respect of subsection (3).

(7) This Section is without prejudice to the generality of Section 34(1)(c).

(Amended E.R. 1 of 2013)

Section 53 Discriminatory Training by Certain Bodies

(1) Nothing in Part 3, 4 or 5 shall render unlawful any act done in relation to particular work by any person in, or in connection with —

(a) affording women only, or men only, access to facilities for training which would help to fit them for that work; or

(b) encouraging women only, or men only, to take advantage of opportunities for doing that work,

where it reasonably appears to that person that at any time within the 12 months immediately preceding the doing of the act there were no persons of the sex concerned doing that work in Hong Kong, or the number of persons of that sex doing the work in Hong Kong was comparatively small.

(2) Nothing in Part 3, 4 or 5 shall render unlawful any act done by any person in, or in connection with, affording persons access to facilities for training which would help to fit them for employment, where it reasonably appears to that person that those persons are in special need of training by reason of the period for which they have been discharging domestic or family responsibilities to the exclusion of regular full time employment.

(3) For the avoidance of doubt, it is hereby declared that the discrimination in relation to which subsection (2) applies may result from confining the training to persons who have been discharging domestic or family responsibilities, or from the way persons are selected for training, or both.

(4) This Section shall not apply in relation to any discrimination which is rendered unlawful by Section 11.

(Amended E.R. 1 of 2013)

Section 54 Other Discriminatory Training, etc.

(1) Nothing in Part 3, 4 or 5 shall render unlawful any act done by an employer in relation to particular work in his employment, being an act done in, or in connection with —

(a) affording his female employees only, or his male employees only, access to facilities for training which would help to fit them for that work; or

(b) encouraging women only, or men only, to take advantage of opportunities for doing that work,

where at any time within the 12 months immediately preceding the doing of the act there were no persons of the sex concerned among those doing that work or the number of persons of that sex doing the work was comparatively small.

(2) Nothing in Section 16 shall render unlawful any act done by an organization to which that Section applies in, or in connection with —

(a) affording female members of the organization only, or male members of the organization only, access to facilities for training which would help to fit them for holding a post of any kind in the organization; or

(b) encouraging female members only, or male members only, to take advantage of opportunities for holding such posts in the organization,

where at any time within the 12 months immediately preceding the doing of the act there were no persons of the sex concerned among persons holding such posts in the organization or the number of persons of that sex holding such posts was comparatively small.

(3) Nothing in Part 3, 4 or 5 shall render unlawful any act done by an organization to which Section 16 applies in, or in connection with, encouraging women only, or men only, to become members of the organization where at any time within the 12 months immediately preceding the doing of the act there were no persons of the sex concerned among those members or the number of persons of that sex among the members was comparatively small.

(Amended E.R. 1 of 2013)

Section 55 Trade Unions, etc.: Elective Bodies

(1) If an organization to which Section 16 applies comprises a body the membership of which is wholly or mainly elected, nothing in that Section shall render unlawful provision which ensures that a minimum number of persons of one sex are members of the body —

(a) by reserving seats on the body for persons of that sex; or

(b) by making extra seats on the body available (by election or co-option or otherwise) for persons of that sex on occasions when the number of persons of that sex in the other seats is below the minimum,

where in the opinion of the organization the provision is in the circumstances needed to secure a reasonable lower limit to the number of members of that sex serving on the body; and nothing in Part 3, 4 or 5 shall render unlawful any act done in order to give effect to such a provision.

(2) This Section shall not be taken as making lawful —

(a) discrimination in the arrangements for determining the persons entitled to vote in an election of members of the body, or otherwise to choose the persons to serve on the body; or

(b) discrimination in any arrangements concerning membership of the organization itself.

(Amended E.R. 1 of 2013)

Section 56 Indirect Access to Benefits, etc.

(1) References in this Ordinance to the affording by any person of access to benefits, facilities or services are not limited to benefits, facilities or services provided by that person himself, but include any means by which it is in that person's power to facilitate access to benefits, facilities or services provided by any other person (***actual provider***).

(2) Where by any provision of this Ordinance the affording by any person of access to benefits, facilities or services in a discriminatory way is in certain circumstances prevented from being unlawful, the effect of the provision shall extend also to the liability under this Ordinance of any actual provider.

Section 56A Double Benefits for Married Persons

(1) For avoidance of doubt, it is hereby declared that nothing in Part 3, 4 or 5 renders it unlawful for a person to refuse or omit to provide a benefit or allowance relating to housing, education, air-conditioning, passage or baggage to a married person if the married person's spouse receives or has received the same or a similar benefit or allowance, whether from the first-mentioned person or from another.

(2) In this Section —

allowance (津貼) includes part of an allowance;

benefit (福利) includes part of a benefit.

(Added 71 of 1997 s. 5. Amended E.R. 1 of 2013)

Section 56B Reproductive Technology

(1) Nothing in Part 4 or 5 renders unlawful any discrimination between persons of different marital status arising from the provision of any reproductive technology procedure.

(2) In this Section, ***reproductive technology procedure*** (生殖科技程序) has the meaning assigned to it by Section 2(1) of the Human Reproductive Technology Ordinance (Cap. 561). *(Replaced 47 of 2000 s. 48)*

(Added 71 of 1997 s. 5. Amended E.R. 1 of 2013)

Section 56C Adoption

Nothing in Part 3, 4 or 5 renders unlawful any discrimination between persons of different marital status arising from the provision of any facilities or services relating to the adoption of any infant within the meaning of Section 2 of the Adoption Ordinance (Cap. 290).

(Added 71 of 1997 s. 5. Amended E.R. 1 of 2013)

Section 57 Acts Done for Purposes of Protection of Women

(1) Nothing in —

(a) the provisions of Part 3;

(b) the provisions of Part 4 so far as it applies to vocational training; or

(c) the provisions of Part 5 so far as it has effect in relation to any of the provisions referred to in paragraph (a) or (b),

shall render unlawful any act done by a person in relation to a woman if —

(i) it was necessary for that person to do it in order to comply with a requirement of an existing statutory provision concerning the protection of women. *(Amended 18 of 2014 s. 17)*

(ii) *(Repealed 18 of 2014 s. 17)*

(2) In subsection (1) —

(a) the reference in paragraph (i) of that subsection to an existing statutory provision concerning the protection of women is a reference to any such provision having effect for the purpose of protecting women as regards —

(i) pregnancy or maternity; or

(ii) other circumstances giving rise to risks specifically affecting women,

whether the provision relates only to such protection or to the protection of any other class of persons as well. *(Amended 18 of 2014 s. 17)*

(b) *(Repealed 18 of 2014 s. 17)*

(3)–(4)*(Repealed 18 of 2014 s. 17)*

(Amended E.R. 1 of 2013)

Section 58 Acts Done under Statutory Authority to be Exempt from Certain Provisions of Part 4

(1) Nothing in —

(a) the relevant provisions of Part 4; or

(b) Part 5 so far as it has effect in relation to those provisions, shall render unlawful any act done by a person if it was necessary for that person to do it in order to comply with a requirement of an existing statutory provision.

(2) In subsection (1), ***the relevant provisions of Part 4*** (第4部的有關條文) means the provisions of Part 4 except so far as they apply to vocational training or sexual harassment.

(Amended E.R. 1 of 2013)

Section 59 Acts Safeguarding Security of Hong Kong

(1) Nothing in Part 3, 4 or 5 shall render unlawful an act done for the purpose of safeguarding the security of Hong Kong.

(2) A certificate purporting to be signed by or on behalf of the Chief Secretary for Administration and certifying that an act specified in the certificate was done for the purpose of safeguarding the security of Hong Kong shall be conclusive evidence that it was done for that purpose. *(Amended L.N. 362 of 1997)*

(3) A document purporting to be a certificate referred to in subsection (2) shall be received in evidence and, in the absence of evidence to the contrary, shall be deemed to be such a certificate.

(4) Subsections (2) and (3) shall not have effect in relation to the determination of the question whether any act is rendered unlawful by —

- (a) Part 3;
- (b) Part 4 so far as it applies to vocational training; or
- (c) Part 5 as read with —
  - (i) Part 3; or
  - (ii) Part 4 so far as it applies to vocational training.

(Amended E.R. 1 of 2013)

Section 60 Construction of References to Vocational Training

In Sections 57 and 58, ***vocational training*** (職業訓練) includes —

- (a) retraining; and
- (b) vocational guidance.

Section 61 Application to New Territories Land

Nothing in Part 4 or 5 shall —

- (a) be construed as affecting the operation of any of the provisions of —
  - (i) the New Territories Ordinance (Cap. 97); or
  - (ii) the New Territories Leases (Extension) Ordinance (Cap. 150); or
- (b) render unlawful any act done by any person in, or in connection with, the operation of any of those provisions.

(Amended E.R. 1 of 2013)

Section 62 Further Exceptions

(1) No provision or Part of this Ordinance specified in column 1 of Part 2 of Schedule 5 shall render unlawful any discrimination specified opposite thereto in column 2 of that Part.

(2) Nothing in Part 3, 4 or 5 shall render unlawful any act done by any person —

(a) in connection with any discrimination which is not unlawful by virtue of the operation of subsection (1); and

(b) to the extent that it is done for the purposes of that discrimination.

(Amended E.R. 1 of 2013)

Part 7 Equal Opportunities Commission

General

Section 63 Establishment of Commission

(1) There is hereby established a body corporate to be called the Equal Opportunities Commission.

(2) The Commission shall have perpetual succession and a common seal and shall be capable of suing and being sued.

(3) The Chief Executive shall appoint to be members of the Commission — *(Amended 66 of 1999 s. 3)*

(a) a Chairperson; and

(b) not less than 4 or more than 16 other members,

each being an individual who is not a public officer.

(4) The members of the Commission shall form its governing body with authority, in the name of the Commission, to perform the functions and exercise the powers of the Commission.

(5) The members of the Commission may be appointed on a full-time or part-time basis as the Chief Executive thinks fit except that the Chairperson shall be appointed on a full-time basis. *(Amended 66 of 1999 s. 3)*

(6) The relevant provisions of Schedule 6 shall have effect with respect to the Commission and its members.

(7) The Commission shall not be regarded as a servant or agent of the Government or as enjoying any status, immunity or privilege of the Government.

(8) Part VII of the Interpretation and General Clauses Ordinance (Cap. 1) shall apply to the Commission and appointments to the Commission except in so far as that Part is inconsistent with the provisions of this Ordinance.

(9) Every appointment under subsection (3) shall be notified in the Gazette.

(10) The Chief Executive in Council may, by notice in the Gazette, amend subsection (3)(b) by substituting another number for any number appearing in that subsection. *(Amended 66 of 1999 s. 3)*

Section 64 Functions and Powers of Commission

(1) The Commission shall —

(a) work towards the elimination of discrimination;

(b) promote equality of opportunity between men and women generally;

(c) work towards the elimination of sexual harassment;

(d) in the case of any act alleged to be unlawful by virtue of this Ordinance, encourage persons who are concerned with the matter to which the act relates to effect a settlement of the matter by conciliation, whether under Section 84 or otherwise;

(e) keep under review the working of this Ordinance and, when it is so required by the Chief Executive or otherwise thinks it necessary, draw up and submit to the Chief Executive proposals for amending this Ordinance; and *(Amended 66 of 1999 s. 3)*

(f) perform such other functions as are imposed on it under this Ordinance or any other enactment.

(2) The Commission may do all such things as are necessary for, or incidental or conducive to, the better performance of its functions and in particular but without prejudice to the generality of the foregoing, may —

(a) establish such committees as it thinks fit;

(b) acquire and hold property of any description if in the opinion of the Commission such property is necessary for —

(i) the accommodation of the Commission or of any committee; or

(ii) the performance of any function which the Commission may perform,

and, subject to the terms and conditions upon which such property is held, dispose of it;

(c) enter into, carry out, assign or accept the assignment of, vary or rescind, any contract, agreement or other obligation;

(d) employ such persons as it thinks fit to carry out any matter relating to the performance of its functions or the exercise of its powers;

(e) without prejudice to the generality of paragraph (d), engage the services of such persons as it thinks fit to carry out any matter relating to the performance of its functions or the exercise of its powers under Section 84;

(f) engage the services of such technical and professional advisers as it thinks fit to advise the Commission on any matter relating to the performance of its functions or the exercise of its powers;

(g) undertake and execute any lawful trust which has as an object the furtherance of any function which the Commission is required or is permitted by this Ordinance to perform or any other similar object;

(h) accept and solicit gifts and donations, whether subject to any trust or not;

(i) with the prior approval of the Chief Executive, become a member of or affiliate to any international body concerned with (whether in whole or in part) the elimination of discrimination; *(Amended 66 of 1999 s. 3)*

(j) exercise such other powers as are conferred on it under this Ordinance or any other enactment.

(3) The relevant provisions of Schedule 6 shall have effect with respect to a committee and its members.

(4) Part VII of the Interpretation and General Clauses Ordinance (Cap. 1) shall apply to a committee and appointments to the committee except in so far as that Part is inconsistent with the provisions of this Ordinance.

Section 65 Research and Education

(1) The Commission may undertake or assist (financially or otherwise) the undertaking by other persons of any research, and any educational activities, which appear to the Commission necessary or expedient for the performance of its functions.

(2) The Commission may impose reasonable charges for educational or other facilities or services made available by it.

(3) The Commission shall not provide any financial assistance under subsection (1) except with the prior approval of the Secretary for Constitutional and Mainland Affairs given, after consulting with the Secretary for Financial Services and the Treasury, generally or in any particular case. *(Amended L.N. 106 of 2002; L.N. 130 of 2007)*

Section 66 Review of Schedule 5

(Amended 18 of 2014 s. 18)

(1) Without prejudice to the generality of Section 64(1), the Commission, pursuant to its functions under paragraphs (a) and (b) of that Section, shall keep Schedule 5 under review. *(Amended 18 of 2014 s. 18)*

(2) Whenever the Commission thinks it necessary, it shall draw up and submit to the Chief Executive proposals for — *(Amended 66 of 1999 s. 3)*

- (a) *(Repealed 18 of 2014 s. 18)*
- (b) amending Schedule 5.

Section 67 Delegations

(1) Subject to subsection (2), the Commission may, with or without restrictions as it thinks fit, delegate in writing any of its functions or powers to —

- (a) any member of the Commission;
- (b) any committee;
- (c) any employee of the Commission;
- (d) any conciliator.

(2) The Commission shall not delegate any of its functions or powers under —

- (a) subsection (1) or Section 64(2)(a) or 88;
- (b) any provisions of any regulations made under Section 89 which are specified in the regulations as provisions which shall not be subject to subsection (1);
- (c) any provisions of any rules made under Section 88 which are specified in the rules as provisions which shall not be subject to subsection (1);
- (d) any provisions of Schedule 6 which are specified in that Schedule as provisions which shall not be subject to subsection (1).

(3) A delegate of the Commission —

- (a) shall perform the delegated functions and may exercise the delegated powers as if the delegate were the Commission; and
- (b) shall be presumed to be acting in accordance with the relevant delegation in the absence of evidence to the contrary.

Section 68 Protection of Members of Commission, etc.

(1) No person to whom this subsection applies, acting in good faith, is personally liable in damages for any act done or default made in the performance or purported performance of any function, or the exercise or purported exercise of any power, imposed or conferred on the Commission under this Ordinance.

(2) The protection conferred by subsection (1) on any person to whom that subsection applies in respect of any act or default does not in any way affect the liability of the Commission for that act or default.

(3) Subsection (1) applies to the following persons — *(Amended 18 of 2014 s. 19)*

(a) a member of the Commission or a committee;

(b) an employee of the Commission;

(c) a conciliator.

(Amended 18 of 2014 s. 19)

Codes of Practice

Section 69 Codes of Practice

(1) The Commission may issue codes of practice containing such practical guidance as it thinks fit for the purposes of —

(a) the elimination of discrimination;

(b) the promotion of equality of opportunity between men and women generally;

(c) the elimination of sexual harassment.

(2) When the Commission proposes to issue a code of practice, it shall prepare and publish (otherwise than in the Gazette) the code, shall consider any representations made to it about the code and may modify the code accordingly.

(3) In the course of preparing any code of practice for eventual publication under subsection (2), the Commission shall, where the code relates (whether in whole or in part) to the elimination of discrimination in the field of employment, consult with —

(a) such organizations or associations of organizations representative of employers or of workers; and

(b) such other organizations, or bodies,

as appear to the Commission to be appropriate.

(4) If the Commission determines to proceed with a code of practice published under subsection (2), it shall cause the code to be —

(a) published in the Gazette; and

(b) laid on the table of the Legislative Council at the next sitting after its publication in the Gazette.

(5) Where a code of practice has been laid on the table of the Legislative Council under subsection (4), the Legislative Council may, by Resolution passed at a sitting of the Legislative Council held before the expiration of a period of 28 days after the sitting at which it was so laid, provide that the code of practice shall be amended in any manner consistent with this Section.

(6) If the period referred to in subsection (5) would but for this subsection expire —

(a) after the end of a session of the Legislative Council or a dissolution thereof; but

(b) on or before the day of the second sitting of the Legislative Council in the next following session thereof,

that period shall be deemed to extend to and expire on the day after that second sitting.

(7) Before the expiration of the period referred to in subsection (5) or that period as extended by virtue of subsection (6), the Legislative Council may by Resolution in relation to a code of practice specified therein —

(a) in the case of the period referred to in subsection (5), extend that period to the first sitting of the Legislative Council held not earlier than the twenty-first day after the day of its expiration;

(b) in the case where the period referred to in subsection (5) has been extended by virtue of subsection (6), extend that period as so extended to the first sitting of the Legislative Council held not earlier than the twenty-first day after the day of the second sitting in that next following session. *(Replaced 8 of 2002 s. 18)*

(8) A Resolution passed by the Legislative Council in accordance with this Section shall be published in the Gazette not later than 14 days after the passing thereof or within such further period as the Chief Executive may allow in any particular case. *(Amended 66 of 1999 s. 3)*

(9) A code of practice issued under this Section shall come into operation —

(a) in the case where before the expiration of the period referred to in subsection (5), or before the expiration of that period as extended under subsection (6) or (7), the Legislative Council does not pass a Resolution amending the code of practice, upon the expiration of that period, or upon the expiration of that period as so extended, as the case may be; and

(b) in the case where the Legislative Council passes a Resolution amending the code of practice, upon the expiration of the day next preceding the day of the publication in the Gazette of such Resolution under subsection (8).

(10) A code of practice issued under this Section may contain such transitional provisions or savings as appear to the Commission to be necessary or expedient in connection with the matters the subject of the code.

(11) The Commission may from time to time revise the whole or any part of a code of practice issued under this Section and issue that revised code, and subsections (2) to (10) shall apply (with appropriate modifications) to such a revised code as they apply to the first issue of a code.

(12) Without prejudice to the generality of subsection (1), a code of practice issued under this Section may include such practical guidance as the Commission thinks fit as to what steps it is reasonably practicable for employers to take for the purpose of preventing their employees from doing in the course of their employment acts made unlawful by this Ordinance.

(13) Without prejudice to the generality of subsection (1), a code of practice issued under this Section, in so far as it relates to the elimination of discrimination between men and women as regards terms of employment, may —

(a) make reference to any of the provisions of any enactment (howsoever described) of any place outside Hong Kong where such enactment relates (whether in whole or in part) to the elimination of such discrimination;

(b) incorporate any of those provisions;

(c) both make reference to and incorporate any of those provisions,

as the Commission thinks fit and subject to such modifications, if any, to those provisions as the Commission thinks fit and specified in the code.

(14) A failure on the part of any person to observe any provision of a code of practice shall not of itself render him liable to any proceedings; but in any proceedings under this Ordinance before any court any code of practice issued under this Section shall be admissible in evidence, and if any provision of such a code appears to the court to be relevant to any question arising in the proceedings it shall be taken into account in determining that question.

(15) In this Section, ***sitting*** (會議), when used to calculate time, means the day on which the sitting commences and only includes a sitting at which subsidiary legislation is included on the order paper.

Investigations

Section 70 Power to Conduct Formal Investigations

Without prejudice to the generality of Section 64(1), the Commission may if it thinks fit, and shall if required by the Chief Secretary for Administration, conduct a formal investigation for any purpose connected with the carrying out of any of its functions under that Section.

(Amended L.N. 362 of 1997)

Section 71 Terms of Reference

(1) The Commission shall not embark on a formal investigation unless the requirements of this Section have been complied with.

(2) Terms of reference for the formal investigation shall be drawn up by the Commission or, if the Commission was required by the Chief Secretary for Administration to conduct the investigation, by the Chief Secretary for Administration after consulting the Commission. *(Amended L.N. 362 of 1997)*

(3) It shall be the duty of the Commission to give general notice of the holding of the formal investigation unless the terms of reference confine it to activities of persons named in them, but in such a case the Commission shall in the prescribed manner give those persons notice of the holding of the investigation.

(4) Where the terms of reference of the formal investigation confine it to activities of persons named in them and the Commission in the course of it proposes to investigate any act made unlawful by this Ordinance which it believes that a person so named may have done, the Commission shall —

(a) inform that person of its belief and of its proposal to investigate the act; and

(b) offer him an opportunity of making oral or written representations with regard to it (or both oral and written representations if he thinks fit),

and a person so named who avails himself of an opportunity under this subsection of making oral representations may be represented —

(i) by counsel or a solicitor; or

(ii) by some other person of his choice, not being a person to whom the Commission objects on the ground that he is unsuitable.

(5) The Commission or, if the Commission was required by the Chief Secretary for Administration to conduct the formal investigation, the Chief Secretary for Administration after consulting the Commission may from time to time revise the terms of reference; and subsections (1), (3) and (4) shall apply to the revised investigation and terms of reference as they applied to the original. *(Amended L.N. 362 of 1997)*

Section 72 Power to Obtain Information

(1) For the purposes of a formal investigation the Commission, by a notice in the prescribed form served on him in the prescribed manner —

(a) may require any person to furnish such written information as may be described in the notice, and may specify the time at which, and the manner and form in which, the information is to be furnished;

(b) may require any person to attend at such time and place as is specified in the notice and give oral information about, and produce all documents in his possession or control relating to, any matter specified in the notice.

(2) Except as provided by Section 79, a notice shall be served under subsection (1) only where —

(a) service of the notice was authorized in writing by or on behalf of the Chief Secretary for Administration; or *(Amended L.N. 362 of 1997)*

(b) the terms of reference of the formal investigation state that the Commission believes that a person named in them may have done or may be doing acts of all or any of the following descriptions —

(i) unlawful discriminatory acts;

(ii) unlawful acts of sexual harassment;

(iii) contraventions of Section 42;

(iv) contraventions of Section 43, 44 or 45,

and confine the investigation to those acts.

(3) A notice under subsection (1) shall not require a person —

(a) to give information, or produce any documents, which he could not be compelled to give in evidence, or produce, in civil proceedings before the Court of First Instance; or *(Amended 25 of 1998 s. 2)*

(b) to attend at any place unless the necessary expenses of his journey to and from that place are paid or tendered to him.

(4) If a person fails to comply with a notice served on him under subsection (1) or the Commission has reasonable cause to believe that he intends not to comply with it, the Commission may apply to the District Court for an order requiring him to comply with it or with such directions for the like purpose as may be contained in the order; and Section 66A of the District Court Ordinance (Cap. 336) shall apply to failure without reasonable excuse to comply with any such order as it applies in the cases there provided.

(5) A person commits an offence if he —

(a) wilfully alters, suppresses, conceals or destroys a document which he has been required by a notice or order under this Section to produce; or

(b) in complying with such a notice or order, knowingly or recklessly makes any statement which in a material respect is false or misleading,

and is liable on conviction to a fine at level 4.

Section 73 Recommendations and Reports on Formal Investigations

(1) If in the light of any of its findings in a formal investigation it appears to the Commission necessary or expedient, whether during the course of the investigation or after its conclusion —

(a) to make to any persons, with a view to promoting equality of opportunity between men and women who are affected by any of their activities, recommendations for changes in their policies or procedures, or as to any other matters; or

(b) to make to the Chief Secretary for Administration any recommendations, whether for changes in the law or otherwise, *(Amended L.N. 362 of 1997)*

the Commission shall make those recommendations accordingly.

(2) The Commission shall prepare a report of its findings in any formal investigation conducted by it.

(3) If the formal investigation is one required by the Chief Secretary for Administration —

(a) the Commission shall deliver the report to the Chief Secretary for Administration; and

(b) the Chief Secretary for Administration shall cause the report to be published in such manner as he thinks fit, and unless required by the Chief Secretary for Administration the Commission shall not publish the report. *(Amended L.N. 362 of 1997)*

(4) If the formal investigation is not one required by the Chief Secretary for Administration, the Commission shall publish the report or make it available for inspection in accordance with subsection (5). *(Amended L.N. 362 of 1997)*

(5) Where under subsection (4) a report is to be made available for inspection, any person shall be entitled, on payment of such reasonable fee, if any, as may be determined by the Commission —

(a) to inspect the report during ordinary office hours and take copies of all or any part of the report; or

(b) to obtain from the Commission a copy, certified by the Commission to be correct, of the report.

(6) The Commission may if it thinks fit determine that the right conferred by subsection (5)(a) shall be exercisable in relation to a copy of the report instead of, or in addition to, the original.

(7) The Commission shall give general notice of the place or places where, and the times when, reports may be inspected under subsection (5).

Section 74 Restrictions on Disclosure of Information

(1) No information given to the Commission by any person (***the informant***) in connection with a formal investigation shall be disclosed by the Commission, any member of the Commission or a committee, any employee of the Commission, any conciliator, or any person who has been such a member, employee or conciliator, except —

(a) on the order of any court;

(b) with the informant's consent;

(c) in the form of a summary or other general statement published by the Commission which does not identify the informant or any other person to whom the information relates;

(d) in a report of the investigation published by the Commission or made available for inspection under Section 73(5);

(e) to members of the Commission or a committee, employees of the Commission or conciliators or, so far as may be necessary for the proper performance of the functions of the Commission, to other persons;

(f) for the purpose of any civil proceedings under this Ordinance to which the Commission is a party, or any criminal proceedings.

(2) Any person who discloses information in contravention of subsection (1) commits an offence and is liable on conviction to a fine at level 4.

(3) In preparing any report for publication or for inspection the Commission shall exclude, so far as is consistent with its functions and the object of the report, any matter which relates to the private affairs of any individual or business interests of any person where the publication of that matter might, in the opinion of the Commission, prejudicially affect that individual or person.

Part 8 Enforcement

General

Section 75 Restrictions of Proceedings for Contravention of Ordinance

(1) Except as provided by this Ordinance no proceedings, whether civil or criminal, shall lie against any person in respect of an act by reason that the act is unlawful by virtue of a provision of this Ordinance.

(2) Subsection (1) shall not preclude the making of an order of certiorari, mandamus or prohibition.

Section 76 Claims under Part 3 or 4

(1) A claim by any person (***the claimant***) that another person (***the respondent***) —

(a) has committed an act of discrimination against the claimant which is unlawful by virtue of Part 3 or 4;

(b) *(Repealed 29 of 2008 s. 95)*

(c) has committed an act of sexual harassment against the claimant which is unlawful by virtue of Part 3 or 4; or *(Amended 29 of 2008 s. 95)*

(d) is to be treated, by virtue of Section 46, 46A or 47, as having committed an act of discrimination or sexual harassment referred to in paragraph (a) or (c) against the claimant, *(Added 29 of 2008 s. 95. Amended 8 of 2020 s. 23)*

may be made the subject of civil proceedings in like manner as any other claim in tort.

(2) Subsection (1) shall not apply to a claim under Section 17(1) of an act in respect of which an appeal, or proceedings in the nature of an appeal, may be brought under any enactment.

(3) Proceedings under subsection (1) shall be brought in the District Court but all such remedies shall be obtainable in such proceedings as, apart from this subsection and Section 75(1), would be obtainable in the Court of First Instance. *(Amended 25 of 1998 s. 2)*

(3A) Without limiting the generality of the power conferred by subsection (3), the District Court may—

(a) make a declaration that the respondent has engaged in conduct, or committed an act, that is unlawful under this Ordinance, and order that the respondent shall not repeat or continue such unlawful conduct or act;

(b) order that the respondent shall perform any reasonable act or course of conduct to redress any loss or damage suffered by the claimant;

(c) order that the respondent shall employ or re-employ the claimant;

(d) order that the respondent shall promote the claimant;

(e) order that the respondent pay to the claimant damages by way of compensation for any loss or damage suffered by reason of the respondent's conduct or act;

(f) order that the respondent shall pay to the claimant punitive or exemplary damages; or

(g) make an order declaring void in whole or part and either ab initio or from such date as may be specified in the order, any contract or agreement made in contravention of this Ordinance. *(Added 71 of 1997 s. 7)*

(4) By virtue of this subsection and notwithstanding any law, the District Court shall have jurisdiction to hear and determine any proceedings under subsection (1) and shall have all such powers as are necessary or expedient for it to have in order to provide, grant or make any remedy, injunction or order mentioned in this Ordinance. *(Replaced 71 of 1997 s. 6)*

(5) In respect of an unlawful act of discrimination falling within Section 5(1)(b), 7(1)(b) or 8(b), no award of damages shall be made if the respondent proves that the requirement or condition concerned was not applied with the intention of treating the claimant unfavourably on the ground of the claimant's sex, marital status or pregnancy, as the case may be.

(5A) Subsection (5) does not apply in relation to an unlawful act of discrimination falling within Section 5(1)(b), 7(1)(b) or 8(b) that is committed on or after the commencement date* of

* Commencement date: 19 June 2020.

Part 9 of the Discrimination Legislation (Miscellaneous Amendments) Ordinance 2020 (8 of 2020). *(Added 8 of 2020 s. 42)*

(6) For the avoidance of doubt, it is hereby declared that damages in respect of an unlawful act of discrimination or sexual harassment may include compensation for injury to feelings whether or not they include compensation under any other head.

(7)–(8)*(Repealed 71 of 1997 s. 6)*

(Amended E.R. 1 of 2013)

Enforcement Notices

Section 77 Issue of Enforcement Notices

(1) This Section applies to any act which is —

(a) an unlawful discriminatory act;

(b) an unlawful act of sexual harassment;

(c) a contravention of Section 42; or

(d) a contravention of Section 43, 44 or 45,

and so applies whether or not proceedings have been brought in respect of the act.

(2) If in the course of a formal investigation the Commission becomes satisfied that a person is committing, or has committed, any acts to which this Section applies, the Commission may in the prescribed manner serve on him a notice in the prescribed form requiring him —

(a) not to commit any such acts (which may include discontinuing or changing any of his practices or other arrangements which occasioned those acts, in particular to avoid any repetition thereof); and

(b) where compliance with paragraph (a) involves changes in any of his practices or other arrangements —

(i) to inform the Commission that he has effected those changes and what those changes are; and

(ii) to take such steps as may be reasonably required by the notice for the purpose of affording that information to other persons concerned.

(3) An enforcement notice may also require the person on whom it is served to furnish the Commission with such other information as may be reasonably required by the notice in order to verify that the notice has been complied with.

(4) An enforcement notice may specify the time at which, and the manner and form in which, any information is to be furnished to the Commission, but the time at which any information is to be furnished in compliance with the notice shall not be later than 5 years after the notice has become final.

(5) Section 72(4) shall apply to requirements under subsections (2)(b), (3) and (4) contained in an enforcement notice which has become final as it applies to requirements in a notice served under Section 72(1).

Section 78 Appeal against Enforcement Notice

(1) Not later than 45 days after an enforcement notice is served on any person he may appeal against any requirement of the notice to the District Court.

(2) Where the District Court considers a requirement in respect of which an appeal is brought under subsection (1) to be unreasonable because it is based on an incorrect finding of fact or for any other reason, the Court shall quash the requirement.

(3) On quashing a requirement under subsection (2), the District Court may direct that the enforcement notice shall be treated as if, in place of the requirement quashed, it had contained a requirement in terms specified in the direction.

(4) Subsection (1) shall not apply to a requirement treated as included in an enforcement notice by virtue of a direction under subsection (3).

Section 79 Investigation as to Compliance with Enforcement Notice

(1) If—

(a) the terms of reference of a formal investigation state that its purpose is to determine whether any requirements of an enforcement notice are being or have been carried out, but Section 72(2)(b) does not apply; and

(b) Section 71(3) is complied with in relation to the investigation on a date (***the commencement date***) not later than the expiration of the period of 5 years beginning when the enforcement notice became final,

the Commission may within the relevant period serve notices under Section 72(1) for the purposes of the investigation without needing to obtain the consent of the Chief Secretary for Administration. *(Amended L.N. 362 of 1997)*

(2) In subsection (1), ***relevant period*** (有關期間) means the period beginning on the commencement date and ending on the later of the following dates —

(a) the date on which the period of 5 years referred to in subsection (1)(b) expires;

(b) the date 2 years after the commencement date.

Section 80 Register of Enforcement Notices

(1) The Commission shall establish and maintain a register (***the register***) of enforcement notices which have become final.

(2) Any person shall be entitled, on payment of such reasonable fee, if any, as may be determined by the Commission —

(a) to inspect the register during ordinary office hours and take copies of any entry; or

(b) to obtain from the Commission a copy, certified by the Commission to be correct, of any entry in the register.

(3) The Commission may, if it thinks fit, determine that the right conferred by subsection (2)(a) shall be exercisable in relation to a copy of the register instead of, or in addition to, the original.

(4) The Commission shall give general notice of the place or places where, and the times when, the register or a copy of it may be inspected.

Other Enforcement by Commission

Section 81 Persistent Discrimination or Sexual Harassment

If, during the period of 5 years beginning on the date on which either of the following became final in the case of any person, namely —

(a) an enforcement notice served on him;

(b) a finding by the District Court under Section 76 that he has done an unlawful discriminatory act or unlawful act of sexual harassment,

it appears to the Commission that unless restrained he is likely to do one or more acts falling within paragraph (b), or contravening Section 42, the Commission may apply to the District Court for an injunction restraining him from doing so; and the District Court, if satisfied that the application is well-founded, may grant the injunction in the terms applied for or in more limited terms.

Section 82 Enforcement of Sections 43, 44 and 45

(1) Proceedings in respect of a contravention of Section 43, 44 or 45 shall be brought only by the Commission in accordance with the provisions of this Section.

(2) The proceedings shall be —

(a) an application for a decision whether the alleged contravention occurred; or

(b) an application under subsection (4),

or both.

(3) An application under subsection (2)(a) shall be made to the District Court.

(4) If it appears to the Commission —

(a) that a person has done an act which by virtue of Section 43, 44 or 45 was unlawful; and

(b) that unless restrained he is likely to do further acts which by virtue of that Section are unlawful,

the Commission may apply to the District Court for an injunction restraining him from doing so; and the District Court, if satisfied that the application is well-founded, may grant the injunction in the terms applied for or in more limited terms.

(5) Without prejudice to subsection (4), if it appears to the Commission that a person has done an act which was unlawful by virtue of Section 43, the Commission may apply to the District Court for an order imposing a financial penalty on such person; and the District Court, if satisfied that the application is well-founded, may make such an order.

(6) The financial penalty imposed under subsection (5) shall not exceed $10,000 for the first occasion on which a penalty is imposed, and $30,000 for the second and any subsequent occasion on which a penalty is imposed in respect of the same person.

Help for Persons Suffering Discrimination or Sexual Harassment

Section 83 Help for Aggrieved Persons in Obtaining Information, etc.

(1) With a view to helping a person (***the person aggrieved***) who considers he may have been discriminated against or sexually harassed in contravention of this Ordinance to decide whether to institute proceedings and, if he does so, to formulate and present his case in the most effective manner, the Commission may prescribe —

(a) forms by which the person aggrieved may question the respondent on his reasons for doing any relevant act, or on any other matter which is or may be relevant;

(b) forms by which the respondent may if he so wishes reply to any questions.

(2) Where the person aggrieved questions the respondent (whether or not in accordance with forms referred to in subsection (1)) —

(a) the question, and any reply by the respondent (whether or not in accordance with such a form) shall, subject to subsections (3), (4) and (5), be admissible as evidence in the proceedings;

(b) if it appears to the District Court that the respondent deliberately, and without reasonable excuse, omitted to reply within a reasonable period or that his reply is evasive or equivocal, the Court may draw any inference from that fact it considers it just and equitable to draw, including an inference that he committed an unlawful act.

(3) The Commission may —

(a) prescribe the period within which questions must be served in order to be admissible under subsection (2)(a);

(b) prescribe the manner in which a question, and any reply by the respondent, may be served.

(4) Rules under the District Court Ordinance (Cap. 336) may enable the District Court entertaining a claim under Section 76 to determine, before the date fixed for the hearing of the claim, whether a question or reply is admissible under this Section or not.

(5) This Section is without prejudice to any other enactment or rule of law regulating interlocutory and preliminary matters in proceedings before the District Court, and has effect subject to any enactment or rule of law regulating the admissibility of evidence in such proceedings.

(6) In this Section, ***respondent*** (答辯人) includes a prospective respondent.

Section 84 Assistance by Way of Conciliation

(1) A person may lodge with the Commission a complaint in writing alleging that another person has done an act which is unlawful by virtue of a provision of this Ordinance.

(2) A representative complaint may be lodged under subsection (1) in accordance with rules made under Section 88.

(3) Subject to subsection (4), where a complaint is lodged under subsection (1), the Commission shall —

(a) conduct an investigation into the act the subject of the complaint; and

(b) endeavour, by conciliation, to effect a settlement of the matter to which the act relates.

(4) The Commission may decide not to conduct, or to discontinue, an investigation into an act the subject of a complaint lodged under subsection (1) if —

(a) it is satisfied that the act is not unlawful by reason of a provision of this Ordinance;

(b) it is of the opinion that the person aggrieved by the act does not desire (or, in a case to which subsection (2) applies, none of the persons aggrieved by the act desires) that the investigation be conducted or continued;

(c) a period of more than 12 months has elapsed beginning when the act was done;

(d) in a case to which subsection (2) applies, it determines, in accordance with rules made under Section 88, that the complaint should not be a representative complaint; or

(e) it is of the opinion that the complaint is frivolous, vexatious, misconceived or lacking in substance.

(5) Where the Commission decides not to conduct, or to discontinue, an investigation into an act the subject of a complaint lodged under subsection (1), it shall by notice served on the person who lodged the complaint advise him of —

(a) that decision; and

(b) the reasons for that decision.

(6) Evidence of anything said or done by any person in the course of conciliation under this Section (including anything said or done at any conference held for the purposes of such

conciliation) is not admissible in evidence in any proceedings under this Ordinance except with the consent of that person.

(7) For the avoidance of doubt, it is hereby declared that subsection (6) shall not apply where —

(a) a complaint is lodged under subsection (1); and

(b) a settlement has been effected of the matter to which the act the subject of the complaint relates.

Section 85 Assistance Other Than by Way of Conciliation

(1) Where a complaint has been lodged under Section 84(1) but, for whatever reason, there has not been a settlement of the matter to which the act the subject of the complaint relates, then any person who may institute proceedings under this Ordinance in respect of that act may make an application to the Commission for assistance in respect of those proceedings.

(2) The Commission shall consider an application under subsection (1) and may grant it if it thinks fit to do so, in particular where —

(a) the case raises a question of principle; or

(b) it is unreasonable, having regard to the complexity of the case or the applicant's position in relation to the respondent or another person involved or any other matter, to expect the applicant to deal with the case unaided.

(3) Assistance by the Commission under this Section may include —

(a) giving advice;

(b) arranging for the giving of advice or assistance by a solicitor or counsel;

(c) arranging for representation by any person including all such assistance as is usually given by a solicitor or counsel in the steps preliminary or incidental to any proceedings, or in arriving at or giving effect to a compromise to avoid or bring to an end any proceedings;

(d) any other form of assistance which the Commission may consider appropriate,

but paragraph (c) shall not affect the law and practice regulating the descriptions of persons who may appear in, conduct, defend and address a court in, any proceedings except to the extent permitted under rules made in accordance with Section 73B of the District Court Ordinance (Cap. 336).

(4) In so far as expenses are incurred by the Commission in providing the applicant with assistance under this Section the recovery of those expenses (as taxed or assessed in such manner as may be prescribed by relevant rules) shall constitute a first charge for the benefit of the Commission —

(a) on any costs or expenses which (whether by virtue of a judgment or order of the District Court or an agreement or otherwise) are payable to the applicant by any other person in respect of the matter in connection with which the assistance is given; and

(b) so far as relates to any costs or expenses, on his rights under any compromise or settlement arrived at in connection with that matter to avoid or bring to an end any proceedings.

(5) The charge conferred by subsection (4) shall be subject to any charge under the Legal Aid Ordinance (Cap. 91) and to any provision in that Ordinance for payment of any sum into the Supplementary Legal Aid Fund established under that Ordinance.

(6) In this Section —

relevant rules (有關規則) means any rules made under the District Court Ordinance (Cap. 336);

respondent (答辯人) includes a prospective respondent.

Period within Which Proceedings to be Brought

Section 86 Period within Which Proceedings to be Brought

(1) The District Court shall not consider a claim under Section 76 unless proceedings in respect of the claim are instituted before the end of the period of 24 months beginning —

(a) when the act complained of was done; or

(b) if there is a relevant report in relation to that act, with the day on which the report is published or made available for inspection under Section 73,

whichever is the later.

(2) The District Court shall not consider an application under —

(a) Section 82(2)(a) unless it is made before the end of the period of 24 months beginning when the act to which it relates was done;

(b) Section 82(4) unless it is made before the end of the period of 5 years so beginning.

(2A) For the purposes of determining the period under subsection (1) within which proceedings may be brought, where an act to which the claim relates was the subject of a complaint lodged under Section 84(1), then the period that elapsed between the date when the complaint was lodged and the date when the complaint was disposed of under Section 84(3) or (4), as certified in writing by the Commission, shall be disregarded. *(Added 71 of 1997 s. 8. Amended 29 of 2008 s. 96)*

(3) Notwithstanding subsections (1) and (2), the District Court may consider any claim or application which is out of time if, in all the circumstances of the case, it considers that it is just and equitable to do so.

(4) For the purposes of subsection (3), the circumstances of the case include, in relation to any claim, whether the act to which the claim relates was the subject of a complaint lodged under Section 84(1) and, if so, the period that elapsed between when the act was done and when that complaint was so lodged.

(5) For the purposes of this Section —

(a) where the inclusion of any term in a contract renders the making of the contract an unlawful act, that act shall be treated as extending throughout the duration of the contract;

(b) any act extending over a period shall be treated as done at the end of that period; and

(c) a deliberate omission shall be treated as done when the person concerned decided upon it,

and, in the absence of evidence to the contrary, a person shall be taken for the purposes of this Section to decide upon an omission when he does an act inconsistent with doing the omitted act or, if he has done no such inconsistent act, when the period expires within which he might reasonably have been expected to do the omitted act if it was to be done.

(6) The Chief Executive in Council may, by notice in the Gazette, amend subsection (1) by substituting a longer period for the period specified in that subsection. *(Amended 66 of 1999 s. 3)*

(7) In this Section, ***relevant report*** (有關報告), in relation to an act referred to in subsection (1), means a report —

(a) published or made available for inspection under Section 73; and

(b) from which it can reasonably be construed (and whether or not the report mentions, or was in any way prepared in consequence of, the act) that the Commission is of the opinion that the act, or the class of acts to which the act belongs, is unlawful under a provision of Part 3, 4 or 5.

(Amended E.R. 1 of 2013)

Part 9 Miscellaneous

Section 87 Validity and Revision of Contracts

(1) A term of a contract is void where —

(a) its inclusion renders the making of the contract unlawful by virtue of this Ordinance;

(b) it is included in furtherance of an act rendered unlawful by this Ordinance; or

(c) it provides for the doing of an act which would be rendered unlawful by this Ordinance.

(2) Subsection (1) shall not apply to a term the inclusion of which constitutes, or is in furtherance of, or provides for, unlawful discrimination against a party to the contract, but the term shall be unenforceable against that party.

(3) A term in a contract which purports to exclude or limit any provision of this Ordinance is unenforceable by any person in whose favour the term would operate apart from this subsection.

(4) Subsection (3) shall not apply to a contract settling a claim to which Section 76 applies.

(5) On the application of any person interested in a contract to which subsection (2) applies, the District Court may make such order as it thinks just for removing or modifying any term made unenforceable by that subsection; but such an order shall not be made unless all persons affected have been given notice of the application (except where under rules made under the District Court Ordinance (Cap. 336) notice may be dispensed with) and have been afforded an opportunity to make representations to the Court.

(6) An order under subsection (5) may include provision as respects any period before the making of the order.

Section 88 Rules

(1) The Commission may make rules —

(a) prescribing the persons, or persons belonging to a class of persons, who may lodge a representative complaint under Section 84(1);

(b) prescribing the bodies and positions for the purposes of Section 35;

(c) prescribing the matters to be taken into account by the Commission for the purposes of a determination under Section 84(4)(d);

(d) to enable the Commission to require such persons, or persons belonging to such class of persons, as are specified in the rules to furnish information to the Commission for the purposes of Section 84;

(e) restricting the disclosure of any information referred to in paragraph (d) furnished to the Commission;

(f) to enable the Commission to direct persons to attend any conference held for the purposes of Section 84;

(g) regulating the procedure of any conference held for the purposes of Section 84;

(h) prescribing any other thing that is required or permitted to be prescribed under this Ordinance.

(2) Any rules made under subsection (1) may —

(a) make different provisions for different circumstances and provide for a particular case or class of cases;

(b) be made so as to apply only in such circumstances as are prescribed by the rules;

(c) specify forms for the purposes of the rules;

(d) be made generally for the better or more effectual carrying out of the provisions of this Ordinance, including incidental, consequential, evidential and supplemental provisions.

(3) Any rules made under this Section may prescribe offences in respect of contraventions of the rules, and may provide for the imposition of a fine not exceeding level 4 and of imprisonment for a period not exceeding 2 years.

Section 89 Regulations to Empower Commission to Bring Certain Proceedings

(1) The Secretary for Constitutional and Mainland Affairs may make regulations — *(Amended L.N. 130 of 2007)*
   (a) where any person may bring proceedings under Section 76(1) but has not done so, empowering the Commission, in such circumstances as are specified in the regulations, to bring and maintain those proceedings as if the Commission were that person;
   (b) specifying which of the remedies referred to in Section 76(3) shall be obtainable by the Commission in any such proceedings;
   (c) for the purposes of enabling the Commission to bring and maintain any such proceedings (including any related purposes), specifying modifications to which any provisions of this Ordinance (including any subsidiary legislation) shall be read.

(2) Any regulations made under this Section shall be subject to the approval of the Legislative Council.

(3) This Section is without prejudice to the Commission's power to bring proceedings by way of judicial review, in relation to this Ordinance or any other law, pursuant to its functions under Section 64(1). *(Added 71 of 1997 s. 9)*

Section 90 Amendment of Schedules

(1) The Chief Executive in Council may, by notice in the Gazette, amend Schedule 1, 4 or 5 but any notice to amend Schedule 5 shall be subject to the approval of the Legislative Council. *(Amended 71 of 1997 s. 10; 66 of 1999 s. 3; 18 of 2014 s. 20)*

(2) The Legislative Council may, by Resolution, amend Schedule 6.

Section 91 Transitional Provisions

(1) The provisions of Schedule 7 shall have effect as transitional provisions for the purposes of this Ordinance.

(2) *(Omitted as spent — E.R. 1 of 2013)*

Schedule 1

[ss. 2(1) and 90]

Educational Establishments and Their Responsible Bodies

	Educational establishment	Responsible body
1.	The University of Hong Kong established by the University of Hong Kong Ordinance (Cap. 1053)	The Court, the Council, the Senate or the Convocation, within the meaning of Section 2 of the University of Hong Kong Ordinance (Cap. 1053), according to which of them has the function concerned

2.	The Chinese University of Hong Kong established by The Chinese University of Hong Kong Ordinance (Cap. 1109)	The Council, the Senate, the Convocation, the Faculties, the School of Studies or the Board of Studies, within the meaning of Section 2 of The Chinese University of Hong Kong Ordinance (Cap. 1109), according to which of them has the function concerned
3.	The Hong Kong Polytechnic University established by The Hong Kong Polytechnic University Ordinance (Cap. 1075)	The Council of The Hong Kong Polytechnic University established under Section 5 of The Hong Kong Polytechnic University Ordinance (Cap. 1075) *(Amended 18 of 2014 s. 21)*
4.	Any post-secondary college registered under the Post Secondary Colleges Ordinance (Cap. 320)	The Board of Governors (or Board of Trustees where no Board of Governors exists) or the College Council, according to which of them has the function concerned
5.	Any technical college or technical institute defined in Section 2 of the Vocational Training Council Ordinance (Cap. 1130)	The Vocational Training Council established by Section 4 of the Vocational Training Council Ordinance (Cap. 1130)
6.	Any industrial training centre or skills centre defined in Section 2 of the Vocational Training Council Ordinance (Cap. 1130)	The Vocational Training Council established by Section 4 of the Vocational Training Council Ordinance (Cap. 1130)
7.	The Hong Kong Baptist University established by the Hong Kong Baptist University Ordinance (Cap. 1126)	The Board of Governors or the Council, within the meaning of Section 2 of the Hong Kong Baptist University Ordinance (Cap. 1126), according to which of them has the function concerned *(Amended 18 of 2014 s. 21)*
8.	The City University of Hong Kong established by the City University of Hong Kong Ordinance (Cap. 1132)	The Council or the Academic Board, within the meaning of Section 2 of the City University of Hong Kong Ordinance (Cap. 1132), according to which of them has the function concerned *(Amended 18 of 2014 s. 21)*
9.	The Hong Kong Academy for Performing Arts established by The Hong Kong Academy for Performing Arts Ordinance (Cap. 1135)	The Council or the Academic Board, within the meaning of Section 2 of The Hong Kong Academy for Performing Arts Ordinance (Cap. 1135), according to which of them has the function concerned
10.	The Hong Kong University of Science and Technology established by The Hong Kong University of Science and Technology Ordinance (Cap. 1141)	The Court, the Council, the Senate or the Convocation, within the meaning of Section 2 of The Hong Kong University of Science and Technology Ordinance (Cap. 1141), according to which of them has the function concerned
11.	The Open University of Hong Kong established by The Open University of Hong Kong Ordinance (Cap. 1145)	The Council or the Senate, within the meaning of Section 2 of The Open University of Hong Kong

		Ordinance (Cap. 1145), according to which of them has the function concerned *(Replaced 50 of 1997 s. 29)*
12.	Lingnan University established by the Lingnan University Ordinance (Cap. 1165)	The Court, the Council or the Senate, within the meaning of Section 2 of the Lingnan University Ordinance (Cap. 1165), according to which of them has the function concerned *(Replaced 54 of 1999 s. 33)*
13.	The Education University of Hong Kong established by The Education University of Hong Kong Ordinance (Cap. 444)	The Council or the Academic Board, within the meaning of Section 2 of The Education University of Hong Kong Ordinance (Cap. 444), according to which of them has the function concerned *(Amended 6 of 2016 s. 2)*
14.	Any school which is registered or provisionally registered under the Education Ordinance (Cap. 279)	The management committee, within the meaning of Section 3 of the Education Ordinance (Cap. 279), of the school
15.	Any school, within the meaning of Section 3 of the Education Ordinance (Cap. 279), entirely maintained and controlled by the Government	The Permanent Secretary for Education *(Amended 3 of 2003 s. 41; L.N. 130 of 2007)*

Schedule 2

(Repealed 71 of 1997 s. 11)

Schedule 3

(Repealed 18 of 2014 s. 22)

Schedule 4

[ss. 34(3) and 90]

Discrimination to Which Sections 28(1) and 29 Shall Not Apply

Provision creating illegality	Exception
Part 3	Sections 11(3), 12(1)(b), 19(3) and 22 Sections 1 and 2 of Schedule 7
Section 25	Sections 26 and 27 Section 3 of Schedule 7

(Amended E.R. 1 of 2013)

Schedule 5

[ss. 62, 66 and 90]

Further Exceptions to this Ordinance

Part 1 Interpretation

Section 1 Interpretation

In this Schedule—

allowance (津貼) includes part of an allowance;

benefit (利益) includes part of a benefit;

indigenous villager (原居村民) means indigenous villager within the meaning of Section 2 of the Government Rent (Assessment and Collection) Ordinance (Cap. 515); *(Amended 53 of 1997 s. 60)*

relevant office (有關職位) means any office (howsoever described) of—

(a) the police force; *(Amended 58 of 1999 s. 9)*

(b) the Hong Kong Auxiliary Police Force within the meaning of the Hong Kong Auxiliary Police Force Ordinance (Cap. 233); *(Amended L.N. 362 of 1997; 76 of 1999 s. 3)*

(c) the Immigration Service within the meaning of the Immigration Service Ordinance (Cap. 331);

(d) the Fire Services Department within the meaning of the Fire Services Ordinance (Cap. 95);

(e) the Correctional Services Department within the meaning of the Prisons Ordinance (Cap. 234);

(f) the Customs and Excise Service within the meaning of the Customs and Excise Service Ordinance (Cap. 342). *(Amended 18 of 2014 s. 23)*

(Amended 18 of 2014 s. 23)

Part 2 Exceptions

	Provision creating illegality	Exception
1.	Parts 3, 4 and 5	Any discrimination between men and women seeking to hold, or holding, any relevant office— (a) as to requirements relating to height or weight; or *(Amended 18 of 2014 s. 23)* (b) so far as there is a difference between the total number of persons of each sex recruited to, or holding, any such office or class of such office. *(Amended 18 of 2014 s. 23)* (c)–(d) *(Repealed 18 of 2014 s. 23)*
2.	Part 4	Any discrimination between men and women arising from that policy of the Government— (a) known as the small house policy; and (b) pursuant to which benefits relating to land in the New Territories are granted to indigenous villagers who are men.

3.	Parts 3, 4 and 5	Any discrimination between persons of different marital status (but excluding any discrimination against a person who is not single as compared with a person who is single) arising from a provision — (a) of — (i) the Civil Service Regulations; (ii) any contract of service or apprenticeship; or (iii) any contract personally to execute any work or labour; and *(Amended 18 of 2014 s. 23)* (b) relating to — (i) housing; (ii) education; (iii) air-conditioning; (iv) passage; or (v) baggage, benefits or allowances.
4–5.	*(Repealed 18 of 2014 s. 23)*	
6.	Parts 4 and 5	Any discrimination between persons of different marital status arising from the public housing scheme known as the Home Ownership Scheme or Private Sector Participation Scheme.
7.	Parts 3, 4 and 5	Any discrimination between men and women arising from — (a) Section 2(5)(a) of the Surviving Spouses' and Children's Pensions Ordinance (Cap. 79); (b) Section 18(1A) of the Pensions Ordinance (Cap. 89); (c) Section 19 of the Widows and Orphans Pension Ordinance (Cap. 94); (d) Section 19(4) of the Pension Benefits Ordinance (Cap. 99); or (e) Section 20(4) of the Pension Benefits (Judicial Officers) Ordinance (Cap. 401).
8.	*(Repealed 18 of 2014 s. 23)*	

(Amended E.R. 1 of 2013)

Schedule 6

Provisions with Respect to the Commission and Committees and their Members

Members and Procedure of Commission

Section 1 Terms and Conditions of Appointment of Chairperson, etc.

(1) Subject to subsection (2), the Chief Executive shall determine the remuneration and the terms and conditions of appointment of the Chairperson. *(Amended 66 of 1999 s. 3)*

(2) The Chairperson shall not, without the specific approval of the Chief Executive — *(Amended 66 of 1999 s. 3)*

(a) hold any office of profit other than his office as Chairperson; or

(b) engage in any occupation for reward outside the functions of his office.

(3) This Section shall apply to any other member of the Commission who is appointed on a full-time basis as it applies to the Chairperson.

Section 2 Terms of Appointment of Members of Commission

(1) Subject to Sections 1 and 5 and subsection (2), a member of the Commission shall hold and vacate his office in accordance with the terms of his appointment and shall, on ceasing to be a member, be eligible for reappointment.

(2) A member of the Commission shall be appointed for a term not exceeding 5 years.

(3) A member of the Commission may at any time by notice in writing to the Chief Executive resign his office. *(Amended 66 of 1999 s. 3)*

Section 3 Members of Commission to Disclose Interests in Respect of Certain Contracts

(1) A member of the Commission who is in any way directly or indirectly interested in a contract made or proposed to be made by —

(a) the Commission;

(b) a committee; or

(c) an employee or agent of the Commission,

shall disclose the nature of his interest at a meeting of the Commission.

(2) The Commission shall record the disclosure in the minutes of the meeting of the Commission.

(3) A member who has an interest in a contract referred to in subsection (1) —

(a) shall not without the permission of the Chairperson or other member presiding take any part in any deliberation of the Commission with respect to that contract; and

(b) shall not in any event vote on any matter concerning it.

(4) For the purposes of subsection (1), a member may give a notice in writing at a meeting of the Commission to the effect that he is a member of a company or firm and is to be regarded as interested in any contract which may, after the date of the notice, be made with the company or firm and the notice shall be regarded as a sufficient disclosure of his interest in relation to any contract so made or proposed to be so made.

(5) A member of the Commission need not attend in person at a meeting of the Commission to make a disclosure which he is required to make under this Section if he takes reasonable steps to secure that the disclosure is made by a notice in writing which is brought up and read at the meeting.

Section 4 Fees and Allowances Payable to Members of Commission

The Commission may pay its members such fees and allowances as the Secretary for Constitutional and Mainland Affairs, after consulting with the Secretary for Financial Services and the Treasury, determines.

(Amended L.N. 106 of 2002; L.N. 130 of 2007)

Section 5 Chief Executive May in Certain Circumstances Declare Office of Member of Commission to be Vacant

If the Chief Executive is satisfied that a member of the Commission —

(a) has been absent from 3 consecutive meetings of the Commission without the permission of the Commission;

(b) has become bankrupt or made an arrangement with his creditors;

(c) is incapacitated by physical or mental illness; or

(d) is otherwise unable or unfit to discharge the functions of a member,

the Chief Executive may declare his office as a member of the Commission to be vacant, and shall notify the fact in such manner as the Chief Executive thinks fit; and upon such declaration the office shall become vacant.

(Amended 66 of 1999 s. 3)

Section 6 Quorum of Commission, etc.

(1) The quorum of the Commission shall be not less than half the members thereof for the time being and, while a member is disqualified from taking part in a decision or deliberation of the Commission in respect of a matter, he shall be disregarded for the purpose of constituting a quorum of the Commission for deciding, or deliberating on, that matter.

(2) All matters for determination at a meeting of the Commission shall be decided by a majority of votes of the members present and voting and where there is an equality of votes the Chairperson or other member presiding shall have a casting vote in addition to his original vote.

Section 7 Fixing of Seal of Commission

The fixing of the seal of the Commission shall be —

(a) authorized by the Commission; and

(b) authenticated by the signatures of —

(i) the Chairperson; and

(ii) any other member of the Commission authorized by the Commission, either generally or specifically, to act for that purpose.

Section 8 Documents of Commission

(1) The Commission may make and execute any document in the performance of its functions or the exercise of its powers or in connection with any matter reasonably incidental to or consequential upon the performance of its functions or the exercise of its powers.

(2) Any document purporting to be executed under the seal of the Commission shall be admitted in evidence and shall, in the absence of evidence to the contrary, be deemed to have been duly executed.

Section 9 Certain Documents Not Required to be Sealed

Any contract or instrument which, if entered into or executed by a person not being a body corporate, would not be required to be under seal may be entered into or executed on behalf of the Commission by any member of the Commission generally or specifically authorized by the Commission for that purpose.

Section 10 Procedure of Commission

Subject to the provisions of this Schedule, the Commission shall have power to regulate its own procedure including the manner in which decisions of the Commission may be made by a quorum of its members otherwise than at a meeting of the Commission.

Staff of Commission

Section 11 Employees, etc. of Commission

(1) The Commission shall determine —

- (a) the remuneration and the terms and conditions of employment of its employees; and
- (b) the standards of work and conduct of its employees, and matters relating to their suspension or dismissal from office.

(2) The Commission shall determine the remuneration and the terms and conditions of engagement of technical and professional advisers, and of conciliators, and the manner of their engagement.

(3) The Commission may —

- (a) grant, or make provision for the grant of, pensions, gratuities and retirement benefits to employees;
- (b) provide other benefits for the welfare of employees and their dependants;
- (c) authorize payments, whether or not legally due, to the personal representatives of a deceased employee or to any person who was dependent on such employee at his death.

(4) The Commission may —

- (a) establish, manage and control; or
- (b) enter into an arrangement with any company or association for the establishment, management and control by that company or association either alone or jointly with the Commission of,

any fund or scheme for the purpose of providing for the pensions, gratuities, benefits and payments referred to in subsection (3).

(5) The Commission may make contributions to and may require employees to make contributions to any fund or scheme referred to in subsection (4).

(6) In this Section, ***employees*** (僱員) includes any class of employee which the Commission specifies and in subsection (3) includes former employees.

Committees

Section 12 Members of Committees

The Commission —

- (a) may appoint members of the Commission, and persons who are not such members, to be members of a committee; and
- (b) shall appoint the chairman of a committee and determine the number of members of a committee.

Section 13 Members of Committee to Disclose Interests in Respect of Certain Contracts

(1) A member of a committee who is in any way directly or indirectly interested in a contract made or proposed to be made by —

(a) the Commission;

(b) the committee; or

(c) an employee or agent of the Commission,

shall disclose the nature of his interest at a meeting of the committee.

(2) The committee shall record the disclosure in the minutes of the meeting of the committee.

(3) A member who has an interest in a contract referred to subsection (1) —

(a) shall not without the permission of the chairperson of the committee or other member presiding take any part in any deliberation of the committee with respect to that contract; and

(b) shall not in any event vote on any matter concerning it.

(4) For the purposes of subsection (1), a member may give a notice in writing at a meeting of a committee to the effect that he is a member of a company or firm and is to be regarded as interested in any contract which may, after the date of the notice, be made with the company or firm and the notice shall be regarded as a sufficient disclosure of his interest in relation to any contract so made or proposed to be so made.

(5) A member of a committee need not attend in person at a meeting of the committee to make a disclosure which he is required to make under this Section if he takes reasonable steps to secure that the disclosure is made by a notice in writing which is brought up and read at the meeting.

Section 14 Fees and Allowances Payable to Members of Committee

(1) The Commission may pay to the members of a committee such fees and allowances as the Secretary for Constitutional and Mainland Affairs, after consulting with the Secretary for Financial Services and the Treasury, determines.

(2) The provisions of this Section shall —

(a) not apply in the case of any member of a committee who is a public officer; and

(b) apply in the case of a member of a committee who is a member of the Commission only to such extent as the Secretary for Constitutional and Mainland Affairs, after consulting with the Secretary for Financial Services and the Treasury, determines.

(Amended L.N. 106 of 2002; L.N. 130 of 2007)

Finances, etc. of Commission

Section 15 Resources of Commission

(1) The resources of the Commission shall consist of —

(a) all money —

(i) paid by the Government to the Commission and appropriated for that purpose by the Legislative Council; and

(ii) otherwise provided to the Commission by the Government; and

(b) all other money and property, including gifts, donations, fees, rent, interest and accumulations of income received by the Commission.

(2) The Secretary for Financial Services and the Treasury may give directions in writing of a general or specific character to the Commission in relation to the amount of money which may be expended by the Commission in any financial year and the Commission shall comply with those directions. *(Amended L.N. 106 of 2002)*

Section 16 Borrowing Powers

(1) Subject to subsection (2), the Commission may borrow by way of overdraft such money as it may require for meeting its obligations or performing its functions under this Ordinance.

(2) The Secretary for Constitutional and Mainland Affairs may, after consulting with the Secretary for Financial Services and the Treasury, give directions in writing of a general or specific character to the Commission in relation to the amount of money which may be borrowed under subsection (1) and the Commission shall comply with those directions. *(Amended L.N. 106 of 2002; L.N. 130 of 2007)*

(3) The Commission may with the approval of the Secretary for Constitutional and Mainland Affairs given after the Secretary has consulted with the Secretary for Financial Services and the Treasury borrow, otherwise than by way of overdraft, such money as it may require for meeting its obligations or performing its functions under this Ordinance. *(Amended L.N. 106 of 2002; L.N. 130 of 2007)*

(4) A person lending money to the Commission shall not be concerned to inquire whether the borrowing of the money is legal or regular or whether the money raised has been properly applied and shall not be prejudiced by any illegality or irregularity or by misapplication or non-application of the money.

Section 17 Investment of Surplus Funds

(1) Subject to subsection (2), the Commission may invest money that is not immediately required to be expended.

(2) The Commission shall not invest money pursuant to subsection (1) except in such forms of investment as the Secretary for Constitutional and Mainland Affairs, after consulting with the Secretary for Financial Services and the Treasury, approves. *(Amended L.N. 106 of 2002; L.N. 130 of 2007)*

Section 18 Accounts, Audit and Annual Report of Commission

(1) The Commission shall cause proper accounts to be kept of all its financial transactions.

(2) The Commission shall, as soon as practicable after the expiry of a financial year, prepare a statement of the accounts of the Commission, which statement shall include an income and expenditure account and a balance sheet.

(3) The Commission shall appoint an auditor who shall, as soon as practicable, audit the accounts required under subsection (1) and the statement of accounts required under subsection (2) and shall submit a report on the statement to the Commission.

(4) The Commission shall, as soon as practicable and in any case not later than 9 months after the expiry of a financial year (or such further period as the Chief Secretary for Administration allows), furnish —

(a) a report on the activities of the Commission during that year including a general survey of developments, during that year, in respect of matters falling within the scope of the Commission's functions;

(b) a copy of the statement of accounts required under subsection (2); and

(c) the auditor's report on the statement,

to the Chief Secretary for Administration who shall cause the same to be tabled in the Legislative Council. *(Amended L.N. 362 of 1997)*

Section 19 Director of Audit's Examination

(1) The Director of Audit may, in respect of any financial year, conduct an examination into the economy, efficiency and effectiveness with which the Commission has expended its resources in performing its functions and exercising its powers.

(2) Subject to subsection (3), the Director of Audit shall have a right of access at all reasonable times to all such documents as he may reasonably require for conducting an examination under this Section and shall be entitled to require from any person holding or being accountable for any such document such information and explanation as he considers reasonably necessary for that purpose.

(3) Subsection (2) applies only to documents in the custody and control of the Commission.

(4) Without prejudice to the power of the Director of Audit to conduct an examination under this Section, this Section applies to any sum of money paid by the Commission in the exercise of its power under Section 65(1) of this Ordinance.

(5) Subsection (1) shall not operate to entitle the Director of Audit to question the merits of the policy objectives of the Commission.

Section 20 Exemption from Taxation

The Commission shall be exempt from taxation under the Inland Revenue Ordinance (Cap. 112).

Delegations

Section 21 Provisions to Which Section 67(1) Shall Not Apply

Sections 4, 11(1)(a), (4) and (5), 16(1) and (3), 17(1) and 18 shall not be subject to Section 67(1) of this Ordinance.

Schedule 7

[s. 91(1) and Sch. 4]

Transitional Provisions

(1) Section 16 of this Ordinance shall not apply, in respect of any organization —

  (a) to contributions or other payments falling to be made to the organization by its members or by persons seeking membership; or

  (b) to financial benefits accruing to members of the organization by reason of their membership,

  where the payment falls to be made, or the benefit accrues, as the case may be —

  (i) under rules of the organization made before this Ordinance was enacted; and

  (ii) before the 3rd anniversary of the day on which that Section comes into operation.

(2) Until the 3rd anniversary of the day on which Section 16 of this Ordinance comes into operation,* Section 16(2) of this Ordinance shall not apply to any organization of members of the teaching profession where on the enactment of this Ordinance —

(a) the organization is an incorporated company with articles of association;

(b) the articles of association restrict membership to persons of one sex (disregarding any minor exceptions); and

(c) there exists another organization to which paragraphs (a) and (b) apply which is for persons of the opposite sex and has objects, as set out in the articles of association, which are substantially the same as those of the first-mentioned organization, subject only to differences consequential on the difference of sex. *(Amended 28 of 2012 ss. 912 and 920)*

(3) If the responsible body for any educational establishment which (apart from this Section) would be required to comply with the provisions of Section 25(b) of this Ordinance from the commencement† of those provisions, is of the opinion that it would be impracticable for it to do so, it may before that commencement serve on the Commission a notice referred to in Section 27(1) of this Ordinance as if that opinion were a determination referred to in Section 27(1) of this Ordinance and, in any such case, the provisions of Section 27 of this Ordinance shall, with all necessary modifications, apply as if such opinion were such a determination.

Schedule 8

(Omitted as spent — E.R. 1 of 2013)

DISABILITY DISCRIMINATION ORDINANCE (CAP. 487)

An Ordinance to render unlawful discrimination against persons on the ground of their or their associates' disability in respect of their employment, accommodation, education, access to partnerships, membership of trade unions and clubs, access to premises, educational establishments, sporting activities and the provision of goods, services and facilities; to make provision against harassment and vilification of persons with a disability and their associates; to extend the jurisdiction of the Equal Opportunities Commission to include discrimination against persons on the ground of their or their associates' disability, and for connected purposes.

[20 May 1996]

(Enacting provision omitted — E.R. 1 of 2013)

* Commencement date: 20 September 1996.

† Commencement date: 20 September 1996.

Part 1 Preliminary

(Format changes — E.R. 1 of 2013)

Section 1 Short Title

(1) This Ordinance may be cited as the Disability Discrimination Ordinance.

(2) *(Omitted as spent — E.R. 1 of 2013)*

Section 2 Interpretation

(1) In this Ordinance, unless the context otherwise requires —

access (獲得、享用) means access as construed in accordance with Section 56;

act (作為) includes a deliberate omission;

advertisement (廣告) includes every form of advertisement, whether to the public or not, and whether —

(a) in a newspaper or other publication;

(b) by television or radio;

(c) by display of notices, signs, labels, showcards or goods;

(d) by distribution of samples, circulars, catalogues, price lists or other material;

(e) by exhibition of pictures, models or films; or

(f) in any other way,

and references to the publishing of advertisements shall be construed accordingly;

associate (有聯繫人士), in relation to a person, includes —

(a) a spouse of the person;

(b) another person who is living with the person on a genuine domestic basis;

(c) a relative of the person;

(d) a carer of the person; and

(e) another person who is in a business, sporting or recreational relationship with the person;

carer (照料者) includes —

(a) the Director of Social Welfare;

(b) any officer of the Social Welfare Department authorized in writing by the Director of Social Welfare;

(c) any person specified in Schedule 1;

club (會社) means an association, incorporate or unincorporate, of not less than 30 persons associated together for social, literary, cultural, political, sporting, athletic or other lawful purposes and which provides and maintains its facilities, in whole or in part, from the funds of the association; *(Amended 29 of 2008 s. 97)*

Commission (平等機會委員會) has the same meaning as in the relevant Ordinance;

commission agent (佣金經紀人) means commission agent as construed in accordance with Section 20;

committee (小組委員會) has the same meaning as in the relevant Ordinance;

committee of management (管理委員會), in relation to a club, means the group or body of persons (however described) that manages the affairs of that club;

conciliator (調停人) has the same meaning as in the relevant Ordinance; *(Amended 15 of 2012 s. 11)*

contract worker (合約工作者) means contract worker as construed in accordance with Section 13;

disability (殘疾), in relation to a person, means —

(a) total or partial loss of the person's bodily or mental functions;

(b) total or partial loss of a part of the person's body;

(c) the presence in the body of organisms causing disease or illness;

(d) the presence in the body of organisms capable of causing disease or illness;

(e) the malfunction, malformation or disfigurement of a part of the person's body;

(f) a disorder or malfunction that results in the person learning differently from a person without the disorder or malfunction; or

(g) a disorder, illness or disease that affects a person's thought processes, perception of reality, emotions or judgment or that results in disturbed behaviour,

and includes a disability that —

(i) presently exists;

(ii) previously existed but no longer exists;

(iii) may exist in the future; or

(iv) is imputed to a person;

discrimination (歧視) means any discrimination falling within Sections 6, 7, 9 or 10, and related expressions shall be construed accordingly;

discriminator (歧視者) includes a prospective discriminator;

dispose (處置), in relation to premises, includes granting a right to occupy the premises, and any reference to acquiring premises shall be construed accordingly;

dynamically supported craft (藉動力而獲得支承的航行器) has the same meaning as in the Shipping and Port Control Ordinance (Cap. 313);

education (教育) includes any form of training or instruction;

educational establishment (教育機構) has the same meaning as in the relevant Ordinance;

employment (僱用) means employment under —

(a) a contract of service or of apprenticeship; or

(b) a contract personally to execute any work or labour,

and related expressions shall be construed accordingly;

employment agency (職業介紹所) means a person who, for profit or not, provides services for the purpose of finding employment for workers or supplying employers with workers;

enforcement notice (執行通知) means a notice under Section 73(2);

estate agent (地產代理) has the same meaning as in the Estate Agents Ordinance (Cap. 511); *(Replaced 29 of 2008 s. 97)*

firm (商號) means a firm within the meaning of the Partnership Ordinance (Cap. 38);

formal investigation (正式調查) means an investigation under Section 66;

general notice (一般通告), in relation to any person, means a notice published by him at a time and in a manner appearing to him suitable for securing that the notice is seen within a reasonable time by persons likely to be affected by it;

genuine occupational qualification (真正的職業資格) means genuine occupational qualification as construed in accordance with Section 12(3);

harass (騷擾) shall be construed in accordance with subsection (6);

intern (實習人員) — see Section 22A(2); *(Added 8 of 2020 s. 24)*

internship (實習) — see Section 22A(2); *(Added 8 of 2020 s. 24)*

near relative (近親), in relation to a person, means —

(a) the person's spouse;

(b) a parent of the person or of the spouse;

(c) a child of the person or the spouse of such a child;

(d) a brother or sister (whether of full blood or half blood) of the person or of the spouse or the spouse of such a brother or sister;

(e) a grandparent of the person or of the spouse; or

(f) a grandchild of the person or the spouse of such a grandchild,

and, in determining the above relationships, children born out of wedlock are to be included, an adopted child is to be regarded as a child of both the natural parents and the adoptive parent or parents and a step child as the child of both the natural parents and any step parent; *(Added 29 of 2008 s. 97)*

notice (通知、通告) means a notice in writing;

palliative or therapeutic device or auxiliary aid (具減輕患情或治療作用的裝置或輔助器材) includes a device or aid specified in Schedule 2;

prescribed (訂明) means prescribed in rules made under Section 85;

profession (專業) includes any vocation or occupation;

pupillage (見習職位) — see Section 33(4); *(Added 8 of 2020 s. 24)*

registered (註冊) includes licenced;

relevant Ordinance (《性別歧視條例》) means the Sex Discrimination Ordinance (Cap. 480);

responsible body (負責組織) has the same meaning as in the relevant Ordinance;

trade (行業) includes any business;

training (訓練) includes any form of education or instruction;

unjustifiable hardship (不合情理的困難) means unjustifiable hardship as construed in accordance with Section 4; *(Amended 8 of 2020 s. 24)*

volunteer (義工) — see Section 22A(2). *(Added 8 of 2020 s. 24)*

(2) References in this Ordinance to the dismissal of a person from employment or to the expulsion of a person from a position as partner include references —

(a) to the termination of that person's employment or partnership by the expiration of any period (including a period expiring by reference to an event or circumstance), not being a termination immediately after which the employment or partnership is renewed on the same terms;

(b) to the termination of that person's employment or partnership by any act of his (including the giving of notice) in circumstances such that he is entitled to terminate it without notice by reason of the conduct of the employer, or the other partners, as the case may be.

(3) References in this Ordinance to the provision of facilities shall be construed to include references to making those facilities available or making arrangements for the provision of those facilities or to the provision of those facilities in buildings or premises.

(4) For the purposes of this Ordinance, an enforcement notice or a finding by the District Court becomes final when an appeal against the notice or finding is dismissed, withdrawn or abandoned or when the time for appealing expires without an appeal having been brought; and for this

purpose an appeal against an enforcement notice shall be taken to be dismissed if, notwithstanding that a requirement of the notice is quashed on appeal, a direction is given in respect of it under Section 74(3).

(5) *(Repealed 29 of 2008 s. 97)*

(6) For the purposes of this Ordinance, a person (howsoever described) harasses another person if that first-mentioned person engages in unwelcome conduct (which may include an oral or written statement) on account of that second-mentioned person's disability, or on account of the disability of an associate of that second-mentioned person, in circumstances in which a reasonable person, having regard to all the circumstances, would have anticipated that the second-mentioned person would be offended, humiliated or intimidated by that conduct.

(7) For the purposes of Section 6(c), references in this Ordinance to —

(a) a person with a disability (or words to the like effect) shall be construed to mean a person (and whether or not he has a disability) with an associate with a disability;

(b) a person without a disability (or words to the like effect) shall be construed to mean a person without an associate with a disability.

(8) For the purposes of any of the provisions of Sections 22, 22A, 23, 37, 38, 38A, 39, 46 and 47, references to a person with a disability (or words to the like effect) shall be construed to include a person (and whether or not he has a disability) with an associate with a disability. *(Amended 8 of 2020 ss. 24 and 40)*

(9) Subject to subsection (10), in this Ordinance ***existing statutory provision*** (現有法例條文) means any provision of —

(a) any Ordinance enacted before this Ordinance was enacted;

(b) any subsidiary legislation made —

(i) under an Ordinance enacted before this Ordinance was enacted; and

(ii) before, on or after this Ordinance was enacted.

(10) Where an Ordinance enacted after this Ordinance was enacted re-enacts (with or without modifications) a provision of an Ordinance enacted before this Ordinance was enacted, then that provision as re-enacted shall be treated for the purposes of subsection (9) as if it continued to be contained in an Ordinance enacted before this Ordinance was enacted.

Section 3 Act Done Because of Disability and for Other Reason

If —

(a) an act is done for 2 or more reasons; and

(b) one of the reasons is the disability of a person (whether or not it is the dominant or a substantial reason for doing the act),

then, for the purposes of this Ordinance, the act is taken to be done for the reason specified in paragraph (b).

Section 4 Unjustifiable Hardship

For the purposes of this Ordinance, in determining what constitutes unjustifiable hardship, all relevant circumstances of the particular case are to be taken into account including —

(a) the reasonableness of any accommodation to be made available to a person with a disability;

(b) the nature of the benefit or detriment likely to accrue or be suffered by any persons concerned;

(c) the effect of the disability of a person concerned; and

(d) the financial circumstances of and the estimated amount of expenditure (including recurrent expenditure) required to be made by the person claiming unjustifiable hardship.

Section 5 Application

This Ordinance binds the Government.

Part 2 Discrimination to Which Ordinance Applies

(Format changes — E.R. 1 of 2013)

Section 6 Discrimination against Persons with Disability, etc.

A person discriminates against another person in any circumstances relevant for the purposes of any provision of this Ordinance if—

(a) on the ground of that other person's disability he treats him less favourably than he treats or would treat a person without a disability;

(b) he applies to that other person a requirement or condition which he applies or would apply equally to a person without a disability but—

(i) which is such that the proportion of persons with a disability who can comply with it is considerably smaller than the proportion of persons without a disability who can comply with it;

(ii) which he cannot show to be justifiable irrespective of the disability or absence of the disability of the person to whom it is applied; and

(iii) which is to that person's detriment because he cannot comply with it; or

(c) on the ground of the disability of an associate of that other person he treats him less favourably than he treats or would treat a person without such a disability.

Section 7 Discrimination by Way of Victimization

(1) A discriminator discriminates against another person (***the person victimized***) in any circumstances relevant for the purposes of any provision of this Ordinance if he treats the person victimized less favourably than in those circumstances he treats or would treat other persons, and does so by reason that the person victimized or any other person (***the third person***) has—

(a) brought proceedings against the discriminator or any other person under this Ordinance;

(b) given evidence or information in connection with proceedings brought by any person against the discriminator or any other person under this Ordinance;

(c) otherwise done anything under or by reference to this Ordinance in relation to the discriminator or any other person; or

(d) alleged that the discriminator or any other person has committed an act which (whether or not the allegation so states) would amount to a contravention of this Ordinance,

or by reason that the discriminator knows the person victimized or the third person, as the case may be, intends to do any of those things, or suspects the person victimized or the third person, as the case may be, has done, or intends to do, any of them.

(2) Subsection (1) shall not apply to treatment of a person by reason of any allegation made by him if the allegation was false and not made in good faith.

Section 8 Comparison of Cases under Section 6

A comparison of the cases of persons with or without a disability under Section 6 shall be such that the relevant circumstances in the one case are the same, or not materially different, in the other.

Section 9 Discrimination (Palliative or Therapeutic Devices and Auxiliary Aids)

For the purposes of this Ordinance, a discriminator discriminates against another person on the ground of that other person's disability if the discriminator treats that other person less favourably because of—

(a) the fact that other person is accompanied by, or possesses a palliative or therapeutic device or auxiliary aid that is used by that other person; or

(b) any matter related to that fact, whether or not it is the discriminator's practice to treat less favourably any person who is accompanied by, or is in possession, and is the user, of such a palliative or therapeutic device or auxiliary aid.

Section 10 Discrimination (Interpreters, Readers and Assistants)

For the purposes of this Ordinance, a discriminator discriminates against another person on the ground of that other person's disability if the discriminator treats that other person less favourably because of—

(a) the fact that other person is accompanied by—

  (i) an interpreter;

  (ii) a reader;

  (iii) an assistant; or

  (iv) a carer,

  who provides interpretive, reading or other services to that other person because of the disability; or

(b) any matter related to that fact, whether or not it is the discriminator's practice to treat less favourably any person who is accompanied by such—

  (i) an interpreter;

  (ii) a reader;

  (iii) an assistant; or

  (iv) a carer.

Part 3 Discrimination and Harassment in Employment Field

(Format changes — E.R. 1 of 2013)

Discrimination by Employers

Section 11 Discrimination against Applicants and Employees

(1) It is unlawful for a person (***the employer***), in relation to employment by him at an establishment in Hong Kong, to discriminate against another person with a disability—

  (a) in the arrangements the employer makes for the purpose of determining who should be offered that employment;

  (b) in the terms on which the employer offers that other person that employment; or

(c) by refusing or deliberately omitting to offer that other person that employment.

(2) It is unlawful for the employer, in the case of a person with a disability employed by him at an establishment in Hong Kong, to discriminate against that person —

(a) in the way he affords that person access to opportunities for promotion, transfer or training, or to any other benefits, services or facilities, or by refusing or deliberately omitting to afford that person access to them;

(b) in the terms of employment he affords that person; or

(c) by dismissing that person, or subjecting him to any other detriment.

(3) Except in relation to discrimination falling within Section 7, subsections (1) and (2) shall not apply to employment where the number of persons employed by the employer, added to the number employed by any associated employers of his, does not exceed 5 (disregarding any persons employed for the purposes of a private home).

(4) Subsection (2) shall not apply to benefits, services or facilities of any description if the employer is concerned with the provision (for payment or not) of benefits, services or facilities of that description to the public, or to a section of the public comprising the person with a disability concerned, unless —

(a) that provision differs in a material respect from the provision of the benefits, services or facilities by the employer to his employees without a disability; or

(b) the benefits, services or facilities relate to training.

(5) Subsection (3) shall expire on the 3rd anniversary of the day on which this Ordinance is enacted.

(6) For the purposes of subsection (3), 2 employers are to be treated as associated if one is a company of which the other (directly or indirectly) has control or if both are companies of which a third person (directly or indirectly) has control.

(7) The Chief Executive in Council may, by notice in the Gazette — *(Amended 66 of 1999 s. 3)*

(a) amend subsection (3) by substituting another number for the last number appearing in that subsection;

(b) amend subsection (5) by substituting another anniversary for the anniversary appearing in that subsection.

Section 12 Exception Where Absence of Disability Is Genuine Occupational Qualification

(1) In relation to discrimination —

(a) Section 11(1)(a) or (c) shall not apply to any employment where being a person without a disability is a genuine occupational qualification for the job;

(b) Section 11(2)(a) shall not apply to opportunities for promotion or transfer to, or training for, such employment.

(2) Section 11(1)(a) and (c) and (2)(c) shall not apply to an employer who discriminates against a person with a disability, if taking into account —

(a) the person's past training, qualifications and experience relevant to the particular employment;

(b) where the person is already employed by the employer, the person's performance as an employee; and

(c) all other relevant factors that it is reasonable to so take into the account,

the person because of the person's disability —

(i) would be unable to carry out the inherent requirements of the particular employment; or

(ii) would, in order to carry out those requirements, require services or facilities that are not required by persons without a disability and the provision of which would impose an unjustifiable hardship on the employer.

(3) Being a person without a disability is a genuine occupational qualification for a job only where —

(a) the essential nature of the job calls for a person without a disability for reasons of physiology or, in dramatic performances or other entertainment, for reasons of authenticity, so that the essential nature of the job would be materially different if carried out by a person with a disability;

(b) the nature or location of the establishment makes it impracticable for the holder of the job to live elsewhere than in premises provided by the employer, and the only such premises which are available for persons holding that kind of job are lived in, or normally lived in, by persons without a disability and, subject to subsection (5), are not equipped with accommodation and facilities for persons with a disability where the alteration of those premises to be so equipped would impose an unjustifiable hardship on the employer; or

(c) the job needs to be held by a person without a disability because of restrictions imposed by a provision specified in Schedule 3.

(4) Subsection (3) applies where some only of the duties of the job fall within any paragraph of that subsection as well as where all of them do.

(5) Paragraph (b) of subsection (3) shall not apply in relation to the filling of a vacancy where the applicant for that vacancy, being a person with a disability, proposes to the employer that, on appointment to the vacancy, he will make reasonable alterations to that part of the premises to be occupied by him as accommodation if—

(a) the applicant undertakes to restore the premises to their condition before alteration on leaving the premises;

(b) in all the circumstances it is likely that the applicant will perform the undertaking;

(c) in all the circumstances, the action required to restore the premises to their condition before alteration is reasonably practicable;

(d) the alteration is at that applicant's expense; and

(e) the alteration does not involve alteration of other premises occupied by any other person.

(6) Paragraph (a), (b) or (c) of subsection (3) shall not apply in relation to the filling of a vacancy at a time when the employer already has employees without a disability —

(a) who are capable of carrying out the duties falling within that paragraph;

(b) whom it would be reasonable to employ on those duties; and

(c) whose numbers are sufficient to meet the employer's likely requirements in respect of those duties without undue inconvenience.

Section 13 Discrimination against Contract Workers

(1) This Section applies to any work for a person (***the principal***) which is available for doing by individuals (***contract workers***) who are employed not by the principal himself but by a contractor or sub-contractor of the principal. *(Amended 29 of 2008 s. 98)*

(2) Subject to subsections (3) and (4), it is unlawful for the principal, in relation to work to which this Section applies, to discriminate against a contract worker with a disability —

(a) in the terms on which he allows the contract worker to do that work;

(b) by not allowing the contract worker to do it or continue to do it;

(c) in the way he affords the contract worker access to any benefits, services or facilities or by refusing or deliberately omitting to afford the contract worker access to them; or

(d) by subjecting the contract worker to any other detriment.

(3) Subsection (2)(b) shall not apply to a principal who does any act in relation to a contract worker with a disability at a time when if the work were to be done by a person taken into his employment being a contract worker without a disability would be a genuine occupational qualification for the job.

(4) Subsection (2)(b) shall not apply to a principal who discriminates against a contract worker with a disability, if taking into account —

(a) the contract worker's past training, qualifications and experience relevant to working as a contract worker;

(b) where the person is already working for the principal as a contract worker, the contract worker's performance as a contract worker; and

(c) all other relevant factors that it is reasonable to so take into the account,

the contract worker because of the contract worker's disability —

(i) would be unable to carry out the inherent requirements of a contract worker; or

(ii) would, in order to carry out those requirements, require services or facilities that are not required by persons without a disability and the provision of which would impose an unjustifiable hardship on the principal.

(5) Subsection (2)(c) shall not apply to benefits, services or facilities of any description if the principal is concerned with the provision (for payment or not) of benefits, services or facilities of that description to the public, or to a section of the public to which the contract worker with a disability belongs, unless that provision differs in a material respect from the provision of the benefits, services or facilities by the principal to his contract workers without a disability.

(6) In this Section —

contractor (承判商) means a person who undertakes any work for the principal under a contract that is entered into by the person directly with the principal;

sub-contractor (次承判商) means a person who enters into a contract with another person (whether or not a contractor of the principal) to undertake all or any part of the work that a contractor of the principal has undertaken. *(Added 29 of 2008 s. 98)*

Section 14 Meaning of Employment at Establishment in Hong Kong

(1) For the purposes of this Ordinance (***the relevant purposes***), employment is to be regarded as being at an establishment in Hong Kong unless the employee does his work wholly or mainly outside Hong Kong.

(2) Subsection (1) shall not apply to —

(a) employment on board a ship registered in Hong Kong; or

(b) employment on aircraft or dynamically supported craft registered in Hong Kong and operated by a person who has his principal place of business, or is ordinarily resident, in Hong Kong,

but for the relevant purposes such employment is to be regarded as being at an establishment in Hong Kong unless the employee does his work wholly outside Hong Kong.

(3) In the case of employment on board a ship registered in Hong Kong (except where the employee does his work wholly outside Hong Kong) the ship shall for the relevant purposes be deemed to be the establishment.

(4) Where work is not done at an establishment it shall be treated for the relevant purposes as done at the establishment from which it is done or (where it is not done from any establishment) at the establishment with which it has the closest connection.

Discrimination by Other Bodies

Section 15 Partnerships

(1) It is unlawful for a firm consisting of not less than 6 partners, in relation to a position as partner in the firm, to discriminate against a person with a disability —

(a) in the arrangements the firm makes for the purpose of determining who should be offered that position;

(b) in the terms on which the firm offers him that position;

(c) by refusing or deliberately omitting to offer him that position; or

(d) in a case where he already holds that position —

(i) in the way the firm affords him access to any benefits, services or facilities, or by refusing or deliberately omitting to afford him access to them; or

(ii) by expelling him from that position or subjecting him to any other detriment.

(2) Subsection (1) shall apply in relation to persons proposing to form themselves into a partnership as it applies in relation to a firm.

(3) Subsection (1)(a) and (c) shall not apply to a position as partner where, if it were employment, being a person without a disability would be a genuine occupational qualification for the job.

(4) Subsection (1)(a), (c) and (d)(ii) shall not apply to a person who discriminates against another person with a disability, if taking into account —

(a) that other person's past training, qualifications and experience relevant to the proposed firm or firm, as the case may be;

(b) where that other person is already a partner, that other person's performance as a partner; and

(c) all other relevant factors that it is reasonable to so take into account,

that other person because of that other person's disability —

(i) would be unable to carry out the inherent requirements of a partner in the proposed firm or firm, as the case may be; or

(ii) would, in order to carry out those inherent requirements, require services or facilities that are not required by partners without a disability and the provision of which would impose an unjustifiable hardship on the proposed firm or firm, as the case may be.

(5) In the case of a limited partnership references in subsection (1) to a partner shall be construed as references to a general partner within the meaning of Section 2 of the Limited Partnerships Ordinance (Cap. 37).

(6) The Chief Executive in Council may, by notice in the Gazette, amend subsection (1) by — *(Amended 66 of 1999 s. 3)*

(a) substituting another number for the number appearing in that subsection; or

(b) repealing the words and number appearing after "for a firm" and before ", in relation to".

Section 16 Trade Unions, etc.

(1) This Section applies to an organization of workers, an organization of employers, or any other organization whose members carry on a particular profession or trade for the purposes of which the organization exists.

(2) It is unlawful for an organization to which this Section applies, in the case of a person with a disability who is not a member of the organization, to discriminate against him —

(a) in the terms on which it is prepared to admit him to membership; or

(b) by refusing or deliberately omitting to accept his application for membership.

(3) It is unlawful for an organization to which this Section applies, in the case of a person with a disability who is a member of the organization, to discriminate against him —

(a) in the way it affords him access to any benefits, services or facilities, or by refusing or deliberately omitting to afford him access to them;

(b) by depriving him of membership, or varying the terms on which he is a member; or

(c) by subjecting him to any other detriment.

Section 17 Qualifying Bodies

(1) It is unlawful for an authority or body which can confer an authorization or qualification which is needed for, or facilitates, engagement in a particular profession or trade to discriminate against a person with a disability —

(a) in the terms on which it is prepared to confer on him that authorization or qualification;

(b) by refusing or deliberately omitting to grant his application for it; or

(c) by withdrawing it from him or varying the terms on which he holds it.

(2) Where an authority or body is required by law to satisfy itself as to his good character before conferring on a person an authorization or qualification which is needed for, or facilitates, his engagement in any profession or trade then, without prejudice to any other duty to which it is subject, that requirement shall be taken to impose on the authority or body a duty to have regard to any evidence tending to show that he, or any of his employees or agents (whether past or present), has —

(a) practised unlawful discrimination;

(b) engaged in unlawful harassment; or

(c) engaged in acts which contravene Section 46 or 47,

in, or in connection with, the carrying on of any profession or trade.

(3) Subsection (1) shall not apply to an authority or body which discriminates against a person on the ground of the person's disability, if taking into account —

(a) that person's past training, qualifications and experience relevant to the particular profession, trade or occupation;

(b) where that person is already a member of the profession, carrying on the trade or engaged in the occupation, that person's performance in the profession, trade or occupation; and

(c) all other relevant factors that it is reasonable to so take into the account,

that person because of that person's disability, would be unable to carry out the inherent requirements of the profession, trade or occupation.

(4) Subsection (1) shall not apply to discrimination which is rendered unlawful by Section 24.

(5) In this Section —

authorization or qualification (授權或資格) includes recognition, licensing, registration, enrolment, approval and certification;

confer (授予) includes renew or extend.

Section 18 Persons Concerned with Provision of Vocational Training

(1) It is unlawful, in the case of a person with a disability seeking or undergoing training which would help fit him for any employment, for any person (***the trainer***) who provides facilities for such training to discriminate against him —

(a) in the terms on which the trainer affords him access to any training course or other facilities concerned with such training;

(b) by refusing or deliberately omitting to afford him such access;

(c) by terminating his training; or

(d) by subjecting him to any other detriment during the course of his training.

(2) Subsection (1) shall not apply to —

(a) discrimination which is rendered unlawful by any of the provisions of Section 11(1) or (2) or 24; or

(b) discrimination which would be rendered unlawful by any of those provisions but for the operation of any other provision of this Ordinance.

Section 19 Employment Agencies

(1) It is unlawful for an employment agency to discriminate against a person with a disability —

(a) in the terms on which the agency offers to provide any of its services;

(b) by refusing or deliberately omitting to provide any of its services; or

(c) in the way it provides any of its services.

(2) References in subsection (1) to the services of an employment agency include guidance on careers and any other services related to employment.

(3) Subsection (1) shall not apply if the discrimination only concerns employment which the employer could lawfully refuse to offer the person with a disability concerned.

(4) Subsection (1) shall not apply to an employment agency which discriminates against a person with a disability, if taking into account —

(a) that person's past training, qualifications and experience relevant to the work sought; and

(b) all other relevant factors that it is reasonable to take into account,

that person because of that person's disability, would be unable to carry out the inherent requirements of the employment sought.

(5) An employment agency shall not be subject to any liability under this Section if it proves —

(a) that it acted in reliance on a statement made to it by the employer to the effect that, by reason of the operation of subsection (3), its action would not be unlawful; and

(b) that it was reasonable for it to rely on the statement.

(6) A person who knowingly or recklessly makes a statement of the kind referred to in subsection (5)(a) which in a material respect is false or misleading commits an offence and is liable on conviction to a fine at level 4.

Section 20 Discrimination against Commission Agents

(1) This Section applies to any work for a person (***the principal***) which is available for doing by individuals (***commission agents***) as the agents of the principal and who are remunerated, whether in whole or in part, by commission.

(2) It is unlawful for the principal, in relation to work to which this Section applies, to discriminate against a person with a disability who is a commission agent —

(a) in the terms on which he allows the person with a disability to do that work;

(b) by not allowing that person to do it or continue to do it;

(c) in the way he affords that person access to any benefits, services or facilities or by refusing or deliberately omitting to afford that person access to them; or

(d) by subjecting that person to any other detriment.

(3) The principal does not contravene subsection (2)(b) by doing any act in relation to a person with a disability at a time when if the work were to be done by a person taken into his employment being a person without a disability would be a genuine occupational qualification for the job.

(4) Subsection (2)(b) shall not apply to a principal who discriminates against a commission agent with a disability, if taking into account —

(a) the commission agent's past training, qualifications and experience relevant to working as a commission agent;

(b) where the person is already working for the principal as a commission agent, the commission agent's performance as a commission agent; and

(c) all other relevant factors that it is reasonable to so take into the account,

the commission agent because of the commission agent's disability —

(i) would be unable to carry out the inherent requirements of a commission agent; or

(ii) would, in order to carry out those requirements, require services or facilities that are not required by persons without a disability and the provision of which would impose an unjustifiable hardship on the principal.

(5) Subsection (2)(c) shall not apply to benefits, services or facilities of any description if the principal is concerned with the provision (for payment or not) of benefits, services or facilities of that description to the public, or to a section of the public to which the person with a disability belongs, unless that provision differs in a material respect from the provision of the benefits, services or facilities by the principal to his commission agents.

Government

Section 21 Government

(1) Subject to subsection (2), without prejudice to the operation of the other provisions of this Part in relation to the Government, it is unlawful for the Government to discriminate against a person with a disability in the performance of its functions or the exercise of its powers.

(2) Subsection (1) shall not render unlawful —

(a) as regards a person with a disability not having the right to enter and remain in Hong Kong, any act done under any immigration legislation governing entry into, stay in and departure from Hong Kong; or

(b) any act done in relation to a person with a disability if it was necessary for that act to be done in order to comply with a requirement of an existing statutory provision.

Harassment

Section 22 Employees, etc.

(1) It is unlawful for a person, in relation to employment by him at an establishment in Hong Kong, to harass a person with a disability who is seeking to be employed by the first-mentioned person.

(2) It is unlawful for a person, in the case of a person with a disability employed by him at an establishment in Hong Kong, to harass that second-mentioned person.

(3) It is unlawful for a person who is employed by another person at an establishment in Hong Kong to harass a third person with a disability who is seeking to be, or who is, employed by that second-mentioned person.

(4) It is unlawful for the principal, in relation to work to which Section 13 applies, to harass a person with a disability who is a contract worker.

(5) It is unlawful for a contract worker to harass a person with a disability who is a fellow contract worker.

(6) It is unlawful for a partner in a firm to harass a person with a disability who is seeking to be, or who is, a partner in the firm.

(7) Subsection (6) shall apply in relation to persons proposing to form themselves into a partnership as it applies in relation to a firm.

(8) Section 15(5) shall apply to subsection (6) as it applies to Section 15(1).

(9) It is unlawful for the principal, in relation to work to which Section 20 applies, to harass a person with a disability who is a commission agent.

(10) It is unlawful for a commission agent to harass a person with a disability who is a fellow commission agent.

(11) It is unlawful for a person who is seeking to be, or who is, employed by a person with a disability at an establishment in Hong Kong to harass that person.

(12) It is unlawful for a person residing in any premises to harass a person with a disability —

(a) employed by another person at an establishment in Hong Kong (and whether or not that other person also resides in those premises or those premises are that establishment); and

(b) carrying out in those premises all or part of that person's work in relation to that person's employment (and whether or not that person also resides in those premises).

Section 22A Harassment at Workplace

(1) It is unlawful for a person who is a workplace participant to harass a person with a disability who is also a workplace participant at a workplace of them both.

(2) In this Section —

intern (實習人員) means a person who is engaged by another person for an internship but is not an employee of that other person;

internship (實習) means —

(a) a period of work the completion of which is required for attaining a professional or academic qualification and includes a pupillage; or

(b) any other work that is usually described as an internship;

volunteer (義工) means a person who performs volunteer work other than in the capacity of an employer or employee;

workplace (工作場所), in relation to a person, means a place —

(a) at which the person works as a workplace participant; or

(b) that the person attends as a workplace participant;

workplace participant (場所使用者) means —

(a) an employee;

(b) an employer;

(c) a contract worker;

(d) the principal, within the meaning of Section 13(1), of a contract worker;

(e) a commission agent;

(f) the principal, within the meaning of Section 20(1), of a commission agent;

(g) a partner in a firm;

(h) an intern; or

(i) a volunteer.

(Added 8 of 2020 s. 25)

Section 23 Other Harassment

(1) It is unlawful for a member of an organization to which Section 16 applies to harass a person with a disability who is seeking to be, or who is, a member of the organization.

(2) It is unlawful for a member of an authority or body referred to in Section 17 to harass a person with a disability seeking an authorization or qualification (within the meaning of that Section) which can be conferred by the authority or body, as the case may be.

(3) It is unlawful for a person to harass a person with a disability seeking or undergoing training which would help fit the second-mentioned person for any employment if that first-mentioned person provides facilities for such training.

(4) It is unlawful for a person who —

(a) operates an employment agency; or

(b) is a member of the staff of an employment agency,

to harass a person with a disability in the course of offering to provide, or providing, any of the agency's services to him.

Part 4 Discrimination and Harassment in Other Fields

(Format changes — E.R. 1 of 2013)

Education

Section 24 Education

(1) Subject to subsections (3), (4) and (5), it is unlawful for an educational establishment to discriminate against a person with a disability —

(a) by refusing or failing to accept that person's application for admission as a student; or

(b) in the terms or conditions on which it is prepared to admit that person as a student.

(2) Subject to subsections (3), (4) and (5), it is unlawful for an educational establishment to discriminate against a student with a disability —

(a) by denying that student's access, or limiting that student's access, to any benefit, service or facility provided by the educational establishment;

(b) by expelling that student; or

(c) by subjecting that student to any other detriment.

(3) Subsections (1) and (2) shall not apply to an educational establishment which discriminates against a person with a disability in respect of admission to an educational establishment established wholly or primarily for students who have a particular disability where that person does not have that particular disability.

(4) Subsections (1) and (2) shall not apply to an educational establishment which refuses or fails to accept a person's application for admission as a student at an educational establishment where that person, if admitted as a student by the educational establishment, would require services or facilities that are not required by students who do not have a disability and the provision of which would impose unjustifiable hardship on the educational establishment.

(5) Subsections (1) and (2) shall not apply to an educational establishment which discriminates against a person with a disability —

(a) if that person is not reasonably capable of performing the actions or activities reasonably required by the educational establishment in relation to students at that educational establishment; or

(b) if the students who participate in or are to participate in those actions or activities are selected by a method which is reasonable on the basis of their skills and abilities relevant to those actions or activities and relative to each other.

Premises, Goods, Services and Facilities

Section 25 Access to Premises

(1) Subject to subsection (2), it is unlawful for a person to discriminate against another person with a disability —

(a) by refusing to allow that other person access to, or the use of, any premises that the public or a section of the public is entitled or allowed to enter or use (whether for payment or not);

(b) in the terms or conditions on which the first-mentioned person is prepared to allow that other person access to, or the use of, any such premises;

(c) in relation to the provision of means of access to such premises;

(d) by refusing to allow that other person the use of any facilities in such premises that the public or a section of the public is entitled or allowed to use (whether for payment or not);

(e) in the terms or conditions on which the first-mentioned person is prepared to allow that other person the use of any such facilities; or

(f) by requiring the other person to leave such premises or cease to use such facilities.

(2) Subsection (1) shall not apply to a person who discriminates against another person with a disability in relation to the provision of access to premises if —

(a) the premises are so designed or constructed as to be inaccessible to a person with a disability; and

(b) any alteration to the premises to provide such access would impose unjustifiable hardship on the first-mentioned person who would have to provide that access.

Section 26 Goods, Services and Facilities

(1) Subject to subsection (2), it is unlawful for a person who, whether for payment or not, provides goods, services or facilities, to discriminate against another person with a disability —

(a) by refusing to provide that other person with those goods, services or facilities;

(b) in the terms or conditions on which the first-mentioned person provides that other person with those goods, services or facilities; or

(c) in the manner in which the first-mentioned person provides that other person with those goods, services or facilities.

(2) Subsection (1) shall not apply to a person who discriminates against another person with a disability if —

(a) the provision of the goods, services or facilities would impose unjustifiable hardship on the person who would have to provide those goods, services or facilities; and

(b) in the case of the facilities described in paragraphs (c), (d), (e) or (f) of Section 27 (or facilities of a like nature to the facilities so described) and to the extent that those facilities are physical in nature, those facilities are so designed or constructed as to be inaccessible to a person with a disability.

Section 27 Examples of Services and Facilities

The following are examples of the services and facilities referred to in Section 26 —

(a) access to and use of any place which members of the public or a section of the public are permitted to enter;

(b) accommodation in a hotel, guesthouse or other similar establishment;

(c) facilities by way of banking or insurance or for grants, loans, credit or finance;

(d) facilities for education, including the conduct of public examinations;

(e) facilities for entertainment, recreation or refreshment;

(f) facilities for transport or travel;

(g) the services relating to transport or travel;

(h) the services relating to telecommunications;

(i) the services of any profession or trade;

(j) the services of —

(i)–(ii)*(Repealed 78 of 1999 s. 7)*

(iii) any department of the Government; or

(iv) any undertaking by or of the Government.

Section 28 Discrimination in Disposal or Management of Premises

(1) It is unlawful for a person (***the disposer***), in relation to premises in Hong Kong of which he has power to dispose, to discriminate against another person with a disability or any other person providing, or intending to provide, services or facilities on those premises (and who for this purpose is to be treated as an associate of that other person with a disability) to persons with a disability —

(a) in the terms on which the disposer offers him those premises;

(b) by refusing his application for those premises; or

(c) in his treatment of him in relation to any list of persons in need of premises of that description.

(2) It is unlawful for a person (***the manager***), in relation to premises managed by him, to discriminate against another person with a disability occupying the premises —

(a) in the way the manager affords him access to any benefits or facilities, or by refusing or deliberately omitting to afford him access to them; or

(b) by evicting him, or subjecting him to any other detriment.

(3) Subsection (1) shall not apply to a person who owns an estate or interest in the premises and wholly occupies them unless he uses the services of an estate agent for the purposes of the disposal of the premises, or publishes or causes to be published an advertisement in connection with the disposal.

(4) Subsection (2) shall not apply to a person who discriminates against another person with a disability if the affording of access to any benefits or facilities would impose unjustifiable hardship on the person affording such access.

(5) In this Section, in relation to premises, ***power to dispose*** (有權處置) includes the power to sell, rent, let, sub-let or otherwise part with possession of those premises.

Section 29 Discrimination: Consent for Assignment or Sub-letting

(1) Where the licence or consent of the landlord or of any other person (***the disposer***) is required for the disposal to any person of premises in Hong Kong comprised in a tenancy, it is unlawful for the disposer to discriminate against another person with a disability by withholding the licence or consent for disposal of the premises to that other person.

(2) It is unlawful for the disposer to discriminate against another person with a disability —

(a) by evicting that other person from the premises occupied by that other person;

(b) by subjecting that other person to any other detriment in relation to the premises occupied by that other person; or

(c) by refusing to permit that other person to make reasonable alterations to the premises occupied by that person if —

(i) that other person has undertaken to restore the premises to their condition before alteration on leaving the premises;

(ii) in all the circumstances it is likely that that other person will perform the undertaking;

(iii) in all the circumstances, the action required to restore the premises to their condition before alteration is reasonably practicable;

(iv) the alteration is at that other person's own expense; and

(v) the alteration does not involve alteration of other premises occupied by any other person.

(3) Subsection (1) shall not apply —

(a) if —

(i) the disposer, or a near relative of his (***the relevant occupier***) resides, and intends to continue to reside, on the premises;

(ii) there is on the premises, in addition to the accommodation occupied by the relevant occupier, accommodation (not being storage accommodation or means of access) shared by the relevant occupier with other persons residing on the premises who are not members of his household; and

(iii) the premises are small premises as construed in accordance with Section 30(2); or

(b) to a disposer who discriminates against another person with a disability if the granting of the licence or consent for disposal of the premises by the disposer would impose unjustifiable hardship on the disposer.

(4) For the avoidance of doubt, it is hereby declared that this Section applies to tenancies created before the enactment of this Ordinance as well as to tenancies created on or after the enactment of this Ordinance.

(5) In this Section —

disposal (處置), in relation to premises comprised in a tenancy, includes assignment of the tenancy and sub-letting or parting with possession of the premises or any part of the premises;

tenancy (租賃) means a tenancy created —

(a) by a lease or sub-lease;

(b) by an agreement for a lease or sub-lease;

(c) by a tenancy agreement; or

(d) pursuant to any enactment.

Section 30 Exceptions for Small Dwellings

(1) Sections 26(1) and 28 shall not apply to the provision by a person of accommodation in any premises, or the disposal of premises by him, if —

(a) that person or a near relative of his (***the relevant occupier***) resides, and intends to continue to reside, on the premises;

(b) there is on the premises, in addition to the accommodation occupied by the relevant occupier, accommodation (not being storage accommodation or means of access) shared by the relevant occupier with other persons residing on the premises who are not members of his household; and

(c) the premises are small premises.

(2) Premises shall be treated for the purposes of subsection (1) as small premises if —

(a) in the case of premises comprising residential accommodation for one or more households (under separate letting or similar agreements) in addition to the accommodation occupied by the relevant occupier, there is not normally residential accommodation for more than 2 such households and only the relevant occupier and any members of his household reside in the accommodation occupied by him;

(b) in the case of premises not falling within paragraph (a), there is not normally residential accommodation on the premises for more than 6 persons in addition to the relevant occupier and any members of his household.

(3) The Chief Executive in Council may, by notice in the Gazette, amend subsection (2)(b) by substituting another number for the number appearing in that subsection. *(Amended 66 of 1999 s. 3)*

Section 31 Exceptions for Voluntary Bodies

(1) Subject to subsection (5), this Section applies to a body the activities of which are carried on otherwise than for profit.

(2) Sections 26(1), 28 and 29 shall not be construed as rendering unlawful —

(a) the restriction of membership of any body to which this Section applies to persons without a disability (disregarding any minor exceptions) where such restriction is reasonable having regard to the main object of the body; or

(b) the provision of benefits, services or facilities to members of any body to which this Section applies where the membership is so restricted,

even though membership of the body is open to the public, or to a section of the public.

(3) Nothing in Section 26, 28 or 29 shall —

(a) be construed as affecting a provision to which this subsection applies; or

(b) render unlawful an act which is done in order to give effect to such a provision.

(4) Subsection (3) applies to a provision for conferring benefits on persons without a disability (disregarding any benefits to persons with a disability which are exceptional or are relatively insignificant), being a provision which constitutes the main object of a body to which this Section applies.

(5) This Section shall not apply to a body whose recurrent expenditure is funded wholly or in part by the Government.

Section 32 Further Exceptions from Sections 26(1) and 28

Sections 26(1) and 28 shall not apply —

(a) to discrimination which is rendered unlawful by any provision or Part of this Ordinance specified in column 1 of Schedule 4; or

(b) to discrimination which would be so unlawful but for any provision or Part of this Ordinance specified in column 2 of that Schedule.

Barristers

Section 33 Discrimination by, or in Relation to, Barristers

(1) It is unlawful for a barrister or barrister's clerk, in relation to any offer of a pupillage or tenancy, to discriminate against a person with a disability —

(a) in the arrangements which are made for the purpose of determining to whom it should be offered;

(b) in respect of any terms on which it is offered; or

(c) by refusing or deliberately omitting to offer it to him.

(2) It is unlawful for a barrister or barrister's clerk, in relation to a person with a disability who is a pupil or tenant in the chambers concerned, to discriminate against him —

(a) in respect of any terms applicable to him as a pupil or tenant;

(b) in the opportunities for training, or gaining experience, which are afforded or denied to him;

(c) in the benefits, services or facilities which are afforded or denied to him; or

(d) by terminating his pupillage or by subjecting him to any pressure to leave the chambers or other detriment.

(3) It is unlawful for any person, in relation to the giving, withholding or acceptance of instructions to a barrister, to discriminate against a person with a disability.

(4) In this Section —

barrister's clerk (大律師書記) includes any person carrying out any of the functions of a barrister's clerk;

pupil (見習大律師), ***pupillage*** (見習職位), ***tenancy*** (租賃) and ***tenant*** (承租人) have the meanings commonly associated with their use in the context of a set of barristers' chambers.

Clubs and Sporting Activities

Section 34 Clubs

(1) Subject to subsection (4), it is unlawful for a club, the committee of management of a club or a member of the committee of management of a club to discriminate against a person with a disability who is not a member of the club —

(a) by refusing or failing to accept that person's application for membership; or

(b) in the terms or conditions on which the club is prepared to admit that person to membership.

(2) Subject to subsections (3) and (4), it is unlawful for a club, the committee of management of a club or a member of the committee of management of a club to discriminate against a person with a disability who is a member of the club —

(a) in the terms or conditions of membership that are afforded to that member;

(b) by refusing or failing to accept that member's application for a particular class or type of membership;

(c) by denying that member's access, or limiting that member's access, to any benefit, service or facility provided by the club;

(d) by depriving that member of membership or varying the terms of membership; or

(e) by subjecting that member to any other detriment.

(3) Subsection (2)(c) shall not apply to a club, the committee of management of a club or a member of the committee of management of a club which discriminates against a person with a disability where, because of that person's disability, that person requires the benefit, service or facility to be provided in a special manner and the benefit, service or facility cannot without unjustifiable hardship be so provided by the club.

(4) Subsections (1) and (2) shall not apply to a club, the committee of management of a club or a member of the committee of management of a club which discriminates against a person with a disability if membership (however described) of the club is restricted only to persons who have a particular disability and that first-mentioned person does not have that disability.

Section 35 Sport

(1) Subject to subsection (3), it is unlawful for a person to discriminate against another person with a disability by excluding that other person from a sporting activity.

(2) In subsection (1), a reference to a sporting activity includes a reference to an administrative or coaching activity in relation to any sport.

(3) Subsection (1) shall not apply to a person who discriminates against another person with a disability —

(a) if that other person is not reasonably capable of performing the actions reasonably required in relation to the sporting activity;

(b) if the persons who participate or are to participate in the sporting activities are selected by a method which is reasonable on the basis of their skills and abilities relevant to the sporting activity and relative to each other; or

(c) if a sporting activity is conducted only for persons who have a particular disability and that other person does not have that disability.

Government

Section 36 Government

(1) Subject to subsection (2), without prejudice to the operation of the other provisions of this Part in relation to the Government, it is unlawful for the Government to discriminate against a person with a disability in the performance of its functions or the exercise of its powers.

(2) Subsection (1) shall not render unlawful —

(a) as regards a person with a disability not having the right to enter and remain in Hong Kong, any act done under any immigration legislation governing entry into, stay in and departure from Hong Kong; or

(b) any act done in relation to a person with a disability if it was necessary for that act to be done in order to comply with a requirement of an existing statutory provision.

Harassment

Section 37 Educational Establishments

(1) It is unlawful for a student of an educational establishment, or a person who is, or is a member of, the responsible body for an educational establishment, as the case may be, to harass a person with a disability who is seeking to be, or who is, a student of that educational establishment.

(2) It is unlawful for a person who is a member of the staff of an educational establishment to harass a person with a disability who is seeking to be, or who is, a student of that educational establishment.

(3) It is unlawful for a person who is seeking to be, or who is, a student of an educational establishment to harass a person with a disability —

(a) who is, or is a member of, the responsible body for; or

(b) who is a member of the staff of,

the establishment.

Section 38 Harassment in Relation to the Provision of Goods, Services and Facilities

(1) It is unlawful for a person who, whether for payment or not, provides goods, services or facilities, to harass another person with a disability who — *(Amended 8 of 2020 s. 35)*

(a) wants to acquire the goods or services;

(b) is in the course of acquiring the goods or services;

(c) wants to make use of the facilities; or

(d) is in the course of making use of the facilities. *(Amended 8 of 2020 s. 35)*

(1A) It is unlawful for a person who —

(a) wants to acquire goods or services;

(b) is in the course of acquiring goods or services;

(c) wants to make use of facilities; or

(d) is in the course of making use of facilities,

to harass another person with a disability who, whether for payment or not, provides the goods, services or facilities. *(Added 8 of 2020 s. 35)*

(2) It is unlawful for a person to —

(a) interfere with the provision of goods, services or facilities to another person with a disability; or

(b) prevent or to attempt to prevent another person who, whether for payment or not, provides goods, services or facilities, or wishes to provide goods, services or facilities from providing those goods, services or facilities to a third person with a disability.

Section 38A Harassment by Clubs

It is unlawful for a club, the committee of management of a club or a member of the committee of management of a club to harass a person with a disability who is, or has applied to be, a member of the club.

(Added 8 of 2020 s. 41)

Section 39 Other Harassment

(1) It is unlawful for a person, in relation to premises managed by him, to harass a person with a disability occupying the premises.

(2) Where the licence or consent of the landlord or of any other person is required for the disposal to any person of premises in Hong Kong comprised in a tenancy, it is unlawful for the landlord or other person to harass a person with a disability seeking the licence or consent for disposal of the premises to him.

(3) Section 29(5) shall apply to subsection (2) as it applies to Section 29.

(4) It is unlawful for a barrister or barrister's clerk, in relation to any chambers, to harass a person with a disability —

(a) in the course of offering to provide to him pupillage or tenancy in the chambers; or

(b) who is a pupil or tenant in the chambers.

(5) It is unlawful for any person, in the course of the giving, withholding or acceptance of instructions to a barrister, to harass a person with a disability who is a barrister.

(6) Section 33(4) shall apply to subsections (4) and (5) as it applies to Section 33.

Extent

Section 40 Extent of Part 4

(1) Section 26(1) —

(a) shall not apply to goods, services or facilities outside Hong Kong except as provided in subsections (2) and (3); and

(b) shall not apply to facilities by way of banking or insurance or for grants, loans, credit or finance, where the facilities are for a purpose to be carried out, or in connection with risks wholly or mainly arising, outside Hong Kong.

(2) Section 26(1) applies to the provision of facilities for travel outside Hong Kong where the refusal or omission occurs in Hong Kong or on a ship, aircraft or dynamically supported craft referred to in subsection (3).

(3) Section 26(1) applies on and in relation to —

(a) any ship registered in Hong Kong;

(b) any aircraft or dynamically supported craft registered in Hong Kong and operated by a person who has his principal place of business, or is ordinarily resident, in Hong Kong;

(c) any ship, aircraft or dynamically supported craft belonging to or possessed by the Government,

even if the ship, aircraft or dynamically supported craft is outside Hong Kong.

(4) This Section shall not render unlawful an act done in or over a place outside Hong Kong, or in or over that place's territorial waters, if any, for the purpose of complying with the laws of that place.

(5) Section 24 shall not apply to benefits, services or facilities outside Hong Kong except —

(a) travel on a ship registered in Hong Kong;

(b) benefits, services or facilities provided on a ship so registered.

(6) Section 38(1) and (1A) does not apply to an act of harassment that is committed outside Hong Kong except as provided in subsection (7). *(Added 8 of 2020 s. 37)*

(7) Section 38(1) and (1A) applies to an act of harassment that is committed on a ship, aircraft or dynamically supported craft referred to in subsection (3)(a), (b) or (c) even if it is outside Hong Kong when the act is committed. *(Added 8 of 2020 s. 37)*

(Amended E.R. 1 of 2013)

Part 5 Other Unlawful Acts

(Format changes — E.R. 1 of 2013)

Section 41 Discriminatory Practices

(1) In this Section, ***discriminatory practice*** (歧視性的做法) means the application of a requirement or condition which results in an act of discrimination which is unlawful by virtue of any provision of Part 3 or 4 as read with Section 6(b) or which would be likely to result in such an act of discrimination if the persons to whom it is applied were not all persons with a disability.

(2) A person acts in contravention of this Section if and so long as —

(a) he applies a discriminatory practice; or

(b) he operates practices or other arrangements which in any circumstances would call for the application by him of a discriminatory practice.

(3) Proceedings in respect of a contravention of this Section shall be brought only by the Commission in accordance with the provisions of Sections 73, 74, 75, 76 and 77.

(Amended E.R. 1 of 2013)

Section 42 Requests for Information

(1) If, because of another provision of Part 3 or 4, it would be unlawful, in particular circumstances, for a person to discriminate against another person, in doing a particular act, it is unlawful for the first-mentioned person to request or require that other person to provide, in connection with or for the purposes of the doing of the act, information (whether by completing a form or otherwise) that persons who do not have a disability would not, in circumstances that are the same or are not materially different, be requested or required to provide.

(2) Subject to subsection (3), if, because of Section 11(1), it would be unlawful, in particular circumstances, for a person to discriminate against another person, in doing a particular act, it is unlawful for the first-mentioned person to request or require that other person to provide information of a medical nature (whether by completing a form or otherwise) in connection with or for the purposes of the doing of the act.

(3) Nothing in subsection (2) shall render it unlawful for a person to request or require another person to provide information of a medical nature that is necessary to determine if that other person would be unable to carry out the inherent requirements of the job or would require services or facilities that are not required by persons without a disability.

(Amended E.R. 1 of 2013)

Section 43 Discriminatory Advertisements

(1) It is unlawful to publish or cause to be published an advertisement which indicates, or might reasonably be understood as indicating, an intention by a person to do any act which is or might be unlawful by virtue of Part 3 or 4.

(2) Subsection (1) shall not apply to an advertisement if the intended act would not in fact be unlawful.

(3) The publisher of an advertisement made unlawful by subsection (1) shall not be subject to any liability under that subsection in respect of the publication of the advertisement if he proves —

(a) that the advertisement was published in reliance on a statement made to him by the person who caused it to be published to the effect that, by reason of the operation of subsection (2), the publication would not be unlawful; and

(b) that it was reasonable for him to rely on the statement.

(4) A person who knowingly or recklessly makes a statement of the kind referred to in subsection (3) which in a material respect is false or misleading commits an offence and is liable on conviction to a fine at level 4.

(Amended E.R. 1 of 2013)

Section 44 Instructions to Discriminate

It is unlawful for a person —

(a) who has authority over another person; or

(b) in accordance with whose wishes that other person is accustomed to act,

to instruct him to do any act which is unlawful by virtue of Part 3 or 4, or procure or attempt to procure the doing by him of any such act.

(Amended E.R. 1 of 2013)

Section 45 Pressure to Discriminate

(1) It is unlawful to induce, or attempt to induce, a person to do any act which contravenes Part 3 or 4 by —

(a) providing or offering to provide him with any benefit, service or facility; or

(b) subjecting or threatening to subject him to any detriment.

(2) An offer or threat is not prevented from falling within subsection (1) because it is not made directly to the person concerned, if it is made in such a way that he is likely to hear of it.

(Amended E.R. 1 of 2013)

Section 46 Vilification

(1) It is unlawful for a person, by any activity in public, to incite hatred towards, serious contempt for, or severe ridicule of, another person with a disability or members of a class of persons with a disability.

(1A) For the purposes of subsection (1), it is immaterial whether a person is actually incited, by an activity, to —

(a) hatred towards;

(b) serious contempt for; or

(c) severe ridicule of,

another person with a disability or members of a class of persons with a disability. *(Added 29 of 2008 s. 99)*

(2) Nothing in this Section renders unlawful —

(a) a fair report of an activity in public;

(b) an activity in public that —

(i) is a communication or the distribution or dissemination of any matter; and

(ii) consists of a publication which is subject to a defence of absolute privilege in proceedings for defamation; or *(Replaced 29 of 2008 s. 99)*

(c) an activity in public done reasonably and in good faith, for academic, artistic, scientific or research purposes in the public interest, including discussions about and expositions of any matter.

(3) In this Section and Section 47, ***activity in public*** (公開活動) includes —

(a) any form of communication to the public, including speaking, writing, printing, displaying notices, broadcasting, screening and playing of tapes or other recorded material;

(b) any conduct (not being a form of communication referred to in paragraph (a)) observable by the public, including actions and gestures and the wearing or display of clothing, signs, flags, emblems and insignia;

(c) the distribution or dissemination of any matter to the public.

Section 47 Offence of Serious Vilification

(1) A person commits an offence if —

(a) the person, by any activity, incites hatred towards, serious contempt for, or severe ridicule of, another person (***the second-mentioned person***) with a disability or members of a class of persons with a disability;

(b) the person intentionally incites such hatred, serious contempt or severe ridicule; and

(c) the activity is an activity in public and consists of threatening physical harm, or inciting others to threaten physical harm —

(i) towards, or towards any premises or property of, the second-mentioned person or the members of the class of persons; or

(ii) towards the premises or property of any other person to which the second-mentioned person or the members of the class of persons have access.

(2) For the purposes of subsection (1)(a), it is immaterial whether a person is actually incited, by an activity, to —

(a) hatred towards;

(b) serious contempt for; or

(c) severe ridicule of,

another person with a disability or members of a class of persons with a disability.

(3) A person who commits an offence under subsection (1) is liable on conviction to a fine at level 6 and to imprisonment for 2 years.

(Replaced 29 of 2008 s. 100)

Section 48 Liability of Employers and Principals

(1) Anything done by a person in the course of his employment shall be treated for the purposes of this Ordinance as done by his employer as well as by him, whether or not it was done with the employer's knowledge or approval.

(2) Anything done by a person as agent for another person with the authority (whether express or implied, and whether precedent or subsequent) of that other person shall be treated for the purposes of this Ordinance as done by that other person as well as by him.

(3) In proceedings brought under this Ordinance against any person in respect of an act alleged to have been done by an employee of his it shall be a defence for that person to prove that he took such steps as were reasonably practicable to prevent the employee from doing that act, or from doing in the course of his employment acts of that description.

(4) For the avoidance of doubt, it is hereby declared that this Section shall not apply for the purposes of any criminal proceedings.

Section 48A Liability of Persons Engaging Interns and Volunteers

(1) This Section applies for the purposes of Section 22A.

(2) For the avoidance of doubt, this Section does not apply for the purposes of any criminal proceedings.

(3) An act done by an intern in the course of an internship is to be treated as an act done —

(a) by the intern; and

(b) by the person who engaged the intern for the internship, whether or not the act was done with the knowledge or approval of that person.

(4) In proceedings brought under this Ordinance against a person in respect of an act alleged to have been done by an intern engaged by the person, it is a defence for the person to prove that the person took reasonably practicable steps to prevent the intern —

(a) from doing that act; or

(b) from doing acts of that description in the course of the internship

(5) Subsections (6) and (7) apply if a volunteer is engaged by another person to perform volunteer work.

(6) An act done by a volunteer in the course of performing volunteer work is to be treated as an act done —

(a) by the volunteer; and

(b) by the person who engaged the volunteer to perform the work, whether or not the act was done with the knowledge or approval of that person.

(7) In proceedings brought under this Ordinance against a person in respect of an act alleged to have been done by a volunteer engaged by the person, it is a defence for the person to prove that the person took reasonably practicable steps to prevent the volunteer —

(a) from doing that act; or

(b) from doing acts of that description in the course of performing volunteer work.

(Added 8 of 2020 s. 26)

Section 49 Aiding Unlawful Acts

(1) A person who knowingly aids another person to do an act made unlawful by this Ordinance shall be treated for the purposes of this Ordinance as himself doing an unlawful act of the like description.

(2) For the purposes of subsection (1), an employee or agent for whose act the employer or principal is liable under Section 48 (or would be so liable but for Section 48(3)) shall be deemed to aid the doing of the act by the employer or principal.

(2A) For the purposes of subsection (1), if a person who engaged an intern —

(a) is liable under Section 48A for an act done by the intern; or

(b) would be liable under Section 48A for the act but for Section 48A(4),

the intern is deemed to aid the doing of the act by that person. *(Added 8 of 2020 s. 27)*

(2B) For the purposes of subsection (1), if a person who engaged a volunteer —

(a) is liable under Section 48A for an act done by the volunteer; or

(b) would be liable under Section 48A for the act but for Section 48A(7),

the volunteer is deemed to aid the doing of the act by that person. *(Added 8 of 2020 s. 27)*

(3) A person does not under this Section knowingly aid another to do an unlawful act if —

(a) he acts in reliance on a statement made to him by that other person that, by reason of any provision of this Ordinance, the act which he aids would not be unlawful; and

(b) it is reasonable for him to rely on the statement.

(4) A person who knowingly or recklessly makes a statement of the kind referred to in subsection (3)(a) which in a material respect is false or misleading commits an offence and is liable on conviction to a fine at level 4.

Part 6 General Exceptions from Parts 3 to 5

(Amended L.N. 391 of 1996)

(Format changes — E.R. 1 of 2013)

Section 50 Special Measures

Nothing in Part 3, 4 or 5 shall render unlawful an act that is reasonably intended to —

(a) ensure that persons with a disability have equal opportunities with other persons in circumstances in relation to which a provision is made by this Ordinance;

(b) afford persons with a disability or a particular disability, goods or access to services, facilities or opportunities to meet their special needs in relation to —

(i) employment, education, clubs or sport;

(ii) the provision of premises, goods, services or facilities; or

(iii) their capacity to live independently;

(c) afford persons with a disability or a particular disability, grants, benefits or programmes, whether direct or indirect, to meet their special needs in relation to —

(i) employment, education, clubs or sport;

(ii) the provision of premises, goods, services or facilities; or

(iii) their capacity to live independently.

(Amended E.R. 1 of 2013)

Section 51 Charities

(1) Nothing in Part 3, 4 or 5 shall —

(a) be construed as affecting a provision to which this subsection applies; or

(b) render unlawful an act which is done in order to give effect to such a provision.

(2) Subsection (1) applies to a provision for conferring benefits on persons who have a disability or a particular disability (disregarding any benefits to other persons which are exceptional or are relatively insignificant), being a provision which is contained in a charitable instrument.

(3) In applying this Section, account shall be taken of Section 88 of the Inland Revenue Ordinance (Cap. 112).

(4) In this Section —

charitable instrument (慈善文書) means an enactment or other instrument so far as it relates to charitable purposes;

charitable purposes (慈善目的) means purposes which are exclusively charitable according to any enactment or rule of law.

(Amended E.R. 1 of 2013)

Section 52 Insurance, etc.

Nothing in Part 3, 4 or 5 shall render unlawful the treatment of a person in relation to any class of insurance business, or similar matter involving the assessment of risk, where the treatment —

(a) was effected by reference to actuarial or other data from a source on which it was reasonable to rely; and

(b) was reasonable having regard to the data and any other relevant factors.

(Amended E.R. 1 of 2013)

Section 53 Discriminatory Training by Certain Bodies

(1) Nothing in Part 3, 4 or 5 shall render unlawful any act done in relation to particular work by any person in, or in connection with —

(a) affording persons with a disability only, or persons without a disability only, access to facilities for training which would help to fit them for that work; or

(b) encouraging persons with a disability only, or persons without a disability only, to take advantage of opportunities for doing that work,

where it reasonably appears to that person that at any time within the 12 months immediately preceding the doing of the act there were no persons with or without a disability, as the case may be, doing that work in Hong Kong, or the number of persons with or without a disability, respectively, doing the work in Hong Kong was comparatively small.

(2) This Section shall not apply in relation to any discrimination which is rendered unlawful by Section 11.

(Amended E.R. 1 of 2013)

Section 54 Other Discriminatory Training, etc.

(1) Nothing in Part 3, 4 or 5 shall render unlawful any act done by an employer in relation to particular work in his employment, being an act done in, or in connection with —

(a) affording his employees with a disability only, or his employees without a disability only, access to facilities for training which would help to fit them for that work; or

(b) encouraging persons with a disability only, or persons without a disability only, to take advantage of opportunities for doing that work,

where at any time within the 12 months immediately preceding the doing of the act there were no persons with or without a disability, as the case may be, among those doing that work or the number of persons with or without a disability, respectively, doing the work was comparatively small.

(2) Nothing in Section 16 shall render unlawful any act done by an organization to which that Section applies in, or in connection with —

(a) affording members with a disability of the organization only, or members without a disability of the organization only, access to facilities for training which would help to fit them for holding a post of any kind in the organization; or

(b) encouraging members with a disability only, or members without a disability only, to take advantage of opportunities for holding such posts in the organization,

where at any time within the 12 months immediately preceding the doing of the act there were no persons with or without a disability, as the case may be, among persons holding such posts in the organization or the number of persons with or without a disability, respectively, holding such posts was comparatively small.

(3) Nothing in Part 3, 4 or 5 shall render unlawful any act done by an organization to which Section 16 applies in, or in connection with, encouraging persons with a disability only, or persons without a disability only, to become members of the organization where at any time within the 12 months immediately preceding the doing of the act there were no persons with or without a disability, as the case may be, among those members or the number of persons with or without a disability, respectively, among the members was comparatively small.

(Amended E.R. 1 of 2013)

Section 55 Elections in Respect of Trade Unions, etc.

(1) If an organization to which Section 16 applies comprises a body the membership of which is wholly or mainly elected, nothing in that Section shall render unlawful provision which ensures that a minimum number of persons with or without a disability are members of the body —

(a) by reserving seats on the body for those persons respectively; or

(b) by making extra seats on the body available (by election or co-option or otherwise) for those persons respectively on occasions when the number of those persons respectively in the other seats is below the minimum,

where in the opinion of the organization the provision is in the circumstances needed to secure a reasonable lower limit to the number of members with or without a disability, as the case may be, serving on the body; and nothing in Part 3, 4 or 5 shall render unlawful any act done in order to give effect to such a provision.

(2) This Section shall not be taken as making lawful —

(a) discrimination in the arrangements for determining the persons entitled to vote in an election of members of the body, or otherwise to choose the persons to serve on the body; or

(b) discrimination in any arrangements concerning membership of the organization itself.

(Amended E.R. 1 of 2013)

Section 56 Indirect Access to Benefits, etc.

(1) References in this Ordinance to the affording by any person of access to benefits, services or facilities are not limited to benefits, services or facilities provided by that person himself, but include any means by which it is in that person's power to facilitate access to benefits, services or facilities provided by any other person (***actual provider***).

(2) Where by any provision of this Ordinance the affording by any person of access to benefits, services or facilities in a discriminatory way is in certain circumstances prevented from being unlawful, the effect of the provision shall extend also to the liability under this Ordinance of any actual provider.

Section 57 Acts Done for Purposes of Protection of Persons with Disability

(1) Nothing in —

(a) the provisions of Part 3;

(b) the provisions of Part 4 so far as it applies to vocational training; or

(c) the provisions of Part 5 so far as it has effect in relation to any of the provisions referred to in paragraph (a) or (b),

shall render unlawful any act done by a person in relation to a person with a disability if —

(i) it was necessary for that first-mentioned person to do it in order to comply with a requirement of an existing statutory provision concerning the protection of persons with a disability; or

(ii) it was necessary for that first-mentioned person to do it in order to comply with a requirement of a provision specified in Schedule 3 and it was done by that person for the purpose of the protection of the second-mentioned person (or of any class of persons with a disability that included that second-mentioned person).

(2) In subsection (1) —

(a) the reference in paragraph (i) of that subsection to an existing statutory provision concerning the protection of persons with a disability is a reference to any such provision having effect for the purpose of protecting those persons as regards circumstances giving rise to risks specifically affecting those persons (or any class of those persons) whether the provision relates only to such protection or to the protection of any other persons as well;

(b) the reference in paragraph (ii) of that subsection to the protection of a particular person with a disability or class of persons with a disability is a reference to the protection of that person or those persons as regards any circumstances falling within paragraph (a).

(3) Subject to subsection (4), the provisions of subsections (1)(ii) and (2)(b), Section 12(3)(c) and Schedule 3 shall expire on the 1st anniversary of the day on which this Ordinance is enacted.

(4) Prior to the expiry of the provisions referred to in subsection (3), the Legislative Council may, by Resolution, amend that subsection to extend those provisions for a period of 1 year.

(Amended E.R. 1 of 2013)

Section 58 Acts Done under Statutory Authority to be Exempt from Certain Provisions of Part 4

(1) Nothing in —

(a) the relevant provisions of Part 4; or

(b) Part 5 so far as it has effect in relation to those provisions,

shall render unlawful any act done by a person if it was necessary for that person to do it in order to comply with a requirement of an existing statutory provision.

(2) In subsection (1), ***the relevant provisions of Part 4*** (第4部的有關條文) means the provisions of Part 4 except so far as they apply to vocational training or harassment.

(Amended E.R. 1 of 2013)

Section 59 Construction of References to Vocational Training

In Sections 57 and 58, ***vocational training*** (職業訓練) includes —

(a) retraining; and

(b) vocational guidance.

Section 60 Further Exceptions

(1) No provision or Part of this Ordinance specified in column 1 of Schedule 5 shall render unlawful any discrimination specified opposite thereto in column 2 of that Schedule.

(2) Nothing in Part 3, 4 or 5 shall render unlawful any act done by any person —

(a) in connection with any discrimination which is not unlawful by virtue of the operation of subsection (1); and

(b) to the extent that it is done for the purposes of that discrimination.

(Amended E.R. 1 of 2013)

Section 61 Infectious Diseases

(1) Subject to subsection (2), nothing in this Ordinance shall apply to a person who discriminates against another person with a disability if —

(a) that person's disability is an infectious disease; and

(b) the discriminatory act is reasonably necessary to protect public health.

(2) For the avoidance of doubt, it is hereby declared that subsection (1) has no application to a person who is HIV-positive or has acquired immune deficiency syndrome (commonly known as "AIDS") merely because of the fact that the person has such a condition.

(3) In this Section, ***infectious disease*** (傳染病) includes —

(a) any scheduled infectious disease, or a disease caused by a scheduled infectious agent, within the meaning of the Prevention and Control of Disease Ordinance (Cap. 599); and *(Replaced 14 of 2008 s. 18)*

(b) any communicable disease specified by the Director of Health by notice in the Gazette.

Part 7 Commission

(Format changes — E.R. 1 of 2013)

Section 62 Functions and Powers of Commission

(1) The Commission shall —

(a) work towards the elimination of discrimination;

(b) promote equality of opportunity between persons with a disability and persons without a disability;

(c) work towards the elimination of harassment and vilification;

(d) in the case of any act alleged to be unlawful by virtue of this Ordinance, encourage persons who are concerned with the matter to which the act relates to effect a settlement of the matter by conciliation, whether under Section 80 or otherwise;

(e) keep under review the working of this Ordinance and, when it is so required by the Chief Executive or otherwise thinks it necessary draw up and submit to the Chief Executive proposals for amending this Ordinance; and *(Amended 66 of 1999 s. 3)*

(f) perform such other functions as are imposed on it under this Ordinance or any other enactment.

(2) The Commission may do all such things as are necessary for, or incidental or conducive to, the better performance of its functions and in particular but without prejudice to the generality of the foregoing, may —

(a) with the prior approval of the Chief Executive, become a member of or affiliate to any international body concerned with (whether in whole or in part) the elimination of discrimination; *(Amended 66 of 1999 s. 3)*

(b) exercise such other powers as are conferred on it under this Ordinance.

Section 63 Review of Schedules 2, 3 and 5

(1) Without prejudice to the generality of Section 62(1), the Commission, pursuant to its functions under paragraphs (a) and (b) of that Section, shall keep Schedules 2, 3 and 5 under review.

(2) Whenever the Commission thinks it necessary, it shall draw up and submit to the Chief Executive proposals for — *(Amended 66 of 1999 s. 3)*

- (a) amending Schedules 2 and 5;
- (b) amending the provisions specified in Schedule 3.

Section 64 Delegations

The Commission shall not under Section 67 of the relevant Ordinance delegate any of its functions or powers under —

- (a) Section 85;
- (b) any provisions of any regulations made under Section 86 which are specified in the regulations as provisions which shall not be subject to Section 67 of the relevant Ordinance;
- (c) any provisions of any rules made under Section 85 which are specified in the rules as provisions which shall not be subject to Section 67 of the relevant Ordinance.

(Amended 80 of 1997 s. 102)

Section 64A Protection of Members of Commission, etc.

(1) No person to whom this subsection applies, acting in good faith, is personally liable in damages for any act done or default made in the performance or purported performance of any function, or the exercise or purported exercise of any power, imposed or conferred on the Commission under this Ordinance.

(2) The protection conferred by subsection (1) on any person to whom that subsection applies in respect of any act or default does not in any way affect the liability of the Commission for that act or default.

(3) Subsection (1) applies to the following persons —

- (a) a member of the Commission or a committee;
- (b) an employee of the Commission;
- (c) a conciliator.

(Added 18 of 2014 s. 32)

Codes of Practice

Section 65 Codes of Practice

(1) The Commission may issue codes of practice containing such practical guidance as it thinks fit for the purposes of —

- (a) the elimination of discrimination;
- (b) the promotion of equality of opportunity between persons with a disability and persons without a disability generally;
- (c) the elimination of harassment and vilification.

(2) When the Commission proposes to issue a code of practice, it shall prepare and publish (otherwise than in the Gazette) the code, shall consider any representations made to it about the code and may modify the code accordingly.

(3) In the course of preparing any code of practice for eventual publication under subsection (2), the Commission shall consult with such associations, organizations, associations of organizations or bodies as appear to the Commission to be appropriate, including any of the associations, organizations, associations of organizations or bodies specified by the Secretary for Labour and Welfare by notice in the Gazette. *(Amended L.N. 106 of 2002; L.N. 130 of 2007)**

(4) If the Commission determines to proceed with a code of practice published under subsection (2), it shall cause the code to be —

(a) published in the Gazette; and

(b) laid on the table of the Legislative Council at the next sitting after its publication in the Gazette.

(5) Where a code of practice has been laid on the table of the Legislative Council under subsection (4), the Legislative Council may, by Resolution passed at a sitting of the Legislative Council held before the expiration of a period of 28 days after the sitting at which it was so laid, provide that the code of practice shall be amended in any manner consistent with this Section.

(6) If the period referred to in subsection (5) would but for this subsection expire —

(a) after the end of a session of the Legislative Council or a dissolution thereof; but

(b) on or before the day of the second sitting of the Legislative Council in the next following session thereof,

that period shall be deemed to extend to and expire on the day after that second sitting.

(7) Before the expiration of the period referred to in subsection (5) or that period as extended by virtue of subsection (6),† the Legislative Council may by Resolution in relation to a code of practice specified therein —

(a) in the case of the period referred to in subsection (5), extend that period to the first sitting of the Legislative Council held not earlier than the twenty-first day after the day of its expiration;

(b) in the case where the period referred to in subsection (5) has been extended by virtue of subsection (6), extend that period as so extended to the first sitting of the Legislative Council held not earlier than the twenty-first day after the day of the second sitting in that next following session. *(Replaced 8 of 2002 s. 20)*

(8) A Resolution passed by the Legislative Council in accordance with this Section shall be published in the Gazette not later than 14 days after the passing thereof or within such further period as the Chief Executive may allow in any particular case. *(Amended 66 of 1999 s. 3)*

(9) A code of practice issued under this Section shall come into operation —

(a) in the case where before the expiration of the period referred to in subsection (5), or before the expiration of that period as extended under subsection (6) or (7), the Legislative Council does not pass a Resolution amending the code of practice, upon the expiration of that period, or upon the expiration of that period as so extended, as the case may be; and

(b) in the case where the Legislative Council passes a Resolution amending the code of practice, upon the expiration of the day next preceding the day of the publication in the Gazette of such Resolution under subsection (8).

---

* For the saving and transitional provisions relating to the amendments made by the Resolution of the Legislative Council (L.N. 130 of 2007), see paragraph (12) of that Resolution.

† For the transitional provision relating to this subsection as amended by Section 20 of the Extension of Vetting Period (Legislative Council) Ordinance 2002 (8 of 2002), see Section 21 of that Ordinance.

(10) A code of practice issued under this Section may contain such transitional provisions or savings as appear to the Commission to be necessary or expedient in connection with the matters the subject of the code.

(11) The Commission may from time to time revise the whole or any part of a code of practice issued under this Section and issue that revised code, and subsections (2) to (10) shall apply (with appropriate modifications) to such a revised code as they apply to the first issue of a code.

(12) Without prejudice to the generality of subsection (1), a code of practice issued under this Section may include such practical guidance as the Commission thinks fit as to what steps it is reasonably practicable for employers to take for the purpose of preventing their employees from doing in the course of their employment acts made unlawful by this Ordinance.

(13) A failure on the part of any person to observe any provision of a code of practice shall not of itself render him liable to any proceedings; but in any proceedings under this Ordinance before any court any code of practice issued under this Section shall be admissible in evidence, and if any provision of such a code appears to the court to be relevant to any question arising in the proceedings it shall be taken into account in determining that question.

(14) In this Section, ***sitting*** (會議), when used to calculate time, means the day on which the sitting commences and only includes a sitting at which subsidiary legislation is included on the order paper.

Investigations

Section 66 Power to Conduct Formal Investigations

Without prejudice to the generality of Section 62(1), the Commission may if it thinks fit, and shall if required by the Chief Secretary for Administration, conduct a formal investigation for any purpose connected with the carrying out of any of its functions under that Section.

(Amended L.N. 362 of 1997)

Section 67 Terms of Reference

(1) The Commission shall not embark on a formal investigation unless the requirements of this Section have been complied with.

(2) Terms of reference for the formal investigation shall be drawn up by the Commission or, if the Commission was required by the Chief Secretary for Administration to conduct the investigation, by the Chief Secretary for Administration after consulting the Commission. *(Amended L.N. 362 of 1997)*

(3) It shall be the duty of the Commission to give general notice of the holding of the formal investigation unless the terms of reference confine it to activities of persons named in them, but in such a case the Commission shall in the prescribed manner give those persons notice of the holding of the investigation.

(4) Where the terms of reference of the formal investigation confine it to activities of persons named in them and the Commission in the course of it proposes to investigate any act made unlawful by this Ordinance which it believes that a person so named may have done, the Commission shall —

(a) inform that person of its belief and of its proposal to investigate the act; and

(b) offer him an opportunity of making oral or written representations with regard to it (or both oral and written representations if he thinks fit), and a person so named who avails himself of an opportunity under this subsection of making oral representations may be represented —

(i) by counsel or a solicitor; or

(ii) by some other person of his choice, not being a person to whom the Commission objects on the ground that he is unsuitable.

(5) The Commission or, if the Commission was required by the Chief Secretary for Administration to conduct the formal investigation, the Chief Secretary for Administration after consulting the Commission may from time to time revise the terms of reference; and subsections (1), (3) and (4) shall apply to the revised investigation and terms of reference as they applied to the original. *(Amended L.N. 362 of 1997)*

Section 68 Power to Obtain Information

(1) For the purposes of a formal investigation the Commission, by a notice in the prescribed form served on him in the prescribed manner —

(a) may require any person to furnish such written information as may be described in the notice, and may specify the time at which, and the manner and form in which, the information is to be furnished;

(b) may require any person to attend at such time and place as is specified in the notice and give oral information about, and produce all documents in his possession or control relating to, any matter specified in the notice.

(2) Except as provided by Section 75, a notice shall be served under subsection (1) only where —

(a) service of the notice was authorized in writing by or on behalf of the Chief Secretary for Administration; or *(Amended L.N. 362 of 1997)*

(b) the terms of reference of the formal investigation state that the Commission believes that a person named in them may have done or may be doing acts of all or any of the following descriptions —

(i) unlawful discriminatory acts;

(ii) unlawful acts of harassment;

(iii) contraventions of Section 41, 42, 43, 44, 45, 46 or 47,

and confine the investigation to those acts.

(3) A notice under subsection (1) shall not require a person —

(a) to give information, or produce any documents, which he could not be compelled to give in evidence, or produce, in civil proceedings before the Court of First Instance; or *(Amended 25 of 1998 s. 2)*

(b) to attend at any place unless the necessary expenses of his journey to and from that place are paid or tendered to him.

(4) If a person fails to comply with a notice served on him under subsection (1) or the Commission has reasonable cause to believe that he intends not to comply with it, the Commission may apply to the District Court for an order requiring him to comply with it or with such directions for the like purpose as may be contained in the order; and Section 66A of the District Court Ordinance (Cap. 336) shall apply to failure without reasonable excuse to comply with any such order as it applies in the cases there provided.

(5) A person commits an offence if he —

(a) wilfully alters, suppresses, conceals or destroys a document which he has been required by a notice or order under this Section to produce; or

(b) in complying with such a notice or order, knowingly or recklessly makes any statement which in a material respect is false or misleading,

and is liable on conviction to a fine at level 4.

Section 69 Recommendations and Reports on Formal Investigations

(1) If in the light of any of its findings in a formal investigation it appears to the Commission necessary or expedient, whether during the course of the investigation or after its conclusion —

(a) to make to any persons, with a view to promoting equality of opportunity between persons with a disability and persons without a disability who are affected by any of their activities, recommendations for changes in their policies or procedures, or as to any other matters; or

(b) to make to the Chief Secretary for Administration any recommendations, whether for changes in the law or otherwise, *(Amended L.N. 362 of 1997)*

the Commission shall make those recommendations accordingly.

(2) The Commission shall prepare a report of its findings in any formal investigation conducted by it.

(3) If the formal investigation is one required by the Chief Secretary for Administration —

(a) the Commission shall deliver the report to the Chief Secretary for Administration; and

(b) the Chief Secretary for Administration shall cause the report to be published in such manner as he thinks fit,

and unless required by the Chief Secretary for Administration the Commission shall not publish the report. *(Amended L.N. 362 of 1997)*

(4) If the formal investigation is not one required by the Chief Secretary for Administration, the Commission shall publish the report or make it available for inspection in accordance with subsection (5). *(Amended L.N. 362 of 1997)*

(5) Where under subsection (4) a report is to be made available for inspection, any person shall be entitled, on payment of such reasonable fee, if any, as may be determined by the Commission —

(a) to inspect the report during ordinary office hours and take copies of all or any part of the report; or

(b) to obtain from the Commission a copy, certified by the Commission to be correct, of the report.

(6) The Commission may if it thinks fit determine that the right conferred by subsection (5)(a) shall be exercisable in relation to a copy of the report instead of, or in addition to, the original.

(7) The Commission shall give general notice of the place or places where, and the times when, reports may be inspected under subsection (5).

Section 70 Restrictions on Disclosure of Information

(1) No information given to the Commission by any person (the informant) in connection with a formal investigation shall be disclosed by the Commission, any member of the Commission or a committee, any employee of the Commission, any conciliator, or any person who has been such a member, employee or conciliator, except —

(a) on the order of any court;

(b) with the informant's consent;

(c) in the form of a summary or other general statement published by the Commission which does not identify the informant or any other person to whom the information relates;

(d) in a report of the investigation published by the Commission or made available for inspection under Section 69(5);

(e) to members of the Commission or a committee, employees of the Commission or conciliators or, so far as may be necessary for the proper performance of the functions of the Commission, to other persons;

(f) for the purpose of any civil proceedings under this Ordinance to which the Commission is a party, or any criminal proceedings.

(2) Any person who discloses information in contravention of subsection (1) commits an offence and is liable on conviction to a fine at level 4.

(3) In preparing any report for publication or for inspection the Commission shall exclude, so far as is consistent with its functions and the object of the report, any matter which relates to the private affairs of any individual or business interests of any person where the publication of that matter might, in the opinion of the Commission, prejudicially affect that individual or person.

Part 8 Enforcement

(Format changes — E.R. 1 of 2013)

General

Section 71 Restrictions of Proceedings for Contravention of Ordinance

(1) Except as provided by this Ordinance no proceedings, whether civil or criminal, shall lie against any person in respect of an act by reason that the act is unlawful by virtue of a provision of this Ordinance.

(2) Subsection (1) shall not preclude the making of an order of certiorari, mandamus or prohibition.

Section 72 Claims under Part 3 or 4

(1) A claim by or on behalf of any person (***the claimant***) that another person (***the respondent***) —

(a) has committed an act of discrimination against the claimant which is unlawful by virtue of Part 3 or 4;

(b) has committed an act of harassment against the claimant which is unlawful by virtue of Part 3 or 4;

(c) has committed an act which is unlawful by virtue of Section 46; or

(d) is to be treated, by virtue of Section 48, 48A or 49, as having committed an act of discrimination or harassment referred to in paragraph (a) or (b) against the claimant or an act referred to in paragraph (c), *(Replaced 29 of 2008 s. 101. Amended 8 of 2020 s. 28)*

may be made the subject of civil proceedings in like manner as any other claim in tort.

(2) Subsection (1) shall not apply to a claim under Section 17(1) of an act in respect of which an appeal, or proceedings in the nature of an appeal, may be brought under any enactment.

(3) Proceedings under subsection (1) shall be brought in the District Court but all such remedies shall be obtainable in such proceedings as, apart from this subsection and Section 71(1), would be obtainable in the Court of First Instance. *(Replaced 71 of 1997 s. 12. Amended 25 of 1998 s. 2)*

(4) Without limiting the generality of the power conferred by subsection (3), the District Court may —

(a) make a declaration that the respondent has engaged in conduct, or committed an act, that is unlawful under this Ordinance, and order that the respondent shall not repeat or continue such unlawful conduct or act;

(b) order that the respondent shall perform any reasonable act or course of conduct to redress any loss or damage suffered by the claimant;

(c) order that the respondent shall employ or re-employ the claimant;

(d) order that the respondent shall promote the claimant;

(e) order that the respondent shall pay to the claimant damages by way of compensation for any loss or damage suffered by reason of the respondent's conduct or act;

(f) order that the respondent shall pay to the claimant punitive or exemplary damages; or

(g) make an order declaring void in whole or in part either ab initio or from such date as may be specified in the order, any contract or agreement made in contravention of this Ordinance.

(4A) By virtue of this subsection and notwithstanding any law, the District Court shall have jurisdiction to hear and determine any proceedings under subsection (1) and shall have all such powers as are necessary or expedient for it to have in order to provide, grant or make any remedy, injunction or order mentioned in this Ordinance. *(Added 71 of 1997 s. 12)*

(5) For the avoidance of doubt, it is hereby declared that damages in respect of an unlawful act of discrimination or harassment, or an act which is unlawful under Section 46, may include compensation for injury to feelings whether or not they include compensation under any other head. *(Amended E.R. 1 of 2013)*

Enforcement Notices

Section 73 Issue of Enforcement Notices

(1) This Section applies to any act which is —

(a) an unlawful discriminatory act;

(b) an unlawful act of harassment; *(Amended 18 of 2014 s. 33)*

(ba) a contravention of Section 41; or *(Added 18 of 2014 s. 33)*

(c) a contravention of Section 42, 43, 44, 45, 46 or 47,

and so applies whether or not proceedings have been brought in respect of the act.

(2) If in the course of a formal investigation the Commission becomes satisfied that a person is committing, or has committed, any acts to which this Section applies, the Commission may in the prescribed manner serve on him a notice in the prescribed form requiring him —

(a) not to commit any such acts (which may include discontinuing or changing any of his practices or other arrangements which occasioned those acts, in particular to avoid any repetition thereof); and

(b) where compliance with paragraph (a) involves changes in any of his practices or other arrangements —

(i) to inform the Commission that he has effected those changes and what those changes are; and

(ii) to take such steps as may be reasonably required by the notice for the purpose of affording that information to other persons concerned.

(3) An enforcement notice may also require the person on whom it is served to furnish the Commission with such other information as may be reasonably required by the notice in order to verify that the notice has been complied with.

(4) An enforcement notice may specify the time at which, and the manner and form in which, any information is to be furnished to the Commission, but the time at which any information is to be furnished in compliance with the notice shall not be later than 5 years after the notice has become final.

(5) Section 68(4) shall apply to requirements under subsections (2)(b), (3) and (4) contained in an enforcement notice which has become final as it applies to requirements in a notice served under Section 68(1).

Section 74 Appeal against Enforcement Notice

(1) Not later than 45 days after an enforcement notice is served on any person he may appeal against any requirement of the notice to the District Court.

(2) Where the District Court considers a requirement in respect of which an appeal is brought under subsection (1) to be unreasonable because it is based on an incorrect finding of fact or for any other reason, the Court shall quash the requirement.

(3) On quashing a requirement under subsection (2), the District Court may direct that the enforcement notice shall be treated as if, in place of the requirement quashed, it had contained a requirement in terms specified in the direction.

(4) Subsection (1) shall not apply to a requirement treated as included in an enforcement notice by virtue of a direction under subsection (3).

Section 75 Investigation as to Compliance with Enforcement Notice

(1) If—

(a) the terms of reference of a formal investigation state that its purpose is to determine whether any requirements of an enforcement notice are being or have been carried out, but Section 68(2)(b) does not apply; and

(b) Section 67(3) is complied with in relation to the investigation on a date (***the commencement date***) not later than the expiration of the period of 5 years beginning when the enforcement notice became final,

the Commission may within the relevant period serve notices under Section 68(1) for the purposes of the investigation without needing to obtain the consent of the Chief Secretary for Administration. *(Amended L.N. 362 of 1997)*

(2) In subsection (1), ***relevant period*** (**有關期間**) means the period beginning on the commencement date and ending on the later of the following dates —

(a) the date on which the period of 5 years referred to in subsection (1)(b) expires;

(b) the date 2 years after the commencement date.

Section 76 Register of Enforcement Notices

(1) The Commission shall establish and maintain a register (***the register***) of enforcement notices which have become final.

(2) Any person shall be entitled, on payment of such reasonable fee, if any, as may be determined by the Commission —

(a) to inspect the register during ordinary office hours and take copies of any entry; or

(b) to obtain from the Commission a copy, certified by the Commission to be correct, of any entry in the register.

(3) The Commission may, if it thinks fit, determine that the right conferred by subsection (2)(a) shall be exercisable in relation to a copy of the register instead of, or in addition to, the original.

(4) The Commission shall give general notice of the place or places where, and the times when, the register or a copy of it may be inspected.

Other Enforcement by Commission

Section 77 Persistent Discrimination, Harassment or Vilification

If, during the period of 5 years beginning on the date on which either of the following became final in the case of any person, namely —

(a) an enforcement notice served on him;

(b) a finding by the District Court under Section 72 that he has done an unlawful discriminatory act, an unlawful act of harassment or acts contravening Section 46 or 47,

it appears to the Commission that unless restrained he is likely to do one or more acts falling within paragraph (b), or contravening Section 41, the Commission may apply to the District Court for an injunction restraining him from doing so; and the District Court, if satisfied that the application is well-founded, may grant the injunction in the terms applied for or in more limited terms.

Section 78 Enforcement of Sections 42, 43, 44 and 45

(1) Proceedings in respect of a contravention of Section 42, 43, 44 or 45 shall be brought only by the Commission in accordance with the provisions of this Section.

(2) The proceedings shall be —

(a) an application for a decision whether the alleged contravention occurred; or

(b) an application under subsection (4),

or both.

(3) An application under subsection (2)(a) shall be made to the District Court.

(4) If it appears to the Commission —

(a) that a person has done an act which by virtue of Section 42, 43, 44 or 45 was unlawful; and

(b) that unless restrained he is likely to do further acts which by virtue of that Section are unlawful,

the Commission may apply to the District Court for an injunction restraining him from doing so; and the District Court, if satisfied that the application is well-founded, may grant the injunction in the terms applied for or in more limited terms.

(5) Without prejudice to subsection (4), if it appears to the Commission that a person has done an act which was unlawful by virtue of Section 43, the Commission may apply to the District Court for an order imposing a financial penalty on such person; and the District Court, if satisfied that the application is well-founded, may make such an order.

(6) The financial penalty imposed under subsection (5) shall not exceed $10,000 for the first occasion on which a penalty is imposed, and $30,000 for the second and any subsequent occasion on which a penalty is imposed in respect of the same person.

Help for Persons Suffering Discrimination, Harassment or Vilification

Section 79 Help for Aggrieved Persons in Obtaining Information, etc.

(1) With a view to helping a person (***the person aggrieved***) who considers he may have been discriminated against or harassed in contravention of this Ordinance, or the subject of an unlawful

act under Section 46 or 47, to decide whether to institute proceedings and, if he does so, to formulate and present his case in the most effective manner, the Commission may prescribe —

(a) forms by which the person aggrieved may question the respondent on his reasons for doing any relevant act, or on any other matter which is or may be relevant;

(b) forms by which the respondent may if he so wishes reply to any questions.

(2) Where the person aggrieved questions the respondent (whether or not in accordance with forms referred to in subsection (1)) —

(a) the question, and any reply by the respondent (whether or not in accordance with such a form) shall, subject to subsections (3), (4) and (5), be admissible as evidence in the proceedings;

(b) if it appears to the District Court that the respondent deliberately, and without reasonable excuse, omitted to reply within a reasonable period or that his reply is evasive or equivocal, the Court may draw any inference from that fact it considers it just and equitable to draw, including an inference that he committed an unlawful act.

(3) The Commission may —

(a) prescribe the period within which questions must be served in order to be admissible under subsection (2)(a);

(b) prescribe the manner in which a question, and any reply by the respondent, may be served.

(4) Rules under the District Court Ordinance (Cap. 336) may enable the District Court entertaining a claim under Section 72 to determine, before the date fixed for the hearing of the claim, whether a question or reply is admissible under this Section or not.

(5) This Section is without prejudice to any other enactment or rule of law regulating interlocutory and preliminary matters in proceedings before the District Court, and has effect subject to any enactment or rule of law regulating the admissibility of evidence in such proceedings.

(6) In this Section, ***respondent*** (答辯人) includes a prospective respondent.

Section 80 Assistance by Way of Conciliation

(1) A person may lodge with the Commission a complaint in writing alleging that another person has done an act which is unlawful by virtue of a provision of this Ordinance.

(2) A representative complaint may be lodged under subsection (1) in accordance with rules made under Section 85.

(3) Subject to subsection (4), where a complaint is lodged under subsection (1), the Commission shall —

(a) conduct an investigation into the act the subject of the complaint; and

(b) endeavour, by conciliation, to effect a settlement of the matter to which the act relates.

(4) The Commission may decide not to conduct, or to discontinue, an investigation into an act the subject of a complaint lodged under subsection (1) if —

(a) it is satisfied that the act is not unlawful by reason of a provision of this Ordinance;

(b) it is of the opinion that the person aggrieved by the act does not desire (or, in a case to which subsection (2) applies, none of the persons aggrieved by the act desires) that the investigation be conducted or continued;

(c) a period of more than 12 months has elapsed beginning when the act was done;

(d) in a case to which subsection (2) applies, it determines, in accordance with rules made under Section 85, that the complaint should not be a representative complaint; or

(e) it is of the opinion that the complaint is frivolous, vexatious, misconceived or lacking in substance.

(5) Where the Commission decides not to conduct, or to discontinue, an investigation into an act the subject of a complaint lodged under subsection (1), it shall by notice served on the person who lodged the complaint advise him of —

(a) that decision; and

(b) the reasons for that decision.

(6) Evidence of anything said or done by any person in the course of conciliation under this Section (including anything said or done at any conference held for the purposes of such conciliation) is not admissible in evidence in any proceedings under this Ordinance except with the consent of that person.

(7) For the avoidance of doubt, it is hereby declared that subsection (6) shall not apply where —

(a) a complaint is lodged under subsection (1); and

(b) a settlement has been effected of the matter to which the act the subject of the complaint relates.

Section 81 Assistance Other Than by Way of Conciliation

(1) Where a complaint has been lodged under Section 80(1) but, for whatever reason, there has not been a settlement of the matter to which the act the subject of the complaint relates, then any person who may institute proceedings under this Ordinance in respect of that act may make an application to the Commission for assistance in respect of those proceedings.

(2) The Commission shall consider an application under subsection (1) and may grant it if it thinks fit to do so, in particular where —

(a) the case raises a question of principle; or

(b) it is unreasonable, having regard to the complexity of the case or the applicant's position in relation to the respondent or another person involved or any other matter, to expect the applicant to deal with the case unaided.

(3) Assistance by the Commission under this Section may include —

(a) giving advice;

(b) arranging for the giving of advice or assistance by a solicitor or counsel;

(c) arranging for representation by any person including all such assistance as is usually given by a solicitor or counsel in the steps preliminary or incidental to any proceedings, or in arriving at or giving effect to a compromise to avoid or bring to an end any proceedings;

(d) any other form of assistance which the Commission may consider appropriate,

but paragraph (c) shall not affect the law and practice regulating the descriptions of persons who may appear in, conduct, defend and address a court in, any proceedings except to the extent permitted under rules made in accordance with Section 73C of the District Court Ordinance (Cap. 336).

(4) In so far as expenses are incurred by the Commission in providing the applicant with assistance under this Section the recovery of those expenses (as taxed or assessed in such manner as may be prescribed by relevant rules) shall constitute a first charge for the benefit of the Commission —

(a) on any costs or expenses which (whether by virtue of a judgment or order of the District Court or an agreement or otherwise) are payable to the applicant by any other person in respect of the matter in connection with which the assistance is given; and

(b) so far as relates to any costs or expenses, on his rights under any compromise or settlement arrived at in connection with that matter to avoid or bring to an end any proceedings.

(5) The charge conferred by subsection (4) shall be subject to any charge under the Legal Aid Ordinance (Cap. 91) and to any provision in that Ordinance for payment of any sum into the Supplementary Legal Aid Fund established under that Ordinance.

(6) In this Section —

relevant rules (有關規則) means any rules made under the District Court Ordinance (Cap. 336);

respondent (答辯人) includes a prospective respondent.

Period within Which Proceedings to be Brought

Section 82 Period within Which Proceedings to be Brought

(1) The District Court shall not consider a claim under Section 72 unless proceedings in respect of the claim are instituted before the end of the period of 24 months beginning —

(a) when the act complained of was done; or

(b) if there is a relevant report in relation to that act, with the day on which the report is published or made available for inspection under Section 69,

whichever is the later.

(2) The District Court shall not consider an application under —

(a) Section 78(2)(a) unless it is made before the end of the period of 24 months beginning when the act to which it relates was done;

(b) Section 78(4) unless it is made before the end of the period of 5 years so beginning.

(2A) For the purposes of determining the period under subsection (1) within which proceedings may be brought, where an act to which the claim relates was the subject of a complaint lodged under Section 80(1), then the period that elapsed between the date when the complaint was lodged and the date when the complaint was disposed of under Section 80(3) or (4), as certified in writing by the Commission, shall be disregarded. *(Added 71 of 1997 s. 13. Amended 29 of 2008 s. 102)*

(3) Notwithstanding subsections (1) and (2), the District Court may consider any claim or application which is out of time if, in all the circumstances of the case, it considers that it is just and equitable to do so.

(4) For the purposes of subsection (3), the circumstances of the case include, in relation to any claim, whether the act to which the claim relates was the subject of a complaint lodged under Section 80(1) and, if so, the period that elapsed between when the act was done and when that complaint was so lodged.

(5) For the purposes of this Section —

(a) where the inclusion of any term in a contract renders the making of the contract an unlawful act, that act shall be treated as extending throughout the duration of the contract;

(b) any act extending over a period shall be treated as done at the end of that period; and

(c) a deliberate omission shall be treated as done when the person concerned decided upon it,

and, in the absence of evidence to the contrary, a person shall be taken for the purposes of this Section to decide upon an omission when he does an act inconsistent with doing the omitted act or, if he has done no such inconsistent act, when the period expires within which he might reasonably have been expected to do the omitted act if it was to be done.

(6) The Chief Executive in Council may, by notice in the Gazette, amend subsection (1) by substituting a longer period for the period specified in that subsection. *(Amended 66 of 1999 s. 3)*

(7) In this Section, ***relevant report*** (有關報告), in relation to an act referred to in subsection (1), means a report —

(a) published or made available for inspection under Section 69; and

(b) from which it can reasonably be construed (and whether or not the report mentions, or was in any way prepared in consequence of, the act) that the Commission is of the opinion that the act, or the class of acts to which the act belongs, is unlawful under a provision of Part 3, 4 or 5.

(Amended E.R. 1 of 2013)

Part 9 Miscellaneous

(Format changes — E.R. 1 of 2013)

Section 83 Validity and Revision of Contracts

(1) A term of a contract is void where —

(a) its inclusion renders the making of the contract unlawful by virtue of this Ordinance;

(b) it is included in furtherance of an act rendered unlawful by this Ordinance; or

(c) it provides for the doing of an act which would be rendered unlawful by this Ordinance.

(2) Subsection (1) shall not apply to a term the inclusion of which constitutes, or is in furtherance of, or provides for, unlawful discrimination against a party to the contract, but the term shall be unenforceable against that party.

(3) A term in a contract which purports to exclude or limit any provision of this Ordinance is unenforceable by any person in whose favour the term would operate apart from this subsection.

(4) Subsection (3) shall not apply to a contract settling a claim to which Section 72 applies.

(5) On the application of any person interested in a contract to which subsection (2) applies, the District Court may make such order as it thinks just for removing or modifying any term made unenforceable by that subsection; but such an order shall not be made unless all persons affected have been given notice of the application (except where under rules made under the District Court Ordinance (Cap. 336) notice may be dispensed with) and have been afforded an opportunity to make representations to the Court.

(6) An order under subsection (5) may include provision as respects any period before the making of the order.

Section 84 Building Approvals

(1) Notwithstanding any provision in any other Ordinance (whether enacted before or after the commencement of this Ordinance) but subject to subsection (3), a public authority which has the power to approve building works shall not, in respect of those works, approve building plans, whether for a new building or for the alterations or additions to an existing building unless the person seeking approval satisfies the public authority that such access as is reasonable in the circumstances to the building or premises will be provided for persons with a disability.

(2) In considering whether reasonable access will be provided under subsection (1), the public authority may take into account —

(a) whether it is practicable to provide such access within the curtilage of the building, bearing in mind the physical location and immediate environs of the building; and

(b) whether providing such access would impose unjustifiable hardship on the person seeking approval or on any other person.

(3) Subsection (1) has no application to —

(a) buildings of 13 m or less in height above ground level which are used, or intended to be used, for occupation by a single family; or

(b) temporary buildings or contractor's sheds referred to in Part VII of the Building (Planning) Regulations (Cap. 123 sub. leg. F).

(4) In this Section, ***public authority*** (公共主管當局) includes —

(a) the Director of Lands;

(b) the Building Authority;

(c) the Housing Authority;

(d) the Director of Architectural Services.

(Amended E.R. 1 of 2013)

Section 85 Rules

(1) The Commission may make rules —

(a) to enable the Commission to make any arrangements necessary to assist any person with a disability to attend before it and provide information pursuant to Section 68;

(b) prescribing the persons, or persons belonging to a class of persons, who may lodge a representative complaint under Section 80(1);

(c) prescribing the matters to be taken into account by the Commission for the purposes of a determination under Section 80(4)(d);

(d) to enable the Commission to require such persons, or persons belonging to such class of persons, as are specified in the rules to furnish information to the Commission for the purposes of Section 80;

(e) restricting the disclosure of any information referred to in paragraph (d) furnished to the Commission;

(f) to enable the Commission to direct persons to attend any conference held for the purposes of Section 80;

(g) regulating the procedure of any conference held for the purposes of Section 80;

(h) prescribing any other thing that is required or permitted to be prescribed under this Ordinance.

(2) Any rules made under subsection (1) may —

(a) make different provisions for different circumstances and provide for a particular case or class of cases;

(b) be made so as to apply only in such circumstances as are prescribed by the rules;

(c) specify forms for the purposes of the rules;

(d) be made generally for the better or more effectual carrying out of the provisions of this Ordinance, including incidental, consequential, evidential and supplemental provisions.

(3) Any rules made under this Section may prescribe offences in respect of contraventions of the rules, and may provide for the imposition of a fine not exceeding level 4 and of imprisonment for a period not exceeding 2 years.

Section 86 Regulations to Empower Commission to Bring Certain Proceedings *

(1) The Secretary for Labour and Welfare may make regulations — *(Amended L.N. 106 of 2002; L.N. 130 of 2007)*

(a) where any person may bring proceedings under Section 72(1) but has not done so, empowering the Commission, in such circumstances as are specified in the regulations, to bring and maintain those proceedings as if the Commission were that person;

* For the saving and transitional provisions relating to the amendments made by the Resolution of the Legislative Council (L.N. 130 of 2007), see paragraph (12) of that Resolution.

(b) specifying which of the remedies referred to in Section 72(3) shall be obtainable by the Commission in any such proceedings;

(c) for the purposes of enabling the Commission to bring and maintain any such proceedings (including any related purposes), specifying modifications to which any provisions of this Ordinance (including any subsidiary legislation) shall be read.

(2) Any regulations made under this Section shall be subject to the approval of the Legislative Council.

(3) This Section is without prejudice to the Commission's power to bring proceedings by way of judicial review, in relation to this Ordinance or any other law, pursuant to its functions under Section 62(1). *(Added 71 of 1997 s. 14)*

*Section 87 Amendment of Schedules**

(1) The Secretary for Labour and Welfare may, by notice in the Gazette, amend Schedule 1 or 2. *(Amended L.N. 106 of 2002; L.N. 130 of 2007)*

(2) The Chief Executive in Council may, by notice in the Gazette, amend Schedule 3, 4 or 5 but any notice to amend Schedule 5 shall be subject to the approval of the Legislative Council. *(Amended 66 of 1999 s. 3)*

Section 88 (Omitted as spent—E.R. 1 of 2013)

Schedule 1

[ss. 2 and 87]

Persons Specified as Carers

(Format changes — E.R. 1 of 2013)

Schedule 2

[ss. 2, 63 and 87]

Devices or Aids Specified as Palliative or Therapeutic Devices or Auxiliary Aids

(Format changes — E.R. 1 of 2013)

Item	Description of device or aid (including trade or manufacturer's name if applicable)
1.	Optacon reading aid for persons with visual impairment
2.	Braille writing device
3.	Low vision aid
4.	Hearing aid
5.	A telecommunications device for persons with hearing impairment
6.	Wheelchair or buggy

* For the saving and transitional provisions relating to the amendments made by the Resolution of the Legislative Council (L.N. 130 of 2007), see paragraph (12) of that Resolution.

7.	Prosthesis
8.	Orthosis
9.	Walking aid
10.	Aid for dialysis therapy
11.	Speech aid
12.	Oxygen unit
13.	Aid for any activities of a personal nature, including a feeding aid and an aid in respect of toilet needs
14.	Urinary bag
15.	Stoma bag

Schedule 3

[ss. 12, 57, 63 and 87]

Provisions Specified for Purposes of Section 12(3)(c)

(Format changes — E.R. 2 of 2012)

Schedule 4

[ss. 32 and 87]

Discrimination to Which Sections 26(1) and 28 Shall Not Apply

(Format changes — E.R. 2 of 2012)

Provision creating illegality	Exception
Part 3	Sections 11(3), 12(1)(b) and 19(3)

(Amended E.R. 1 of 2013)

Schedule 5

[ss. 60, 63 and 87]

Further Exceptions to This Ordinance

(Format changes — E.R. 2 of 2012)

	Provision creating illegality	Exception
1.	Part 3	Only a person who holds a valid Registration Card for People with Disabilities issued by the Central Registry for Rehabilitation established by the Government being allowed to have his or her degree of productivity assessed under Schedule 2 to the Minimum Wage Ordinance (Cap. 608). *(Added 15 of 2010 s. 24)*

<table>
<tr><td>2.</td><td>Part 3</td><td>An employer, in accordance with the Minimum Wage Ordinance (Cap. 608), paying a minimum wage to a person with a disability that is less than that payable to a person without such a disability. (Added 15 of 2010 s. 24)</td></tr>
<tr><td>3.</td><td>Part 3</td><td>An employer dismissing a person with a disability on account of the outcome of an assessment made under Schedule 2 to the Minimum Wage Ordinance (Cap. 608). (Added 15 of 2010 s. 24)</td></tr>
<tr><td>4.</td><td>Parts 4 and 5</td><td>Providing fare concessions to persons —
(a) who —
(i) receive assistance under the Comprehensive Social Security Assistance Scheme administered by the Director of Social Welfare; and
(ii) are medically certified under the Scheme to be 100% disabled for the purposes of the Scheme; or
(b) who receive an allowance described as Disability Allowance under the Social Security Allowance Scheme administered by the Director of Social Welfare,
in respect of —
(c) a public transport service operated by the MTR Corporation Limited;
(d) a public transport service operated by a company pursuant to a franchise granted under Section 5 of the Public Bus Services Ordinance (Cap. 230); (Amended L.N. 4 of 2015)
(e) a public transport service operated by a company or person pursuant to a franchise or licence granted under Section 6 or 28 of the Ferry Services Ordinance (Cap. 104); or (Added L.N. 223 of 2009. Amended 15 of 2010 s. 24; L.N. 131 of 2012; L.N. 4 of 2015)
(f) a public transport service operated by a person pursuant to a passenger service licence issued under Section 27 of the Road Traffic Ordinance (Cap. 374) in respect of a public light bus which is on a scheduled service (as defined by regulation 2(1) of the Road Traffic (Public Service Vehicles) Regulations (Cap. 374 sub. leg. D)). (Added L.N. 4 of 2015)</td></tr>
</table>

(Amended E.R. 1 of 2013)

Schedule 6

(Omitted as spent — E.R. 2 of 2012)

FAMILY STATUS DISCRIMINATION ORDINANCE (CAP. 527)

An Ordinance to render unlawful discrimination against persons on the ground of family status and to extend the jurisdiction of the Equal Opportunities Commission to include such discrimination and for connected purposes.

(Enacting provision omitted — E.R. 1 of 2013)

[21 November 1997] *L.N. 552 of 1997*

Part I Preliminary

(Format changes — E.R. 1 of 2013)

Section 1 Short Title

(Amended E.R. 5 of 2018)

(1) This Ordinance may be cited as the Family Status Discrimination Ordinance.

(2) *(Omitted as spent — E.R. 1 of 2013)*

Section 2 Interpretation

(1) In this Ordinance unless the context otherwise requires —

access (獲得、享用) means access as construed in accordance with Section 40;

act (作為) includes a deliberate omission;

advertisement (廣告) includes every form of advertisement, whether to the public or not, and whether —

(a) in a newspaper or other publication;

(b) by television or radio;

(c) by display of notices, signs, labels, showcards or goods;

(d) by distribution of samples, circulars, catalogues, price lists or other material;

(e) by exhibition of pictures, models or films; or

(f) in any other way,

and references to the publishing of advertisements shall be construed accordingly;

club (會社) means an association, incorporate or unincorporate, of not less than 30 persons associated together for social, literary, cultural, political, sporting, athletic or other lawful purposes and which provides and maintains its facilities, in whole or in part, from the funds of the association; *(Amended 29 of 2008 s. 103)*

Commission (委員會) has the same meaning as in the relevant Ordinance;

commission agent (佣金經紀人) means commission agent as construed in accordance with Section 16;

committee (小組委員會) has the same meaning as in the relevant Ordinance; *(Added 18 of 2014 s. 35)*

committee of management (管理委員會) in relation to a club, means the group or body of persons (howsoever described) that manages the affairs of that club;

conciliator (調停人) has the same meaning as in the relevant Ordinance; *(Amended 15 of 2012 s. 11)*

contract worker (合約工作者) means a contract worker as construed in accordance with Section 9;

discrimination (歧視), in relation to a person —

(a) who has family status, means discrimination falling within Section 5; and

(b) who is victimized, means discrimination falling within Section 6,

and related expressions shall be construed accordingly;

dispose (處置), in relation to premises, includes granting a right to occupy the premises, and any references to acquiring premises shall be construed accordingly;

dynamically supported craft (動力承托的航行器) has the same meaning as in the Shipping and Port Control Ordinance (Cap. 313);

education (教育) includes any form of training or instruction;

educational establishment (教育機構) means an educational establishment specified in column 1 of Schedule 1;

employment (僱用) means employment under —

(a) a contract of service or of apprenticeship; or

(b) a contract personally to execute any work or labour,

and related expressions shall be construed accordingly;

employment agency (職業介紹所) means a person who, for profit or not, provides services for the purpose of finding employment for workers or supplying employers with workers;

enforcement notice (執行通知) means a notice under Section 55(2);

estate agent (地產代理) has the same meaning as in the Estate Agents Ordinance (Cap. 511);

family status (家庭崗位), in relation to a person, means the status of having responsibility for the care of an immediate family member;

firm (商號) means firm within the meaning of the Partnership Ordinance (Cap. 38);

formal investigation (正式調查) means an investigation under Section 48;

general notice (一般通告), in relation to any person, means a notice published by him at a time and in a manner appearing to him suitable for securing that the notice is seen within a reasonable time by persons likely to be affected by it;

immediate family member (直系家庭成員), in relation to a person, means a person who is related to the person by blood, marriage, adoption or affinity;

near relative (近親), in relation to a person, means —

(a) the person's spouse;

(b) a parent of the person or of the spouse;

(c) a child of the person or the spouse of such a child;

(d) a brother or sister (whether of full blood or half blood) of the person or of the spouse or the spouse of such a brother or sister;

(e) a grandparent of the person or of the spouse; or

(f) a grandchild of the person or the spouse of such a grandchild,

and, in determining the above relationships, children born out of wedlock are to be included, an adopted child is to be regarded as a child of both the natural parents and the adoptive parent or parents and a step child as the child of both the natural parents and any step parent; *(Added 29 of 2008 s. 103)*

notice (通告、通知) means a notice in writing;

prescribed (訂明) means prescribed in rules made under Section 66;

profession (專業) includes any vocation or occupation;

relevant Ordinance (有關條例) means the Sex Discrimination Ordinance (Cap. 480);

responsible body (負責組織), in relation to an educational establishment, means the body specified in column 2 of Schedule 1 opposite that establishment;

trade (行業) includes any business;

training (訓練) includes any form of education or instruction;

vocational training (職業訓練) includes retraining and vocational guidance.

(2) References in this Ordinance to the dismissal of a person from employment or to the expulsion of a person from a position as partner include references —

(a) to the termination of that person's employment or partnership by the expiration of any period (including a period expiring by reference to an event or circumstance), not being a termination immediately after which the employment or partnership is renewed on the same terms;

(b) to the termination of that person's employment or partnership by any act of his (including the giving of notice) in circumstances such that he is entitled to terminate it without notice by reason of the conduct of the employer, or the other partners, as the case may be.

(3) For the purposes of this Ordinance, an enforcement notice or a finding by the District Court becomes final when an appeal against the notice or finding is dismissed, withdrawn or abandoned or when the time for appealing expires without an appeal having been brought; and for this purpose an appeal against an enforcement notice shall be taken to be dismissed if, notwithstanding that a requirement of the notice is quashed on appeal, a direction is given in respect of it under Section 56(3).

(4) *(Repealed 29 of 2008 s. 103)*

(5) Subject to subsection (6), in this Ordinance, ***existing statutory provision*** (現有法例條文) means any provision of —

(a) any Ordinance enacted before this Ordinance was enacted;

(b) any subsidiary legislation made —

(i) under an Ordinance enacted before this Ordinance was enacted; and

(ii) before, on or after this Ordinance was enacted.

(6) Where an Ordinance enacted after this Ordinance was enacted re-enacts (with or without modifications) a provision of an Ordinance enacted before this Ordinance was enacted, then that provision as re-enacted shall be treated for the purposes of subsection (5) as if it continued to be contained in an Ordinance enacted before this Ordinance was enacted.

Section 3 Application

This Ordinance binds the Government.

Section 4 Act Done for Two or More Reasons

If an act is done for 2 or more reasons and one of the reasons is the family status of a person (whether or not it is the dominant or a substantial reason for doing the act), then for the purposes of this Ordinance, the act shall be taken to be done for the reason of the person's family status.

Part II Discrimination to Which Ordinance Applies

(Format changes — E.R. 5 of 2018)

Section 5 Discrimination against a Person Who Has Family Status

A person discriminates against a person who has family status in any circumstances relevant for the purposes of any provision of this Ordinance if—

(a) on the ground of the second-mentioned person's family status or that person's particular family status (***the relevant family status***) he treats that person less favourably than he treats or would treat another person who does not have family status or the relevant family status, as the case may be; or

(b) he applies to that person a requirement or condition which he applies or would apply equally to a person who does not have family status or the relevant family status, as the case may be, but—

(i) which is such that the proportion of persons with family status or the relevant family status, as the case may be, who can comply with it is considerably smaller than the proportion of persons who does not have family status or the relevant family status who can comply with it;

(ii) which he cannot show to be justifiable irrespective of whether or not the person to whom it is applied has family status or the relevant family status, as the case may be; and

(iii) which is to that person's detriment because he cannot comply with it.

Section 6 Discrimination by Way of Victimization

(1) A person (***the discriminator***) discriminates against another person (***the person victimized***) in any circumstances relevant for the purposes of any provision of this Ordinance if he treats the person victimized less favourably than in those circumstances he treats or would treat other persons, and does so by reason that the person victimized or any other person (***the third person***) has—

(a) brought proceedings against the discriminator or any other person under this Ordinance;

(b) given evidence or information in connection with proceedings brought by any person against the discriminator or any other person under this Ordinance;

(c) otherwise done anything under or by reference to this Ordinance in relation to the discriminator or any other person; or

(d) alleged that the discriminator or any other person has committed an act which (whether or not the allegation so states) would amount to a contravention of this Ordinance,

or by reason that the discriminator knows the person victimized or the third person, as the case may be, intends to do any of those things, or suspects the persons victimized or the third person, as the case may be, has done, or intends to do, any of them.

(2) Subsection (1) does not apply to the treatment of a person by reason of any allegation made by him if the allegation was false and not made in good faith.

Section 7 Comparison of Cases under Section 5

A comparison of the cases of persons with a particular family status with those who do not have that family status or any family status as the case may require, shall be such that the relevant circumstances in the one case are the same, or not materially different, in the other.

Part III Discrimination in Employment Field

(Format changes — E.R. 5 of 2018)

Discrimination by Employers

Section 8 Discrimination against Applicants and Employees

(1) It is unlawful for a person (***the employer***), in relation to employment by him at an establishment in Hong Kong, to discriminate against a person who has family status —

(a) in the arrangements the employer makes for the purpose of determining who should be offered that employment;

(b) in the terms on which the employer offers that other person employment; or

(c) by refusing or deliberately omitting to offer that other person that employment.

(2) It is unlawful for the employer, in the case of a person who has family status employed by him at an establishment in Hong Kong, to discriminate against that person —

(a) in the way he affords that person access to opportunities for promotion, transfer or training, or to any other benefits, facilities or services, or by refusing or deliberately omitting to afford him access to them;

(b) in the terms of employment he affords that person; or

(c) by dismissing that person or subjecting him to any other detriment.

(3) Subsections (1) and (2) shall not apply to employment where the number of persons employed by the employer, added to the number employed by any associated employers of his, does not exceed 5 (disregarding any persons employed for the purposes of a private home).

(4) Nothing in subsection (1) or (2) renders it unlawful for an employer to restrict the employment of a person if —

(a) that person is an immediate family member of an employee of the employer; or

(b) that person is an immediate family member of an employee of another employer,

and the first-mentioned employer can demonstrate, after making reasonable enquiries, that there is a significant likelihood of collusion between that person and the employee which would result in damage to the business of the first-mentioned employer.

(5) Subsection (2) shall not apply to benefits, facilities or services of any description if the employer is concerned with the provision (for payment or not) of benefits, facilities or services of that description to the public comprising the person concerned, unless —

(a) that provision differs in a material respect from the provision of the benefits, facilities or services by the employer to his employees; or

(b) the benefits, facilities or services relate to training.

(6) Subsection (3) shall expire on the 3rd anniversary of the day on which this Ordinance is enacted.

(7) For the purposes of subsection (3), 2 employers are to be treated as associated if one is a company of which the other (directly or indirectly) has control or if both are companies of which a third person (directly or indirectly) has control.

(8) The Chief Executive in Council may, by notice in the Gazette — *(Amended 66 of 1999 s. 3)*

(a) amend subsection (3) by substituting another number for the last number appearing in that subsection;

(b) amend subsection (6) by substituting another anniversary for the anniversary appearing in that subsection.

(9) Subsection (1)(b) or (2)(b) shall not apply to any term of employment under which an employer affords, or omits to afford, any immediate family member of the person concerned direct or indirect access to benefits, facilities or services. *(Added 40 of 2000 s. 2)*

(10) Subsection (2)(a) or (c) shall not apply to any arrangement under which an employer affords, or omits to afford, any immediate family member of the person concerned direct or indirect access to benefits, facilities or services. *(Added 40 of 2000 s. 2)*

Section 9 Discrimination against Contract Workers

(1) This Section applies to any work for a person (***the principal***) which is available for doing by individuals (***contract workers***) who are employed not by the principal himself but by a contractor or sub-contractor of the principal. *(Amended 29 of 2008 s. 104)*

(2) It is unlawful for the principal, in relation to work to which this Section applies, to discriminate against a contract worker who has family status —

(a) in the terms on which he allows the contract worker to do that work;

(b) by not allowing the contract worker to do it or continue to do it;

(c) in the way he affords the contact worker access to any benefits, facilities or services or by refusing or deliberately omitting to afford the contract worker access to them; or

(d) by subjecting the contract worker to any other detriment.

(3) Subsection (2)(c) shall not apply to benefits, facilities or services of any description if the principal is concerned with the provision (for payment or not) of benefits, facilities or services of that description to the public, or to a section of the public to which the contract worker belongs, unless that provision differs in a material respect from the provision of the benefits, facilities or services by the principal to his contract workers.

(4) Subsection (2)(a) shall not apply to any term under which a principal affords, or omits to afford, any immediate family member of a contract worker direct or indirect access to benefits, facilities or services. *(Added 40 of 2000 s. 3)*

(5) Subsection (2)(c) or (d) shall not apply to any arrangement under which a principal affords, or omits to afford, any immediate family member of a contract worker direct or indirect access to benefits, facilities or services. *(Added 40 of 2000 s. 3)*

(6) In this Section —

contractor (承判商) means a person who undertakes any work for the principal under a contract that is entered into by the person directly with the principal;

sub-contractor (次承判商) means a person who enters into a contract with another person (whether or not a contractor of the principal) to undertake all or any part of the work that a contractor of the principal has undertaken. *(Added 29 of 2008 s. 104)*

Section 10 Meaning of Employment at Establishment in Hong Kong

(1) For the purposes of this Ordinance (***the relevant purposes***), employment is to be regarded as being at an establishment in Hong Kong unless the employee does his work wholly or mainly outside Hong Kong.

(2) Subsection (1) shall not apply to —

(a) employment on board a ship registered in Hong Kong; or

(b) employment on aircraft or dynamically supported craft registered in Hong Kong and operated by a person who has his principal place of business, or is ordinarily resident, in Hong Kong, but for the relevant purposes such employment is to be regarded as being at an establishment in Hong Kong unless the employee does his work wholly outside Hong Kong.

(3) In the case of employment on board a ship registered in Hong Kong (except where the employee does his work wholly outside Hong Kong) the ship shall for the relevant purposes be deemed to be the establishment.

(4) Where work is not done at an establishment it shall be treated for the relevant purposes as done at the establishment from which it is done or (where it is not done from any establishment) at the establishment with which it has the closest connection.

Discrimination by Other Bodies

Section 11 Partnerships

(1) It is unlawful for a firm consisting of not less than 6 partners, in relation to a position as partner in the firm, to discriminate against a person who has family status —

- (a) in the arrangements the firm makes for the purpose of determining who should be offered that position;
- (b) in the terms on which the firm offers that person that position;
- (c) by refusing or deliberately omitting to offer that person that position; or
- (d) in a case where that person already holds that position —
  - (i) in the way the firm affords him access to any benefits, facilities or services, or by refusing or deliberately omitting to afford him access to them; or
  - (ii) by expelling him from that position or subjecting him to any other detriment.

(2) Subsection (1) shall apply in relation to persons proposing to form themselves into a partnership as it applies in relation to a firm.

(3) In the case of a limited partnership references in subsection (1) to a partner shall be construed as references to a general partner within the meaning of Section 2 of the Limited Partnerships Ordinance (Cap. 37).

(4) The Chief Executive in Council may, by notice in the Gazette, amend subsection (1) by — *(Amended 66 of 1999 s. 3)*

- (a) substituting another number for the number appearing in that subsection; or
- (b) repealing the words and number appearing after "for a firm" and before ", in relation to".

Section 12 Trade Unions, etc.

(1) This Section applies to an organization of workers, an organization of employers, or any other organization whose members carry on a particular profession or trade for the purposes of which the organization exists.

(2) It is unlawful for an organization to which this Section applies, in the case of a person who has family status and who is not a member of the organization, to discriminate against that person —

- (a) in the terms on which it is prepared to admit that person to membership; or
- (b) by refusing, or deliberately omitting to accept, his application for membership.

(3) It is unlawful for an organization to which this Section applies, in the case of a person who has family status and who is a member of the organization, to discriminate against that person —

- (a) in the way it affords that person access to any benefits, facilities or services, or by refusing or deliberately omitting to afford him access to them;

(b) by depriving that person of membership, or varying the terms on which he is a member; or

(c) by subjecting that person to any other detriment.

Section 13 Qualifying Bodies

(1) It is unlawful for an authority or body which can confer an authorization or qualification which is needed for, or facilitates, engagement in a particular profession or trade to discriminate against a person who has family status —

(a) in the terms on which it is prepared to confer on that person that authorization or qualification;

(b) by refusing or deliberately omitting to grant that person's application for it; or

(c) by withdrawing it from that person or varying the terms on which he holds it.

(2) Where an authority or body is required by law to satisfy itself as to his good character before conferring on a person an authorization or qualification which is needed for, or facilitates, his engagement in any profession or trade then, without prejudice to any other duty to which it is subject, that requirement shall be taken to impose on the authority or body a duty to have regard to any evidence tending to show that he, or any of his employees or agents (whether past or present), has practised unlawful discrimination in, or in connection with, the carrying on of any profession or trade.

(3) Subsection (1) shall not apply to discrimination which is rendered unlawful by Section 18.

(4) In this Section —

authorization or qualification (授權或資格) includes recognition, licensing, registration, enrolment, approval and certification;

confer (授予) includes renew or extend.

Section 14 Persons Concerned with Provision of Vocational Training

(1) It is unlawful, in the case of a person who has family status seeking or undergoing training which would help that person fit for employment, for any person (***the trainer***) who provides, or makes arrangements for the provision of, facilities for such training to discriminate against the first-mentioned person —

(a) in the terms on which the trainer affords the first-mentioned person access to any training course or other facilities concerned with such training;

(b) by refusing or deliberately omitting to afford him such access;

(c) by terminating his training; or

(d) by subjecting him to any other detriment during the course of his training.

(2) Subsection (1) shall not apply to —

(a) discrimination which is rendered unlawful by any of the provisions of Section 8(1) or (2) or 18; or

(b) discrimination which would be rendered unlawful by any of those provisions but for the operation of any other provision of this Ordinance.

Section 15 Employment Agencies

(1) It is unlawful for an employment agency to discriminate against a person who has family status —

(a) in the terms on which the agency offers to provide any of its services;

(b) by refusing or deliberately omitting to provide any of its services; or

(c) in the way it provides any of its services.

(2) References in subsection (1) to the services of an employment agency include guidance on careers and any other services related to employment.

(3) This Section shall not apply if the discrimination only concerns employment which the employer could lawfully refuse to offer the person concerned.

(4) An employment agency shall not be subject to any liability under this Section if it proves —

(a) that it acted in reliance on a statement made to it by the employer to the effect that, by reason of the operation of subsection (3), its action would not be unlawful; and

(b) that it was reasonable for it to rely on the statement.

(5) A person who knowingly or recklessly makes a statement of the kind referred to in subsection (4)(a) which in a material respect is false or misleading commits an offence and is liable on conviction to a fine at level 4.

Section 16 Discrimination against Commission Agents

(1) This Section applies to any work for a person (***the principal***) which is available for doing by individuals (***commission agents***) as the agents of the principal and who are remunerated, whether in whole or in part, by commission.

(2) It is unlawful for the principal, in relation to work to which this Section applies, to discriminate against a person who has family status who is a commission agent —

(a) in the terms on which he allows that person to do that work;

(b) by not allowing that person to do or continue to do that work;

(c) in the way he affords that person access to any benefits, facilities or services or by refusing or deliberately omitting to afford him access to them; or

(d) by subjecting that person to any other detriment.

(3) Subsection (2)(c) shall not apply to benefits, facilities or services of any description if the principal is concerned with the provision (for payment or not) of benefits, facilities, or services of that description to the public, or to a section of the public to which the person who is the commission agent belongs, unless that provision differs in a material respect from the provision of the benefits, facilities or services by the principal to his commission agents.

(4) Subsection (2)(a) shall not apply to any term under which a principal affords, or omits to afford, any immediate family member of a commission agent direct or indirect access to benefits, facilities or services. *(Added 40 of 2000 s. 4)*

(5) Subsection (2)(c) or (d) shall not apply to any arrangement under which a principal affords, or omits to afford, any immediate family member of a commission agent direct or indirect access to benefits, facilities or services. *(Added 40 of 2000 s. 4)*

Government

Section 17 Government

(1) Subject to subsection (2), without prejudice to the operation of the other provisions of this Part in relation to the Government, it is unlawful for the Government to discriminate against a person who has family status, in the performance of its functions or the exercise of its powers.

(2) Subsection (1) shall not render unlawful —

(a) as regards a person not having the right to enter and remain in Hong Kong, any act done under any immigration legislation governing entry into, stay in and departure from Hong Kong; or

(b) any act done in relation to a person if it was necessary for that act to be done in order to comply with a requirement of an existing statutory provision.

Part IV Discrimination in Other Fields

(Format changes — E.R. 5 of 2018)

Education

Section 18 Discrimination by Responsible Bodies for Educational Establishments

(1) It is unlawful for the responsible body for an educational establishment to discriminate against a person who has family status —

(a) in the terms on which it offers to admit that person to the establishment as a student;

(b) by refusing or deliberately omitting to accept an application for that person's admission to the establishment as a student; or

(c) where that person is a student of the establishment —

(i) in the way it affords him access to any benefits, facilities or services, or by refusing or deliberately omitting to afford him access to them; or

(ii) by excluding him from the establishment or subjecting him to any other detriment.

(2) For the avoidance of doubt, it is hereby declared that subsection (1) does not apply to any act done by the responsible body for an educational establishment in order to comply with —

(a) the system commonly known as the Primary One Admission System or any scheme, system or programme that replaces that System in whole or in part;

(b) the system commonly known as the Secondary School Places Allocation System or any scheme, system or programme that replaces that System in whole or in part; or

(c) any provision of a law, being a provision relating to the admission of students.

Goods, Facilities, Services and Premises

Section 19 Discrimination in Provision of Goods, Facilities or Services

(1) It is unlawful for any person concerned with the provision (for payment or not) of goods, facilities or services to the public or a section of the public to discriminate against a person who has family status who seeks to obtain or use those goods, facilities or services —

(a) by refusing or deliberately omitting to provide that person with any of them; or *(Amended 29 of 2008 s. 105)*

(b) by refusing or deliberately omitting to provide that person with goods, facilities or services of the like quality, in the like manner and on the like terms as are normal in his case in relation to members of the public who do not have family status or a particular family status or (where that person belongs to a section of the public) to members of that section who do not have family status or a particular family status.

(2) The following are examples of the facilities and services referred to in subsection (1) —

(a) access to and use of any place which members of the public or a section of the public are permitted to enter;

(b) accommodation in a hotel, guesthouse or other similar establishment;

(c) facilities by way of banking or insurance or for grants, loans, credit or finance;

(d) facilities for education;

(e) facilities for entertainment, recreation or refreshment;

(f) facilities for transport or travel;

(g) the services of any profession or trade;

(h) the services of —

(i)–(ii)*(Repealed 78 of 1999 s. 7)*

(iii) any department of the Government; or

(iv) any undertaking by or of the Government.

Section 20 Discrimination in Disposal or Management of Premises

(1) It is unlawful for a person, in relation to premises in Hong Kong of which he has power to dispose, to discriminate against a person who has family status —

(a) in the terms on which he offers that person those premises;

(b) by refusing that person's application for those premises; or

(c) in his treatment of that person in relation to any list of persons in need of premises of that description.

(2) It is unlawful for a person, in relation to premises managed by him, to discriminate against a person who has family status occupying the premises —

(a) in the way he affords that person access to any benefits or facilities, or by refusing or deliberately omitting to afford him access to them; or

(b) by evicting that person, or subjecting him to any other detriment.

(3) Subsection (1) shall not apply to a person who owns an estate or interest in the premises and wholly occupies them unless he uses the services of an estate agent for the purposes of the disposal of the premises, or publishes or causes to be published an advertisement in connection with the disposal.

(4) In this Section, in relation to premises, ***power to dispose*** (有權處置) includes the power to sell, rent, let, sub-let or otherwise part with possession of those premises.

Section 21 Discrimination: Consent for Assignment or Sub-letting

(1) Where the licence or consent of the landlord or of any other person is required for the disposal to any person of premises in Hong Kong comprised in a tenancy, it is unlawful for the landlord or other person to discriminate against a person who has family status by withholding the licence or consent for disposal of the premises to that person.

(2) Subsection (1) shall not apply if —

(a) the person withholding a licence or consent, or a near relative of his (***the relevant occupier***) resides, and intends to continue to reside, on the premises;

(b) there is on the premises, in addition to the accommodation occupied by the relevant occupier, accommodation (not being storage accommodation or means of access) shared by the relevant occupier with other persons residing on the premises who are not members of his household; and

(c) the premises are small premises as construed in accordance with Section 22(2).

(3) For the avoidance of doubt, it is hereby declared that this Section applies to tenancies created before the enactment of this Ordinance as well as to tenancies created on or after the enactment of this Ordinance.

(4) In this Section —

disposal (處置), in relation to premises comprised in a tenancy, includes assignment of the tenancy and sub-letting or parting with possession of the premises or any part of the premises;

tenancy (租賃) means a tenancy created —

(a) by a lease or sub-lease;

(b) by an agreement for a lease or sub-lease;

(c) by a tenancy agreement; or

(d) pursuant to any enactment.

Section 22 Exceptions for Small Dwellings

(1) Sections 19(1) and 20 shall not apply to the provision by a person of accommodation in any premises, or the disposal of premises by him, if —

(a) that person or a near relative of his (***the relevant occupier***) resides, and intends to continue to reside, on the premises;

(b) there is on the premises, in addition to the accommodation occupied by the relevant occupier, accommodation (not being storage accommodation or means of access) shared by the relevant occupier with other persons residing on the premises who are not members of his household; and

(c) the premises are small premises.

(2) Premises shall be treated for the purpose of subsection (1) as small premises if —

(a) in the case of premises comprising residential accommodation for one or more households (under separate letting or similar agreements) in addition to the accommodation occupied by the relevant occupier, there is not normally residential accommodation for more than 2 such households and only the relevant occupier and any member of his household reside in the accommodation occupied by him;

(b) in the case of premises not falling within paragraph (a), there is not normally residential accommodation on the premises for more than 6 persons in addition to the relevant occupier and any members of his household.

(3) The Chief Executive in Council may, by notice in the Gazette, amend subsection (2)(b) by substituting another number for the number appearing in that subsection. *(Amended 66 of 1999 s. 3)*

Section 23 Exceptions for Voluntary Bodies

(1) This Section applies to a body the activities of which are carried on otherwise than for profit.

(2) Sections 19(1) and 20 shall not be construed as rendering unlawful —

(a) the restriction of membership of any body to which this Section applies with reference to family status or a particular family status; or

(b) the provision of benefits, facilities or services to members of any body to which this Section applies where the membership is so restricted,

even though membership of the body is open to the public, or to a section of the public.

(3) Nothing in Section 19 or 20 shall —

(a) be construed as affecting a provision to which this subsection applies; or

(b) render unlawful an act which is done in order to give effect to such a provision.

(4) Subsection (3) applies to a provision for conferring benefits on persons of a particular family status (disregarding any benefits to others which are exceptional or are relatively insignificant), being a provision which constitutes the main object of a body to which this Section applies.

Section 24 Further Exceptions from Sections 19(1) and 20

(1) Sections 19(1) and 20 shall not apply —

(a) to discrimination which is rendered unlawful by Part III or Section 18; or

(b) to discrimination which would be so unlawful but for Section 8(3) or 15(3).

(2) A person who provides at any place facilities or services restricted with reference to family status or a particular family status, does not contravene Section 19(1) if the place is, or is part of a reception centre or other establishment for persons requiring special care, supervision or attention.

Advisory Bodies

Section 25 Discrimination in Eligibility to Vote for and to be Elected or Appointed to Advisory Bodies

(1) In this Section, a reference to a relevant body means a public body, a public authority, a statutory advisory body, or a prescribed body.

(2) In this Section, a reference to a relevant position includes membership of a public body, a public authority and a prescribed position.

(3) It is unlawful to discriminate against a person who has family status in —

(a) determining the eligibility of a person to stand for election to a relevant body or relevant position, or to be selected for a relevant position;

(b) the terms or conditions on which a person is considered eligible to stand for election to a relevant body or relevant position, or to be selected for a relevant position;

(c) determining the eligibility of a person to vote in elections of members of a relevant body or the holder of a relevant position, or to take part in the selection of the holder of a relevant position;

(d) the terms or conditions on which a person is considered eligible to vote in elections of members of a relevant body or the holder of a relevant position, or to take part in the selection of the holder of a relevant position;

(e) considering whether a person should be appointed as a member of a relevant body, where some or all of the members of that body are appointed; or

(f) considering whether a person should be appointed to a relevant position, approved as a member of a relevant body or recognized as holding a relevant position.

(4) This Section shall have effect, notwithstanding the provisions of any Ordinance which provide that a person who has family status or a particular family status is not eligible to stand for election, or to be selected for, a relevant body or position, or to vote in elections for or to take part in the selection of members of a relevant body or the holder of a relevant position.

Barristers

Section 26 Discrimination by, or in Relation to, Barristers

(1) It is unlawful for a barrister or barrister's clerk, in relation to any offer of a pupillage or tenancy, to discriminate against a person who has family status —

(a) in the arrangements which are made for the purpose of determining to whom it should be offered;

(b) in respect of any terms on which it is offered; or

(c) by refusing, or deliberately omitting, to offer it to the person.

(2) It is unlawful for a barrister or barrister's clerk to discriminate against a person who has family status who is a pupil or a tenant in the chambers concerned —

(a) in respect of any terms applicable to that person as a pupil or tenant;

(b) in the opportunities for training, or gaining experience, which are afforded or denied to that person;

(c) in the benefits, facilities or services which are afforded or denied to that person; or

(d) by terminating that person's pupillage or subjecting him to any pressure to leave the chambers or other detriment.

(3) It is unlawful for any person, in relation to the giving, withholding or acceptance of instructions to a barrister, to discriminate against a person who has family status.

(4) In this Section —

barrister's clerk (大律師書記) includes any person carrying out any of the functions of a barrister's clerk;

pupil (見習大律師), ***pupillage*** (見習職位), ***tenancy*** (租賃) and ***tenant*** (承租人) have the meanings commonly associated with their use in the context of a set of barristers' chambers.

Clubs

Section 27 Discrimination by Clubs

(1) It is unlawful for a club, the committee of management of a club or a member of the committee of management of a club to discriminate against a person who has family status and who is not a member of the club —

(a) by refusing or failing to accept that person's application for membership; or

(b) in the terms or conditions on which the club is prepared to admit that person to membership.

(2) It is unlawful for a club, the committee of management of a club or a member of the committee of management of a club to discriminate against a person who has family status and who is a member of the club —

(a) in the terms or conditions of membership that are afforded to that person;

(b) by refusing or failing to accept that person's application for a particular class of membership;

(c) by denying that person access or limiting his access, to any benefit, service or facility provided by the club;

(d) by depriving that person of membership or varying the terms of membership; or

(e) by subjecting that person to any other detriment.

(3) Nothing in subsection (1) or (2) renders it unlawful to discriminate against a person who has family status if the discrimination occurs in relation to the use or enjoyment of any benefit provided by the club where it is not practicable for the benefit to be used or enjoyed simultaneously or to the same extent by persons —

(a) who do not have family status and those who have family status; or

(b) who have a particular family status and those who do not have that family status.

Government

Section 28 Government

(1) Subject to subsection (2), without prejudice to the operation of the other provisions of this Part in relation to the Government, it is unlawful for the Government to discriminate against a person who has family status in the performance of its functions or the exercise of its powers.

(2) Subsection (1) shall not render unlawful —

(a) as regards a person not having the right to enter and remain in Hong Kong, any act done under any immigration legislation governing entry into, stay in and departure from Hong Kong; or

(b) any act done in relation to a person if it was necessary for that act to be done in order to comply with a requirement of an existing statutory provision.

Extent

Section 29 Extent of Part IV

(1) Section 19(1) —

(a) shall not apply to goods, facilities or services outside Hong Kong except as provided in subsections (2) and (3); and

(b) shall not apply to facilities by way of banking or insurance or for grants, loans, credit or finance, where the facilities are for a purpose to be carried out, or in connection with risks wholly or mainly arising, outside Hong Kong.

(2) Section 19(1) applies to the provision of facilities for travel outside Hong Kong where the refusal or omission occurs in Hong Kong or on a ship, aircraft or dynamically supported craft referred to in subsection (3).

(3) Section 19(1) applies on or in relation to —

(a) any ship registered in Hong Kong;

(b) any aircraft or dynamically supported craft registered in Hong Kong and operated by a person who has his principal place of business, or is ordinarily resident, in Hong Kong; or

(c) any ship, aircraft or dynamically supported craft belonging to or possessed by the Government,

even if the ship, aircraft or dynamically supported craft is outside Hong Kong.

(4) This Section shall not render unlawful an act done in or over a place outside Hong Kong, or in or over that place's territorial waters, if any, for the purpose of complying with the laws of that place.

(5) Section 18 shall not apply to benefits, facilities or services outside Hong Kong except —

(a) travel on a ship registered in Hong Kong;

(b) benefits, facilities or services provided on a ship so registered.

Part V Other Unlawful Acts

(Format changes — E.R. 5 of 2018)

Section 30 Discriminatory Practices

(1) In this Section, ***discriminatory practice*** (歧視性的做法) means the application of a requirement or condition which results in an act of discrimination which is unlawful by virtue of any provision

of Part III or IV as read with Section 5(b) or which would be likely to result in such an act of discrimination if the persons to whom it is applied were not all of a particular family status.

(2) A person acts in contravention of this Section if and so long as —

(a) he applies a discriminatory practice; or

(b) he operates practices or other arrangements which in any circumstances would call for the application by him of a discriminatory practice.

(3) Proceedings in respect of a contravention of this Section shall be brought only by the Commission in accordance with the provisions of Sections 55, 56, 57, 58 and 59.

Section 31 Discriminatory Advertisements

(1) It is unlawful to publish or cause to be published an advertisement which indicates, or might reasonably be understood as indicating, an intention by a person to do any act which is or might be unlawful by virtue of Part III or IV.

(2) Subsection (1) shall not apply to an advertisement if the intended act would not in fact be unlawful.

(3) For the purposes of subsection (1), use of a job description which is specific to a particular family status or the absence of family status shall be taken to indicate an intention to discriminate, unless the advertisement contains an indication to the contrary.

(4) The publisher of an advertisement made unlawful by subsection (1) shall not be subject to any liability under that subsection in respect of the publication of the advertisement if he proves —

(a) that the advertisement was published in reliance on a statement made to him by the person who caused it to be published to the effect that, by reason of the operation of subsection (2), the publication would not be unlawful; and

(b) that it was reasonable for him to rely on the statement.

(5) A person who knowingly or recklessly makes a statement of the kind referred to in subsection (4) which in a material respect is false or misleading commits an offence and is liable on conviction to a fine at level 4.

Section 32 Instruction to Discriminate

It is unlawful for a person —

(a) who has authority over another person; or

(b) in accordance with whose wishes that other person is accustomed to act,

to instruct him to do any act which is unlawful by virtue of Part III or IV, or procure or attempt to procure the doing by him of any such act.

Section 33 Pressure to Discriminate

(1) It is unlawful to induce, or attempt to induce, a person to do any act which contravenes Part III or IV by —

(a) providing or offering to provide that person with any benefit; or

(b) subjecting or threatening to subject that person to any detriment.

(2) An offer or threat is not prevented from falling within subsection (1) because it is not made directly to the person concerned, if it is made in such a way that he is likely to hear of it.

Section 34 Liability of Employees and Principals

(1) Anything done by a person in the course of his employment shall be treated for the purposes of this Ordinance as done by his employer as well as by him, whether or not it was done with the employer's knowledge or approval.

(2) Anything done by a person as agent for another person with the authority (whether express or implied, and whether precedent or subsequent) of that other person shall be treated for the purpose of this Ordinance as done by that other person as well as by him.

(3) In proceedings brought under this Ordinance against any person in respect of an act alleged to have been done by an employee of his it shall be a defence for that person to prove that he took such steps as were reasonably practicable to prevent the employee from doing that act, or from doing in the course of his employment acts of that description.

(4) For the avoidance of doubt, it is hereby declared that this Section shall not apply for the purposes of any criminal proceedings.

Section 35 Aiding Unlawful Acts

(1) A person who knowingly aids another person to do an act made unlawful by this Ordinance shall be treated for the purposes of this Ordinance as himself doing an unlawful act of the like description.

(2) For the purposes of subsection (1), an employee or agent for whose act the employer or principal is liable under Section 34 (or would be so liable but for Section 34(3)) shall be deemed to aid the doing of the act by the employer or principal.

(3) A person does not under this Section knowingly aid another to do an unlawful act if—

  (a) he acts in reliance on a statement made to him by that other person that, by reason of any provision of this Ordinance, the act which he aids would not be unlawful; and

  (b) it is reasonable for him to rely on the statement.

(4) A person who knowingly or recklessly makes a statement of the kind referred to in subsection (3)(a) which in a material respect is false or misleading commits an offence and is liable on conviction to a fine at level 4.

Part VI General Exceptions from Parts III to V

(Format changes — E.R. 5 of 2018)

Section 36 Special Measures

Nothing in Part III, IV or V shall render unlawful an act that is reasonably intended to —

  (a) ensure that persons who have family status or a particular family status have equal opportunities with other persons in circumstances in relation to which a provision is made by this Ordinance;

  (b) afford persons who have family status or a particular family status goods or access to services, facilities or opportunities to meet their special needs in relation to —

    (i) employment, education, welfare or clubs; or

    (ii) the provision of premises, goods, services or facilities;

  (c) afford persons who have family status or a particular family status, grants, benefits, or programmes, whether direct or indirect, to meet their special needs in relation to —

    (i) employment, education, welfare or clubs; or

(ii) the provision of premises, goods, services or facilities.

Section 37 Charities

(1) Nothing in Part III, IV or V shall —

(a) be construed as affecting a provision to which this subsection applies; or

(b) render unlawful an act which is done in order to give effect to such a provision.

(2) Subsection (1) applies to a provision for conferring benefits on persons of a particular family status (disregarding any benefits to others which are exceptional or are relatively insignificant), being a provision which is contained in a charitable instrument.

(3) In applying this Section, account shall be taken of Section 88 of the Inland Revenue Ordinance (Cap. 112).

(4) In this Section —

charitable instrument (慈善文書) means an enactment or other instrument so far as it relates to charitable purposes;

charitable purposes (慈善目的) means purposes which are exclusively charitable according to any enactment or rule of law.

Section 38 Insurance, etc.

Nothing in Part III, IV or V shall render unlawful the treatment of a person in relation to any class of insurance business, or similar matter involving the assessment of risk, where the treatment —

(a) was effected by reference to actuarial or other data from a source on which it was reasonable to rely; and

(b) was reasonable having regard to the data and any other relevant factors.

Section 39 Discriminatory Training by Certain Bodies

(1) Nothing in Part III, IV or V shall render unlawful any act done by any person in, or in connection with, affording persons access to facilities for training which would help to fit them for employment, where it reasonably appears to that person that those persons are in special need of training by reason of the period for which they have been discharging domestic or family responsibilities to the exclusion of regular full time employment.

(2) For the avoidance of doubt, it is hereby declared that the discrimination in relation to which subsection (1) applies may result from confining the training to persons who have been discharging domestic or family responsibilities, or from the way persons are selected for training, or both.

(3) This Section shall not apply to any discrimination which is rendered unlawful by Section 8.

Section 40 Indirect Access to Benefits, etc.

(1) References in this Ordinance to the affording by any person of access to benefits, facilities or services are not limited to benefits, facilities or services provided by that person himself, but include any means by which it is in that person's power to facilitate access to benefits, facilities or services provided by any other person (***actual provider***).

(2) Where by any provision of this Ordinance the affording by any person of access to benefits, facilities or services in a discriminatory way is in certain circumstances prevented from being unlawful, the effect of the provision shall extend also to the liability under this Ordinance of any actual provider.

Section 41 Acts Done under Statutory Authority to be Exempt from Provisions of Part III or IV

Nothing in –

(a) Part III or IV;

(b) Part V so far as it has effect in relation to provisions in those parts,

shall render unlawful any act done by a person if it was necessary for that person to do it in order to comply with a requirement of an existing statutory provision.

Section 42 Application to New Territories Ordinance

Nothing in Part IV or V shall –

(a) be construed as affecting the operation of any of the provisions of the New Territories Ordinance (Cap. 97); or

(b) render unlawful any act done by any person in, or in connection with, the operation of any of those provisions.

Section 43 Further Exceptions

(1) No provision or Part of this Ordinance specified in column 1 in Part 2 of Schedule 2 shall render unlawful any discrimination specified opposite thereto in column 2 of that Schedule.

(2) Nothing in Part III, IV or V shall render unlawful any act done by any person –

(a) in connection with any discrimination which is not unlawful by virtue of the operation of subsection (1); and

(b) to the extent that it is done for the purposes of that discrimination.

Part VII Commission

(Format changes — E.R. 1 of 2013)

Section 44 Functions and Powers of Commission

(1) The Commission shall –

(a) work towards the elimination of discrimination;

(b) promote equality of opportunity between persons irrespective of family status;

(c) in the case of any act alleged to be unlawful by virtue of this Ordinance, encourage persons who are concerned with the matter to which the act relates to effect a settlement of the matter by conciliation, whether under Section 62 or otherwise;

(d) keep under review the working of this Ordinance and, when it is so required by the Chief Executive or otherwise thinks it necessary, draw up and submit to the Chief Executive proposals for amending this Ordinance; and *(Amended 66 of 1999 s. 3)*

(e) perform such other functions as are imposed on it under this Ordinance or any other enactment.

(2) The Commission may do all such things as are necessary for, or incidental or conducive to, the better performance of its functions and in particular but without prejudice to the generality of the foregoing, may –

(a) with the prior approval of the Chief Executive, become a member of or affiliate to any international body concerned with (whether in whole or in part) the elimination of discrimination; *(Amended 66 of 1999 s. 3)*

(b) exercise such other powers as are conferred on it under this Ordinance.

Section 45 Review of Schedule 2

(1) Without prejudice to the generality of Section 44(1), the Commission, pursuant to its functions under paragraphs (a) and (b) of that Section, shall keep Schedule 2 under review.

(2) Whenever the Commission thinks it necessary, it shall draw up and submit to the Chief Executive proposals for amending Schedule 2. *(Amended 66 of 1999 s. 3)*

Section 46 Delegations

The Commission shall not under Section 67 of the relevant Ordinance delegate any of its functions or powers under —

(a) Section 66;

(b) any provisions of any regulations made under Section 67 which are specified in the regulations as provisions which shall not be subject to Section 67 of the relevant Ordinance;

(c) any provisions of any rules made under Section 66 which are specified in the rules as provisions which shall not be subject to Section 67 of the relevant Ordinance.

Section 46A Protection of Members of Commission, etc.

(1) No person to whom this subsection applies, acting in good faith, is personally liable in damages for any act done or default made in the performance or purported performance of any function, or the exercise or purported exercise of any power, imposed or conferred on the Commission under this Ordinance.

(2) The protection conferred by subsection (1) on any person to whom that subsection applies in respect of any act or default does not in any way affect the liability of the Commission for that act or default.

(3) Subsection (1) applies to the following persons —

(a) a member of the Commission or a committee;

(b) an employee of the Commission;

(c) a conciliator.

(Added 18 of 2014 s. 37)

Section 47 Codes of Practice

(1) The Commission may issue codes of practice containing such practical guidance as it thinks fit for the purposes of —

(a) the elimination of discrimination;

(b) the promotion of equality of opportunity between persons irrespective of family status.

(2) The provisions of Section 69(2) to (15) of the relevant Ordinance apply to and in relation to a code of practice proposed to be issued or issued under subsection (1) subject to the modifications described in subsection (3).

(3) The modifications referred to in subsection (2) are as follows —

(a) any references to discrimination in the provisions referred to in subsection (2) shall be construed as references to discrimination under this Ordinance;

(b) any reference to discrimination between men and women in those provisions shall be construed as a reference to discrimination under this Ordinance;

(c) the references in those provisions to a code of practice shall be construed as references to a code of practice prepared, published or issued under this Section, as the case may require; and

(d) any reference in those provisions to another provision of Section 69 of the relevant Ordinance shall be construed as a reference to the corresponding provision of this Section incorporated by virtue of subsection (2).

Investigations

Section 48 Power to Conduct Formal Investigations

Without prejudice to the generality of Section 44(1), the Commission may if it thinks fit, and shall if required by the Chief Secretary for Administration, conduct a formal investigation for any purpose connected with the carrying out of any of its functions under that Section.

(Amended L.N. 362 of 1997)

Section 49 Terms of Reference

(1) The Commission shall not embark on a formal investigation unless the requirements of this Section have been complied with.

(2) Terms of reference for the formal investigation shall be drawn up by the Commission, or if the Commission was required by the Chief Secretary for Administration to conduct the investigation, by the Chief Secretary for Administration after consulting the Commission. *(Amended L.N. 362 of 1997)*

(3) It shall be the duty of the Commission to give general notice of the holding of the formal investigation unless the terms of reference confine it to activities of persons named in them, but in such a case the Commission shall in the prescribed manner give those persons notice of the holding of the investigation.

(4) Where the terms of reference of the formal investigation confine it to activities of persons named in them and the Commission in the course of it proposes to investigate any act made unlawful by this Ordinance which it believes that a person so named may have done, the Commission shall —

(a) inform that person of its belief and of its proposal to investigate the act; and

(b) offer him an opportunity of making oral or written representations with regard to it (or both oral and written representations if he thinks fit),

and a person so named who avails himself of an opportunity under this subsection of making oral representations may be represented —

(i) by counsel or a solicitor; or

(ii) by some other person of his choice, not being a person to whom the Commission objects on the ground that he is unsuitable.

(5) The Commission or, if the Commission was required by the Chief Secretary for Administration to conduct the formal investigation, the Chief Secretary for Administration after consulting the Commission may from time to time revise the terms of reference; and subsections (1), (3) and (4) shall apply to the revised investigation and terms of reference as they applied to the original. *(Amended L.N. 362 of 1997)*

Section 50 Power to Obtain Information

(1) For the purposes of a formal investigation the Commission, by a notice in the prescribed form served on him in the prescribed manner —

(a) may require any person to furnish such written information as may be described in the notice, and may specify the time at which, and the manner and form in which, the information is to be furnished;

(b) may require any person to attend at such time and place as specified in the notice and give oral information about, and produce all documents in his possession or control relating to, any matter specified in the notice.

(2) Except as provided by Section 57, a notice shall be served under subsection (1) only where —

(a) service of the notice was authorized in writing by or on behalf of the Chief Secretary for Administration; or *(Amended L.N. 362 of 1997)*

(b) the terms of reference of the formal investigation state that the Commission believes that a person named in them may have done or may be doing acts of all or any of the following descriptions —

(i) unlawful discriminatory acts;

(ii) contraventions of Section 30;

(iii) contraventions of Sections 31, 32 or 33,

and confine the investigation to those acts.

(3) A notice under subsection (1) shall not require a person —

(a) to give information, or produce documents, which he could not be compelled to give in evidence, or produce, in civil proceedings before the Court of First Instance; *(Amended 25 of 1998 s. 2)*

(b) to attend at any place unless the necessary expenses of his journey to and from that place are paid or tendered to him.

(4) If a person fails to comply with a notice served on him under subsection (1) or the Commission has reasonable cause to believe that he intends not to comply with it, the Commission may apply to the District Court for an order requiring him to comply with it or with such directions for the like purpose as may be contained in the order; and Section 66A of the District Court Ordinance (Cap. 336) shall apply to failure without reasonable excuse comply with any such order as it applies to the cases there provided.

(5) A person commits an offence if he —

(a) wilfully alters, suppresses, conceals or destroys a document which he has been required by a notice or order under this Section to produce; or

(b) in complying with such a notice or order, knowingly or recklessly makes any statement which in a material respect is false or misleading,

and is liable to a fine at level 4.

Section 51 Recommendations and Reports on Formal Investigations

(1) If in the light of its findings in a formal investigation it appears to the Commission necessary or expedient, whether during the course of the investigation or after its conclusion —

(a) to make to any persons, with a view to promoting equality of opportunity between persons irrespective of family status who are affected by any of their activities, recommendations for changes in their policies or procedures, or as to any other matters; or

(b) to make to the Chief Secretary for Administration any recommendations, whether for changes in the law or otherwise, *(Amended L.N. 362 of 1997)*

the Commission shall make those recommendations accordingly.

(2) The Commission shall prepare a report of its findings in any formal investigation conducted by it.

(3) If the formal investigation is one required by the Chief Secretary for Administration —

(a) the Commission shall deliver the report to the Chief Secretary for Administration;

(b) the Chief Secretary for Administration shall cause the report to be published in such manner as he thinks fit,

and unless required by the Chief Secretary for Administration the Commission shall not publish the report. *(Amended L.N. 362 of 1997)*

(4) If the formal investigation is not one required by the Chief Secretary for Administration, the Commission shall publish the report or make it available for inspection in accordance with subsection (5). *(Amended L.N. 362 of 1997)*

(5) Where under subsection (4) a report is to be made available for inspection, any person shall be entitled, on payment of such reasonable fee, if any, as may be determined by the Commission —

(a) to inspect the report during ordinary office hours and take copies of all or any part of the report; or

(b) to obtain from the Commission a copy, certified by the Commission to be correct, of the report.

(6) The Commission may if it thinks fit determine that the right conferred by subsection (5)(a) shall be exercisable in relation to a copy of the report instead of, or in addition to, the original.

(7) The Commission shall give general notice of the place or places where, and the times when, reports may be inspected under subsection (5).

Section 52 Restrictions on Disclosure of Information

(1) No information given to the Commission by any person (***the informant***) in connection with a formal investigation shall be disclosed by the Commission, any member of the Commission or a committee, any employee of the Commission, any conciliator, or any person who has been such a member, employee or conciliator, except —

(a) on the order of any court;

(b) with the informant's consent;

(c) in the form of a summary or other general statement published by the Commission which does not identify the informant or any other person to whom the information relates;

(d) in a report of the investigation published by the Commission or made available for inspection under Section 51(5);

(e) to members of the Commission or a committee, employees of the Commission or conciliators or, so far as may be necessary for the proper performance of the functions of the Commission, to other persons;

(f) for the purpose of any civil proceedings under this Ordinance to which the Commission is a party, or any criminal proceedings.

(2) Any person who discloses information in contravention of subsection (1) commits an offence and is liable on conviction to a fine at level 4.

(3) In preparing any report for publication or for inspection the Commission shall exclude, so far as it consistent with its functions and the object of the report, any matter which relates to the private affairs of any individual or business interests of any person where the publication of that matter might, in the opinion of the Commission, prejudicially affect that individual or person.

Part VIII Enforcement

(Format changes — E.R. 1 of 2013)

General

Section 53 Restrictions on Proceedings for Contravention of Ordinance

(1) Except as provided by this Ordinance no proceedings, whether civil or criminal, shall lie against any person in respect of an act by reason that the act is unlawful by virtue of a provision of this Ordinance.

(2) Subsection (1) shall not preclude the making of an order of certiorari, mandamus or prohibition.

Section 54 Claims under Part III or IV

(1) A claim by any person (***the claimant***) that another person (***the respondent***) —

- (a) has committed an act of discrimination against the claimant which is unlawful by virtue of Part III or IV; or
- (b) is by virtue of Section 34 or 35 to be treated as having committed such an act of discrimination against the claimant,

may be made the subject of civil proceedings in like manner as any other claim in tort.

(2) Subsection (1) shall not apply to a claim under Section 13(1) of an act in respect of which an appeal, or proceedings in the nature of an appeal, may be brought under any enactment.

(3) Proceedings under subsection (1) shall be brought in the District Court but all such remedies shall be obtainable in such proceedings as, apart from this subsection and Section 53(1), would be obtainable in the Court of First Instance. *(Amended 25 of 1998 s. 2)*

(4) Without limiting the generality of the power conferred by subsection (3), the District Court may —

- (a) make a declaration that the respondent has engaged in conduct, or committed an act, that is unlawful under this Ordinance, and order that the respondent shall not repeat or continue such unlawful conduct or act;
- (b) order that the respondent shall perform any reasonable act or course of conduct to redress any loss or damage suffered by the claimant;
- (c) order that the respondent shall employ or re-employ the claimant;
- (d) order that the respondent shall promote the claimant;
- (e) order that the respondent pay to the claimant damages by way of compensation for any loss or damage suffered by reason of the respondent's conduct or act;
- (f) order that the respondent shall pay to the claimant punitive or exemplary damages; or
- (g) make an order declaring void in whole or part and either ab initio or from such date as may be specified in the order, any contract or agreement made in contravention of this Ordinance.

(5) By virtue of this subsection and notwithstanding any law, the District Court shall have jurisdiction to hear and determine any proceedings under subsection (1) and shall have all such powers as are necessary or expedient for it to have in order to provide, grant or make any remedy, injunction or order mentioned in this Ordinance.

(6) In respect of an unlawful act of discrimination falling within Section 5(b), no award of damages shall be made if the respondent proves that the requirement or condition concerned was not applied with the intention of treating the claimant unfavourably on the ground of the claimant's family status.

(6A) Subsection (6) does not apply in relation to an unlawful act of discrimination falling within Section 5(b) that is committed on or after the commencement date* of Part 9 of the Discrimination Legislation (Miscellaneous Amendments) Ordinance 2020 (8 of 2020). *(Added 8 of 2020 s. 43)*

(7) For the avoidance of doubt, it is hereby declared that damages in respect of an unlawful act of discrimination may include compensation for injury to feelings whether or not they include compensation under any other head.

Enforcement Notices

Section 55 Issue of Enforcement Notices

(1) This Section applies to any act which is —

(a) an unlawful discriminatory act;

(b) a contravention of Section 30; or

(c) a contravention of Section 31, 32 or 33,

and so applies whether or not proceedings have been brought in respect of the act.

(2) If in the course of a formal investigation the Commission becomes satisfied that a person is committing, or has committed, any acts to which this Section applies, the Commission may in the prescribed manner serve on him a notice in the prescribed form requiring him —

(a) not to commit any such acts (which may include discontinuing or changing any of his practices or other arrangements which occasioned those acts, in particular to avoid any repetition thereof); and

(b) where compliance with paragraph (a) involves changes in any of his practices or other arrangements —

(i) to inform the Commission that he has effected those changes and what those changes are;

(ii) to take such steps as may be reasonably required by the notice for the purpose of affording that information to other persons concerned.

(3) An enforcement notice may also require the person on whom it is served to furnish the Commission with such other information as may be reasonably required by the notice in order to verify that the notice has been complied with.

(4) An enforcement notice may specify the time at which, and the manner and form in which, any information is to be furnished to the Commission, but the time at which any information is to be furnished in compliance with the notice shall not be later than 5 years after the notice has become final.

(5) Section 50(4) shall apply to requirements under subsections (2)(b), (3) and (4) contained in an enforcement notice which has become final as it applies to requirements in a notice served under Section 50(1).

Section 56 Appeal against Enforcement Notices

(1) Not later than 45 days after an enforcement notice is served on any person he may appeal against any requirement of the notice to the District Court.

---

* Commencement date: 19 June 2020.

(2) Where the District Court considers a requirement in respect of which an appeal is brought under subsection (1) to be unreasonable because it is based on an incorrect finding of fact or for any other reason, the Court shall quash the requirement.

(3) On quashing a requirement under subsection (2), the District Court may direct that the enforcement notice shall be treated as if, in place of the requirement quashed, it had contained a requirement in terms specified in the direction.

(4) Subsection (1) shall not apply to a requirement treated as included in an enforcement notice by virtue of a direction under subsection (3).

Section 57 Investigation as to Compliance with Enforcement Notices

(1) If —

(a) the terms of reference of a formal investigation state that its purpose is to determine whether any requirements of an enforcement notice are being or have been carried out, but Section 50(2)(b) does not apply; and

(b) Section 49(3) is complied with in relation to the investigation on a date (***the commencement date***) not later than the expiration of the period of 5 years beginning when the enforcement notice became final,

the Commission may within the relevant period serve notices under Section 50(1) for the purposes of the investigation without needing to obtain the consent of the Chief Secretary for Administration. *(Amended L.N. 362 of 1997)*

(2) In subsection (1), ***relevant period*** (有關期間) means the period beginning on the commencement date and ending on the later of the following dates —

(a) the date on which the period of 5 years referred to in subsection (1)(b) expires;

(b) the date 2 years after the commencement date.

Section 58 Register of Enforcement Notices

(1) The Commission shall establish and maintain a register (***the register***) of enforcement notices which have become final.

(2) Any person shall be entitled, on payment of such reasonable fee, if any, as may be determined by the Commission —

(a) to inspect the register during ordinary office hours and take copies of any entry; or

(b) to obtain from the Commission a copy, certified by the Commission to be correct, of any entry in the register.

(3) The Commission may, if it thinks fit, determine that the right conferred by subsection (2)(a) shall be exercisable in relation to a copy of the register instead of, or in addition to, the original.

(4) The Commission shall give general notice of the place or places where, and the times when, the register or a copy may be inspected.

Other Enforcement by Commission

Section 59 Persistent Discrimination

If, during the period of 5 years beginning on the date on which either of the following became final in the case of any person, namely —

(a) an enforcement notice served on him;

(b) a finding by the District Court under Section 54 that he has done an unlawful discriminatory act,

it appears to the Commission that unless restrained he is likely to do an act falling within paragraph (b), or contravening Section 30, the Commission may apply to the District Court for an injunction restraining him from doing so; and the District Court, if satisfied that the application is well-founded, may grant the injunction in the terms applied for or in more limited terms.

Section 60 Enforcement of Sections 31, 32 and 33

(1) Proceedings in respect of a contravention of Section 31, 32 or 33 shall be brought only by the Commission in accordance with the provisions of this Section.

(2) The proceedings shall be —

(a) an application for a decision whether the alleged contravention occurred; or

(b) an application under subsection (4),

or both.

(3) An application under subsection (2)(a) shall be made to the District Court.

(4) If it appears to the Commission —

(a) that a person has done an act which by virtue of Section 31, 32 or 33 was unlawful; and

(b) that unless restrained he is likely to do further acts which by virtue of that Section was unlawful,

the Commission may apply to the District Court for an injunction restraining him from doing so; and the District Court, if satisfied that the application is well-founded, may grant the injunction in the terms applied for or in more limited terms.

(5) Without prejudice to subsection (4), if it appears to the Commission that a person has done an act which was unlawful by virtue of Section 31, the Commission may apply to the District Court for an order imposing a financial penalty on such person; and the District Court, if satisfied that the application is well-founded, may make such an order.

(6) The financial penalty imposed under subsection (5) shall not exceed $10,000 for the first occasion on which a penalty is imposed, and $30,000 for the second and any subsequent occasion on which a penalty is imposed in respect of the same person.

Help for Persons Suffering Discrimination

Section 61 Help for Aggrieved Persons in Obtaining Information, etc.

(1) With a view to helping a person (***the person aggrieved***) who considers he may have been discriminated against in contravention of this Ordinance to decide whether to institute proceedings and, if he does so, to formulate and present his case in the most effective manner, the Commission may prescribe —

(a) forms by which the person aggrieved may question the respondent on his reasons for doing any relevant act, or on any other matter which is or may be relevant;

(b) forms by which the respondent may if he so wishes reply to any questions.

(2) Where the person aggrieved questions the respondent (whether or not in accordance with the forms referred to in subsection (1)) —

(a) the question, and any reply by the respondent (whether or not in accordance with such a form) shall, subject to subsections (3), (4) and (5), be admissible as evidence in the proceedings;

(b) if it appears to the District Court that the respondent deliberately, and without reasonable excuse, omitted to reply within a reasonable period or that his reply is evasive or equivocal, the court may draw any inference from that fact it considers just and equitable to draw, including an inference that he committed an unlawful act.

(3) The Commission may —

(a) prescribe the period within which questions must be served in order to be admissible under subsection (2)(a);

(b) prescribe the manner in which a question, and any reply by the respondent, may be served.

(4) Rules under the District Court Ordinance (Cap. 336) may enable the District Court entertaining a claim under Section 54 to determine, before the date fixed for the hearing of the claim, whether a question or reply is admissible under this Section or not.

(5) This Section is without prejudice to any other enactment or rule of law regulating interlocutory and preliminary matters in proceedings before the District Court, and has effect subject to any enactment or rule of law regulating the admissibility of evidence in such proceedings.

(6) In this Section, ***respondent*** (答辯人) includes a prospective respondent.

Section 62 Assistance by Way of Conciliation

(1) A person may lodge with the Commission a complaint in writing alleging that another person has done an act which is unlawful by virtue of a provision of this Ordinance.

(2) A representative complaint may be lodged under subsection (1) in accordance with rules made under Section 66.

(3) Subject to subsection (4), where a complaint is lodged under subsection (1), the Commission shall —

(a) conduct an investigation into the act the subject of the complaint; and

(b) endeavour, by conciliation, to effect a settlement of the matter which the act relates.

(4) The Commission may decide not to conduct, or to discontinue, an investigation into an act the subject of a complaint lodged under subsection (1) if —

(a) it is satisfied that the act is not unlawful by reason of a provision of this Ordinance;

(b) it is of the opinion that the person aggrieved by the act does not desire (or, in a case to which subsection (2) applies, none of the persons aggrieved by the act desires) that the investigation be conducted or continued;

(c) a period of more than 12 months has elapsed beginning when the act was done;

(d) in a case to which subsection (2) applies, it determines, in accordance with rules made under Section 66, that the complaint should not be a representative complaint; or

(e) it is of the opinion that the complaint is frivolous, vexatious, misconceived or lacking in substance.

(5) Where the Commission decides not to conduct, or to discontinue, an investigation into an act the subject of a complaint lodged under subsection (1), it shall by notice served on the person who lodged the complaint advise him of —

(a) that decision; and

(b) the reasons for that decision.

(6) Evidence of anything said or done by any person in the course of conciliation under this Section (including anything said or done at any conference held for the purposes of such conciliation) is not admissible in evidence in any proceedings under this Ordinance except with the consent of that person.

(7) For the avoidance of doubt, it is hereby declared that subsection (6) shall not apply where —

(a) a complaint is lodged under subsection (1); and

(b) a settlement has been effected of the matter to which the act the subject of the complaint relates.

Section 63 Assistance Other Than by Way of Conciliation

(1) Where a complaint has been lodged under Section 62(1) but, for whatever reason, there has not been a settlement of the matter to which the act the subject of the complaint relates, then any person who may institute proceedings under this Ordinance in respect of that act may make an application to the Commission for assistance in respect of those proceedings.

(2) The Commission shall consider an application under subsection (1) and may grant it if it thinks fit to do so, in particular where —

(a) the case raises a question of principle; or

(b) it is unreasonable, having regard to the complexity of the case or the applicant's position in relation to the respondent or another person involved or any other matter, to expect the applicant to deal with the case unaided.

(3) Assistance by the Commission under this Section may include —

(a) giving advice;

(b) arranging for the giving of advice or assistance by a solicitor or counsel;

(c) arranging for representation by any person including all such assistance as is usually given by a solicitor or counsel in the steps preliminary or incidental to any proceedings, or in arriving at or giving effect to a compromise to avoid or bring to an end any proceedings;

(d) any other form of assistance which the Commission may consider appropriate,

but paragraph (c) shall not affect the law and practice regulating the descriptions of persons who may appear in, conduct, defend and address a court in, any proceedings except to the extent permitted under rules made (for the purposes of this Ordinance) in accordance with Section 73D of the District Court Ordinance (Cap. 336).

(4) In so far as expenses are incurred by the Commission in providing the applicant with assistance under this Section the recovery of those expenses (as taxed or assessed in such manner as may be prescribed by relevant rules) shall constitute a first charge for the benefit of the Commission —

(a) on any other costs or expenses which (whether by virtue of a judgment or order of the District Court or an agreement or otherwise) are payable to the applicant by any other person in respect of the matter in connection with which the assistance is given; and

(b) so far as relates to any costs or expenses, on his rights under any compromise or settlement arrived at in connection with that matter to avoid or bring to an end any proceedings.

(5) The charge conferred by subsection (4) shall be subject to any charge under the Legal Aid Ordinance (Cap. 91) and to any provision in that Ordinance for payment of any sum into the Supplementary Legal Aid Fund established under that Ordinance.

(6) In this Section —

relevant rules (有關規則) means any rules made under the District Court Ordinance (Cap. 336);

respondent (答辯人) includes a prospective respondent.

Period within Which Proceedings Are to be Brought

Section 64 Period within Which Proceedings Are to be Brought

(1) The District Court shall not consider a claim under Section 54 unless proceedings in respect of the claim are instituted before the end of the period of 24 months beginning —

(a) when the act complained of was done; or

(b) if there is a relevant report in relation to that act, with the day on which the report is published or made available for inspection under Section 51,

whichever is later.

(2) The District Court shall not consider an application under —

(a) Section 60(2)(a) unless it is made before the end of the period of 24 months beginning when the act to which it relates was done;

(b) Section 60(4) unless it is made before the end of the period of 5 years so beginning.

(3) For the purposes of determining the period under subsection (1) within which proceedings may be brought, where an act to which the claim relates was the subject of a complaint lodged under Section 62(1), then the period that elapsed between the date when the complaint was lodged and the date when the complaint was disposed of under Section 62(3) or (4), as certified in writing by the Commission, shall be disregarded. *(Amended 29 of 2008 s. 106)*

(4) Notwithstanding subsections (1) and (2), the District Court may consider any claim or application which is out of time if, in all the circumstances of the case, it considers that it is just and equitable to do so.

(5) For the purposes of subsection (4), the circumstances of the case include, in relation to any claim, whether the act to which the claim relates was the subject of a complaint lodged under Section 62(1) and, if so, the period that elapsed between when the act was done and when the complaint was so lodged.

(6) For the purposes of this Section —

(a) where the inclusion of any term in a contract renders the making of the contract an unlawful act, that act shall be treated as extending throughout the duration of the contract;

(b) any act extending over a period shall be treated as done at the end of that period; and

(c) a deliberate omission shall be treated as done when the person concerned decided upon it,

and, in the absence of evidence to the contrary, a person shall be taken for the purposes of this Section to decide upon an omission when he does an act inconsistent with doing the omitted act or, if he has done no such inconsistent act, when the period expires within which he might reasonably have been expected to do the omitted act if it was to be done.

(7) The Chief Executive in Council may, by notice in the Gazette, amend subsection (1) by substituting a longer period for the period specified in that subsection. *(Amended 66 of 1999 s. 3)*

(8) In this Section, ***relevant report*** (有關報告), in relation to an act referred to in that subsection (1), means a report —

(a) published or made available for inspection under Section 51; and

(b) from which it can reasonably be construed (and whether or not the report mentions, or was in any way prepared in consequence of, the act) that the Commission is of the opinion that the act, or the class of acts to which the act belongs, is unlawful under a provision of Part III, IV or V.

Part IX Miscellaneous

(Format changes — E.R. 5 of 2018)

Section 65 Validity and Revision of Contracts

(1) Section 87 of the relevant Ordinance applies in relation to the validity and revision of contracts, for the purposes of this Ordinance, subject to the modifications described in subsection (2).

(2) The modifications referred to in subsection (1) are as follows —

(a) the references in that Section —

(i) to the relevant Ordinance shall be construed as references to this Ordinance;

(ii) to any subsection of that Section shall be construed as references to the corresponding subsection of this Section incorporated by reference under subsection (1); and

(b) the reference in that Section to Section 76 of that Ordinance shall be construed as a reference to Section 54.

Section 66 Rules

(1) For the purposes of this Ordinance, the Commission shall have the same power to make rules as it has under the relevant Ordinance and accordingly Section 88 of that Ordinance applies to this Ordinance subject to the modifications described in subsection (2).

(2) The modifications referred to in subsection (1) are as follows —

(a) the references in that Section —

(i) to Section 84, 84(1) and 84(4)(d) of that Ordinance shall be construed as references respectively to Section 62, 62(1) and 62(4)(d);

(ii) to rules shall be construed as a reference to rules made under this Section;

(iii) to that Section, a subsection or paragraph of that Section shall be construed as a reference respectively to this Section, the corresponding subsection or paragraph of this Section incorporated by reference under subsection (1);

(b) the reference in that Section —

(i) to Section 35 of that Ordinance shall be construed as a reference to Section 25; and

(ii) to that Ordinance shall be construed as a reference to this Ordinance.

Section 67 Regulations to Empower Commission to Bring Certain Proceedings

(1) The Secretary for Constitutional and Mainland Affairs shall have the same powers to make regulations for the purposes of this Ordinance as he has under the relevant Ordinance and accordingly Section 89 of that Ordinance shall apply subject to the modification that the references to Section 76(1) and 76(3) of that Ordinance shall be construed as references respectively to Section 54(1) and 54(3). *(Amended L.N. 130 of 2007)*

(2) Any regulations made under this Section shall be subject to the approval of the Legislative Council.

Section 68 Amendment of Schedules

The Chief Executive in Council may, by notice in the Gazette, amend Schedule 1 or 2 but any notice to amend Schedule 2 shall be subject to the approval of the Legislative Council.

(Amended 66 of 1999 s. 3)

Section 69 (Omitted as spent—E.R. 5 of 2018)

Schedule 1

[ss. 2(1) and 68]

Educational Establishments and Their Responsible Bodies

(Format changes — E.R. 1 of 2013)

	Educational establishment	Responsible body
1.	The University of Hong Kong established by the University of Hong Kong Ordinance (Cap. 1053)	The Court, the Council, the Senate or the Convocation, within the meaning of Section 2 of the University of Hong Kong Ordinance (Cap. 1053), according to which of them has the function concerned
2.	The Chinese University of Hong Kong established by The Chinese University of Hong Kong Ordinance (Cap. 1109)	The Council, the Senate, the Convocation, the Faculties, the School of Studies or the Board of Studies, within the meaning of Section 2 of The Chinese University of Hong Kong Ordinance (Cap. 1109), according to which of them has the function concerned
3.	The Hong Kong Polytechnic University established by The Hong Kong Polytechnic University Ordinance (Cap. 1075)	The Council or Senate, within the meaning of Section 2 of The Hong Kong Polytechnic University Ordinance (Cap. 1075), according to which of them has the function concerned
4.	Any post secondary college registered under the Post Secondary Colleges Ordinance (Cap. 320)	The Board of Governors (or Board of Trustees where no Board of Governors exists) or the College Council, according to which of them has the function concerned
5.	Any technical college or technical institute defined in Section 2 of the Vocational Training Council Ordinance (Cap. 1130)	The Vocational Training Council established by Section 4 of the Vocational Training Council Ordinance (Cap. 1130)
6.	Any industrial training centre or skills centre defined in Section 2 of the Vocational Training Council Ordinance (Cap. 1130)	The Vocational Training Council established by Section 4 of the Vocational Training Council Ordinance (Cap. 1130)
7.	The Hong Kong Baptist University established by the Hong Kong Baptist University Ordinance (Cap. 1126)	The Council, Court or Senate, within the meaning of Section 2 of the Hong Kong Baptist University Ordinance (Cap. 1126), according to which of them has the function concerned
8.	The City University of Hong Kong established by the City University of Hong Kong Ordinance (Cap. 1132)	The Council, Court or Senate, within the meaning of Section 2 of the City University of Hong Kong Ordinance (Cap. 1132), according to which of them has the function concerned
9.	The Hong Kong Academy for Performing Arts established by The Hong Kong Academy for Performing Arts Ordinance (Cap. 1135)	The Council or the Academic Board, within the meaning of Section 2 of The Hong Kong Academy for Performing Arts Ordinance (Cap. 1135), according to which of them has the function concerned

10.	The Hong Kong University of Science and Technology established by The Hong Kong University of Science and Technology Ordinance (Cap. 1141)	The Court, the Council, the Senate or the Convocation, within the meaning of Section 2 of The Hong Kong University of Science and Technology Ordinance (Cap. 1141), according to which of them has the function concerned
11.	The Open University of Hong Kong established by The Open University of Hong Kong Ordinance (Cap. 1145)	The Council, the Court or the Senate, within the meaning of Section 2 of The Open University of Hong Kong Ordinance (Cap. 1145), according to which of them has the function concerned
12.	Lingnan University established by the Lingnan University Ordinance (Cap. 1165)	The Council, the Court or the Senate, within the meaning of Section 2 of the Lingnan University Ordinance (Cap. 1165), according to which of them has the function concerned *(Replaced 54 of 1999 s. 35)*
13.	The Education University of Hong Kong established by The Education University of Hong Kong Ordinance (Cap. 444)	The Council or the Academic Board, within the meaning of Section 2 of The Education University of Hong Kong Ordinance (Cap. 444), according to which of them has the function concerned *(Amended 6 of 2016 s. 2)*
14.	Any school which is registered or provisionally registered under the Education Ordinance (Cap. 279)	The management committee, within the meaning of Section 3 of the Education Ordinance (Cap. 279), of the school
15.	Any school, within the meaning of Section 3 of the Education Ordinance (Cap. 279), entirely maintained and controlled by the Government	The Permanent Secretary for Education *(Amended 3 of 2003 s. 41; L.N. 130 of 2007)*

Schedule 2

[ss. 43(1), 45(1) and (2) and 68]

Further Exceptions to This Ordinance

(Format changes — E.R. 1 of 2013)

Part 1 Interpretation

Section 1 Interpretation

In this Schedule —

allowance (津貼) includes part of an allowance;

benefit (利益) includes part of a benefit.

Part 2 Exceptions

	Provision creating illegality	Exception
1.	Parts III, IV and V	Any discrimination against a person who has family status arising from a provision — (a) of — (i) the Civil Service Regulations; (ii) any contract of service or apprenticeship; or (iii) any contract personally to execute any work or labour; and *(Amended 18 of 2014 s. 38)* (b) relating to — (i) housing; (ii) education; (iii) air-conditioning; (iv) passage; or (v) baggage, benefits or allowances.

Schedule 3

(Omitted as spent — E.R. 1 of 2013)

RACE DISCRIMINATION ORDINANCE (CAP. 602)

An Ordinance to render discrimination, harassment and vilification, on the ground of race, unlawful; to prohibit serious vilification of persons on that ground; to extend the jurisdiction of the Equal Opportunities Commission to include such unlawful acts; to confer on the Commission the function of eliminating such discrimination, harassment and vilification and promoting equality and harmony between people of different races; to amend certain definitions, and the provisions on discrimination against contract workers, in existing anti-discrimination legislation as well as the provision on unlawful sexual harassment by creating a hostile or intimidating environment in the Sex Discrimination Ordinance for alignment with corresponding provisions in this Ordinance; to make other consequential and related amendments to enactments; and for related purposes.

[3 October 2008] L.N. 222 *of* 2008

(Enacting provision omitted — E.R. 1 of 2013)

Part 1 Interpretation, Application, etc.

(Format changes — E.R. 1 of 2013)

Section 1 Short Title

(Amended E.R. 5 of 2018)

(1) This Ordinance may be cited as the Race Discrimination Ordinance.

(2) *(Omitted as spent — E.R. 1 of 2013)*

Section 2 Interpretation

(1) In this Ordinance, unless the context otherwise requires —

access (獲得、享用) means access as construed in accordance with Section 53;

act (作為) includes a deliberate omission;

advertisement (廣告) includes every form of advertisement, whether to the public or not, and whether —

(a) in a newspaper or other publication;

(b) by television or radio;

(c) by display of notices, signs, labels, showcards or goods;

(d) by distribution of samples, circulars, catalogues, price lists or other material;

(e) by exhibition of pictures, models or films; or

(f) in any other way;

associate (有聯繫者), in relation to a person, includes —

(a) a spouse of the person;

(b) another person who is living with the person on a genuine domestic basis;

(c) a relative of the person;

(d) a carer of the person; and

(e) another person who is in a business, sporting or recreational relationship with the person; *(Added 8 of 2020 s. 12)*

carer (照料者) includes —

(a) the Director of Social Welfare;

(b) any officer of the Social Welfare Department authorized in writing by the Director of Social Welfare;

(c) any person specified in Schedule 6; *(Added 8 of 2020 s. 12)*

club (會社) means an association, incorporate or unincorporate, of not less than 30 persons associated together for social, literary, cultural, political, sporting, athletic or other lawful purposes and which provides and maintains its facilities, in whole or in part, from the funds of the association;

commencement date (生效日期), except in Section 73, in relation to any provision of this Ordinance, means —

(a) the date appointed under Section 1(2) for that provision to come into operation; or

(b) if different dates are appointed for the provision to commence for different purposes, the date appointed for that provision to come into operation for the relevant purpose;

Commission (平機會) means the Equal Opportunities Commission established under Section 63(1) of the Sex Discrimination Ordinance (Cap. 480);

commission agent (佣金經紀人) means a commission agent as construed in accordance with Section 22;

committee (委員會) means a committee established under Section 64(2)(a) of the Sex Discrimination Ordinance (Cap. 480);

committee of management (管理委員會), in relation to a club, means the group or body of persons (howsoever described) that manages the affairs of the club;

conciliator (調停人) means any person engaged by the Commission under Section 64(2)(e) of the Sex Discrimination Ordinance (Cap. 480); *(Amended 15 of 2012 s. 11)*

contract worker (合約工作者) means a contract worker as construed in accordance with Section 15;

discrimination (歧視) means any discrimination falling within Section 4, 5 or 6 and related expressions are to be construed accordingly;

dispose (處置), in relation to premises, includes granting a right to occupy the premises, and any reference to acquiring premises are to be construed accordingly;

dynamically supported craft (動力承托的航行器) has the same meaning as in the Shipping and Port Control Ordinance (Cap. 313);

education (教育) includes any form of training or instruction;

educational establishment (教育機構) means an educational establishment specified in column 2 of Schedule 1;

employment (僱用) means employment under —

(a) a contract of service or of apprenticeship; or

(b) a contract personally to execute any work or labour;

employment agency (職業介紹所) means a person who, for profit or not, provides services for the purpose of —

(a) finding employment for workers; or

(b) supplying employers with workers;

enforcement notice (執行通知) means a notice served under Section 71(2);

estate agent (地產代理) has the same meaning as in the Estate Agents Ordinance (Cap. 511);

firm (商號) means a firm within the meaning of the Partnership Ordinance (Cap. 38);

formal investigation (正式調查) means an investigation conducted under Section 64;

general notice (一般通告), in relation to a person, means a notice published by the person at a time and in a manner appearing to the person suitable for securing that the notice is seen within a reasonable time by persons likely to be affected by it;

genuine occupational qualification (真正的職業資格) means a genuine occupational qualification as construed in accordance with Section 11(2);

harass (騷擾) means to harass within the meaning of Section 7(1) or (2);

intern (實習人員) — Section 24A(2); *(Added 8 of 2020 s. 29)*

internship (實習) — Section 24A(2); *(Added 8 of 2020 s. 29)*

near relative (近親), in relation to a person, means —

(a) the person's spouse;

(b) a parent of the person or of the spouse;

(c) a child of the person or the spouse of such a child;

(d) a brother or sister (whether of full blood or half blood) of the person or of the spouse or the spouse of such a brother or sister;

(e) a grandparent of the person or of the spouse; or

(f) a grandchild of the person or the spouse of such a grandchild,

and, in determining the above relationships, children born out of wedlock are to be included, an adopted child is to be regarded as a child of both the natural parents and the adoptive parent or parents and a step child as the child of both the natural parents and any step parent;

notice (通告、通知) means a notice in writing;

prescribed (訂明) means prescribed in rules made under Section 82;

profession (專業) includes any vocation or occupation;

pupillage (見習職位) — see Section 35(4); *(Added 8 of 2020 s. 29)*

responsible body (負責組織), in relation to an educational establishment, means the body specified in column 3 of Schedule 1 opposite to that establishment;

retirement (退休) includes retirement (whether voluntary or not) on grounds of age, length of service or incapacity;

trade (行業) includes any business;

training (訓練) includes any form of education or instruction; *(Amended 8 of 2020 s. 29)*

volunteer (義工) — see Section 24A(2). *(Added 8 of 2020 s. 29)*

(2) References in this Ordinance to ***race, on the ground of race and racial group*** shall be construed in accordance with Section 8.

(3) References in this Ordinance to the dismissal of a person from employment or to the expulsion of a person from a position as partner include references —

(a) to the termination of that person's employment or partnership by the expiration of any period (including a period expiring by reference to an event or circumstance), not being a termination immediately after which the employment or partnership is renewed on the same terms;

(b) to the termination of that person's employment or partnership by any act of that person (including the giving of notice) in circumstances such that that person is entitled to terminate it without notice by reason of the conduct of the employer, or the other partners, as the case may be.

(4) For the purposes of this Ordinance, an enforcement notice or a finding by the District Court becomes final when an appeal against the notice or finding is dismissed, withdrawn or abandoned or when the time for appealing expires without an appeal having been brought; and for this purpose an appeal against an enforcement notice is taken to be dismissed if, notwithstanding that a requirement of the notice is quashed on appeal, a direction is given in respect of it under Section 72(3).

(5) Subject to subsection (6), in this Ordinance, ***existing statutory provision*** (現有法例條文) means a provision of —

(a) an Ordinance enacted before this Ordinance was enacted; or

(b) any subsidiary legislation made —

(i) under an Ordinance enacted before this Ordinance was enacted; and

(ii) before, on or after the enactment of this Ordinance.

(6) Where an Ordinance, enacted after this Ordinance was enacted, re-enacts (with or without modifications) a provision of an Ordinance enacted before this Ordinance was enacted, then that provision as re-enacted is to be treated for the purposes of subsection (5) as if it continued to be contained in an Ordinance enacted before this Ordinance was enacted.

(7) The Secretary for Justice may, by notice published in the Gazette, amend this Ordinance by substituting, for a reference to the commencement date of a provision, the actual calendar date appointed for the commencement of that provision.

Section 3 Application to Government

This Ordinance binds the Government.

Part 2 Discrimination and Harassment to Which This Ordinance Applies

(Format changes — E.R. 5 of 2018)

Section 4 Racial Discrimination

(1) In any circumstances relevant for the purposes of any provision of this Ordinance, a person (***the discriminator***) discriminates against another person if —

(a) on the ground of the race of that other person, the discriminator treats that other person less favourably than the discriminator treats or would treat other persons; or

(b) the discriminator applies to that other person a requirement or condition which the discriminator applies or would apply equally to persons not of the same racial group as that other person but —

(i) which is such that the proportion of persons of the same racial group as that other person who can comply with it is considerably smaller than the proportion of persons not of that racial group who can comply with it;

(ii) which the discriminator cannot show to be justifiable irrespective of the race of the person to whom it is applied; and

(iii) which is to the detriment of the other person because that person cannot comply with it.

(2) For the purposes of subsection (1)(b)(ii), a requirement or condition is justifiable if it serves a legitimate objective and bears a rational and proportionate connection to the objective.

(3) It is declared that, for the purposes of this Ordinance, segregating a person from other persons on the ground of the race of that person is treating that person less favourably than the other persons are treated.

Section 5 Discrimination on the Ground of Race of Associate

In any circumstances relevant for the purposes of any provision of this Ordinance, a person (***the discriminator***) discriminates against another person (***the relevant person***) if, on the ground of the race of an associate of the relevant person, the discriminator treats the relevant person less favourably than the discriminator treats or would treat another person not having an associate of the same racial group as the associate of the relevant person.

(Replaced 8 of 2020 s. 13)

Section 6 Discrimination by Way of Victimization

(1) A person (***the discriminator***) discriminates against another person (***the person victimized***) in any circumstances relevant for the purposes of any provision of this Ordinance if the discriminator treats the person victimized less favourably than in those circumstances the discriminator treats or would treat other persons, and does so —

(a) by reason that the person victimized or any other person (***the third person***) has —

(i) brought proceedings against the discriminator or any other person under this Ordinance;

(ii) given evidence or information in connection with proceedings brought by any person against the discriminator or any other person under this Ordinance;

(iii) otherwise done anything under or by reference to this Ordinance in relation to the discriminator or any other person; or

(iv) alleged that the discriminator or any other person has committed an act which (whether or not the allegation so states) would amount to a contravention of this Ordinance; or

(b) by reason that the discriminator —

(i) knows the person victimized or the third person, as the case may be, intends to do any of those things; or

(ii) suspects the person victimized or the third person, as the case may be, has done, or intends to do, any of them.

(2) Subsection (1) does not apply to treatment of a person by reason of any allegation made by that person if the allegation was false and not made in good faith.

Section 7 Racial Harassment

(1) In any circumstances relevant for the purposes of any provision of this Ordinance, a person harasses another person if, on the ground of the race of that other person or an associate of that other person, the first-mentioned person engages in unwelcome conduct (which may include an oral or a written statement), in circumstances in which a reasonable person, having regard to all the circumstances, would have anticipated that the other person would be offended, humiliated or intimidated by that conduct.

(2) In any circumstances relevant for the purposes of any provision of this Ordinance, a person (***the first-mentioned person***) harasses another person (***the second-mentioned person***) if, on the ground of the race of the second-mentioned person or his or her associate, the first-mentioned person, alone or together with other persons, engages in conduct (which may include an oral or a written statement) that creates a hostile or intimidating environment for the second-mentioned person.

(Amended 8 of 2020 s. 14)

Section 8 Meaning of Race, on the Ground of Race, Racial Group and Comparison of Cases of Persons or Different Racial Groups

(1) In this Ordinance and subject to subsections (2) and (3) —

(a) ***race*** (種族), in relation to a person, means the race, colour, descent or national or ethnic origin of the person, and includes a race, colour, descent or national or ethnic origin that is imputed to the person;

(b) a reference to an act done on the ground of the race of a person is a reference to an act done on the ground of — *(Amended 8 of 2020 s. 18)*

(i) the race, colour, descent or national or ethnic origin of the person; or

(ii) the race, colour, descent or national or ethnic origin that is imputed to the person;

(c) an act constitutes discrimination on the ground of descent only if it constitutes discrimination against members of communities based on forms of social stratification such as caste and analogous systems of inherited status which nullify or impair their equal enjoyment of human rights; and

(d) ***racial group*** (種族群體) means a group of persons defined by reference to race, colour, descent or national or ethnic origin, and references to a person's racial group refer to any racial group into which the person falls or is imputed to fall. *(Amended 8 of 2020 s. 18)*

(2) An act done on the ground of any matter specified in subsection (3) does not constitute an act done on the ground of the race, colour, descent or national or ethnic origin of a person; and Section 4(1)(b) does not apply to a requirement or condition as to any matter specified in subsection (3).

(3) The matters specified in this subsection are —

(a) that the person —

(i) is or is not an indigenous inhabitant of the New Territories; or

(ii) is or is not a person who was in 1898 a resident of an established village in Hong Kong or a person descended through the male line from such person;

(b) that the person —

(i) is or is not a Hong Kong permanent resident;

(ii) has or has not the right of abode or the right to land in Hong Kong;

(iii) is or is not subject to any restriction or condition of stay imposed under the Immigration Ordinance (Cap. 115); or

(iv) has or has not been given the permission to land or remain in Hong Kong under the Immigration Ordinance (Cap. 115);

(c) the length of residence in Hong Kong of the person; or

(d) the nationality, citizenship or resident status of the person under the law of any country or place concerning nationality, citizenship, resident status or naturalization of or in that country or place.

(4) The fact that a racial group comprises 2 or more distinct racial groups does not prevent it from constituting a particular racial group for the purposes of this Ordinance.

(5) A comparison under Section 4(1) of the case of a person of a particular racial group with that of a person not of that group must be such that the relevant circumstances in the one case are the same, or not materially different, in the other.

(6) A comparison of the cases under Section 5 of —

(a) a person having an associate who is of a particular racial group; and

(b) a person not having an associate who is of that group,

must be such that the relevant circumstances in the one case are the same as, or not materially different from, those in the other. *(Replaced 8 of 2020 s. 15)*

Section 9 Act Done for Racial and Other Reason

If —

(a) an act is done for 2 or more reasons; and

(b) one of the reasons is the race of a person (whether or not it is the dominant reason or a substantial reason for doing the act),

then, for the purposes of this Ordinance, the act is taken to be done for the reason of the race of the person.

Part 3 Discrimination and Harassment in Employment Field

(Format changes — E.R. 5 of 2018)

Discrimination by Employers

Section 10 Discrimination against Applicants and Employees

(1) It is unlawful for a person (***the employer***), in relation to employment by the employer at an establishment in Hong Kong, to discriminate against another person —

(a) in the arrangements the employer makes for the purpose of determining who should be offered that employment;

(b) in the terms on which the employer offers that other person employment; or

(c) by refusing, or deliberately omitting to offer, the other person that employment.

(2) It is unlawful for an employer, in the case of a person employed by that employer at an establishment in Hong Kong, to discriminate against that employee —

(a) in the terms of employment which the employer affords that employee;

(b) in the way the employer affords the employee access to opportunities for promotion, transfer or training, or to any other benefits, facilities or services, or by refusing or deliberately omitting to afford the employee access to them; or

(c) by dismissing the employee, or subjecting him or her to any other detriment.

(3) Except in relation to discrimination falling within Section 6, subsections (1) and (2) do not apply to employment when the number of persons employed by the employer, added to the number employed by any associated employers of that employer, does not exceed 5. This subsection does not apply to the employment by a person of another person to perform domestic duties on the premises on which the first-mentioned person or his or her near relative resides.

(4) Subject to subsection (5), subsections (1)(b) and (2) do not apply to provision in relation to death or retirement for a person made before the commencement date* in so far as any such provision continues for that person on and after that date.

(5) Subsections (1)(b) and (2) apply to provision made in relation to retirement of the kind mentioned in subsection (4) in so far as, in their application to such provision, they render it unlawful for a person (***the employer***) to discriminate against another person —

(a) in such of the terms on which the employer offers that other person employment as make provision in relation to the way in which the employer will afford that other person access to opportunities for promotion, transfer or training or as provide for that other person's dismissal or demotion;

(b) in the way the employer affords that other person opportunities for promotion, transfer or training, or by refusing or deliberately omitting to afford that other person access to any such opportunities; or

(c) by dismissing that other person or subjecting that other person to any detriment which results in that other person's dismissal or consists in or involves that other person's demotion.

(6) Subsection (2) does not apply to benefits, facilities or services of any description if the employer is concerned with the provision (for payment or not) of benefits, facilities or services of that description to the public, or to a section of the public comprising the employee in question, unless —

(a) that provision differs in a material respect from the provision of the benefits, facilities or services by the employer to his or her employees;

(b) the provision of the benefits, facilities or services to the employee in question is regulated by the employee's contract of employment; or

(c) the benefits, facilities or services relate to training.

(7) Except in relation to discrimination falling within Section 5 or 6, nothing in subsection (1)(a) or (c) renders it unlawful for a person to discriminate against another person on the ground of the race of that other person, in connection with employment to perform domestic duties on the premises on which the first-mentioned person or his or her near relative resides.

(8) Subsection (3) expires on the third anniversary of the day on which this Ordinance is enacted.

(9) For the purposes of subsection (3), 2 employers are to be treated as associated if one is a company of which the other (directly or indirectly) has control or if both are companies of which a third person (directly or indirectly) has control.

---

* Commencement date: 10 July 2009.

(10) The Chief Executive in Council may, by notice published in the Gazette, do either or both of the following —

(a) amend subsection (3) by substituting another number for the number appearing after the word "exceed" in that subsection;

(b) amend subsection (8) by substituting another anniversary for the anniversary appearing in that subsection.

Section 11 Exception for Genuine Occupational Qualification

(1) In relation to discrimination falling within Section 4 —

(a) Section 10(1)(a) and (c) does not apply to any employment where being of a particular racial group is a genuine occupational qualification for the job; and

(b) Section 10(2)(b) does not apply to opportunities for promotion or transfer to, or training for, such employment.

(2) Being of a particular racial group is a genuine occupational qualification only where —

(a) the job involves participation in a dramatic performance or other entertainment in a capacity for which a person of that racial group is required for reasons of authenticity;

(b) the job involves participation as an artist's or photographic model in the production of a work of art, visual images or sequence of visual images for which a person of that racial group is required for reasons of authenticity;

(c) the job involves working in a place where food or drink is (for payment or not) provided to and consumed by members of the public or a section of the public in a particular setting for which, in that job, a person of that racial group is required for reasons of authenticity;

(d) the holder of the job provides persons of that racial group with personal services promoting their welfare, and those services can most effectively be provided by a person of that racial group; or

(e) the job involves providing persons of that racial group with personal services of such nature or in such circumstances as to require familiarity with the language, culture and customs of and sensitivity to the needs of that racial group, and those services can most effectively be provided by a person of that racial group.

Section 12 Exception for Employment Intended to Provide Training in Skills to be Exercised Outside Hong Kong

Without prejudice to Section 8(2) and (3), nothing in Section 10 renders unlawful any act done by an employer for the benefit of a person not ordinarily resident in Hong Kong in or in connection with employing the person at an establishment in Hong Kong, where the purpose of that employment is to provide the person with training in skills which the person appears to the employer to intend to exercise wholly outside Hong Kong.

Section 13 Exception for Employment of Person with Special Skills, Knowledge or Experience

(1) Nothing in Section 10 renders unlawful any act done by an employer for the benefit of any person in or in connection with employing the person at an establishment in Hong Kong, where —

(a) the employment requires special skills, knowledge or experience not readily available in Hong Kong;

(b) the person –

(i) possesses those skills, knowledge or experience; and

(ii) is recruited or transferred from a place outside Hong Kong; and

(c) the act is reasonably done for a person so recruited or transferred, having regard to –

(i) the prevailing terms of employment offered to persons with those skills, knowledge or experience in places outside Hong Kong; and

(ii) any other relevant circumstances (other than the race of the person).

(2) Where in an employment of a person to which subsection (1) or this subsection applies –

(a) the employment terminates and is immediately followed by renewal or re-engagement (whether or not on the same terms);

(b) the person is promoted; or

(c) the person is transferred within the same group of companies,

nothing in Section 10 renders unlawful any act done, by the employer or the employer upon transfer (as the case may be), for the benefit of the person in or in connection with the renewal, re-engagement, promotion or transfer, or in or in connection with the employment pursuant to it, so long as the act is reasonably done for the person having regard to the matters referred to in subsection (1)(c).

(3) In this Section –

(a) ***group of companies*** (公司集團) means a group of companies within the meaning of the Companies Ordinance (Cap. 622); *(Amended 28 of 2012 ss. 912 and 920)*

(b) an employee is transferred within the same group of companies if the termination of the employment of the employee by one employer is immediately followed by the employment of the employee by another employer, both employers being at that time within the same group of companies; and a reference to transfer of employment within the same group of companies shall be construed accordingly.

(4) Nothing in this Section shall prejudice the operation of Section 8(2) and (3).

Section 14 Exception for Existing Employment on Local and Overseas Terms of Employment

(1) Nothing in Section 10 renders unlawful –

(a) any differential treatment by an employer in or in connection with employing an employee on local terms of employment on the one hand and employing another employee on overseas terms of employment on the other hand in accordance with those two sets of terms respectively; or

(b) any differential treatment by an employer in or in connection with employing on overseas terms of employment an employee who is a national or citizen of a country or place on the one hand and employing also on those terms another employee who is a national or citizen of another country or place on the other hand in accordance with those terms.

(2) Subsection (1) applies only to an employee in an existing employment as specified in Schedule 2.

(3) In this Section, ***local terms of employment*** (本地僱用條款) and ***overseas terms of employment*** (海外僱用條款) have the meanings assigned to them respectively by Section 11 of Schedule 2.

(4) Nothing in this Section shall prejudice the operation of Section 8(2) and (3).

Section 15 Discrimination against Contract Workers

(1) This Section applies to any work for a person (***the principal***) that is available for doing by individuals (***contract workers***) who are employed not by the principal himself or herself but by a contractor or sub-contractor of the principal.

(2) It is unlawful for the principal, in relation to work to which this Section applies, to discriminate against a contract worker —

(a) in the terms on which the principal allows that contract worker to do that work;

(b) by not allowing the contract worker to do it or continue to do it;

(c) in the way the principal affords the contract worker access to any benefits, facilities or services, or by refusing or deliberately omitting to afford him or her access to them; or

(d) by subjecting the contract worker to any other detriment.

(3) The principal does not contravene subsection (2)(b) by doing any act in relation to a person not of a particular racial group at a time when, if the work were to be done by a person taken into the principal's employment, being of that racial group would be a genuine occupational qualification for the job.

(4) Without prejudice to Section 8(2) and (3), nothing in this Section renders unlawful any act done by the principal for the benefit of a contract worker not ordinarily resident in Hong Kong in or in connection with allowing the contract worker to do work to which this Section applies, where the purpose of the contract worker's being allowed to do that work is to provide him or her with training in skills which he or she appears to the principal to intend to exercise wholly outside Hong Kong.

(5) Without prejudice to Section 8(2) and (3), nothing in this Section renders unlawful any act done by the principal for the benefit of any contract worker in or in connection with allowing the contract worker to do work to which this Section applies, where —

(a) the work requires special skills, knowledge or experience not readily available in Hong Kong;

(b) the contract worker —

(i) possesses those skills, knowledge or experience; and

(ii) comes to do the work from a place outside Hong Kong; and

(c) the act is reasonably done for a person who comes from that place, having regard to —

(i) the prevailing terms of employment offered to persons with those skills, knowledge or experience in places outside Hong Kong; and

(ii) any other relevant circumstances (other than the race of the person).

(6) Subsection (2)(c) does not apply to benefits, facilities or services of any description if the principal is concerned with the provision (for payment or not) of benefits, facilities or services of that description to the public, or to a section of the public to which the contract worker in question belongs, unless that provision differs in a material respect from the provision of the benefits, facilities or services by the principal to his or her contract workers.

(7) In this Section —

contractor (承判商) means a person who undertakes any work for the principal under a contract that is entered into by the person directly with the principal;

sub-contractor (次承判商) means a person who enters into a contract with another person (whether or not a contractor of the principal) to undertake all or any part of the work that a contractor of the principal has undertaken.

Section 16 Meaning of Employment at Establishment in Hong Kong

(1) For the purposes of this Ordinance (***the relevant purposes***), employment is to be regarded as being at an establishment in Hong Kong unless the employee does his or her work wholly or mainly outside Hong Kong.

(2) Subsection (1) does not apply to —

(a) employment on board a ship registered in Hong Kong; or

(b) employment on an aircraft or a dynamically supported craft registered in Hong Kong and operated by a person whose principal place of business is in Hong Kong or who is ordinarily resident in Hong Kong,

but for the relevant purposes such employment is to be regarded as being at an establishment in Hong Kong unless the employee does his or her work wholly outside Hong Kong.

(3) In the case of employment on board a ship registered in Hong Kong (except where the employee does his or her work wholly outside Hong Kong) the ship is deemed for the relevant purposes to be the establishment.

(4) Where work is not done at an establishment it is to be treated for the relevant purposes as done at the establishment from which it is done or (where it is not done from any establishment) at the establishment with which it has the closest connection.

Discrimination by Other bodies

Section 17 Partnerships

(1) It is unlawful for a firm consisting of not less than 6 partners, in relation to a position as partner in the firm, to discriminate against a person —

(a) in the arrangements they make for the purpose of determining who should be offered that position;

(b) in the terms on which they offer the person that position;

(c) by refusing, or deliberately omitting to offer, the person that position; or

(d) in a case where the person already holds that position —

(i) in the way they afford the person access to any benefits, facilities or services, or by refusing or deliberately omitting to afford him or her access to them; or

(ii) by expelling the person from that position, or subjecting him or her to any other detriment.

(2) Subsection (1) applies in relation to persons proposing to form themselves into a partnership as it applies in relation to a firm.

(3) Subsection (1)(a) and (c) does not apply to a position as partner, where, if it were employment, being of a particular racial group would be a genuine occupational qualification for the job.

(4) Subject to subsection (5), subsection (1)(b) and (d) does not apply to provision in relation to death or retirement for a person made before the commencement date* in so far as any such provision continues for that person on and after that date.

---

* Commencement date: 10 July 2009.

(5) Subsection (1)(b) and (d) applies to provision made in relation to retirement of the kind mentioned in subsection (4) in so far as, in its application to such provision, it renders it unlawful for a firm to discriminate against a person —

(a) in such of the terms on which the firm offers the person a position as partner as provide for his or her expulsion from that position; or

(b) by expelling the person from a position as partner or subjecting him or her to any detriment which results in his or her expulsion from such a position.

(6) In the case of a limited partnership, references in subsection (1) to a partner shall be construed as references to a general partner within the meaning of Section 2(1) of the Limited Partnerships Ordinance (Cap. 37).

(7) The Chief Executive in Council may, by notice published in the Gazette, amend subsection (1) by —

(a) substituting another number for the number appearing in that subsection; or

(b) repealing the words and number appearing after "for a firm" and before ", in relation to".

Section 18 Organizations of Workers or Employers or Professional or Trade Organizations, etc.

(1) This Section applies to an organization of workers, an organization of employers, an organization of both workers and employers, or any other organization whose members carry on a particular profession or trade for the purposes of which the organization exists.

(2) It is unlawful for an organization to which this Section applies, in the case of a person who is not a member of the organization, to discriminate against the person —

(a) in the terms on which it is prepared to admit the person to membership; or

(b) by refusing, or deliberately omitting to accept, the person's application for membership.

(3) It is unlawful for an organization to which this Section applies, in the case of a person who is a member of the organization, to discriminate against the person —

(a) in the way it affords the person access to any benefits, facilities or services, or by refusing or deliberately omitting to afford him or her access to them;

(b) by depriving the person of his or her membership, or varying the terms on which he or she is a member; or

(c) by subjecting the person to any other detriment.

(4) This Section does not apply to provision in relation to the death or retirement from work of a member made before the commencement date* in so far as any such provision continues for that member on and after that date.

(5) Where, immediately before the enactment of this Ordinance, the main object of an organization to which this Section applies was to enable the benefits of membership to be enjoyed by persons of a particular racial group (defined otherwise than by reference to colour), then, in so far as that continues to be its main object, this Section is not to be construed as affecting that object and does not render unlawful an act which is done in order to give effect to that object.

(6) In determining whether the main object of an organization to which this Section applies is as stated in subsection (5), regard shall be had to —

(a) the essential character of the organization;

---

* Commencement date: 10 July 2009.

(b) the extent to which the affairs of the organization are so conducted that the persons primarily enjoying the benefits of membership are of the racial group in question; and

(c) any other relevant circumstances.

Section 19 Qualifying Bodies

(1) It is unlawful for an authority or body which can confer an authorization or qualification which is needed for, or facilitates, engagement in a particular profession or trade to discriminate against a person —

(a) in the terms on which it is prepared to confer on the person that authorization or qualification;

(b) by refusing, or deliberately omitting to grant, the person's application for it; or

(c) by withdrawing it from the person or varying the terms on which he or she holds it.

(2) Subsection (1) does not render unlawful any requirement for proficiency in either Chinese or English, or in both of them (whether or not to equivalent or comparable levels) imposed for the conferment of an authorization or qualification if —

(a) the requirement is reasonable, having regard to the demands of, or associated with, the profession or trade concerned; or

(b) without prejudice to paragraph (a), the authorization or qualification is one specified in Schedule 3.

(3) Where an authority or body is required by law to satisfy itself as to a person's good character before conferring on the person an authorization or qualification which is needed for, or facilitates, the person's engagement in any profession or trade then, without prejudice to any other duty to which it is subject, that requirement shall be taken to impose on the authority or body a duty to have regard to any evidence tending to show that the person, or any of his or her employees or agents (whether past or present), has —

(a) practised unlawful discrimination;

(b) engaged in unlawful harassment; or

(c) engaged in acts which contravene Section 45,

in, or in connection with, the carrying on of any profession or trade.

(4) Subsection (1) does not apply to discrimination which is rendered unlawful by Section 26.

(5) In this Section —

authorization or qualification (授權或資格) includes recognition, licensing, registration, enrolment, approval and certification;

confer (授予) includes renew or extend.

Section 20 Persons Concerned with Provision of Vocational Training

(1) It is unlawful, in the case of a person (***the first-mentioned person***) seeking or undergoing training which would help to fit him or her for employment, for any person (***the second-mentioned person***) who provides, or makes arrangements for the provision of, facilities for such training to discriminate against the first-mentioned person —

(a) in the terms on which the second-mentioned person affords the first-mentioned person access to any training course or other facilities concerned with such training;

(b) by refusing, or deliberately omitting to afford, the first-mentioned person such access;

(c) by terminating the first-mentioned person's training; or

(d) by subjecting the first-mentioned person to any other detriment during the course of his or her training.

(2) Nothing in subsection (1) is to be construed as requiring a person who provides, or makes arrangements for the provision of, facilities for such training —

(a) to modify for persons of any racial group its arrangements regarding holidays or medium of instruction; or

(b) to make different arrangements regarding holidays or medium of instruction for persons of any racial group.

(3) Subsection (1) does not apply to —

(a) discrimination which is rendered unlawful by any of the provisions of Section 10 or 26; or

(b) discrimination which would be rendered unlawful by any of those provisions but for the operation of any other provision of this Ordinance.

Section 21 Employment Agencies

(1) It is unlawful for an employment agency to discriminate against a person —

(a) in the terms on which the agency offers to provide any of its services;

(b) by refusing, or deliberately omitting to provide, any of its services; or

(c) in the way it provides any of its services.

(2) References in subsection (1) to the services of an employment agency include guidance on careers and any other services related to employment.

(3) This Section does not apply if the discrimination only concerns employment which the employer could lawfully refuse to offer the person.

(4) An employment agency is not subject to any liability under this Section if it proves —

(a) that it acted in reliance on a statement made to it by the employer to the effect that, by reason of the operation of subsection (3), its action would not be unlawful; and

(b) that it was reasonable for it to rely on the statement.

(5) A person who knowingly or recklessly makes a statement of the kind referred to in subsection (4)(a) which in a material respect is false or misleading commits an offence and is liable on conviction to a fine at level 4.

Section 22 Discrimination against Commission Agents

(1) This Section applies to any work for a person (***the principal***) that is available for doing by individuals (***commission agents***) as the agents of the principal and who are remunerated, whether in whole or in part, by commission.

(2) It is unlawful for the principal, in relation to work to which this Section applies, to discriminate against a person who is a commission agent —

(a) in the terms on which he or she allows the person to do that work;

(b) by not allowing the person to do it or continue to do it;

(c) in the way he or she affords the person access to any benefits, facilities or services, or by refusing or deliberately omitting to afford the person access to them; or

(d) by subjecting the person to any other detriment.

(3) The principal does not contravene subsection (2)(b) by doing any act in relation to a person not of a particular racial group at a time when, if the work were to be done by a person taken into the

principal's employment, being of that racial group would be a genuine occupational qualification for the job.

(4) Subsection (2)(c) does not apply to benefits, facilities or services of any description if the principal is concerned with the provision (for payment or not) of benefits, facilities or services of that description to the public, or to a section of the public to which the person belongs, unless that provision differs in a material respect from the provision of the benefits, facilities or services by the principal to his or her commission agents.

Special Cases

Section 23 Employment, etc. for Religion

(1) Nothing in this Part applies to employment for the purposes of an organized religion where the employment is limited to a particular racial group so as to comply with the doctrines of the religion or to avoid offending the religious susceptibilities common to its followers.

(2) Nothing in Section 19 applies to an authorization or qualification (within the meaning of that Section) for the purposes of an organized religion where the authorization or qualification is limited to a particular racial group so as to comply with the doctrines of the religion or to avoid offending the religious susceptibilities common to its followers.

Harassment

Section 24 Employees, etc.

(1) It is unlawful for a person, in relation to employment by that person at an establishment in Hong Kong, to harass a person who is seeking to be employed by that person.

(2) It is unlawful for a person (***the first-mentioned person***), in the case of a person employed by that first-mentioned person at an establishment in Hong Kong, to harass that other person.

(3) It is unlawful for a person, who is employed by another person (***the second-mentioned person***) at an establishment in Hong Kong to harass a person who is seeking to be, or who is, employed by that second-mentioned person.

(4) It is unlawful for the principal, in relation to work to which Section 15 applies, to harass another person who is a contract worker.

(5) It is unlawful for a contract worker to harass another person who is a fellow contract worker.

(6) It is unlawful for a partner of a firm to harass a person who is seeking to be, or who is, a partner in the firm.

(7) Subsection (6) applies in relation to persons proposing to form themselves into a partnership as it applies in relation to a firm.

(8) Section 17(6) applies to subsection (6) as it applies to Section 17(1).

(9) It is unlawful for the principal, in relation to work to which Section 22 applies, to harass a person who is a commission agent.

(10) It is unlawful for a commission agent to harass a person who is a fellow commission agent.

(11) It is unlawful for a person who is seeking to be, or who is, employed by a person at an establishment in Hong Kong to harass the second-mentioned person.

(12) It is unlawful for a person residing in any premises to harass another person who is —

(a) employed by a third person at an establishment in Hong Kong (whether or not the third person also resides in those premises and whether or not those premises are that establishment); and

(b) carrying out in those premises all or part of his or her work in relation to the employment (whether or not he or she resides in those premises).

Section 24A Harassment at Workplace

(1) It is unlawful for a person who is a workplace participant to harass another person who is also a workplace participant at a workplace of them both.

(2) In this Section —

intern (實習人員) means a person who is engaged by another person for an internship but is not an employee of that other person;

internship (實習) means —

(a) a period of work the completion of which is required for attaining a professional or academic qualification and includes a pupillage; or

(b) any other work that is usually described as an internship;

volunteer (義工) means a person who performs volunteer work other than in the capacity of an employer or employee;

workplace (工作場所), in relation to a person, means a place —

(a) at which the person works as a workplace participant; or

(b) that the person attends as a workplace participant;

workplace participant (場所使用者) means —

(a) an employee;

(b) an employer;

(c) a contract worker;

(d) the principal, within the meaning of Section 15(1), of a contract worker;

(e) a commission agent;

(f) the principal, within the meaning of Section 22(1), of a commission agent;

(g) a partner in a firm;

(h) an intern; or

(i) a volunteer.

(Added 8 of 2020 s. 30)

Section 25 Other Harassment

(1) It is unlawful for a member of an organization to which Section 18 applies to harass a person who is seeking to be, or who is, a member of that organization.

(2) It is unlawful for a member of an authority or body referred to in Section 19 to harass a person who is seeking an authorization or qualification (within the meaning of that Section) which can be conferred by the authority or body or to harass a person holding such an authorization or qualification. This subsection does not apply to harassment which is rendered unlawful by Section 38.

(3) It is unlawful for a person to harass another person who is seeking or undergoing training which would help to fit that other person for any employment if the person provides, or makes arrangements for the provision of, facilities for such training. This subsection does not apply to harassment which is rendered unlawful by Section 24(1) or (2) or 38.

(4) It is unlawful for a person who —

(a) operates an employment agency; or

(b) is a member of the staff of an employment agency,

to harass a person to whom the agency provides any of the agency's services or who is seeking the provision of such services.

Part 4 Discrimination and Harassment in Other Fields

(Format changes — E.R. 5 of 2018)

Education

Section 26 Discrimination by Responsible Bodies for Educational Establishments

(1) It is unlawful for the responsible body for an educational establishment to discriminate against a person —

(a) in the terms on which it offers to admit that person to the establishment as a student;

(b) by refusing, or deliberately omitting to accept, an application for that person's admission to the establishment as a student; or

(c) where the person is a student of the establishment —

(i) in the way it affords the person access to any benefits, facilities or services, or by refusing or deliberately omitting to afford the person access to them; or

(ii) by expelling the person from the establishment or subjecting him or her to any other detriment.

(2) Nothing in subsection (1) is to be construed as requiring the responsible body for an educational establishment —

(a) to modify for persons of any racial group arrangements of the establishment regarding holidays or medium of instruction; or

(b) to make different arrangements regarding holidays or medium of instruction for persons of any racial group.

Goods, Facilities, Services and Premises

Section 27 Discrimination in Provision of Goods, Facilities or Services

(1) It is unlawful for any person (***the first-mentioned person***) concerned with the provision (for payment or not) of goods, facilities or services to the public or a section of the public to discriminate against another person (***the second-mentioned person***) who seeks to obtain or use those goods, facilities or services —

(a) by refusing, or deliberately omitting to provide, the second-mentioned person with any of them; or

(b) by refusing or deliberately omitting to provide the second-mentioned person with goods, facilities or services of the like quality, in the like manner and on the like terms as are normal in the first-mentioned person's case in relation to other members of the public or (where the second-mentioned person belongs to a section of the public) to other members of that section.

(2) The following are examples of the facilities and services referred to in subsection (1) —

(a) access to and use of any place which members of the public or a section of the public are permitted to enter;

(b) accommodation in a hotel, guesthouse or other similar establishment;
(c) facilities by way of banking or insurance or for grants, loans, credit or finance;
(d) facilities for education;
(e) facilities for entertainment, recreation or refreshment;
(f) facilities for transport or travel;
(g) the services of any profession or trade;
(h) the services of —
  (i) any department of the Government; or
  (ii) any undertaking by or of the Government.

Section 28 Discrimination in Disposal or Management of Premises

(1) It is unlawful for a person, in relation to premises in Hong Kong of which that person has power to dispose, to discriminate against another person —
  (a) in the terms on which the person offers that other person the premises;
  (b) by refusing the other person's application for those premises; or
  (c) in the person's treatment of the other person in relation to any list of persons in need of the premises of that description.

(2) It is unlawful for a person, in relation to premises managed by that person, to discriminate against another person (***the second-mentioned person***) —
  (a) in the way he or she affords the second-mentioned person access to any benefits or facilities, or by refusing or deliberately omitting to afford the second-mentioned person access to them; or
  (b) by evicting the second-mentioned person, or subjecting him or her to any other detriment.

(3) Subsection (1) does not apply to a person who owns an estate or interest in the premises and wholly occupies them unless the person uses the services of an estate agent for the purposes of the disposal of the premises, or publishes or causes to be published, an advertisement in connection with the disposal.

(4) In this Section, ***power to dispose*** (有權處置), in relation to premises, includes the power to sell, rent, let, sub-let or otherwise part with possession of those premises.

Section 29 Discrimination: Consent for Assignment or Sub-letting

(1) Where the licence or consent of a landlord or of any other person is required for the disposal to any person of premises in Hong Kong comprised in a tenancy, it is unlawful for the landlord or other person to discriminate against a person (***assignee/sublettee***) by withholding the licence or consent for disposal of the premises to the assignee/sublettee.

(2) Subsection (1) does not apply if —
  (a) the person withholding the licence or consent or a near relative of that person (***the relevant occupier***) resides, and intends to continue to reside, on the premises;
  (b) there is on the premises, in addition to the accommodation occupied by the relevant occupier, accommodation (not being storage accommodation or means of access) shared by the relevant occupier with other persons residing on the premises who are not members of the relevant occupier's household; and
  (c) the premises are small premises as construed according to Section 30(2).

(3) For the avoidance of doubt, it is declared that this Section applies to tenancies created before the enactment of this Ordinance as well as to tenancies created on or after the enactment of this Ordinance.

(4) In this Section —

disposal (處置), in relation to premises comprised in a tenancy, includes assignment of the tenancy and sub-letting or parting with possession of the premises or any part of the premises;

tenancy (租賃) means a tenancy created —

(a) by a lease or sub-lease;

(b) by a tenancy agreement; or

(c) pursuant to any agreement.

Section 30 Exceptions for Small Dwellings

(1) Sections 27(1) and 28 do not apply to the provision by a person of accommodation in any premises, or the disposal of premises, by the person, if—

(a) that person or a near relative of that person (***the relevant occupier***) resides, and intends to continue to reside, on the premises;

(b) there is on the premises, in addition to the accommodation occupied by the relevant occupier, accommodation (not being storage accommodation or means of access) shared by the relevant occupier with other persons residing on the premises who are not members of the relevant occupier's household; and

(c) the premises are small premises.

(2) Premises are to be treated for the purposes of subsection (1) as small premises if—

(a) in the case of premises comprising residential accommodation for one or more households (under separate letting or similar agreements) in addition to the accommodation occupied by the relevant occupier —

(i) there is not normally residential accommodation on the premises for more than 2 such households; and

(ii) only the relevant occupier and any member of his or her household reside in the accommodation occupied by the relevant occupier; and

(b) in the case of premises not falling within paragraph (a), there is not normally residential accommodation on the premises for more than 6 persons in addition to the relevant occupier and any members of his or her household.

(3) The Chief Executive in Council may, by notice published in the Gazette, amend subsection (2)(b) by substituting another number for the number appearing in that subsection.

Section 31 Exceptions for Voluntary Bodies

(1) Sections 27(1) and 28 are not to be construed as rendering unlawful —

(a) the restriction of membership of any voluntary body to persons of a particular racial group (disregarding any minor exceptions); or

(b) the provision of benefits, facilities or services to members of any voluntary body where the membership is so restricted,

even though membership of the body is open to the public, or to a section of the public.

(2) Nothing in Section 27(1) or 28 —

(a) is to be construed as affecting a specified provision; or

(b) renders unlawful an act which is done in order to give effect to a specified provision.

(3) In this Section –

specified provision (指明規定) means a provision for conferring benefits on persons of a particular racial group (disregarding any benefits to persons of another racial group which are exceptional or are relatively insignificant), being a provision which constitutes the main object of a voluntary body;

voluntary body (志願團體) means a body the activities of which are carried on otherwise than for profit.

Section 32 Exceptions for Cemeteries

Nothing in Section 27(1), 28 or 29(1) renders unlawful –

(a) any act to set aside or allocate a cemetery, crematorium or columbarium (in whole or in part) for the reception of human remains of persons belonging to any particular community, race or religion;

(b) any act to provide goods, facilities or services in a cemetery, crematorium or columbarium, or part of it, that is so set aside or allocated; or

(c) any act done in connection with an act referred to in paragraph (a) or (b).

Section 33 Further Exceptions

(1) Section 27(1) does not apply to anything done by a person as a participant in arrangements under which he or she (for reward or not) takes into his or her home, and treats as if they were members of his or her family, any children, elderly persons or persons requiring a special degree of care and attention.

(2) Sections 27(1) and 28 do not apply –

(a) to discrimination which is rendered unlawful by any provision or Part of this Ordinance specified in column 2 of Schedule 4; or

(b) to discrimination which would be so unlawful but for any provision or Part of this Ordinance specified in column 3 of that Schedule.

Public Bodies, etc.

Section 34 Discrimination in Eligibility to Stand for Election, etc.

(1) It is unlawful for a person to discriminate against another person in –

(a) determining the eligibility of a person to stand for election to a relevant body or relevant position, or to be selected for a relevant position;

(b) the terms or conditions on which a person is considered eligible to stand for election to a relevant body or relevant position, or to be selected for a relevant position;

(c) determining the eligibility of a person to vote in elections of members of a relevant body or the holder of a relevant position;

(d) the terms or conditions on which a person is considered eligible to vote in elections of members of a relevant body or the holder of a relevant position, or to take part in the selection of the holder of a relevant position;

(e) considering whether a person should be appointed as a member of a relevant body, where some or all of the members of that body are appointed; or

(f) considering whether a person should be appointed to a relevant position, approved as a member of a relevant body or recognized as holding a relevant position.

(2) In this Section —

(a) a reference to a relevant body means a public body, a public authority, a statutory advisory body, or a prescribed body;

(b) a reference to a relevant position includes membership of a public body, a public authority, and a prescribed position.

Barristers

Section 35 Discrimination by, or in Relation to, Barristers

(1) It is unlawful for a barrister or barrister's clerk, in relation to any offer of a pupillage or a tenancy, to discriminate against a person —

(a) in the arrangements which are made for the purpose of determining to whom it should be offered;

(b) in respect of any terms on which it is offered; or

(c) by refusing, or deliberately omitting, to offer it to that person.

(2) It is unlawful for a barrister or barrister's clerk, in relation to a person who is a pupil or a tenant in the chambers concerned, to discriminate against that person —

(a) in respect of any terms applicable to that person as a pupil or a tenant;

(b) in the opportunities for training, or gaining experience, which are afforded or denied to that person;

(c) in the benefits, facilities or services which are afforded or denied to that person; or

(d) by terminating that person's pupillage or by subjecting him or her to any pressure to leave the chambers or other detriment.

(3) It is unlawful for any person, in relation to the giving, withholding or acceptance of instructions to a barrister, to discriminate against a person.

(4) In this Section —

barrister's clerk (大律師書記) includes any person carrying out any of the functions of a barrister's clerk;

pupil (見習大律師), ***pupillage*** (見習職位), ***tenancy*** (租賃) and ***tenant*** (承租人) have the meanings commonly associated with their use in the context of a set of barrister's chambers.

Clubs

Section 36 Discrimination by Clubs

(1) It is unlawful for a club, the committee of management of a club or a member of the committee of management of a club to discriminate against a person who is not a member of the club —

(a) by refusing or failing to accept the person's application for membership; or

(b) in the terms or conditions on which the club is prepared to admit the person to membership.

(2) It is unlawful for a club, the committee of management of a club or a member of the committee of management of a club to discriminate against a person who is a member of the club —

(a) by refusing or failing to accept the person's application for a particular class or type of membership;

(b) in the terms or conditions of membership that is afforded to the person;

(c) by denying the person access, or limiting his or her access, to any benefits, services or facilities provided by the club;

(d) by depriving the person of membership or varying the terms of membership; or

(e) by subjecting the person to any other detriment.

Section 37 Exception from Section 36 for Certain Clubs

(1) Section 36 does not apply to, or in relation to, a club the main object of which is to enable the benefits of membership to be enjoyed by persons of a particular racial group defined otherwise than by reference to colour.

(2) In determining whether the main object of a club is as stated in subsection (1), regard shall be had to —

(a) the essential character of the club;

(b) the extent to which the affairs of the club are so conducted that the persons primarily enjoying the benefits of membership are of the racial group in question; and

(c) any other relevant circumstances.

(3) Where the main object of a club is to enable the benefits of membership to be enjoyed by persons of a number of different racial groups defined otherwise than by reference to colour —

(a) nothing in Section 36 shall render unlawful any arrangements concerning membership which is designed to give effect to such object; and

(b) nothing in Section 36 shall render unlawful a provision to which this paragraph applies or any act done in order to give effect to such a provision.

(4) Subsection (3)(b) applies to a provision which is designed to ensure that the committee of management of the club includes, in relation to each of the relevant racial groups, a minimum number of members, and —

(a) which for that purpose —

(i) reserves seats for each of those racial groups on that committee; or

(ii) makes extra seats available for persons of any such racial group when the number of persons of that racial group in the other seats falls below the minimum; and

(b) which, in the opinion of the club or its committee of management, is needed in the circumstances to secure a reasonable lower limit to the number of members of each of those racial groups serving on the committee.

(5) In determining whether the main object of a club is as stated in subsection (3), regard shall be had to —

(a) the essential character of the club;

(b) the extent to which the affairs of the club are so conducted that the persons primarily enjoying the benefits of membership are of the different racial groups in question; and

(c) any other relevant circumstances.

Harassment

Section 38 Educational Establishments

(1) It is unlawful for a person who is, or is a member of, the responsible body for an educational establishment to harass a person who is seeking to be, or who is, a student of the establishment.

(2) It is unlawful for a person who is a member of the staff of an educational establishment to harass a person who is seeking to be, or who is, a student of the establishment.

(3) It is unlawful for a person who is a student of an educational establishment to harass a person who is seeking to be, or who is, a student of the establishment.

(4) It is unlawful for a person who is seeking to be, or who is, a student of an educational establishment to harass a person —

(a) who is, or is a member of, the responsible body for the establishment; or

(b) who is a member of the staff of the establishment.

Section 39 Other Harassment

(1) It is unlawful for a person concerned with the provision of goods, facilities or services to harass another person who seeks to obtain or use those goods, facilities or services or to whom the person provides those goods, facilities or services.

(1A) It is unlawful for a person who —

(a) seeks to obtain or use goods, facilities or services; or

(b) is provided with goods, facilities or services,

to harass another person who is concerned with the provision of the goods, facilities or services. *(Added 8 of 2020 s. 36)*

(2) It is unlawful for a person, in relation to premises in Hong Kong of which that person has power to dispose, to harass another person who applies for those premises.

(3) It is unlawful for a person, in relation to premises managed by that person, to harass a person occupying the premises.

(4) Where the licence or consent of the landlord or of any other person is required for the disposal to any person of premises in Hong Kong comprised in a tenancy, it is unlawful for the landlord or other person to harass a person seeking the licence or consent for the disposal of the premises to him or her, or a person from whom the licence or consent is withheld.

(5) Subsections (1), (1A), (2), (3) and (4) do not apply to harassment which is rendered unlawful by Section 24, 24A, 25 or 38. *(Amended 8 of 2020 ss. 31 and 36)*

(6) Section 29(4) applies to subsection (4) as it applies to Section 29.

(7) It is unlawful for a barrister or barrister's clerk, in relation to any chambers, to harass a person who is, or has applied to be, a pupil or tenant in the chambers.

(8) It is unlawful for any person, in the course of giving, withholding or acceptance of instructions to a barrister, to harass a person.

(9) Section 35(4) applies to subsections (7) and (8) as it applies to Section 35.

(10) It is unlawful for a club, the committee of management of a club or a member of the committee of management of a club to harass a person who is, or has applied to be, a member of the club.

Extent

Section 40 Extent of Part 4

(1) Section 27(1) —

(a) does not apply to goods, facilities or services outside Hong Kong except as provided in subsections (2) and (3); and

(b) does not apply to facilities —

(i) by way of banking or insurance; or

(ii) for grants, loans, credit or finance,

where the facilities are for a purpose to be carried out, or in connection with risks wholly or mainly arising, outside Hong Kong.

(2) Section 27(1) applies to the provision of facilities for travel outside Hong Kong where the refusal or omission occurs in Hong Kong or on a ship, aircraft or dynamically supported craft referred to in subsection (3).

(3) Section 27(1) applies on and in relation to —

(a) any ship registered in Hong Kong;

(b) any aircraft or dynamically supported craft registered in Hong Kong and operated by a person whose principal place of business is in Hong Kong or who is ordinarily resident in Hong Kong; or

(c) any ship, aircraft or dynamically supported craft belonging to or possessed by the Government,

even if the ship, aircraft or craft is outside Hong Kong.

(4) This Section does not render unlawful an act done in or over a place outside Hong Kong, or in or over that place's territorial waters for the purpose of complying with the laws of that place.

(5) Section 26 does not apply to benefits, facilities or services outside Hong Kong except —

(a) travel on a ship registered in Hong Kong; or

(b) benefits, facilities or services provided on a ship so registered.

(6) Section 39(1) and (1A) does not apply to an act of harassment that is committed outside Hong Kong except as provided in subsection (7). *(Added 8 of 2020 s. 38)*

(7) Section 39(1) and (1A) applies to an act of harassment that is committed on a ship, aircraft or dynamically supported craft referred to in subsection (3)(a), (b) or (c) even if it is outside Hong Kong when the act is committed. *(Added 8 of 2020 s. 38)*

Part 5 Other Unlawful Acts

(Format changes — E.R. 5 of 2018)

Section 41 Discriminatory Practices

(1) In this Section, ***discriminatory practice*** (歧視性的做法) means the application of a requirement or condition

(a) which results in an act of discrimination which is unlawful by virtue of any provision of Part 3 or 4 as read with Section 4(1)(b); or

(b) which would be likely to result in such an act of discrimination if the persons to whom it is applied were not all of the same racial group.

(2) A person acts in contravention of this Section if and so long as the person —

(a) applies a discriminatory practice; or

(b) operates practices or other arrangements which in any circumstances would call for the application by the person of a discriminatory practice.

(3) Proceedings in respect of a contravention of this Section may be brought only by the Commission and any such proceedings must be brought in accordance with Sections 71, 72, 73, 74 and 75.

Section 42 Discriminatory Advertisements

(1) It is unlawful to publish or cause to be published an advertisement which indicates, or might reasonably be understood as indicating, an intention by a person to do any act which is or might be unlawful by virtue of Part 3 or 4.

(2) Subsection (1) does not apply to an advertisement if the intended act would not in fact be unlawful.

(3) For the purposes of subsection (1), use of a job description which is specific with reference to race is to be taken to indicate an intention to discriminate, unless the advertisement contains an indication to the contrary.

(4) The publisher of an advertisement made unlawful by subsection (1) is not subject to any liability under that subsection in respect of the publication of the advertisement if the publisher proves —

(a) that the advertisement was published in reliance on a statement made to the publisher by the person who caused it to be published to the effect that, by reason of the operation of subsection (2), the publication would not be unlawful; and

(b) that it was reasonable for the publisher to rely on the statement.

(5) A person who knowingly or recklessly makes a statement of the kind referred to in subsection (4)(a) which in a material respect is false or misleading commits an offence and is liable on conviction to a fine at level 4.

Section 43 Instructions to Discriminate

It is unlawful for a person —

(a) who has authority over another person; or

(b) in accordance with whose wishes that other person is accustomed to act,

to instruct that other person to do any act which is unlawful by virtue of Part 3 or 4, or procure or attempt to procure the doing by him or her of any such act.

Section 44 Pressure to Discriminate

(1) It is unlawful to induce, or attempt to induce, a person to do any act which contravenes Part 3 or 4 by —

(a) providing or offering to provide the person with any benefit; or

(b) subjecting or threatening to subject the person to any detriment.

(2) An offer or threat is not prevented from falling within subsection (1) because it is not made directly to the person concerned, if it is made in such a way that he or she is likely to hear of it.

Section 45 Vilification

(1) It is unlawful for a person, by any activity in public, to incite hatred towards, serious contempt for, or severe ridicule of, another person or members of a class of persons on the ground of the race of the person or members of the class of persons.

(2) For the purposes of subsection (1), it is immaterial whether a person is actually incited, by an activity, to —

(a) hatred towards;

(b) serious contempt for; or

(c) severe ridicule of,

another person or members of a class of persons on the ground of the race of the person or members of the class of persons.

(3) Nothing in this Section renders unlawful —

(a) a fair report on an activity in public;

(b) an activity in public that —

(i) is a communication or the distribution or dissemination of any matter; and

(ii) consists of a publication which is subject to a defence of absolute privilege in proceedings for defamation; or

(c) an activity in public done reasonably and in good faith, for academic, artistic, scientific or research purposes or for other purposes in the public interest, including discussions about and expositions of any matter.

(4) In this Section and Section 46, ***activity in public*** (公開活動) includes any of the following activities, whether or not the person carrying out the activity is in a public place while carrying out the activity —

(a) any form of communication to the public, including speaking, writing, printing, displaying notices, broadcasting, screening and playing of tapes or other recorded material;

(b) any conduct (not being a form of communication referred to in paragraph (a)) observable by the public, including actions and gestures and the wearing or display of clothing, signs, flags, emblems and insignia;

(c) the distribution or dissemination of any matter to the public.

Section 46 Offence of Serious Vilification

(1) A person commits an offence if —

(a) the person, by any activity, incites hatred towards, serious contempt for, or severe ridicule of, another person (***the second-mentioned person***) or members of a class of persons, on the ground of the race of the second-mentioned person or the members of the class of persons;

(b) the person intentionally incites such hatred, serious contempt or severe ridicule on such ground; and

(c) the activity is an activity in public and consists of threatening physical harm, or inciting others to threaten physical harm —

(i) towards, or towards any premises or property of, the second-mentioned person or the members of the class of persons; or

(ii) towards the premises or property of any other person to which the second-mentioned person or the members of the class of persons have access.

(2) For the purposes of subsection (1)(a), it is immaterial whether a person is actually incited, by an activity, to —

(a) hatred towards;

(b) serious contempt for; or

(c) severe ridicule of,

another person or members of a class of persons on the ground of the race of the person or members of the class of persons.

(3) A person who commits an offence under subsection (1) is liable on conviction to a fine at level 6 and to imprisonment for 2 years.

Section 47 Liability of Employers and Principals

(1) Anything done by a person in the course of the person's employment is to be treated for the purposes of this Ordinance as done by that person's employer as well as by that person, whether or not it was done with the employer's knowledge or approval.

(2) Anything done by a person (***the first-mentioned person***) as agent for another person (***the second-mentioned person***) with the authority (whether express or implied, and whether precedent or subsequent) of the second-mentioned person is to be treated for the purposes of this Ordinance as done by the second-mentioned person as well as the first-mentioned person.

(3) In proceedings brought under this Ordinance against any other person in respect of an act alleged to have been done by an employee of that person, it is a defence for that other person to prove that he or she took such steps as were reasonably practicable to prevent the employee from doing that act, or from doing in the course of the employee's employment acts of that description.

(4) For the avoidance of doubt, it is declared that this Section does not apply for the purposes of any criminal proceedings.

Section 47A Liability of Persons Engaging Interns and Volunteers

(1) This Section applies for the purposes of Section 24A.

(2) For the avoidance of doubt, this Section does not apply for the purposes of any criminal proceedings.

(3) An act done by an intern in the course of an internship is to be treated as an act done —

(a) by the intern; and

(b) by the person who engaged the intern for the internship, whether or not the act was done with the knowledge or approval of that person.

(4) In proceedings brought under this Ordinance against a person in respect of an act alleged to have been done by an intern engaged by the person, it is a defence for the person to prove that the person took reasonably practicable steps to prevent the intern —

(a) from doing that act; or

(b) from doing acts of that description in the course of the internship.

(5) Subsections (6) and (7) apply if a volunteer is engaged by another person to perform volunteer work.

(6) An act done by a volunteer in the course of performing volunteer work is to be treated as an act done —

(a) by the volunteer; and

(b) by the person who engaged the volunteer to perform the work, whether or not the act was done with the knowledge or approval of that person.

(7) In proceedings brought under this Ordinance against a person in respect of an act alleged to have been done by a volunteer engaged by the person, it is a defence for the person to prove that the person took reasonably practicable steps to prevent the volunteer —

(a) from doing that act; or

(b) from doing acts of that description in the course of performing volunteer work.

(Added 8 of 2020 s. 32)

Section 48 Aiding Unlawful Acts

(1) A person who knowingly aids another person to do an act made unlawful by this Ordinance is to be treated for the purposes of this Ordinance as himself or herself doing an unlawful act of the like description.

(2) For the purposes of subsection (1), an employee or agent for whose act the employer or principal is liable under Section 47 (or would be so liable but for Section 47(3)) is deemed to aid the doing of the act by the employer or principal.

(2A) For the purposes of subsection (1), if a person who engaged an intern —

(a) is liable under Section 47A for an act done by the intern; or

(b) would be liable under Section 47A for the act but for Section 47A(4),

the intern is deemed to aid the doing of the act by that person. *(Added 8 of 2020 s. 33)*

(2B) For the purposes of subsection (1), if a person who engaged a volunteer —

(a) is liable under Section 47A for an act done by the volunteer; or

(b) would be liable under Section 47A for the act but for Section 47A(7),

the volunteer is deemed to aid the doing of the act by that person. *(Added 8 of 2020 s. 33)*

(3) A person (***the first-mentioned person***) does not under this Section knowingly aid another person (***the second-mentioned person***) to do an unlawful act if —

(a) the first-mentioned person acts on a statement made to him or her by the second-mentioned person that, by reason of any provision of this Ordinance, the act which the first-mentioned person aids would not be unlawful; and

(b) it is reasonable for the first-mentioned person to rely on that statement.

(4) A person who knowingly or recklessly makes a statement of the kind referred to in subsection (3)(a) which in a material respect is false or misleading commits an offence and is liable on conviction to a fine at level 4.

Part 6 Matters Not Affected by Parts 3, 4 and 5

(Format changes — E.R. 5 of 2018)

Section 49 Special Measures

Nothing in Part 3, 4 or 5 renders unlawful an act that is reasonably intended to —

(a) ensure that persons of a particular racial group have equal opportunities with other persons in circumstances in relation to which a provision is made by this Ordinance;

(b) afford persons of a particular racial group goods or access to services, facilities or opportunities to meet their special needs in relation to —

(i) employment, education, welfare or clubs; or

(ii) the provision of premises, goods, services or facilities; or

(c) afford persons of a particular racial group grants, benefits or programmes, whether direct or indirect, to meet their special needs in relation to —

(i) employment, education, welfare or clubs; or

(ii) the provision of premises, goods, services or facilities.

Section 50 Charities

(1) Nothing in Part 3, 4 or 5 —

(a) is to be construed as affecting a provision to which this subsection applies; or

(b) renders unlawful an act which is done in order to give effect to such a provision.

(2) Subsection (1) applies to a provision for conferring benefits on persons of a particular racial group (disregarding any benefits to persons of another racial group which are exceptional or relatively insignificant), being a provision which is contained in a charitable instrument.

(3) In applying this Section —

charitable instrument (慈善文書) means an enactment or other instrument so far as it relates to charitable purposes;

charitable purposes (慈善目的) means purposes which are exclusively charitable according to any enactment or rule of law.

Section 51 Discriminatory Training by Certain Bodies

(1) Nothing in Part 3, 4 or 5 renders unlawful any act done in relation to particular work by any person in, or in connection with —

(a) affording only persons of a particular racial group access to facilities for training which would help to fit them for that work; or

(b) encouraging only persons of a particular racial group to take advantage of opportunities for doing that work,

where it reasonably appears to that person that at any time within the 12 months immediately preceding the doing of the act —

(c) there were no persons of the racial group concerned doing that work in Hong Kong; or

(d) the number of persons of that racial group doing the work in Hong Kong was comparatively small.

(2) Subsection (1) does not apply in relation to any discrimination that is rendered unlawful by Section 10.

Section 52 Discriminatory Training by Employers, Organizations of Workers or Employers or Professional or Trade Organizations, etc.

(1) Nothing in Part 3, 4 or 5 renders unlawful any act done by an employer in relation to a particular work in his or her employment at a particular establishment in Hong Kong, being an act done in, or in connection with —

(a) affording only those of his or her employees working at that establishment who are of a particular racial group access to facilities for training which would help to fit them for that work; or

(b) encouraging only persons of a particular racial group to take advantage of opportunities for doing that work at that establishment,

where at any time within the 12 months immediately preceding the doing of the act —

(c) there were no persons of the racial group concerned among those doing that work at that establishment; or

(d) the number of persons of that racial group among those doing that work was comparatively small.

(2) Nothing in Section 18 renders unlawful any act done by an organization to which that Section applies in, or in connection with —

(a) affording only members of the organization who are of a particular racial group access to facilities for training which would help to fit them for holding a post of any kind in the organization; or

(b) encouraging only members of a particular racial group to take advantage of opportunities for holding such posts in the organization,

where at any time within the 12 months immediately preceding the doing of the act —

(c) there were no persons of the racial group concerned among persons holding such posts in the organization; or

(d) the number of persons of that racial group holding such posts was comparatively small.

(3) Nothing in Part 3, 4 or 5 renders unlawful any act done by an organization to which Section 18 applies in, or in connection with, encouraging persons of a particular racial group to become members of the organization where at any time within the 12 months immediately preceding the doing of the act —

(a) no persons of the racial group were members of that organization; or

(b) the proportion of persons of the racial group among members of that organization was comparatively small.

Section 53 Indirect Access to Benefits, etc.

(1) References in this Ordinance to the affording by any person of access to benefits, facilities or services —

(a) are not limited to benefits, facilities or services provided by that person himself or herself; but

(b) include any means by which it is in that person's power to facilitate access to benefits, facilities or services provided by any other person (***actual provider***).

(2) Where by any provision of this Ordinance the affording by any person of access to benefits, facilities or services in a discriminatory way is in certain circumstances prevented from being unlawful, the effect of the provision is to extend also to the liability under this Ordinance of any actual provider.

Section 54 Nationality Law, etc. Not Affected

Nothing in this Ordinance —

(a) is to be construed as affecting in any way any law concerning nationality, citizenship, resident status or naturalization; or

(b) renders unlawful any act done by any person in, or in connection with, the operation of any such law.

Section 55 Immigration Legislation

Nothing in Part 3, 4 or 5 affects, as regards a person not having the right to enter and remain in Hong Kong, any immigration legislation governing entry into, stay in and departure from Hong Kong, or the application of any such legislation.

Section 56 Acts Done under Statutory Authority Not Affected by Parts 3, 4 and 5

Nothing in Part 3, 4 or 5 renders unlawful any act done by a person if it was necessary for that person to do it in order to comply with a requirement of an existing statutory provision.

Section 57 Application to New Territories Land

Nothing in Part 4 or 5 —

(a) is to be construed as affecting the operation of any of the provisions of —

(i) the New Territories Ordinance (Cap. 97); or

(ii) the New Territories Leases (Extension) Ordinance (Cap. 150); or

(b) renders unlawful any act done by any person in, or in connection with, the operation of any of those provisions.

Section 58 Other Matters Not Affected

(1) No provision or Part of this Ordinance specified in column 2 of Schedule 5 renders unlawful any discrimination specified opposite thereto in column 3 of that Schedule.

(2) Nothing in Part 3, 4 or 5 renders unlawful any act done by any person —

(a) in connection with any discrimination which is not unlawful by virtue of the operation of subsection (1); and

(b) to the extent that it is done for the purposes of that discrimination.

Part 7 Commission

(Format changes — E.R. 1 of 2013)

Commission

Section 59 Functions and Powers of Commission

(1) The Commission shall —

(a) work towards the elimination of discrimination;

(b) promote equality of opportunity and harmony between persons of different racial groups generally;

(c) work towards the elimination of harassment and vilification;

(d) in the case of any act alleged to be unlawful by virtue of this Ordinance, encourage persons who are concerned with the matter to which act relates to effect a settlement of the matter by conciliation, whether under Section 78 or otherwise;

(e) keep under review the working of this Ordinance and when required to do so by the Chief Executive, or when it otherwise thinks fit, draw up and submit to the Chief Executive proposals for amending this Ordinance; and

(f) perform such other functions as are imposed on it under this Ordinance or any other enactment.

(2) The Commission may do all such things as are necessary for, or incidental or conducive to, the better performance of its functions.

(3) Without limiting subsection (1), the Commission may in particular —

(a) with the prior approval of the Chief Executive, become a member of or affiliate to any international body concerned (whether in whole or in part) with the elimination of discrimination; or

(b) exercise such powers as are conferred on it under this Ordinance.

Section 60 Review of Schedule 5

(1) Without limiting Section 59(1), the Commission, pursuant to its powers under paragraphs (a) and (b) of that Section, shall keep Schedule 5 under review.

(2) Whenever the Commission thinks it necessary, it shall draw up and submit to the Chief Executive proposals for amending Schedule 5.

Section 61 Restrictions on Delegation by Commission

The Commission may not under Section 67(1) of the Sex Discrimination Ordinance (Cap. 480) delegate any of its functions or powers under —

(a) Section 82;

(b) any provisions of any regulations made under Section 83 which are specified in the regulations as provisions which are not subject to Section 67 of the Sex Discrimination Ordinance (Cap. 480); or

(c) any provisions of any rules made under Section 82 which are specified in the rules as provisions which are not subject to that Section 67.

Section 62 Protection of Members of Commission, etc.

(1) No person to whom this subsection applies, acting in good faith, is personally liable in damages for any act done or default made in the performance or purported performance of any function, or the exercise or purported exercise of any power, imposed or conferred on the Commission under this Ordinance.

(2) The protection conferred by subsection (1) on any person to whom that subsection applies in respect of any act or default does not in any way affect the liability of the Commission for that act or default.

(3) Subsection (1) applies to the following persons — *(Amended 18 of 2014 s. 41)*

(a) a member of the Commission or a committee;

(b) an employee of the Commission;

(c) a conciliator.

(Amended 18 of 2014 s. 41)

Codes of Practice

Section 63 Codes of Practice

(1) The Commission may issue codes of practice containing such practical guidance as it thinks fit for the purposes of —

(a) the elimination of discrimination;

(b) the promotion of equality of opportunity and harmony between persons of different racial groups; or

(c) the elimination of harassment and vilification.

(2) When the Commission proposes to issue a code of practice, it shall prepare and publish (otherwise than in the Gazette) the code; it shall consider any representations made to it about the code and may modify the code accordingly.

(3) In the course of preparing any code of practice for eventual publication under subsection (2), the Commission shall consult such associations, organizations, associations of organizations or bodies as appear to the Commission to be appropriate including any associations, organizations, associations of organizations or bodies specified by the Secretary for Constitutional and Mainland Affairs by notice published in the Gazette.

(4) If the Commission determines to proceed with a code of practice published under subsection (2), it shall cause the code to be —

(a) published in the Gazette; and

(b) laid on the table of the Legislative Council at the next sitting after its publication in the Gazette.

(5) The Legislative Council may, by Resolution passed at a sitting of the Legislative Council held not later than 28 days after the sitting at which a code of practice is laid on the table of that Council (***the relevant period***), provide that the code of practice shall be amended in any manner consistent with this Section.

(6) If the relevant period would but for this Section expire after the end of a session or a dissolution of the Legislative Council, but on or before the day of its second sitting in the next session, the period for amending the code is deemed to be extended and expire on the day after that second sitting.

(7) The Legislative Council may, before the expiration of the relevant period, by Resolution extend the period for amending the code of practice to the first sitting of that Council held not earlier than the twenty-first day after the day of such expiration.

(8) Where the relevant period is extended under subsection (6), the Legislative Council may, before the expiration of the extended period, by Resolution extend that extended period to the first sitting of that Council held not earlier than the twenty-first day after the day of the second sitting in the next session referred to in that subsection.

(9) A Resolution passed by the Legislative Council in accordance with this Section shall be published in the Gazette not later than 14 days after the passing of the Resolution or within such further period as the Chief Executive may allow in a particular case.

(10) A code of practice shall come into operation —

(a) if on the expiration of the relevant period or that period as extended under subsection (6), (7) or (8), the Legislative Council has not passed a Resolution amending the code of practice, on the expiration of the relevant period or that period as so extended (as the case may be); and

(b) if the Legislative Council passes a Resolution amending the code of practice, at midnight on the day before the day on which the Resolution is published in the Gazette.

(11) A code of practice may contain such transitional provisions or savings as appear to the Commission to be necessary or expedient in connection with the matters which are the subject of the code.

(12) The Commission may from time to time revise the whole or any part of a code of practice and issue the revised code, and subsections (2), (3), (4), (5), (6), (7), (8), (9), (10) and (11) apply (with appropriate modifications) to a revised code.

(13) Without limiting subsection (1), a code of practice may include such practical guidance as the Commission thinks fit as to what steps it is reasonably practicable for employers to take for the purpose of preventing their employees from doing in the course of their employment acts made unlawful by this Ordinance.

(14) A failure on the part of any person to observe any provision of a code of practice shall not of itself render the person liable to any proceedings; but in any proceedings under this Ordinance before any court any code of practice issued under this Section shall be admissible in evidence, and if any provision of such a code appears to the court to be relevant to any question arising in the proceedings it shall be taken into account in determining that question.

(15) In this Section, ***sitting*** (會議), when used to calculate time, means the day on which the sitting commences and only includes a sitting at which subsidiary legislation is included in the order paper.

Investigations

Section 64 Power to Conduct Formal Investigations

Without limiting Section 59 —

(a) if the Commission thinks fit, it may conduct a formal investigation for any purpose connected with the carrying out of any of its functions under that Section; and

(b) if required by the Chief Secretary for Administration, the Commission shall conduct a formal investigation for any purpose connected with the carrying out of any of its functions under that Section.

Section 65 Terms of Reference

(1) The Commission shall not embark on a formal investigation unless the requirements of this Section have been complied with.

(2) The terms of reference for the formal investigation are to be drawn up by the Commission or, where the Chief Secretary for Administration requires the Commission to conduct the investigation, by the Chief Secretary for Administration after consulting the Commission.

(3) The Commission shall give general notice of the holding of the formal investigation unless the terms of reference confine it to activities of persons named in them, but in such a case the Commission shall in the prescribed manner give those persons notice of the holding of the investigation.

(4) Where the terms of reference of the formal investigation confine it to activities of persons named in them and the Commission in the course of the investigation proposes to investigate any act made unlawful by this Ordinance which it believes a person so named may have done, the Commission shall —

(a) inform that person of its belief and its proposal to investigate the act; and

(b) offer that person an opportunity of making oral or written representations with regard to it (or both oral and written representations as that person thinks fit).

(5) A person who avails himself of an opportunity to make oral representations under subsection (4)(b) may be represented —

(a) by counsel or a solicitor; or

(b) by some other person of the person's choice, not being a person to whom the Commission objects on the ground that he or she is unsuitable.

(6) The Commission may or, if the Commission was required by the Chief Secretary for Administration to conduct the formal investigation, the Chief Secretary for Administration after consulting the Commission may, from time to time, revise the terms of reference.

(7) Subsections (1), (3), (4) and (5) apply to the revised investigation and terms of reference as they apply to the original.

Section 66 Power to Obtain Information

(1) For the purposes of a formal investigation, the Commission, by a notice in the prescribed form served on a person in the prescribed manner, may —

(a) require the person to furnish such written information as may be described in the notice;

(b) specify the time at which, and the manner and form in which, the information is to be furnished; and

(c) require the person to attend at the time and place specified in the notice and give oral information about, and produce all documents in the person's possession or control relating to, any matter specified in the notice.

(2) Except as provided in Section 73, a notice may be served under subsection (1) only where —

(a) service of the notice has been authorized in writing by or on behalf of the Chief Secretary for Administration; or

(b) the terms of reference of the formal investigation —

(i) state that the Commission believes that a person named in them may have done or may be doing all or any of the acts described in subsection (3); and

(ii) confine the investigation to those acts.

(3) The acts referred to in subsection (2)(b)(i) are acts of the following descriptions —

(a) unlawful discriminatory acts;

(b) unlawful acts of harassment;

(c) contraventions of Section 41, 42, 43, 44 or 45.

(4) A notice under subsection (1) may not require a person —

(a) to give information, or produce any documents, which the person could not be compelled to give in evidence, or produce, in civil proceedings before the Court of First Instance; or

(b) to attend at any place unless the necessary expenses of the person's journey to and from that place are paid or tendered to him or her.

(5) If—

(a) a person fails to comply with a notice served on that person under subsection (1); or

(b) the Commission has reasonable cause to believe that that person intends not to comply with it,

the Commission may apply to the District Court for an order requiring the person to comply with the notice or with such directions for the like purpose as may be contained in the order; and Section 66A of the District Court Ordinance (Cap. 336) applies to failure without reasonable excuse to comply with any such order as it applies in the cases there provided.

(6) A person who —

(a) wilfully alters, suppresses, conceals or destroys a document which he or she has been required by a notice or order under this Section to produce; or

(b) in complying with such a notice or order, knowingly or recklessly makes any statement which in a material respect is false or misleading,

commits an offence.

(7) A person who commits an offence under subsection (6) is liable on conviction to a fine at level 4.

Section 67 Recommendations and Reports on Formal Investigations

(1) If in the light of its findings in a formal investigation it appears to the Commission necessary or expedient, whether during the course of the investigation or after its conclusion —

(a) to make to any persons, with a view to promoting equality of opportunity and harmony between persons of different racial groups who are affected by any of their activities, recommendations for changes in their policies or procedures, or as to any other matters; or

(b) to make to the Chief Secretary for Administration any recommendations, whether for changes in the law or otherwise, the Commission shall make those recommendations accordingly.

(2) The Commission shall prepare a report of its findings in any formal investigation conducted by it.

(3) If the formal investigation is one required by the Chief Secretary for Administration, the following applies —

(a) the Commission shall deliver the report to the Chief Secretary for Administration;

(b) the Chief Secretary for Administration shall cause the report to be published in such manner as he or she thinks fit; and

(c) unless required by the Chief Secretary for Administration, the Commission shall not publish the report.

(4) If the formal investigation is not one required by the Chief Secretary for Administration, the Commission shall publish the report or make it available for inspection in accordance with subsection (5).

(5) Where under subsection (4) a report is to be made available for inspection, any person shall be entitled, on payment of a reasonable fee, if any, as may be determined by the Commission —

(a) to inspect the report during ordinary office hours and take copies of the whole report or any part of it; or

(b) to obtain from the Commission a copy, certified by the Commission to be correct, of the report.

(6) The Commission may, if it thinks fit, determine that the right conferred by subsection (5)(a) is exercisable in relation to a copy of the report, instead of, or in addition to, the original.

(7) The Commission shall give general notice of the place or places where, and the times when, the report or a copy of it may be inspected.

Section 68 Restrictions on Disclosure of Information

(1) No information given to the Commission by any person (***the informant***) in connection with a formal investigation shall be disclosed by the Commission, any member of the Commission or a committee, any employee of the Commission, any conciliator, or any person who has been such a member, employee or conciliator, except —

(a) on the order of any court;

(b) with the informant's consent;

(c) in the form of a summary or other general statement published by the Commission which does not identify the informant or any other person to whom the information relates;

(d) in a report of the investigation published by the Commission or made available for inspection under Section 67(5);

(e) to members of the Commission or a committee, employees of the Commission or conciliators or, so far as may be necessary for the proper performance of the functions of the Commission, to other persons; or

(f) for the purpose of any civil proceedings under this Ordinance to which the Commission is a party, or any criminal proceedings.

(2) Any person who discloses information in contravention of subsection (1) commits an offence and is liable on conviction to a fine at level 4.

(3) In preparing any report for publication or for inspection, the Commission shall exclude, so far as it is consistent with its functions and the object of the report, any matter which relates to the private affairs of any individual or business interests of any person where the publication of that matter might, in the opinion of the Commission, prejudicially affect that individual or person.

Part 8 Enforcement

(Format changes — E.R. 1 of 2013)

General

Section 69 Restrictions on Proceedings for Contravention of Ordinance

(1) Except as otherwise provided by this Ordinance, no proceedings, whether civil or criminal, lie against any person in respect of an act by reason that the act is unlawful by virtue of a provision of this Ordinance.

(2) Subsection (1) does not preclude the making of an order of certiorari, mandamus or prohibition.

Section 70 Claims in Respect of Discrimination, Harassment and Vilification

(1) A claim by or on behalf of any person (***the claimant***) that another person (***the respondent***) —

(a) has committed an act of discrimination against the claimant which is unlawful by virtue of Part 3 or 4;

(b) has committed an act of harassment against the claimant which is unlawful by virtue of Part 3 or 4;

(c) has committed an act which is unlawful by virtue of Section 45; or

(d) is to be treated, by virtue of Section 47, 47A or 48, as having committed an act of discrimination or harassment referred to in paragraph (a) or (b) against the claimant or an act referred to in paragraph (c), *(Amended 8 of 2020 s. 34)*

may be made the subject of civil proceedings in like manner as any other claim in tort.

(2) Subsection (1) does not apply to a claim under Section 19(1) of an act in respect of which an appeal, or proceedings in the nature of an appeal, may be brought under any enactment.

(3) Proceedings under subsection (1) are to be brought in the District Court but all such remedies shall be obtainable in such proceedings as, apart from this subsection and Section 69(1), would be obtainable in the Court of First Instance.

(4) Without limiting the power conferred by subsection (3), the District Court may —

(a) make a declaration that the respondent has engaged in conduct, or committed an act, that is unlawful under this Ordinance and order that the respondent shall not repeat or continue such unlawful conduct or act;

(b) order that the respondent shall perform any reasonable act or course of conduct to redress any loss or damage suffered by the claimant;

(c) order that the respondent shall employ or re-employ the claimant;

(d) order that the respondent shall promote the claimant;

(e) order that the respondent shall pay to the claimant damages by way of compensation for any loss or damage suffered by reason of the respondent's conduct or act;

(f) order that the respondent shall pay to the claimant punitive or exemplary damages; or

(g) make an order declaring void in whole or in part and either ab initio or from such date as may be specified in the order, any contract or agreement made in contravention of this Ordinance.

(5) By virtue of this subsection and notwithstanding any law, the District Court has jurisdiction to hear and determine any proceedings under subsection (1) and has all such powers as are necessary or expedient for it to have in order to provide, grant or make any remedy, injunction or order mentioned in this Ordinance.

(6) In respect of an unlawful act of discrimination falling within Section 4(1)(b), no award of damages is to be made if the respondent proves that the requirement or condition concerned was not applied with the intention of treating the claimant unfavourably on the ground of the race of the claimant.

(6A) Subsection (6) does not apply in relation to an unlawful act of discrimination falling within Section 4(1)(b) that is committed on or after the commencement date* of Part 9 of the Discrimination Legislation (Miscellaneous Amendments) Ordinance 2020 (8 of 2020). *(Added 8 of 2020 s. 44)*

(7) For the avoidance of doubt, it is declared that damages in respect of an unlawful act of discrimination or harassment, or an act which is unlawful by virtue of Section 45, may include compensation for injury to feelings whether or not they include compensation under any other head.

Enforcement Notices

Section 71 Issue of Enforcement Notices

(1) This Section applies to any act which is —

- (a) an unlawful discriminatory act;
- (b) an unlawful act of harassment;
- (c) a contravention of Section 41; or
- (d) a contravention of Section 42, 43, 44 or 45,

and so applies whether or not the proceedings have been brought in respect of the act.

(2) If in the course of a formal investigation the Commission becomes satisfied that a person is committing, or has committed, any acts to which this Section applies, the Commission may in the prescribed manner serve on the person a notice in the prescribed form requiring the person —

- (a) not to commit any such acts (which may include discontinuing or changing any of the person's practices or other arrangements which occasioned those acts, in particular to avoid any repetition thereof); and
- (b) where compliance with paragraph (a) involves changes in any of the person's practices or other arrangements —
  - (i) to inform the Commission that he or she has effected changes and what those changes are; and
  - (ii) to take such steps as may be reasonably required by the notice for the purpose of affording that information to other persons concerned.

(3) An enforcement notice may also require the person on whom it is served to furnish the Commission with such other information as may be reasonably required by the notice in order to verify that the notice has been complied with.

(4) An enforcement notice may specify the time at which, and the manner and form in which, any information is to be furnished to the Commission, but the time at which any information is to be furnished in compliance with the notice must not be later than 5 years after the notice has become final.

---

* Commencement date: 19 June 2020.

(5) Section 66(5) applies to requirements under subsections (2)(b), (3) and (4) contained in an enforcement notice which has become final as it applies to requirements in a notice served under Section 66(1).

Section 72 Appeal against Enforcement Notice

(1) Not later than 45 days after an enforcement notice is served on any person, he or she may appeal to the District Court against any requirement in the notice.

(2) Where the District Court considers a requirement in respect of which an appeal is brought under subsection (1) to be unreasonable because it is based on an incorrect finding of fact or for any other reason, the Court shall quash the requirement.

(3) On quashing a requirement under subsection (2), the District Court may direct that the enforcement notice shall be treated as if, in place of the requirement quashed, it had contained a requirement in terms specified in the direction.

(4) Subsection (1) does not apply to a requirement treated as included in an enforcement notice by virtue of a direction under subsection (3).

Section 73 Investigation as to Compliance with Enforcement Notice

(1) If—

(a) the terms of reference of a formal investigation state that its purpose is to determine whether any requirements of an enforcement notice are being or have been carried out, but Section 66(2)(b) does not apply; and

(b) Section 65(3) is complied with in relation to the investigation on a date (***commencement date***) not later than the expiration of the period of 5 years beginning when the enforcement notice became final,

the Commission may within the relevant period serve notices under Section 66(1) for the purposes of the investigation without needing to obtain the consent of the Chief Secretary for Administration.

(2) In subsection (1), ***relevant period*** (有關期間) means the period beginning on the commencement date and ending on the later of the following dates —

(a) the date on which the period of 5 years referred to in subsection (1)(b) expires;

(b) the date 2 years after the commencement date.

Section 74 Register of Enforcement Notices

(1) The Commission shall establish and maintain a register (***the register***) of enforcement notices which have become final.

(2) A person is entitled, on payment of a reasonable fee, if any, as may be determined by the Commission —

(a) to inspect the register during ordinary office hours and take copies of any entry; or

(b) to obtain from the Commission a copy, certified by the Commission to be correct, of any entry in the register.

(3) The Commission may, if it thinks fit, determine that the right conferred by subsection (2)(a) is exercisable in relation to a copy of the register, instead of, or in addition to, the original.

(4) The Commission shall give general notice of the place or places where, and the times when, the register or a copy of it may be inspected.

Other Enforcement by Commission

Section 75 Persistent Discrimination, Harassment or Vilification

If, during the period of 5 years beginning on the date on which either of the following became final in the case of any person, namely —

(a) an enforcement notice served on the person;

(b) a finding by the District Court that the person has done —

(i) an unlawful discriminatory act;

(ii) an unlawful act of harassment; or

(iii) an act contravening Section 45,

it appears to the Commission that unless restrained the person is likely to do one or more acts falling within paragraph (b), or contravening Section 41, the Commission may apply to the District Court for an injunction restraining the person from doing so; and the District Court, if satisfied that the application is well-founded, may grant the injunction in the terms applied for or in more limited terms.

Section 76 Enforcement of Sections 42, 43 and 44

(1) Proceedings in respect of a contravention of Section 42, 43 or 44 may be brought only by the Commission and in accordance with this Section.

(2) The proceedings must be —

(a) an application for a decision whether the alleged contravention occurred; or

(b) an application under subsection (4),

or both.

(3) An application under subsection (2)(a) must be made to the District Court.

(4) If it appears to the Commission —

(a) that a person has done an act which by virtue of Section 42, 43 or 44 was unlawful; and

(b) that unless restrained the person is likely to do further acts which by virtue of that Section are unlawful,

the Commission may apply to the District Court for an injunction restraining the person from doing so; and the District Court, if satisfied that the application is well-founded, may grant the injunction in the terms applied for or in more limited terms.

(5) Without prejudice to subsection (4), if it appears to the Commission that a person has done an act which was unlawful by virtue of Section 42, the Commission may apply to the District Court for an order imposing a financial penalty on such person; and the District Court, if satisfied that the application is well-founded, may make such an order.

(6) The financial penalty imposed under subsection (5) shall not exceed $10,000 for the first occasion on which a penalty is imposed, and $30,000 for the second and any subsequent occasion on which a penalty is imposed in respect of that person.

Help for Persons Suffering Discrimination, Harassment or Vilification

Section 77 Help for Aggrieved Persons in Obtaining Information, etc.

(1) With a view to helping a person (***the person aggrieved***) who considers he or she may have been discriminated against or harassed in contravention of this Ordinance, or the subject of an unlawful act under Section 45 —

(a) to decide whether to institute proceedings; and

(b) if the person does so, to formulate and present his or her case in the most effective manner,

the Commission may prescribe —

(c) forms by which the person aggrieved may question the respondent on the respondent's reasons for doing any relevant act, or on any other matter which is or may be relevant; and

(d) forms by which the respondent may if he or she so wishes reply to any questions.

(2) Where the person aggrieved questions the respondent (whether or not in accordance with a form referred to in subsection (1)) —

(a) the question, and any reply by the respondent (whether or not in accordance with such a form) is, subject to subsections (3), (4) and (5), admissible as evidence in the proceedings; and

(b) if it appears to the District Court that the respondent deliberately, and without reasonable excuse, omitted to reply within a reasonable period or that the respondent's reply is evasive or equivocal, the Court may draw any inference from that fact it considers it just and equitable to draw, including an inference that the respondent committed an unlawful act.

(3) The Commission may —

(a) prescribe the period within which questions must be served in order to be admissible under subsection (2)(a); and

(b) prescribe the manner in which a question, and any reply by the respondent, may be served.

(4) Rules under the District Court Ordinance (Cap. 336) may enable the District Court entertaining a claim under Section 70 to determine, before the date fixed for the hearing of the claim, whether a question or reply is admissible under this Section or not.

(5) This Section is without prejudice to any other enactment or rule of law regulating interlocutory and preliminary matters in proceedings before the District Court, and has effect subject to any enactment or rule of law regulating the admissibility of evidence in such proceedings.

(6) In this Section, ***respondent*** (答辯人) includes a prospective respondent.

Section 78 Assistance by Way of Conciliation

(1) A person may lodge with the Commission a complaint in writing alleging that another person has done an act which is unlawful by virtue of a provision of this Ordinance.

(2) A representative complaint may be lodged under subsection (1) in accordance with rules made under Section 82.

(3) Subject to subsection (4), where a complaint is lodged under subsection (1), the Commission shall —

(a) conduct an investigation into the act the subject of the complaint; and

(b) endeavour, by conciliation, to effect a settlement of the matter to which the act relates.

(4) The Commission may decide not to conduct, or to discontinue, an investigation into an act the subject of a complaint lodged under subsection (1) if —

(a) it is satisfied that the act is not unlawful by reason of a provision of this Ordinance;

(b) it is of the opinion that the person aggrieved by the act does not desire (or, in a case to which subsection (2) applies, none of the persons aggrieved by the act desires) that the investigation be conducted or continued;

(c) a period of more than 12 months has elapsed beginning when the act was done;

(d) in a case to which subsection (2) applies, it determines, in accordance with rules made under Section 82, that the complaint should not be a representative complaint; or

(e) it is of the opinion that the complaint is frivolous, vexatious, misconceived or lacking in substance.

(5) Where the Commission decides not to conduct, or to discontinue, an investigation into an act the subject of a complaint lodged under subsection (1), it shall by notice served on the person who lodged the complaint advise the person of —

(a) that decision; and

(b) the reason for that decision.

(6) Evidence of anything said or done by any person in the course of conciliation under this Section (including anything said or done at any conference held for the purposes of such conciliation) is not admissible in evidence in any proceedings under this Ordinance except with the consent of that person.

(7) For the avoidance of doubt, it is declared that subsection (6) does not apply where —

(a) a complaint is lodged under subsection (1); and

(b) a settlement has been effected of the matter to which the act the subject of the complaint relates.

Section 79 Assistance Other Than by Way of Conciliation

(1) Where —

(a) a complaint has been lodged under Section 78(1); but

(b) for whatever reason, there has not been a settlement of the matter to which the act the subject of the complaint relates,

then any person who may institute proceedings under this Ordinance in respect of that act may make an application to the Commission for assistance in respect of those proceedings.

(2) The Commission shall consider an application under subsection (1) and may grant it if it thinks fit to do so, in particular where —

(a) the case raises a question of principle; or

(b) it is unreasonable, having regard to the complexity of the case or the applicant's position in relation to the respondent or another person involved or any other matter, to expect the applicant to deal with the case unaided.

(3) Assistance by the Commission under this Section may include —

(a) giving advice;

(b) arranging for the giving of advice or assistance by a solicitor or counsel;

(c) arranging for representation by any person including all such assistance as is usually given by a solicitor or counsel in the steps preliminary or incidental to any proceedings, or in arriving at or giving effect to a compromise to avoid or bring to an end any proceedings;

(d) any other form of assistance which the Commission may consider appropriate, but paragraph (c) does not affect the law and practice regulating the descriptions of persons who may appear in, conduct, defend and address a court in, any proceedings except to the extent permitted under rules made in accordance with Section 73E of the District Court Ordinance (Cap. 336).

(4) In so far as expenses are incurred by the Commission in providing the applicant with assistance under this Section the recovery of those expenses (as taxed or assessed in such manner as may be prescribed by relevant rules) constitutes a first charge for the benefit of the Commission —

(a) on any costs or expenses which (whether by virtue of a judgment or order of the District Court or an agreement or otherwise) are payable to the applicant by any other person in respect of the matter in connection with which the assistance is given; and

(b) so far as relates to any costs or expenses, on his or her rights under any compromise or settlement arrived at in connection with that matter to avoid or bring to an end any proceedings.

(5) The charge conferred by subsection (4) is subject to any charge under the Legal Aid Ordinance (Cap. 91) and to any provision in that Ordinance for payment of any sum into the Supplementary Legal Aid Fund established under that Ordinance.

(6) In this Section —

relevant rules (有關規則) means any rules made under the District Court Ordinance (Cap. 336);

respondent (答辯人) includes a prospective respondent.

Period within Which Proceedings to be Brought

Section 80 Period within Which Proceedings to be Brought

(1) The District Court shall not consider a claim under Section 70 unless proceedings in respect of the claim are instituted within the period of 24 months beginning —

(a) when the act complained of was done; or

(b) if there is a relevant report in relation to that act, with the day on which the report is published or made available for inspection under Section 67,

whichever is the later.

(2) The District Court —

(a) shall not consider an application under Section 76(2)(a) unless it is made within the period of 24 months beginning when the act to which it relates was done; and

(b) shall not consider an application under Section 76(4) unless it is made within the period of 5 years so beginning.

(3) For the purposes of determining the period under subsection (1) within which proceedings may be brought, where an act to which the claim relates was the subject of a complaint lodged under Section 78(1), then the period that elapsed between the date when the complaint was lodged and the date when the complaint was disposed of under Section 78(3) or (4), as certified in writing by the Commission, shall be disregarded.

(4) Notwithstanding subsections (1) and (2), the District Court may consider any claim or application which is out of time, if, in all the circumstances of the case, it considers that it is just and equitable to do so.

(5) For the purposes of subsection (4), the circumstances of the case include, in relation to any claim —

(a) whether the act to which the claim relates was the subject of a complaint lodged under Section 78(1); and

(b) if so, the period that elapsed between when the act was done and when that complaint was so lodged.

(6) For the purposes of this Section —

(a) where the inclusion of any term in a contract renders the making of the contract an unlawful act, that act shall be treated as extending throughout the duration of the contract;

(b) any act extending over a period shall be treated as done at the end of that period; and

(c) a deliberate omission shall be treated as done when the person concerned decided upon it.

(7) In the absence of evidence to the contrary, a person shall be taken for the purposes of this Section to decide upon an omission, that is deciding upon omitting to do an act (*relevant act*) —

(a) when the person does an act inconsistent with doing the relevant act; or

(b) if the person has done no such inconsistent act, when the period expires within which he or she might reasonably have been expected to do the relevant act if it were to be done.

(8) The Chief Executive in Council may, by notice published in the Gazette, amend subsection (1) by substituting a longer period for the period specified in that subsection.

(9) In this Section, ***relevant report*** (有關報告), in relation to an act referred to in subsection (1), means a report —

(a) published or made available for inspection under Section 67; and

(b) from which it can reasonably be construed (whether or not the report mentions the act or the report was in any way prepared in consequence of the act) that the Commission is of the opinion that the act, or the class of acts to which the act belongs, is unlawful under a provision of Part 3, 4 or 5.

Part 9 Miscellaneous

(Format changes — E.R. 5 of 2018)

Section 81 Validity and Revision of Contracts

(1) A term of a contract is void where —

(a) its inclusion renders the making of the contract unlawful by virtue of this Ordinance;

(b) it is included in furtherance of an act rendered unlawful by this Ordinance; or

(c) it provides for the doing of an act which would be rendered unlawful by this Ordinance.

(2) Subsection (1) does not apply to a term the inclusion of which constitutes, or is in furtherance of, or provides for, unlawful discrimination against a party to the contract, but the term shall be unenforceable against that party.

(3) A term in a contract which purports to exclude or limit any provision of this Ordinance is unenforceable by any person in whose favour the term would operate apart from this subsection.

(4) Subsection (3) does not apply to a contract settling a claim to which Section 70 applies.

(5) On the application of any person interested in a contract to which subsection (2) applies, the District Court may make such order as it thinks just for removing or modifying any term made unenforceable by that subsection; but such an order shall not be made unless all persons affected —

(a) have been given notice of the application (except where under rules made under the District Court Ordinance (Cap. 336) notice may be dispensed with); and

(b) have been afforded an opportunity to make representations to the Court.

(6) An order under subsection (5) may include provision as respects any period before making the order.

Section 82 Rules

(1) The Commission may make rules —

(a) prescribing the persons, or persons belonging to a class of persons, who may lodge a representative complaint under Section 78(1);

(b) prescribing the bodies and positions for the purposes of Section 34;

(c) prescribing the matters to be taken into account by the Commission for the purposes of a determination under Section 78(4)(d);

(d) to enable the Commission to require such persons, or persons belonging to such class of persons, as are specified in the rules to furnish information to the Commission for the purposes of Section 78;

(e) restricting the disclosure of any information referred to in paragraph (d) furnished to the Commission;

(f) to enable the Commission to direct persons to attend any conference held for the purposes of Section 78;

(g) regulating the procedure of any conference held for the purposes of Section 78;

(h) prescribing any other thing that is required or permitted to be prescribed under this Ordinance.

(2) Any rules made under subsection (1) may —

(a) make different provisions for different circumstances and provide for a particular case or class of cases;

(b) be made so as to apply only in such circumstances as are prescribed by the rules;

(c) specify forms for the purposes of the rules;

(d) be made generally for the better or more effectual carrying out of the provisions of this Ordinance, including incidental, consequential, evidential and supplemental provisions.

(3) Any rules made under this Section may prescribe offences in respect of contraventions of the rules, and may provide for the imposition of a fine not exceeding level 4 and of imprisonment for a period not exceeding 2 years.

Section 83 Regulations to Empower Commission to Bring Certain Proceedings

(1) The Secretary for Constitutional and Mainland Affairs may make regulations —

(a) where any person may bring proceedings under Section 70 but has not done so, empowering the Commission, in such circumstances as are specified in the regulations, to bring and maintain those proceedings as if the Commission were that person;

(b) specifying which of the remedies referred to in Section 70(3) shall be obtainable by the Commission in any such proceedings;

(c) for the purposes of enabling the Commission to bring and maintain any such proceedings (including any related purposes), specifying modifications to which any provisions of this Ordinance (including any subsidiary legislation) shall be read.

(2) Any regulations made under this Section shall be subject to the approval of the Legislative Council.

(3) This Section is without prejudice to the Commission's power to bring proceedings by way of judicial review, in relation to this Ordinance or any other law, pursuant to its functions under Section 59(1).

Section 84 Amendment of Schedules

(Amended 8 of 2020 s. 16)

(1) The Chief Executive in Council may, by notice published in the Gazette, amend Schedule 1, 2, 3, 4 or 5 but any notice to amend Schedule 2, 3, 4 or 5 shall be subject to the approval of the Legislative Council. *(Amended 8 of 2020 s. 16)*

(2) The Secretary for Constitutional and Mainland Affairs may, by notice published in the Gazette, amend Schedule 6. *(Added 8 of 2020 s. 16)*

Section 85 (Omitted as spent—E.R. 5 of 2018)

Section 86 (Omitted as spent—E.R. 5 of 2018)

Section 87 (Omitted as spent—E.R. 5 of 2018)

Section 88 (Omitted as spent—E.R. 5 of 2018)

Section 89 (Omitted as spent—E.R. 5 of 2018)

Section 90 (Omitted as spent—E.R. 5 of 2018)

Section 91 (Omitted as spent—E.R. 5 of 2018)

Section 92 (Omitted as spent—E.R. 5 of 2018)

Section 93 (Omitted as spent—E.R. 5 of 2018)

Section 94 (Omitted as spent—E.R. 5 of 2018)

Section 95 (Omitted as spent—E.R. 5 of 2018)

Section 96 (Omitted as spent—E.R. 5 of 2018)

Section 97 (Omitted as spent—E.R. 5 of 2018)

Section 98 (Omitted as spent—E.R. 5 of 2018)

Section 99 (Omitted as spent—E.R. 5 of 2018)

Section 100 (Omitted as spent—E.R. 5 of 2018)

Section 101 (Omitted as spent—E.R. 5 of 2018)

Section 102 (Omitted as spent—E.R. 5 of 2018)

Section 103 (Omitted as spent—E.R. 5 of 2018)

Section 104 (Omitted as spent—E.R. 5 of 2018)

Section 105 (Omitted as spent—E.R. 5 of 2018)

Section 106 (Omitted as spent—E.R. 5 of 2018)

Schedule 1

[ss. 2(1) and 84]

Educational Establishments and Their Responsible Bodies

(Format changes — E.R. 5 of 2018)

Item	Educational establishment	Responsible body
1.	The University of Hong Kong established by the University of Hong Kong Ordinance (Cap. 1053)	The University of Hong Kong established by the University of Hong Kong Ordinance (Cap. 1053)
2.	The Chinese University of Hong Kong established by The Chinese University of Hong Kong Ordinance (Cap. 1109)	The Chinese University of Hong Kong established by The Chinese University of Hong Kong Ordinance (Cap. 1109)
3.	The Hong Kong Polytechnic University established by The Hong Kong Polytechnic University Ordinance (Cap. 1075)	The Hong Kong Polytechnic University established by The Hong Kong Polytechnic University Ordinance (Cap. 1075)
4.	Any Post Secondary College registered under the Post Secondary Colleges Ordinance (Cap. 320)	The Board of Governors (or the Board of Trustees where no Board of Governors exists) or the College Council, according to which of them has the function concerned
5.	The Vocational Training Council established by the Vocational Training Council Ordinance (Cap. 1130)	The Vocational Training Council established by the Vocational Training Council Ordinance (Cap. 1130)
6.	The Hong Kong Baptist University established by the Hong Kong Baptist University Ordinance (Cap. 1126)	The Hong Kong Baptist University established by the Hong Kong Baptist University Ordinance (Cap. 1126)
7.	The City University of Hong Kong established by the City University of Hong Kong Ordinance (Cap. 1132)	The City University of Hong Kong established by the City University of Hong Kong Ordinance (Cap. 1132)
8.	The Hong Kong Academy for Performing Arts established by The Hong Kong Academy for Performing Arts Ordinance (Cap. 1135)	The Council or the Academic Board, within the meaning of Section 2 of The Hong Kong Academy for Performing Arts Ordinance (Cap. 1135), according to which of them has the function concerned
9.	The Hong Kong University of Science and Technology established by The Hong Kong University of Science and Technology Ordinance (Cap. 1141)	The Hong Kong University of Science and Technology established by The Hong Kong University of Science and Technology Ordinance (Cap. 1141)
10.	The Open University of Hong Kong established by The Open University of Hong Kong Ordinance (Cap. 1145)	The Open University of Hong Kong established by The Open University of Hong Kong Ordinance (Cap. 1145)
11.	The Lingnan University established by the Lingnan University Ordinance (Cap. 1165)	The Lingnan University established by the Lingnan University Ordinance (Cap. 1165)
12.	The Education University of Hong Kong established by The Education University of Hong Kong Ordinance (Cap. 444) *(Amended 6 of 2016 s. 2)*	The Education University of Hong Kong established by The Education University of Hong Kong Ordinance (Cap. 444)

13.	Any school which is registered or provisionally registered under the Education Ordinance (Cap. 279)	The management committee, incorporated management committee or school management company (as the case may be), within the meaning of Section 3(1) of the Education Ordinance (Cap. 279), of the school
14.	Any school, within the meaning of Section 3(1) of the Education Ordinance (Cap. 279), entirely maintained and controlled by the Government	The Permanent Secretary for Education
15.	The Clothing Industry Training Authority established by the Industrial Training (Clothing Industry) Ordinance (Cap. 318)	The Clothing Industry Training Authority established by the Industrial Training (Clothing Industry) Ordinance (Cap. 318)
16.	The Construction Industry Council established by the Construction Industry Council Ordinance (Cap. 587)	The Construction Industry Council established by the Construction Industry Council Ordinance (Cap. 587)

Schedule 2

[ss. 14 and 84]

Employee in Existing Employment

(Format changes — E.R. 5 of 2018)

(1) An employee specified in Section 2, 3, 4, 5 or 6 is an employee in an existing employment for the purposes of Section 14 of this Ordinance.

(2) An employee specified in this Section is an employee (other than a public officer or specified English teacher) of an employer where —

(a) the employee —

(i) began his or her employment with the employer pursuant to an offer of employment made to him or her before the commencement date;* and

(ii) continues to be employed by the employer without a break in service since he or she began service pursuant to the offer; or

(b) the employee is employed by the employer following one or more transfers of employment, all being transfers within the same group of companies within the meaning of Section 13(3)(b) of this Ordinance, where the employment immediately preceding the first transfer was pursuant to an offer of employment made to him or her before the commencement date* and there is no break in the employee's service since he or she began his or her employment pursuant to the offer.

(3) An employee specified in this Section is a judicial officer —

(a) who —

(i) began serving as a judicial officer pursuant to an offer of employment made to him or her before 27 November 1997; and

(ii) continues to serve as such officer without a break in service since he or she began service pursuant to the offer; or

* Commencement date: 10 July 2009.

(b) who —

(i) began serving as a public officer (other than a judicial officer) pursuant to an offer of employment made to him or her before 1 January 1999;

(ii) had continued to serve as a public officer without a break in service since he or she began service pursuant to the offer and until he or she began serving as a judicial officer; and

(iii) continues to serve as a judicial officer without a break in service since beginning serving as such.

(4) An employee specified in this Section is an ICAC officer —

(a) who —

(i) began serving as an ICAC officer pursuant to an offer of employment made to him or her before 1 January 1999; and

(ii) continues to serve as such officer without a break in service since he or she began service pursuant to the offer; or

(b) who —

(i) began serving as a public officer (other than an ICAC officer) pursuant to an offer of employment made to him or her before 1 January 1999;

(ii) had continued to serve as a public officer without a break in service since he or she began service pursuant to the offer and until he or she began serving as an ICAC officer; and

(iii) continues to serve as an ICAC officer without a break in service since beginning serving as such.

(5) An employee specified in this Section is a public officer (other than a judicial officer or an ICAC officer) who —

(a) began serving as such officer pursuant to an offer of employment made to him or her before 1 January 1999; and

(b) continues to serve as such officer without a break in service since he or she began service pursuant to the offer.

(6) An employee specified in this Section is a specified English teacher who —

(a) began his or her employment as such pursuant to an offer of employment made to him or her before the commencement date*; and

(b) continues to be employed as such without a break in service since he or she began service pursuant to the offer.

(7) An employee (other than a public officer or specified English teacher) who is an employee specified in Section 2 remains an employee so specified, whether or not the employment of the employee by the employer concerned, or (where Section 2(b) applies) by any of the employers within the group of companies concerned, was or is pursuant to any extension, any renewal or re-engagement after termination and whether or not the employee was or has been promoted.

(8) A judicial officer, an ICAC officer or any other public officer, who is an employee specified in Section 3, 4 or 5 remains an employee so specified, whether or not the service of the officer was or is pursuant to any extension, any renewal or re-engagement after termination and whether or not the officer was or has been promoted.

(9) A specified English teacher who is an employee specified in Section 6 remains an employee so specified whether or not the service of the specified English teacher was or is pursuant to —

(a) any extension, any renewal or re-engagement after termination; or

(b) any transfer from one primary or secondary school to another, or from a primary or secondary school to the Native-speaking English Teacher Section of the Education Bureau or vice versa.

(10) Provisions of this Schedule apply irrespective of whether or not an employee is or has become a Hong Kong permanent resident.

(11) For the purposes of this Ordinance —

ICAC officer (廉署人員) means a public officer who is an officer within the meaning of Section 2 of the Independent Commission Against Corruption Ordinance (Cap. 204);

judicial officer (司法人員) means a judicial officer holding a judicial office specified in Schedule 1 to the Judicial Officers Recommendation Commission Ordinance (Cap. 92);

local terms of employment (本地僱用條款) and ***overseas terms of employment*** (海外僱用條款) —

(a) in relation to any employee (other than a public officer), mean respectively —

(i) such conditions or terms of service as apply, from time to time, primarily to the appointment or employment by the employer concerned of a person who is a Hong Kong permanent resident; and

(ii) such conditions or terms of service as apply, from time to time, primarily to the appointment or employment by the employer concerned of a person who is not a Hong Kong permanent resident;

(b) in relation to a judicial officer, an ICAC officer or any other public officer, respectively mean the local conditions or terms of service and overseas conditions or terms of service within the meaning of such regulations, administrative rules, circulars and circular memoranda as apply, from time to time, generally to the appointment or employment of judicial officers, ICAC officers or other public officers (as the case may be);

public officer (公職人員) does not include a specified English teacher who is employed —

(a) in a primary or secondary school entirely maintained and controlled by the Government; or

(b) in the Native-speaking English Teacher Section of the Education Bureau;

specified English teacher (指明英語教師) means a teacher —

(a) who is a native-speaker of English or possesses native-speaker English competency;

(b) who is normally first recruited from a place outside Hong Kong; and

(c) who —

(i) is employed in a secondary school under the "Enhanced Native-speaking English Teacher Scheme" administered by the Education Bureau;

(ii) is employed in a primary school under the "Native-speaking English Teacher Scheme" administered by that Bureau; or

(iii) is employed as an Advisory Teacher or a Regional Native-speaking English Teacher Coordinator in the Native-speaking English Teacher Section of that Bureau. *(Amended E.R. 5 of 2018)*

Schedule 3

[ss. 19(2) and 84]

Authorization or Qualification Specified for the Purposes of Section 19(2) of This Ordinance

(Format changes — E.R. 5 of 2018)

Any authorization or qualification conferred for the purposes of —

(a) the Professional Accountants Ordinance (Cap. 50);

(b) the Pharmacy and Poisons Ordinance (Cap. 138);
(c) the Dentists Registration Ordinance (Cap. 156);
(d) the Legal Practitioners Ordinance (Cap. 159);
(e) the Medical Registration Ordinance (Cap. 161);
(f) the Midwives Registration Ordinance (Cap. 162);
(g) the Nurses Registration Ordinance (Cap. 164);
(h) the Supplementary Medical Professions Ordinance (Cap. 359);
(i) the Chiropractors Registration Ordinance (Cap. 428);
(j) the Civil Aviation Ordinance (Cap. 448); or
(k) the Chinese Medicine Ordinance (Cap. 549).

Schedule 4

[ss. 33(2) and 84]

Discrimination to Which Sections 27(1) and 28 of This Ordinance Do Not Apply

(Format changes — E.R. of 5 of 2018)

Item	Provision creating illegality	Exception
1.	Part 3 and Section 26	Sections 10(3), (4) and (7), 11(1)(b), 12, 13, 14, 15(4) and (5) and 21(3).

Schedule 5

[ss. 58(1), 60 and 84]

Other Matters Not Affected by This Ordinance

(Format changes — E.R. of 5 of 2018)

Item	Provision creating illegality	Matter
1.	Part 4	Any discrimination between persons of different racial groups arising from that policy of the Government known as the "Portable Comprehensive Social Security Assistance Scheme" under which eligibility for certain assistance is extended only to persons who take up permanent residence in certain places outside Hong Kong. *(Amended E.R. 5 of 2018)*

Schedule 6

[ss. 2 and 84]

Persons Specified as Carers

(Schedule 6 added 8 of 2020 s. 17)

Index

C

D

J

K

L

M

N

O

P

Q

R

V

W